The Communist International
in Lenin's Time

THE GERMAN REVOLUTION
AND THE DEBATE ON
SOVIET POWER

Documents: 1918-1919
Preparing the Founding Congress

Edited by John Riddell

A PATHFINDER BOOK
Anchor Foundation/New York

Library of Congress Number 86-060845
ISBN cloth 0-937091-00-6; ISBN paper 0-937091-01-4

Manufactured in the United States of America
First edition 1986

Published by the Anchor Foundation
Distributed by Pathfinder Press
410 West Street, New York, New York 10014
Africa, Europe, and the Middle East:
    Pathfinder Press, 47 The Cut, London SE1 8LL England
Asia, Australia, and the Pacific:
    Pathfinder Press, P.O. Box 37, Leichhardt, Sydney, NSW 2040 Australia
Canada:
    DEC Book Distribution, 229 College St., Toronto, Ontario M5T 1R4 Canada
New Zealand:
    Pilot Books, Box 8730, Auckland, New Zealand

Contents

Part One

Part Two

Photographs

Preface

In the first days of November 1918, while war still raged across Europe, German workers and soldiers rose in revolt, forming revolutionary councils across the country. Their uprising toppled the German Empire on November 9 and brought Germany's participation in the war to an abrupt end two days later, thereby halting the world interimperialist slaughter.

The overthrow of the kaiser's regime, coming a little more than a year after that of the Russian tsar, opened a second front in the struggle against the international imperialist system. It helped lessen the imperialists' attempts to isolate the Russian workers' and peasants' republic established under Bolshevik leadership in November 1917.

Ever since the outbreak of World War in August 1914, when the leaders of most parties of the Second International had betrayed the working class and its internationalist principles, the Bolsheviks had advanced the call for a new, Communist International. Now the German revolution was helping to create the political conditions in which, in the view of the Bolshevik leaders of Soviet Russia, this new organization could be officially launched.

In November 1918 German working people confronted the same alternative paths that Russian workers and peasants had faced in 1917: forward, to the replacement of capitalist and landlord rule by a revolutionary government of the exploited toilers, or back to restabilized rule by the exploiters, those responsible for the horrors of the World War. The debate and struggle over this question in the German and international workers' movement is the central thread running through the documents in this book.

Many of these documents recount the struggle by German revolutionists for leadership of the working class against both the open and the veiled supporters of capitalist rule inside the workers' movement. Others tell the story of the debates at the founding congress of the German Communist Party (KPD) in December 1918. The second part of the book records the international debate on Soviet power and the

---

Footnotes to the preface begin on page xix.

process that led to launching the Communist International (Comintern) in March 1919.

The political record of the German revolution aids in understanding the events that led to founding the Comintern. Moreover, the successes and failures of working-class strategy and tactics in the German revolution were to figure among the key experiences drawn on by the Comintern as it hammered out its perspectives at its first four congresses held between 1919 and 1922.

Russian Communist leader V.I. Lenin held that the new International was born as a living movement in the months of November and December 1918, when Communist parties were formed in several European countries. He placed special importance on the formation of the Communist Party in Germany, where the workers' movement was strong and had a Marxist political heritage. The revolutionary wing of the German movement was now in the center of a deep-going challenge to rule by the big industrial and landowning capitalists. In January 1919 Lenin explained:

"The *foundation* of a genuinely proletarian, genuinely internationalist, genuinely revolutionary Third International, the *Communist International,* became *a fact* when the German Spartacus League, with such world-known and world famous leaders, with such staunch working-class champions as [Karl] Liebknecht, Rosa Luxemburg, Clara Zetkin and Franz Mehring, made a clean break with ... social-chauvinists (socialists in words, but chauvinists in deeds) who have earned eternal shame by their alliance with the predatory, imperialist German bourgeoisie and [Kaiser] Wilhelm II. It became a fact when the Spartacus League changed its name to the Communist Party of Germany. Though it has not yet been officially inaugurated, the Third International actually exists."[1]

The Spartacus League had originated as a revolutionary current in the Social Democratic Party of Germany (SPD), initiating and spearheading opposition to the SPD majority leadership's open support in August 1914 to German imperialist war policy. The Spartacists called on workers around the world to conduct a revolutionary class struggle against the imperialist bourgeoisie, which was responsible for the war. At first the Spartacists were only a small handful. But as discontent mounted against the war and against the German imperial government that was waging it, their stand won increasing working-class support.

Wider layers of the SPD ranks and a growing minority of its leaders soon began to oppose the party leadership's war policies. Most oppositionists within the SPD leadership, however, were centrists, who shared the class-collaborationist outlook of their colleagues in top party bodies. Prodded into action by mounting working-class discontent, these oppositionist leaders had become convinced that the threat of social revolution could be averted only through bringing a halt to Germany's participation in the war, a perspective they shared with a growing layer of petty-bourgeois and bourgeois pacifists.

These oppositional forces were expelled from the SPD in January 1917 and formed the centrist-led Independent Social Democratic Party of Germany (USPD). The Spartacists joined the USPD and carried on their fight for revolutionary policies as a public faction within the new party.

The Spartacists' revolutionary agitation and resistance to the war had won them the respect of broad layers of German workers and soldiers. They became the most authoritative current outside Russia to stand up against the chauvinist war effort of the government of their own country and to attempt to put the international workers' movement on a revolutionary course.

When the workers and soldiers overthrew the kaiser and his regime on November 9, 1918, the SPD and USPD leaders formed a provisional government committed to preserving the existing capitalist state. The Spartacus League advocated replacing this government with one resting on the mass-based councils of workers and soldiers that had arisen during the uprising. Only such a government, they argued, could advance the interests of the exploited German working people. They fought the efforts by the SPD and USPD leaderships to reconsolidate capitalist rule. Their work to establish a revolutionary government and lessen the isolation of the world's first workers' and peasants' government in Russia was hailed by the Bolsheviks and other revolutionists around the world.

The Spartacists gained further authority among German workers as outspoken defenders of the Soviet government of Russia. Inspired by the victory in Russia, working people in Germany, like those in many other countries, looked to the October 1917 revolution as the first successful example of how to overturn capitalist political rule and begin the construction of a new society.

In Russia the workers' and peasants' government was based on mass, delegated councils of the exploited — *soviets* in the Russian language. These soviets had arisen in the course of the 1917 revolution as democratic bodies through which workers, peasants, and soldiers could centralize their struggle against the war, landlordism, and capitalist exploitation. Revolutionary-minded workers and peasants outside Russia began to look to the soviets as an embodiment of their own demand for a government that would represent their class interests against those of their exploiters. The call for a "council republic" or "Soviet republic" became a popular way of expressing the desire to "do what the Russians did."

During 1918, a Communist current began to take shape in the international workers' movement. It was made up of revolutionary internationalists committed to the conquest of state power by the proletariat and its allies and to the establishment of governments of the soviet type.

A few days before the victory of the German workers and soldiers, a revolutionary tide had broken apart the Austro-Hungarian Empire, and workers' and soldiers' councils had been formed in many areas. Poland and other countries of eastern Europe were swept by revolutionary struggles in November and subsequent months. In western Europe and North America, where such major explosions had not yet erupted, revolutionary currents who looked to the Bolsheviks gained in strength.

The Communist movement was also attracting revolutionary fighters from the oppressed peoples of Asia. Inspired by the Russian revolution to deepen their struggle against imperialist colonial domination, these revolutionists sought assistance from the Bolshevik leadership in hammering out a strategy to advance this goal. Throughout vast regions of Asia that had been colonized and nationally oppressed by the old tsarist empire, militants looked to the Bolshevik-led Soviet government for help in carrying out democratic, antifeudal revolutions against local landlords and profiteers. Here too, governments based on soviets of the peasants and other exploited toilers arose.

The Communist International thus took shape in the fight to defend and consolidate the workers' and peasants' republic in Russia, to establish Soviet governments in a number of other countries in central and eastern Europe and in the Asian regions of the old tsarist empire, and to extend this revolutionary process to new sections of the globe.

"The most characteristic feature of this International," Lenin stated in an article written shortly after the Comintern's formation, was that it *"has already begun to develop,* to a certain extent, into a *union of Soviet Socialist Republics."*

The International Working Men's Association (First International) — founded in 1864 and led by Karl Marx and Frederick Engels during its decade-long existence — "laid the foundation of the proletarian, international struggle for socialism," Lenin wrote.

The Socialist (Second) International, founded in 1889, in which Engels played a leading role until his death in 1895, "marked a period in which the soil was prepared for the broad, mass spread of the movement in a number of countries." The growth of this International, Lenin said, "proceeded in *breadth*, at the cost of a temporary drop in the revolutionary level, a temporary strengthening of opportunism, which in the end led to the disgraceful collapse of this International.

"The Third International actually emerged in 1918," Lenin continued, "when the long years of struggle against opportunism and social-chauvinism, especially during the war, led to the formation of Communist Parties in a number of countries. . . .

"The Third International has gathered the fruits of the work of the Second International, discarded its opportunist, social-chauvinist, bourgeois and petty-bourgeois dross, and *has begun to implement* the dictatorship of the proletariat."[2]

The establishment in Russia of a revolutionary government of the workers and exploited peasants in October 1917 and the expropriation of the landlords and capitalists over the following year polarized the world working-class movement. As Lenin noted, "working people all over the world have instinctively grasped the significance of the Soviets as an instrument in the proletarian struggle and as a form of the proletarian state. But the 'leaders', corrupted by opportunism, still continue to worship bourgeois democracy, which they still call 'democracy' in general."[3]

The struggle between proponents of these counterposed views irreversibly deepened the split in the German workers' movement. Before 1914, the SPD and the trade unions linked with it had been the most powerfully organized and politically authoritative contingent of the international workers' movement. By the end of 1918, the SPD had broken apart, giving birth to three rival parties.

The "majority" SPD defended the rule of the industrialists, bankers, and landowners and had assumed responsibility for administering the German capitalist state. The Spartacists, along with other revolutionists, formed the Communist Party of Germany, which strove to overthrow capitalist rule and establish a state defending the interests of the working class and its allies.

Between them stood the USPD. After the November revolution the majority of its leaders quickly realigned themselves with the SPD; together with a minority of the USPD ranks, these centrist leaders were to rejoin the SPD within four years. The majority of the USPD's working-class ranks, on the other hand, and a minority of its leaders radicalized after November 1918 and were won in 1920 to a fusion with the KPD.

In January 1919 the German government, now headed by the SPD alone, unleashed right-wing military units against the revolutionary workers of Berlin, dealing them a sharp defeat. Workers in other regions of Germany were subjected to similar armed attacks in subsequent months. The impact of this confrontation sped the polarization of the international workers' movement into two opposed camps. Taken together with the example of the Russian revolution, the German experience convinced millions of workers of the need for a new, Communist International.

*   *   *

The Communist International in Lenin's Time, the series of volumes of which this book is a part, aims to make more accessible to today's readers the example and lessons of the international Communist movement that grew out of the Russian revolution and that was led by the Bolshevik Party (renamed the Russian Communist Party [Bolsheviks] in March 1918). The series seeks to trace the historic continuity of revolutionary Marxism through the struggle to launch the Communist International and the first five years of its activity — the years during which its policies were shaped by Lenin and the team of Marxist revolutionists led by him. The program, strategy, and organizational conceptions hammered out at that time remain the foundation for all those seeking to chart a revolutionary course in the changed conditions of today's world, more than half a century later.

The volumes of *The Communist International in Lenin's Time* will present the discussion and debates within this worldwide movement — debates that were shaped by the great political upheavals of the first quarter of this century. It will include the key exchanges between the leaders of the new International and various reformist, centrist, and anarcho-syndicalist currents.

A previously published volume of the series, *Lenin's Struggle for a Revolutionary International,* covers the years of preparatory struggle from 1907 through 1916. A forthcoming volume will include materials from the years 1917-18, focusing on the impact of the victorious October revolution in Russia on the prospects for forming a new, revolutionary International.

The series will follow the Comintern's development from its foundation until the end of 1923. Seven volumes will publish the complete resolutions and proceedings of the first four Comintern congresses, held in March 1919, July-August 1920, June-July 1921, and November-December 1922. Companion volumes will record the decisions, debates, and activity of the Comintern's elected Executive Committee (ECCI) during the years between these congresses, as well as key developments in various national Communist parties that shaped the course of deliberations at the congresses. Another volume will cover the year following the Fourth Congress, including the expanded ECCI plenum of June 1923. The Communist International's work among trade unionists, women, anti-imperialist fighters from colonial countries, and young workers will be the topics of additional books.

*   *   *

The present volume is divided into two parts. The first focuses on the German revolution and the founding of the German Communist Party. The second takes up the international debate on Soviet power, as well as the preparations by the Bolsheviks for the March 1919 founding congress of the Communist International.

Part one, "The German Revolution," takes up the first two months of the German revolution leading to the confrontation of the revolutionary workers with the SPD-led capitalist government in the Berlin uprising of January 1919. It also records the attempt of the Russian Soviet government after the November 9 revolution to form a united front with the new German republic against international capitalist reaction and to come to the aid of the embattled workers, soldiers, and peasants who had overturned the kaiser's regime.

Chapters 4 and 5 focus on the strategic and tactical debate among German Communists. These chapters include extensive excerpts from the stenographic record of the German Communist Party's founding congress. The formation of this party posed the question of how vanguard revolutionary forces should be organized, whether they should take the name *Communist*, and under what conditions they would favor organizing a new International. The KPD congress also discussed counterposed positions on Communist participation in the national assembly elections called by the SPD-led government and on the broader question of revolutionists' participation in elections in capitalist countries. It debated whether and how to form a strategic alliance with the exploited peasantry in Germany. All of these problems were discussed extensively in subsequent years in the world Communist movement.

The German Communists' policies diverged markedly on many questions from those advocated and carried out by the Russian Com-

munist Party. The newly formed German party's political strengths
and weaknesses were sharply tested in the January 1919 Berlin uprising.

The story of the KPD's formation also sheds light on the evolution
of the Spartacist forces led by Luxemburg and Liebknecht. This important revolutionary current increasingly moved toward the Bolsheviks politically through the experience of the First World War,
the October 1917 revolution in Russia, and the 1918-19 revolutionary events in Germany.

Luxemburg, Liebknecht, and their followers had waged a sharp
struggle against the SPD majority leadership, whom they branded as
enemies of the workers' movement. The Spartacists were also sharply critical of the centrist current in the SPD, personified by Karl
Kautsky, which later led the USPD. While the USPD leaders opposed many of the majority SPD leadership's policies on the war,
they supported the principle of "national defense" and aimed at no
more than a return to the prewar unity and practice of the SPD and
the Second International. Nonetheless, during the war the Spartacists
resisted making a clean political break with the Kautskyist current
and held back from beginning to build a new, revolutionary party.

Like the Zimmerwald Left, the international revolutionary Marxist
current established in 1915 under the leadership of the Bolsheviks,
the Spartacists called for a new International. Unlike the Bolsheviks,
however, they did not see the necessity of insisting that this International must be purged of all forms of opportunism, including its centrist form. They also disagreed with other aspects of Bolshevik policy regarding the party and its role in the revolutionary struggle and
with the Bolsheviks' stand on the worker-peasant alliance, land reform, and the national and colonial liberation movements.[4]

During the initial months of the 1918-19 German revolution, the
forces around Luxemburg and Liebknecht came to view themselves
more as a Communist current pursuing the same goals as the Bolsheviks. Although the Spartacists lacked political homogeneity, and
although all wings of their movement disagreed with many important
policies of the Soviet Communist leadership, they were clearly
evolving politically toward Bolshevism. This process was still unfolding when Liebknecht and Luxemburg were murdered in January
1919 by right-wing armed detachments launched against the Berlin
workers by the SPD-led government. Subsequent volumes will record how the German Communists were won to the Comintern and
became members of its leadership bodies.

In part two of this volume, "Toward Launching the Communist

International," the framework broadens to the international preparations led by the Bolsheviks in late 1918 and early 1919 to launch the new, Communist International.

Chapter 7 focuses on the exchange between Lenin and Kautsky on the Russian workers' and peasants' government and its lessons regarding the dictatorship of the proletariat.

Chapter 8 contains selections from the debate on Bolshevism at the international conference organized by procapitalist Social Democratic currents in Bern, Switzerland, in February 1919 in an attempt to revive the defunct Second International.

The final chapter traces the Bolsheviks' work to prepare the launching of the new, Communist International and records the German Communist leaders' initial opposition to its formation at that time. It will be left to a companion volume, *The Founding of the Communist International,* to show how these objections were overcome in the course of the March 1919 international Communist congress. The congress proceedings published in that volume will also include Lenin's resolution and report "Bourgeois Democracy and the Dictatorship of the Proletariat," which is his concise assessment of the central issue debated throughout the documents in the present volume.

Leaving aside articles by Lenin, 65 percent of the documents in this book have never before been published in English. Others of these documents exist only in hard-to-obtain translations published more than fifty years ago. The availability of documents in other English-language editions has been taken into account in selecting material for this volume. Lenin's pamphlet, *The Proletarian Revolution and the Renegade Kautsky,* although widely available in English translation, has nonetheless been included in full because of its centrality to the political debate on Soviet power recorded in this volume.

The present volume also includes as an appendix the 1919 program of the Russian Communist Party, adopted in the same month as the Comintern founding congress.

*   *   *

Except for articles by Lenin, the documents in this collection have been newly translated. Occasional interpolations by the editor have been enclosed in square brackets. The writings of Lenin have been reproduced from the most recent English-language edition of the *Collected Works* published by Progress Publishers in Moscow. One item by Lenin not found in that edition has been newly translated from the fifth Russian edition of his collected works.[5]

The aim of this work is not solely to provide a documentary record, but to do so in such a way as to tell the story of the Communist International through its decisions, polemics, and major experiences in struggle.

A running commentary by the editor explains the historical background to the documents and provides a brief account of the main events that shaped them. The editor has made no attempt to provide a historical balance sheet or assessment of the events described. Where appropriate, however, the commentary indicates the subsequent assessment of elected bodies and central leaders of the Communist International during its first five years.

Footnotes by the editor, giving the source of documents and explanatory information, are printed at the end of each chapter. In some cases the authors of documents provided footnotes; these are indicated by asterisks (*) and are printed at the bottom of the page.

Ellipsis points (. . .) indicate the omission of material from a translated document. In the text of articles by Lenin, however, we have retained the Progress Publishers' style of using ellipsis points, as in Russian, to show a pause in the author's thought.

A glossary is provided of individuals, publications, and political currents mentioned in this volume. A chronology lists important dates relating to documents in this collection. Existing English-language editions of related material are indicated in a brief bibliography and in the footnotes.

*   *   *

This book was made possible by a large number of collaborators who helped to collect source material, research historical questions, and translate documents into English.

Robert Dees was responsible for a large part of the research for this volume, helped draft chapter 5, and assisted in writing the commentary as a whole. Bruce Marcus of Pathfinder Press lent editorial assistance and organized the final copyediting and production. Wilfried Dubois of Frankfurt, Germany, helped resolve many of the most obstinate research problems.

Research and interpretation of documents of the German revolution was greatly assisted by Rudolf Segall and his colleagues Helmut Dahmer and Reiner Tosstorff of the Verein zur wissenschaftlichen Erforschung und Aufarbeitung historischen Kulturguts (Association for Scholarly Research and Presentation of the Historical Heritage), Frankfurt. Wolrad Bode and Lüko Willms helped locate important source material.

Others who assisted research work included Fritz Keller in Austria; David Bowie in Britain; Kay Riddell in Canada; Derek Jeffers and Nat London in France; Mehdi Assar and H. Siamak for Iran; Alejandro Gálvez in Mexico; Joost Kircz and Pierre Rousset in the Netherlands; Gérard Donzé and Pierre Hirsch in Switzerland; Fuat Orçun for Turkey; and Jeff Hamill, John Keillor, Ron Richards, and Bob Wilkinson in the United States.

We wish to acknowledge the help of Pierre Broué, Richard Debo, Yoichi Murata, and Hermann Weber, who advised us on aspects of Communist history.

The translations, commentary, and choice of documents, of course, are the responsibility of the editor alone.

Among the many librarians and libraries who were of substantial assistance in locating documents were Geneviève Dreyfus and the Bibliothèque de Documentation Internationale Contemporaine in Paris; Francesca Gorri and the Fondazione Giangiacomo Feltrinelli of Milan; Hilja Kukk and the Hoover Institution of Stanford, California; Marcel van der Linden and the late Vilém Kahan of the International Institute of Social History, Amsterdam; Jane Cooper and the University of Toronto Library, Toronto; and Ethel Lobman and the Tamiment Library, New York.

Staff translators were Robert Dees from French and German, Bob Cantrick from German, and Sonja Franceta from Russian. Other translators for this volume were Ron Allen, Jeff Hamill, George Myland, and Rebecca Park (from Russian); John Hawkins (from German); and Mehdi Assar (from Farsi). Alix Holt, Denis Peillard, and Rudolf Segall also advised us regarding difficult points in the translation.

John Riddell
May 1986 □

Notes

1. V.I. Lenin, "Letter to the Workers of Europe and America," in *Collected Works* (Moscow: Progress Publishers, 1974), vol. 28, pp. 429-30.
2. Lenin, "The Third International and Its Place in History," in *Collected Works,* vol. 29, pp. 306-7.
3. Ibid., p. 308.
4. Many of the Spartacists' differences with the Bolsheviks are explained in documents in this volume. For the Spartacists' and Bolsheviks' contrasting attitudes to the centrists and their differences regarding the right of oppressed peoples to self-determination, see John Riddell, ed., *Lenin's Struggle for a Rev-*

olutionary International: Documents 1907-16, the Preparatory Years (New York: Monad Press, 1984), a volume of *The Communist International in Lenin's Time*.

5. See "Remarks on Theses 'Foundations of the Third International,'" printed in chapter 9, page 456.

Prologue:

Letter to the Workers
of Europe and America[1]
by V.I. Lenin

January 21, 1919

Comrades, at the end of my letter to American workers dated August 20, 1918,[2] I wrote that we are in a besieged fortress so long as the other armies of the world socialist revolution do not come to our aid. I added that the workers are breaking away from their social-traitors, the Gomperses and Renners. The workers are slowly but surely coming round to communist and Bolshevik tactics.

Less than five months have passed since those words were written, and it must be said that during this time, in view of the fact that workers of various countries have turned to communism and Bolshevism, the maturing of the world proletarian revolution has proceeded very rapidly.

Then, on August 20, 1918, only our Party, the Bolshevik Party, had resolutely broken with the old, Second International of 1889-1914 which so shamefully collapsed during the imperialist war of 1914-18. Only our Party had unreservedly taken the new path, from the socialists and social-democracy which had disgraced themselves by alliance with the predatory bourgeoisie, to communism; from petty-bourgeois reformism and opportunism, which had thoroughly permeated, and now permeate, the official Social-Democratic and socialist parties, to genuinely proletarian, revolutionary tactics.

Now, on January 12, 1919, we already see quite a number of communist proletarian parties, not only within the boundaries of the former tsarist empire—in Latvia, Finland and Poland, for example—but also in Western Europe—Austria, Hungary, Holland and, lastly, Germany. The *foundation* of a genuinely proletarian, genuinely internationalist, genuinely revolutionary Third International, the *Communist International*, became *a fact* when the German Spartacus

---

Footnotes to the prologue begin on page 5.

League, with such world-known and world-famous leaders, with such staunch working-class champions as Liebknecht, Rosa Luxemburg, Clara Zetkin and Franz Mehring, made a clean break with socialists like Scheidemann and Südekum, social-chauvinists (socialists in words, but chauvinists in deeds) who have earned eternal shame by their alliance with the predatory, imperialist German bourgeoisie and Wilhelm II. It became a fact when the Spartacus League changed its name to the Communist Party of Germany. Though it has not yet been officially inaugurated, the Third International actually exists.

No class-conscious worker, no sincere socialist can now fail to see how dastardly was the betrayal of socialism by those who, like the Mensheviks and "Socialist-Revolutionaries" in Russia, the Scheidemanns and Südekums in Germany, the Renaudels and Vanderveldes in France, the Hendersons and Webbs in Britain, and Gompers and Co. in America, supported "their" bourgeoisie in the 1914–18 war. That war fully exposed itself as an imperialist, reactionary, predatory war both on the part of Germany and on the part of the capitalists of Britain, France, Italy and America. The latter are now beginning to quarrel over the spoils, over the division of Turkey, Russia, the African and Polynesian colonies, the Balkans, and so on. The hypocritical phrases uttered by Wilson and his followers about "democracy" and "union of nations" are exposed with amazing rapidity when we see the capture of the left bank of the Rhine by the French bourgeoisie, the capture of Turkey (Syria, Mesopotamia) and part of Russia (Siberia, Archangel, Baku, Krasnovodsk, Ashkhabad, and so on) by the French, British and American capitalists, and the increasing animosity over the division of the spoils between Italy and France, France and Britain, Britain and America, America and Japan.

Beside the craven, half-hearted "socialists" who are thoroughly imbued with the prejudices of bourgeois democracy, who yesterday defended "their" imperialist governments and today limit themselves to platonic "protests" against military intervention in Russia — beside these there is a growing number of people in the Allied countries who have taken the communist path, the path of Maclean, Debs, Loriot, Lazzari and Serrati. These are men who have realised that if imperialism is to be crushed and the victory of socialism and lasting peace ensured, the bourgeoisie must be overthrown, bourgeois parliaments abolished, and Soviet power and the dictatorship of the proletariat established.

Then, on August 20, 1918, the proletarian revolution was confined to Russia, and "Soviet government", i.e., the system under which *all* state power is vested in Soviets of Workers', Soldiers' and Peasants' Deputies, still seemed to be (and actually was) only a Russian institution.

Now, on January 12, 1919, we see a mighty "Soviet" movement not only in parts of the former tsarist empire, for example, in Latvia, Poland and the Ukraine, but also in West-European countries, in neutral countries (Switzerland, Holland and Norway) and in countries which have suffered from the war (Austria and Germany). The revolution in Germany — which is particularly important and characteristic as one of the most advanced capitalist countries — at once assumed "Soviet" forms. The whole course of the German revolution, and particularly the struggle of the Spartacists, i.e., the true and only representatives of the proletariat, against the alliance of those treacherous scoundrels, the Scheidemanns and Südekums, with the bourgeoisie — all this clearly shows how history has *formulated* the question in relation to Germany:

"Soviet power" or the bourgeois parliament, no matter under what signboard (such as "National" or "Constituent" Assembly) it may appear.

That is how *world history* has formulated the question. Now, this can and must be said without any exaggeration.

"Soviet power" is the second historical step, or stage, in the development of the proletarian dictatorship. The first step was the Paris Commune. The brilliant analysis of its nature and significance given by Marx in his *The Civil War in France* showed that the Commune had created a *new type* of state, a *proletarian state*. Every state, including the most democratic republic, is nothing but a machine for the suppression of one class by another. The proletarian state is a machine for the suppression of the bourgeoisie by the proletariat. Such suppression is necessary because of the furious, desperate resistance put up by the landowners and capitalists, by the entire bourgeoisie and all their hangers-on, by all the exploiters, who stop at nothing when their overthrow, when the expropriation of the expropriators, begins.

The bourgeois parliament, even the most democratic in the most democratic republic, in which the property and rule of the capitalists are preserved, is a machine for the suppression of the working millions by small groups of exploiters. The socialists, the fighters for the emancipation of the working people from exploitation, had to utilise the bourgeois parliaments as a platform, as a base, for propaganda, agitation, and organisation *as long as our struggle was confined to the framework of the bourgeois system*: Now that world history has brought up the question of destroying the whole of that system, of overthrowing and suppressing the exploiters, of passing from capitalism to socialism, it would be a shameful betrayal of the proletariat, deserting to its class enemy, the bourgeoisie, and being a traitor and a renegade to confine oneself to bourgeois parliamentarism, to bourgeois democracy, to present it as "democracy" in general, to obscure its *bourgeois* character, to forget that as long as capitalist property exists universal suffrage is an instrument of the bourgeois state.

The three trends in world socialism, about which the Bolshevik press has been speaking incessantly since 1915, stand out with particular distinctness today, against the background of the bloody struggle and civil war in Germany.

Karl Liebknecht is a name known to the workers of all countries. Everywhere, and particularly in the Allied countries, it is the symbol of a leader's devotion to the interests of the proletariat and loyalty to the socialist revolution. It is the symbol of really sincere, really self-sacrificing and ruthless struggle against capitalism. It is a symbol of uncompromising struggle against imperialism not in words, but in deeds, of self-sacrificing struggle precisely in the period when "one's own" country is flushed with imperialist victories. With Liebknecht and the Spartacists are all those German socialists who have remained honest and really revolutionary, all the best and dedicated men among the proletariat, the exploited masses who are seething with indignation and among whom there is a growing readiness for revolution.

Against Liebknecht are the Scheidemanns, the Südekums and the whole gang of despicable lackeys of the Kaiser and the bourgeoisie. They are just as much traitors to socialism as the Gomperses and Victor Bergers, the Hendersons and Webbs, the Renaudels and Vanderveldes. They represent that top section of workers who have been bribed by the bourgeoisie, those whom we Bolsheviks called (applying the name to the Russian Südekums, the Mensheviks) "agents of the bourgeoisie in the working-class movement", and to whom the best socialists in America gave the magnificently expressive and very fitting title: "labour lieutenants of the capitalist class". They represent *the latest*, "modern", *type* of socialist treachery, for in all the civilised, advanced countries the bourgeoisie rob—either by colonial oppression or by financially extracting "gain" from formally independent weak countries—they rob a population many times larger than that of "their own" country. This is the economic factor that enables the imperialist bourgeoisie to obtain superprofits, part of which is used to bribe the top section of the proletariat and convert it into a reformist, opportunist petty bourgeoisie that fears revolution.

Between the Spartacists and the Scheidemann men are the wavering, spineless "Kautskyites", who in words are "independent", but in deeds are entirely, and all along the line, *dependent* upon the bourgeoisie and the Scheidemann men one day, upon the Spartacists the next, some following the former and some the latter. These are people without ideas, without backbone, without policy, without honour, without conscience, the living embodiment of the bewilderment of philistines who stand for socialist revolution in words, but are actually incapable of understanding it when it has begun and, in renegade fashion, defend "democracy" in general, that is, *actually* defend *bourgeois* democracy.

In every capitalist country, every thinking worker will, in the situation varying with national and historical conditions, perceive these three main trends among the socialists and among the syndicalists, for the imperialist war and the incipient world proletarian revolution engender identical ideological and political trends all over the world. ☐

Notes

1. Excerpted from V.I. Lenin, *Collected Works* (Moscow: Progress Publishers, 1974), vol. 28, pp. 429-34.

2. Lenin, *Collected Works*, vol. 28, pp. 62-75.

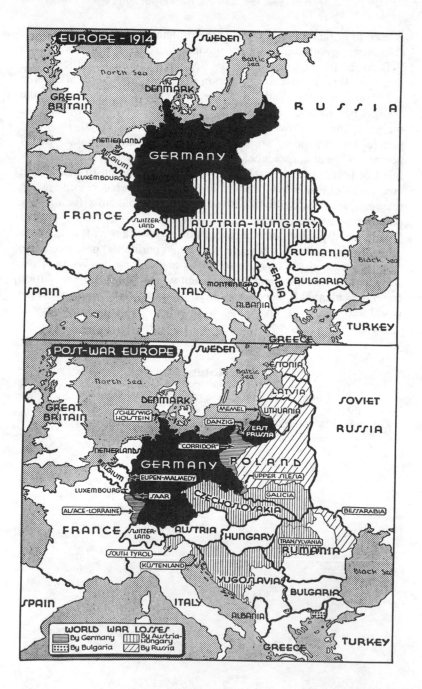

EUROPE - 1914

SWEDEN
North Sea
Baltic Sea
DENMARK
GREAT BRITAIN
NETHERLAND
BELGIUM
LUXEMBOURG
GERMANY
RUSSIA
FRANCE
SWITZERLAND
AUSTRIA-HUNGARY
RUMANIA
Black Sea
SPAIN
ITALY
MONTENEGRO
SERBIA
BULGARIA
ALBANIA
TURKEY
GREECE

POST-WAR EUROPE

SWEDEN
North Sea
Baltic Sea
ESTONIA
LATVIA
GREAT BRITAIN
DENMARK
SCHLESWIG HOLSTEIN
MEMEL
LITHUANIA
DANZIG
EAST PRUSSIA
SOVIET RUSSIA
NETHERLAND
"CORRIDOR"
BELGIUM
GERMANY
POLAND
LUXEMBOURG
EUPEN-MALMEDY
UPPER SILESIA
SAAR
GALICIA
ALSACE-LORRAINE
CZECHOSLOVAKIA
BESSARABIA
SWITZERLAND
AUSTRIA
FRANCE
HUNGARY
TRANSYLVANIA
SOUTH TYROL
RUMANIA
KÜSTENLAND
YUGOSLAVIA
Black Sea
SPAIN
ITALY
BULGARIA
ALBANIA
TURKEY
GREECE

WORLD WAR LOSSES
By Germany   By Austria-Hungary
By Bulgaria   By Russia

6

Introduction

For millions of working people locked in the First World War, the Russian October revolution of 1917 offered a hopeful new perspective of how the slaughter could be brought to an end.[1] Its example showed that mass action by workers, soldiers, and peasants could install a revolutionary government committed to ending the war and abolishing capitalist exploitation and oppression. The spread of such revolutionary action to all the warring countries could restore the international solidarity of the toilers. It could make possible the building of a new world revolutionary organization in place of the politically bankrupt Socialist "Second" International, which had been shattered by the war's outbreak in August 1914.

The new Soviet government's first decree appealed to the governments and peoples of the world for an immediate armistice and a democratic peace based on national self-determination and a renunciation of annexationist goals.[2] The Soviet government published the secret agreements of the tsarist regime and capitalist Provisional Government with their wartime allies and repudiated the territories these treaties had promised to Russia. The Soviet government announced that it was leaving the war. When its proposal for peace talks among all warring countries was rejected, it concluded an armistice, and subsequently a peace treaty, with the German government and its allies. The Communist Party of Russia (Bolsheviks) (RCP), which had organized and led the Russian workers and peasants to power, called on the world's toilers to not rely on the governments of their exploiters to achieve peace. Instead they should follow the Russian road, and win peace, land, and bread through a workers' and peasants' revolution.

In August 1914 the Second International had collapsed in ruins. Most leaders of its component parties had betrayed its working-class principles by allying with their respective capitalist classes in herding the workers and peasants to slaughter. Since that time, the Bolsheviks had called on the Socialist movement to break with the right-

---

Footnotes to the introduction begin on page 20.

wing opportunist and centrist currents that had led the mass workers' parties to this disaster. They called for a new, revolutionary International that could unite workers' organizations in renewing the world struggle for socialism and liberation of the colonial peoples. Achievement of this goal became possible with the Bolsheviks' victory in Russia, which gave their program authority among hundreds of thousands of working people throughout Europe and the world.

Before the new International could be founded, however, revolutionary action had to spread beyond Russia's frontiers. During its first year, the Soviet republic was blockaded and invaded by both of the warring imperialist alliances, who now joined forces with the counterrevolutionary armies of the Russian landlords and capitalists. The workers' and peasants' government waged a desperate struggle for survival. Although it had won the sympathy of millions in central and western Europe, workers and farmers there had not yet been able to break the yoke of their ruling classes' war machine. Struggles by these working people, although increasing in scope, did not yet significantly ease the pressure on the Soviet regime. Revolution remained confined to the territory of the Russian Soviet republic, which initially shrank under the blows of internal civil war and foreign invasion.

The Bolsheviks' supporters outside Russia were organized in small and isolated nuclei, without mass influence. No other Communist parties had yet been organized beyond the borders of the old tsarist empire. The Bolsheviks still fought alone.

The Soviet republic's isolation was finally broken in October and November 1918 by the outbreak of revolution in Germany, Austria-Hungary, and Bulgaria. These upheavals forced the governments of these countries, who with Turkey made up the Central Powers, to sue for peace. The Allies (Entente),[3] the rival war alliance of the governments of Britain, France, the United States, Japan, Italy, and some smaller states, was triumphant. Yet the November 11 armistice did not halt the revolutionary upsurge. It deepened in Germany and parts of the former Austro-Hungarian Empire, as workers and peasants fought to shake off capitalist exploitation. It spread to Poland, where workers' councils were formed in all major centers. Within a few months, Communist parties were organized in several European countries. Above all the German revolution and the founding of the German Communist Party in December 1918 signaled to the Bolsheviks in Russia that the time to organize the new International had arrived. Its founding congress was held in Moscow in March 1919.

Second to the events in Russia, the key revolutionary experience for the new International was the struggle opened by the overthrow of the kaiser's regime in Germany in November 1918. The German revolution accelerated the divisions in the workers' movement in that country. The Social Democratic Party of Germany (SPD) and its allies sought to preserve the German capitalist state and reform it; the German Communists strove to establish a revolutionary government based on workers' and soldiers' councils.[4] In early 1919 the conflict came to civil war, in which the German proletariat was defeated. There were additional revolutionary opportunities during the subsequent four years, but the German workers were unable to achieve victory. The experiences and errors of German Communists, however, were central in the debates through which the Communist International hammered out the program and strategy for the struggle for a revolutionary government of workers and farmers.

Imperial Germany: the Road to Revolution

The German revolution of 1918 was shaped by the outcome of the bourgeois-democratic uprising that had erupted seventy years earlier. In 1848 Germany was still an economically backward assembly of feudal kingdoms, principalities, and "free cities." It was shaken that year by a democratic revolution under liberal bourgeois leadership, aimed at achieving German national unification and sweeping away other feudal barriers to capitalist development. The more radical wing of this movement was composed of the middle-class democracy, which, in the first stages of the revolution, united under its banner the peasantry and the young, still small German proletariat.

But the irresolution of both the bourgeois leadership and most of its democratic left wing isolated the proletarian and peasant fighters and brought the revolution to defeat in 1849. Frightened by this taste of popular revolution, the majority of the German bourgeoisie subsequently moved into an alliance with the landowning class that ruled Prussia, the largest and strongest of the German states. German national unity was achieved in 1871 under the government of Baron Otto von Bismarck. The bourgeoisie won a unified state, and its industrial and financial holdings expanded rapidly. But the industrial and banking capitalists were still far from exercising unchallenged hegemony. The German state preserved a substantial part of the power and privileges of the Prussian monarchy and the junkers, the landlord nobility of Germany east of the Elbe river, who were now becoming rich capitalist farmers. In 1873 Karl Marx summed up the new German Empire as "nothing but a police-guarded military despotism, embellished with parliamentary forms, alloyed with feudal admixture."[5]

The Prussian king became kaiser (emperor) of Germany, but the other feudal dynasties preserved their thrones. In 1914 Germany still encompassed four kingdoms, five grand duchies, twelve other principalities, and three "free cities." In Germany's eastern provinces, a subject Polish national minority, composed in large part of laborers on the farms of German landowners, struggled for its national rights. In Alsace-Lorraine, annexed from France in 1871, grievances against German imperial rule were strongly felt. A substantial fraction of the German nationality, on the other hand, remained outside its borders, chiefly in the Austro-Hungarian Empire. A parliament, the Reichstag, existed, but the government and army were responsible only to the German kaiser. The officer corps of the army was drawn almost entirely from the landed aristocracy, and it held significant power in its own right, strongly influencing the kaiser. The junkers were also predominant in the imperial state bureaucracy.

Forty-three of Germany's 100 richest families were from the aristocracy. On their great estates in Prussia and Mecklenburg, the junkers enjoyed an absolute authority inherited from feudalism over a work force composed of landless proletarians and peasants possessing only tiny plots. Here the "law on domestic servants" (*Gesindeordnung*) subjected laborers utterly to their master's every whim and denied them the right to any legal recourse.[6]

The junkers' domination of the state was especially firm in Prussia, the kingdom containing a majority of Germany's population. In 1916, of 516 high Prussian officials, 315 were nobles. There the junkers were even able to maintain the three-class system of voting for the Prussian assembly, by which representation was made proportional to the taxes paid by each economic layer of the citizenry. This granted disproportionate representation to the ruling classes and enabled the junkers to dominate the assembly.

This hidebound state structure presided over what was quickly becoming the most modern capitalist economy in Europe. Industrial production had multiplied six times in the four decades before the war, leaving Germany second only to the United States both in industrial production as a whole and in production of iron and steel. Germany ranked first in exports of machinery and electrical equipment. It was emerging as a major imperialist power, whose economic dynamism only heightened the contradictions within its state structure.

Yet German imperialism was at a great disadvantage: it had

emerged too late to build a colonial empire. All wings of the German ruling class allied in a political and military offensive to achieve world-power status and possessions in Europe and in the African and Asian colonies proportionate to the nation's economic strength. This brought Germany into a head-on clash with British and French imperialism in the First World War. The war, in turn, plunged the German empire into social and political crisis.

The Crisis of the German SPD

The explosive development of German industry created a powerful working class. During the last decades of the nineteenth century and the first decade of the twentieth, this class had constructed a mass political party, the Social Democratic Party of Germany (SPD). By 1914 the SPD was a million members strong and the Social Democratic trade unions were even larger.

The SPD was Marxist in its formal program and in its best traditions. But decades of peaceful capitalist expansion had fostered the formation of a privileged layer of the working class — a labor aristocracy. Under conditions of German capitalism's rapid military and economic advance toward world-power status, this layer had been able to make gains giving it a more privileged and secure living standard. Many workers in this layer had come to identify their interests with the success of German imperialism. Basing itself on this layer of the working class, a reformist bureaucracy increasingly strengthened its position in the leadership of the SPD and the trade unions. It joined forces with middle-class elements in the SPD apparatus to begin eroding the revolutionary practice of the party. The SPD was more and more marked by a profound contradiction between word and deed. While still formally committed to revolutionary socialism, the party came to limit its activities in large measure to electioneering and a parliamentary struggle for limited reforms within the framework of the capitalist economic order.

As early as the latter half of the 1890s the initial signs of this degenerative process sparked an intense political struggle within the party. The clash between the revolutionaries and the expanding reformist current in the SPD persisted and grew in sharpness in the years before the war.[7]

Matters were brought abruptly to a head on August 4, 1914. On that day the SPD's deputies in the national parliament, the Reichstag, responded to the declaration of war by declaring their loyalty in this conflict to the German state and by voting unanimously for credits authorizing the war expenses. To symbolize this new status, the party fraction stood for the first time for the traditional "three cheers" for Kaiser Wilhelm II. Henceforth the SPD functioned in close alliance with the imperialist government. The SPD leadership, headed by Friedrich Ebert, worked to block strikes. Many SPD deputies voted for a compulsory labor law. When the Reichstag approved the March 1918 peace of Brest-Litovsk with the Soviet republic, by which German militarism seized vast territories of the former tsarist empire, the SPD managed only an abstention. As German military power flagged, the SPD leadership joined with liberal bourgeois and middle-class forces in encouraging the government to seek a compromise peace in order to avert revolution.

By such actions the SPD was converted from an instrument of working-class struggle into a prop for capitalist rule. While the SPD's new, harmonious collaboration with Germany's rulers brought party and union bureaucrats increased influence and social prestige, it also set them on a collision course with the German working class.

The Second International Collapses

The same process of degeneration gripped the Second International, the association of Social Democratic parties founded in 1889. In case of war, the International was pledged by its 1907 Stuttgart congress decision not only to intervene for the war's speedy termination, but also to strive "to utilize the economic and political crisis created by the war to rouse the masses and thereby hasten the downfall of capitalist class rule."[8] This pledge was reaffirmed at the International's emergency antiwar congress at Basel in 1912. Yet when war was declared, the leaders of the Social Democratic parties in Germany, Austria-Hungary, Britain, France, and Belgium voted for the war budgets, joined in the xenophobic flag-waving, entered informal or formal governmental coalitions to prosecute the war effort, and transformed their parties and the Socialist-led trade unions into instruments of the governmental assault on working people at home and abroad. The International's leading bodies ceased to function. The pro-war leaderships of parties in Germany, Austria-Hungary, Britain, and France broke off all contact with their counterparts on the opposite side of the trenches and did not renew ties while the war lasted.

In launching the war, the capitalist ruling classes had dealt the working-class movement a severe defeat from which it was not to recover for several years. The depth of this defeat was due in part to the impact of the war itself: the incessant patriotic propaganda, the mobilization of millions of worker-conscripts, the vast fratricidal slaughter, the drastic fall in living standards, the elimination of political rights, and the imprisonment of those who resisted. But even more damaging was the impact of the betrayal by the Second International's most authoritative leaders and parties in almost all the warring countries.

Only after a year of war, and against the fierce opposition of the pro-war leaders, was it possible to hold the Zimmerwald conference, the first gathering of Socialist currents that opposed the pro-war course of the majority leadership of the Second International.[9] The Zimmerwald Manifesto's ringing denunciation of the war's imperialist character, its call to workers to renew struggle for their interests as a class, and the mere fact of Socialist unity across the battle lines, inspired workers to renewed activity. Yet the manifesto issued no call for mass revolutionary struggle against the warring imperialist regimes and made serious concessions to petty-bourgeois pacifism. It contained no call for a new, revolutionary International, thereby leaving the door open to reconciliation with the chauvinist betrayers. The movement that issued from the Zimmerwald conference was increasingly divided between two irreconcilable perspectives: that of its centrist majority wing, which more and more sought to resurrect the old International as changes in the wartime situation created openings to pursue this goal, and that of its revolutionary left wing, led by the Bolsheviks and their central leader, V.I. Lenin.

It was not the Zimmerwald movement itself, but a tendency within it — the Bolshevik-led Zimmerwald Left — that provided the nucleus for a revived revolutionary International. The manifesto it proposed at the Zimmerwald conference called for a complete break with the chauvinists within the Socialist parties, including the centrist current led by Karl Kautsky, and for preparations to launch a new, third International, cleansed of opportunism. It proposed a revolutionary struggle to overthrow the capitalist governments as the road to a lasting peace and the liberation of humanity from the system of exploitation and oppression responsible for war.[10] The Zimmerwald Left won increasing support over the year and a half leading up to the opening of the democratic revolution in Russia in March 1917.

The Spartacus Tendency

It took the German workers' movement many months to begin to recover from the demoralizing impact of the August 1914 betrayal. At first there was no public indication of the deep disagreements within the party. In an internal meeting of the party's parliamentary fraction on August 3, a minority of fourteen SPD deputies had opposed the party's decision to vote for war credits. Nonetheless, all had submitted to discipline in the Reichstag vote. Then on December 2, SPD Deputy Karl Liebknecht voted alone in the Reichstag against the second set of war credits. "It is an imperialist war," he declared, "fought for capitalist domination of the world market. . . . We must demand a speedy peace, a peace without conquest."[11] A small group of revolutionists in the SPD, led by Liebknecht and Rosa Luxemburg, began that month to publish an underground newsletter. Their publication later adopted the name *Spartacus,* and that became the popular name for their current.

Before the war Luxemburg had headed a revolutionary current that had functioned largely within the party's full-time apparatus, with little independent base among the working-class ranks of the party. Now it began to develop links with militants seeking to build a new leadership in the factories. By mid-1915, the Spartacists were in touch with activists in 300 localities and had established a substantial network for distributing underground literature.

As the number of war dead grew and the social consequences of the war were felt more acutely, opposition to the SPD leadership's policy mounted in the party ranks and in the working class. A centrist current in the party apparatus moved to take the leadership of this opposition and channel it in directions they hoped could head off a revolutionary crisis. Twenty-two SPD Reichstag deputies joined Liebknecht on December 29, 1915, in violating party discipline by voting against war credits. This broad opposition current soon won massive support in the party membership, taking the leadership of the party organizations in Berlin, Leipzig, Bremen, and other key industrial centers. The SPD majority leadership moved to safeguard its control of the party machinery, expelling thirty-three oppositional deputies from the Reichstag fraction in March 1916.

The first national conference of the opposition, in January 1917, took only a very limited decision to maintain communications and to work to "preserve party principles and party statutes . . . against the threatening conduct of the party Executive Committee."[12] Nevertheless, they were promptly expelled. The SPD was left with only 170,000 members, while 120,000 went with the opposition to form the Independent Social Democratic Party of Germany (USPD).

Far from constituting a revolutionary party, the USPD was a

heterogeneous bloc formed in opposition to the majority leadership's war policy, which its various wings opposed for widely divergent reasons. The USPD included Eduard Bernstein, who since 1899 had advocated revising the fundamental tenets of Marxism and had opposed socialist revolution; Karl Kautsky, the best-known defender of Marxism against the revisionists in the first decade of the century but now a supporter of German national defense in the war; and many leaders who sought no more than for the SPD to return to the good old days of prewar unity and stability. But the USPD also attracted many militant workers who were seeking a revolutionary alternative to the SPD betrayers.

Revolutionary Socialists divided over how to respond to the USPD's formation. The goal of the Spartacus group was to build a revolutionary party. But its leaders feared that they were still too small to do this and that if they tried to launch the new party at that time they would be overwhelmed by repression, cut off from the USPD's working-class base, and reduced to an insignificant sect. They therefore worked within the USPD as an informally organized public faction, hoping to win a majority in its ranks. A smaller and less influential revolutionary current, the Bremen Left, remained outside the USPD and developed relations with like-minded groups in some other cities. The Bremen Left called for forming a separate revolutionary party immediately, but was still too weak to undertake this task alone.

The Soviet Republic Under Siege

In November 1917 Russian workers and peasants took the helm of a country utterly exhausted by war. Millions of soldiers had been killed or crippled, and a growing majority of the worker and peasant ranks were unwilling to continue fighting and dying. With the economy in ruins, working people faced spreading hunger. When the Soviet appeal for general peace negotiations met no response and the German government opened a new offensive on the Russian front, the Soviet republic was compelled to conclude a separate peace with Germany and the other Central Powers. By the terms of the peace of Brest-Litovsk, signed March 3, 1918, Germany occupied territories containing one third of the population, 73 percent of coal production, and 89 percent of the iron ore production of the former tsarist empire. German generals then marched beyond the limits set by the treaty, occupying independent Finland and the Ukraine as well as territories the treaty had allocated to Russia. Independent Soviet governments in the Ukraine, Belorussia, Latvia, Estonia, and Finland were over-thrown by German imperialism.

Meanwhile, the rival imperialist alliance, the Entente, landed armies on Russia's coasts. The British and Japanese governments occupied the eastern port of Vladivostok, while London and Washington took the northern ports of Murmansk, Arkhangelsk, and surrounding territory. The Entente's agents also promoted counterrevolution against the Soviet regime. In May 1918 their clients, the Czech Legion, rebelled in central Russia and linked up with White Guard armies of the landlords and capitalists.[13] Russia was plunged into full-scale civil war.

The Russian capitalists, who still owned much of the industry, began widespread sabotage in support of the White armies. Many rich peasants went over to the counterrevolution. In response, beginning in mid-1918, the Bolsheviks organized poor peasants' committees in the countryside and in the latter half of that year expropriated the remaining industrial capitalists and consolidated the basis for centralized economic planning. In the face of mounting counterrevolutionary violence, these measures could not halt the drastic decline of production. Yet Soviet power survived. The continuing World War still prevented the rival imperialist powers from undertaking a direct, large-scale invasion of the Soviet republic. And the newly organized Red Army was able in September 1918 to halt for a time the advance of the counterrevolutionary armies and win a respite for the beleaguered Soviet state.

The Approach of Revolution in the West

In August 1918, the World War entered its fifth year. The workers' movement had not yet been able, in any country outside Russia, to challenge capitalist rule or to force their rulers to conclude peace. The war remained a deadlock between the rival imperialist alliances. It had become a battle of attrition, in which neither side was able to secure a decisive advantage on the battlefield, and each sought to exhaust the human reserves and productive capacity of its adversaries. Germany had secured the majority of military victories, particularly on the eastern front against Russia, but had won no strategic advantage. Meanwhile the superiority of the Allied powers in raw materials, productive capacity, and labor power had increased, particularly after the U.S. government officially declared war on Germany in 1917.

The same pressures that had exhausted Russian imperialism now bore down on the overmatched Central Powers. By the war's end, Germany alone had absorbed a casualty list of almost seven million, including 1.7 million dead. Many small peasants were ruined by the impact of war. Workers' real wages fell by a third, and soon there was little food for them to buy. By a conservative estimate, 700,000 in Germany died during the war of the effects of hunger. Only the rich benefited. In near-famine conditions, the owners of the great estates reaped superprofits from rising food prices. The war doubled the profits of Krupp's steel and munitions concern and increased ten times over the holdings of the Stinnes empire in heavy industry and transport. These trends increased social conflicts in Germany and all the other warring countries.

In 1917 and 1918 mass action against the war and its effects on working people spread across Europe. Many struggles after November 1917 expressed strong support for the Soviet republic and its stand against the war. The strike wave in Britain in 1918 embraced more than one million workers. In 1917 a massive mutiny affected fifty-four divisions of the French army. In December of that year a wave of strikes began that led the following May to a walkout by 250,000 Paris workers.

Seven hundred thousand workers in Austria-Hungary joined a general strike in January 1918 sparked by opposition to the Central Powers' harsh demands on Soviet Russia and by support for the Soviet decree on peace. Austro-Hungarian sailors joined the struggle on February 1, temporarily gaining control of half the war fleet. F. Rasch, an Austro-Hungarian sailor condemned to death for his participation in the revolt, said before his execution, "What happened in Russia emboldened us. Over there, a new sun has risen that will shine not only for the Slavs but for all the nations, and it will bring them peace and justice."[14]

The workers' movement in Japan was still weak and subject to intense repression. The Japanese army's intervention in eastern Russia in 1918, however, led to speculative hoarding of rice; the "rice revolts" against the ensuing shortages spread across the country in the summer of 1918, revealing the instability of Japanese militarism.

Only in the United States, which officially entered the war three years after it had begun, was the ruling class offensive able to forestall massive workers' resistance until after the war's conclusion. Even there, however, opposition to the war gave an impulse to the development of revolutionary currents in the labor movement and in the Socialist Party.

The war brought particularly great hardship to small and medium peasants throughout Europe. Conscription took away fathers and sons who performed much of the labor on these small landholdings. Draft animals were directed to the army. The general economic breakdown caused by the war prevented peasants as well as working people in the cities from obtaining the products they needed. The massive casualty lists were a disaster for peasant families. In these ways, the war promoted an alliance of working people in the countryside with the proletariat, while the huge conscript armies served as the instrument where this unity could most readily be forged in action.

Mass protest against the war and its effects, combined with the impact of the Russian revolution, weakened the grip of pro-war chauvinist leaderships on the Socialist movement. The Italian party, whose majority had always opposed the war, moved left under the impact of the Bolshevik revolution, and a revolutionary current began to develop in its ranks. A revolutionary left also gained strength in the U.S. Socialist Party, where right-wing leaders were disregarding the party's official position against U.S. participation in the war.[15] While the German party split in 1917, in France a centrist opposition won a majority at the July 1918 party conference. Most leaders of the growing opposition in these and other countries were centrists, who opposed a revolutionary policy and aimed only to restore the International as it had existed before 1914. But the ranks they led were moving beyond these limited positions, and the revolutionary currents among them, while still small, were winning increasing authority.

The chauvinist leaderships of the trade unions succeeded by and large in maintaining their grip on these organizations. While the war lasted, they prevented workers from using the unions as instruments of struggle against the bosses and the bosses' government. As a result, working-class militancy often flowed into new channels, forging new coordinating and leadership bodies. In Britain, for example, shop stewards' committees united militant and revolutionary-minded workers into a loose national association.

Small Communist nuclei formed in many European countries. While these revolutionists identified with the Bolsheviks, they often had little knowledge of the Soviet party's Marxist program and strategy. The first layers to break from the opportunist leaderships were frequently ultraleftists influenced by anarcho-syndicalism. Other forces attracted to Bolshevism brought with them pacifist and reformist attitudes common in the Social Democratic parties.

Mass protests against hunger broke out in Germany as early as

Above, "We want world peace," demonstration in Czechoslovakia against war and monarchy on October 14; below, revolutionary workers and soldiers in Budapest, October 29.

1916. In May of that year, 50,000 Berlin metal workers went on strike to demand the release of Karl Liebknecht, leader of the revolutionary wing of German socialism, who had been arrested while speaking at an antiwar May Day rally.[16] Revolutionary sailors organized protests in the summer of 1917, hoping that a sailors' general strike could force the conclusion of peace. The movement was crushed and two of its leaders executed. On January 28, 1918, a strike began in Berlin that spread to encompass a million workers in fifty cities. Even the SPD leaders, who since 1914 had been doing everything to promote the war effort, had to send representatives into the strike committee. A workers' council was formed in Berlin, whose demands read in part: "Rapid conclusion of peace without annexations or reparations, on the basis of the peoples' right to self-determination . . . as formulated by the Russian people's representatives at Brest-Litovsk."[17] The strike was broken, and 50,000 strikers were drafted and sent to the front. Lenin commented, "this action of the proletariat in a country doped by the fumes of nationalism and intoxicated with the poison of chauvinism is a fact of cardinal importance and marks a turn of sentiment among the German proletariat.

"We cannot say what course the revolutionary movement in Germany will take. One thing is certain, and that is the existence of a tremendous revolutionary force there that must by iron necessity make its presence felt."[18]

Notes

1. The date of the Bolshevik revolution's triumph was October 25, 1917, by the Old Style (Julian) calendar used in prerevolutionary Russia, and it has therefore become universally known as the October revolution. By the more modern Gregorian calendar then used in the other imperialist countries, it was victorious on November 7. The Gregorian calendar was introduced in Soviet Russia in February 1918. All dates in this book are given by the Gregorian calendar. For events in countries where the Julian calendar was then in use, the Old Style date is given in parentheses.

2. V.I. Lenin, *Collected Works* (hereinafter *CW*) (Moscow: Progress Publishers, 1972), vol. 26, pp. 249-53.

3. While the Triple Entente was the alliance of Britain, France, and Russia, the word *Entente* was also generally used to refer to the Allied powers as a whole.

4. The workers', soldiers', and peasants' councils that were formed across eastern and central Europe in 1918 outside the Soviet republic are referred to in this volume as *councils*, while the corresponding bodies within the Soviet republic are designated by the name by which they have gone down in history: *soviets*.

No such distinction was made by the writers whose works are translated in this volume. They referred to these bodies by the word for councils in their language: *sovety* in Russian; *Räte* in German.

5. Karl Marx and Frederick Engels, *Selected Works* (Moscow: Progress Publishers, 1977), vol. 3, p. 27. An analysis of class relations in Germany in the wake of the 1871 unification and of the consolidation of the German Empire under Bismarck can be found in Engels, "The Role of Force in History," in Marx and Engels, *Selected Works*, vol. 3, pp. 416-28.

6. *Dokumente und Materialien zur Geschichte der deutschen Arbeiterbewegung* (Berlin: Dietz Verlag, 1957), series 2, vol. 2, p. 365.

7. For an outline of the last years of this conflict, see John Riddell, ed., *Lenin's Struggle for a Revolutionary International: Documents, 1907-1916; The Preparatory Years* (New York: Monad Press, 1984), pp. 54-108, a volume of *The Communist International in Lenin's Time*.

8. Ibid., p. 35.

9. Meetings of oppositional Socialist women and youth had preceded the September 1915 Zimmerwald gathering. The resolutions of these three conferences and proceedings of the Zimmerwald conference are printed in Riddell, *Lenin's Struggle*, pp. 276-301.

10. Ibid., pp. 298-301.

11. Ibid., p. 175.

12. Eugen Prager, *Geschichte der U.S.P.D.* (Glashütten im Taunus: Detlev Auvermann, 1970), p. 126. (Reprint of 1922 edition.)

13. In 1914 the tsarist government began to recruit an army of Czechs and Slovaks, the Czech Legion, among prisoners of war and deserters from the Austro-Hungarian army held in Russia. Members of oppressed nationalities within the Austro-Hungarian Empire, these soldiers fought in the Russian army, supposedly for the liberation of their homeland. After the Brest-Litovsk peace, the Allies requested that the Czech Legion, now about 50,000 strong, be sent through Siberia to the western front in France. The Soviet government agreed. In May, when the legion was strung out along hundreds of miles of the Trans-Siberian Railroad, it came into conflict with Soviet authorities and launched a revolt. The Czech Legion's offensive against the Soviet republic was turned back in September 1918.

14. *The International Working-Class Movement: Problems of History and Theory* (Moscow: Progress Publishers, 1984), vol. 4, p. 156.

15. See Farrell Dobbs, *Birth of the Communist Movement 1918-1922*, vol. 2 of *Revolutionary Continuity: Marxist Leadership in the U.S.* (New York: Monad Press, 1983), pp. 19-39.

16. Liebknecht's arrest is described in a Spartacist leaflet printed in Riddell, *Lenin's Struggle*, pp. 452-54.

17. Jörg Berlin, ed., *Die deutsche Revolution 1918/19: Quellen und Dokumente* (Cologne: Pahl-Rugenstein, 1979), p. 102.

18. Lenin, *CW*, vol. 27, p. 546-47.

Revolutionary soldiers in Munich, November 1918.

Part One:
The German Revolution

-1-

The Russian Soviet Republic and the German Revolution of November 1918

On November 9, 1918, a revolutionary upsurge in Germany triumphed, overturning the German Empire and forcing the kaiser to take flight. This victory, following that of the Russian October revolution a year earlier, spurred other revolutionary struggles by the working class and its allies in several countries of central Europe, hastened the formation of Communist parties across the continent, and made the Bolsheviks' perspective of a new, Communist International an immediate organizational possibility.

The stage was set for the German revolution by the failure of the German High Command's summer 1918 offensive in France. The spirit of insurgency in the German army, already evident among its troops in Russia, now spread to its armies on the western front. Whole units began to refuse to fight. Lenin remarked in August:

"German imperialists have been unable to stifle the socialist revolution. The price Germany had to pay for crushing the revolution in Red Latvia, Finland and the Ukraine was the demoralisation of her army. The defeat of Germany on the Western front is largely due to the fact that her old army no longer exists. What the German diplomats joked about — the 'Russification' of the German soldiers — now turns out to be no joke at all, but the bitter truth. The spirit of protest is rising, 'treason' is becoming a common thing in the German army."[1]

Germany's main ally, the decrepit Hapsburg monarchy of the Austro-Hungarian Empire, was even more immediately threatened by the rebellion of its armies and its peoples, and in September it unilaterally appealed to the Allied powers for peace. Another German ally, Bulgaria, was gripped in September by a peasant rebellion. Its army, largely peasant in composition, began to crumble, and the Bulgarian

---

Footnotes to this chapter begin on page 68.

government sued for peace on September 26. No German forces were available to reconstruct the collapsed Bulgarian front. The crisis of Germany's military regime could no longer be delayed.

On October 1, 1918, Lenin raised the urgency of Soviet Russia keeping pace with the events in Germany in the following letter to two of his closest collaborators in the Bolshevik party, Y.M. Sverdlov, head of the Central Committee secretariat, and Leon Trotsky, the leader of the Red Army.

To Y.M. Sverdlov and L.D. Trotsky[2]
by V.I. Lenin

Things have so "accelerated" in Germany that we must not fall behind either. But today we are already behind.

We should call *tomorrow* a joint session of the

> Central Executive Committee
> Moscow Soviet
> District Soviets
> Trade unions, etc., etc.

A *number* of reports must be made on *the beginning of the revolution in Germany*.

(Victory of *our* tactics of struggle against German imperialism. And so forth.)

A resolution to be adopted.

The international revolution has come so close in *one week* that it has to be reckoned with as an event of the *next few days*.

No alliances either with the government of Wilhelm, or with the government of Wilhelm II + Ebert and the other scoundrels.

But for the German worker masses, the German working people in their millions, once they have begun with their spirit of revolt (so far *only* a spirit), we

are beginning to prepare

a fraternal alliance, *bread*, military aid.

We are all ready to die to help the German workers advance the revolution which has begun in Germany.

The conclusion: (1) ten times more effort to secure grain (clean out *all* stocks both for ourselves *and for the German* workers).

(2) Ten times more *enrollments* for the army. We must have *by the spring* an army of three millions to help the international workers' revolution.

This resolution should go out to the whole world by cable on Wednesday night. □

Two days later, on October 3, Lenin wrote as follows to a joint meeting of leading bodies of the Soviet state: the All-Russian Central Executive Committee of the Soviets, the Moscow Soviet, and representatives of factory committees and trade unions.

"Everything to Help the German Workers"[3]
by V.I. Lenin

Germany is in the throes of a political crisis. The panicky bewilderment both of the government and of all the exploiting classes in general has become abundantly clear to the whole people. The hopelessness of the military situation and the lack of support for the ruling classes among the working people have been exposed at one go. This crisis means either that the revolution has begun or at any rate that the people have clearly realised it is inevitable and imminent.

The government has morally resigned and is in a state of hysterical indecision, wavering between a military dictatorship and a coalition cabinet. But a military dictatorship has, virtually speaking, been under test ever since the outbreak of the war, and now it has ceased to be feasible because the army has become unreliable. And the admission of Scheidemann and Co. to the cabinet would only hasten the revolutionary outburst and make it more widespread, more conscious, more firm and determined after the thorough exposure of the pitiful impotence of these lackeys of the bourgeoisie, of these corrupt individuals, who are just like our Mensheviks and Socialist-Revolutionaries, like the Hendersons and Sidney Webbs in Britain, the Albert Thomas and Renaudels in France, and so on.

The crisis in Germany has only begun. It will inevitably end in the transfer of political power to the German proletariat. The Russian proletariat is following events with the keenest attention and enthusiasm. Now even the blindest workers in the various countries will see that the Bolsheviks were right in basing their whole tactics on the support of the world workers' revolution, and in not fearing to bear all sorts of heavy sacrifices. Today even the most ignorant will see how unspeakably vile the betrayal of socialism by the Mensheviks and Socialist-Revolutionaries was when they formed an alliance with the predatory British and French bourgeoisie, ostensibly to secure the annulment of the Brest-Litovsk Peace Treaty. And the Soviet government will certainly not help the German imperialists by attempting to violate the Brest-Litovsk Peace Treaty, to tear it up at a moment when the anti-imperialist forces in Germany are beginning to seethe and boil, and when the spokesmen for the German bourgeoisie are beginning to excuse themselves to their people for having concluded such a peace treaty, and to search for a way of "changing" their policy.

But the workers of Russia are not merely following events with attention and enthusiasm. They are demanding that everything be done to *help the German workers*, who have the gravest trials ahead of them, a most difficult transition from slavery to freedom, a most stubborn *struggle against their own and British imperialism*. The defeat of German imperialism will for a while have the effect of increasing the insolence, brutality, reaction, and annexatory attempts of British and French imperialism.

The Bolshevik working class of Russia has always been internationalist in action, unlike those scoundrels, the heroes and leaders of the Second International, who either resorted to outright betrayal by forming an alliance with their bourgeoisie, or tried, by phrase-mongering and excuses (as Kautsky, Otto Bauer and Co. did), to avoid revolution, and opposed all bold and great revolutionary action, all sacrifice of narrow national interests for the sake of furthering the workers' revolution.

The Russian workers will understand that very soon they will have to make the greatest sacrifices in the cause of internationalism. The time is approaching when circumstances may require us to come to the aid of the German people, who are struggling for their liberation from their own imperialism, against British and French imperialism.

Let us begin to prepare at once. Let us show that the Russian worker is capable of working much harder, of fighting and dying much more self-sacrificingly, when the world workers' revolution is at stake, as well as the Russian revolution.

First of all, let us multiply our efforts in storing up grain stocks. Let us resolve that every large elevator will put aside some grain to help the German workers should they be hard pressed in their struggle for emancipation from the imperialist monsters and brutes. Let every Party organisation, every trade union, every factory and workshop, etc., form special connections with several rural areas of their own selection with the object of strengthening the alliance with the peasants, helping and enlightening them, vanquishing the kulaks, and gathering up all surpluses of grain to the last ounce.

Let us, similarly, multiply our efforts in creating a proletarian Red Army. The turning-point has arrived—we all know it, we all see and feel it. The workers and labouring peasants have had a respite from the horrors of imperialist slaughter, they have realised and learnt from experience that war must be waged against the oppressors in defence of the gains of their revolution, the revolution of the working people, of their government, the Soviet government. An army is being created, a Red Army of workers and poor peasants, who are prepared to make any sacrifice in defending socialism. The army is growing in strength and is being tempered in battle with the Czechs and whiteguards. A firm foundation has been laid, and we must now hurry to erect the edifice itself.

We had decided to have an army of one million men by the spring; now we need an army of three million. We can have it. *And we shall have it.*

In these past few days world history has given tremendous momentum to the world workers' revolution. The most kaleidoscopic changes are possible, there may be attempts to form an alliance between German and Anglo-French imperialism against the Soviet government.

And we too must speed up our preparations. We must multiply our efforts.

Let this be the slogan for the anniversary of the Great October Workers' Revolution!

Let it be a pledge to the coming victories of the world workers' revolution! □

October 1918: Germany Seeks an Armistice

Faced with a collapsing army at the front and growing signs of revolt at home, Germany's rulers moved swiftly to salvage what they could. On September 29 the foreign secretary, Hintze, bluntly presented the alternatives to Paul von Hindenburg, army chief of staff, and Quartermaster General Erich Ludendorff, who was the real power in both army and government. Military dictatorship was not possible, Hintze explained, because "its success was tied to the prospect of military victory, which was now excluded." Thus, to avert a "revolution from below," Hintze proposed a "revolution from above": democratic reform, a coalition government based on bourgeois liberals and the Social Democrats, an armistice, and peace.[4] The plan offered an added advantage: the High Command could transfer blame for the military defeat to the new government. The High Command approved the plan and prevailed on the kaiser to agree. On October 3 the new government, headed by Prince Max von Baden and including Philipp Scheidemann as representative of the Social Democratic Party, took office.

This new coalition government, however, could not halt the crisis of the German ruling class nor quell the anger of the masses of working people. The Allied powers granted no armistice; instead, U.S. President Woodrow Wilson engaged in a repeated exchange of notes with Berlin, demanding German concessions. The war raged on, demanding sacrifices all the more intolerable now that Germany's rulers had admitted defeat.

Workers and soldiers waited in tense anticipation, seeking an opening to resolve the crisis in their own manner. October was punctuated by workers' strikes and demonstrations. These were organized by a working-class vanguard that had begun to emerge in the mass strikes and antigovernment protests of 1917 and 1918. In most areas these cadres were aligned with the USPD. In Berlin elected worker representatives who had led the January 1918 strike wave continued throughout 1918 to function together in a current that took the name Revolutionary Shop Stewards of the Large Factories of Greater Berlin (Die revolutionäre Obleute und Vertrauensmänner der Grossbetriebe Gross-Berlins). These delegates collaborated with the Berlin USPD, led by Georg Ledebour, which was the stronghold of that party's left wing. These currents shifted to the left during 1918 under the impact of the Russian October revolution and the rising mass struggles in Germany. In the summer, the Shop Stewards began active preparations for an insurrection. With financial assistance from the Russian embassy, they began arming groups of workers.

In October, the Bolsheviks sent one of their central leaders, Nikolai Bukharin, to work incognito in Berlin with the USPD and Spartacus leaders. While there is no record of his activity in Berlin, it was clearly aimed at prodding forward the revolutionary current within the USPD. Bukharin later reported that he talked with the central USPD leaders and all twenty-four USPD Reichstag deputies. He even met the revisionist theorist and USPD member Eduard Bernstein, who had maintained for twenty years that socialism would come not through revolution but through gradual change. Bukharin told him, "You are on the verge of revolution." Bernstein ridiculed the suggestion.[5]

The Spartacus and Bremen Left currents remained small nuclei. In Berlin the Spartacists had only fifty adherents. Only in a few cities, such as Bremen and Stuttgart, did these revolutionists have substantial influence in the factories. A major step was taken toward the unification of the revolutionary Socialist currents on October 7, when the Spartacus group held a small underground national conference, which was also attended by members of the Bremen Left current. The conference resolution analyzed German reaction as an "alliance of princes and junkers with finance capital," who had found a common interest in high tariffs and militarism. The defeat of these forces in the war and the consequent "collapse of German imperialism" had created "a revolutionary situation, in which all the problems that the German bourgeoisie was not able to solve in 1848 are posed anew." The program advanced a series of democratic and socialist demands including putting an end to all forms of antiworker repression, abolishing all ruling royal dynasties and creating a unified republic, transferring disciplinary power in the army from officers to soldiers' committees, and expropriating bank capital, the mines and mills, and "all large and medium-sized agricultural holdings."

The task of the German proletariat, the resolution maintained, was: "to link up with the revolutionary program of the Communist Party of 1848, proclaim the German socialist republic, standing in solidarity with the Russian Soviet republic, and thereby to unleash the world proletarian struggle against the world bourgeoisie for a proletarian dictatorship against the capitalist League of Nations."[6]

Most importantly, the conference decided that the Spartacists would work actively to form workers' and soldiers' councils everywhere that they did not already exist.

Lenin responded to the news of the Spartacus conference with the following letter.

To the Members of the Spartacus Group[7]
by V.I. Lenin

October 18, 1918

Dear Comrades,

We have had news today that the Spartacus group, together with the Bremen Left Radicals, has taken the most energetic steps to promote the setting up of Workers' and Soldiers' Councils throughout Germany. I take this opportunity to send our best wishes to the German revolutionary internationalist Social-Democrats. The work of the German Spartacus group, which has carried on systematic revolutionary propaganda in the most difficult conditions, has really saved the honour of German socialism and the German proletariat. Now the decisive hour is at hand: the rapidly maturing German revolution calls on the Spartacus group to play the most important role, and we all firmly hope that before long the German socialist proletarian republic will inflict a decisive blow on world imperialism.

I hope that the book by the renegade Kautsky against the dictatorship of the proletariat will also bring certain benefits.[8] It will prove the correctness of what the Spartacus group always said against the Kautskians, and the masses will the more quickly be freed from the corrupting influence of Mr. Kautsky and Co.

With best greetings and firm hopes that in the very near future it will be possible to hail the victory of the proletarian revolution in Germany. □

During these tense days of October, the SPD called on workers to avoid any disruption of law and order and to have confidence in its efforts to influence the new coalition government. All Germans should patiently "withstand the hard days to come," the SPD declared on October 17, promising that patience would soon be rewarded with peace and democracy.[9]

But the workers' patience was now exhausted. *Vorwärts,* the Berlin SPD daily, reported anxiously that talk in the factories was of a government of Ledebour and Hugo Haase (the two cochairmen of the USPD), workers' councils on the Russian model, and the dictatorship of the proletariat.[10] At a demonstration called by the USPD in Berlin October 16, more than 5,000 workers resisted police attacks and broke through police lines to reach the Reichstag building. They chanted, "Down with the war; down with the government; long live Liebknecht!" The demonstrators then made their way to the Soviet embassy where, as an outraged minister of the interior told his colleagues, the embassy staff joined in the protest, many of them leaning from embassy windows to wave red flags.[11]

Faced with the rising tide of such resistance and with its inability to secure an immediate armistice, the government hurriedly made further concessions.

On October 23 Karl Liebknecht was released from prison and greeted by 20,000 militant Berlin workers. He proceeded to a gathering at the Soviet embassy, where he received greetings from the Bolshevik Central Committee. "The liberation from prison of the representative of the revolutionary workers of Germany," the Bolshevik message to him read, "is the portent of a new era, the era of victorious socialism, which is now opening up both for Germany and for the whole world."[12]

Ludendorff was dismissed October 26, and two days later the kaiser ratified a face-lift of the constitution eliminating his personal political authority in government and purporting to make the government responsible to parliamentary control.

That same day the government decided to hinder collaboration between revolutionary-minded German workers and Soviet Russia by expelling the Soviet embassy. It was Scheidemann, the SPD representative, who suggested to the cabinet how a pretext could be found. "We must avoid a flagrant violation of [the embassy's] extraterritorial rights," Scheidemann said. "But if, for example, a suspicious diplomatic crate were accidentally to break open while in transport, then perhaps the recall of the present ambassador could be demanded."[13] The "accident" was organized; police "discovered" revolutionary leaflets that they themselves had planted; the entire embassy staff was packed onto a train November 6 and expelled from the country.

Events moved more swiftly in Austria-Hungary. Under the impact of widespread soldier revolts, the Hapsburgs' army in Italy crumbled during the last week of October. The non-German national territories of the empire declared their independence, and Austria-Hungary disintegrated. On October 30 a massive demonstration of workers and soldiers assembled in front of the parliament building in Vienna, demanding proclamation of a republic. The alarmed parliamentary deputies appointed a provisional government headed by the right-wing Social Democrat Karl Renner. The Austrian revolution had begun.

Karl Radek, a Bolshevik leader with long experience in the German Socialist movement, recalled in 1925 the impact on workers in Russia of the news from Austria and Germany in October and early November 1918.

"Our Isolation Has Ended"[14]
by Karl Radek

Comrade Joffe, our ambassador in Berlin, called me on the Hughes [teleprinter] machine: "I have just heard that the German government has decided to approach the Allies with a proposal for a truce and for peace negotiations."

The very fact that he was reporting this directly on the Hughes machine, uncoded, not only removed all doubt in my mind about the authenticity of this news; it also showed that Joffe felt no need for restraint. Nevertheless, I cautiously asked him: "Are you aware of the seriousness of your information and its possible consequences?"

Joffe answered: "I take complete responsibility for the report."

Naturally, I quickly passed this information on to the Soviet government. Its effect was that of liberation.

In the last few months the situation had deteriorated very much. Our intelligence reports showed that the noose around Soviet Russia's neck was getting tighter every day. The Germans were not only occupying the Ukraine but were making contact with Krasnov and Denikin. White detachments were training in Pskov. Rakovsky, as he passed through Vienna, saw a completely undisguised sign for a recruitment office in a hotel. The Germans were growing stronger in Finland, and Petrograd was exposed to attack.

In our assessment, the Germans, reckoning with the possibility of returning Belgium to the Allies, were therefore planning to capture Moscow and Petrograd in order to have a bargaining chip in their hands. These apprehensions were fully confirmed by a series of memoirs that came out later, after the German revolution. And minutes of German government deliberations of the time, published in 1919, show in black and white that General Hoffmann was demanding permission to tighten the noose.

But now the Germans were offering peace negotiations. Obviously their situation at the front was worse than we thought. Nevertheless Comrade Sverdlov told the workers at the People's Commissariat for Foreign Affairs and the People's Commissariat for War: "Be on your guard. Autumn flies bite hard."

Tensely we awaited developments. Every day brought more news of the growing panic in Berlin. The cat and mouse game began. Combining the Hoffmann method of threats with the agitational methods of Trotsky,[15] Wilson began to drop the most overt hints that the Hohenzollerns should be removed as a precondition for peace negotiations. The Allied governments were informing the whole world by radio of Wilson's communications with the German government. These broadcasts were dealing the German front blows no less dangerous than those of the American and French guns.

Bukharin, who had been in Berlin, reported growing ferment among the workers, and the crystallization of a revolutionary left wing among the Independents [USPD]. News came of the release of Liebknecht and we received a few glowing lines from him.[16] We felt that the German revolution had a leader. The Independents asked us to reject payment of the debt imposed on us by the Brest peace, but Vladimir Ilyich [Lenin] opposed this. "It is worth paying this so that Joffe can remain in Berlin," he said. So we sent the gold.

Suddenly news came of the breakthrough at the Bulgarian front.

This was followed by the news that Austria was surrendering unconditionally to the enemy. . . .

The glad news came of the beginning of revolution in Austria. This was Saturday night [November 2]. The newspaper galleys were already locked up for the next printing. Ilyich and Sverdlov instructed me to write an appeal. "But where shall we print it? There are no typesetters around." "There will be," said Béla Kun. "Just give us some bread and sausage." So together with the students of the Hungarian party school, he quickly went to look for typesetters among the prisoners of war. At 4:00 a.m. he rushed in to get the text of the appeal. And when I came out on the street in the morning, leaflets with the news of the revolution in Austria were already being passed from hand to hand.

From every corner of the city demonstrations were marching toward the Moscow soviet. From the balcony at the soviet we looked onto a sea of heads that came in waves from Strastnaya Square and Mokhovaya Street. Suddenly there was shouting that grew like a hurricane. A car was slowly moving through the crowd. We realized that Ilyich, unable to stay any longer in the Kremlin, had come out for the first time since he had been wounded.[17] Kun and I went running up to him. His face showed excitement and at the same time he seemed profoundly worried. At that moment I did not understand why this champion of the revolution should be worried.[18] When Ilyich appeared on the balcony tens of thousands of workers burst into cheers.

I have never seen such a sight. Workers, both men and women, and Red Army soldiers filed past until late evening. The world revolution had arrived. The masses of people were listening to its iron step. Our isolation had ended. □

The Moscow newspaper *Pravda* summarized Lenin's address, made on November 3, as follows.

Speech on Austro-Hungarian Revolution[19]
by V.I. Lenin

Events have shown that the people's sufferings have not been in vain.

We are not only fighting Russian capitalism. We are fighting the capitalism of all countries, world capitalism — we are fighting for the freedom of all workers.

Hard as it was for us to cope with famine and our enemies, we now see that we have millions of allies.

They are the workers of Austria, Hungary and Germany. While we are gathered here, Friedrich Adler is very likely on his way to Vienna after his release from prison.[20] The first day of the Austrian workers' revolution is probably being celebrated on the squares of Vienna.

The time is near when the first day of the world revolution will be celebrated everywhere.

Our labour and sufferings have not been in vain! The world revolution will triumph!

Long live the world proletarian revolution! (*Stormy applause*) ☐

———————

Revolution was ignited in Germany by a mutiny of the North Sea fleet. When the admirals decided to send it out October 30 on a final, hopeless assault on the British navy, the sailors acted to prevent the ships from leaving port. Their commanders responded by throwing more than 1,000 sailors in jail. A mass solidarity movement sprung up to defend the arrested sailors, encompassing the sailors aboard ship, the workers of Kiel and nearby cities, and soon, the soldiers sent to subdue them.

On November 3, officers opened fire on a massive, unarmed demonstration, killing eight. The next day the workers responded with a general strike. The imprisoned sailors were released by their comrades; sailors raised the red flag over most ships; an armed demonstration of 20,000 soldiers and sailors marched through Kiel; and a newly formed workers' and soldiers' council took control of the city.

The government sent SPD leader Gustav Noske to take the situation in hand. Most sailors considered their actions no more than loyal implementation of the SPD's statements favoring peace and democracy and looked to Noske for leadership. He prevailed on them to moderate their demands and thus regained some degree of temporary control. But this did not prevent revolutionary detachments in Kiel from fanning out to nearby cities. News of the revolt spread quickly, spurring workers and soldiers into action all across Germany.

By November 6 the revolution had spread to the big cities of the North Sea coast; by November 8, to major centers across the nation. In some areas the authorities resisted, and key buildings were stormed by

"Brothers, don't shoot!" Revolutionary workers win support of soldiers at barracks in Berlin, November 9, 1918.

armed workers and soldiers. In others, there was no bloodshed. On the whole the revolutionary wave overwhelmed the resistance.

In almost all the great industrial centers the uprising followed a common pattern. First, mass strikes and demonstrations by the workers broke out. Then, soldiers joined the revolt. Finally, a joint workers' and soldiers' council assumed de facto control. In some cities the SPD managed to include bourgeois forces in the workers' and soldiers' councils, or set up "citizens' councils" to compete with them.

Meanwhile, the SPD continued its efforts to hold back the mass movement and defuse the revolutionary crisis through negotiations. The November 4 appeal of its Executive Committee announced that the abdication of the kaiser was under discussion. It called on workers "not to frustrate these negotiations through reckless intervention," and to reject all calls to action by an "irresponsible minority."[21] But the negotiations resolved nothing. Scheidemann was compelled on November 7 to place an ultimatum before the government. "You, my good sirs, and the imperial chancellor must realize that we have done everything we could to keep the masses in line," he told the war cabinet. If the kaiser did not abdicate immediately, he insisted, the German state itself would collapse.[22] On November 8 news arrived that a republic based on workers', soldiers', and peasants' councils had been declared in Bavaria, headed by USPD leader Kurt Eisner. The authorities fought desperately to maintain their hold on Berlin, cutting off its communications with the outside, and even issuing an edict prohibiting formation of "workers' and soldiers' councils of the Russian type."[23]

A provisional Berlin workers' council established by the Revolutionary Shop Stewards held meetings to discuss a date for the insurrection. Following Liebknecht's release from prison, the Spartacists and the Shop Stewards agreed to unite their efforts. Liebknecht and Wilhelm Pieck represented the Spartacists in the stewards' leadership, and they argued for launching mass actions in support of the advancing revolution. A majority of the council rejected this, insisting that it must first finish the technical preparations for the insurrection. November 11 was finally chosen as the date for the rising. But by November 8, the rising tide of revolution across Germany made further delay impossible, and the word went out for general strike the following day.[24]

The Executive Committee of the council issued a call for a general strike for "peace, freedom, and bread." It also called for "a socialist republic with all that that implies."[25] The following is the text of another leaflet, issued on November 8 by the Internationale Group, the formal name of the Spartacus organization,[26] which called for revolutionary action and explained what kind of government should replace that of the kaiser.

"The Time for Action Has Arrived"[27]

Workers and soldiers!

Your hour has come. After long and silent suffering you have moved into action. It is no exaggeration to say that at this moment the eyes of the world are upon you, and you hold its fate in your hands.

Workers and soldiers! Now that the time for action has arrived, there can be no retreat. The same "Socialists" who for four years served as the government's pimps have in recent weeks been stalling you day after day with promises of a "people's government," a parliamentary state, and other such rubbish. Now they are trying everything to weaken your struggle and pacify the movement.

Workers and soldiers! Follow the lead of your comrades and fellow soldiers and sailors in Kiel, Hamburg, Bremen, Lübeck, Rostock, Flensburg, Hannover, Magdeburg, Braunschweig, Munich, and Stuttgart. What they have done, you too must do. What you win through the tenacity and success of your struggles here will settle the fate of your brothers elsewhere in Germany and that of the proletariat of the entire world.

Soldiers! Do as the sailors from the fleet have done. Join with your brothers in work clothes. Do not let yourselves be used against your brothers. Do not obey the officers' orders. Do not fire on freedom fighters.

Workers and soldiers! The next goals of your struggle must be:

1. Free all civilian and military prisoners.

2. End Germany's division into separate states and abolish the royal dynasties.

3. Elect workers' and soldiers' councils. Elect delegates to them from all factories and military units.

4. Establish relations immediately with other German workers' and soldiers' councils.

5. Transfer all governmental power to representatives of the workers' and soldiers' councils.

6. Establish immediate contact with the international proletariat, especially with the Russian workers' republic.

Workers and soldiers! Now prove that you are strong enough and that you are capable enough to wield power.

Long live the socialist republic!

Long live the International!

> The Internationale Group
> (Spartacus Group)
> Karl Liebknecht
> Ernst Meyer □

———————

By November 8, Imperial Chancellor Max von Baden was convinced that only the kaiser's abdication and an SPD-led government could salvage the situation for the ruling capitalist and landholding families. "If I manage to convince the kaiser," he asked SPD leader Ebert, "do I have you on my side in the fight against the social revolution?" Ebert replied, "If the kaiser does not abdicate, then social revolution is unavoidable. But I do not want it; no, I hate it like sin."[28] Nonetheless, the kaiser once more refused to abdicate.

November 9 dawned with mass demonstrations in Berlin, as workers marched on the city center, and entire military units joined their ranks. The demonstrators' main slogan was that of the workers' committee leaflet: "Peace, freedom, and bread!" Max von Baden later recalled that as the marchers approached, he reasoned as follows: "The revolution is on the verge of winning. We cannot crush it, but perhaps we can strangle it. . . . If Ebert is presented to me from the streets as the people's leader, then we will have a republic; if it is Liebknecht, then Bolshevism. But if the abdicating kaiser appoints Ebert Reich chancellor, then there is still a small hope for the monarchy. Perhaps it will be possible to divert the revolutionary energies into the legal channels of an election campaign."[29] The kaiser still refused to budge, but his chancellor could delay no longer. About noon, after discussions with Ebert, Max von Baden unilaterally declared that "the kaiser . . . has decided to abdicate the throne . . . [and] proposes that the regent nominate Deputy Ebert as Reich chancellor and present a bill to hold elections immediately to a German national assembly. . . ."[30] Wilhelm had actually decided nothing of the kind, and Max von Baden had not been named regent. Ebert's first act as chancellor was to ask Max von Baden to accept the regent's office, hoping thereby to salvage the monarchy; but he refused. Ebert then made yet another appeal to the masses to cease their intervention into the business of government.

"Leave the Streets"[31]

Berlin, November 9, 1918

Fellow citizens! The former Reich chancellor, Prince Max von Baden, in agreement with all the ministers, has entrusted me with the responsibility of the Reich chancellorship. In consultation with the political parties I shall organize the new government and report the results to the public shortly.

The new government will be a people's government. Its goal can only be to bring peace to the German people as quickly as possible and to secure the freedom they have won.

Fellow citizens! I call on you all for support in the difficult work that awaits us. You know how seriously the war has jeopardized the people's food supply, which is the first prerequisite of political life.

The political upheaval must not disrupt the population's food supply.

The prime duty of all in city and country must still be to assist, not hinder, the production of food supplies and their delivery into the cities. Food shortages mean plunder and robbery, with misery for all. The poorest would suffer the most; the industrial worker would be hit the hardest.

Anyone who misappropriates food supplies or other necessities, or the means of transportation needed to distribute them, terribly wrongs all society.

Fellow citizens! I urgently appeal to you: leave the streets!

Maintain law and order!

Reich Chancellor Ebert □

Ebert favored retaining some form of monarchy, and Max von Baden was still working to that end. But as the workers and soldiers of Berlin took full control of the city, Scheidemann, speaking at 2:00 p.m. before a revolutionary throng, decided on his own to proclaim a republic. Ebert is reported to have been dismayed by Scheidemann's unilateral declaration,[32] but it had committed the SPD to the abolition of the monarchy.

Scheidemann Proclaims the Republic[33]

The German people have won across the board. Everything old and rotten has collapsed; militarism is finished! The Hohenzollerns have abdicated![34] Long live the German republic! Reichstag Deputy Ebert has been proclaimed Reich chancellor. He has been called upon to put together a new government; all Socialist parties will be part of it.

Our task now is to not allow this shining victory, this complete victory of the German people, to be sullied. Therefore, I urge you to see to it that there is no disruption of public order. We must be able to be proud of this day forever. Nothing must happen that could be held against us later. What we need now is law, order, and security. Representatives will be assigned to work with the army commanders on the borders and with Minister of War Scheüch. The Reichstag deputy, Comrade Göhre, will countersign all decrees by Minister of War Scheüch. Therefore effective immediately orders signed by Ebert and all proclamations signed with the names Göhre and Scheüch should be respected. Help see to it that the new German republic we will establish is not endangered.

Long live the German republic! □

Two hours after Scheidemann spoke, Karl Liebknecht and a large crowd in front of the royal palace also pledged to struggle for a republic, but one with an opposite class character — one headed by a government of workers and soldiers. The following is the account of a Berlin newspaper, the *Vossische Zeitung.*

Liebknecht Proclaims the Socialist Republic[35]

"The day of revolution has come. We have forced them to make peace. As of this moment peace is achieved. The old order is no more. The reign of the Hohenzollerns, who lived in this palace for centuries, is finished. We now proclaim the free socialist republic of Germany. We greet our Russian brothers, who were shamefully chased out four days ago."[36]

Liebknecht then pointed to the main entrance to the palace and, raising his voice, cried out: "Through this gate the new socialist freedom of the workers and soldiers will enter. There where the kaiser's banner once flew, we will raise the red flag of the free German republic!"

The soldiers of the palace guard, who could be seen on the roof, waved their helmets and greeted the throng below, which pushed toward the gate. Slowly it opened, allowing Liebknecht's car to enter. The crowd was prevented from following. In a few minutes the soldiers of the palace guard appeared, without arms or gear, to a tumultuous cheer from the crowd. Shortly thereafter Liebknecht stepped onto the balcony with his supporters. A broad piece of red cloth stood out against their gray uniforms.

"Comrades," Liebknecht began, "this is the dawning of our freedom. Never again will a Hohenzollern set foot here. Seventy years ago Friedrich Wilhelm IV stood on this same spot,[37] and had to doff his hat to the procession with those fifty blood-covered bodies, fallen on the barricades of Berlin for freedom's cause. A different procession moves by here today. It is the spirits of the millions who have given their lives for the sacred cause of the proletariat. With split skulls, bathed in blood, these victims of tyranny stagger past, followed by the spirits of millions of women and children, consumed by grief and misery for the cause of the proletariat. After them come the millions upon millions of bloody victims of this world war.

"Today an immense multitude of impassioned proletarians stands at this same place, to pay homage to the new freedom. Comrades, I proclaim the free German socialist republic, which will embrace all Germans, in which there will be no more servants, in which every honest worker will receive an honest wage for his labor. The reign of capitalism, which turned Europe into a swamp of blood, is broken.

"We call our Russian brothers back. When they left, they told us: 'If within one month you haven't accomplished what we did, then we will turn our backs on you.' But it took only four days.

"But even if the old order has been torn down," Liebknecht continued, "we must not think that our task is finished. We must strain every nerve and muscle to build the workers' and soldiers' government and to create a new proletarian political system, a system of peace, of happiness, and of freedom for our German brothers and our brothers around the world. We stretch our hands out to them and call on them to complete the world revolution.

"All of you who want to see a free socialist republic of Germany and the world revolution, raise your hands and take an oath." All hands rose and the call resounded, "Long live the republic!" After the cheers subsided, a soldier standing near Liebknecht waved the red flag he was carrying and cried, "Long live its first president: Liebknecht."

Liebknecht concluded: "We are not that far yet. Whether president or not, we must all stand together, in order to make the revolutionary ideal come true. For freedom and happiness and peace!"

Shortly thereafter the red flag was raised on the kaiser's flagpole. □

As Scheidemann's address indicated, the SPD was pressing the USPD to join in a coalition government. SPD leaders knew that USPD participation was essential to give the new regime the authority to contain the revolutionary mass upsurge. In addition, they reckoned that the lure of seats and influence in government would win over the USPD's national leadership, encouraging it to rein in the party's unruly ranks and discipline its revolutionary left wing. Haase and other national leaders stood much closer to the SPD than did the USPD as a whole.

Ebert named Scheidemann and Otto Landsberg to serve with him as SPD members of the new government. Pending an agreement with the USPD, the three SPD leaders explained their aims in the following declaration.

Our Liberation Is Now Complete[38]

November 9, 1918

Countrymen!

Today the liberation of the people was completed. The kaiser has abdicated; his oldest son has renounced the throne. The Social Democratic Party has assumed responsibility for the government and invited the Independent Social Democratic Party to join it on a wholly equal basis.

The new government will organize elections to a national constituent assembly in which all citizens of both sexes over twenty years of age will participate with completely equal rights. After that the government will relinquish power to the new people's representatives. Until then the government has the responsibility to conclude an armistice and conduct peace negotiations, secure food for the people, and ensure the return of our countrymen under arms to their families and to gainful employment in the most rapid, orderly manner possible. The democratic administration must get right to work on this. Only if it functions flawlessly can havoc be avoided. All must be conscious of their responsibility to the whole.

Human life is sacred. Property must be protected from arbitrary usurpation. Whoever dishonors this magnificent movement with foul criminal acts is an enemy of the people and must be treated as such. Our whole future depends upon the success of our endeavor. Everyone who, with honest dedication, helps to achieve it will have the right to say that in that greatest moment in world history he was there, working for the common good. Enormous tasks stand before us.

Toiling men and women in city and country; men in uniform and in work clothes: join in our common work!

Ebert, Scheidemann,
Landsberg □

After his address at the royal palace, Liebknecht found his way to the USPD fraction chambers in the Reichstag. The executive committees of the USPD and the Shop Stewards had been in session there for some time, considering Chancellor Ebert's request that the USPD join the SPD in a coalition government of Socialist parties. At first, the USPD leaders were hesitant. But as one delegation after another arrived, chiefly from SPD-led workers' and soldiers' councils, urging the USPD to join the government, opinion swung toward participation. Liebknecht, the best known opponent of the war in Germany and internationally, was asked to join in, but he remained firm in his refusal.

Spartacus leader Wilhelm Pieck, who also took part in these discussions, later recalled that "the workers' and soldiers' delegations arriving in our room one after another exerted extraordinarily strong pressure on Comrade Liebknecht to join the government. They explained that his name in particular would help achieve an immediate armistice and that he was delaying the signing of the armistice by his categorical refusal. He could not justify causing the death of a single soldier by this stand, they said. From all appearances the SPD had designed this line of argument. Liebknecht found himself in an extremely difficult situation and therefore decided to formulate conditions under which the formation of a joint government would be possible, although only for three days, until an armistice could be concluded."[39] The USPD leaders initially concurred with Liebknecht's conditions and proposed them to the SPD. The following reply from the SPD Executive Committee was received within a couple of hours.

SPD Reply to USPD Conditions for Coalition Government[40]

Berlin, November 9, 1918,
8:30 p.m.

To the Executive Committee of the Independent Social Democratic Party:

Guided by a genuine desire to arrive at an agreement, we wish to explain our basic position on your conditions.

You demand:

1. Germany should be a socialist republic.[41]

This demand is the goal of our own policy. However, the people must decide on this through the constituent assembly.

2. All executive, legislative, and judicial power in this republic should rest exclusively in the hands of elected representatives of the entire toiling population and the soldiers.

If by this demand you mean the dictatorship of one class, which does not have the support of the majority of the people, then we must reject this condition, because it contradicts our democratic principles.

3. Exclude all bourgeois members from the government.

We must reject this condition, because fulfilling it would seriously jeopardize our capacity to feed the people, if not make that task impossible.

4. The Independents shall participate for only three days, as a temporary measure in order to form a government able to conclude an armistice.

We consider the collaboration of the Socialist currents necessary at least until the convening of the constituent assembly.

5. The departmental ministers shall serve only as technical assistants to the cabinet proper, which shall make the decisions.

We agree to this condition.

6. The two cabinet heads shall have equal rights.

We favor all cabinet members having the same status. However, the constituent assembly must decide this.

The Executive Committee
of the Social Democratic
Party of Germany. □

Following the SPD's rejection of the key conditions drafted by Liebknecht, the USPD leadership retreated to safer ground. On November 10 it issued a new set of proposals, this time without Liebknecht's agreement. While this statement asserted that in theory the councils were to hold political power, in reality it accepted that all government ministries would remain in the hands of the ministers inherited from the kaiser's government. By implication, the entire imperial governmental machine would continue to function with its authority unimpaired by revolution.

The USPD proposals aimed at making a rapid accord with the SPD possible and included three nominations for the cabinet. The USPD leadership had originally favored choosing Haase, Ledebour, and Liebknecht, in order that all three of the party's major factions would bear responsibility for the governmental venture and its outcome. When Ledebour and Liebknecht refused, Wilhelm Dittmann and Emil Barth were proposed. Both had reputations as left-wingers that were now to dissolve quickly; Barth was the only leader of the Shop Stewards who could be persuaded to serve.

The following are the USPD's November 10 proposals.

USPD Enters Government[42]

To the Executive Committee of the Social Democratic Party of Germany.

The following is in response to your letter of November 9, 1918.

In order to safeguard the gains of the socialist revolution, the Independent Social Democratic Party is willing to join the cabinet under the following conditions:

The cabinet must be composed only of Social Democrats, who, as people's commissioners, shall have equal status.

This restriction does not apply to the departmental ministers. They are only technical assistants for the cabinet, which makes the decisions. Two Social Democrats, one from each party, with equal status, shall be assigned to work alongside each departmental minister.

The duration of the Independent Social Democrats' participation in the cabinet is not limited. Each party shall assign three members to it.

Political power lies in the hands of the workers' and soldiers' councils. A general congress of councils in all of Germany shall be called immediately.

The constituent assembly question shall be posed only after the gains of the revolution have been consolidated; it is therefore reserved for further discussion.

These conditions are dictated by the desire for united proletarian action. In the event they are accepted, we have delegated our members Haase, Dittmann, and Barth to the cabinet.

> The Executive Committee
> of the Independent Social
> Democratic Party.
> signed: Haase □

On the afternoon of November 10, the leaderships of the SPD and USPD came to agreement on constituting a six-member cabinet, which they named the "Council of People's Representatives" (Rat der Volksbeauftragten). The same day a meeting of the Berlin Workers' and Soldiers' Council, acting on behalf of the revolutionary councils across the nation, took up the new government's composition.

The underground workers' council that prepared the insurrection had been no more than an extension of the Shop Stewards' structure. The November 10 meeting, however, was attended by about 3,000 elected representatives of councils newly formed in factories and regiments across the city. Held at a large Berlin arena, the Busch Circus, it was a tumultuous assembly. SPD organizers had fanned out to the factories and barracks to influence the assembly's makeup. They seized on a very strong feeling for workers' unity and used it to win support for an SPD-USPD government. SPD influence was predominant in the soldiers' councils, and soldier representatives were in the majority at the Busch Circus assembly.

Left-wing delegates proposed that the government be composed of the forces that had fought to organize and launch the revolution: the USPD and the Spartacists. But this suggestion was hooted down by the majority with shouts of "parity": that is, equal representation of the USPD and SPD.

After Ebert and Haase had spoken, Karl Liebknecht rose to warn the assembly of the dangers to the revolution that were hidden beneath the cloak of "unity." One participant recorded his comments as follows.

"Enemies Surround Us"[43]
by Karl Liebknecht

I am afraid that I must try to pour cold water on your enthusiasm. The counterrevolution is already on the march; it is already in action! (*Shouts: "Where is that?"*) It is already among us. Those who have spoken to you, were they friends of the revolution? (*Shouts: "No!" Loud retorts: "Yes!"*) Read what Reich Chancellor Ebert (*Shout: "Without him you would not even be here!"*) had printed in *Vorwärts*. It is a slander of the revolution carried out yesterday.

Dangers to the revolution threaten us from many sides. (*Shouts: "From you!"*) Danger threatens not only from those circles that up to now have held the reins — the demagogues, big landowners, junkers, capitalists, imperialists, monarchists, princes, and generals — but also from those who today support the revolution, but were still opposing it the day before yesterday. (*Stormy interruptions: "Unity, unity!" Retorts: "No!" Shouts: "Sit down!"*)

Be careful whom you choose for the government and whom you

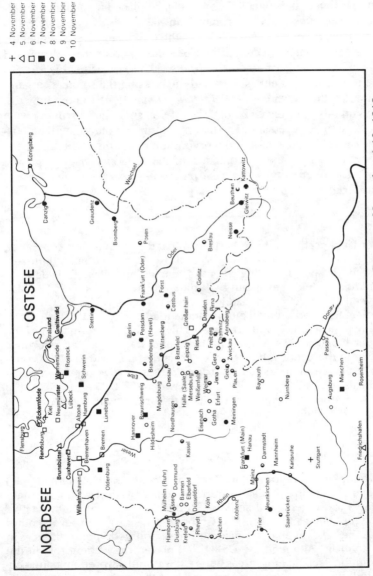

Spread of the workers' and soldiers' councils through Germany, November 4-10, 1918.

+	4 November
◁	5 November
□	6 November
■	7 November
○	8 November
◑	9 November
●	10 November

NORDSEE

OSTSEE

Königsberg

Danzig

Graudenz

Bromberg

Posen

Stralsund

Greifswald

Warnemünde

Rostock

Schwerin

Stettin

Frank'urt (Oder)

Forst

Cottbus

Breslau

Neisse

Beuthen

Gleiwitz

Kattowitz

Görlitz

Großenhain

Dresden

Pirna

Freiberg

Chemnitz

Annaberg

Grei.

Zwickau

Plauer

Flensburg

Rendsburg

Eckernförde

Kiel

Neumünster

Lübeck

Altona

Hamburg

Lüneburg

Brunsbüttel

Cuxhaven

Wilhelmshaven

Bremerhaven

Bremen

Oldenburg

Hannover

Braunschweig

Magdeburg

Hildesheim

Nordhausen

Dessau

Bitterfeld

Wittenberg

Berlin

Potsdam

Brandenburg (Havel)

Halle (Saale)

Merseburg

Weißenfels

Riesa

Leipzig

Weimar

Eisenach

Gotha

Erfurt

Jena

Gera

Meiningen

Bayreuth

Nürnberg

Kassel

Frankfurt (Main)

Hanau

Darmstadt

Mannheim

Karlsruhe

Stuttgart

Augsburg

München

Rosenheim

Friedrichshafen

Passau

Mainz

Koblenz

Neunkirchen

Saarbrücken

Trier

Aachen

Köln

Rheydt

Krefeld

Düsseldorf

Elberfeld

Barmen

Essen

Mulheim (Ruhr)

Dortmund

Duisburg

Hamborn

Weichsel

Oder

Elbe

Weser

Rhein

Donau

trustingly elect to the soldiers' councils. The soldiers' councils must be in the vanguard of the defense of the councils' power. No significant portion of the councils' power can be placed in the hands of officers. The reins must be primarily in the hands of the simple soldiers. (*Loud shouts: "They are!"*) In the provinces several higher officers have been elected chairmen of soldiers' councils. (*Protests*) I tell you: Enemies surround us! (*Shouts: "You're twisting the facts!"*) The revolution's enemies are insidiously using the soldiers' organizations to their own ends. (*Persistent commotion*) I know how unpleasant this disturbance is, but even if you shoot me, I will say what I believe to be necessary. The triumph of the revolution will be possible only if it becomes a social revolution. Only then will it have the strength to ensure the socialization of the economy, happiness, and peace for all eternity. (*Applause from some, persistent uproar, renewed shouts: "Unity"*) □

After Liebknecht's speech, Barth proposed that an action committee of eighteen be elected, composed of those who had prepared the revolution in the preceding months, including himself, Ledebour, Liebknecht, and Luxemburg. (Released from prison in Breslau November 9, Luxemburg had just arrived in Berlin.) The SPD, and the soldiers they had brought along, demanded "unity" and "parity," and finally imposed their will. The assembly ratified the formation of the Council of People's Representatives and transferred all executive power to this council. It elected an Executive Committee of the councils (Vollzugsrat) made up of fourteen representatives of the workers' councils, divided on a parity basis between the SPD and USPD, and fourteen from the soldiers' councils, a majority of whom were inclined to the SPD. The Executive Committee then issued a decree dissolving its component councils across Berlin; this was modified the following day by instructions acknowledging their existence but instructing them to limit their activity to local affairs.[44]

Governments were formed in Germany's component states and main industrial cities in a similar fashion. In most areas the revolution established the workers' and soldiers' councils as the only authoritative force. But in Bielefeld, Breslau, Cologne, Duisburg, and several other areas the SPD was able to win inclusion of bourgeois political forces in the councils. Although the USPD had played the leading role in the revolution itself, in most areas where it was initially predominant it accepted the parity notion and granted half the council executive seats to the SPD. The USPD took a majority only in Bremen, Düsseldorf, Halle, and Leipzig, the few cities where the SPD was not a significant factor in the councils. Wherever the SPD was dominant, however, it took the majority.[45]

In the few areas where revolutionaries led the councils, they took action to dismantle some of the old capitalist machinery of government. In Bremen, Chemnitz, Hamburg, and Leipzig, for example, the old city councils or legislative bodies were dissolved. In some areas within Berlin and elsewhere, action was taken to dissolve the old police force. In Berlin, Bremen, Hamburg, Halle, Frankfurt, and a few other areas, the councils established Red Guards, security forces, or other armed bodies under their control. In the small state of Brunswick, one of the most radical provisional regimes set up tribunals for black marketeers and other economic criminals, unilaterally demobilized returning soldiers, and expropriated some factories.

Such examples gave a taste of what the councils could and did achieve when they exerted their authority, but they remained isolated exceptions. In general, the councils delegated all power to the provisional governments and left themselves with little authority in the daily business of government. The provisional regimes, in turn, confirmed the authority of the old capitalist administrators, judges, police, and officer corps, and left government by and large in the hands of the old imperial state apparatus.

The Council of Peoples' Representatives, while nominally controlled by the Executive Committee of the councils, in fact acted as what it was — the legitimate successor of the imperial government of Max von Baden. It acted to preserve rule by the capitalists and landlords. In theory, each technical assistant in charge of a ministry worked under two supervisors, one each chosen by the SPD and USPD. But the technical assistants were none other than the ministers inherited from Max von Baden's government. Fully in command of their ministries, they continued the work of the imperial government and had strong leverage over the decisions of the People's Representatives. As for the Social Democratic "supervisors," very few were actually appointed, and many of those who were named were never integrated into the work of the ministry they supposedly controlled. Karl Kautsky, for example, was appointed by the USPD to the foreign office. However, the kaiser's foreign secretary, Wilhelm Solf, cut him off from the ministry's real business and shunted him into examining ministry archives on the causes of the war. The USPD never bothered to name its supervisor to the crucial ministry of war.[46]

In this way, behind the masquerade of an all-Socialist government, the coalition of bourgeois parties with the SPD established under Max von Baden continued in office, its composition changed only by the inclusion of the right wing of the USPD.

The continuing independent authority of the imperial officer corps was another key pillar of continuity of the old state apparatus of the junkers and big capital. Having begun by a decision to maintain the High Command, the Ebert cabinet soon came to rely upon it. Their relationship began November 10 with a telephone call from Gen. Wilhelm Groener, successor to Ludendorff, which Groener later described as the conclusion of "an alliance to fight against the revolution, to fight against Bolshevism."[47]

By this agreement, the High Command acknowledged the authority of the new provisional republican government. In return, the Ebert government confirmed the authority of the officer corps and its disciplinary powers within the army. The officers, Ebert claimed, were the only force that could organize the army's return to Germany without mishap and demobilize it quickly. In December he backed Groener's attempt to use returning army detachments against the revolution.

Despite its hatred of the soldiers' councils, the High Command did not yet dare challenge their existence. Instead, it tried to influence them, seeking to promote officers into positions of leadership and even actively encouraging the formation of counterfeit "soldiers' councils" under officer control.

The officer caste also tried to limit the councils' authority and the scope of their activity, and here they called on the government for assistance. On November 12 the six cabinet members, responding to a request from the High Command, sent it a telegram designed to shore up the officers' authority. Their message, which they had published in *Vorwärts* the following day, read in part:

"2. Officers' disciplinary authority remains in force. Unconditional obedience while in service is of decisive importance if the army's return to the German homeland is to succeed. Military order and discipline in the army must therefore be maintained under all circumstances.

"3. In order to maintain trust between officers and men, the soldiers' councils have a consultative voice in questions of supply, leave, and disciplinary measures. Their highest duty is to work to prevent disorder and mutiny."[48]

Although the new government was working to preserve the old state structure with only cosmetic changes, it could not openly advertise its intentions. Its authority was based on workers' and soldiers' belief that it was building a democratic republic that would represent their interests. Thus, to the masses the government claimed to be institutionalizing and extending the gains won by the November revolution. The following November 12 decree enumerated basic reforms, which for the most part had already been achieved by the revolution itself.

Reform Program Enacted[49]

To the German People:

The government that emerged from the revolution, exclusively socialist in leadership, sees its mission as implementing the socialist program. It therefore proclaims the following immediate measures, which have the force of law:

1. Martial law is lifted.
2. The rights of association and assembly shall not be limited, including for public employees.
3. Censorship is abolished. Censorship of the theater is lifted.
4. Freedom of expression and of the press shall not be limited.[50]
5. Freedom of religion is guaranteed. No one may be required to participate in religious rites.[51]
6. Amnesty is declared for all political offenses. Legal proceedings pending for such offenses are cancelled.
7. The Law on Patriotic Service is abrogated,[52] with the exception of those provisions dealing with mediation of disputes.
8. The laws on servants and the exceptional laws against farm workers are suspended.[53]
9. Protective legislation for workers that was suspended at the beginning of the war is reinstated.

Additional decrees on social policy will be published shortly. The eight-hour day will take effect no later than January 1, 1919. The government will do everything to promote sufficient job opportunities. An unemployment compensation decree has been prepared; its cost shall be shared by national, state, and local governments.

Obligatory health insurance will be increased above the present level of 2,500 marks.

The housing shortage will be combated by making more housing available.

The government will try to ensure a regulated food supply for the population.

The government will maintain orderly production and protect property and personal freedom and safety against encroachment by individuals.

All men and women aged twenty and over shall have the right to vote. All elections to public bodies shall henceforth be by universal, secret, and direct suffrage with proportional representation.

These voting rights apply also to the constituent assembly, for which specific regulations will follow.

> Berlin, November 12, 1918
> Ebert, Haase, Scheidemann,
> Landsberg, Dittmann,
> Barth □

An SPD poster from those days drove home the message:

"Already, in only a few days!

"A people's republic. Equal suffrage. Women's suffrage. The right to vote at twenty years.

"All dynasties and royal courts have vanished. A Socialist national government.

"Workers' and soldiers' councils everywhere. The privileged House of Lords eliminated. The three-class parliament dissolved.

"Freedom of assembly. Freedom of association. Freedom of the press. Freedom of religion.

"Militarism smashed. Dismissal of all personages from the past. Soldiers' salaries increased.

"The eight-hour day. The law on servants abolished. Workers and employers have equal rights.

"So much has already been gained. Much more must still be achieved.

"Close your ranks. Do not let yourselves be divided.

"Unity!"[54]

On November 12 the USPD Executive Committee made the following appeal to the party membership to support the newly formed Council of People's Representatives, which it portrayed as the instrument of rule by the councils.

"We Hold Decisive Influence"[55]

To the Party:
Comrades!
We are happy and proud to address you.
The fortress of Prussian-German militarism, seemingly buttressed against all storms, has collapsed.

The crowns of the German princely dynasties and that of the German emperor have shattered like glass.

Glowing with promise, the socialist republic has replaced the monarchy.

The revolutionary people made short shrift of the old governmental power's representatives — the generals and the bureaucrats. The people broke the power of the army officers, the control of the junker caste in the administration, and the command of the capitalist clique over public life. The people seized governmental power.

Today the workers' and soldiers' councils wield this power.

When the walls of the old administration crumbled, the foundations were laid for the vigorous construction of the new socialist system. Now we must make the supreme effort to safeguard peace, cement the gains of the revolution, and complete not only the political but also the economic liberation of the working class.

From its first day the Independent Social Democratic Party of Germany heralded the impending end of militarism and imperialism and did everything to unleash the revolutionary forces of the working class. The Social Democratic Party, dazed by the outbreak of the revolution, vilified the first revolutionary fighters and fought us at every turn.

The situation urgently required the establishment of a government that would put an end to the slaughter, pursue the armistice negotiations to a successful conclusion, and secure peace; a government that would push forcefully for the realization of socialist principles.

But the only guarantee of this was for our party to have decisive influence in the government. Therefore, we demanded that the new cabinet had to be exclusively socialist, with equal representation and status for both Social Democratic parties.

This government could receive its power only from the hands of the workers' and soldiers' councils. Therefore, it came into being at the moment when the first plenary assembly of the Berlin workers' and soldiers' councils sanctioned the formation of a provisional cabinet with this composition.

Imbued with a strong belief in the practicability of our ultimate goal, we begin the hard work of redressing the war's calamity and misery, rebuilding the destroyed economy, thoroughly transforming all aspects of public life, and eliminating all power positions of the propertied minority that has ruled up to now.

This can come to pass only if the workers in their masses stand by us and help advance our work.

We will call a party congress as soon as comrades can leave the posts where they are standing guard for the revolution. Comrades will then judge the steps that we have taken.

And now we must throw ourselves into the work, bringing the proletariat together under the banner of the party that coolly and clearly led the masses to the revolutionary goal that we have reached.

Long live revolutionary Social Democracy, true to its principles: the Independent Social Democratic Party of Germany!

Long live the Socialist International!

> The Executive Committee
> of the Independent Social
> Democratic Party of
> Germany □

On November 11, a conference of the Internationale Group in Berlin constituted the current as a membership organization and changed its name to the Spartacus League. The previous day it had published the following program in its newly founded Berlin newspaper, *Die Rote Fahne* (The red flag), indicating the essential measures necessary to open the road to a true socialist government. These measures, it stressed, required the SPD's exclusion from government.

"Organize the Power Anew from Below"[56]

Safeguard the power you have won.

The first democratic virtue is distrust!

The red flag flies over Berlin! You have earned your rightful place among the cities in which the proletariat and the soldiers have already taken power. But just as the world watched to see whether you would accomplish your mission, now the world watches to see *how* you will accomplish it. You must spare no effort to carry out a revolutionary socialist program.

The abdication of a couple of Hohenzollerns will not do the job. Nor will placing a couple more Socialists at the head of the government. They have supported the bourgeoisie for four long years. They cannot do otherwise; they can only give us more of the same. Distrust those in chancellor's and ministers' posts who think they can direct your destiny from on high. It is not a question of replacing those in office from the top down but of organizing the power anew from below. Take care that the power you have seized does not slip out of your hands, and make sure that you use it to realize your goal. For your goal is the immediate conclusion of a proletarian, socialist peace, directed against world imperialism, and the socialist transformation of society.

In order to attain these goals, it is necessary above all that the Berlin proletariat, both in and out of uniform, declare its indomitable willingness to fight resolutely for the following demands:

1. Disarm all the police, the entire officer corps, and those soldiers not on the side of the new order. Arm the people. All armed soldiers and proletarians must keep their weapons.

2. Appointees of the workers' and soldiers' council must take charge of all military and civil administration and positions of authority.

3. Turn over all arms and munitions supplies and all arms factories to the workers' and soldiers' council.

4. The workers' and soldiers' council must control all means of transportation.

5. Abolish military courts. Replace military blind obedience with the voluntary discipline of soldiers under the control of the workers' and soldiers' council.

6. Eliminate the Reichstag and all parliaments as well as the existing imperial government. The Berlin workers' and soldiers' council must assume governmental power and establish a national workers' and soldiers' council.

7. Elect workers' and soldiers' councils throughout Germany with exclusive legislative and executive power. The entire adult urban and rural working population, regardless of sex, shall be eligible to vote for the workers' and soldiers' councils.

8. Abolish all dynasties and separate states. Our slogan is "For a unified socialist German republic."

9. Immediately establish relations with all existing workers' and soldiers' councils in Germany and with socialist sister parties abroad.

10. Immediately recall the Russian embassy to Berlin.

Workers and soldiers! Our bondage of thousands of years is coming to an end. Out of the unspeakable suffering of the war a new freedom is arising. For four long years the Scheidemanns and governmental Socialists drove you through the horrors of war, explaining that you must defend the "fatherland," when only imperialism's predatory interests were at stake. Now that German imperialism is collapsing, they are trying to save what they can for the bourgeoisie and to throttle the revolutionary energy of the masses.

No "Scheidemann" must be allowed to sit in the government. Socialists must not enter the government so long as a governmental

Socialist is still there. No cooperation with those who have betrayed you these four long years.

Down with capitalism and its agents!

Long live the revolution!

Long live the International! □

Soviet Russia Responds to the Revolution

When the imperial German government expelled the Soviet embassy November 6, the Bolsheviks concluded that Kaiser Wilhelm must be seeking an agreement with the Entente against the Soviet republic. Addressing the Sixth All-Russian Congress of Soviets, Lenin stated:

"Things have reached a state where British and French capitalists, who had proclaimed they were Wilhelm's enemies, are now on the verge of joining forces with this same Wilhelm in an effort to strangle the Socialist Soviet Republic. For they have come to realise that it is no longer a curiosity or an experiment in socialism, but the hotbed, the really genuine hotbed, of the world socialist revolution. Hence, the number of our enemies has increased along with the successes of our revolution. We must realise what is lying in store for us, without in any way concealing the gravity of the situation. We shall go to meet it not alone but with the workers of Vienna and Berlin, who are moving into the same fight, and who will perhaps bring greater discipline and class-consciousness to our common cause."[57]

When news reached Russia of the kaiser's overthrow, the Soviet government anxiously sought contact with the new revolutionary regime, hoping to establish a bloc to counter the plans of the Entente. At the same time it sought ways, as through the following appeal, to reach the working-class fighters who had carried out the revolution and encourage them to struggle to put power in the hands of the workers and peasants.

Soviet Appeal to the German Councils[58]

Tsarskoe Selo [Pushkin],
November 11

To all German workers', soldiers', and sailors' councils:

We have heard by radio from Kiel that Germany's workers, soldiers, and sailors have taken power. The Russian Soviet government congratulates you with all our heart and joins you in mourning those who have fallen in the glorious struggle for the workers' liberation. Unfortunately they will not be the last victims. We also learned from these broadcasts that Prince Max von Baden still heads the government, and Ebert, who supported Wilhelm and the capitalists for four years, is to become Reich chancellor.

Workers, soldiers, and sailors of Germany: so long as you tolerate a government consisting of princes, capitalists, and Scheidemanns, then you do not really have power. The Scheidemanns together with the Erzbergers will sell you out to capital.[59] In the armistice agreement they will arrange with the English and French capitalists for you to surrender your weapons. Soldiers and sailors, do not give up your arms, or the united capitalists will rout you. It is essential that you genuinely take power everywhere, arms in hand, and build a workers', soldiers', and sailors' government headed by Liebknecht. Do not allow them to foist a national assembly upon you. You know what the Reichstag got you.

Only the workers', soldiers', and sailors' councils and a workers' government will inspire the trust of the workers and sailors of other countries. Such a government will propose an honorable peace to the English and French workers. We are firmly convinced that they will follow your and our examples and settle accounts with their capitalists and generals. Then an honorable people's peace will be signed.

It is essential to link the fight for peace and freedom with the fight for bread. In Russia there is enough bread for you and us in the Ukraine, in the Kuban, and on the Don. That is why the English government is trying to get quickly through the Black Sea to south Russia, where it will help Generals Denikin, Krasnov, and Skoropadsky snatch the workers' bread. Our Red Army is fighting heroically against the bands of workers' enemies, who are also supported by your generals and the Scheidemann government. If you want bread, then it is essential to act quickly, before the British steal it away. The German workers', soldiers', and sailors' councils must immediately give the German soldiers in the Ukraine the order, by radio and by sending delegations. Krasnov's forces are very weak. While the Red Army attacks these bands from the north, together we can crush them in a few weeks, and then there will be bread for you.

Workers', soldiers', and sailors' councils: the Scheidemann government chased the Russian Soviet government's envoy out of Berlin for fear that he would be able to establish the link between German and Russian soldiers. We cannot send delegates to you immediately, until you have reined in Generals Hoffmann and Beseler, because the German generals in Lithuania and Poland block our way. Contact us by radio, call the Moscow and Tsarskoe Selo radio stations and let us know what is happening in Berlin. We are doing everything possible to send bread to you as quickly as we can.

Long live international solidarity of workers and soldiers!

Long live the alliance between the free Russian workers and the German soldiers and sailors!

Long live the German Soviet republic!

The Russian workers',
peasants', and soldiers'
Soviet government. □

Radek's 1925 memoirs describe the reaction among Russian workers to the victory in Germany:

"In the factories it was indescribable; I had never seen such enthusiasm. I spoke at the Prokhorov textile factory. I said that the German revolution was not only our greatest victory but at the same time our greatest duty. Only that summer had we learned what hunger was. But they, the German workers, had lived for three years on a couple of ounces of bread and beets. I told them we had to help the German revolution with bread even out of what little we had. I watched the faces of the audience very closely. At meetings, in a difficult moment, my eyes invariably search for the weakest link in the chain. I always choose the most backward worker and speak exclusively to him or her, because if you convince that listener then you can be sure you have convinced them all. But now before me were faces full of enthusiasm. I could not find anyone indifferent or tired. 'Even if we starve, we will help our German brothers!' My exclamation was unanimously picked up by the masses of women workers."[60]

The November 11 armistice obliged Germany to evacuate its troops on the western front immediately, but to keep its forces in eastern Europe to "maintain order." The German generals aimed to use these troops against the advancing Soviet revolution.

Meanwhile, the Soviet Commissariat of Foreign Affairs tried repeatedly to contact the new German government via the Hughes teleprinter. Finally, on November 14, Radek and the commissar of foreign affairs, Georgiy Chicherin, succeeded in reaching Haase, the German cabinet member assigned to foreign affairs. Also present was Julian Marchlewski, a Polish Communist with long experience in the German revolutionary left.

The following is from the text of their exchange with Haase.

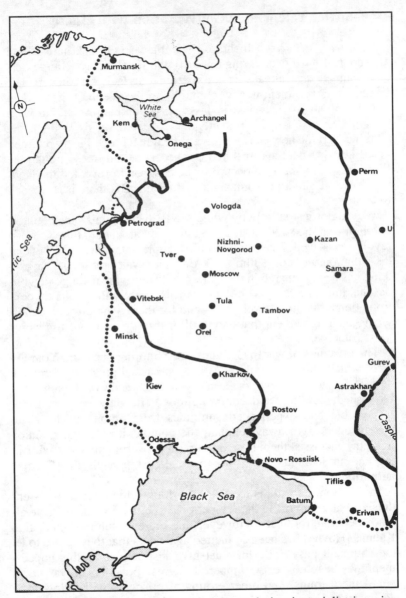

Territory controlled by Soviet government during imperialist invasion and civil war, November 1918.

Soviet Teleprinter Conversation with Haase[61]

Georgiy Chicherin: Chicherin, Marchlewski, Radek here. Good afternoon. I have been trying to reach you for five days. Immeasurable damage has already resulted from our lack of contact. The Ukrainian government is now preparing to receive the Entente fleet in Odessa and Novorossisk; in Jassy [Iasi], an entire plan has been worked out to have the Entente forces march on us through the Ukraine.[62] If the new German government had immediately returned our Black Sea fleet and restored our access to rail lines through the Ukraine, we might have occupied the coast and prevented the landing. Now the situation is much more difficult. But there is still much to be done.

We cannot just sit idly by while the British organize the counterrevolution in the south. It is aimed not only at us but at the German revolution as well. Even an Ebert must appreciate that — the logic of his situation will force him to. We cannot wait any longer: everything has been prepared in the Ukraine.[63] However, if we go in without making agreement with the Germans, there will be bloody confrontations, disastrous both for us and for them. Therefore, we must secure their agreement that they will instruct their troops to receive us as friends. . . .

The prisoners of war in Germany are a burning question. Your decree, which leaves everything as it was, caused great consternation here.[64] In using force of arms you will achieve nothing but bloodshed, conflict, and confrontations. The only solution is for responsible and experienced comrades from among us to go to the prisoners right away, explain the complexities of the situation to them, and assist them in setting up self-government and establishing an autonomous and smooth relationship with the German authorities.

In addition, two trains loaded with flour, which our workers enthusiastically sent off to the revolutionary German workers, have already departed for Orsha. However, the supreme soldiers' council in Kaunas [Kovno] has been so incited against us that they refuse to let the shipment pass.[65] Berlin must give instructions so this impediment may be removed. A number of German prisoners of war are on board these trains, and other groups of prisoners will follow. The desire to go home is enormous. Appropriate instructions must be issued so that they are not denied permission to reenter. These matters all show how essential it is that we now remain in close communication.

The Soviet Central Executive Committee has delegated several leading comrades to go to Berlin. We request that those carrying papers bearing my signature be allowed through the lines. There will also be a number of French and British agitators traveling to work among prisoners of war and on the western front. Naturally, it is most important that our [diplomatic] delegation, which is waiting in Borisov under humiliating conditions, be returned to Berlin immediately, as the Berlin workers' and soldiers' council decided.[66] After we received the telegram signed by you and Ebert, we inquired whether you adhere to the position of the old German government on breaking diplomatic relations with Russia. . . .

Finally, I would like to ask whether you received the numerous telegrams and radiotelegrams we sent you. We know very well from our experiences during the Kerensky period how privy councillors and other officials of the old regime behave toward a new government.

My friends standing here with me will speak with you later. We would be most grateful if you would respond to me now. End. Chicherin.

Hugo Haase: I deeply regret that we have not been in touch before now. I did receive telegrams from you, which prompted me to seek contact with you by teleprinter today. I understand your situation perfectly. I ask you and your friends to consider our internal and external situation. Our troops will no longer fight under any circumstances. Soldiers' councils everywhere are tumultuously demanding that peace be concluded as quickly as possible. They would rebel against anyone responsible for the armistice being broken off. They demand the most scrupulous adherence to the conditions of the armistice so that hostilities are not renewed. The troops are in such a state that no power can mobilize them for military action. . . .

On behalf of the workers I warmly thank you for the two trainloads of flour that the Russian workers are sending to ease our food situation. I will relay the information about the soldiers' council in Kaunas to the cabinet so that the necessary instructions can be sent. Similarly, I will immediately report on the return of prisoners of war so that no problems arise. Your proposal to send French and British agitators to propagandize among prisoners of war and on the western front was flatly rejected here. Any activity of that nature would lead to prolonging the war with the Entente and cutting off delivery of desperately needed foodstuffs. The cabinet will rule on diplomatic relations after it has clarified the matter of the consul general.[67] I will urge that this be done right away. You know my position.[68] I will speak with Joffe today. . . .

Karl Radek: Radek here. Good afternoon, Comrade Haase. . . .

Chicherin's proposals took into account the war-weariness of the German soldiers. All we ask of the German government is that it instruct its military authorities in the Ukraine and the occupied territories to offer no resistance to possible movements of our troops, which will not be directed against the German army. If the German troops are not capable of fighting against the Entente, that implies that they are also incapable of fighting against us. The German government would need only to discretely impress this upon its commanders and appoint special commissioners to ensure that individual commanders do not just happen to be more zealous about fighting us than the Entente. . . .

Your response to the question of the return of the Russian legation astonishes us.

Hauschild and all the rest of Kaiser Wilhelm's representatives are well and unharmed. The government has no objection to their unrestricted return. If the German prisoners of war felt that their consuls were not fitting representatives of revolutionary Germany, we were hardly in a position to tell them otherwise. We will for our part in no way interfere if the German revolutionary government sends Privy Councillor Schiemann.[69] But we would consider it a transgression against the interests of the German and Russian peoples if the foreign office makes the return of the representatives of the Russian workers and soldiers dependent on whether every ceremonial nicety toward Wilhelm's servants was properly observed. This is especially so since we know, just as you do, that the German consuls were involved in spiriting away Russian gold and jewels — as we will soon publicly demonstrate. Now that we have officially declared that the consuls may depart as soon as their staff has arrived, we ask you to order the German authorities in Borisov, Kaunas, and wherever else it may be necessary, to allow Joffe to return to Berlin.

We also request permission for Rakovsky and Bukharin to travel to Vienna and we request safe-conduct for our couriers to Switzerland and Sweden.

We hope the Entente will not cut off your bread supply for that. . . .

We believe that despite all the differences dividing the Communist government of Russia from Scheidemann's party and yours, we can and should attend to current interests that we hold in common by reaching agreements in order to spare the German soldiers and the population in the occupied territories hardship and misery. For that reason, we urgently and most strongly request that you get answers now to all these questions. We are not accustomed to waiting around when the situation calls for quick and vigorous action. And should the German government fail to do everything possible to quickly reach agreement with us on resolving these questions, we shall be compelled to act independently on our own initiative and do whatever the situation demands.

We are quite certain that if we do so, we can count not only on the support of our cothinkers in Germany, but also on help from part of the German occupation armies. In that event, responsibility for dividing the German occupation army would rest with the provisional government of Germany, which apparently does not grasp that this situation requires concerted, prompt, and vigorous action by the proletariat of both countries.

Finally, I would like to communicate a request of Karski [Marchlewski] to you: in the event that you permit Polish comrades to travel to Warsaw, Karski — who would be heading their group — wishes to go on to Berlin to meet with the government. We also request that you grant us the opportunity to speak with Liebknecht, Rosa Luxemburg, and Tyszka [Jogiches] on the Hughes machine.

Regards. Together with Chicherin, who wants to add a few words, I await your reply. Radek. . . .

Haase: Please bear in mind that I am not in charge of the foreign ministry but am a member of the six-person political directorate and in that context am answerable for foreign affairs. The Reich chancellery does not have a Hughes machine. I am speaking to you on the one in the foreign ministry, and as you can imagine, there are restrictions on its use. Naturally, I will take the matters you and Comrade Chicherin raise to the cabinet and discuss them from the same principled point of view I have always held.

We are only in our fifth day as a government. Day and night we are beset by a storm of questions, all of them demanding immediate answers. The questions pertaining to the Russian ambassador and withdrawal from the occupied territories have been discussed promptly on more than one occasion. In light of our conversation, I will raise the question today once again. I advise that you personally recommend that the staff of the consulate general who are under house arrest be released unconditionally. I have received no word whatever about the staff in the consulate general in Petersburg [Leningrad]. Be sure to send information as soon as possible by telegraph. Unfortunately, I now have to leave for a conference that cannot be put off; therefore, I cannot respond in more detail to Radek's and Chicherin's comments. You may rest assured, however, that I will submit everything I have heard to the cabinet for quick action. Best regards. □

Haase's response confirmed that the new German government was opposed to any collaboration with Soviet Russia that might displease the Allied powers. Chicherin later recorded, "as soon as I read the ribbon of my conversation with Haase to Vladimir Ilyitch, he said, 'nothing will come of it, this must be stopped.' "[70] Haase never resumed the conversation.

Two days later Berlin telegraphed the Soviet government, rejecting the offer of Soviet grain. It valued this offer "all the higher, since we know, as does the whole world, that the people in Petersburg and Moscow are themselves victims of the most bitter poverty." Nevertheless, the telegram continued, "Fortunately the steps we have taken with President Wilson have opened the possibility that we can be supplied from overseas."[71]

On receiving this message, Radek recalled, "I saw the face of the old woman textile worker from the Prokhorov factory who, even with hungry children at home, willingly sacrificed a piece of bread to help the German brothers. Her outstretched hand hung in midair. Haase, leader of the German revolution, was receiving bread and fats from Wilson, the leader of the American plutocracy. He did not need help from the Russian revolution. It was August 4 again: Judas Iscariot had committed his second betrayal."[72]

The U.S. government offer was published November 15 in German newspapers. It attached a significant proviso: food shipments could be considered only "on condition that public order in Germany is genuinely reestablished and maintained and a just distribution of food supplies guaranteed."[73] SPD propagandists underlined the meaning of this message: if the revolution marched forward to further conquests, Wilson would cut off food shipments.

On November 16, however, the French daily *Le Temps* revealed that, "It was not Mr. Wilson who thought up the condition that he set. It was urged on him by the German Reich chancellor himself [Ebert]. When he asked America to quickly supply Germany with food, he took the trouble to add: under the condition that public order be preserved in Germany and equitable food distribution be guaranteed."[74]

In early December, the Spartacists publicized the report from *Le Temps*, commenting:

"The specter of hunger stalks Germany. Without food supplies from abroad, in the near future we will experience very serious difficulties feeding the people. Wilson and other governments have repeatedly promised to supply us with food, on the disgraceful condition that 'law and order' be preserved in Germany. In other words, the German proletariat must renounce the revolution and socialism.

"Horror and indignation grip the German working masses as the international capitalist clique's conspiracy against the revolution cracks the whip of hunger at the German proletariat. "And what do we discover? The threat of hunger's whip comes not from Wilson and his imperialist wolf pack. It was Ebert who requested this infamy from them!"[75]

The Ebert government denounced this as slander, and *Vorwärts* denied that any such message from Ebert existed. But the Ebert telegram subsequently turned up in published U.S. diplomatic papers, proposing the precise condition found in the U.S. reply — that food be sent "if public order is maintained."[76]

On November 18, the German cabinet discussed whether to permit the Soviet ambassador to return to Berlin. Invited to sit in on the meeting were Kautsky from the USPD; Eduard David, a leader of the SPD's proimperialist right wing; and Rudolf Nadolny, held over from the kaiser's government as head of the foreign office's Russian section.

The cabinet minutes on this point follow.

German Government Denies Recognition to Soviets[77]

November 18, 1919

Friedrich Ebert chairs. Present are the cabinet members, plus Dr. David, Kautsky, and Privy Councillor Nadolny.

(Continuation of the discussion of Germany's relationship to the Soviet republic.)

Haase: I recommend a policy of delay. (*Reads reports from embassies in The Hague, Bern, and Stockholm.*) These reports indicate that the Entente is prepared to compromise with the current citizens' socialist republic on peace terms and on the delivery of food supplies, providing that and so long as the government continues in its present composition under Ebert. But confronted with a rise of Bolshevism they would intervene immediately with all available means. Joffe's return alone would be enough to alter the prospects for peace.

(Landsberg and Nadolny remind the meeting of the radio broadcasts in which the Soviet government insulted the German government and urged the workers to overthrow it and of other broadcasts proclaiming solidarity between the German revolution and the Russian Soviet republic.)

Kautsky: (Agrees with Haase) The decision must be delayed. The Soviet government will not last long; in a few weeks it will be finished. We do have a few questions in dispute with them, for example, the arrest of the consuls general in Moscow and Petersburg. We can negotiate on this, thereby winning time. After a week or two, when Joffe agrees to the terms — no agitation among English and French prisoners of war — then perhaps his return would be possible. . . .

Haase: If the purpose of the anti-Bolshevik campaign is to unite all countries in a common fight against the socialist revolution, then we cannot go along with it.

David: Very true!

Haase: The French and English Socialists are also unanimously against sending troops to Russia. We could not justify spilling even one drop of German blood in that way.

Ebert: A Danish comrade urgently cautioned me that the Bolsheviks were about to be expelled from Denmark as well. Their collapse is imminent. This government's most important task is to conclude peace. Anything that interferes with peace must be deferred.

Nadolny: Our opponents are very effectively using against us the declaration in support of Russia by the workers' and soldiers' councils, passed at Busch Circus. . . .

Barth: I presented our current position on the Russian question to the [Berlin councils'] Executive Committee. It was approved without opposition.

Kautsky: We want to live with the whole world in peace and friendship, even with the Russian republic. No one can begrudge us such a peaceful position.

(The following agreement was reached:)

We will demand that the Russian government state its position on the radio messages casting aspersions on the present government. We will investigate the circumstances surrounding the arrest of the Petersburg and Moscow consuls general. A member of the workers' and soldiers' council from there should be invited here.[78] By then our consuls general should have arrived back here. □

Although the Petersburg and Moscow consuls general soon returned

V.I. Lenin and Y.M. Sverdlov, November 7, 1918.

to Germany, the Soviet ambassador still did not receive permission to return to Berlin. Soviet representatives were prevented from entering Germany to attend the December congress of German councils. German generals continued activities in the east hostile to the Red Army. Although thrust into office by workers and soldiers inspired by the Russian revolution, the government headed by Ebert, Scheidemann, and Haase had nonetheless joined the imperialist blockade against Soviet Russia.

Notes

1. V.I. Lenin, *Collected Works* (hereinafter *CW*) (Moscow: Progress Publishers, 1974), vol. 28, p. 86.

2. Lenin, *CW*, vol. 35, p. 364-65.

3. V.I. Lenin, "Letter to a Joint Session of the All-Russia Central Executive Committee, the Moscow Soviet and Representatives of Factory Committees and Trade Unions," in *CW*, vol. 28, pp. 101-4.

4. Ya.S. Drabkin, *Die Novemberrevolution 1918 in Deutschland* (Berlin [GDR]: Deutscher Verlag der Wissenschaften, 1968), pp. 75-78.

5. A.G. Löwy, *Die Weltgeschichte ist das Weltgericht* (Vienna: Europa Verlag, 1969), p. 106-7.

6. *Dokumente und Materialien zur Geschichte der deutschen Arbeiterbewegung* (Berlin [GDR]: Dietz Verlag, 1957), series 2, vol. 2, pp. 228-33.

7. Lenin, *CW*, vol. 35, p. 369.

8. See Karl Kautsky, *The Dictatorship of the Proletariat* (Ann Arbor, Mich.: University of Michigan Press, 1964). Excerpts of Kautsky's pamphlet are printed in chapter 7 of the present work.

9. *Dokumente und Materialien*, pp. 251-54.

10. Drabkin, *Novemberrevolution*, pp. 100-101.

11. *Dokumente und Materialien*, pp. 247, 256.

12. Lenin, *CW*, vol. 35, p. 371. The statement was signed by Lenin, Ya.M. Sverdlov, and Joseph Stalin.

13. Drabkin, *Novemberrevolution*, p. 129.

14. Excerpted from Karl Radek, "Noyabr'," in *Krasnaya Nov'*, October 1926, pp. 139-40.

15. Radek is referring to the contrast of methods at the Brest-Litovsk peace negotiations in early 1918, where Gen. Max Hoffmann, representing the German High Command, specialized in blunt statements of Germany's expansionist goals, while Trotsky, head of the Soviet delegation, used the negotiations as a platform to win mass support internationally for the Soviet regime's position on peace and self-determination.

16. Liebknecht's message is not available. His subsequent greetings on November 6 to the Sixth All-Russian Congress of Soviets read in part, "The Russian Soviet republic has become the banner of the fighting International. It is arousing the laggards, filling the hesitant with courage and multiplying ten times over everyone's power and determination. Besieged by hatred and slander, it towers above this river of filth as a magnificent achievement filled with

stupendous energy and the noblest ideals. A new and better world has begun."
(Karl Liebknecht, *Gesammelte Reden und Schriften* [Berlin (GDR): Dietz Verlag, 1974], vol. 9, pp. 588-89.)

17. On August 30, 1918, Lenin had been wounded in an assassination attempt by a member of a Socialist Revolutionary terrorist group.

18. Lenin expressed the perils to Soviet Russia posed by the collapse of German imperialism in a resolution he drafted for an October 27 meeting of the executive committee of the soviets:

"Soviet power finds itself in the following peculiar situation: on the one hand, we have never been so close to an international proletarian revolution as we are now; on the other hand, we have never been in such a perilous position as we are now. There are no longer two approximately equal groups of imperialist plunderers, devouring and weakening each other. There remains a single group of victors, the Anglo-French imperialists, which intends to divide the whole world among the capitalists. It intends to overthrow Soviet power in Russia at all costs and replace it by bourgeois power. It is preparing now to attack Russia from the South, through the Dardanelles and the Black Sea, for example, or through Bulgaria and Rumania. Moreover, at least a part of the Anglo-French imperialists evidently hope that the German Government, by a direct or tacit agreement with them, will withdraw its troops from the Ukraine only as the latter becomes occupied by Anglo-French troops, so as not to allow the otherwise inevitable victory of the Ukrainian workers and peasants and their establishment of a Ukrainian workers' and peasants' government.

"Behind the back of the Krasnov and whiteguard counter-revolutionaries, preparations are being made for an attack against us by a much more dangerous force, the force of the international counter-revolutionary bourgeoisie, with the Anglo-American and French bourgeoisie in first place." (Lenin, *CW*, vol. 28, p. 129.)

19. Lenin, *CW*, vol. 28, p. 131.

20. Friedrich Adler, the most prominent Austrian Social Democratic opponent of the war, had assassinated Austrian Prime Minister Stürgkh in 1916 as a protest against the war.

21. *Dokumente und Materialien*, p. 290.

22. Jörg Berlin, ed., *Die deutsche Revolution 1918/19: Quellen und Dokumente* (Cologne: Pahl-Rugenstein Verlag, 1979), pp. 162-63.

23. *Dokumente und Materialien*, p. 320.

24. Both Liebknecht's and Pieck's diaries kept during these events were published. See Liebknecht, "Tagebuch," in *Gesammelte Reden*, vol. 9, pp. 580-85, and Wilhelm Pieck, "Erinnerungen an die Novemberrevolution in Berlin," in *Gesammelte Reden und Schriften*, (Berlin [GDR]: Dietz Verlag, 1959) vol. 1, pp. 412-83.

25. *Dokumente und Materialien*, p. 326.

26. In 1915 the current around Liebknecht and Luxemburg published a single issue of a revolutionary Marxist magazine, *Die Internationale*. It was immediately suppressed. When this current formed a national organization in January 1916, it took the name of this journal, and called itself the Internationale Group. That same month its underground circulars, which had been published since December 1914, first appeared with the signature Spartacus, and the group soon became popularly known as the Spartacus current.

27. *Dokumente und Materialien*, pp. 324-25.

28. Max von Baden, *Erinnerungen und Dokumente* (Stuttgart: Deutsche Ver-

lags-Anstalt, 1927), p. 618.

29. Ibid., 632.

30. *Vorwärts,* November 9, 1918, 2d special edition, cited in Berlin, *Die deutsche Revolution,* p. 165.

31. *Dokumente und Materialien,* p. 333. The text of this appeal was written at Ebert's request by two members of the kaiser's government, Konrad Haussmann and Walter Simons.

32. Philipp Scheidemann, *Memoiren eines Sozialdemokraten* (Dresden: Carl Reissner Verlag, 1928), p. 313.

33. Gerhard A. Ritter and Susanne Miller, eds., *Die deutsche Revolution 1918-1919: Dokumente* (Frankfurt: Fischer Taschenbuch Verlag, 1983), pp. 77-78. This text is a stenographic record of Scheidemann's speech. A somewhat different version of the speech was given by Scheidemann in his memoirs, published in 1928. See Scheidemann, *Memoiren,* pp. 311-12.

34. Kaiser Wilhelm did not formally abdicate until November 28.

35. Ritter and Miller, *Die deutsche Revolution,* pp. 78-79.

36. The reference is to the expulsion from Germany of the Soviet embassy.

37. Following the democratic revolution in Berlin of March 18, 1848, the population carried the bodies of its fallen into the palace courtyard and forced Prussian King Friedrich Wilhelm IV to pay homage to those killed by his troops in the street fighting.

38. Ritter and Miller, *Die deutsche Revolution,* pp. 80-81.

39. Pieck, *Gesammelte Reden,* p. 429.

40. Ritter and Miller, *Die deutsche Revolution,* pp. 89-90.

41. Emphasis in this document has been added by the editor.

"Socialist republic" was Liebknecht's expression, as recorded by Pieck, in formulating the conditions. The SPD reply used the term "social republic." See Pieck, *Gesammelte Reden,* p. 429.

42. *Dokumente und Materialien,* p. 346.

43. Liebknecht, "Feinde ringsum!", in *Gesammelte Reden,* pp. 596-97.

44. *Dokumente und Materialien,* p. 359; Drabkin, *Novemberrevolution,* p. 230.

45. Pierre Broué, *Révolution en Allemagne: (1917-1923)* (Paris: Les Editions de Minuit, 1971), p. 165.

46. David W. Morgan, *The Socialist Left and the German Revolution* (Ithaca: Cornell University Press, 1975), pp. 143-44.

47. Cited in Lothar Berthold and Helmut Neef, *Militarismus und Opportunismus gegen die Novemberrevolution* (Frankfurt/Main: Verlag Marxistische Blätter, 1978), p. 434.

48. Ibid., 167.

49. *Dokumente und Materialien,* pp. 365-66.

50. While legal restrictions on freedom of the press were ended, limitations continued in other forms. It took the Spartacists eight days after November 9 before they could find a publisher for their daily newspaper, *Die Rote Fahne* — at an exhorbitant price. Under government restrictions on paper supplies, they were alloted only enough paper for four pages a day, while the SPD's *Vorwärts* received enough for sixteen to thirty-two pages daily. Meanwhile, well-financed right-wing agencies flooded the country with unrestricted propaganda in press runs of millions.

Although freed from official censorship, *Rote Fahne* still enjoyed no secure right to publish; its offices were occupied briefly by the military on December

6. After January 15 *Rote Fahne* was shut down repeatedly and was closed during most of 1919.

51. In accordance with this provision, compulsory religious instruction in Prussian schools was abolished. After protests from religious authorities, however, the decree was withdrawn December 28.

52. The Law on Patriotic Service was a wartime measure that subjected all men ages 17 to 60 to military service and empowered the war ministry to regulate labor in broad areas of the economy. It was used to outlaw strikes and bind workers to their jobs.

53. The laws on domestic servants, which dated in part from the eighteenth century and earlier, subjected farm hands, maids, coachmen, gardeners, and other servants of the big landowners totally to their "master's" command. Servants had no recourse against the master's will.

The exceptional laws against farm workers permitted the landowners to dictate the terms of labor contracts for farm laborers, deduct fines from farmworkers' pay for the slightest infringement of these provisions, and terminate employment at will without paying outstanding wages. In cases of dispute, the farmworker had no recourse.

Legal reforms enacted in 1918 and 1919 fell far short of ending the subjugation of these rural wage laborers.

54. *Illustrierte Geschichte der Deutschen Revolution* (Berlin: Internationaler Arbeiter-Verlag, 1929), p. 216.

55. "An die Partei!", in *Dokumente und Materialien*, pp. 362-63.

56. "Arbeiter und Soldaten von Berlin!", ibid., pp. 341-42.

57. Lenin, *CW*, vol. 28, pp. 146-47.

58. "An alle Arbeiter-, Soldaten- und Matrosenräte Deutschlands!", in *Dokumente und Materialien*, pp. 360-61.

59. The SPD leadership had collaborated with Matthias Erzberger, a leader of the Catholic Center Party and a prominent critic of the kaiser's government, in the latter stages of the war.

60. Radek, "Noyabr'," pp. 141-42.

61. Excerpted from Ritter and Miller, *Die deutsche Revolution*, pp. 343-50. A different English translation by Richard K. Debo of the complete document can be found in *Canadian-American Slavic Studies*, vol. 14, no. 4 (Winter 1980), pp. 524-34.

62. The Jassy conference brought representatives of all major anti-Bolshevik factions together with agents of the Allied powers from whom they were seeking assistance. The French and British representatives gave assurances that Soviet power would be kept out of the Ukraine either by the German troops stationed there at the time or by an invading Anglo-French army.

63. The puppet regime of P.P. Skoropadsky in the Ukraine was maintained only by Germany's army of occupation and would clearly fall as soon as this support ended. Revolutionary forces in the Ukraine, led by the Bolsheviks, were readying a bid to reestablish the Soviet government that the Germans had ousted. The Entente had already landed troops on the Ukraine's Black Sea coast and stood ready to support counterrevolutionary armies, while the Red Army was prepared to intervene. Under these conditions, securing the neutrality of German occupation forces was vital to prevent their clashing with Ukrainian workers and their Red Army supporters.

64. More than a million Russian prisoners of war remained in Germany in

November 1918. With the outbreak of revolution their German camp guards opened the gates and allowed them to leave. On November 11, a subcommittee of the Berlin councils issued a decree ordering that all prisoners, including those from Russia, be arrested at once and taken to the nearest place of detention.

65. The Kaunas soldiers' council was one of those organized by the High Command and led by officers; it was the supreme soldiers' council for the eastern front.

66. A statement of the November 10 assembly of the Workers' and Soldiers' Councils of Greater Berlin instructed the German government to restore immediately diplomatic relations with the Soviet republic and recall the Soviet ambassador to Berlin.

67. On hearing of the overthrow of the kaiser in Berlin, revolutionary German prisoners of war in Moscow and Leningrad occupied the German consulates in those cities and arrested Herbert Hauschild, the consul general representing the deposed imperial government.

68. Haase had been on record as favoring German collaboration with the Soviet republic.

69. Theodor Schiemann was an imperial official especially known for his hostility to Russia.

70. Richard K. Debo, *Revolution and Survival: the Foreign Policy of Soviet Russia, 1917-18* (Toronto: University of Toronto Press, 1979), p. 404.

71. *Akten zur deutschen auswärtigen Politik 1918-1945*, series A: 1918-1925, vol. 1, p. 31.

72. Radek, "Noyabr'," p. 142.

73. Drabkin, *Novemberrevolution*, p. 190.

74. Quoted in the Spartacist leaflet, "Wer schwingt die Hungerpeitsche," *Dokumente und Materialien*, p. 523.

75. Ibid.

76. Arno J. Mayer, *Politics and Diplomacy of Peacemaking: Containment and Counterrevolution at Versailles 1918-1919* (New York: Alfred A. Knopf, 1967), p. 97; Drabkin, *Novemberrevolution*, p. 190.

77. Excerpted from Ritter and Miller, *Die deutsche Revolution*, pp. 351-53.

78. The reference is to the councils established by German prisoners of war in Russia.

-2-

Germany: Power to the Exploited or Restored Bourgeois Rule?

Although the six-member cabinet led by Ebert and Haase had reached an accommodation with the old state bureaucracy and the officer corps, the working people, whose revolutionary action had established a "German Socialist Republic" and brought the war to an end, still looked to the the workers' and soldiers' councils for leadership. These bodies constituted a representative structure on which a government of the workers and peasants of Germany could rest. In that sense, they were the embryo of a new revolutionary state.

A debate on the role of these councils broke out in the workers' movement in the weeks after November 9 between revolutionary socialists, who called for a workers' government based on the councils, and the SPD-led forces, who sought to consolidate a stable capitalist state with a parliamentary system.

While bourgeois political currents openly assailed the councils, the SPD-USPD government did not openly challenge the councils' formal authority. Instead it insisted that the formal sovereignty of the councils must be only a temporary stage toward establishing the rule of the "whole people." The government sought to restrict the scope of the councils' activity, while reestablishing the authority of the old capitalist state institutions.

The People's Representatives claimed to have no mandate to carry out basic social change on behalf of the workers and soldiers who had raised them to power. They postponed any such action until a national assembly was convened. In seeking a mandate from the "whole people," the SPD officials aimed in reality at openly bringing into the government political representatives of the capitalists and their petty-bourgeois hangers-on. But the term *whole people* was an intentionally slippery one. It was presented to the base of the party as meaning that in order to consolidate a revolutionary socialist republic, the working

---

Footnotes to this chapter begin on page 109.

class in Berlin and other major cities had to involve growing layers of workers and exploited peasants throughout Germany — an irrefutable truth.

Friedrich Stampfer, editor of *Vorwärts*, put forward the government's case in the following lead article, printed on November 13.

The Reich Government and the Workers' and Soldiers' Councils[1]
by Friedrich Stampfer

Like a snowman in the spring sun, the old monarchical-militaristic police state of Prussian Germany has melted away. This has created the need for the entire Social Democracy, as constituted before the war, to assume political power. It has achieved unity, if not organizationally, then in action. But our joy at this fact must not blind us to the shadows that darken the path.

Social Democrats of both tendencies had just [before November 9] approved a change in the Reich constitution stipulating that no government that did not have the confidence of the people could remain in office, and that the military authorities were to be subordinate to democratically organized civil authorities.[2] These provisions were directed against the now-fallen monarchical system. But that now raises the question of whether they should apply universally. To this, Social Democracy says "yes"; it has to, in accord with the Erfurt program, which both tendencies have in common.[3]

The members of the new government call themselves "People's Representatives," a much more distinguished title than that of a minister, who is addressed as "your excellency." But first they must earn this title, because they have not yet received any sort of regular mandate from the people.

Who are "the people"? They are the entirety of adult male and female citizens. How can the people confer the appropriate mandate? Only through orderly majority rule, through general elections or referenda, which must be safeguarded against any fraud or improper influence. The new government can receive its mandate only from the whole people.

Since the government still lacks such a mandate, in my opinion it must consider its position provisional, yet to be confirmed by the people. It may preempt the people's final decision only insofar as their immediate interests dictate. Before it acts, the government must ask itself whether it is prepared to accept responsibility for its actions before the entire people, so that on the day of reckoning it can render accounts with a clear conscience.

Consequently, the government cannot be bound by mandates that are not clearly from the entire people. Furthermore, it must work to shorten the transition period: just as soon as humanly possible, it must provide for parliamentary representation, for election of a national constituent assembly to whom the government can return its power, retaking it only by decision of that assembly.

The new national leadership called for such an assembly with commendable clarity in its recently published program. In addition, all of south Germany — Austria, Bavaria, Baden, Württemberg, and Hesse — has declared for the constituent assembly.

Opposed to this conception is another, which in its sharpest form could well be summarized as follows:

The People's Representatives should not represent the entire people, but only the workers and soldiers, whose organs are the workers' and soldiers' councils. The latter constitute the real power, and all must bow unquestioningly to their orders, including the People's Representatives, the new national leadership.

This is supposed to be not a transitional, but rather a permanent arrangement. It means the "dictatorship of the proletariat," that is, the realization of socialism through a ruthless power struggle against all obstacles, whether they arise from class interests or even from differences of opinion among Socialists.

So these are the opposing positions, more or less: democracy through the national constituent assembly, or dictatorship through the workers' and soldiers' councils. Their common goal is to achieve socialism. But one side would achieve it carefully through the general will of the people, while the other would do it through the commanding will of their party. They would smash through, without regard for the suffering that might be caused by erroneous measures, especially to the workers, as has in fact happened in Russia.

These questions, and thereby the whole future of our people, must be decided by those workers and soldiers who have taken an active part in the revolution. Their victory will shine with that much more glowing brilliance, the more clearly it is explained that this is a victory not of force, but of general democratic rights of the people, which the workers and soldiers have won for the people as a whole.

So let the workers and soldiers be conscious of the enormous responsibility that they now bear. Let them take care that the movement that has begun so magnificently not end in confusion and unbearable suffering. I believe they must be told as clearly as possible that the Social Democratic Party, which sent Ebert, Scheidemann, and Landsberg to the government, will under no circumstances let itself be swept along on a course that leads not to a socialist order, but to the Russian chaos.

The government of socialist unity can remain in power only if the workers and soldiers recognize and support it as the real, authoritative central power. The government should examine all its measures to ensure that they are tailored to ease the terrible suffering that now weighs upon the working population. The government must be shielded from all unnecessary interference so that it can act, and it must understand that the people expect from it not only words, but resolute actions. Finally, the government must always be prepared to account for its actions before those appointed by the whole people, and it must not arbitrarily postpone that reckoning, but hasten it as much as possible.

It is essential that we forswear renewed fratricidal strife among the workers and soldiers, avoid quarreling, infighting, and chaos. Do not think that there exists a panacea that can quickly bring the people happiness and well-being. Our population now resembles someone who has been wounded who must first learn to walk with crutches before he can run and dance again.

Above all we must conclude peace. Only the new government can do that. Therefore, it must strive to obtain a just, lasting peace through the League of Nations, a peace that will allow us to live, breathe, and work. The government must provide for feeding the people — a frightfully difficult task, as anyone knows who is familiar with the armistice conditions. It must return the soldiers to their families and to gainful employment. An outstanding, smoothly functioning organization is necessary to accomplish this. Otherwise there will be a general catastrophe.

This government has not yet received the mandate of the entire people, but we must do everything to ensure that it does. Right now it is only our government, the workers' and soldiers' government, the government of the Socialists, who came together in the hour of need for common action. We are completely dependent on its viability and success. We and the government must go forward with a clear conscience toward that day — which is certain to come — when the whole people will call us to account through its national constituent assembly. □

Rosa Luxemburg, writing in the November 18 issue of *Rote Fahne*, presented a perspective that was the polar opposite of Stampfer's class-collaborationist approach. She cautioned that the principal enemy of Germany's laboring majority had not yet been defeated, and that the main struggle still lay ahead.

The Beginning[4]
by Rosa Luxemburg

The revolution has begun. What we need now is not rejoicing over its accomplishments, not celebrations of victory over the prostrate foe, but rigorous self-criticism and strict marshaling of our strength so the work now begun can go forward. For little has been attained and the enemy is *not* defeated.

What has been accomplished? The monarchy has been swept away. Supreme governmental power has been handed over to the workers' and soldiers' representatives. But the monarchy was never the real enemy. It was only the cover, the figurehead for imperialism. It was not the Hohenzollern who ignited the World War, spread fire to the four corners of the earth, and brought Germany to the brink of the abyss. Like all bourgeois governments, the monarchy was only an administrator for the ruling classes. The criminals who must be held responsible for the genocide are the imperialist bourgeoisie, the capitalist ruling class.

Abolition of capital's domination and achievement of a socialist order: that and nothing less is the historic theme of the current revolution. A massive task, this cannot be dispatched in a twinkling by a few decrees from on high, but can be set in motion only through the conscious action of the urban and rural working people. It can be carried through all tempests and brought safely to port only by the highest intellectual maturity and unflagging idealism of the popular masses.

The revolution's goal clearly points out its course, and its tasks indicate the needed methods. *All power to the toiling masses, and to the workers' and soldiers' councils; safeguard the revolution's accomplishments from the enemies that lie in wait for it.* These are the guidelines for all measures of the revolutionary government.

Every step, every action of the government must point like a compass in this direction:

• Expand and reelect local workers' and soldiers' councils to replace the chaotic and impulsive character of their initial actions through a conscious process of understanding the revolution's goals, tasks, and course.

- Maintain representative bodies of the masses in permanent session. Real political power should be transferred from the Executive Committee of the councils, a small body, to the broader basis of the workers' and soldiers' councils.
- Immediately convoke a national parliament of the workers and soldiers in order to organize all of Germany's proletariat as a class, a solid political power, the bulwark and driving force of the revolution.
- Immediately organize not the "peasants," but the farm workers and small peasants, a layer that has not participated in the revolution up to now.
- Build a proletarian Red Guard for ongoing defense of the revolution and train a workers' militia in order to organize the entire proletariat to be on guard at all times.
- Expel the surviving organs of the absolutist militaristic police state from the administration, judiciary, and army.
- Immediately confiscate dynastic fortunes and property and large landed estates as an initial, preliminary measure to secure the people's food supply, since hunger is the most dangerous ally of counterrevolution.
- Immediately convene in Germany a world congress of workers to loudly and clearly proclaim the socialist and international character of the revolution, because the future of the German revolution is anchored in the International and in the world proletarian revolution.

We have listed only the first, most necessary steps. What is the present revolutionary government doing?

It simply leaves the state as an administrative organism, from top to bottom, in the hands of yesterday's supporters of Hohenzollern absolutism and tomorrow's tools of the counterrevolution.

It convenes the national constituent assembly, thereby creating a bourgeois counterweight to the workers' and soldiers' power, shunting the revolution onto the rails of a bourgeois revolution, and conjuring away the socialist goals of the revolution.

It does nothing to demolish the continuing power of capitalist class rule.

It does everything to reassure the bourgeoisie, to preach the sacredness of private property, and to ensure the inviolability of capitalist property relations.

It retreats before the constantly advancing counterrevolution without appealing to the masses, without sharply warning the people.

Law and order! Law and order! These words reverberate from all sides and from all government statements and are jubilantly echoed from all wings of the bourgeoisie. The clamor against the specter of "anarchy" and "putschism," the familiar infernal whine of the capitalist worried about his safes, property, and profits: this is the overriding theme song of today, and the revolutionary workers' and soldiers' government calmly tolerates the sounding of the rallying cry for the assault on socialism. Worse — it participates in word and deed.

The results of the revolution's first week are as follows: in the land of the Hohenzollern, basically nothing has changed. The workers' and soldiers' government functions as a stand-in for the bankrupt imperialist government. All its acts — of commission and omission — are based on a fear of the working masses. Before the revolution could develop power and momentum, its life blood, which is its socialist and proletarian character, was drained.

Everything is as you would expect. The most reactionary country in the civilized world does not become a revolutionary people's republic in twenty-four hours. Soldiers who yesterday killed revolutionary proletarians in Finland, Russia, the Ukraine, and in the Baltics — and workers who quietly allowed this to happen — have not in twenty-four hours become conscious fighters for socialism.

The state of the German revolution reflects the maturity of German political conditions. Scheidemann-Ebert are the government befitting the German revolution in its present stage. And the Independents, who believe they can build socialism together with Scheidemann-Ebert and who solemnly certify in *Die Freiheit* that with them they are forming an "exclusively socialist government,"[5] thereby become the authorized corporate partners in this first, provisional stage.

But revolutions do not stand still. It is a fundamental law that they constantly move forward and outgrow themselves. The first stage is already pressing against its internal contradictions. The situation is understandable as a beginning, but untenable in the long run. The masses must be on guard if the counterrevolution is not to win across the board.

We have made a beginning. What remains is not in the hands of the petty creatures who want to block the flow of the revolution and stop the wheel of world history. World history's order of the day calls for achieving the final goals of socialism. The German revolution is on the path of this guiding light. Step by step, through storm and stress, through struggle and anguish, misery and victory, the revolution will triumph.

It must! □

When Luxemburg's article appeared, most workers were still skeptical toward assertions that the new government was acting against the revolution. The outcome of the November 9 uprising appeared to them as the achievement of the goal for which the German labor movement, organized politically in the SPD, had been fighting since the 1880s: the overturn of kaiserism and landlord-capitalist rule and their replacement by a socialist republic. After long decades of struggle, the Social Democratic movement seemed at last to have achieved governmental power. Moreover, many workers associated the SPD-USPD coalition cabinet with the working-class unity in struggle that had won the victory of November 9. The SPD sought to channel this desire for unity in action into support of the government's program of capitalist reconstruction.

During the war, growing numbers of working people had come to scorn the SPD for its support to the kaiser's military regime. Close to half the SPD's remaining members had rallied to the USPD in the 1917 split. By the final stages of the slaughter, however, the SPD had begun to salvage its authority by identifying itself with the mounting sentiment for peace and democratic reform. Now, with the war over and the kaiser gone, the SPD sought to convince workers that there was no longer a basis, if there ever had been, for division in the Social Democratic camp.

An editorial in *Vorwärts* November 10 said, "*The working class must remain united.* . . . If group works against group, and sect against sect, then we will fall into *the Russian chaos,* a general collapse, *misery* instead of happiness."

Such "unity," *Vorwärts* said, was vital to achieving the revolution's remaining goals, which it summarized as "concluding peace, organizing food supplies for the people, demobilizing ten million soldiers in an orderly fashion, organizing economic activity."

Vorwärts warned against "certain small groups led by unknown and irresponsible forces who are trying to go their own way." From across Germany had come news that "on the day of the revolution the old party and the Independents had found their way together again and have reconstituted the old united party," *Vorwärts* continued. "This unity must be achieved here as well."[6] In fact, there was no such reunification in any part of Germany. But the SPD won support for its "unity" line.

On November 10, recounted Revolutionary Shop Stewards' leader Richard Müller, *Vorwärts* "was the newspaper that every worker tried to obtain. . . . What *Vorwärts* wrote had an extraordinary influence among the workers, even among those who yesterday had been its bitterest foes. The entire war policy and its effects on workers' lives, the 'civil peace' with the bourgeoisie, was forgotten. Joy at the victory of the working class and dislike of the long fratricidal struggle within it overcame all hesitations. . . . The majority could not be convinced that the Social Democracy would betray a second time."

The Spartacists and the Shop Stewards argued that the SPD should not be permitted in a revolutionary government. But even in factories where the Shop Stewards had enjoyed workers' political support for years, Müller said, this view now met with little agreement. "Workers wanted the two parties [SPD and USPD] to march together and considered it correct that the workers' council be elected on a parity basis. So in some factories Social Democratic full-timers, who the previous day had been attacked and physically thrown out of the plants because they refused to join the general strike, were now elected as members of the workers' councils."

Elections to the councils showed, in Müller's view, that even in radical Berlin "the right-wing Socialists, the right-wing Independents, and all those who favored the two parties working together and forming a joint government had the majority on their side."[7]

Spartacus writers did not question that the SPD's slogans, for the moment, enjoyed mass support. But the Spartacists held that the new government's procapitalist orientation would prevent it from achieving the November 9 demands for "peace, freedom, and bread," and this would soon bring it into conflict with the workers and soldiers.

The Spartacists explained that SPD appeals in August 1914 and thereafter for sacrifice by the workers in the "national interest" had also been accepted for a time, but soon led to disaster and widespread disaffection from the party. At the outset of the imperialist slaughter, the revolutionists recalled, the German bourgeoisie had enlisted the SPD and trade union leadership in a "civil peace," that is, an abandonment for the duration of the war of the struggle to defend the class interests of workers and their exploited allies. In the following article, published November 19, Karl Liebknecht warned that workers were now being asked by the SPD to abandon class struggle in peacetime as well.

The New "Civil Peace"[8]
by Karl Liebknecht

"We no longer recognize different Socialist parties — only Socialists."[9] That is what they say now at the end of the World War. The flag of a new "civil peace" is raised. Fanatical hatred is sown against those who oppose the latest frenzy for unity. And once again Scheidemann and Company yell the loudest.

They get a good response especially from the soldiers. No wonder. Not all soldiers are proletarians, by a long shot, and the state of siege, censorship, official propaganda, and Stampfer's skills had their effect. Most soldiers are revolutionary against militarism, the war, and the blatant representatives of imperialism. But with respect to socialism they are still divided, vacillating, and immature. Many proletarian soldiers, like workers who were subject for years to the mind-numbing influence of the social imperialists, believe that the revolution is completed, and that it is now only a matter of concluding the peace and demobilizing the army. After a long ordeal the soldiers want quiet.

They overlook the fact that the "revolution," which took place almost with official tolerance, has been no more up to now than a collapse of the autocratic forms left over from the "turbulent year,"[10] no more than the completion of the bourgeois revolution. They forget that while political power has fallen into the hands of the proletariat, this transfer of power can be historically justified only if it is used to accomplish the proletariat's historic task: the overthrow of economic class domination. They fail to understand that the problems of peace, demobilization, and economic recovery can be resolved only if the proletariat proceeds decisively and unwaveringly to its final goal.

Unity! Who could yearn and strive for it more than we? Unity, which gives the proletariat the strength to carry out its historic mission.

But not all "unity" breeds strength. Unity between fire and water extinguishes the fire and turns the water to steam. Unity between wolf and lamb makes the lamb a meal for the wolf. Unity between the proletariat and the ruling classes sacrifices the proletariat. Unity with traitors means defeat.

Only forces pulling in the same direction are made stronger through unity. When forces pull against each other, chaining them together cripples them both.

We strive to combine forces that pull in the same direction. The current apostles of unity, like the unity preachers during the war, strive to unite opposing forces in order to obstruct and deflect the radical forces of the revolution. Politics is action. Working together in action presupposes unity on means and ends. Whoever agrees with us on means and ends is for us a welcome comrade in battle. Unity in thought and attitude, in aspiration and action, that is the only real unity. Unity in words is an illusion, self-deception, or a fraud. The revolution has hardly begun, and the apostles of unity already want to liquidate it. They want to steer the movement onto "peaceful paths" to save capitalist society. They want to hypnotize the proletariat with the catchword of unity in order to wrench power from its hands by reestablishing the class state and preserving economic class rule. They lash out at us because we frustrate these plans, because we are truly serious about the liberation of the working class and the world socialist revolution.

Can we unify with those who are nothing more than substitutes for the capitalist exploiter, dressed as socialists?

Can we, may we join with them without becoming accomplices in their conspiracies?

Unity with them would mean ruin for the proletariat. It would mean renouncing socialism and the International. They are not fit for a fraternal handshake. They should be met not with unity, but with battle.

The toiling masses are the prime movers of social revolution. Clear class consciousness, clear recognition of their historic tasks, a clear will to achieve them, and unerring effectiveness — these are the attributes without which they will not be able to complete their work. Today more than ever the task is to clear away the unity smokescreen, expose half measures and halfheartedness, and unmask all false friends of the working class. Clarity can arise only out of pitiless criticism, unity only out of clarity, and the strength to create the new socialist world only out of unity in spirit, goals, and purpose. □

The charge of disrupting workers' unity had also been flung against the Bolsheviks by reformist and centrist forces, before, during, and after the 1917 revolutions in Russia. After August 1914, the Bolsheviks had argued that a split with the opportunist forces on an international basis was the only road to true working-class unity in action against their oppressors and exploiters. Lenin and Zinoviev wrote in 1915, "Today *unity* with the opportunists *actually* means subordinating the working class to their 'own' national bourgeoisie, and an alliance with the latter for the purpose of oppressing other nations and of fighting for dominant-nation privileges; it means *splitting* the revolutionary proletariat of all countries."[11]

In 1918 German revolutionists moved closer to the Bolsheviks' position on the need for a political and organizational break from the opportunist and centrist currents. But the German revolutionary Marxists lacked the experience and capacity of the Bolsheviks in taking political initiatives to win a hearing from workers still loyal to their traditional organizations and in appealing to their aspiration for unity in struggle against the exploiters.

The workers' and soldiers' councils represented a potential vehicle for such united action by the working class. From their inception, however, they were deformed and hobbled by the political domination of the SPD and its supporters. In the following article, published November 21, Liebknecht analyzed the weaknesses of what he calls the revolution's "political form" — the workers' and soldiers' councils. He explained that real control of the government still lay with the surviving institutions of the capitalist state.

Where Matters Stand[12]
by Karl Liebknecht

Between the political form of the German revolution up to now and its social content lies a gaping contradiction, which cries out for resolution. How it is resolved will determine the future development of the revolution. Its political form is that of proletarian action, its social content that of bourgeois reform.

Granted, its political form was primarily a military action that can be called proletarian only with a grain of salt. The revolution's driving force was not so much proletarian class needs as more or less general social ailments. The victory of the masses of workers and soldiers was thanks not so much to their combative strength as to the internal collapse of the former system. The political form of the revolution was not only proletarian action, but also the ruling classes' flight from their responsibility for the course of events. With a sigh of relief, the ruling classes left the liquidation of their bankruptcy to the proletariat, thereby hoping to escape the social revolution, whose approaching thunder leaves them in a cold sweat.

The present "Socialist" government would like to resolve the contradiction by riveting the proletarian form back onto the bourgeois content. The task of the socialist proletariat is to raise the outdated content to the higher level of the more advanced form, to escalate the revolution to a social revolution.

"The German proletariat now holds political power."

Does this statement reflect reality? It is true that workers' and soldiers' councils have been formed in all major German cities, but bourgeois citizens' councils and the like often stand next to them. In many small towns all has remained as before or has changed only cosmetically. Numerous "peasants' councils" have sprung up, but nowhere are they controlled by the rural proletariat. They are mostly in the hands of middle or large landowners.

The workers' councils are not always composed solely of proletarians and their clearly defined representatives. We know of cases in which workers have allowed themselves to be taken in by clever, ingratiating bosses or other fat capitalists. Often the elected workers are only partially enlightened, barely class conscious, or very insecure, indecisive, or powerless. As a result, the councils either have no revolutionary character or have only illusory political power over the agents of the old regime. Members of every conceivable bourgeois profession present themselves as "fellow workers," and send their representatives into the workers' councils, which are therefore in danger of becoming general people's parliaments organized according to profession — in line with the proposals of Herr von Heydebrandt.

In the soldiers' councils things are even worse. They are the expression of a body of men composed of all classes of society. Proletarians may be the big majority here, but these are hardly the most conscious proletarian fighters, ready for class battles. Their councils are often built from the top down through the intervention of officers and even of circles of the nobility, who seek to retain their control over the soldiers through cunning adaptation and have had themselves elected as the soldiers' representatives.

Add to that the fact that, given the whole character of the revolution, the socially less-differentiated soldiers' councils today naturally hold far stronger influence than the workers' councils. The "Socialist government," to the best of its ability, has preserved or restored the entire bourgeois state and administrative apparatus and the military machinery. It is extremely hard for the workers' and soldiers' councils to get any real control over these institutions. The powerful economic position of the propertied classes has not been touched and some of their sources of social power, for example their superior formal education, are virtually impossible to eliminate in the foreseeable future. Most importantly, the majority of the food supplies are in the hands of the antiproletarian, antisocialist landowners. Consequently, it is clear that one can speak of real political rule by the proletariat only with the greatest of reservations.

Admittedly, the present government — the six-man cabinet — and the Executive Committee of the Workers' and Soldiers' Councils were elected by the Greater Berlin workers' and soldiers' councils, whose political maturity today is probably close to the national average. But that is only for show. Political power consists not of formal mandates or mysteriously conferred powers of attorney, but rather in the firm possession of such strong instruments of power that political ascendancy is safe against all attacks.

The centers of state power were in the hands of the workers and soldiers on November 9. No one could have stopped them from seizing important economic instruments of power. Instead, since November 9 they have allowed the already conquered instruments of power to slip away more and more. Let us not fool ourselves. Even the political power that the proletariat did acquire on the ninth has today mostly dissolved and continues to trickle away hourly.

As the proletariat grows weaker in this way, all its mortal enemies are rapidly assembling. The counterrevolution is organizing with increasingly open cynicism in the countryside and cities. We hear from Schleswig-Holstein and other provinces that district administrators, chief local and regional officials, policemen, municipal officers, teachers, lawyers, manufacturers, peasants, and all sorts of prosperous layers are consolidating into a daily broader and more solid bloc, which is all the more dangerous the longer the rural proletariat is abandoned and accessible to their influence.

Action to starve out the proletariat, and if it comes to that, a *Vendée* against the proletarian centers is clearly being prepared.[13]

The danger is growing by leaps and bounds. There is no time to lose, or else in a few weeks the proletariat will stand before the ruins of its hopes. The working masses must order an immediate halt to the continuing process of weakening the proletariat. They must immediately restrain the government, which is promoting this process, and tell it: "Not one step further!"

They must keep a tight grip on their conquests. They must proceed to conquer the remaining positions of power, to finally overpower the ruling classes and to turn the proletariat's reign into a truth, a reality with flesh and bone.

Hesitating means losing both what has been won and what must be won. Hesitation draws death closer — the death of the revolution. The danger is enormous and pressing. □

Liebknecht had declined nomination to the Executive Committee of the Workers' and Soldiers' Councils of Berlin. He did so, he wrote on

November 15, "as a consequence of my stand on the question of join-ing the present coalition cabinet," for which the Executive Committee was formally responsible.[14] The Spartacists nonetheless participated in the councils in Berlin and elsewhere. They held that the councils, de-spite their weaknesses, had the potential to act as instruments of workers' struggle and to provide the basis for a new, revolutionary government.

Some other revolutionists, however, pulled out of the councils al-together. A small communist group in Dresden, which stood outside the Spartacus League and was allied with the Bremen Left, exemplified this sectarian approach in walking out of the Dresden workers' and soldiers' council on November 16. They explained this action as fol-lows.

"Revolutionary and Counterrevolutionary Currents Cannot Unite"[15]

Dresden,
November 16, 1918

To the United Revolutionary Workers' and Soldiers' Council of Greater Dresden.

Every day the revolution is more and more revealed as a grandiose deceptive maneuver, desired and prepared by the bourgeois govern-ments in order to save capitalist society from threatened doom.

Germany's capitalist class will receive a cheap peace from the En-tente, and in return will undertake with Entente support to strangle communism (Bolshevism) — the only real threat to capitalism. Both Socialist tendencies are helping them. The so-called revolution thereby becomes a counterrevolutionary operation.

The Communists of Greater Dresden joined together on November 9 with the Socialists — dependent and independent — to carry out a socialist revolution.[16]

The experience of one week has been enough for us to realize that this compromise is untenable. Revolutionary and counterrevolution-ary currents cannot unite.

The task of pushing forward, escalating, and completing the incip-ient revolutionary movement can be accomplished only by Com-munists.

Therefore we are withdrawing from the United Revolutionary Workers' and Soldiers' Council of Greater Dresden and resigning from the positions that were assigned to us.

[Signed by Otto Rühle, chairman of the workers' and soldiers' council, by seven members of its executive committee, and by eleven members of the council.] □

As soon as the November revolution posed the threat of overturning capitalist rule, the German bourgeosie, which had supported or tolerated the old monarchical constitution, suddenly began to posture as ardent democrats. The bourgeois political parties, renamed and reorganized, now attacked the workers' and soldiers' councils in the name of representative democracy and the parliamentary system. The SPD carried this position into the working class, calling on the councils to hand over to a national assembly the power and authority they had won in November. As the majority of the population, workers could win a Socialist majority in the assembly, they maintained, and on that basis could build the new social order. The USPD national leadership accepted the essence of this proposition, arguing only that the national assembly elections should be delayed until a full and adequate political debate among the parties had unfolded.

The German workers' movement had long advanced the demand for a constituent national assembly in its struggle to eliminate the autocratic features of the imperial state and institute full democratic rights. The planned assembly elections would also realize other democratic demands of the workers' movement: the voting age was to be reduced to twenty years from twenty-five; women would vote for the first time; the elected assembly would at last be formally sovereign.

As the Spartacists and left-wing members of the USPD pointed out, however, the political context had changed since the days of struggle against the monarchy. The SPD and USPD leaders were no longer advocating a constituent national assembly as a democratic alternative to the imperial regime. Instead, the officialdom of these parties was now counterposing the national assembly demand to the much broader democracy possible in a state based on councils of workers, soldiers, and small peasants, and committed to the socialist transformation of social relations. The demand had been transformed into window dressing for leaving power in the hands of the capitalists and the officer corps.

In response, the revolutionists therefore called on the workers' and soldiers' councils to expand their political authority and move toward constituting a revolutionary government. The following article by Luxemburg, printed in the November 20 *Rote Fahne,* helped launch an educational campaign on this question.

The National Assembly[17]
by Rosa Luxemburg

From the *Deutsche Tageszeitung*, the *Vossische Zeitung*, and *Vorwärts* to the Independents' *Freiheit*; from Reventlow, Erzberger, and Scheidemann to Haase and Kautsky resounds a unanimous call for the national assembly and an equally unanimous cry of fear at the idea of working-class power.

To this end the entire "people," the entire "nation" is to be called upon to decide the subsequent fate of the revolution by majority vote.

It is understandable why the open and disguised agents of the ruling classes use this slogan. But we do not discuss with these watchmen of the capitalist coffers — either *in* the national assembly, or *about* it.

The Independent leaders, however, are lining up with capital's guardians on this decisive question.

As Hilferding explains in *Freiheit*, they want to spare the revolution from using force and experiencing civil war with all its horrors. Petty-bourgeois illusions! They imagine that the course of the mightiest social revolution in the history of humanity will take the form of the various social classes coming together and cultivating a nice, peaceful, and "dignified" discussion with each other, and then staging a vote — perhaps by filing through the parliamentary doors as of old.[18] When the capitalist class sees that it is in the minority, then as a well-disciplined parliamentary party, it will declare with a sigh: "There is nothing to be done. We see that we have been outvoted. Very well, we bow to the majority and turn over our land, factories, mines, all our fireproof safes, and our lovely profits to the workers."

Truly, the spirit of Lamartine, Garnier-Pagès, Ledru-Rollin — the petty-bourgeois illusionists and babblers from 1848 — has not been extinguished. They have risen again — shorn of the luster and talent and charm of newness — in the boring, pedantic, scholarly German edition of Kautsky, Hilferding, and Haase.

These profound Marxists have forgotten the ABCs of socialism.

They have forgotten that the bourgeoisie is not a parliamentary party, but a ruling class in possession of all the economic and social instruments of power.

The gentlemen junkers and capitalists are peaceful only so long as the revolutionary government is content with pasting pretty little bandages onto capitalist wage relations. They are well-behaved only so long as the revolution is well-behaved, that is, so long as their vital nerve, the artery of bourgeois class rule — capitalist private property, wage relations, and profit — remains untouched.

But take profit by the neck, or put private property under the knife, and they turn vicious.

Today's idyllic scene, where wolf and sheep, tiger and lamb graze together as in Noah's ark, will last until the instant socialism is posed in earnest.

The moment that this illustrious national assembly really decides to seriously institute socialism, to eradicate capitalism root and branch, the battle will be joined. Approach the bourgeoisie's heart — and they keep their hearts in safes — and they will fight to the death for their supremacy. A thousand open and hidden obstacles to the socialist measures will spring up.

All this is inevitable. It all must be fought out, defended, beat down — with or without the national assembly. The "civil war" that they are anxiously trying to banish from the revolution cannot be banished. For civil war is just another word for class struggle, and the idea of trying to introduce socialism without class struggle, by parliamentary majority decision, is a ridiculous petty-bourgeois illusion.

So what is gained through this cowardly detour called the national assembly? The bourgeoisie's position is strengthened, the proletariat is weakened and bewildered with empty illusions, time and energy are dissipated and lost in "discussions" between wolf and lamb. In a word, it plays into the hands of all those elements whose good intention is to cheat the proletarian revolution of its socialist aims and to castrate it into a bourgeois-democratic revolution.

But the question of the national assembly is not a tactical question, nor a question of what is "easier." It is a question of principle, of the socialist perception of the revolution.

The first decisive step in the Great French Revolution was the unification of the three separate estates in July 1789 into a common national assembly. This decision stamped the whole subsequent course of events. It was the symbol of the victory of a new, bourgeois social order over the medieval, feudal estate system.[19]

In the same manner, the symbol of the new, socialist order, borne by the present proletarian revolution, is the workers' parliament, representing the urban and rural proletariat. It symbolizes the class character of the actual tasks and the political organs that should carry them out.

The national assembly is an outdated legacy of the bourgeois revolutions, an empty shell, a stage prop from the time of petty-bourgeois illusions of a "united people," of the bourgeois state's "liberty, equality, fraternity."[20]

Those who resort to the national assembly are consciously or unconsciously turning the revolution back to the historical stage of bourgeois revolutions. They are disguised agents of the bourgeoisie or unconscious ideologues for the petty bourgeoisie.

The fight for the national assembly is being conducted under the battle cry: democracy or dictatorship. Obedient Socialist leaders are adopting this slogan of the counterrevolutionary demagogues without noticing that this alternative is a demagogic fraud.

The question today is not democracy or dictatorship. The question that history has put on the agenda reads: *bourgeois* democracy or *socialist* democracy. For the dictatorship of the proletariat is democracy in the socialist sense of the word. Dictatorship of the proletariat does not mean bombs, putsches, riots, and anarchy, as the agents of capitalist profits deliberately and falsely claim. Rather it means using all instruments of political power to achieve socialism, to expropriate the capitalist class, through and in accordance with the will of the revolutionary majority of the proletariat, and thus in the spirit of socialist democracy.

There is no socialism without the conscious will and the conscious action of the majority of the proletariat. A class organ, the national parliament of urban and rural proletarians, is needed to sharpen this consciousness and steel this will and organize this action.

Convening such a workers' government in place of the traditional national assembly of the bourgeois revolutions is in itself already a step in the class struggle; a break with the historical past of bourgeois society; a powerful tool with which to rouse the proletarian masses; a first, open, sharp declaration of war on capitalism.

No evasions, no ambiguities — the die is cast. Yesterday parliamentary cretinism was a weakness. Today it is an ambiguity. Tomorrow it will be a betrayal of socialism. ◻

The task of answering Luxemburg and other German revolutionists was taken up by the leaders of the USPD, especially Karl Kautsky. Although he had been Germany's best-known exponent of Marxism during the decade before and the decade after the turn of the century, by 1914 he had become an outspoken advocate of a reformist course. Kautsky's answer to the Spartacists on the national assembly question, which follows, was printed December 5 and 6 in *Die Freiheit* and then quickly circulated in pamphlet form.

National Assembly and Council Assembly[21]
by Karl Kautsky

I

The Council of People's Representatives has decided, subject to approval by the General Assembly of Workers' and Soldiers' Councils, that the elections to the national assembly shall take place on February 16.

Approval of this decision by many members of the Independent Social Democrats was much more a matter of submitting to necessity than it was an expression of their own view. They mistrust the national assembly, but see it as the only means with which to save the republic from disintegration and to achieve peace. Many among us wanted at least a later date for the elections, so that in the meantime the masses could be better schooled in socialism. But any postponement of the date would negate the most important immediate advantage that the national assembly is supposed to offer: providing the means to achieve peace and hold the nation together.

On the other hand, if you believe that the masses will not be sufficiently mature to vote in February, then how can you believe that they are mature enough today to vote for the workers' and soldiers' councils? Why have confidence in the General Assembly of Workers' and Soldiers' Councils in December, but distrust the national assembly in February? The date really cannot play the decisive role that is being attributed to it.

It is quite a different question whether we recognize the national assembly as necessary at all, or whether it poses a danger. As is known, the Spartacists are strongly convinced it is a danger. The *Rote Fahne* of November 29 explains:

"The national assembly is a device with which to cheat the proletariat out of its power, paralyze its class energy, and make its final goals vanish into thin air. The alternative is to put all power into the hands of the proletariat, develop this incipient revolution into a mighty class struggle for a socialist order, and to this end establish the political supremacy of the working masses, the dictatorship of the workers' and soldiers' councils. For or against socialism, for or against the national assembly. There is no third choice!"

You could not ask that sentences be uttered with more conviction.

For simple minds, such conviction is a substitute for proof — so it must be, because you search in vain for evidence that a national assembly by its nature must oppose socialism, or that a soldiers' council inherently must support socialism.

Of all those who rage that the national assembly is a necessary tool of the counterrevolution, has even one of them considered what the difference is between the assembly and the workers' and soldiers' councils? There is no indication that they have.

Does the difference lie in the scope of who is eligible to vote? Every soldier is eligible to vote for the soldiers' councils, and since we have universal conscription, that includes members of all classes. Social class does not determine who can vote, but rather the military minimum height requirements. Does that offer a guarantee for socialist consciousness?

And as for the worker's councils, it is not only wage workers who are supposed to be represented there. According to the election rules for the Greater Berlin workers' council, included among those with the right to vote are "members of liberal professions (doctors, lawyers, writers, artists, the self-employed, and so forth)."

According to earlier reports, peasants' councils are to exist alongside these workers' councils, to which not only peasants, but also village craftsmen, doctors, and other village professionals are to receive the right to vote. So who is excluded from the franchise?

According to Prussian income tax statistics from 1913, the number of those with an income over 9,500 marks was 132,000; the number of those who made less than that was nearly 16 million (15,885,000), and of these, more than 15 million (15,188,000) had an income of less than 3,000 marks.

Let us count as capitalists all those with an income over 9,500 marks, although many members of the liberal professions, who can vote for the workers' councils, are in that category. We then find that the general franchise gives the vote to very few additional people who would not have it under the occupational franchise of the workers' council constitution. The scope of the franchise is virtually the same either way, provided that the workers' and soldiers' council franchise is fairly applied.

To think that the capitalists exercise any power whatsoever in the elections through strength of numbers, or that with universal, equal suffrage they would thereby receive some kind of weapon, is nothing but superstition. It is all the more strange given that until now our party has always understood perfectly why we advocated universal, equal suffrage as a weapon of the proletariat.

So a significant difference between the national assembly and the council assembly cannot be found in the number of voters. However, we are told, a national assembly would be nothing more than a talk shop. No doubt there have been parliaments that were powerless, had nothing to do, and so produced nothing but a lot of talk. But that depended upon the historical situation and the authority of the parliament, not on the type of franchise. A parliament that stands before great responsibilities and exercises full political power will not be just a talk shop. The national assembly of the Great French Revolution attests to that.

Even there, superfluous speeches will certainly be delivered. But are the advocates of the workers' and soldiers' councils willing to guarantee that such things will never happen in these councils? All assemblies in which speeches are made are plagued with superfluous ones. That is just part of life, all of whose activities are associated with superfluous expenditures of energy.

Recently I had the opportunity to hear a member of the Spartacus group, whose endless speech lost its way in the most diffuse and trivial digressions from his topic. But he still managed to awake his listeners at the end with the thunderous cry: "We will not tolerate a talk shop, we will not tolerate the national assembly!"

So that is not the difference between the national assembly and council assembly, either.

The difference lies in the way elections take place.

The national assembly will be elected through a precisely defined franchise that is equal for the entire population, excluding any doubt over who has the right to vote. All voters vote in the same electoral bodies, all classes together. Since all classes vote alike, the electoral campaign thereby becomes a struggle of classes for power. At the same time it is a contest by each candidate and his party for the voters as a whole. Only the candidates of big parties can make headway in this contest, only representatives of views that rise above limited special interests. The class interests represented by each party win out only in the form of general, social interests, not special occupational or local ones.

Thus by abolishing feudal representation by estates, modern parliamentarism overcomes guild and local particularism and gives rise to the big, modern parties that embrace the entire country. Our own party has always won new strength and new determination in every electoral campaign against the common bourgeois opponent.

At the same time, this universal suffrage shows more clearly than any other method where the majority of the people stand. Therefore, provided that the people's freedom is not restricted by any state power, this general franchise establishes the sole unambiguous authority that is recognized by all. It creates clarity and stability, which we urgently need, as will be shown.

Such is not the case with the council franchise. Here not only each class, but every occupation votes separately. According to the voting regulations for Greater Berlin, the candidate must even be employed as part of the group that is to elect him. The election campaign therefore ceases to be a struggle between classes, where each class proves its intellectual strength and independence. Even before the electoral campaign each occupation and class will be assigned its number of representatives.

Within each occupational electoral body not all parties will try to compete with each other, but only those that have a chance of winning within that occupation. Elections to the councils for industrial wage workers will no longer be electoral campaigns between bourgeois candidates and Socialist candidates, but rather among representatives of various Socialist factions. That will foster not party unity, but sectarian fragmentation. It will also foster fragmentation into occupations and trades, because in the occupational assemblies special interests all too easily outweigh the overall interests of the entire class and entire society.

These days that can be important. In these hard times, wages are for the most part quickly becoming insufficient. There are two ways to raise them. One is at the expense of capital, that is, out of profits. But this approach loses its effectiveness if there is no profit or not enough to allow for further curbs without hurting the business. Then the wages of one layer of workers can be raised only at the expense of others, by increasing the prices of goods.

The view that every wage increase necessitates a price increase and harms the workers is false. In normal times that is certainly not true. Then wage increases are pushed through only during times of good business, when profits are high.

But things are different now. We are experiencing a crisis; profits are currently slim. However, workers have won the power to occasionally push through wage increases. Here the danger exists that these raises will be obtained not at the expense of capital, but at the expense of other, weaker layers of workers. Certain layers of workers can achieve a monopoly position with respect to other workers. The danger of such a division in the working class would be seriously exacerbated if an occupational franchise were the basis for electing the workers' councils, and the state were based on them.

Furthermore, the franchise to the workers' and soldiers' councils is just as obscure and dependent upon changing conditions as universal suffrage is precise and clear. Therefore, the results of the council elections will never have the same moral authority, nor will they stabilize a government of the popular masses as will the voice of universal suffrage. That is why in Russia they felt the need to reinforce the regime with terror.

Originally the council franchise was indeed quite clear and simple. The big industrial enterprises in and of themselves bring together large numbers of workers right from the start. But things get murkier in the case of a disintegrating army and even more so with other layers of the working population that we do not want simply to exclude.

The Berlin election rules that we have repeatedly cited have the following to say on that:

"Members of liberal professions (doctors, lawyers, writers, artists, the self-employed, and so forth) shall be encompassed by their occupational organization."

Here we already see a disturbing uncertainty. One category of voters is designated as "and so forth." Who has the right to vote as an "and so forth"?

And then, what happens to the right to vote of those for whom no occupational organization exists, or perhaps only a loose, inadequate one? Where are they "encompassed"?

Moreover, it is noteworthy that the elections for the General Assembly of Workers' and Soldiers' Councils that are about to take place will not be conducted according to uniform election rules that apply to all. Every locality, every class has its own rules.

How will it be decided which delegates have been legitimately elected, and which have not? We will be very happy if the General Assembly manages to get through the credentials reports successfully. We hope that these difficulties will gradually be overcome. But more likely they will increase as the whole council system expands further and further beyond its origin, the big factory workers' councils in the industrial centers, which is the one solid base it has.

In order for the councils to become organs of state self-government, they would have to be extended to the entire nation and to all levels of the population. Peasants' councils must be formed. Councils must be organized of women working in the home. In fact, why is it that a workers' wife should have no right to vote, just because taking care of the children chains her to the home? Hence the need for housewives' councils and of course councils of servant girls.

The more you proceed in that direction, the closer you come to universal suffrage, the further you get from its clarity and unambiguousness, and the more chaotic the organism becomes.

II

The above observations do not all mean to imply that the workers' and soldiers' councils are inferior to the national assembly. Such an inferiority would be apparent if the question were to choose between the national assembly and the workers' and soldiers' councils. However, to pose the issue on such a general plane is totally false and misleading. Rather the question is: What are the tasks of the national assembly, and what are those of the workers' and soldiers' councils? In which cases should the national assembly act, when and where should the councils act?

The national assembly and the workers' and soldiers' councils are both equally necessary, but each of the two organizations has a different mission. The national assembly is unable to handle many things that are successfully handled by the workers' and soldiers' councils, and vice versa. Each should be assigned its proper place.

The revolution has two stages: overthrowing the old authorities, and consolidating and reconstructing the new political and social order.

The stage of the violent overthrow arises only when a governmental system, using mighty instruments of power, suppresses the popular will that is pressing for change, or when it forces the people down a ruinous path without their knowledge and against their will. In that case the only way to save the people and open the road to future social progress is to set against the government's instruments of power those of the emerging social forces. When the general popular indignation is so great that the emerging new power is predominant, the government collapses and the revolution triumphs.

No national assembly would be capable of fulfilling such a mission. The revolutionary mission arises rather in situations where no national assembly exists, or is powerless, or does not represent the popular masses. The revolution's tasks could only be accomplished by an uprising of the workers and soldiers, and the fact that these insurrectional forces immediately organized themselves into workers' and soldiers' councils was a big advance over previous revolutions.

Earlier revolutions mostly took the form of the angry masses taking to the streets, disorganizing the army and sweeping it along. The old government fell. The new one that took its place was basically self-appointed and consisted of various forces that were popular and nimble enough to grab the power lying fallen in the dust.

The new provisional government was not subject to any supervision besides that of unpredictable, chance street demonstrations, until a definitive situation was created through a national assembly.

This time, as compared with the totally uncontrolled character of earlier revolutions, considerable progress was registered first in Russia, then in Germany. Instead of leaving the masses unorganized, driven only by chance impulses, the revolutionaries organized themselves during the stage of revolutionary action and created a permanent organization that appointed and supervised the provisional government and simultaneously subjected the entire national and local administrative apparatus to its control.

So however indefinite the workers' and soldiers' council franchise may be, however unclear its authority, however chaotic its proceedings may occasionally be as compared to the franchise, authority, and proceedings of normal representative assemblies; if the councils are compared to the mass rallies that in earlier revolutions constituted the only political factor outside of the provisional government, the workers' and soldiers' councils seem very definite, clear, and orderly. (The exception here is the Great French Revolution, in which the Paris sections played for a time a role similar to the workers' and soldiers' councils.)[22]

The councils showed themselves to be indispensable and highly beneficial in the first phase of the revolution, when the overthrow of the old powers was the order of the day.

But the revolution cannot stop there. It must enter the second stage, that of the consolidation and construction of the new order. The councils cannot fulfill this new mission. That can be done only by national, provincial, and municipal assemblies, in which all classes measure their strength in elections, and which are elected according to a clear, definite franchise that assures them universal recognition.

But that does not make the workers' councils superfluous. The class struggle does not cease in the second phase; an idyllic scene of class reconciliation does not arise. So just as a central parliament is necessary to hold the nation together, attend to legislation, and supervise the central executive, it is no less important that the popular masses energetically participate in this activity, strengthening the power of their representatives in parliament and spurring on their zeal with constant pressure from without.

Moreover, the workers' councils are uniquely competent to

safeguard proletarian class interests, at least so long as Social Democracy is split and for that reason cannot present a united proletarian front. The soldiers' councils can only be transitory phenomena; they will disappear of their own accord once the army is demobilized. Peasant councils or artisans' or retailers' or housewives' councils are absolutely superfluous for influencing the national assembly on political questions. If we called them to life, it would be to replace the national assembly with a council assembly. But alongside a national assembly they would be superfluous, whereas the actual workers' councils would retain important political functions.

Therefore, it is not a question of national assembly or workers' councils, but *both*.

III

Now one can see what is behind the position of the *Rote Fahne* people, who flatly equate the national assembly with the counterrevolution. They see only the first phase of the revolution, the overthrow, as the revolution itself. They cannot understand that the second phase of the revolution could be anything but the counterrevolution. To them, the consolidation phase is an abomination, a betrayal of socialism, because they imagine that socialism can be achieved by overthrowing capitalism in the same way that the republic was by overthrowing the monarchy. If the one can be accomplished only by violent conflicts that entail disturbances and disorder, then the same must be true of the other.

But the difference between establishing the republic and establishing socialism becomes apparent here. Whereas the republic can possibly be achieved in a matter of hours, constructing socialism requires decades. Furthermore, the republic and monarchism are mutually exclusive. The entire state must be one or the other. But there is no mode of production that rules exclusively. Capitalism spread only gradually over the course of the last century from one branch of industry to the next. Precapitalist forms of production, even remnants of agrarian communism, survive in capitalism's cracks and crannies even today. Likewise, socialist and capitalist forms of production will coexist for a period of time.

In other words, the social revolution is a completely different process that calls for completely different methods than the political revolution, and what is good for the one is not at all necessarily good for the other.

Whereas the political revolution is not possible without disturbances and disorder, the social revolution presupposes the functioning of the production processes. In fact, the more that law and order is preserved, the more confidence there is in the new regime's stability, the more smoothly the social revolution will be accomplished. The national assembly will achieve this most quickly and is best able to lead the country out of the provisional stage. That is why this assembly is an economic necessity and a precondition to a social revolution that is not limited to mere proclamations, but will actually introduce socialist production. It is high time we got out of this provisional stage of uncertainty.

We must not be misled by references to the Great French Revolution, which remained in this stage for five years, from 1789 to 1794.

At the time there were only the bare beginnings of industrial capitalism in France. The great mass of the population were peasants, who produced almost everything they needed on their own land, even most industrial products. What they could not produce for themselves was supplied by the village craftsman. Their production was not disturbed in times of upheaval in the big cities. On the contrary, during that time they were free of taxes and could improve their farms. And when the civil war jumped back and forth across the countryside, only limited areas were disturbed, and only temporarily. That is how the French peasants, freed from feudal burdens, were able during five years of continual insurrections not only to hold on, but even to improve their situation, so that at the end of the revolutionary period they were a vigorous force. They thus offered an expanded internal market to capitalist industry, which now surged rapidly forward, *after* the period of unrest.

Capitalist industry itself, however, cannot prosper in the midst of unrest. It is built upon a division of labor, on the mutual dependence of the individual businesses, on the international circulation of goods, and on credit. Disruption and uncertainty at any point always immediately produce far-reaching crises.

Today, this mutual dependence has spread to agriculture. The peasant can no longer live or work without industrial products. He no longer does his own spinning and weaving, and the village blacksmith is no longer adequate to produce his tools of production. He needs machines, artificial fertilizers, a supply of animal feed from abroad, and he can no longer farm without credit.

Under such conditions an extended period of unrest has a completely different effect than it did 125 years ago. At that time agriculture could blossom during civil war. That was not the case with industry, which suffered then too. In Lyons, for example, poverty finally made the workers counterrevolutionaries.[23] Today civil war economically ruins even backward Russia. All the less could a highly industrialized country like Germany withstand a period of unrest and uncertainty.

It will of course be argued that what has been said here applies only to *capitalist* industry. But that is simply what we have got, and we cannot replace it with socialism at one fell swoop. And even if that were possible, socialism, being just as much a social form of production, will need security and stability no less than capitalism does. It is a totally ridiculous prejudice to believe that law and order are necessary only in the interests of exploitation. Exploitation can take place in times of unrest and disorder, too. Capital calls for law and order because its exploitation is not founded upon violent plunder and extortion, but rather takes place in the course of the production process. That is why they want law and order. As soon as society replaces the individual capitalists as the owner and manager of the means of production, it also assumes the capitalist's concern for law and order. Law and order are preconditions to accomplishing socialism and the socialist revolution. That is one of the differences between the bourgeois revolution, directed against feudalism, and the proletarian, aimed at defeating capitalism.

We must not be disconcerted by the fact that the national assembly is demanded by bourgeois, capitalist concerns. This fact is the only argument that the national assembly's opponents present in claiming that it must be a tool of the counterrevolution. But the bourgeois parties all yearn for a rich harvest next year. Must we then block the harvest in the interests of the revolution?

On one side of the national assembly issue stand all those who think economically, who have recognized the economic needs of production. On the opposing side stand only the politicians of violence, that peculiar brand of Marxism that we can designate as Tartar.[24] They think that force can accomplish everything and that the needs of the economy can be mastered by the use of force. Wilhelm II and his people were destroyed through overestimating violence and scorning the economy. That should stand as a warning.

IV

We must concede one thing to the opponents of the national assembly. It offers us no guarantee that we will have the majority in it. This is true. But it surely follows that this entails the bounden duty to exert all forces in the election campaign to win this majority. But the Spartacists, with good reason, behave as if the game is lost from the start. Up to now our party has seen revolutionizing people's minds as its duty, since that is the only way to implement socialism. The Spartacists, on the contrary, see their task as concocting some device that will spare them the tedious work, that will assure victory and power whatever the conditions, whether the masses are with us or not.

Unfortunately, this gimmick is like the perpetual motion machine. It would be very nice, if it worked. Unfortunately, nature has ruled that out.

There is no contrivance that will assure power to us Socialists without the majority of the people. Do the workers' and soldiers' councils represent the long-sought-after perpetual motion machine? But already we hear complaints that counterrevolutionary elements are infiltrating into the soldiers' councils, I do not want to even get started on the peasant councils and the councils of "cultural intellectuals." But now it is even the workers' councils themselves! Spartacus identifies itself with the revolution. But how can they be sure that the workers' councils will agree with them and not with the other Socialists, whom they denounce as counterrevolutionaries and as protectors of the money bags?

So now the workers' and soldiers' councils do not look secure enough, either. The Spartacists are already looking for a new safeguard and think they have found it in the arming of the proletariat, that is, those in the work force who think like Spartacus. (*Rote Fahne*, December 2) But the war has just shown us that in the long run, technical methods cannot compensate for numerical inferiority, because what one side can do will quickly be learned by the other. New contrivances only make the conflict more savage and gruesome but do not alter the outcome. A couple of people can be secretly armed, but at best they will mount a putsch that will be crushed by the masses and have no lasting effect. And if a lot of them take up arms, then the other side will catch on and do likewise. So this too shows that mere mechanical means will not save us the trouble of revolutionizing people's minds. Nor will it enable a minority to control the majority over the long haul.

It simply cannot be done without winning over the majority; that must be our consistent goal. We are certainly saying nothing new with this, but only repeating what our predecessors have told us time and again over half a century. But the contrary approach of searching for a way to help a proletarian minority achieve victory and supremacy without winning the majority is even older, and its appearance now is only a revival of the most primitive socialist attitudes. This outlook always springs from feelings of hopelessness.

On the morrow of a workers' revolution that in one blow overthrew two dozen governments in a country in which the proletariat makes up the majority of the population, a Socialist party despairs at ever winning the masses or capturing the majority in the national assembly. They despair at being able to hold their own in a battle of ideas in an arena to which all parties and classes have access.

Such a party could not exhibit stronger proof of its political poverty. We have much more confidence in our cause. The masses of the people now stand on the side of socialism. They have lost all confidence in the parties that ruled up to now. They are expecting from us deliverance, economic deliverance. Economic concerns will dominate the coming months, even years, and therefore the masses demand that we begin constructing socialism rather than perpetuating the unrest or prolonging the war with civil war.

Everything depends upon our conduct. The national assembly is on the march and nothing will stop it. Socialists who pit themselves against it will succeed only in reducing its Socialist majority. And if the national assembly should feature a counterrevolutionary majority, it would be the fault of these Socialists.

Precisely because this possibility is not excluded, we must all the more urgently demand that the struggle *against* the national assembly be ended, and that the struggle *for* the national assembly be taken up with full force. □

Luxemburg and Liebknecht wrote no reply to Kautsky's pamphlet in the short time before they were murdered in mid-January. However, Lenin dealt with the substance of Kautsky's arguments against Soviet power in his pamphlet, *The Proletarian Revolution and the Renegade Kautsky,* written one month previously, which is printed in chapter 7 of this volume. The same topic was discussed in the resolution of the first Comintern congress on "Bourgeois Democracy and the Dictatorship of the Proletariat."[25]

The debate on the councils and the national assembly continued in Germany through November and December. Radical forces within the USPD contested the party leadership's support for the proposed national assembly. But no authoritative national leadership emerged for those opposing the government's plans, and there was no organized political campaign to counter them.

The Executive Committee of the councils had the political authority to lead such a campaign. On November 11 it had claimed "dictatorial power," and in theory it remained the highest political body in Germany. In fact, however, it immediately began to cede this authoritative position. Although it resolved November 12 to build its own defense force, two days later it abandoned the attempt in the face of SPD-instigated opposition in the army. When Däumig presented a motion November 16 specifying that "the revolutionary organizations of the workers' and soldiers' councils embody the new state power" and opposing the national assembly,[26] this motion was voted down. Decrees of the Executive Committee issued November 23 barred the councils from interfering in governmental administration, as for example by taking measures to assure supplies of food or raw materials; the councils were relegated largely to social welfare tasks. Another decree that day attempted to block factory committees from taking up questions such as expropriation or abolition of piece work. When disagreements arose between factory committees and employers, the Executive Committee stated, the trade union officials were to be brought into the negotiations before workers took action to press their demands. When the Executive Committee called a national congress of the councils, to convene December 16, it specified that the authority of the congress was only provisional, pending convocation of a legislative assembly.

While the Berlin leadership of the councils vacillated and gave ground politically in the weeks following the revolution, right-wing forces began to recover their confidence. A massive propaganda campaign was organized to combat "Bolshevism" and to defend the old order. As part of this effort, reactionary forces began to whip up a lynch atmosphere against the alleged terrorism of the revolutionary left. Rosa Luxemburg gave some examples in the November 18 *Rote Fahne* of the slanders circulating in the first days of the revolution.

"Liebknecht has murdered two hundred officers in Spandau.

"The Spartacists have stormed the Marstall.[27]

"The Spartacists have tried to seize the *Berliner Tageblatt* with machine guns.

"Liebknecht is plundering the stores.

"Liebknecht is distributing money to the soldiers in order to rouse them to counterrevolution."[28]

Another story, printed in the capitalist press and reported November

19 to the Berlin councils' assembly, was that Liebknecht would pay 2,000 marks for every dead sailor.[29]

By December, leaflets and posters were appearing calling for the Spartacus leaders to be killed. One regiment of guards put a bounty of 10,000 marks on Liebknecht's head, dead or alive.[30]

Luxemburg sounded the alarm against this campaign in the following article, published November 24.

A Dangerous Game[31]
by Rosa Luxemburg

From the *Kreuz-Zeitung* to *Vorwärts*, the German press reverberates with abuse against "terror," "putschism," "anarchy," and "dictatorship."

Quis tulerit Gracchos de seditione querentes?[32] How touching it is that the palace guard of bourgeois anarchy, those who in four years have turned Europe into a pile of ruins, bewail the anarchy of the proletarian dictatorship.

Over the centuries the propertied classes have not balked at using every form of villainy and violence to protect the citadel of order, private property, and class rule against the slightest rebellion of their slaves. And yet, from time immemorial they wail about the violence and terror of — the slaves. Thiers and Cavaignac, who in the massacre of June 1848 butchered tens of thousands of Parisian proletarians — men, women, and children — howled to high heavens about the supposed atrocities of the Paris Commune.[33]

Reventlow, Friedberg, and Erzberger, who without blinking an eye drove a million and a half German men and boys to the slaughterhouse for the sake of Longwy, Briey, and new colonies;[34] and Scheidemann-Ebert, who for four long years approved all the measures necessary for the greatest bloodletting the world has ever seen, now shriek in raucous chorus against the "terror," the "reign of fear" supposedly represented by the dictatorship of the proletariat. . . .

Thanks to the theory of scientific socialism, the socialist proletariat enters its revolution without any illusions, with a clear picture of the ultimate implications of its historic mission, and bourgeois society's unbridgeable contradictions and deadly hostility to it. The proletariat enters the revolution not to chase after antihistorical, utopian fantasies, but rather, based on the inexorable driving force of history, to accomplish its historic task of making socialism a reality.

The socialist proletariat should move as a bloc, as the overpowering majority of the workers, to fulfill its historic mission.

Therefore, the proletariat does not need to begin by destroying its own illusions with acts of violence or by digging a trench between it and bourgeois society. What it needs is total state political power. It needs to use this power ruthlessly to abolish capitalist private property, wage slavery, bourgeois class rule, and to build a new socialist order.

But today there are those who very much do need terror and anarchy. These are the bourgeois gentlemen, all the parasites of the capitalist economy who tremble for their property, their privileges, their profits, and their sovereign rights. These are the ones who falsely accuse the socialist proletariat of anarchy and putsches so that at the opportune moment their agents can unleash real anarchy to strangle the proletarian revolution, bring the socialist dictatorship down in chaos, and erect capital's class dictatorship forever on the ruins of the revolution.

Capital in its struggle to survive is the heart and soul of today's hysteria against the proletariat's revolutionary vanguard. Its hands and tools are the dependent Social Democrats, whose servile role has survived the revolution unchanged. The only change is that masters and servants alike have now pinned red badges on their vests.

Vorwärts, the central organ of the dependent Social Democrats, is today the central organ of the counterrevolutionary witch-hunt against Spartacus.

The dependent Berlin city commander has armed the security forces with live ammunition to use against imaginary Spartacus "attacks."[35] The lackeys of Wels and Company are inciting the more backward elements among the soldiers against Liebknecht and his friends. We are receiving a constant barrage of threatening letters and warnings.

With cold-blooded smiles we watch the show from a historical vantage point. We see through the play, actors, production, and casting.

But what, one wonders, would the masses of the revolutionary proletarians do if the hate campaign were to accomplish its goal and were to muss one hair on the heads of those whom the proletariat carried out of prison on their shoulders and recognized as their natural leaders? Who would then have the power to calm these masses?

You bourgeois gentlemen and you *Vorwärts* flunkies of doomed capital, you gamble on the masses' ignorance and political inexperience like a bankrupt man playing his last card. You are waiting for your chance, thirsting for the laurels of Thiers, Cavaignac, and Galliffet.

That is a dangerous game. The hour of the dictatorship of the proletariat and of socialism has come. Whoever stands in the path of socialist revolution's stormy assault will be left lying shattered and broken on the ground. □

Notes

1. *Vorwärts*, November 13, 1918.
2. The reference is to the reform of the imperial constitution ratified by the kaiser on October 28, 1918.
3. The Erfurt program of the SPD was adopted in 1891. While recognizing many of its weaknesses, revolutionary Marxists in the SPD and throughout the Second International had looked to it since its adoption as a generally correct political guide. Engels's comments on the weaknesses of the Erfurt program at the time of its adoption can be found in "A Critique of the Draft Social-Democratic Programme of 1891," in Karl Marx and Frederick Engels, *Selected Works* (Moscow: Progress Publishers, 1977), vol. 3, pp. 429-39. V.I. Lenin refers at some length to Engels's critique in his "State and Revolution," in *Collected Works* (hereinafter *CW*) (Moscow: Progress Publishers, 1974), vol. 25, pp. 447-54.

Lenin summarized his historical balance sheet on this program in a speech at the Second Comintern Congress in 1920: "The Erfurt Programme says nothing about the dictatorship of the proletariat, and history has proved that this was not due to chance. . . . The Erfurt Programme's failure to mention the dictatorship of the proletariat was . . . in practice, a cowardly concession to the opportunists. The dictatorship of the proletariat has been in our programme [of the Russian party] since 1903." ("Speech on Terms of Admission into the Communist International," in Lenin, *CW*, vol. 31, p. 246-47.)

4. Rosa Luxemburg, *Gesammelte Werke* (Berlin [GDR]: Dietz Verlag, 1974), vol. 4, pp. 397-400.
5. See "USPD Enters Government" in chapter 1 of the present volume.
6. "Kein Brüderkampf," in *Vorwärts*, November 10, 1918.
7. Richard Müller, *Die Novemberrevolution*, vol. 2 of *Geschichte der deutschen Revolution* (West Berlin: Olle und Wolter, 1973), pp. 35-36.
8. Excerpted from Karl Liebknecht, *Gesammelte Reden und Schriften*, (Berlin [GDR]: Dietz Verlag, 1974) vol. 9, pp. 601-3.
9. On August 4, 1914, Kaiser Wilhelm had told the Reichstag, "We no longer recognize parties — only Germans."
10. The "turbulent year" was the revolutionary year of 1848.
11. Lenin and Gregory Zinoviev, "Socialism and War," in Lenin, *CW*, vol. 21, p. 311.
12. Liebknecht, "Das, was ist," in *Gesammelte Reden*, pp. 604-7.
13. In 1793 the Vendée, a department of France, was the center of a wide-ranging and persistent royalist insurrection against the French revolution.

Counterrevolutionary clerics in this region were able to rally support from small peasants, whose opposition to oppressive feudal land relations was a bulwark of the revolution in France as a whole.

14. Liebknecht, *Gesammelte Reden*, p. 598. According to Wilhelm Pieck, Liebknecht explained that he declined nomination because he could not collaborate with the "governmental Socialists." (Wilhelm Pieck, "Erinnerungen an die Novemberrevolution in Berlin," in *Gesammelte Reden und Schriften* [Berlin (GDR): Dietz Verlag, 1959], vol. 1, p. 434.)

15. *Dokumente und Materialien zur Geschichte der deutschen Arbeiterbewegung* (Berlin [GDR]: Dietz Verlag, 1957), series 2, vol. 2, pp. 403-4.

16. The "independent" Socialists referred to are those of the USPD (from the party's name, the Independent Social Democratic Party). SPD members, by contrast, were often referred to pejoratively as the "dependent" Socialists, that is, dependent upon the bourgeoisie.

17. Luxemburg, *Gesammelte Werke*, pp. 407-10.

18. This refers to a method of voting by which Reichstag deputies left the hall and were counted as they returned through one of three doors designated "yes," "no," or "abstention."

19. In the Estates General convoked in 1789 in Paris, representatives of each of the "three estates" were to meet separately with an equal voice. The nobility and clergy were the first two estates; the third estate included the bourgeoisie as well as the rural and urban masses. Revolutionary action by the plebeians provided the impetus for unification of the estates that year in a Constituent Assembly.

20. "Liberty, equality, fraternity" was the motto of the French revolution of 1789.

21. Karl Kautsky, "Nationalversammelung und Räteverfassung," in *Die Freiheit*, December 5 and 6, 1918.

22. The Paris "sections" were elected bodies from plebeian districts of the city during the Great French Revolution that took measures to defend and promote the revolution.

23. One of the great manufacturing centers of eighteenth century France, Lyons specialized in the production of luxury goods. During the revolution these industries came to a standstill. Workers lost their livelihood and sank into destitution, while the well-to-do bourgeoisie turned against the revolution and its base of support narrowed. In May 1793 reactionary forces were able to gain the upper hand in Lyons, take control of the city, and fortify it against the revolutionary government.

24. *Tartar* referred to the Turkic inhabitants of the tsarist empire. The term was also used as a racist epithet meaning violent and brutal.

25. See John Riddell, ed., *The Founding of the Communist International* (New York: Monad Press, 1986), chapter 5, a volume of *The Communist International in Lenin's Time*.

26. Hermann Müller, *Die Novemberrevolution* (Berlin, 1931), p. 127.

27. The Marstall was the headquarters of revolutionary sailors organized in the People's Naval Division.

28. Luxemburg, *Gesammelte Werke*, p. 401.

29. Drabkin, *Novemberrevolution*, p. 242.

30. Ibid., p. 333.

31. Excerpted from Luxemburg, "Ein gewagtes Spiel," in *Gesammelte Werke*, pp. 411-14.

32. The Latin saying can be translated, "Who can tolerate the Gracchi, who complain about uprisings?" Its meaning is "Who will listen to those who rail against what they themselves do." The Gracchi were tribunes in republican Rome in the second century B.C. who roused the plebeians to demand agrarian reform. The Roman nobility denounced them as seditious and ultimately both Gracchi fell victim to patrician violence.

33. Following the February 1848 revolution in France, Louis-Adolphe Thiers and Louis-Eugène Cavaignac organized the bourgeoisie's June massacre of Paris working people. Thiers went on to lead the attack on the Paris Commune of 1871; Cavaignac died in 1857.

34. The annexation of the iron-mining region near Longwy and Briey in eastern France had been among the war aims of German imperialism.

35. SPD leader Otto Wels had been appointed military commander of the city of Berlin.

Der Rat der Volksbeauftragten

Council of People's Representatives: Dittman, Landsberg, Haase, Ebert, Barth, and Scheidemann.

-3-

The Counterrevolution Gathers Strength

As the German bourgeoisie began its preparations to liquidate the revolution, the working class was mounting a stepped-up struggle to advance its interests. Socialist political parties and trade unions mushroomed in size after November 9, and the working-class press flourished. Millions of soldiers, some demobilized and some still in their units, were returning from battle, looking for food, work — and for a better future for Germany. In the second half of November strikes flared in the Berlin metal industry, the Ruhr and Silesian coal fields, and elsewhere, demanding higher wages, shorter hours, and, in several cases, immediate expropriation of these industries. The new government's active and vocal opposition to these strikes revealed, for the first time to many workers, its hostility to their interests.

Challenged by this wave of strikes, the government began to praise the virtues of hard work. Its propaganda agency produced a leaflet that read:

"German worker, have you considered? . . . Today you are a free man, *the freest of workers in the whole world.* . . . And at this precise moment you stop working? Are you so dim- witted? *Stop and think.* . . . The state, your family, and you yourself must live. Therefore *you must work and work hard.* . . . And yet you put your hands in your lap? *Shame on you, German worker.* You do not deserve your freedom. You preferred carrying out shameful deeds under the whip of militarism to laboring today of your own free will. *German worker, get to work."*[1]

"Truckloads of this leaflet were sent to workers' and soldiers' councils across Germany," explains the German Communist Party's 1929 history of the revolution. "The SPD councils tried to hide them and have them pulped. So the leaflet was reset and printed again, but without the words, 'Shame on you, German worker.' "[2]

Footnotes to this chapter begin on page 153.

Rosa Luxemburg commented on the significance of the strike wave in the following article printed in the November 27 *Rote Fahne*.

"The Ice is Breaking Up"[3]
by Rosa Luxemburg

All the fine plans for a dignified, tame, "constitutional," German revolution that preserves "law and order" and sees protecting capitalist private property as its first and most important task — all these little plans are being swept away. *The ice is breaking up*. While in government circles on high an amicable, harmonious arrangement with the bourgeoisie is upheld by any means necessary, down below the masses of proletarians are rising up and shaking a threatening fist: *the strikes have begun*. There are strikes in Upper Silesia, at Daimler, and elsewhere. This is only the beginning. The movement's waves will naturally grow ever bigger and more powerful.

How could it be otherwise? A revolution has taken place. It was made by workers, proletarians in and out of uniform. Socialists, workers' representatives, sit in the government.

And what has changed for the masses of workers in their daily wages and living standards? Nothing at all or very little. Barely were a few meager concessions made here and there, and the employers are trying to conjure away even that little bit.

The masses are put off with promises of the golden fruits that allegedly will fall into their laps from the national assembly. Supposedly, we will slide softly and "peacefully" into the promised land of socialism by way of long debates, speeches, and parliamentary majority decisions.

The proletariat's healthy class instinct recoils from this schema of parliamentary cretinism. The Communist Manifesto says that the liberation of the working class must be accomplished by the working class itself.[4] And the "working class" is not a few hundred elected representatives, who direct society's destiny with their arguments and refutations. Even less is it two or three dozen leaders who occupy government posts. The working class is the broadest masses themselves. The socialization of the economy can be prepared only with their active participation in the overthrow of capitalist relations.

Instead of waiting for the magical decrees of the government or the decisions of this wonderful national assembly, the masses are instinctively wielding the only sure weapon that leads to socialism: *the struggle against capital*. Up to now the government has done everything to emasculate the revolution, reducing it to a purely political overturn, and to forge class harmony with its clamor against any menace to "law and order."

The proletarian masses are calmly collapsing the house of cards called revolutionary class harmony and waving the feared banner of class struggle. . . .

The strikes now breaking out are not just "trade union" bickering for baubles, for the crumbs off the table of the wage system. They represent the masses' natural response to the powerful jolt that capitalist relations received with the collapse of German imperialism and the brief workers' and soldiers' political revolution. They are the very beginnings of a general confrontation between labor and capital in Germany. The strikes herald the birth of a mighty class confrontation whose outcome can be only the abolition of wage relations and the introduction of a socialist economy. They release the living social power of the present revolution: the revolutionary class energy of the proletarian masses. They inaugurate the period of direct involvement by the broadest masses, an involvement to which socialization decrees and the measures taken by any representative body or the government can be only background music. . . .

By its mere appearance onto the scene of the class struggle, the proletarian mass has skipped over all the revolution's shortcomings, indecisiveness, and cowardice and taken up the tasks of the day. The ice is breaking up, and the dwarfs promoting their little game at the head of the revolution will either topple, or they will finally come to understand the colossal scope of the earth-shaking historic drama they are cast in. □

———————

In late November, the army High Command put into motion its plans to subdue the revolution. Nine divisions of handpicked "loyal" troops, commanded by Gen. Arnold Lequis, were to occupy the capital and "reestablish a firm government." The plans, which were discussed with Ebert,[5] included occupying all public buildings, disarming the workers, shooting anyone found with an unlicensed weapon, and searching "insecure" districts of the city.

An attempt at a military coup took place just before these divisions began to arrive in Berlin. On December 6 groups of soldiers and sailors marched on the Reich chancellery and, when Ebert appeared on a balcony, proclaimed him president. Ebert responded that he could not accept this post until he had discussed the matter with his government colleagues. Some of these troops then invaded the *Rote Fahne* premises in hopes of arresting "the whole gang of Spartacists." Meanwhile, another unit of soldiers set up machine guns and fired on a legal Spartacus demonstration, killing fourteen. Yet a third group arrested the entire Executive Committee of the councils. Crowds of indignant sailors and workers gathered quickly, forced the right-wing soldiers to release their prisoners, and foiled the attempted coup.

Once more at liberty, an angry Executive Committee protested to the cabinet against its inaction in the face of the counterrevolutionary danger. Suspicion was especially raised at the attempt to "proclaim" Ebert president. Moreover, when police chief Emil Eichhorn, a USPD member, arrested one of the coup organizers, the cabinet insisted on his release. Discussions were held between the Executive Committee and the cabinet, but the only outcome was a joint statement reaffirming the authority of both and promising continued "trusting collaboration."[6] *Vorwärts* dismissed the attempted putsch as the work of "a couple of petty officials of the Foreign Ministry," and attacked the Spartacists as the real danger.[7]

The Berlin working class, on the other hand, was outraged by the attempted coup. In response to a call by the Spartacus League, several major factories were struck December 7, and a giant protest demonstration took place. One of the speakers at the rally that day, Wilhelm Pieck, recalled in 1920, "Liebknecht and I . . . demanded the overthrow of the government, which was responsible for the growing strength of the counterrevolution. The masses then marched in an enormous procession to the Soviet Russian embassy on Unter den Linden," where they expressed their solidarity with the Soviet government by demanding that the government led by Friedrich Ebert and Philipp Scheidemann recall the Soviet ambassador to Berlin.[8] It was the first major action the Spartacists had organized in their own name.

On December 8 the Spartacists called the first armed demonstration since the overthrow of the kaiser, and 150,000 gathered in an impressive display of the Spartacists' growing influence. According to *Rote Fahne*, the rally demanded that the Ebert-Scheidemann government be ousted, all officers disarmed, workers' defense guards formed, and that the councils assume all power.

On December 9, *Rote Fahne* warned that the troops of General Lequis were now drawn up in a menacing ring around Berlin, and made the following call:

"Workers! Soldiers! Comrades! Attention! The revolution stands in great danger! Be on guard! Our most vital interests are at stake! Everything for the revolution and socialism!

"Everything — even life!

"Defeat the attack!

"Down with the conspirators!

"Long live socialism!

"Then the future, the final victory will be ours!"[9]

The divisions began their entry into Berlin on December 10. Ebert addressed them, praising their heroism in battle, and declaring, "No enemy has defeated you."[10] His provocative words contributed to the reactionary legend that Germany had been beaten only by a "stab in the back" by internal enemies.

Rote Fahne warned December 10 that the danger of military action against the working class was still present, for "the December 6 plotters have not given up their game, only put it off." A campaign was required, *Rote Fahne* explained, to fraternize with and educate the soldiers, who "are flesh of our flesh and blood of our blood. . . . Direct contact with the masses of Berlin workers will make these troops, who were supposed to be degraded into our enemies and oppressors, into our loyal comrades in battle."[11] Such efforts were carried out during the following days by revolutionary-minded workers in Berlin and succeeded in winning over or neutralizing the frontline troops. Lequis's divisions melted away.

The Spartacists took an important step toward constituting themselves as a political party on December 14 by publishing their political program, drafted by Rosa Luxemburg, in *Rote Fahne*. It was quickly republished as a pamphlet entitled *What the Spartacus League Wants*. The Spartacist program was a clear call for workers to take power and for a socialist transformation of society, linked with a series of demands around which workers could organize. It provided a revolutionary alternative to the vacillating statements of the USPD and a pole around which the forces for a new party could rally.

While the Spartacists' program had important inadequacies from the Bolsheviks' point of view, they hailed it as the first major programmatic document to come from a Communist movement outside Russia. On the Bolsheviks' suggestion, prominent mention of the Spartacus League program was made in the January 1919 letter of invitation to the founding congress of the Communist International as providing a starting point in laying a programmatic foundation for the new International.[12]

What the Spartacus League Wants[13]
by Rosa Luxemburg

I

On November 9, the workers and soldiers of Germany smashed the old regime. The blood-soaked illusion that the Prussian saber could rule the world had expired on the battlefields of France. The gang of crooks who had ignited the global conflagration and driven Germany into the sea of blood had reached the end of their rope. The people, betrayed for four years, who had forgotten their duty toward culture, honor, and humanity to serve the bloodthirsty god, Moloch, and who had let themselves be used for every imaginable crime, awoke from their four-year stupor — at the brink of the abyss.

On November 9, the German proletariat rose up to cast off the shameful yoke. The Hohenzollerns were put to flight; workers' and soldiers' councils were elected.

But the Hohenzollerns were never anything more than administrators for the imperialist bourgeoisie and the junkers. Bourgeois class rule is the real guilty party responsible for the World War — in Germany as much as in France, in Russia as well as Britain, in both Europe and America. The capitalists of all countries are the real instigators of the mass slaughter. International capital is the insatiable god, Baal, into whose bloody maw are thrown millions upon millions of steaming human sacrifices.

The World War has given society a choice: either the continuation of capitalism, with new wars, and rapid decline into chaos and anarchy; or the abolition of capitalist exploitation.

With the end of the World War, the system of bourgeois class rule has forfeited its right to existence. It is no longer capable of leading society out of the frightful state of economic collapse that the imperialist orgy left behind.

The means of production have been destroyed on a gigantic scale and millions of producers slaughtered, the finest and strongest sons of the working class. Those who survived are greeted on their return by the ghastly spectre of poverty and unemployment, while famine and disease threaten to cut off the nation's energy at its roots. National bankruptcy brought on by the enormous burden of war debts is inevitable.

There is no way out of the bloody confusion, no way back from the yawning abyss, no help or salvation, except through socialism. Only the proletarian world revolution can bring order into this chaos; provide work and bread for all; put a halt to mutual destruction of peoples; and bring peace, freedom, and genuine culture to tortured humanity. Down with the wage system! — that is the slogan of the hour. Cooperative labor shall replace wage labor and class domination. The tools of production must cease to be the monopoly of a single class; they must become the common property of all. No more exploiters and no more exploited! Regulate the production and distribution of goods in the interests of all. Abolish both the existing mode of production, which is exploitation and plunder, and the existing system of trade, which is nothing but fraud.

Instead of employers and their wage slaves: the free association of all workers! Work shall be no one's torment because it shall be everyone's duty. A decent, human existence for all who fulfill their obligation to society. Henceforth, hunger shall no longer be the curse of those who work but the punishment for those who do not.

Only a society such as this can eradicate bondage and hatred among nations. Only under a society such as this will the earth no longer be desecrated by killing. Only then will we be able to say, *"That was the last war."*

In this hour, socialism is humanity's only hope. Above the collapsing walls of capitalist society, the words of the *Communist Manifesto* glow in fiery warning:

"Socialism or collapse into barbarism!" [14]

II

Bringing the socialist system into being is the most momentous task ever inherited by any class or revolution in world history. It will require totally rebuilding the state and completely transforming the economic and social foundations of society.

This rebuilding and transformation cannot be decreed by any agency, commission, or parliament; it can be taken in hand and carried out only by the people themselves.

In all previous revolutions, a small minority of the people led the revolutionary struggle, set its goals, gave it direction, and used the masses as a tool to achieve its own interests, the interests of a minority. The socialist revolution is the first one to triumph in the interests of the vast majority and the first one that can succeed only with the participation of the great majority of the toilers.

Not only are the proletarian masses called upon to act with clear understanding in defining the goals and giving leadership to the revolution, but they must also bring about socialism, step by step, by their own active intervention.

The essence of socialist society is that the vast, laboring masses cease to be ruled over and instead begin to experience every aspect of political and economic life for themselves — to run it and to acquire free and conscious control over their own destiny.

Therefore, from the highest state offices to the smallest community, the proletarian masses must replace the inherited institutions of class rule — federal councils, parliaments, town councils — with their own class institutions: the workers' and soldiers' councils. They must occupy every post, oversee every function, and measure every requirement of state by the standard of their own class interests and the goals of socialism. Furthermore, only constant, living interaction between the popular masses and their institutions, the councils, will enable them to imbue the government with the spirit of socialism.

By the same token, the economic transformation can be accomplished only if it is carried out by proletarian mass action. Mere decrees for socialization handed down by the highest revolutionary offices are in themselves empty phrases. Only action by the working class can turn words into reality. The workers can gain control of production and ultimately take over its management through intransigent hand-to-hand struggle against capital in every factory, through applying direct mass pressure, through strikes, and through creating their own, permanent, representative institutions.

The working masses must learn to transform themselves from lifeless automatons that capitalists insert into the production process, into free, thinking, self-activating administrators of that process. They have to acquire the sense of responsibility of functioning members of a community who as a whole are the sole proprietors of all social wealth. They must develop industriousness without the employers' whip, maximum productivity without a capitalist slave driver, discipline without the yoke, and order without bosses. The moral foundations of socialist society are the masses' high idealism about the interests of the collectivity, their strict self-discipline, and their genuine public spirit, just as apathy, egotism, and corruption are the moral foundations of capitalist society.

The working masses can acquire these socialist civic virtues, as well as the knowledge and ability to direct socialist enterprises, only through their own participation and experience.

The socialization of society can become a reality only if the working masses in their entirety fight for it stubbornly and tirelessly everywhere that labor and capital, the people and bourgeois class rule, square off face to face. The liberation of the working class must be undertaken by the working class itself.

III

In the bourgeois revolutions, the weapons of bloodshed, terror, and political assassination were indispensable for the rising classes.

The proletarian revolution needs no terror to achieve its goals; it hates and abhors killing. It has no need of those methods of struggle because it is fighting institutions, not individuals, and because it does not enter the arena with naive illusions that shatter and must then be avenged. It is not a desperate attempt by a minority to impose its ideals upon the world by force; instead, it is an act by the great multimillioned mass of the people, who are called to fulfill a historic mission and to translate historical necessity into reality.

However, the proletarian revolution is also the death knell for all forms of servitude and oppression. Therefore, all capitalists, junkers, petty proprietors, officers, and all the beneficiaries and parasites of exploitation and class rule rise up in unison against the proletarian revolution for a battle to the death.

It is an insane illusion to imagine that the capitalists will submit good-naturedly to a decision by a socialist parliament or national assembly and calmly agree to give up their property, profit, privileges, and their right to exploit. Everywhere the ruling classes have always fought desperately to defend their privileges to the bitter end: from the Roman patricians to the medieval feudal barons; from English cavaliers to the American slaveowners; the Walachian boyars and the silk manufacturers of Lyons alike — each one caused torrents of blood to be shed.[15] They walked over corpses, they murdered and burned, and they instigated civil war and treason in order to defend their privileges and power.

The imperialist bourgeoisie, the last of the exploiting classes, exceeds all of its predecessors in brutality, unabashed cynicism, and depravity. It will defend tooth and nail what is most sacred to it, its profit and its right to exploit, with the same cold malice displayed through the history of its colonial policies and in the last war. Against the proletariat it will move heaven and hell. It will mobilize the peasantry against the cities. It will incite backward layers of the working class against the socialist vanguard. Its officers will organize massacres. It will try to cripple every socialist measure with a thousand kinds of passive resistance. It will tie down the revolution with a score of *Vendées*. It will call in the foreign enemy — the murder machines of Clemenceau, Lloyd George, and Wilson — to save the country. It would rather turn the country into a smoking heap of rubble than voluntarily give up its system of wage slavery.

All this resistance must be broken, step by step, with an iron hand and relentless force. The violence of the bourgeois counterrevolution must be met by the revolutionary violence of the proletariat. The proletarian masses must respond to the attacks, intrigues, and conspiracies of the bourgeoisie with their own unshakable clarity, vigilance, and activity, always at the ready. They must reply to the everpresent danger of counterrevolution by arming the people and disarming the ruling classes; to the bourgeoisie's obstructionist parliamentary maneuvering they must counterpose the vigorous organization of associated workers and soldiers — the concentrated, united, and heightened power of the working class. Only the united front of the entire German proletariat, south and north, urban and rural, workers and soldiers; only living, intellectual contact between the German revolution and the International; and only the extension of the German revolution to a world proletarian revolution can lay the granite foundation upon which the house of the future can be erected.

The battle for socialism is the most violent civil war world history has ever witnessed, and the proletarian revolution must prepare the weapons it will need, and learn how to use them: it must learn how to fight and to win.

Arming the united mass of working people in this way with all the political power they need for the tasks of revolution — that is the dictatorship of the proletariat. It is therefore true democracy. There is no democracy when the wage slave sits with the capitalist nor when the rural proletarian sits with the junker in fake equality for parliamentary debates about questions that affect their lives. When the proletarian masses in their millions lay hold of all state power with their calloused hands and, wielding it like the hammer of the god Thor, smash it down upon the head of the ruling classes, then that alone is democracy, that alone is no deception of the people.

The Spartacus League proposes the following program of demands that will make it possible for the proletariat to fulfill its tasks:

A. Immediate Measures to Defend the Revolution

1. Disarm all police, all officers, and all nonproletarian soldiers; and all members of the ruling classes;
2. Seizure of all supplies of weapons and ammunition and all

arms manufacturing enterprises by the workers' and soldiers' councils;

3. Arm the entire adult male proletarian population as a *workers' militia;* form a Red Guard of proletarians as an active part of the militia to defend the revolution against counterrevolutionary attacks and conspiracies;

4. Terminate the authority of commissioned and noncommissioned officers; replace blind military obedience by the voluntary discipline of the soldiers themselves; elect all officers by the troops, subject at all times to recall; abolish courts-martial;

5. Remove officers and capitulators from the soldiers' councils;

6. Replace all political institutions and agencies of the former regime by representatives of the workers' and soldiers' councils;

7. Establish a revolutionary tribunal and bring to justice the principal parties guilty of starting and prolonging the war: both Hohenzollerns, Ludendorff, Hindenburg, Tirpitz, their accomplices, and all co-conspirators in the counterrevolution;

8. Seize all food supplies to ensure that the people are fed.

B. In the Political and Social Arena

1. Abolish the system of separate states; form a unified German socialist republic;

2. Abolish all parliaments and city councils; transfer their functions to the workers' and soldiers' councils and their commissions and organs;

3. Election of the workers' councils throughout Germany by the entire adult working-class population of both sexes in both city and countryside, voting by place of work; election of soldiers' councils by vote of the troops, excluding officers and capitulators; the right of the workers and soldiers to recall their representatives at any time;

4. Elect delegates from the workers' and soldiers' councils throughout the country to a central council of workers and soldiers; it in turn shall elect an executive committee as the highest legislative and executive organ;

5. Convoke the central council at least every three months for the time being; reelect its delegates before each meeting, so that it may continuously monitor the activities of the executive committee and maintain living ties between the mass workers' and soldiers' councils in the country and their highest governing body; right of the local workers' and soldiers' councils to recall and replace their central council representatives whenever they fail to represent the interests

of those electing them; right of the executive committee to appoint and remove both the Peoples' Representatives and also all national governmental departments and bureaus;

6. Abolish all distinctions of rank; abolish all orders and titles; establish complete legal and social equality between the sexes;

7. Enact radical social legislation; shorten the workweek both to combat unemployment and to make up for the physical exhaustion of the working class by the World War; limit the working day to six hours;

8. Immediately and fundamentally restructure the systems of food distribution, housing, and education in line with the spirit and meaning of the proletarian revolution.

C. Immediate Economic Demands

1. Confiscate all dynastic fortunes and incomes for the benefit of society as a whole;

2. Cancel all state and other public debts and all war loans, except for obligations of less than a certain amount to be determined by the workers' and soldiers' councils;

3. Expropriate the land of all large and middle-sized agricultural enterprises; form socialist agricultural cooperatives with a unified central administration for the whole country; small peasants' enterprises to remain the property of their owners until they voluntarily decide to join the socialist cooperatives;

4. Expropriation of all banks, mines, mills, and smelters and all large-scale industrial and commercial enterprises by the republic of workers' and soldiers' councils;

5. Confiscate all wealth above a certain level to be determined by the central council;

6. Takeover of the entire public transportation system by the republic of workers' and soldiers' councils;

7. In every enterprise, elect factory councils whose responsibility it shall be, in consultation with workers' councils, to organize the internal affairs of the enterprise, regulate working conditions, oversee production, and, ultimately, assume management of the enterprise;

8. Appoint a central strike commission to work with the factory councils to give the incipient nationwide strike movement a unified leadership, a socialist direction, and the strongest support that the power of the workers' and soldiers' councils can provide.

D. International Tasks

Immediately establish ties with fraternal parties in other countries in order to give the socialist revolution an international character and to ensure that peace is shaped and secured by international brotherhood and by the revolutionary uprising of the world proletariat.

IV.

That is what the Spartacus League wants.

And because it wants these things, because it is the socialist conscience of the revolution, because it warns and urges the revolution onward, it is hated, persecuted, and slandered by all open and secret enemies of the proletariat.

"Crucify them!" cry the capitalists, trembling over their cash boxes.

"Crucify them!" cry the petty bourgeoisie, officers, anti-Semites, and lackeys of the bourgeois press, fearing for their place at the table of bourgeois class domination.

"Crucify them!" echo all the swindled, betrayed, and misused layers of the working class and soldiers, who still do not realize that they are railing against their own flesh and blood when they rail against the Spartacus League.

Everything that is counterrevolutionary, hostile to the people, antisocialist, ambiguous, underhanded, and confused is uniting in hatred and slander against the Spartacus League. That proves that the revolution's heart beats in the breast of the Spartacus League and the future belongs to it.

The Spartacus League is not a party that aspires to have power over the heads of the working masses nor to attain power by using them. The Spartacus League is nothing but the most conscious component of the proletariat, and at every turn it points out to the broad working-class masses their historic tasks. At every stage of the revolution, the Spartacus League shows the working class the way forward toward the ultimate socialist goal, and in every national question it represents the interests of the world proletarian revolution.

The Spartacus League refuses to share governmental power with those hirelings of the bourgeoisie, Scheidemann-Ebert, because it recognizes that kind of collaboration as a betrayal of the basic principles of socialism, and because it understands that that would strengthen the counterrevolution and cripple the revolution.

The Spartacus League would also refuse to take power simply because Scheidemann-Ebert had exhausted their political capital and the Independents, through their complicity in this, had reached a dead end.

The Spartacus League will never take governmental power until that is the clear, unambiguous will of the great majority of the proletarian masses of Germany. It will never take power until the masses are in conscious agreement with its aims, goals, and methods of struggle.

The proletarian revolution will arrive at complete understanding and maturity only in stages, step by step, on the road to Calvary of its own bitter experience, and through a process of defeats and victories.

The victory of the Spartacus League comes not at the beginning, but at the end of the revolution. It coincides with the victory of the multimillioned masses of the socialist proletariat.

Proletarians arise! To arms! There is a world to win and a world to defeat. In this, the final class battle of world history, with humanity's highest ideal at stake, our war cry will be: "Thumb in his eye and knee on his chest."[16] □

The same day this program appeared, December 14, elections were held for the Berlin delegation to the General Congress of Workers' and Soldiers' Councils of Germany, which was to convene two days later. The SPD won a clear majority, gaining more than 75 percent of the Berlin delegates, while the USPD was held to fewer than 20 percent.

Although the revolutionary opponents of the government still led only a small minority of workers, they were growing in numbers and confidence in response to the mounting threat of counterrevolution. Conflicts between militant workers and the government led to increased strain in the USPD, which had a foot in both camps. The USPD had held no national party conference following the revolution, and the Hugo Haase leadership had no party mandate for its governmental alliance with the SPD and the capitalist ruling class.

Since late November, the Spartacists had campaigned for a congress of the USPD to rule on its participation in the government and its support for the national assembly. Whether they could win enough support in the USPD ranks and party apparatus to win the demand for a convention was tested on December 15 by a special conference of the Greater Berlin USPD, which was the stronghold of the party's left wing. Haase gave the report for the party leadership, and Luxemburg gave the counterreport. The following are excerpts from the discussion.

The Berlin USPD Debate
on the National Assembly[17]

Hugo Haase: . . . It is really splitting hairs to say that it is permissible to work together [with the SPD] in the Executive Committee of the Berlin councils but not in the government. The Executive Committee, which can appoint and dismiss the government, is the highest authority, to which the government is subordinate. (*Protests*)

We could not just abandon the government to Ebert, Scheidemann, and Company alone. But what does the Spartacus League now say in *Rote Fahne?* "The Spartacus League will never take governmental power until that is the clear, unambiguous will of the great majority of the proletarian masses of Germany. It will never take power until the masses are in conscious agreement with its aims, goals, and methods of struggle."

Well, the big majority was not in agreement on tactical and programmatic questions, but it was united in support of the two parties working together. If the majority of the people are not yet won over to socialism, what are we supposed to do in the meantime, until they are? Should we just turn the government over to the bourgeoisie? Yes, they would like that; to govern as they please and so undo the revolution. Yet that is exactly what the Spartacus League proposes to do: to just watch and wait until the proletariat has the majority. (*Commotion among the Spartacists*) . . .

As evidence of my view I wish to inform you of the most recent events at the Schwartzkopff factory. As you know, the workers there have always fought in the front lines. . . . An assembly of shop stewards has stated that if the leaders do not unify, the workers will do so over their heads. We see the same trend in Hamburg. . . . We do not have to agree with this trend; but it is a symptom of the proletariat's mood that we cannot simply disregard.

What is our political situation? From all sides we hear the call for the national assembly, especially from the bourgeoisie and the majority Socialists.

The national assembly is unavoidable. We must accept that. I do not oppose the national assembly. The only question is: when?

The Spartacists say, "Down with the national assembly," and point to the example of the Bolsheviks. But that was not the Bolsheviks' line at first. Rather, they sharply attacked the Kerensky government because it wanted to postpone the national assembly. And the Bolsheviks did not boycott the national assembly elections at all. They participated, in the hopes that they would win a majority together with the Left Socialist Revolutionaries. So it cannot be counterrevolutionary to seek the same goal in Germany. The Soviet government, this new, proletarian state form, did not appear until the second stage of the Russian revolution, although workers' and soldiers' soviets had already existed in Russia in the 1905 revolution and right from the beginning of the 1917 revolution. It was not until nine months after the revolution, after the Bolsheviks had seized state power, that they came out against the national assembly and in favor of the Soviet government.[18]

Liebknecht: Because they had learned from experience!

Haase: No, because a majority of right-wing Socialists had been elected.

We cannot slavishly imitate the Bolshevik revolution here, because the objective conditions are completely different. Russia is a peasant country, and an overwhelming majority of the peasants are poor. Only 10 percent of the population are industrial workers. Germany, on the other hand, is a developed, industrialized state, which needs food supplies. The majority of its population are proletarians.

I have always supported democracy and socialism. We know very well that for socialists, the western democracies are anything but ideal. Exploitation and repression reign there, too. But as we proceed to the national assembly elections, we are guaranteed that voting will be absolutely free. In the past the authorities cheated us — our meetings were banned, our comrades thrown in prison, our newspapers suppressed. The bourgeoisie still controls the big majority of the newspapers. All the more important, therefore, is the educational work ahead of us. We are for postponing the national assembly until this work is completed. . . .

The Spartacus League calls for a boycott. The Russian comrades, who boycotted the 1905 Duma elections, later regretted this as an error.[19] You can be certain that 99 percent of the proletariat will not heed their call to boycott, to wait for the next act of the revolution. Should we just stand by with folded arms, watching and waiting for the proletariat's conditions of struggle to worsen? Should we refrain from using the weapons we have and thereby allow the bourgeoisie to seize governmental power? If we do not prepare for the national assembly, then we have abdicated as a party. . . .

It is unacceptable that the Spartacus League, while belonging to our party, has its own organization, and fights us from within. At the Gotha congress Heckert explained:[20] "we differentiate ourselves from the Independents, but we will use their party as a protective cover while the war lasts." I objected to that then and still say that it would be better if we separated from them. . . .

Rosa Luxemburg: Comrade Haase has just delivered the indictment against policies that he himself devised and the defense attorney's plea for the Ebert-Scheidemann policies. He said that Liebknecht was ready to enter the government, but he forgot to mention the condition that Liebknecht set: that the new government carry out principled socialist policies. Even today we are ready, under this condition, to enter the government. As for the events at Schwartzkopff, that unity vote was mainly the result of manipulation, as a comrade will report to you.

Five weeks have passed since November 9. Since then the picture has changed completely. Reaction is much stronger than on the first day. And Haase tells us: see how wonderfully far we have brought things. His duty should have been to show us the progress of the counterrevolution fostered by the government in which Haase sits. This government, rather than preventing the counterrevolution, has strengthened the bourgeoisie and reaction. The bourgeoisie could not wish for a government more beneficial to them. It is a fig leaf for their counterrevolutionary goals.

The present government has not taken even the most elementary measures. Has it repudiated the war loans? Has it armed the people to defend the revolution? It banned the Red Guard and recognized Wels's White Guard. Ebert and Wels together pulled all the counterrevolutionary strings behind the December 6 putsch. All the officers and generals, Lequis and Hindenburg, support the government, and Haase tells us that it is a socialist government. It is precisely these government measures that confuse the proletariat. After December 6 the Independents should have left the government, refusing responsibility for what happened in order to rouse the masses and tell them that the revolution was in danger. Their failure to do this lulls the masses into a false sense of security. Haase's speech today only continued this policy.

Haase enumerated the great works of the new government — nothing but bourgeois reforms that prove to us just how backward Germany was. These merely settle the bourgeoisie's back debts, instead of making the revolutionary proletarian conquests that were in order.

Haase furthermore said that we shouldn't slavishly copy the Russians' tactics, since Germany is economically more advanced. We should learn from them, however. The Bolsheviks had to start by acquiring experience. We can pick the ripe fruit of this experience for ourselves.

Socialism is not a question of parliamentary elections, but a question of power. Breast to breast and toe to toe the proletariat must wage the class struggle with the bourgeoisie, and for that it must be properly equipped. Discussions and majority resolutions will no longer get us anywhere. Haase has come out for postponing the national assembly, but he nonetheless sees it as an arena for the political struggle. After the Independents' party leadership settled on April as the date for the national assembly, their representatives in the government capitulated and shifted the date to February 16.

Haase praised the principle of democracy. Now, if the principle of democracy is supposed to apply, then it should apply especially within the party itself. Therefore, a party congress must be called immediately so that the masses can say whether they still want this government.

If the USPD has suffered a defeat in the Berlin elections, then the real cause is Haase's policies in the government. (*Loud objections*) How absurd it is to blame the Spartacus group, when we worked to rouse the masses' socialist conscience! For four years Haase and his friends battled the social patriots, only in the end to make peace with the culprits. And that is why they are the real culprits.

Haase wants to reproach us for subordinating ourselves to the will of the masses because we will take charge of the government only with the approval of the masses. We do not subordinate, we do not temporize. But we want to denounce your halfhearted measures, your weaknesses. If Haase and his friends leave the government, they will thereby arouse and enlighten the masses. But if they continue to cover for the government, the masses will rise up and sweep them away. In the revolution today, speeches and pamphlets cannot accomplish the educational work that is required. Now it is a matter of education through action.

Yes, the situation in the USPD is untenable. Forces are united here that do not belong together. You must decide either to make common cause with the social patriots, or to go with the Spartacus League. The party congress should decide that. But in asking for a congress, we find that Haase is just as deaf now as Scheidemann was to the same demand during the war.

I propose the following resolution to the conference:

The December 15, 1918, Special Conference of the Greater Berlin USPD:

1. Demands that the USPD representatives immediately withdraw from the Ebert-Scheidemann government;

2. Rejects convening a national assembly, which can only strengthen the counterrevolution and cheat the revolution of its socialist goals;

3. Demands that the workers' and soldiers' councils immediately assume all political power. Disarm the counterrevolution! Arm the working population! Dissolve the Ebert government of People's Representatives! Vest supreme state power in the Executive Committee of the Workers' and Soldiers' Councils!

4. Demands that a USPD party congress be immediately called.

We now face a moment of world-historic importance, just before the proceedings of the general congress [of workers' and soldiers' councils]. The revolution has already been brought almost to the edge of disaster. With an iron hand the proletariat must pull it back. The government has done everything to wrench power from the general congress in advance. It has disarmed the civilian population and the proletariat. It has adopted measures that are contrary to the revolution and that confuse the masses. We must fight against this relentlessly. (*Loud applause*)

Emil Barth: I object strongly to Comrade Luxemburg's remarks. The demand to repudiate the war loans would mean the immediate collapse of Germany. Foch would march in and the Ruhr would be lost. We stand here stark naked and are the debtors of the Entente. Furthermore, when I'm up to something, I do not trumpet it about; I just do it. The Spartacists should consider that when they demand arming the proletariat. And what's more, the decree by the Council of People's Representatives relates to handing over army equipment.

The Spartacists reproach us for not preventing the troops from entering Berlin. If we had done that, we would have knocked heads with a hundred thousand soldiers, who are still organized in structured units. Today the soldiers just want to go home. But tomorrow, once they have put their feet up, they will certainly think as we do.

The struggle today is quite different from the struggle yesterday, because since then the revolution has taken place. No one did more for the revolution than I, (*Noisy disturbance*) procuring arms and agitating among the soldiers. But when I called on the Spartacists to help me, they were the ones who said, there is nothing we can do. (*Loud uproar*)

Karl Liebknecht: Barth has presented a very one-sided and narrow view of the revolution by speaking of those who *made* the revolution. Its fate did not depend on the distribution of Brownings, but rather on the mass movement and will of the people. The masses know better than the leaders what is necessary.

Barth says that there are things you simply do, without talking about them. That is the rotten approach of a diplomat. We openly, not secretly, demand the arming of the proletariat and disarming of the bourgeoisie, so that the socialist republic can become a reality, not just a phrase, and so that the proletarians will be capable of taking over all the seats of power. In addition, Barth portrayed the actions of the Spartacus League as buffoonery. That's quite a statement, when a People's Representative views huge mass rallies in such a way.

Who duped the people with the illusion that everything was going just fine? Who stirred up the troops against Bolshevism? The culprits are Ebert, Scheidemann, and Company. Haase and Barth are accomplices. The government should have undertaken the political education of the masses. They should have sent envoys to the frontline troops to fan the flames of revolution there. If the government had ended the officer corps' authority and not left the generals in their positions, then they would not be openly organizing the counterrevolution today. Making the troops pledge allegiance to the government is a blunt rebuff to the Executive Committee of the councils. At the same time, the government has restored the power of the bureaucracy and stationed itself protectively in front of capital's coffers by disarming the proletariat and arming the bourgeoisie.

We see that the relationship of forces between the government and the Executive Committee has completely shifted. The Executive Committee was born out of the will of the masses, but step by step its power has been taken away, until the attempted coup against it on December 6 reduced it to an object of pity. With Haase's assistance, the cabinet's policies snatched power away from the proletariat. *We demand the withdrawal of the Independents from the cabinet.* We summon the proletariat to a new revolution, to the real revolution, which will crush the social patriots. (*Loud applause*) . . .

Hugo Eberlein: It is not the ballot, but rather the economic relationship of forces that is decisive. Just as before, capital will bring its dominant influence to bear in the national assembly elections as elsewhere. The new German parliamentarism will resemble the French as one rotten egg resembles another. We demand not collaboration between capital and labor under democracy, but rather continuation of the class struggle. And for that, we need a workers' parliament in which the bourgeois class is no longer represented. . . .

Rudolf Hilferding: . . . The general congress, which will convene tomorrow, will have a completely different majority than the Spartacists would like to see. And its first decision will likely be to move the date for the national assembly elections to sooner than previously planned. The national assembly will come, no doubt about it. Therefore, politically it is a waste of time to continue a lengthy discussion on the theoretical question: council government or national assembly?

They say that we are now in the first phase of the revolution. But if that is so, it means that we must do what is called for in the first phase. In Russia too they were for the national assembly in the first phase. That is not to say, by the way, that I think things will develop here like the Russian model. The Kerensky government was overthrown because it launched a new offensive, while the soldiers wanted peace. But no government here even thinks of continuing the war. Thus the impulse that existed in Russia for the soldiers to rise up against the government is lacking here.

The mood on November 9 forced us to participate in the government. A refusal would have driven Scheidemann's party into a coalition with the bourgeoisie, for which we would then have been responsible. Of course, a situation could arise that would require that our comrades withdraw from the government. But up to now there has been no such serious reason. You can say what you want about the Scheidemanns, but they are not stupid and therefore not counterrevolutionary.

I propose the following resolution:

"The conference declares:

"The most important political task of the USPD at this moment is organizing for the national assembly elections. It is a matter of mobilizing all the forces of the proletariat to ensure the victory of socialism over the bourgeoisie. The USPD considers itself the standard-bearer of the revolution and its driving force. It is prepared to fulfill all duties that flow from this, whether in the Socialist government or in resolute opposition to every counterrevolutionary movement — as the situation demands. It calls upon its representatives in the government to work with all determination and without hesitation to secure and advance the gains of the revolution."

Luxemburg (Summary):[21] Our first duty is to break all links with the present government. That is our demand, and it is correct. Comrade Barth got up here before and listed all his heroic acts in the revolution. For such a great revolutionary, Comrade Barth has certainly gone downhill fast in the last five weeks. Now Comrade Barth participates in all the Ebert government's counterrevolutionary activities. Why did he enter this government? Why did he not stay in the ranks of the proletariat, where a true revolutionary belongs? No, comrades, individuals do not make the revolution. If the revolution does not start with the masses, then it is not worth a brass farthing.

Ströbel argued that the USPD representatives had to participate in the government to work for the revolution. No, comrades. For us Socialists, it is not governing that is important, but overthrowing capitalism, which is not even shaken yet. It is still standing. We are not trying to show that our party is capable of governing, but that we now, in this government, cannot govern as socialists. That is already proven.

We have been told that we must wait a long time before the majority of the proletariat will find its way to our revolutionary perspective. Those who advance that argument totally fail to appreciate the living and dynamic tempo of revolutionary development. What we want is not to take power ourselves. No; we want political power in the hands of the majority of the proletariat. All those who have promoted the national assembly trap have miseducated the masses and set revolutionary developments back months and years.

Hilferding emphasized the democratic principle. But this formal democratic equality is a fake and a fraud so long as capital's economic power persists. We cannot debate with the bourgeoisie and the junkers whether socialism should be introduced. Socialism does not mean sitting down together in parliament and passing laws. For us socialism means suppressing the ruling classes with all the brutality (*Loud laughter*) that the proletarian struggle can bring to bear. The national assembly is supposed to serve to bridge the gap between capital and labor. Now you must decide which way you want to go, either with us or with Scheidemann. Now there is no more evasion — it is one or the other. □

Although the Berlin USPD was considered the bastion of the party's left wing, Hilferding's resolution was adopted by 485 votes to 185 — a serious blow to the Spartacists' hopes to shake the grip of the USPD's right-wing national leadership.

That same day, December 15, Luxemburg appealed to the delegates arriving for the General Congress of Workers' and Soldiers' Councils of Germany. Her article, which follows, called on them to break from their dependence on the Ebert-Scheidemann government and instead to lead the mass workers' struggle that could bring the workers' and soldiers' councils to power.

To the Ramparts![22]
by Rosa Luxemburg

Tomorrow the General Congress of Workers' and Soldiers' Councils from all parts of Germany will convene. This will bring together — organizationally, at any rate — what the revolutionary proletariat of all Germany, worker and soldier alike, regards as the flower of the budding tree of revolution.

It is possible to visualize a very different type of congress. One could imagine the congress coming on the crest of the first, rising wave of proletarian revolution. Then the revolution's star might have illuminated the hour of the congress's birth with the same clear light it shed in the days of the ninth of November, when it lit the proletariat out of the horrible night of war and servitude.

The congress did not take place in those first hours. A substitute appeared in its stead — the Executive Committee of the Berlin Workers' and Soldiers' Council, which took into its hands, its all-too-weak hands, the duties of a central leading body.

Thus, the general congress meets at a moment when the revolution has lost its first, meteoric brilliance, the brilliance that in those first days blinded all enemies of the revolution and, unfortunately, its supporters as well. They too believed, in so many cases, that through the miracles wrought by the ninth of November the business of making the revolution had been completed. Today they have all regained their eyesight. For all who once thought the historic powers, the ruling classes of a centuries-old system, could be unseated by human masses celebrating, soldiers waving, and red flags fluttering on Unter den Linden are now forced to watch as the counterrevolution — capitalism — comes back to life. In those days, like a louse, it was only playing dead. But now it feels the time and opportunity are at hand to suck blood once again.

The counterrevolution's machinations are plain to see. They began the moment it succeeded in appointing Ebert-Scheidemann as its agents in the government, thereby crippling the government's revolutionary vitality and directing its political energy into counterrevolutionary channels.

The things this "socialist" government has accomplished! Every day a new decree: a decree to restore the old governmental agencies; a decree that tried to restore all the district administrators, police chiefs, and mayors who had been chased out; a decree declaring private property inviolable; a decree declaring the courts, those instruments of class law, to be "independent" and giving them a free hand to continue practicing class law; a decree ordering that taxes be paid as always. *Nulla dies sine linea,*[23] not a day without a decree; not a day when a pebble about to fall out of the rotten edifice of capitalist rule is not cemented back into place.

Who could blame the bourgeoisie for feeling strong enough, under circumstances so favorable for them, to try getting rid of their agents, the Ebert-Scheidemann-Haase government, and taking the reins they had lost back into their own hands? They are taking their time, going step by step. First they convinced their agents to slip the power back into their hands via the detour of the national assembly. Ebert-Scheidemann threw themselves into that task with all the zeal of renegades. They worked for the national assembly day and night, in every street and town square. They labored for the bourgeoisie with all their might. They organized putsches and ordered proletarians shot down. They worshipped the military and saluted the black, white, and red flag — and still they did not earn the gratitude of their master, capitalism.

The master has become impatient. He is weary of his servant. Time is getting short. He feels his hour has come again, and he could hardly care less about the national assembly: he wants his old Reichstag back.

Such is the hour when the nationwide congress convenes. Capitalism, reinvigorated, is ready for action.

And the revolution? Make no mistake about it: if the revolution were to continue with the same revolutionary organs it created in those first days, the workers' and soldiers' councils, and if their strength and meaning reflected the condition and significance of the revolution, the revolution's outlook would be bleak indeed.

Unrestrained baiting of the workers' and soldiers' councils has begun. In turbulent times little mistakes are a matter of course. Under the old regime they were an everyday occurrence. Previously they were the daily routine; today they merely show a lack of experience. But now every one is magnified into a capital offense and is stamped as conclusive evidence of the unworkability of the council system.

And to finish it off, they invoke the specter of the Entente. Mr. *Ebert* was the first one. He was the one who *of his own free will* offered America the councils' head on a platter in exchange for food — nay, *begged* that food be delivered only in exchange for their head. The *Ebert-Scheidemann-Haase* government threatened Germany with the specter of famine. The idea was hammered into everyone's head: *either the councils or bread.*

This was followed by news reports that the Entente was about to invade Germany. The reports began to arrive every day: the invasion is beginning; the Entente is at the door; the Entente is about to make a statement; Clemenceau has stated; Lloyd George has declared. Every day another report; every day another hoax.

Because they were all hoaxes. Not a word was true. Every word printed was invented in the foreign ministry or in the Reich chancellery. They even outdid the old regime in this field; even the old regime never lied to the people as unblinkingly, as doggedly, as shamelessly, or as deceitfully as this government.

And the councils found no way to counter this. They left the entire apparatus for influencing public opinion in the hands of the government, of the counterrevolution. They looked on in silence while the government, that den of counterrevolutionaries, daily lobbed flaming firebrands into their house.

But the revolution does not suffer from the same weakness as the councils. *It* cannot be collared and destroyed with those little tricks. *It* is growing and is only now really becoming that which it really is: the proletarian revolution. Strikes are spreading across the country like wildfire. The proletarians are standing up: yesterday in Upper Silesia; today in Berlin; tomorrow in Rhineland-Westphalia, Stuttgart, and Hamburg. They are breaking all the chains forged for them by government, party, and trade union. They are confronting the enemy, capitalism, eye to eye. The "democratic" tinsel that made many a me-too Socialist appear so appealing during the first days of the revolution is now gone. The giant, naked form of the revolution is rising up and flexing the muscles that broke the old order and will form the new one.

There lies the power upon which the councils, assembled for the congress, can base themselves. That is the power they must both obediently serve and lead in action. That is the wellspring from which alone flows their strength and lifeblood.

The revolution will survive without the councils; the councils without the revolution are dead.

Many opportunities have been missed. Often the councils have made their way in hesitation and confusion, prejudiced by outmoded party formulas, their vision artificially narrowed by slogans and rhetoric designed to deceive them about their role in events or their power over them.

There are four very urgent steps the congress can take to make up for past omissions and to assume its rightful role.

1. It must wipe out the counterrevolution's lair, the place where all the threads of counterrevolutionary conspiracy come together. That is, it must eliminate the Ebert-Scheidemann-Haase cabinet.

2. It must demand the disarming of all frontline troops that do not unconditionally recognize the workers' and soldiers' councils as the highest authority. Otherwise, these will become the personal body-guards of the Ebert-Haase cabinet.

3. It must demand the disarming of all officers and of the White Guards formed by the Ebert-Haase government; it must create Red Guards.

4. It must reject the national assembly as an attempt to assassinate both the revolution and the workers' and soldiers' councils.

The workers' and soldiers' councils can still place themselves at the head of the revolution by immediately implementing these four measures. The proletariat is willing to be led by the councils, provided they in turn are willing to lead forcefully against capitalism. The proletariat is ready to give them everything and raise them to the summit with the cry:

"All power to the workers' and soldiers' councils!" □

The SPD laid out its proposals for the congress in the following article from *Vorwärts,* published December 16, the morning the congress opened.

"A Time of Reconstruction"[24]

Today at 10:00 a.m., in the meeting hall of the former three-class parliament, the first congress of the German revolution will meet — the Congress of the Workers' and Soldiers' Councils of all Germany.

When the might of the ruling classes collapsed under the blows of the World War, amid the misfortune of defeat, it was a stroke of good fortune that there was an organized force in Germany able to take charge — the power of the German working class, reared and apprenticed in two generations of struggle. When Wilhelm the Conqueror became a deserter, when junker and bourgeois, immobilized with fear, cowered under their rock, the entire toiling population of Germany looked hopefully toward the sole political force remaining — the power of the workers' movement. They looked to it for their salvation.

It is the proud duty of the congress that begins today to prove worthy of that confidence and to restore it wherever it has been shaken. "All power to the workers' and soldiers' councils!" — that slogan was constantly dinned into the ear of the congress from certain quarters. Today, the congress of workers' and soldiers' councils has that power. It is the parliament of the revolution and has the power to topple the government of the revolution or to lend it the powerful support that it will need to overcome the unforeseeable difficulties that lie ahead.

The congress, which is entrusted with such a great historic mission, will undoubtedly have insight enough — in its majority — to recognize the weaknesses inherent in its composition. The elections that brought it into being were unfortunately not general, not equal, and not direct. Indeed in many cases they were not even secret. They were conducted merely as an emergency measure, born of the necessity of the moment; and the people, steeped in the spirit of democracy, would prefer not to go through that sort of thing a second time. If the credentials commission works in an efficient and nonpartisan fashion, it will be making a valuable contribution to the second question on the agenda: whether the council system deserves to be immortalized as the main pillar of the German constitution.

However, part of that debate will be preempted in discussing the first agenda point, "The Report of the Executive Committee of the Berlin Workers' and Soldiers' Councils." There it will come out that, although the auxiliary and transitional institutions formed by the workers and soldiers have an indispensable function to fulfill, their face is not without some ugly blemishes. It may be said, with no partisan political bias whatever, that the councils have performed flawlessly wherever they consisted of experienced practitioners from the labor movement; objectionable damage occurred only where unorganized masses swept aside the proven leaders. A helping hand will have to be extended in these instances, in keeping with the spirit of the new, liberated social order and in line with the strict integrity which has always characterized the German labor movement. Whenever the revolution is endangered by the malady of internal disruption, it must seek its cure in ruthless self-criticism.

In this way, a certain amount of clarity can be introduced into the discussion of "national assembly or workers' councils," even before that item comes up on the agenda. Social Democracy refuses to recognize this as an alternative, believing instead that its most sacred obligation is to give the whole people their full, democratic right of self-determination by holding elections to the national assembly at the earliest technically possible date. That would be January 19.

Until then, however, the national leadership, supported by the confidence of the people, must have its hands free. It would be intolerable for the cause of socialism, which will undoubtedly face its most severe historic test in only four weeks, to be discredited by rival parallel governments. The national leadership is responsible to the people and to the national assembly and must be called on to resolutely repudiate anything for which it cannot take responsibility or give its approval. Its actions and what the people think of it will determine whether they speak out in the elections for or against Social Democracy. Therefore the government must have the power to prevent blunders and acts of caprice, as these would serve only as grist for reaction's mill.

We may anticipate sharp debates. Three factions are in formation: one Social Democratic, one Independent, and one Left-Independent Spartacist. It is up to the last-mentioned whether the meeting proceeds in a manner in keeping with the movement's dignity and the great significance of its cause. Insofar as a survey is possible at this point, the Social Democrats — in whose ranks we would like to include the right wing of the Independents — have the upper hand by a wide margin, despite all electoral irregularities. Even if the far left experienced significant growth from still undecided forces, they could not pose a threat in the voting. But were they not the ones who raised the slogan, "All power to the workers' and soldiers' councils"? Very well. They have recognized the workers' and soldiers' councils as the highest authority, and like it or not, they will have to abide by the councils' verdict!

We hope the congress of the German revolution will disappoint aesthetes by an absence of theatrics. It does not become the German workers and soldiers to let themselves be made giddy by fancy language. We are not interested in painting grand historic canvasses; we prefer to show our consciousness of the greatness and awesome gravity of the times by doing something of practical value for the welfare of our beleaguered people. That was always the style of the numerous party and trade union comrades whom we will have the pleasure of welcoming to the congress; that is what won them the allegiance of millions. And we rely upon their clarity and firmness of purpose to prevent the congress from degenerating into the hubbub of futile procedural debates and scenes of tumult. Crisp, clear, calm, and determined: that is how the men must conduct themselves who have the great calling of leading the people in such stormy times. We need men of action, not heroic orators.

The revolution is meeting upon the rubble of the Bastille of three-class bloc voting. Let us be glad that rubble here is only a figure of speech! The building is elegantly and exquisitely preserved with its *fauteuils*, mirrored salons, and its comforts all intact. Nothing was plundered or destroyed. Is that not a symbol? We should destroy nothing and waste nothing. We need the little that remains so that we may painstakingly and gradually craft job opportunities and a modicum of well-being for our people. Let the congress of the German revolution convene under the sign of the task of reconstruction! □

Rules for election of delegates to the general congress of the councils were determined by regional council bodies. The selection procedure was weighted to favor sectors where the SPD was strong. Of the 489 delegates, only 187 were wage or salaried workers. No less than 195 delegates were party and trade union full-time functionaries, the vast majority aligned with the SPD. Economists, writers, doctors, lawyers, and other professionals made up 71 of the delegates. Thirteen delegates were officers. Only 2 delegates were women.

Two hundred and ninety delegates registered as SPD supporters; 90 as USPD members; and 25 as supporters of the German Democratic Party, an openly bourgeois formation. Liebknecht attempted to organize a joint fraction of Spartacists and left USPD members, but failed. Only about 10 of the USPD delegates belonged to the Spartacus League. Liebknecht and Luxemburg were barred from participation by a regulation of the Berlin Executive Committee that all candidates had to be employed in the workplace where they were elected. Eleven delegates formed an independent fraction led by Heinrich Laufenberg, a leader of a revolutionary group in Hamburg allied with the Bremen Left.

The makeup of the congress did not reflect the Spartacists' increasing influence in the working class, at least in Berlin. Together with the Revolutionary Shop Stewards, they called a mass rally in front of the congress hall on December 16, the opening day of its sessions. About 250,000 Berlin workers left work to demonstrate for the congress to assume full political power and replace the Ebert cabinet. It was one of the largest rallies Berlin had ever seen, equal in size or somewhat larger than a rally called the same day by the SPD. It showed the prospects for independent action by revolutionists when they acted together. Liebknecht's address to the demonstrators was summarized in *Rote Fahne* as follows.

"The Congress Must Assume
Full Political Power"[25]
by Karl Liebknecht

Comrades, fellow soldiers, and friends. Today, when the first Congress of Workers' and Soldiers' Councils assembles, is a historic moment.

The first task facing the congress is to defend the revolution and defeat the counterrevolution by disarming all generals and officers, abolishing the previously existing military authority, forming a Red Guard to complete the social revolution, and rooting out the remaining counterrevolutionaries. And, I might add, even though it will upset some misguided and misled proletarians, that includes the Ebert-Scheidemann government. (*Loud shouts of "Down with the Scheidemanns!"*) For there is documentary proof that all the threads of the counterrevolution meet in the Ebert-Scheidemann government. Just yesterday, Ebert was demanding broader powers. (*Vociferous shouts of protest against Ebert*)

What we have right now in Germany is not a socialist republic but a capitalist one. The proletariat must still bring the socialist republic into being through struggle against the present government, which is buttressing capitalism. We demand that the congress assume full political power so that it can institute socialism and that it not turn the power over to a national assembly, which would not be an organ of the revolution. We demand that the congress of workers' councils extend the hand of friendship to our Russian brothers and invite them to send their representatives. We want world revolution and the unification of workers of all countries under workers' and soldiers' councils. □

As the congress opened, Ebert brought greetings from the government, asserting that "the victorious proletariat will not institute class rule," and calling for political power to be transferred to the national assembly.[26] A proposal to admit Luxemburg and Liebknecht with voice was voted down. The demonstrators in front of the building then sent a delegation to present their demands to the assembly. Their representative called for "all power to the workers' and soldiers' councils," for "removal of the Ebert Council of People's Representatives," and for election of an Executive Committee of the councils "as the highest legislative and governmental body."[27] The demands also repeated

Liebknecht's call for disarming the counterrevolution and arming the proletariat.

The congress agenda began with reports from Richard Müller for the Executive Committee and Wilhelm Dittmann for the Council of People's Representatives. After a lengthy discussion of these reports, the following resolution was moved by three SPD delegates.

SPD Resolution to Congress of Councils[28]

1. The National Congress of Workers' and Soldiers' Councils of Germany, which holds all political power, turns all legislative and executive power over to the Council of People's Representatives until the national assembly shall rule otherwise.

2. The congress also establishes a Central Committee [Zentralrat] of the workers' and soldiers' councils, which shall be the parliamentary authority overseeing the German and Prussian cabinet. It has authority over the national People's Representatives and — pending a final decision on the state structure — over the People's Representatives of Prussia.

3. The Council of People's Representatives shall appoint deputy ministers who shall supervise administration in the national ministries. Two such deputies shall be assigned to each ministry, chosen from the two Social Democratic parties. The Central Committee shall review the appointments of ministers and deputies.

(signed) Lüdemann,
Kahmann, Severing □

The resolution was approved by a majority of delegates; the vote was not recorded. While tipping its hat to the authority of the councils, the resolution left the supervisory function of the new Central Committee vague and undefined, and delegated all power to the Ebert-Scheidemann-Haase government. In addition, the councils' authority was limited to the two-month period prior to the convocation of the national assembly. Although the next agenda point was to take up the question, "national assembly or a council system?", the question had in effect been settled, and the rest of the congress was an anticlimax. In his report defending the "council system," Ernst Däumig, a left-wing USPD delegate and a leader of the Revolutionary Shop Stewards, asserted that the congress had become "a political suicide club" and had voted its own "death sentence."[29] Däumig's resolution, which called for the retention of "the workers' council system as the basis of the constitution," was defeated 344-98.[30] The USPD fraction thereupon refused to stand for election to the Central Committee of the councils, and it was elected with a purely SPD membership. The congress also adopted an SPD motion to move the date of the national assembly elections up one month to January 19.

The congress deviated from the agenda and proposals of the SPD leadership only on one key point: control of the armed forces. Its first day's session was interrupted by a delegation of representatives of soldiers and sailors in Berlin, who demanded that their proposals be immediately discussed and adopted. They demanded that control of the armed forces be given to elected soldiers' and sailors' councils, that officers be disarmed, symbols of rank abolished, and disciplinary power be transferred to soldiers' councils.[31] The chairman ruled that these proposals be held over for later consideration, but the soldiers insisted they be discussed and adopted at once. The meeting dissolved in an uproar, and the chairman declared it adjourned.

Realizing that the voice of the Berlin soldiers could not be ignored, the SPD the next day moved the adoption of the better-known but less radical demands proposed earlier by the Hamburg soldiers' council. These demands, known as the Hamburg Points, were adopted by the congress with some minor modifications. As amended, they read as follows.

The Hamburg Points[32]

1. The People's Representatives, under the control of the Executive Committee, shall have command of the army, navy, and the republican defense force. In the garrisons, military command shall be exercised by the local workers' and soldiers' councils, in ongoing consultation with the High Command. Military affairs common to all garrisons shall be decided by those responsible for the High Command, jointly with a council of delegates from the garrisons.

2. To symbolize the destruction of militarism and the abolition of blind obedience, all insignias of rank shall be removed, and the practice of carrying weapons when out of uniform shall be discontinued.

3. The soldiers' councils shall be responsible for the reliability of all units and for maintaining discipline. The Congress of Workers' and Soldiers' Councils believes that troops will submit to the discipline of soldiers' councils whom they have themselves elected and to that of superiors on duty. Such discipline is absolutely necessary if

the goals of the socialist revolution are to be realized. Military rank shall not hold among those off duty.

4. Removal of all stripes, NCO gold braid and the like, cockades, epaulets, and sidearms shall be at the sole discretion of the soldiers' councils, not individuals. Excesses hurt the revolution's image and are out of place when our troops are returning home. The congress demands the abolition of all orders, medals of honor, and titles.

5. The soldiers themselves shall elect their leaders. Former officers who enjoy the confidence of the majority of their units are eligible to be reelected.

6. Officers in military administration and civil servants with military rank may remain in their posts in the interest of demobilization if they promise not to act against the interests of the revolution.

7. Abolition of the standing army and organization of a people's militia shall be carried out as rapidly as possible. □

The High Command reacted angrily to the adoption of the Hamburg Points and raised its objections with the cabinet. The Ebert government, while publicly claiming that the Hamburg Points would be applied, met with representatives of the High Command and agreed on a series of restrictions that negated their most essential provisions. The most important of these restrictions was that the Hamburg Points would not apply to the army at the front, that is, to the forces the High Command hoped to use against the revolution.

The final major report to the congress was on "socialization of the economy." Socialization, that is, expropriation of the bourgeoisie, was a persistent demand of workers' demonstrations and strikes in the months following November 9. The government had earlier moved to counter this demand by appointing a commission of economists to study the question. Only after several months of study, and after the defeat of the workers' movement in the armed battles of early 1919, did the commission report, and even its moderate recommendations were then pigeonholed.

Rudolf Hilferding, a USPD leader and one of the commission members, reflected the government's approach in his report to the December congress of councils. Hilferding stressed that the most important task was to get the economy moving again. For the moment, he said, this required excluding some branches of industry, where no disruption could be permitted, from being considered for socialization. Some industries, such as the bakeries, were ripe for socialization, Hilferding said. He also cited coal mining and "the first stages of iron production," industries where the workers themselves were already campaigning strongly for expropriations, among the places where government ownership might be practical. Banking, however, was too indispensable to be taken over, he stressed. Since any nationalizations would be carried out on a step-by-step basis, compensation was required to prevent injustice to those capitalists whose holdings were the first to be taken over, Hilferding said.[33] The congress took no action on this or any other legislative question before it closed on December 21.

Since the major Spartacus leaders were excluded from the congress of the councils, a revolutionary answer to Hilferding and other reformists on this question was largely absent at the gathering itself. But Liebknecht took up these and many other arguments for postponing action against Germany's capitalist rulers in the following speech made December 23 in Berlin.

The Hour of Socialism Is Now[34]
by Karl Liebknecht

Above all we must in these times have absolute clarity in our political objectives. We need clear insight into the course of the revolution. We must recognize what it has been up to now in order to understand what the future tasks will be.

Up to now the German revolution has been nothing more than an attempt to overcome the war and its effects. The revolution's first step therefore was to conclude an armistice with the hostile powers and to overthrow the leaders of the old system. The next task of all determined revolutionaries consists of upholding and extending these gains.

We see that the armistice, about which the present government is now negotiating with the hostile powers, is being used by the latter to strangle Germany. But such an action is irreconcilable with the proletariat's objectives because it would not correspond with the ideal of a peace that is lasting and humane.

The goal of the German and the international proletariat is neither a transitory peace, nor a peace based on violence, but rather one that is lasting and just. But that is not the objective of the present government. Because the government fails to encroach on capital's foundations it is, by its very nature, capable of concluding only an ephemeral peace.

So long as capitalism exists, war is unavoidable. All socialists know that very well. What caused the World War? Capitalist rule means the exploitation of the proletariat, it means the constant and unrestrained extension of capitalism in the world market. Here the capitalist powers representing rival national interests collide sharply. And this economic collision necessarily leads in the end to a political and military clash — to war. Now they seek to placate us with the League of Nations idea, which supposedly will produce a lasting peace between the different countries. As socialists we know perfectly well that such a League of Nations is nothing more than an alliance of the ruling classes of the various countries — an alliance that cannot conceal its capitalist character, is incapable of guaranteeing a lasting peace, and is directed against the international proletariat.

Competition, the essence of capitalist production, means fratricide for us socialists. We therefore demand the opposite: international solidarity among the peoples. The proletariat alone is resolved to win an enduring, humane peace. Entente imperialism can never grant the German proletariat this peace. We must obtain it from our fellow workers in France, America, and Italy. Only ending the World War with a lasting and humane peace deserves the active support of the international proletariat. That is what our socialist principles teach us.

Surely now, after this colossal carnage, we must cast a new world from a single pour. All humanity was thrown into the glowing crucible of the World War. The proletariat holds the hammer in its hand with which to shape a new world.

The proletariat suffers not only from the war and its devastation, but also from the inherent nature of the capitalist social order, the true cause of this war. For the proletariat the only salvation from the dark disaster that is its fate is to abolish capitalism.

But how can this be done? In order to answer this question we must clearly understand that only the proletariat, through its own action, can deliver itself from bondage. We are told that the national assembly is the way to freedom. The national assembly, however, means nothing more than nominal political democracy. That is not at all the democracy that socialism has always demanded. The ballot is certainly not the lever with which the power of the capitalist social order can be dislodged. We know that a large number of countries have long had formal democracy through a national assembly — like France, America, and Switzerland. But capital dominates in these democracies all the same.

There is no question but that capital will make the influence of its organized economic supremacy felt to the utmost in the national assembly elections. Under the pressure and influence of this preeminence, great masses of the population will give their vote to their enemy, despite themselves and contrary to their own true interests. For that reason alone the national assembly can never represent the victory of the socialist will. It is absurd to believe that the prerequisites and conditions necessary to achieve socialism exist in a formal parliamentary democracy. Rather, just the opposite is true: achieving socialism is the fundamental precondition for a true democracy.

The revolutionary German proletariat cannot expect its objectives to be advanced by the old Reichstag reborn in the form of the national assembly, because this national assembly will be the same as the old talk-shop on the Königsplatz.[35] We will certainly find all the same gentlemen there as before, those who prior to and during the war tried to control the fate of the German people, with such disastrous results. And it is also probable that the bourgeois parties will have a majority in the national assembly. But even if, with a socialist majority, the national assembly should resolve to socialize the German economy, such a parliamentary decision would remain a paper decree and would founder on the most vehement opposition from the capitalists. Socialism cannot be achieved in parliament or by using parliamentary methods. Extraparliamentary, revolutionary struggle is the one and only decisive method that will put the proletariat in a position to reshape society according to its will.

By its nature, capitalist society is nothing but the more or less veiled reign of violence. Its intention is to return to the legal conditions of the previous "order," and to discredit and sweep away the revolution that the proletariat made by treating it as a criminal action, a historical aberration. But the proletariat did not make the heaviest of sacrifices during the bloody war for nothing. We, the vanguard of the revolution, will not be driven from our positions. We will survive until we have consolidated socialist power. . . .

The present government has not yet tackled a single one of the most urgent revolutionary tasks. Rather it has done everything to hold back the revolution. Now we hear that, with the government's assistance, peasants' councils are being elected in the countryside, councils of that layer of the population that has been among the most backward and bitter enemies of the proletariat and which even today remains the most vehement foe of the rural proletariat.[36] Revolutionaries must firmly and resolutely oppose all these machinations. We must make use of our power and, most importantly, we must energetically and confidently begin socialization of the economy.

The first step will entail the proletariat confiscating the arms de-

pots and the entire arms industry. Then the large industrial and agricultural enterprises must pass over to social ownership. Given the
advanced and highly centralized structure of the German economy,
this socialist changeover doubtlessly will be relatively easy and quick
to accomplish. Furthermore, we have an already highly developed
system of cooperatives, in which the middle class is especially interested. This is also useful for effectively implementing socialism.

We know very well that this socialization will be a long and massive process. We have not the slightest illusion about the difficulties
that stand in the way of this task, especially given the dangerous situation our people now face. But does anyone seriously believe that
people are able to select at their discretion the best time for a revolution and the realization of socialism? Truly, world history does not
proceed like that. We cannot just declare that the socialist revolution
does not fit into our carefully made plans today or tomorrow, but on
the following day, when we will be better prepared — when we once
again have bread and raw materials and have our capitalist production in full swing — then we will want to discuss socializing the
economy. No, that is a wrong and ridiculous conception of the nature
of historical development. One can neither select the best time for a
revolution to begin, nor adjourn it at will. Because revolutions by
their very nature are nothing other than great and fundamental social
crises, whose eruption and development are not contingent upon the
will of individuals, indeed which take no note of them, bursting upon
them like powerful tempests. As Marx taught us, social revolutions
can take place only during crises of capitalism. Well then, this war is
just such a crisis. Therefore, the hour of socialism strikes now, if at
all.

On that Friday night [November 8], which was the very eve of the
revolution, the leaders of the Social Democratic parties still had no
idea that the revolution was knocking at the door. They did not want
to believe that the revolutionary ferment among the masses of workers and soldiers was already so advanced. But as they realized that
the great battle had already begun, they then all ran in haste to catch
up. Otherwise they feared that the mighty movement would surge
past them.

The decisive moment has arrived. All those who wail about the
revolution coming just now, at such an inopportune moment, are
fools and weaklings. Now it is a question of our willingness to act, of
our revolutionary sincerity and will. The great mission, for which we
have so long prepared, will wait no more. The revolution is here. It
must be! It is no longer a question of whether, only of how. The

question is posed. And just because we now find ourselves in a difficult situation is no reason to conclude that there should be no revolution.

I repeat that we do not underestimate these difficulties. We, above all, are aware of the problem that the German people have no revolutionary experience or tradition. But on the other hand the labor of socialization is considerably lightened for the German proletariat by several circumstances. Opponents of our program argue that now, in such a precarious situation, with unemployment, shortages of food and raw materials, it is impossible to begin socializing the economy. But did not the ruling-class government resort to the most drastic economic measures — measures that fundamentally altered production and consumption — right in the middle of the war, that is in a situation at least as difficult as now? And all these measures were implemented back then for the sake of the war, of holding out to the end, in the interests of militarism and the ruling class.

The war-economy measures could be implemented only through the self-discipline of the German people. At that time this self-discipline stood in the service of the mass slaughter. Its effect was detrimental to the people. But now that it will be in the interests of the people, for their benefit, much greater accomplishments and changes will be possible than ever before. This self-discipline will now come into play for the cause of socialism, for carrying out socialism. It was precisely the social patriots who described the drastic economic war measures as "war socialism." And Scheidemann, that obedient servant of the military dictatorship, enthusiastically supported them. Now we can regard that war socialism as a reconstruction of our economic life that can well serve as preparation for real socialization, under the banner of socialism.

The achievement of socialism is inevitable. It must come because we have to definitively overcome the disorder that has roused such anger. But this disorder is unmanageable so long as yesterday's rulers, the economic and political forces of capitalism that caused this chaos, are at the rudder.

The duty of the present government should have been to intervene, to act quickly and decisively. Yet they have not advanced the task of socialization by a single step. What have they done about food supplies? They tell the people, "You must be nice and well-behaved, and then Wilson will send us food." The entire bourgeoisie chants the same thing day after day, and those who a few months ago could not do enough to curse or besmirch the American president are now enraptured by him and fall at his feet in admiration — to get food from him. Oh yes, for sure, Wilson and his buddies may well help us, but only in the amount and manner that will serve the imperialist interests of Entente capitalism.

Now all the open and secret opponents of the proletarian revolution are hurrying to boost Wilson as a good friend of the German people — the very same humanitarian Wilson who sanctioned Foch's inhuman armistice conditions and thereby contributed to intensifying without limit the people's suffering.[37] No, we revolutionary socialists do not for a moment believe in the fraud of the humane Wilson, for he can and will do nothing other than represent the interests of Entente capital with cool deliberation. What purpose is really served by this counterfeit now being hawked by the bourgeoisie and social patriots? To convince and to entice the proletariat to surrender the power it won in the revolution.

We will not fall for it. We base our socialist policies on the granite foundation of the German proletariat. We base them on the granite foundation of international socialism. For us, who have begun the social revolution, to appeal to Entente capital for compassion is incompatible with the proletariat's dignity and revolutionary mission. Rather, we count on the revolutionary solidarity of the proletariat of France, England, Italy, and America and their readiness to act internationally. The fainthearted and the unbelievers, in whom the spirit of socialism is utterly absent, tell us that we are fools to hope for a social revolution to break out in the countries that emerged victorious from the World War. Is there anything to this? Of course, it would be utterly wrong to believe that the revolution will break out in the Entente countries right away, on command. The world revolution, which is our goal and hope, is much too mighty a historical process to develop in days or weeks in a rapid succession of blows. The Russian Socialists predicted the German revolution as a necessary consequence of the Russian. But after the outbreak of the Russian revolution everything was still quiet here for a full year, until the hour finally did strike.

Today the peoples of the Entente are understandably flushed with victory. The joy over the destruction of German militarism and the liberation of Belgium and France is so great that at this moment we cannot expect a revolutionary echo from the workers of our previous enemies. In any case, the censor, who still holds sway in the Entente countries, violently suppresses any voice that calls for revolutionary unity with the revolutionary proletariat. We must also not overlook the fact that the treasonous and criminal policies of the social patriots during the war ruptured and destroyed the proletariat's international ties.

In addition, just what sort of revolution do we actually expect from the Socialists of France, England, Italy, and America? What goal and what character should this revolution have? The November 9 revolution had a bourgeois program and in its first stage set as its mission the establishment of a democratic republic. We know very well that this has not really been completed even today, in the revolution's present phase. But we do not at all expect a revolution of this sort from the Entente proletariat. This is because France, England, America, and Italy have for decades and centuries had a firm grip on the bourgeois-democratic freedom that we won on November 9. They have a republican constitution of just the kind that the much-lauded national assembly is supposed to bless us with. The English and Italian monarchies are only irrelevant decorative formalities and facades. Thus with good reason we can expect nothing less than a social revolution from the proletariat of the Entente countries. But how can we be justified in having such expectations, how can we demand a social revolution of the proletariat of other countries if we have not yet done so ourselves? So we must take the first step. The more quickly and decisively the German proletariat leads the way, the more quickly and decisively we push our revolution through to socialism, the sooner the proletariat in the Entente will follow us.

But in order to go all the way to socialism, it is absolutely necessary for the proletariat to retain political power. There can be no more vacillating or hesitating, only a clear either-or choice. Either bourgeois capitalism will survive and bless the earth and all humanity with its exploitation and wage slavery and perpetual danger of war, or the proletariat will remember its world historic mission and the class interests that call on it to abolish class rule forevermore.

The social patriots and bourgeoisie now are trying to entice the people away from their historic calling by depicting the revolution as dark and eerie, by describing in the bloodiest terms the suffering and destruction, turmoil and terror that will supposedly accompany the transformation of social relations. But these scare tactics are love's labors lost. For the social conditions themselves — capitalism's inability to rebuild the economic life it destroyed — that is what will, with iron necessity, drive the people down the road of social revolution. When we carefully observe the great strike movement of the these last few days, then we plainly see that even in the middle of the revolution, the conflict between the employers and workers lives on. The proletarian class struggle will not rest so long as the bourgeoisie still resists, clinging to the ruins of its former glory. The proletariat will rest only when the social revolution attains its victorious conclusion.

That is what the Spartacus League wants. □

Notes

1. *Illustrierte Geschichte der deutschen Revolution* (Berlin: Internationaler Arbeiter-Verlag, 1929), p. 218.

2. Ibid.

3. Excerpted from Rosa Luxemburg, "Der Acheron in Bewegung," in *Gesammelte Werke* (Berlin [GDR]: Dietz Verlag, 1974), vol. 4, pp. 419-22. Another translation of the complete article can be found in Robert Looker, ed., *Rosa Luxemburg, Selected Political Writings* (New York: Grove Press, 1974), pp. 271-74.

4. While the *Communist Manifesto* defends this proposition, the formulation given here comes not from the Manifesto but from Karl Marx's "General Rules of the International Working Men's Association." See Karl Marx and Frederick Engels, *Selected Works* (Moscow: Progress Publishers, 1977), vol. 2, p. 19. It is quoted by Engels in his introduction to the 1890 German edition of the Manifesto, ibid., vol. 1, p. 104.

5. In 1925 court testimony, General Groener emphasized that he had consulted with Ebert; no one from the SPD disputed this assertion.

One of the military conspirators close to Groener, Col. Hans von Haeften, later wrote that the coup plans were submitted to Ebert in writing on November 18; Ebert gave no response. They were also discussed with War Minister Heinrich Scheüch and other top government officials. According to Haeften, these plans included that troops would demand dissolution of the councils and proclaim Ebert as president with dictatorial powers. (F.L. Carsten, *Revolution in Central Europe; 1918-1919* [Berkeley and Los Angeles: University of California Press, 1972], p. 60-61.)

6. *Dokumente und Materialien zur Geschichte der deutschen Arbeiterbewegung* (Berlin [GDR]: Dietz Verlag, 1957), series 2, vol. 2, p. 575.

7. Gerhard Ritter and Susanne Miller, *Die deutsche Revolution 1918-1919: Dokumente* (Frankfurt: Fischer Taschenbuch Verlag, 1983), pp. 129-30.

8. Wilhelm Pieck, "Erinnerungen an die Novemberrevolution in Berlin," in *Gesammelte Reden und Schriften* (Berlin [GDR]: Dietz Verlag, 1959), vol. 1, p. 442.

9. *Dokumente und Materialien*, pp. 576-77.

10. Ritter and Miller, *Die deutsche Revolution*, p. 139.

11. *Dokumente und Materialien*, p. 579.

12. See "Letter of Invitation to the First Congress of the Communist International," printed in chapter 9 of this volume.

13. Hermann Weber, *Der Gründungsparteitag der KPD* (Frankfurt: Europäische Verlagsanstalt, 1969), pp. 293-301.

14. These words are not found in the *Communist Manifesto*. The thought, however, is contained in the following passage:

"The history of all hitherto existing society is the history of class struggles.

"Freeman and slave, patrician and plebeian, lord and serf, guild-master and journeyman, in a word, oppressor and oppressed, stood in constant opposition to one another, carried on an uninterrupted, now hidden, now open fight, a fight that each time ended, either in a revolutionary reconstitution of society at large, or in the common ruin of the contending classes."

(Karl Marx and Frederick Engels, "Manifesto of the Communist Party," in Marx and Engels, *Collected Works* [New York: International Publishers, 1976], vol. 6, p. 484.)

15. The Walachian boyars were the feudal lords of what is now southern Romania. In Lyons in 1831 a revolt by silk weavers against their employers was suppressed by French troops.

16. The quoted words are a saying of the pioneer German socialist, Ferdinand Lassalle.

17. Excerpted from *Die Freiheit*, December 16, 1918.

18. Lenin explains in the chapter "The Constituent Assembly and the Soviet Republic" of his reply to Kautsky, printed in chapter 7 of the present volume, that he first called for the establishment of Soviet power in April 1917.

19. In fact, it was the 1906 boycott of the Duma elections that the Bolsheviks later considered to have been an error. They held that in 1905, when revolutionary mass action was on the rise, their boycott of that year's Duma elections was a correct and successful means of working to prevent the convocation of a reactionary parliament to help quell the uprising. See V.I. Lenin, *Collected Works* (Moscow: Progress Publishers, 1966), vol. 31, pp. 62-65.

20. The USPD was founded at a congress in Gotha in April 1917; Fritz Heckert spoke there on behalf of the Spartacus current.

21. Luxemburg, *Gesammelte Werke*, pp. 460-61.

22. Luxemburg, "Auf die Schanzen," in ibid., pp. 452-56.

23. "Not a day without a brushstroke." This saying is recorded as the maxim of Apelles, a Greek painter of the fourth century B.C.

24. "Der Kongress," in *Dokumente und Materialien*, pp. 619-21.

25. Karl Liebknecht, "Zum Reichsrätekongress," in *Gesammelte Reden und Schriften* (Berlin: Dietz Verlag, 1974), vol. 9, p. 646.

26. *Allgemeiner Kongress der Arbeiter- und Soldatenräte Deutschlands* (West Berlin: Verlag Olle und Wolter, 1973), col. 4.

27. Ibid., col. 19-20.

28. Ibid., col. 176.

29. Ibid., col. 227.

30. Ibid., col. 283, 300.

31. Ibid., col. 123.

32. *Dokumente und Materialien*, pp. 632-33.

33. *Allgemeiner Kongress*, col. 312-21.

34. Excerpted from Liebknecht, "Was will der Spartakusbund," in *Gesammelte Reden*, pp. 649-62. The transcript of Liebknecht's speech was first published in a 1921 collection of his writings.

35. Königsplatz is the square on which the Reichstag was located.

36. The sharp difference between the German Communists' approach to the peasantry in 1918 and the emphasis on the need for a strong worker-peasant alliance subsequently adopted by the Communist International is taken up in chapter 5.

37. By the terms of the armistice of November 11, 1918, Germany had to ac-

cept continuation of the Allied blockade and surrender, in addition to military equipment, 5,000 trucks, 5,000 locomotives, and 150,000 railway cars. Both of these provisions worsened the food shortage in the cities.

Above, Gustav Noske; below, Friedrich Ebert welcoming returning troops, Berlin, 1918.

-4-

Founding the German Communist Party

Prospects for launching a Communist Party in Germany were improved in December by a rapprochement between the Spartacists and the Revolutionary Shop Stewards in Berlin. On December 16 the two organizations had rallied 250,000 Berlin workers in front of the congress of the councils. The collaboration of these two currents was strengthened two days later when the Shop Stewards elected two Spartacists, Karl Liebknecht and Wilhelm Pieck, to its five-person leadership body. On December 21 a Shop Stewards' meeting, echoing the Spartacists' demands on the USPD, unanimously called on the USPD Executive Committee to carry out a "clear break from the majority Socialists" and to convene a party congress by the end of the month.[1]

While some leaders of the Revolutionary Shop Stewards, such as Georg Ledebour, were now canvassing possibilities of "launching their own political party, which would stand midway between the USPD and the Spartacus League,"[2] others in the organization were pressing for unity with the Spartacists.

Leaders of the Spartacus League, however, were still divided on whether or not to launch a new party. There is no written record of their discussion. But Wilhelm Pieck recalled in 1920 that, "Leo Jogiches and also Rosa Luxemburg could not be reconciled to this idea. They sought rather to achieve their long-standing goal of influencing workers in the USPD to the point where its adoption of the Spartacists' policies could be secured and the Spartacists could take the leadership of that party."[3] Another German Communist leader, Clara Zetkin, maintained in 1921 that in December 1918 Jogiches, the Spartacists' central organizer, and Luxemburg "still stood by their opinion that only when the USPD held its congress should we break from it and constitute ourselves as a Communist Party."[4]

Other leaders, including Liebknecht, had long been impatient to

Footnotes to this chapter begin on page 204.

157

launch the new party. By late December this view was dominant in the Spartacus leadership. On December 22 a call was issued for a national conference to be held in seven days time to consider the question. That same day the Spartacists sent an ultimatum to the USPD leadership demanding a party congress and insisting on a reply within twenty-four hours. This was a last-ditch appeal aimed at reaching that party's ranks. The USPD's Berlin newspaper responded that this was a "declaration of war," and that a congress was excluded.[5]

After this negative response from the USPD leadership, Luxemburg no longer argued for further work in that party. She wrote to Zetkin on December 25 that the USPD was "dissolving completely," as its rightwing units rallied to the SPD.[6]

Additional support for the founding of a Communist Party came from another revolutionary current, the International Communists of Germany (IKD). This name had been assumed in the month following the November revolution by the Bremen Left and other independent revolutionary groups in Hamburg, Berlin, Dresden, and a few other localities. When the USPD was formed in 1917, these groups had rejected the Spartacists' course of entering the new party and had tried to form an independent, nationwide Communist organization instead. These efforts were hard hit by police repression and did not succeed. It was not until December 15, 1918, that these groups met in their first national conference and formally organized the IKD as a loose federation of autonomous local groups. A week later a second national conference of the IKD voted to unite with the Spartacus League in founding a new party, noting that the "tactical and principled differences" between the two currents had "shrunk to divergent ways of formulating the same ideas."[7]

The key components of what became the IKD had rallied to the Bolshevik-led Zimmerwald Left during the war. Agreement with Bolshevik strategy and methods, however, did not run deep in the IKD. On the question of party organization, for example, the IKD opposed an authoritative central leadership, criticizing even the Spartacists for their "rigid centralization from the top down."[8] The Bremen Left, which was the IKD's strongest component, also advocated replacing the trade unions with a "unified organization" that would combine the functions of both union and party — one of many anarcho-syndicalist notions influencing the IKD.

Many in the IKD were doubtful about uniting with the Spartacists, including Johann Knief, leader of the Bremen group. A key factor in overcoming these hesitations was the intervention of Bolshevik leader Karl Radek, who arrived in Berlin, probably on December 20, after a precarious journey from Russia. Radek was a member of the

Soviet government delegation to the General Congress of Workers' and Soldiers' Councils that had been stopped at the German border. Radek and two companions had continued the journey undercover, only to arrive just as the congress ended. For many years prior to 1917 Radek had played an active role in German Socialist politics, where he had been a longtime associate of Knief and the Bremen Left. Nonetheless, Radek now found himself highly critical of the ultraleftism prevalent in both the IKD and Spartacist organizations. His 1925 memoirs of the German revolution, printed below, recount his first impressions of the German Communists.

In Berlin[9]
by Karl Radek

Dirty and ragged, I feverishly bought a copy of *Rote Fahne*. As I drove to the hotel I looked the paper over. I was seized with alarm. The tone of the paper sounded as if the final conflict were upon us. It could not be more shrill. If only they can avoid overdoing it!

I looked for the address of the editorial office. There it was. I headed for it. Fanny Jezierska opened the door for me. Liebknecht was there, also Luxemburg, Thalheimer, Paul Levi. We had a short initial talk. Liebknecht kept after me; he was agitated "The first congress of councils has called a constituent assembly, and it is now closing. You came here for nothing."

"How many of our people were there?" I asked. There was no Spartacus fraction at all at the congress of councils. Laufenberg and the Hamburg group held some sort of intermediate position, and Rosa spoke of him with suspicion.[10]

"How is it going in the Berlin council?" We didn't have an organized force there either, I was told. Things were better in some of the provinces. Our people, under the leadership of Knief, controlled a significant part of the Bremen council. And Brandler was active in Chemnitz [Karl-Marx-Stadt].

"How many organized members do we have in Berlin?" I asked them.

"We are just starting to assemble forces here. When the revolution began, we had fewer than fifty people in Berlin."

Paul Levi and I drove to the Central Committee office on Friedrichstrasse to visit Tyszka [Leo Jogiches]. The office was like a beehive. Mathilde Jacob came forward to meet me. She was a veteran, a typist who before the war had typed the manuscript of my newspaper correspondence, *World Politics,* and had been a close friend of

Rosa and Tyszka during the war. She led me to Tyszka. My former teacher had grown old. On his shoulders had rested the main burden of underground work during the entire war. After the January 1917 strike they got him, and he spent a year in prison. We greeted each other with a certain tension; we had not spoken since the 1912 split in the Polish Social Democracy.[11] We did not speak of those old times. He asked about Lenin, Trotsky, Zinoviev, Dzerzhinsky. After a few moments he was just as cordial and down-to-carth as ever.

"Well," Tyszka asked, "do you want to be considered merely a representative from the Russian Central Committee or do you want to get down to work like you used to?" Of course I wanted to get to work. The old man was a conspirator to the bone. "Do not put your trust in legality," he told me. "They would not dare arrest you now, but you must go underground; as soon as there is a skirmish they will arrest you. Most likely, the old secret police are quietly continuing their work." We agreed that Rosa, Liebknecht, Levi, he, and I would all meet that evening over supper and have a quiet little talk about where things stood.

Levi brought me to a little working-class restaurant. Rosa and Liebknecht were in the back room; Tyszka arrived a little later. We each got a big bowl of groats with cinnamon. The proprietress poured more into Liebknecht's bowl than ours, gazing at him with loving admiration. At first the debate turned on the terror in Russia. Rosa was upset that Dzerzhinsky had become head of the Cheka. "Their terror never succeeded in crushing us," she said. "How can we rely on terror?"

"Well, by utilizing terror," I replied, "by persecuting us, they threw us back many years. The world revolution is at stake here; we have to gain a few years. How can we deny the importance of the terror in this? Moreover we know that terror is powerless when it is up against the selflessness and fervor of a new class that represents the future progress of society. It is different for a class that is sentenced to death by history and has the crime of the World War on its hands."

Liebknecht backed me up vehemently. Rosa said, "Maybe you're right. But how can Józef [Dzerzhinsky] be so cruel?" Tyszka laughed and said to her: "You would be too if you had to." Rosa had long ago recognized her error on the question of the soviets as a form of dictatorship. She had also recognized that it was wrong to oppose any division of the landed estates.[12]

As for the situation in Germany, we were only at the beginning, she said; the Social Democrats still ruled over the masses, and our task was to organize our forces. When I posed the question of organizing a separate Communist Party, she said that Tyszka thought this was premature but they had convinced him that worker leaders could not fight without their own banner. I asked if they did not think their excessively strong tone inappropriate for a party of their strength. "When a healthy child is born," replied Rosa, "it screams; it does not squeak."

Liebknecht and I went for a walk. Large crowds were gathered on Friedrichstrasse and Unter den Linden, not the usual gapers and idlers but crowds of people discussing politics. Their faces were filled with joy. The war had ended. We bought some chocolate at a stand, the kind with saccharine. I found it empty somehow, and unsatisfying. But people obviously liked it very much. Everywhere pay was being increased, and now you could buy things for yourself.

We crossed the arcade. I said to Liebknecht, "This crowd does not understand at all that the sword of the Entente is hanging over its head."

"Right," replied Liebknecht. "You can speak against the Entente only in an educational way around here. If anyone even attempted to say anything about defending the revolution from the Entente, he would be devoured by the crowd."

We came near the Brandenburg Gate. We stopped at the cab drivers' restaurant where some coachmen and drivers were drinking. Forgetting the groats we had just eaten, we ordered leg of pork with cabbage and peas, a popular meal for Berlin cab drivers. It was on the menu in these restaurants despite the rationing. The waiters did not have a boss, and they knew their customers, so they got all kinds of deals on the sly. A conversation started up among the drivers: "Wilson is a good fellow. He forced the kaiser, that swine, to run for it. Now he is supplying Germany with bread. He is making a good peace."

Paul Levi and I went to a meeting of metal workers far down at the end of Chausseestrasse. Driving through the Tiergarten, we saw huge antigovernment demonstrations. Surprised, I asked Levi if these were really our demonstrations. "No, these are the Independents' demonstrations." "But how is that? The Independents are in the government." "Yes, but the Berlin organization is in the hands of the left-wing Independents. They have an organization of so-called Revolutionary Shop Stewards, who took part in preparations for the revolution. They are against an alliance with Scheidemann and Ebert." I remembered Tyszka's misgivings: would it not be better to postpone the break with the Independent Social Democrats until these masses were confronted with the question of a split?

We came to a large workers' rally. Levi went off somewhere and the communist workers coerced me into speaking. I told them not only of the Russian proletariat's great victories, but also of its hardships, of the civil war and hunger, and of the path to victory. Suddenly I heard a shout: "How much did they pay you to slander Soviet Russia?" It was a worker who had missed the beginning of the speech and just heard about the difficulties of the struggle. They really had no idea what a revolution was.

Preparations for the party congress were under way. Rosa had written a draft of the party program. It was being discussed in the leading circles and was not controversial. It was the question of how to relate to the constituent [national] assembly that sparked controversy. Liebknecht said, "When I wake up in the morning, I am against taking part in the constituent assembly elections, but by evening I am in favor of it." It was a very tempting idea to counterpose the slogan of the councils to that of a constituent assembly. But the congress of councils itself was in favor of the constituent assembly. You could hardly skip over that stage. Rosa and Liebknecht recognized that and Tyszka insisted on it. But the party youth were decidedly against it. "We will break it up with machine guns."

I wired to send for my friend Johann Knief, leader of the Bremen organization, the group closest to the Bolsheviks. Johann was against uniting with the Spartacists and raised all the disputed questions right through to Rosa Luxemburg's theory of accumulation.[13] His perspective was that after the Ebert-Haase bloc would come the Ledebour-Liebknecht-Luxemburg bloc, and only after them would it be our turn. A Bolshevik-type party had to be founded independently of Rosa Luxemburg, he said. He referred to the danger of a dictatorship by Tyszka, who had been educated in conditions of underground work and would suffocate the party in the clutches of centralism. The German revolution could triumph only as a very broad mass movement. The party should not be as centralized as Tyszka wanted.

I pointed out to him that these views had nothing whatsoever in common with Bolshevism. Trade unions and councils are the forms of organization for the broad masses. The party, a vanguard organization, must be strictly centralized. Knief's Hanseatic stubbornness was unyielding.[14] I warned him that I would speak most resolutely against him, and he was forced to give way. He would not oppose the unification of the groups in Bremen, Hamburg, and Hannover, where our influence was the strongest, with the Spartacists.

The first congress of the German Communist Party was held in the Prussian parliament. About one hundred delegates attended, many of them old acquaintances. Pieck, Ernst Meyer, Duncker, and others were there, but young people unknown before the war predominated. Two of them were Russians: Leviné, a former Socialist Revolutionary with a serious pensive face, who was brought up in Germany; and the sharp, young Max Levien, in military garb, the son of a former general in the German consulate in Moscow who finished high school in Moscow and considered himself a Russian. The youth in the congress were ready to storm the heavens. They thought that Karl and Rosa were applying brakes to the movement, and that victory was actually close at hand. Former deputy Rühle stood out in particular.

I took the floor to give greetings from the Russian Central Committee, which caused a great stir with the reporters of the bourgeois press. They rushed to the door to telephone their editors, but the experienced Pieck had ordered that the doors be closed and no one be allowed to leave. The congress listened to me with great intensity. Unity with the Russian Communist Party and the Russian revolution was at the very core of its outlook. Yet the immaturity and inexperience of the German party were shown very clearly there. Its ties to the masses were very weak. The congress also had a sarcastic attitude toward the negotiations with the left Independents. I did not feel that this was a party here before me.

I spent New Year's Eve with Liebknecht. Although very tired, he was happy as a child. "That's no problem; we can deal with it. The Social Democrats are stronger than we, but they are old men. The youth will follow us. They have spirit and passion. The Independents have already been forced out of the government.[15] That will push them into opposition. Matters will move ahead more quickly." □

Radek was not alone in his concern that the revolutionary movement in Germany was out of step with the current thinking of working people. Rosa Luxemburg, for her part, concluded that once the general congress of councils had voted overwhelmingly earlier in December to back the national assembly, the revolutionists had to drop their call for a boycott of the coming assembly elections. Instead, they now had to take part in the election campaign, she believed, using it to influence broader layers of the working masses. She explained this view in a December 23 article on the elections:

"Ebert and company have devised the national assembly as a dam built to contain the revolutionary flood. Thus we must direct this flood in and through the national assembly to sweep away the dam.

"The platform provided by this counterrevolutionary parliament, the election campaign, must become a means to educate, unite, and mobilize the revolutionary masses, and a stage in the struggle to establish a proletarian dictatorship.

"The masses must assault the gates of the national assembly. The clenched fist of the revolutionary proletariat must be raised right in its midst. A banner must be displayed there, on which the fiery letters glow: *All power to the workers and soldiers councils!*

"Proletarians, comrades, on with the job. There is no time to lose. . . . The future belongs to the proletarian revolution, and everything must be harnessed to its service, even the elections to the national assembly."[16]

There was no agreement within the Spartacus League, however, on the need to make this turn. Several Berlin Spartacus groups adopted motions opposing Luxemburg's proposal, and Liebknecht's major address of December 23 (excerpted in chapter 3, above) contained no such shift in line.

The IKD was also divided. Johann Knief, its most prominent leader, favored participating in the elections, but the second IKD national conference rejected his position. This led Knief to decline nomination as a delegate to the fusion congress of the two organizations. A few days later the Revolutionary Shop Stewards voted in favor of participation by the relatively narrow margin of twenty-six to sixteen.

A renewed government assault on the workers was repulsed in the last week of December. Sailors of the People's Naval Division, a republican defense force under government command stationed in Berlin, had grown increasingly radical. These sailors participated in a December 21 demonstration called by the Spartacist-led League of Red Soldiers. In retaliation, the government demanded that 80 percent of the division's troops be discharged and that it evacuate its headquarters. When the outraged sailors refused, they were attacked by pro-government troops. Berlin workers rallied to their defense, however, and they were able to score a hard-fought victory, in which fifty-six of Ebert's guardsmen were killed and only eleven of the sailors.

During the course of this "bloody Christmas," a group of Spartacus members seized the SPD newspaper *Vorwärts* and set about publishing the newspaper under their own editorship. They acted on their own initiative, independently of the Spartacist leadership. On December 25 their *Rote Vorwärts* [Red Vorwärts] proclaimed, "Overthrow the Ebert-Scheidemann government. It must be replaced by real Socialists, that is, by Communists."[17]

Since December 8, the Spartacists had repeatedly made the call, "Down with the government." According to Spartacus leader Clara Zetkin, Luxemburg saw this call as "a propaganda slogan to rally the revolutionary proletariat rather than a tangible object of revolutionary action."[18] The slogan, however, was also open to interpretation as a call for insurrection. The revolutionaries occupying *Vorwärts* had heard it as such a signal and had launched an action that, if persisted in, could only lead to a premature armed showdown with government troops. The Spartacus and Shop Steward leaderships averted this, securing the evacuation of those occupying the *Vorwärts* building on December 26.

Nonetheless, this potentially disastrous episode showed the high price the Spartacists were paying for not having previously forged a politically homogeneous and disciplined party. The Spartacus leadership believed this delay in forming a party was necessitated by their small size and limited political influence. When the war ended, their current still counted only a couple of thousand supporters.[19] Yet the failure to organize these initial cadres in a centralized, revolutionary party had deprived the Spartacus leaders of the instrument they now needed to overcome their isolation and meet the rapidly expanding challenges and opportunities.

During the war years, harsh repression had made building a revolutionary organization particularly difficult. Most Spartacus leaders served time in jail. Nevertheless, the absence of a strong revolutionary party, however small at its origin, was not due primarily to these objective factors but to the political positions of the Spartacus leaders, above all to those of Luxemburg and Jogiches.

In the previous two decades, Luxemburg and Jogiches had participated in the Social Democratic movement not only in Germany, which occupied a part of their native Poland, but also in Russia, which occupied most of the rest of it. Following the 1903 split in the Russian Social Democracy between the Bolshevik and Menshevik factions, Luxemburg and Jogiches vacillated between these two wings on important political questions. These differences with the Bolsheviks were accompanied by opposition to the party-building methods of V.I. Lenin.[20]

At the outbreak of the war in August 1914, Luxemburg and Jogiches took a revolutionary internationalist stand against the SPD leadership's betrayal and condemned the spineless pacifism of the centrist current led by Haase and Kautsky. Neither in the German nor in the international workers' movement, however, did Luxemburg and Jogiches recognize the need for both political and organizational independence from the centrists as well as from the open social patriots. Throughout the war years, the Spartacist current failed to align itself with the Bolshevik-led Zimmerwald Left.[21]

Criticizing in 1916 the shortcomings of Luxemburg's pamphlet published that year under the pseudonym "Junius," Lenin wrote, "A very great defect in revolutionary Marxism in Germany as a whole is its lack of a compact illegal organisation that would systematically pursue its own line and educate the masses in the spirit of the new tasks; such an organisation would also have to take a definite stand on opportunism and Kautskyism."[22] Lenin added, "Junius's pamphlet conjures up in our mind the picture of a *lone* man who has no comrades in an illegal organisation accustomed to thinking out revolutionary slogans to their conclusion and systematically educating the masses in their spirit. But this shortcoming — it would be a grave error to forget this — is not Junius's personal failing, but the result of the weakness of *all* the German Leftists, who have become entangled in the vile net of Kautskyite hypocrisy, pedantry and 'friendliness' for the opportunists." Although Lenin expressed confidence that Luxemburg's adherents, despite their isolation, would "succeed in going further along the right road,"[23] it was nonetheless only after the November 1918 revolution that the Spartacists carried out an organizational break with Kautsky and the USPD.

Luxemburg feared that organizing an independent revolutionary party in Germany would lead to sectarian isolation from the masses of workers who still looked for leadership to the SPD, and later also to the USPD. She overestimated the masses' ability to spontaneously create a new revolutionary leadership at the critical moment and chart a course of action that could lead to the conquest of power.

The Spartacists' failure to consolidate the nucleus of a revolutionary party, rooted in the factories and tested through years of class-struggle experience, meant that leadership initiative during the revolutionary upsurge in 1918-19 passed not only to the most rebellious and self-sacrificing, but also the most impetuous and undisciplined forces. There was no workers' party with a homogeneous communist program and revolutionary-centralist organizational norms. As a result, the Marxists were swept along by revolutionary-minded but inexperienced fighters whose courage and combativity outweighed their grasp of proletarian strategy and tactics.[24]

The Founding Congress Meets

As the Spartacus League national conference convened December 29, 1918, in Berlin, the capital was still tense from the impact of the fierce

Christmas battles. The city and its surroundings were alive with workers' meetings and demonstrations. The growing popular revulsion against the government's repressive moves had finally pressured the USPD to withdraw from the Ebert government early that morning. In 1920 Spartacus leader Paul Levi recalled the spirit of those days:

"The atmosphere in Berlin ... was full of revolutionary tension. ... There was no one who was not convinced that the immediate future would see renewed massive demonstrations and renewed actions. ... The delegates represented masses who until now had been unorganized, and they came to us only through action, in action, and for action. They were completely unable to understand that a new action, which was easy to foresee, could well lead not to victory but to a setback. Even in their dreams they could not conceive of adopting a tactic that would leave room for maneuver in case of a setback."[25]

Eighty-three delegates met in the festival hall of the Prussian parliament; they represented forty-six cities. "As a result of the tumultuous events of those days," another Spartacus leader, Ernst Meyer, later wrote, "the founding congress was as good as completely unprepared. Most delegates were organizers of small local groups. A firm and united ideology was entirely absent."[26] Some key leaders were absent, such as August Merges, chairman of the radical Brunswick workers' and soldiers' council, and Clara Zetkin, who lived in Stuttgart and said some years later that she had not been informed of the conference.[27]

The first day's session was to discuss the question of forming the new party. Unlike the rest of the conference, it was open only to Spartacus League delegates; no stenographic record was kept, and no report published. After a short debate, and despite the continuing opposition of Leo Jogiches and two other delegates, the conference voted to found the new party.

The choice of a name was more difficult. Prior to the congress, the leadership had been divided almost down the middle. Luxemburg and Jogiches had favored the name "Socialist Workers Party," while Liebknecht and Hugo Eberlein had proposed using the designation "Communist." The leadership had voted four to three, with one abstention, against Luxemburg's proposal. Both positions were carried to the conference and debated at its first day's closed session. Eberlein later summarized Luxemburg's viewpoint in these terms:

"The Russian Communist Party remains alone in the International. The parties of the Second International will fight against it without mercy. The duty of Communists is to break the Socialist parties of western Europe away from the Second International in order to found a new revolutionary International. The Russian Communist Party alone will never be able to do that. There is a deep gulf between it and the Socialist parties of the West, particularly of France, Britain, and the United States. It is up to us, the German revolutionaries, to form the link between revolutionaries of eastern Europe and the still reformist Socialists of the West, and thus speed the break of these Socialists with reformism. We can do this better as the 'Socialist Party.' If we call ourselves the 'Communist Party,' the closeness of our ties with the Russians will make our task in the West more difficult."[28]

After discussing the question, the conference established a commission to make a recommendation to the next day's session.

The December 30 session included 29 delegates from the IKD, to bring the total to 127 delegates from fifty-six localities. Three representatives of the League of Red Soldiers were present. There was one delegate from the Free Socialist Youth, an independent revolutionary youth organization that had counted 4,000 members at the time of its founding conference on October 26-27.[29] Three fraternal delegates from Soviet Russia also attended.

Most of the congress delegates were young: three-quarters were under thirty-five and only one (Jogiches) was over fifty years old. About half were workers, mostly in the skilled trades; about one-quarter were professionals; the rest were mostly office workers or independent tradesmen. Five delegates were women.[30]

The first report, by Karl Liebknecht, was on "The Crisis in the USPD." After a survey of the discouraging results of the Spartacists' work in that party, which he termed a "labor of Sisyphus," he read the following resolution, which constituted the new party.

Resolution on Founding the Communist Party of Germany[31]

Although the USPD came out of the generalized crisis in the old German Social Democracy, its composition is the product of the specific contradictions of wartime politics. It was put together from diverse forces who agreed neither on basic principles nor on policy, and whose leading bodies in their majority personify disastrously impotent pseudoradicalism. From the very beginning, the USPD's politics have never displayed socialist clarity, resolute class struggle, or consistent internationalism, but instead opportunist confusion, timid compromise, and accommodation to the pressures of national circumstances. Thus, from the beginning they were doomed to paralysis.

Since the November revolution, their weak and erratic policies have evolved into a complete abandonment of principle. USPD representatives took half the places in the cabinet even though the majority Socialists made perfectly clear from November 9 on that they would continue to reject revolutionary proletarian policies. By that act they made a major contribution to weakening and stalling the worker and soldier masses; they became a fig leaf for the Ebert-Scheidemann government. For eight weeks, whether by toleration or by outright complicity, they have been accomplices to every crime and betrayal by the "Socialist" government, whose goal is to restore and preserve capitalist rule. They helped create the conditions for rapid growth of the counterrevolutionary forces and helped in a most destructive fashion to undermine the revolutionary power of the working masses.

In this way they assumed a share of the responsibility for the tragic events of December 23 and 24.

The recent forced resignation of their representatives from the government will not exonerate or rehabilitate them. Nor does this tardy act in any way guarantee that they will now turn away from the unprincipled and spineless policies they have been following so far. On the contrary, their action is in keeping with those policies.

As a result of the official USPD policy, their members are increasingly linking up with the majority Socialists for the coming elections and are even completely fusing with them.

Every attempt made within the USPD's constitutional framework to have the rank-and-file members of the party rule on this ruinous policy and condemn it; every attempt to force the calling of a party convention that could assert revolutionary proletarian policies and pass judgment on the discredited members of the USPD — all such efforts have been stymied by the resistance of the party's executive bodies. This is yet another striking confirmation of the USPD's confusion and paralysis.

The resulting situation can no longer be tolerated. The USPD has lost its right to be called a party of socialist class struggle.

More than ever, the revolutionary situation demands clarity and decisiveness, unambiguous positions, a break from all lukewarm and opportunist elements, and unity of all honest and determined revolutionary proletarian fighters.

To remain in the USPD any longer would seriously compromise our duty to the proletariat and to the cause of socialism and revolution.

We have never succumbed to illusions about the nature of the

USPD, a by-product of the World War that is destined to disintegrate once the war ends. The time has come when all revolutionary proletarian forces must turn their backs on the USPD and create a new and independent party with a clear program, firm goals, unified policies, and with the highest revolutionary determination and willingness to act as a powerful instrument for carrying out the socialist revolution that is now beginning.

The national conference of the Spartacus League sends fraternal greetings to the fighting proletariat of all countries, and it calls upon them to act together to make the world revolution.

The Spartacus League hereby dissolves its organizational ties with the USPD and constitutes itself as a separate political party that shall be called the Communist Party of Germany (Spartacus League).[32] □

Comment on the Resolution
by Karl Liebknecht

Comrades, I would like to ask you to approve this resolution, thereby announcing to the world that we are determined to put our lives and bodies on the line to defend the revolution. We will carry through to the end the social revolution, which until now has been betrayed and which has been established by the recent weeks and months as our duty and the historic duty of the German proletariat. Let the world know that class rule, the Eberts and Scheidemanns, will be defeated; the fainthearted and false friends of the working class, who are retarding the progress of emancipation, will be defeated. The revolution will be made, and it will inspire the world. By the end of this revolutionary period world imperialism, which believes it has been victorious, will be brought down by the united power of the proletariat of the world. (*Thunderous ovation*) □

Following Liebknecht's remarks, the chairman, Wilhelm Pieck, proposed that the resolution be voted without discussion, and it was adopted with only one negative vote. The IKD had announced that it would immediately join the new party if this resolution was adopted. Following this vote its delegates participated fully in the remainder of the congress.

Three proposals for the new party's name were then placed before the delegates. The commission appointed the previous day recommended the name "Revolutionary Communist Party of Germany (Spartacus League)," while Fritz Heckert, leader of the Chemnitz Spartacists, proposed "Communist Party of Germany (Spartacus League)" (KPD), and another delegate suggested "Communist Workers Party of Germany." Heckert's proposal was adopted by a large majority.

The next agenda item was greetings by Karl Radek, who was introduced as the representative of the Russian Soviet government.

Radek explained that he had been sent to Germany as part of the Soviet government's delegation to the congress of the German councils and brought the KPD the "greetings and solidarity of workers' Russia." He described the jubilation of Russian workers at the news of the German revolution, "not only because [it] killed German imperialism once and for all, breaking the Russian revolution free of encirclement by the imperialist powers, but because the much younger and organizationally much less experienced Russian working class is fully aware that they would not be strong enough on their own, without the German socialist revolution, to build a new house on the rubble left to us by capitalism.

"We feel that our older brother, who has taught us in the past, has now joined us in our liberation struggle, and that the wave of workers' revolution has thus washed over Russia's borders into the West. This fills Russian workers with deep joy."

Radek explained how establishment of workers' power in Germany could frustrate the plans of the Allied powers to rob and oppress Germany. "There is no way to make Germany capable of armed defense against the yoke that the Entente aims to impose on it except to make the German workers masters of Germany," he said.[33]

When Radek had finished, Liebknecht proposed the following statement, which was adopted and sent to the Soviet government.

"The national conference of the Spartacus League, which has today founded the Communist Party of Germany, sends most sincere greetings to the Russian Soviet republic, to our Russian fellow comrades in the common struggle against the enemy of the oppressed of every country. Our knowledge that your hearts are with us gives us strength and power for our struggle. Long live socialism! Long live the world revolution!"[34]

The congress now came to the most contentious point on its agenda, the national assembly elections. Although Levi, the reporter, spoke on behalf of all members of the Spartacists' outgoing Central Committee, his viewpoint found little agreement among the delegates.

Report on the National Assembly[35]
by Paul Levi

I know it will not be easy to speak in favor of the national assembly elections. . . .

The national assembly is the banner of the counterrevolution. It is supposed to be the fortress that the counterrevolution will build for itself and to which it will retreat along with all of its toadies, like Ebert and Scheidemann; with all its generals, like Hindenburg and Groener; and with its economic backers, like Stinnes and Thyssen and the directors of the Deutsche Bank. They all seek shelter in the national assembly. They need the national assembly; it will be the anchor to which they can tie their drifting boats.

Comrades, we understand all of that perfectly well. There is not the slightest difference between us on these issues. We know exactly what road the proletariat must travel to victory: it can only be over the dead body of the national assembly. I use the term "dead body" even though it has acquired a rather bad name in Berlin.[36] There is another point about which we have no doubt: the national assembly will be a pliant tool in the hands of the counterrevolution, just as the bourgeoisie and their agents Ebert and Scheidemann wish it to be.

There is no doubt that representatives of the determined revolutionary tendency within the proletariat will be in the minority in this national assembly. Comrades, we propose to you nevertheless that we not stand aloof from the national assembly elections. Our proposal to you is to intervene in these elections with all our energy. (*Shouts of "Never!" "No!"*)

Let me finish. Say your "never" after I have finished speaking. As I was saying, we propose participating in these elections and fighting them out, I tell you, with all of the anger, energy, and fighting spirit you showed in every battle so far, for all of the positions that the counterrevolution has thrown up before you. (*Shout: "A waste of energy!"*)

Comrade, you say it is a waste of energy. Yes, the comrade is right. If the counterrevolution's positions can be taken without expending any energy, if we do not have to storm them, then Comrade Kahlert is right. As long as the bourgeoisie is not ready to give up, it will keep forcing us to fight; as long as it refuses to retreat a single step of its own free will, and as long as it keeps on fighting, it will continue to be our job to fight the bourgeoisie for every position it occupies. (*Shout: "By making the revolution!"*) . . .

You must force your way into every opening which the

bourgeoisie offers you and take it by storm in bitter, hand-to-hand combat. In this parliament, too, you must fight back again and again and repel every attack, and I am telling you, you must fight differently than before, and not with speeches. You must act with the confidence that the power of the proletariat is behind you. . . .

In Russia, as everyone knows, the Bolsheviks always participated in elections to the national assembly. They did so even though they knew they would be a tiny minority in it. And only when, during the course of the elections, the situation in Russia changed and went beyond the national assembly did they disperse it. (*Shout: "We'll do that right now!"*)

You say you will do it now. How can you know that all of Germany is already today at such an advanced stage of revolution as the comrade believes? Of course, it might be. We can make the revolution in Berlin. In Rhineland-Westphalia the situation is sufficiently advanced,[37] and perhaps it is in Upper Silesia, also. But do these three districts represent Germany? I say no. A force that wants to destroy the national assembly and believes that doing so will lead to the complete political collapse of the bourgeoisie needs more behind it than these three centers, which you believe are representative of the situation everywhere in Germany.

Initially, when the Bolsheviks stood alone, they took part in the national assembly elections. Only when the process of disintegration was far advanced, after a long campaign and the assumption of power, did the Bolsheviks meet the convening of the national assembly with a concerted effort to disperse it. It is not true that the Russians' policy was to say from the very beginning, "If it convenes, we'll break it up." On the contrary, they prepared themselves to enter the national assembly, to speak and act there. . . .

Consider the situation. The national assembly is going to meet. It will dominate the whole political scene in Germany for months to come, and there is no way you can prevent that. It will be at the center of politics in Germany. There is no way you can stop all eyes from being focused on it. Even your best supporters will have to study and observe what goes on in the national assembly and will have to orient toward it, and you will not be able to prevent that. It will affect the consciousness of the German proletariat, and despite these facts, you want to remain on the outside and work from the outside?

Comrades, you want to disband the national assembly. What would you say if the national assembly were to meet in a godforsaken place like Schilda?[38] (*Shout: "They would be cutting their own throats!"*) Nothing that still has as much power as the German bourgeoisie cuts its own throat. The German bourgeoisie is organizing itself, collecting its strength, building an instrument it can use to suppress the revolution, and you claim that it is cutting its own throat. It is not cutting its own throat.

It is our duty to break into that building. We have an obligation to lob firebrands into their fortress. It is our duty to fight this battle just as we would in any other situation in which the bourgeoisie challenges us. What it all comes down to is this: wherever the bourgeoisie takes its stand, wherever it regroups and concentrates its forces and prepares to fight again, are you going to say we should not take them on? Let me tell you, if you do that, you will cause immeasurable harm both to yourselves and our movement. □

Discussion on the National Assembly[39]

Otto Rühle (Pirna): I am against Levi's proposal that we participate in the national assembly. Only a few days ago, I still thought that participating in the elections was completely out of the question for us. To my amazement, I found out otherwise in an article in *Rote Fahne;*[40] and today we hear the outrageous proposal that we participate in the national assembly elections. We spent yesterday and today getting out from under the dead weight we had saddled ourselves with through our decision at Gotha.[41] Now we turn around and march right back into opportunistic, compromise politics. We have had enough of compromises and opportunism. I cannot warn you strongly enough, do not embark upon that road again. Reject participation in the national assembly. It would leave us floating in a vacuum.

It is obvious that when the national assembly is formed, wholesale suppression of the workers' and soldiers' councils will begin. Müller of the party [SPD] Executive Committee and Frässdorf of Dresden have already advanced the idea that convening the national assembly means the end of the councils. We must constantly goad on the living struggle in the streets, and it would be wrong for us to lull the movement by passing out ballots to the workers.

What are we supposed to say to people? Elect us to the national assembly so that we can undermine it and break it up from within? So that we can sabotage it and ridicule it in the eyes of the whole world? People just will not understand that. Someone said we have to give women and youth the opportunity to vote. I do not understand how we are supposed to explain to them that we want them to vote us in.

We can no longer regard this parliamentarism as a tool. We simply do not vote in elections to a national assembly. You will get your chance to vote when it is time to elect representatives from your factories to the councils.

We demanded from bourgeois society the right to universal, equal, and secret elections. Once we are in power, we will want something else, and we will create something else. We are only on the verge of seizing power. When we get power, we will not let it be taken away from us by a national assembly. . . .

Well, comrades, let them move the national assembly to Schilda. Then we will have another government here in Berlin, and its first priority will be to try to disperse their national assembly. And if that fails, let them stay in Schilda. We will establish the new government here in Berlin. We still have fourteen days left. In those fourteen days we can reach out to the most remote areas and explain to the comrades what the stakes are. Let the bourgeoisie have the national assembly as their institution. Our institution is different. Either we will establish our institution after the national assembly is gone, or — if we cannot break it up — ours will exist at the same time as the national assembly. That way we will be able to pursue the struggle in any form.

I urge you not to get involved with the opportunist course presented here. I am not saying that is a deliberately opportunist policy. But it will be opportunist in its effect. For the broad masses of people living in the countryside and small towns it will ultimately mean compromise politics. I strongly appeal to you, do not become involved in it. Stay on the straight course of total political consistency, which requires a single slogan: "For the council system."

Rosa Luxemburg (greeted with loud applause): All of us, including Comrade Levi, responded to the storm of protest generated by his report with inner satisfaction over its source. We all understand and value very highly the revolutionary spirit and determination that is evident in you all, and we will take in stride Comrade Rühle's warning to you about our opportunism. Perhaps we have not worked in vain, if we have a party of such determined comrades. . . .

While I am moved by the spirit you express so vehemently, I also have misgivings. I am happy and yet I am dismayed. I am convinced that you want a sort of radicalism that is a little too quick and easy. In particular, this is shown by the interjections, "Call the question now." That does not display the maturity and seriousness appropriate here. . . . Those qualities by no means exclude revolutionary élan; on the contrary, they should complement it. You are trying to decide impetuously something that requires careful consideration. To illustrate this, I will give you just one example. . . . When the national assembly was rejected in Russia, the situation there was somewhat similar to the one in Germany today. But have you forgotten that before they rejected the national assembly, something else had happened in November: the proletariat had taken power. Do you already have a socialist government today? Do you have a Trotsky-Lenin government? Russia had a long revolutionary history, whereas Germany does not. The Russian revolution did not begin in March 1917 but much earlier, in 1905. Their most recent revolution is nothing but the most recent chapter; preceding it lies the entire period that began in 1905. It produced a level of maturity in the masses very different from what exists in Germany today. You have nothing behind you except the pitiful half-revolution of November 9. . . .

The starting point of your strategy is the assumption that in two weeks, when they all leave Berlin, a new government can be set up here. "In two weeks we will form a new government." I would be very happy if that were to happen. But as a serious politician, I cannot base my strategy on speculation. Of course, no possibility can be excluded. I will discuss later the fact that the recent change in the government will set in motion a major shakeup in the next period.[42] But it is my duty to choose a course based on my understanding of the situation in Germany. The tasks are enormous, and they will lead to the socialist world revolution, but what we have witnessed until now is the immaturity of the masses in Germany. Our immediate task is to educate the masses to carry out those tasks. We will do that through parliamentarism. Words will be decisive. I am telling you, it is precisely because of the masses' immaturity and their resultant inability to achieve the victory of the council system that the counterrevolution has been able to build up the national assembly as a bastion against us. Now our road runs right through that bastion. . . .

There can be no talk of opportunism in this hall. Please take note of that, Comrade Rühle. There is a profound contradiction in your own line of reasoning when you say you are afraid of the adverse effect parliamentarism will have on the masses. On the one hand you are so sure of the revolutionary maturity of the masses that you count on setting up a socialist government here in two weeks, which would signify the final victory of socialism. At the same time you fear that the elections will have dangerous ill effects on those same, mature masses. I must tell you frankly, I am not afraid of anything. I am convinced that everything in the present situation has molded and prepared the masses to correctly understand our policies. We must educate them in the spirit of our policies so that they can use the elections not as a weapon of the counterrevolution, but, as revolutionary, class-conscious masses, use the weapon that has been placed in their hands to strike down the very ones who put it there.

I will close with the following: there are no differences among us over goals and intentions. We all agree that the national assembly is a bastion of the counterrevolution. We all want to call upon and educate the masses to destroy the national assembly. The question is: What is the best and most suitable way to do it? Yours is less complicated and easier, ours is somewhat more complicated; but that is exactly why I value it as a way to further the theoretical revolutionization of the masses. Moreover, your strategy is based on speculation about the tumultuous events in the next few weeks, while ours keeps an eye on the education of the masses, who still have a long way to go. Our policy is to put the immediate tasks into the context of what needs to be done to further the now approaching revolution up to the point where the proletarian masses are able to take the reins into their own hands. . . .

Actions in the streets must always be the controlling factor and will be victorious. We want to raise in the national assembly a victorious standard that is supported by actions on the outside. We want to blow up that bastion from within. We want to have both forums, that of the national assembly and that of the election meetings. Whether you decide one way or the other, you share common ground with us, the common ground of revolutionary struggle against the national assembly.

Gelwitzki (Berlin): . . . I would like to ask you to support Comrade Rühle. I ask you to adopt the following resolution, which has been adopted by several district meetings in Berlin:

"The members of these district organizations oppose participation in the national assembly. Instead they demand that every instrument of force be brought to bear against it. They further call upon all revolutionary workers to see to it that all power is firmly rooted in the workers' and soldiers' councils. They will shed their blood in the streets, if that is what it takes, to win the power and achieve the world revolution."

These two resolutions were unanimously adopted in my district despite all the machinations that were used to lead the workers in a different direction. . . .[43]

Our clarity of purpose has always won the masses to our side, and it must not be compromised by the machinations of any central body. It is gratifying to be able to say now that we have rid ourselves of the authoritarianism of our leaders. They tried to use authoritarian methods to lead the masses in the wrong direction, but the masses did not follow them. You say, if we do not participate in the elections, the votes which we would get will go to the Independents. That is the most illogical argument I have ever heard. That is nothing but vote chasing. Do we want to be vote chasers? No, we do not want votes, we want fighters. Ten men in the streets are worth more than a thousand votes in the elections.

But at the same time, we have an obligation to consider what the alternative is. Our alternative is, "All power to the workers' and soldiers' councils!" This is the slogan which first won the masses to us and which has the support of the revolutionary forces of Greater Berlin. We must see to it that it is put into effect by January 19. . . .

It was said that we have to let developments take their course. Who are these "developments"? Are we not "developments"? We are the active agents, and it is up to us to push developments along. It is our duty to use all available means to assure that the breakthrough we aim for is achieved; namely, "All power to the workers' and soldiers' councils." I ask you to unanimously adopt our resolution. Do not participate in the national assembly elections. . . .

Käte Duncker (Central Committee): As far as I am concerned, participating in the elections is not a question of principle; it is a tactical question. We agree on the analysis of the national assembly. We have no disagreement about that. But comrades, you know our program. You will recall the very clear and unambiguous section at the end which states that we will take power only when the conscious and clear will of the majority of the German proletariat is behind us. Do you believe we are already at that point today? No, we are not. You are quite wrong. They are not even behind us in words. Yet we sit here, rather like children trying to open buds with our fingers instead of waiting until they open by themselves.

How can we get the majority of the proletariat behind us? Only by utilizing every opportunity we can to agitate for our goals. And the election movement is one such opportunity. . . .

I would like to add one thing. We must also remember that more than half the voters are women, who had no political rights until now. They are now getting the political right to vote for the first time. Do you think that women, after having been told for decades that they have to fight for this right, will now follow us when we tell them not to exercise it? A small, enlightened number of them will, but the vast majority, insofar as they think and feel in proletarian terms, will line up behind the USPD and vote the USPD ticket. The majority of women will not support this slogan. It will be different if we have the opportunity to talk to them at our election rallies and educate them at those meetings. . . .

Eugen Leviné (Berlin): Comrades, I wish to begin where Comrade Duncker left off. The question of participation in the national assembly elections is not a principled one, but it is important.

Our comrades who favor participating in the elections are accused of wanting to get involved in parliamentary work again. Obviously that is not the issue, and therefore I will set aside that argument and raise others that speak against participation. . . .

We know that whatever the case, whether we participate or not, a small minority of the working masses will support us. If we participate, only a few will be with us. . . . But also if we boycott, only a few will follow us. Why is that? . . . It is because we are in an early stage of the revolution, and that prevents the masses from coming over to our side. . . . But it is our task to influence the situation so as to make as short as possible the period of time from now until the day when we have the majority.

We must show through propaganda, agitation, and political experience that there is no other way out of all the anarchy of present conditions than to struggle for immediate socialization. . . . But what we learned through the experience of the Russian revolution is that political principles are not acquired and absorbed from edicts and declarations. It takes the lesson of practical experience. Political life, too, has an apprenticeship program, called the councils, where you learn by working with others. We have no other way out of the present political and economic situation than to devote all of our energy to the councils. . . .

The local councils now lead only a shadow existence and are letting themselves be backed against the wall by the Ebert-Haase government. That is precisely why our task is to build the organization up from below and expand the factory councils.

We must turn our attention to gearing up the factory councils for the economic struggles and training every worker to participate. Participation in any election is incompatible with this task of mobilizing the mass organizations from below. . . . We might be able to explain to the comrades here how you can be against the national assembly and still be for participating in the elections. But those same comrades will never be able to explain it to their co-workers in the factories. . . . The minute you tell them to participate in the elections, you blur their strict opposition to the national assembly and you shift the emphasis from the task of building the factory councils to the hope for results from the national assembly. It is therefore very dangerous to use this slogan. . . .

Fritz Heckert (Chemnitz): All opportunism is harmful, the opportunism of "practical" politicians as well as the revolutionary opportunism being practiced by the comrades who speak against participating in the elections. . . .

It has been drummed into the heads of the German people to expect results from a free parliament. For fifty years we who were in the German Social Democracy fought for equal voting rights in Prussia, and we certainly never told the workers that "parliamentarism" was nothing but a meaningless phrase. We told them that the Reichstag was so wretched because policy was decided in the House of Lords of the Prussian state. We fought for equal voting rights for fifty years, and so we must now expect a persistent sentiment on that point among the masses. Just as the experiment was necessary in Russia, so it is necessary in Germany to convince the workers that the national assembly offers no solution. We will not be able to keep the masses away from the elections. All we can do is tell them, "If you elect a national assembly, you are creating a counterrevolutionary institution that will not solve any problems.". . .

I am for participating in the elections because we have to take advantage of every opening. Even the election campaign is an opening. I do not expect that we will win many seats out of it, and those of us who do get elected will not accomplish anything. All we will accomplish is that the German people will perceive that the national assembly is the same sort of hoax as the old Reichstag. (*Loud laughter*) I beg your pardon, you may think that is funny, but it is not the least bit funny to the majority of workers. Most of them believe that things will be different now in the national assembly than they were in the German Reichstag. It is fine with me if you shout into the workers' ears every day of the week that it is not so. But it is not a question of what you tell the masses. What matters is what they themselves believe, and they believe in the national assembly.

(*Voice from the floor: "The masses do not want the national assembly."*)

How little the masses want the national assembly is shown by the fact that the Scheidemannite demonstration was bigger than ours.[44] Our march did not have 160,000, as the Scheidemanns did.

(*Interjection: "You'd better learn how to count." The chair rings for order.*)

Well, my figures may be a bit off, but it does seem to me that there was quite a large crowd of them. . . .

Werner Hirsch (Cuxhaven): . . . The opponents of participating in the elections keep referring to the backwardness of the masses. But that low level is just what proves that we cannot stop the national assembly. In these circumstances the political situation must without any doubt be the determining factor. But the political situation today is one in which we do not have the majority of the proletariat with us. Even if the Spartacus demonstrations here in Berlin were far larger than those of the Scheidemanns, that is only the way things are in Berlin. In most of the country it is still true that we have today only a minority of the proletarian masses on our side. One indication of that is the resolutions from the Berlin Executive Committee calling for a national assembly. We might be able to set up a government here in Berlin as Comrade Rühle believes. But that is not the situation we are striving for. I believe we should only try to take power when we have the majority of the proletariat solidly behind us. We do not want to impose anything on the masses against their will; rather, we want to impose our ideas on their minds until we win them to our side. . . .

Rieger (Berlin): We must rid ourselves of the concept of democracy in the old, tainted sense of the word. Having equal voting rights is not democracy when we have no other equal social rights. The equal right to consumption and enjoyment is far more important than anything else. We have to make a clean break with the hoax of parliamentarism in the bourgeois sense. A majority in the workers' councils will be the most visible expression of true democracy. . . . We must have the courage to expose the reactionary purpose of the national assembly, which is to render the workers' councils irrelevant. Therefore, we cannot tolerate making deals with any bourgeois institutions. So be principled. Do not be diverted; reject any and all participation in the elections. . . .

Karl Liebknecht: . . . There are two ways things may develop in Germany. One possibility is that the entire economy will collapse, rapidly bringing down with it the political hopes the masses had placed in the November revolution, and that this will induce a very rapid evolution. In that case we are on the eve of a swiftly unfolding chain of events that in the next few weeks will lead to the socialist revolution. By no means do I wish to rule out the possibility that we may seize power at the head of the proletariat. There may be surprises in store for us in the days ahead. The development and consciousness of the masses often bypasses that of the so-called leaders. We have just recently seen examples of the masses perceiving ahead of their leaders the right thing to do. I am far from being a pedant.

Nevertheless, I wish to point out that besides that possibility, there is another way things could develop. It is possible that the counter-revolution is being consolidated in the hands of Scheidemann, Ebert, and their friends, in league with the bourgeoisie. We may soon be forced into illegal activity or rounded up or something like that. Such a set of circumstances would force us to adjust our policies for a longer-term perspective. It is the latter possibility rather than the former one that makes a boycott of the elections seem so inadvisable.

Assume for a moment that we still have to reckon with a longer period of development. Take into account that at the present time the great majority of the proletariat is not yet completely prepared for revolution. Given that situation, we would have to use every available means to win over the masses and educate them. . . .

We are in the middle of an election campaign. It is true that we can have rallies and launch bitter attacks against the national assembly and expose it in advance, as we have been doing. . . . The only question is, do we not want to exploit this election struggle in a more positive way so as to make an even stronger impression; to use this campaign to make our opposition to the national assembly even more clear to the masses by saying, "Do not vote for us simply because you happen to have the right to cast ballots. Rather, those of you who want to exercise that right should go ahead and do so, but do it in a way that helps further the revolution by fighting against the national assembly.". . .

To a large extent, they can suppress what we would do in the national assembly by blocking it out of the press. There is one thing that is possible, that cannot be blocked out, and that unfailingly gets into the public eye. That is not long speeches — speeches come and go — but action in parliament that disrupts the proceedings and could lead to violent conflicts and confrontations. If we are not afraid of it, it can also lead toward breaking up the whole thing. So there is a certain value to getting elected.

(*Shout: "That cuts both ways."*)

In my view, it is possible in this way to have an external agitational impact from within parliament, to discredit the national assembly, and so to promote direct action. □

Following further discussion, Rühle's motion for abstention in the national assembly elections was adopted by a vote of sixty-two to twenty-three.[45]

After the vote, the IKD, whose delegates had been prominent in pressing for the boycott, made a declaration that it had dissolved, in order to build a common party with the Spartacus League.

Frölich later wrote that Jogiches was "deeply shocked" at the congress decision to boycott the elections and took it as confirmation of his view "that the decision to form a Communist Party had been premature; but Rosa Luxemburg shrugged her shoulders resignedly, declaring that a new-born babe always squalled first."[46] Pieck noted that "Comrades Luxemburg, Liebknecht, and Jogiches were extremely disappointed by this vote. ... But they did not let it come to a split, because they were convinced that the party membership itself would soon be convinced that the decision was wrong."[47]

In August 1919 Lenin wrote to the British Communist Sylvia Pankhurst that he considered the Spartacus leaders to have been correct both in their stand at the congress and their acceptance of the congress decision:

"It is better to be with the revolutionary workers when they are mistaken over some partial or secondary question than with the 'official' socialists or Social-Democrats, if the latter are not sincere, firm revolutionaries, and are unwilling or unable to conduct revolutionary work among the working masses, but pursue correct tactics in regard to that partial question. And the question of parliamentarism is now a partial, secondary question. Rosa Luxemburg and Karl Liebknecht were, in my opinion, correct when they defended participation in the elections to the German bourgeois parliament, to the constituent national assembly, at the January 1919 Conference of the Spartacists in Berlin, *against* the majority at the Conference. But, of course, they were still more correct when they preferred remaining with the Communist Party, which was making a partial mistake, to siding with the direct traitors to socialism, like Scheidemann and his party, or with those servile souls, doctrinaires, cowards, spineless accomplices of the bourgeoisie, and reformists in practice, such as Kautsky, Haase, Däumig and all this 'party' of German 'Independents'."[48]

The attitude of Scheidemann and his party to the KPD congress was clearly expressed in the SPD's newspaper *Vorwärts* the day following the parliamentarism debate. Distorting some comments by Radek and by delegates who favored the election boycott, *Vorwärts* portrayed the KPD as a party of warmongers and terrorists. The December 31 *Vorwärts* account began with a general assessment of the congress, which read as follows.

Spartacus Aims to Break Up
the National Assembly[49]

Break with the Independents. Boycott the national assembly. Bolsheviks agitate for world war.

At their conference yesterday, the Spartacus League sent the Independents their letter of farewell. Rejecting their leaders' advice by adopting an ever more "radical" stand, they rejected participation in the January 19 elections and indicated they would attempt to disrupt them by force and disperse the national assembly. In so doing they have declared a *power struggle*. We Social Democrats accept the challenge in order to defend the right of the people to self-determination against terrorist oppression. We will fight for the people's *freedom* as we have always done, and we are not worried about the outcome.

After all, these are our own domestic problems. But what are we to think when a representative of the Russian government — *Radek,* whom we know so well here in Germany — has the nerve to come to Berlin to agitate here for another war against Britain? Can we not throw the fellow out? Here we have concluded an armistice with the Entente and are doing our best to attain favorable peace terms quickly, and along comes *an agent of a foreign government* calling upon us to join them in starting the war again! Have the blind followers of the Spartacus League — the honest ones among them — still not noticed where that leads? They never used to have anything good to say about *warmongers,* but now they are cheering a foreign warmonger, who would drive Germany into another completely senseless slaughter.

Civil war at home, another world war abroad: that is the Spartacists' program. At the same time, they are *afraid of the elections,* which would show that not even one hundredth of the population is with them. A group that is too weak even to field candidates will not be able to impose its will on either domestic or foreign policy. The people's good sense will put this madness in a straitjacket and call the criminals to account. □

The national assembly elections were held as scheduled on January 19, 1919, and 83 percent of the electorate voted — a higher percentage than in the last prewar national elections. Their outcome confirmed that the SPD retained a strong hold among the working masses. It gained 37.9 percent of the vote, a record high, while the USPD was able to secure only 7.6 percent. The combined vote of the SPD and USPD thus fell short of 50 percent, and the bourgeois parties gained a majority.

This experience did not, however, overcome the division in the KPD on participation in parliament and on related questions. During the months following the congress, the party's attention was focused on the civil war that spread across Germany, in which it was dealt savage blows. After the fighting ebbed, and the party began to recover its strength, its central leaders set out to win the ranks to the perspective they had defended at the founding congress. The next congress, held in Heidelberg in October 1919, approved by a narrow majority theses that rejected a parliamentary boycott and also for the first time called for revolutionary work in the existing, SPD-led trade unions. The congress then adopted, by a vote of twenty-one to twenty, a motion excluding from the party those who rejected these theses. Although Comintern leaders, including Radek and Lenin, tried to preserve party unity, the breach in the KPD could not be healed, and half the membership, including all but a few dozen in Berlin, left the party.[50] In April 1920 they formed a rival organization, the Communist Workers Party of Germany (KAPD).

The ultraleft positions adopted by the KPD's founding congress, and enshrined as principles by the KAPD, were held in other parties in the young international Communist movement, as well. These views were subsequently taken up and debated in the Communist International. In 1920 the second Comintern congress adopted a report and a resolution presenting a Marxist approach on participation by Communists in bourgeois parliamentary elections. That congress also adopted a resolution on the trade union question, another area where the early KPD committed ultraleft errors. Both questions were also taken up in Lenin's 1920 pamphlet, *"Left-Wing" Communism — an Infantile Disorder.*[51]

The trade union issue surfaced at the KPD congress on the day following the parliamentarism debate. The report that day on "economic struggles" by Paul Lange of the Central Committee evaded the key problem in that regard that was preoccupying the delegates: Communists' attitude toward the unions.

Before 1914, the trade union bureaucracy had been the main prop of the SPD's opportunist right wing. During the war, the Social Democratic union bureaucracy had allied with the government and bosses to stifle, as far as possible, any expressions of worker discontent. As a result, when workers fought back, they had tended to improvise new bodies to coordinate their fight: shop stewards' councils, factory committees, and citywide workers' councils. After November 9, however, the trade union brass moved quickly to reassert its control in the factories as part of the SPD-led drive to break the fighting strength of the new rank-and-file bodies. After four years of efforts to harness the workers to the war machine, the bureaucrats now had to take steps to refurbish the unions' image as organizations fighting to win gains for the workers. They did so in characteristic fashion by a quick deal with the bosses to institutionalize a few of the gains made possible by the workers' victory of November 9. On November 15 the unions obtained an agreement from most of the large employers' associations in which the bosses promised, among other things, to rehire demobilized soldiers, institute the eight-hour day, and, most importantly for the union bureaucrats, to recognize them as the authorized representatives of the work force.[52]

Writing in *Rote Fahne* on November 21, Lange had condemned this agreement as a flagrant revival of the antiworker collaboration of union and employer that prevailed during the war.[53] Nonetheless, in the wake of the strike wave following the November 9 revolution, the unions recruited masses of new workers, while the factory councils began to lose momentum. In the first year after the revolution the unions increased their membership to 5.5 million from 1.7 million. The expanding unions were the key arena for the SPD leadership in rebuilding its base and political authority in the workers' movement.

Most German Communists stayed outside the unions, aiming to replace them with the factory councils. Some who came from the IKD proposed to build a new "unified organization," replacing both unions and parties.

At the German Communists' congress, Lange's report on "economic struggles" focused not on the Communists' trade union policy but on the fight over ownership and control of industry. Workers must not wait for governmental commissions and trade union leaderships to act on the question of expropriation of the bourgeoisie, Lange stated, but must move on the question themselves through mass action. He recommended building up the strength of factory councils, and fighting through them to open the corporate books to workers' inspection and to achieve workers' control of working conditions and of production. Despite Lange's evasion of the problem of trade union policy, however, the question was bluntly posed by the first speaker to take the floor after Lange's opening report.

Trade Union Discussion[54]

Arthur Hammer (Essen): . . . We should have asked Lange to tell us what we should do in practice about the strikes and the unions.

Things are very different out there. You cannot put off the miners by talking about our socialist goals. They want to see action. . . .

In the large mines the workers have already set up factory councils, and they will set up more in the other mines. The union leaders still do not correctly interpret the signs of the times — they are still living in the time before the revolution. It does not occur to them that they need to reassess everything and to take direct control over production as such. It is obvious how extremely backward these people are. We tell the workers that they must build plant and factory councils, and they take our advice. But what are we supposed to say to the workers when they come to us and ask what they should do with the unions and their membership cards? In some cases they are throwing away their membership cards. . . .

Rieger: . . . We must understand that union contracts of one or another type will get us nothing. . . . Syndicalism stands opposed to union contracts. It strives for tactical freedom. Where the contracts make it impossible for workers to conduct sympathy strikes, syndicalism calls for abolishing contracts. It calls instead for short strikes with a revolutionary focus to improve social conditions. The workers must learn through social struggles to give struggles a revolutionary character, so that communist ideas will prevail in the social revolution. . . .

We must note that until that victory, economic struggles will have to be conducted. We must note that the unions too have a function. However, we must break completely with the national union federations. Syndicalism holds that workers in one workplace should not be split up along occupational lines; instead, they have an obligation to struggle together. The individual trades should not have separate organizations; rather, workers of all trades share the common goal of uprooting capitalism. Until that has been done, they have to fight together. Therefore: short, revolutionary strikes with a broad, revolutionary basis; solidarity strikes with the broadest possible basis. . . .

Paul Frölich (Hamburg): . . . It is absolutely essential that we reach a clear decision here on the trade union question. I doubt that we can justify our co-workers remaining in these unions. In Hamburg and in the big cities on the North Sea coast, we have been discussing the trade union problem for many years, since the great miners' strike of 1913.[55] We have come to the conclusion that the old trade union strategy cannot possibly satisfy the workers, and that against the huge concentrations of capital we will get nowhere with the old methods of trade union struggle. We are just knocking our heads against a brick wall. At the same time, experience shows that we cannot go on waging the political struggle in the old manner. In the political struggle, too, all of the workers' economic power must be thrown into the balance. We saw how the two aspects converged. The economic struggle could no longer be waged except by putting pressure on the political institutions. We drew the conclusion that it is necessary to abandon this dichotomy between political and trade union work and combine the two approaches.

I recognize that conditions for this approach are mature only in industries dominated by large enterprises. But I have always felt it was an error on the part of the comrades of the old Spartacus League — who after all still had connections to the USPD press — that they never once dealt with this question and that they allowed the *Leipziger Volkszeitung* to print the slogan, "Not out of the trade unions but into the trade unions." They succumbed to the absurd idea that if we are inside the unions we can destroy them. We found out that that strategy did not work within the old party, and it certainly will not work in the unions. The main reason is that both the union finances and the union staff of functionaries are governed by bourgeois law, and we can fight bourgeois law only with revolutionary methods. We cannot fight it by using it. It is not possible to win over the unions by electing a radical local executive board here or there. The only slogan for us is, "Get out of the unions."

And what then? . . . We [in Hamburg] founded the unitary organization. It looks after our members' economic interests, too. Because we prioritized the factory councils, we are in a position to use the power generated by the economic struggles to benefit the revolutionary movement: we can connect every economic struggle with struggles occurring in other factories. . . . □

Motion by Rieger

The National Conference resolves that the policy of the national union federations in securing wage contracts; their suppression of strikes; the systematic obstruction of the proletariat's struggles for social emancipation by the union bureaucracy; as well as the hands-off and even hostile attitude that the union leadership takes toward immediate action to socialize the means of production, all objectively preserve the state and are therefore antirevolutionary. Membership in such union federations is therefore incompatible with the goals and tasks of the Communist Party of Germany. Rather, to conduct economic struggles and also to take over production after the victory of the social revolution, it will be necessary to form revolutionary, locally organized workers' organizations (unitary organizations). These combat organizations shall carry out their work in close cooperation with the Communist Party and the central strike committees, and they shall assist in initiating and administering communist production. . . . □

A similar resolution introduced by several delegates stated, in part, "the revolutionary proletariat needs a unitary organization of economic and political struggle. That organization is the Communist Party of Germany."

Discussion (Continued)

Heckert: Comrades are giving a facile answer to this question. . . . Comrades are speaking as if they could sweep away everything with a wave of the hand, like a house of cards. But you must put something better in place of what you sweep away. I doubt that you are able to do that. I do not believe that the unions have become superfluous or that it would be useful to raise the slogan of resigning from them and launching a struggle against them, if we do not yet have the resources to immediately replace what we would be tearing down. We have a big task, transforming all of society. This revolution is not only political but social as well. What is the situation in the factory councils? It is not especially favorable for us. We will be involved in many major battles, and the bourgeoisie will unite against us.

In these battles for socialization, the unions will no longer be able to play the same role as they did before. You are thinking in terms of how things were before the revolution, and that confuses the matter. We are now in the revolution and there are new tasks not only for us, but for the trade unions as well. Today they can no longer carry out the same kind of policy they implemented during the war. Once we have established factory councils we can proceed to put the factories in the workers' hands. That essentially takes care of the side of trade union activity that you particularly object to. As soon as you socialize the mines, the miners' union will play an entirely different role than it did before. . . . The fact that the form these unions took was bad and that the people who led them committed many crimes does not mean that they will continue to play such a negative role under new historical conditions. I cannot say.

We will need institutions that take over and run production. We will need cooperation from factory to factory and connections from trade to trade, and for that there has to be some form of federations of workers' unions. In my opinion, we can shift the unions over to fulfilling that function — objective circumstances will force them to. . . . I am not worried that the unions will be able to cause any more damage of that kind; but it would be very damaging to call for leaving the unions now.

Luxemburg: . . . It was obvious that as soon as we began to discuss the economic tasks, we would stumble over the great barrier represented by the unions. The question of the fight for emancipation is inseparable from the question of the fight against the unions. That is ten times more true of Germany than anywhere else, for Germany is the only country where throughout four years of World War, at the behest of the unions, no movement for higher wages occurred. Had the unions done nothing other than that, they would deserve to perish ten times over. The official unions showed during the war, in the revolution, and up to the present that they are organizations of the bourgeois state and of capitalist class rule. It is therefore obvious that in the struggle for socialization in Germany the first task will be to eliminate the obstacles the unions put in the way of socialization. How should that task be carried out? What manner of organization can be put in their place?

I am very definitely opposed to the proposal by the comrades from Bremen presented here in the motion for the so-called unitary organization. There is something they have overlooked. We want to make the workers' and soldiers' councils the vehicles for the political and economic demands and power of the working class. Above all, this concept has to be the starting point for organizations to lead the economic struggle.

Our platform explains the fundamental principle that the workers' councils are the organizations at the factory level that lead and watch over the economic struggles. Factory councils, elected by the work force, cooperate with the workers' councils — which also come from the factories — and are joined at the top in national economic councils.[56]

As you can see, the platform leads straight to completely assuming all the functions of the unions. (*Applause*) We expropriate from the trade unions the functions entrusted to them by the workers, whom they betrayed. We replace the unions with another system that has a new foundation. . . .

I also see one small hitch in the call to resign from the unions: what will become of the enormous power those gentlemen control? That is only a minor technical question. I would not want any angle to be overlooked in the process of liquidating the unions, and I would not be in favor of a split that left even a part of the power in their hands.

I conclude with a motion. I ask you to submit the motions you have introduced to the same economic commission that prepared the platform. It was elected by workers' and soldiers' councils that share the point of view of the Spartacus League, and it works in consultation with members of the Spartacus Central Committee. It does not consider itself authorized to make decisions; instead, it worked out the report for discussion by comrades across the country. . . .

Paul Lange (Central Committee — Summary): . . . If you have followed the movement for higher wages in the past weeks and months, you will have noticed that the unions and bosses were on one side, and the factory councils and workers were on the other. That is why we want to promote and build the factory councils, and that is why we believe that they will continue the work of combating the unions in a most decisive way. But we do not believe that we can stipulate that the workers have to quit the union before they can join us. The Spartacus League does not want to be a political unitary organization in the sense that we are responsible for both political and economic struggles. We are a political organization, and we support the factory councils, which have to carry out the economic struggles. □

Rather than voting on this agenda point, the congress decided to refer all motions to the Program and Organization Commission to be elected later that day. The problem of trade union policy continued to preoccupy Communists in Germany and internationally. At the first Comintern congress, a United States delegate, Boris Reinstein, called for a stand in favor of "revolutionizing and transforming the trade union movement." The congress, however, considered that in view of the widely divergent conditions in different countries it was not possible at that time to work out a line on this question, and Reinstein's motion was referred to the Comintern Executive Committee for further study.[57] Subsequently, the German party leadership, influenced by discussions with Karl Radek and by a pamphlet he wrote while imprisoned in Berlin,[58] won a majority at the October 1919 congress for a clear policy of participation where possible in the trade unions with the goal of transforming them into revolutionary instruments of class struggle.

The trade union discussion at the congress was followed by Rosa Luxemburg's report on "The Party Program and the Political Situation." In the portions of this report printed below, she explained how the Communist program differed from that of the prewar SPD and emphasized the patient educational work required of the KPD in the coming months.

Report on Our Program and the Political Situation[59]
by Rosa Luxemburg

Great historic events provide the basis for our discussion on program today; specifically, we have come to the point where the proletariat's Social Democratic, socialist program must be established on a new foundation. Comrades, in so doing we must pick up the threads of Marx and Engels's thinking exactly seventy years ago when they wrote *The Communist Manifesto*. As you know, *The Communist Manifesto* views socialism, the realization of the ultimate goal of socialism, as the immediate task of the proletarian revolution. . . .

The disappointments of the 1848 revolution led Marx and Engels to abandon the position that the proletariat could directly and immediately bring about socialism. Social Democratic, Socialist parties that had an entirely different perspective were then formed in every country. They declared that their immediate task was to wage the daily struggle for small-scale political and economic goals, thereby gradually constructing a proletarian army that could answer the call to create socialism once capitalist development was ripe for it. The Socialist program thereby shifted abruptly to an entirely different basis; this took a particularly characteristic form in Germany. There, before the August 4 collapse of Social Democracy, the Erfurt program was authoritative.[60] According to that program, the so-called immediate, minimum demands were placed in the foreground, while socialism was only a distant guiding star, set as the ultimate goal. However, what the program said is not all-important; decisive is how that program was interpreted in life. One important document of the workers' movement was authoritative for interpretation of the program; that was Engels's preface to *The Class Struggles in France,* written in 1895. . . .[61]

In this document, Engels makes use of his expert knowledge of military science to explain that, given the level of development of modern militarism, industry, and the big cities, it is pure insanity to think that working people can make a revolution in the streets and win. This thesis had two consequences. First, parliamentary struggle came to be viewed as the opposite of direct revolutionary action by the proletariat and as virtually the sole method of class struggle. This theory yielded outright parliamentarism and nothing else. Second, oddly enough, militarism, the most powerful organization that the class state possesses, the masses of proletarians in uniform, came to be viewed as immune and inaccessible to any and all socialist influence. . . .

From then on, this conception did in fact dominate everything that the German Social Democracy said and did, until that fine day, August 4, 1914. It all began with that declaration of nothing-else-but-parliamentarism. Engels did not live to see the results, the practical consequences, of this application of his preface and his theory. I am certain . . . that Engels — and Marx, too, if he had lived long enough — would have been the first to protest it and to stop the runaway cart with a firm hand. . . .[62]

Comrades, today we have arrived at a point where we can say we have returned to Marx and are marching under his banner again. When we say in our program today that the immediate task of the proletariat — to put it concisely — is nothing less than making socialism come true and exterminating capitalism root and branch, we are taking the position that Marx and Engels took in 1848 and from which they never deviated, in principle. . . .

An examination of the misconceptions and illusions of 1848 led to the belief that the proletariat still had an infinitely long way to go before socialism could be achieved. Of course, no serious theoretician has ever tried to predict a definite date for the collapse of capitalism. But in a general sense it seemed to lie in the far distant future, and that belief is evident in every line of the preface that Engels wrote in 1895. We can now draw the balance sheet. Was it not a very short time compared to the pace at which the class struggle once developed? Seventy years of large-scale capitalist development have sufficed to bring us to the point where we can seriously attempt to wipe capitalism off the face of the earth. Moreover, not only is it possible to carry out that task today, not only is it our duty to the proletariat; but rather, doing so is today the only way to ensure the survival of human society. (*Loud applause*)

Comrades, what did the war leave of bourgeois society but a gigantic rubble heap? Formally, all the means of production and many of the institutions of power — almost all of the decisive institutions of power — remain in the hands of the ruling classes. We have no illusions about that. But the only thing they can do with that power, besides try desperately to restore exploitation through slaughter, is cause anarchy. They have come to the point where the dilemma confronting humanity today is either perish amid chaos or find salvation through socialism. The bourgeois classes cannot find any way forward, out of the wreckage of the World War, within the framework of their class rule and the capitalist system.

Marx and Engels were the first to say that socialism has become a historical necessity, and they recorded this truth for the first time in the great document *The Communist Manifesto* as the scientific basis of socialism. Today we are seeing that proposition proven true in the most literal sense of the word. Socialism has become a necessity not just because the proletariat is no longer willing to live under the conditions provided by the capitalist classes; rather, if the proletariat fails to fulfill its class obligation and realize socialism, we will all perish together.

Comrades, that is the general foundation for the program that we want to adopt officially today and that you already know from the pamphlet *What the Spartacus League Wants*. It is deliberately counterposed to the conception which underlay the old Erfurt program; that is, the division into immediate, so-called minimum demands for political and economic struggle and the ultimate socialist goal or maximum program. In deliberate contrast to that, we are settling the accounts of the last seventy years of development, and of the immediate results of the World War in particular, when we say we no longer have a minimum and maximum program. Socialism is both at the same time — it is the minimum that we have to accomplish today. (*"That's right!"*) . . .

Comrades, what general, practical implications flow from this for us in the immediate future? No doubt, your first reaction will be to hope that the Ebert-Scheidemann government will now fall and be replaced by an openly socialist, proletarian, revolutionary government. However, I would like to direct your attention not upward toward the top, but downward instead. We must not cling to and perpetuate the illusion we held during the first phase of the November 9 revolution, that a socialist revolution can be made by overthrowing the capitalist government and replacing it with a different one. The proletarian revolution will be victorious only if we begin the other way around, by constantly undermining the Ebert-Scheidemann government with a mass revolutionary, proletarian, social struggle. . . .

Above all else, from now on we must extend the system of workers' and soldiers' councils as widely as possible, especially the system of workers' councils. What we inherited from November 9 was scarcely a beginning, and to make matters worse, we even lost major instruments of power in the first stage of the revolution. As you know, the counterrevolution has undertaken to progressively dismantle the workers' and soldiers' council system. The counterrevolutionary government has abolished altogether the workers' and soldiers' councils in Hesse, and elsewhere the instruments of power are being torn from the councils' hands. Therefore, we must not only expand the workers' and soldiers' council system, we must also include rural workers and small peasants in it. We must take power, and for us the question of seizing power is posed as a question before every workers' and soldiers' council throughout Germany: What is it doing? What can it do? What must it do? (*"Bravo!"*)

That is where the power is. Everywhere we must undermine the bourgeois state from below by ending the separation of state power into executive, legislative, and administrative branches. Instead we must unify them in the hands of the workers' and soldiers' councils.

Comrades, that is a huge field to plow. We must work from the bottom up, giving the workers' and soldiers' such power that when the Ebert-Scheidemann government — or any like it — ultimately falls, it will only be the finale. Thus, the seizure of power will not be a one-time operation but an ongoing process in which we work our way into the bourgeois state until we occupy all positions and can defend them tooth and nail.

Furthermore, in my opinion and that of my closest party associates, the economic struggle should also be led by the workers' councils. In addition, the workers' councils should lead the discussion of economic issues and take responsibility for widening that discussion to ever broader circles. The workers' councils should have all state power. We must work toward this goal in the immediate future, and if we make that our task, we may expect to witness an enormous intensification of the struggle in the period ahead. We must fight step by step, toe to toe in every province, city, village, and town, to tear all the instruments of power piece by piece away from the bourgeoisie and transfer them to the workers' and soldiers' councils. However, to do this, our comrades and the proletariat need education. Even where there are workers' and soldiers' councils, there is no consciousness of what their mission is. (*"That's right!"*) . . .

The key thing to remember here is, "In the beginning was the deed," and the deed that must be done is to make the workers' and soldiers' councils the sole governmental authority for the whole country. Only that can undermine the foundations and prepare the overthrow — which will crown all our efforts. Consequently, comrades, it was only after careful deliberation and careful reckoning that we pointed out to you yesterday, and I stress to you again today: Do not take the easy road in this struggle.

Several comrades mistakenly thought I was saying that in boycotting the national assembly they would be standing by with arms folded. I never dreamed of such a thing. I was simply unable to go into it in more detail, whereas I can now do so within the framework and context of this report. I believe that history will not make it as easy for us as it was in the bourgeois revolutions, where overthrowing the official power in the capital and replacing it with a few new individuals, or a few dozen of them, was sufficient. We have to work from the bottom up, and that corresponds precisely to the mass character and the goals of our revolution, which go to the foundations of the social system. It is consistent with the character of the proletarian revolution in our time that we do not conquer political power from above, but from below. November 9 was an attempt to shake state power and class rule. It was a weak, insufficient, unconscious, chaotic attempt. Now it is necessary to direct all of the proletariat's power against the underpinnings of the capitalist system in a fully conscious way. Down where each employer confronts his wage slaves, down where all the administrative institutions of class political rule come face to face with those whom they rule, the masses, that is where we must progressively wrest the institutions of power away from the rulers and take them into our hands.

As I have described it, the process may seem somewhat more tedious than you perhaps first imagined. I believe it is salutary for us to review all of the difficulties and complications of this revolution and understand them very clearly. I hope that frankly discussing the great difficulties and the proliferating tasks will affect you no differently than it does me. I hope that it will not weaken your resolve and spirit. On the contrary, the bigger the job, the greater our energy becomes. Let us not forget, the revolution can work with tremendous speed. I do not presume to prophesy how long the process will take. Who among us keeps track of that? Who cares, as long as we dedicate our life to bringing it about? All that matters is that we understand very clearly what is to be done. And I hope that in my small way I have helped to show you the main outlines of just what lies before us. (*Thunderous applause*) □

Luxemburg's report also took up the agrarian question in Germany and proletarian relations with the peasantry. These remarks, together with further comments made during the congress discussion period on these matters, are printed below in chapter 5.

The discussion also dealt with the conquest of power and the question of "terror," that is, the forcible repression of the armed counterrevolution by a revolutionary government. The following are portions of the debate on these points.

Discussion on Program[63]

Frölich: . . . Comrades, I must say, I believe there is a part of the program that is questionable; I suspect that its authors were a little timid when they wrote it. It says in section three:

"In the bourgeois revolutions, the weapons of bloodshed, terror, and political assassination were indispensable for the rising classes.

"The proletarian revolution needs no terror to achieve its goals; it hates and abhors killing. It has no need of those methods of struggle because it is fighting institutions, not individuals, and because it does not enter the arena with naive illusions that shatter and must then be avenged."

Comrades, I have serious objections to this passage. To begin with, it implies a sharp criticism of the Bolsheviks' policies. (*Objections from the floor*) They explained very plainly: "Yes, we have to use terror." Now of course, comrades, the fact that the Bolsheviks did something a *different* way should not deter us from doing it *our own* way. But before we level that criticism against the Russian revolution, we have to be certain it is justified; we must check carefully whether they were not compelled by the overall situation to use terror. Comrades, if you clearly understand the bitter intensity of the civil war being waged over there, then you will see why it must be waged with every available means, including the use of terror.

In addition, we should all agree that the revolutionary struggles here in Germany will be much more violent than those in Russia. That seems quite certain to me, because capitalism here has a much more solid foundation than it does there, and we do not possess the exceptionally potent weapon of a revolutionary peasantry. On the contrary, as Comrade Luxemburg very correctly pointed out, we have in our peasantry the problem of an unusually resolute and conscious counterrevolutionary force. I therefore feel that we will have to wage an even more bitter class struggle here in Germany.

Now what is the key point here? In all these struggles, the most essential thing for us is to be as tightly organized as possible, while disorganizing the enemy. And comrades, our situation is that every time they chop off our heads, new people immediately step forward from the masses to take matters in hand. However, it is different for the bourgeoisie. In point of fact, their organization is led mostly by indi-

vidual outstanding figures; hence, it is necessary to cut that head off
of their organization — not physically, of course; physically only if
we are forced to. Nevertheless, the head must be removed from the
counterrevolution's organization, and comrades, it has to be said that
so far, on this issue, our whole revolution has shown that it is still in
its infancy, so to speak. . . .

Max Levien (Munich): Comrades, Comrade Frölich has challenged the passage contained in the fourth part of the document *What
the Spartacus League Wants.* The passage says:

"In the bourgeois revolutions, the weapons of bloodshed, terror,
and political assassination were indispensable for the rising classes.

"The proletarian revolution needs no terror to achieve its goals; it
hates and abhors killing."

Against this he appeals to the Bolsheviks' experience. This is a
misunderstanding. No revolutionary party ever fought more vigorously against the kind of terror referred to here than did those same
Bolsheviks. The comrade does not know the history of the Russian
revolution. If he did, he would know that no one fought harder
against the Socialist Revolutionaries, who, as everyone knows, advocate assassinating individuals as well as struggling against individuals. . . .

But what does the Russian example show? The intensity of the
class struggle is not indicated by the quantity of blood that flows, nor
by the number of times terrorist methods are employed; rather, it is
indicated by the pace at which an overthrow proceeds, and the overthrow can take place very quietly if the way has been adequately prepared. So the intensity of the class struggle is not measured in liters
of blood — perhaps none will be shed.

Obviously, the passage is not meant to imply that if we are attacked, we will not defend ourselves. Equally obviously it allows for
a certain amount of initiative in using terrorist methods, if the situation requires it. But I would like to request very specifically that we
retain this particular formulation, because it excludes resorting to any
individual acts of terrorism. . . .

Naturally, that does not prevent us from correctly understanding
the effect that individuals can have on the masses under the present
counterrevolutionary system; on the contrary, it includes that, and I
would be the first to applaud if a revolutionary tribunal were to sentence Scheidemann and Ebert to be strung up. That is up to the revolutionary tribunal, and it will have to be guided by the situation in
deciding which measures to use. In a case like that, whatever measures were taken would really be beyond our control, and, I might

add, they are beyond being influenced by our subjective desires or our impulse to dance the carmagnole. . . .[64]

Now I would like to address something Comrade Rosa Luxemburg said in her speech that could be misinterpreted. Comrade Luxemburg talked about the council system. To be sure, in these times, when coal is in short supply, the council system is the best fuel for the locomotive of history, for the revolution. But I believe misunderstandings could arise if we forget that seizing power also means seizing the center of power. Comrade Rosa Luxemburg said that the revolution will not be made simply by replacing Ebert-Scheidemann with herself and Comrade Liebknecht. True enough. Naturally, that would be another illusion; it would be an illusion just like the one about terrorism. Naturally, you cannot jump over your own shadow, and Comrade Liebknecht cannot perform miracles if the conditions for them are not present. But again, I would like to refer back to what Comrade Rosa Luxemburg said in reference to the national assembly, that we must be prepared and on guard for all eventualities. Well, I would just add that we must also expect the eventuality that, if our actions gain enough momentum, one day the sky will crash down on their heads, and we will be face to face with the question of taking over the central government. . . .

So I think we should not ignore the question of smashing the state machinery, of possibly smashing it by taking control of the central government. Dictatorship of the proletariat does not mean setting yourself up at the head of the state and issuing decrees, not at all. But the dictatorship of the proletariat does not exclude that, as the Bolsheviks have shown us so magnificently. In Russia they had to do it. The situation could arise where it would be necessary for us here, too. It would be most helpful if Comrade Luxemburg would say whether she agrees with what I have said or whether she would perhaps refuse to go along with taking over the central government if that became a necessity. I do not for a moment believe she would.

Liebknecht: . . . Comrades, one speaker stated that the program commission should work rapidly and complete its work in three months because in three months we have to have another party convention to discuss the program. Comrades, I certainly hope we will be spared all that work, (*"That's right!"*) and that the idea of having a party convention in three months and so on will be surpassed by events, which according to my expectations will proceed apace. I wish to refer back to the debate that was reopened by several speakers: if I made a point yesterday of speaking for participation in elections to the national assembly, it was, as one speaker has already pointed out, because I did not want to rule out the possibility of a circuitous or lengthy process of development. But my personal conviction is most assuredly that we should expect a very rapid evolution and must gear everything for that. Therefore, there can be no talk of differences inside the party between us and the majority of the delegates. . . .

Comrades, Comrade Frölich criticized the one passage which expresses opposition to terror as a method of struggle for the proletarian revolution. Comrade Levien has already spoken out against those remarks. I would just like to add that this passage makes quite clear the sense in which its opposition to terror as a proletarian method of struggle is intended. It says that the proletariat itself, if it had the choice, would not want terror and does not need it. However, it continues, we must reckon with the fact that the ruling classes will defend tooth and nail their institutions of power, and that it is the proletariat's task to defeat, ruthlessly and with an iron hand, the ruling classes' resistance along with all counterrevolutionary initiatives. (*"That's right! Bravo!"*) That makes it clear that we do not expect making the revolution to be a Sunday-school picnic, (*"Very true!"*) but rather that we are determined to raise an iron fist and bring it crashing down on anyone who puts up resistance to the proletarian socialist revolution. (*Loud applause*) □

When the discussion closed, Rosa Luxemburg was ill and unable to deliver a summary. All motions regarding the party program were referred to the twenty-five-member Program and Organization Commission to be elected later that day.

The next report, given by Hugo Eberlein for the outgoing leadership, took up the organizational structure of the new party. "We consider that the old system in which local units were subordinated to the Central Committee must be ended," he said. "The individual local groups and the factory organizations must have full autonomy. They must be independent in their activity and must not always wait for whatever is organized from the top down. They must be able to initiate actions without the Central Committee always having the right to say, 'You may do this,' or 'You may not do that.' " The Central Committee's task lay in educating the party, he continued, and in supporting the efforts of the local units to the best of its ability. "Further," Eberlein stated, "we consider that the question of our press cannot be decided centrally. The local organizations everywhere must be able to found their own newspapers and issue their own leaflets and pamphlets."[65]

The congress decided to dispense with discussion on the organizational question and to refer all organizational proposals to the Program and Organization Commission. Statutes based on Eberlein's report were adopted by the October 1919 congress of the KPD.

These statutes were a far cry from the democratic centralist organizational principles adopted by the Communist International. In the early 1920s, the KPD moved toward the concepts outlined in the resolution on the organizational structure of Communist parties adopted by the third Comintern congress in 1921.[66]

The German Communist congress voted to elect a Central Committee composed of all eleven members of the outgoing Spartacus leadership (Hermann Duncker, Käte Duncker, Eberlein, Jogiches, Lange, Levi, Liebknecht, Luxemburg, Ernst Meyer, Pieck, and August Thalheimer) plus Frölich, from the now-dissolved IKD.

The next item on the agenda was the international conference called by the Socialist parties of the Entente countries. The Bolshevik Party had appealed on December 24 to all partisans of a third, revolutionary International to boycott this gathering (the Bolshevik appeal is printed below in chapter 9). The German congress took its stand through the following resolution, which was introduced by Hermann Duncker.

Resolution on the International Conference[67]

The British Labour Party has called an international conference of social patriots, which has now been greeted "with deep satisfaction" by the Scheidemanns. The National Congress of the Communist Party of Germany (Spartacus League) refuses to recognize that conference as in any way representing international socialism.

The conference, convened to enact a mutual amnesty for responsibility for the fratricidal war that claimed millions upon millions of victims and to effect reconciliation among the capitalist interests, cannot conceal the fact that the Second International has collapsed.

The traitors of August 4, 1914, who pimped for their respective national capitalist interests during four years of war by choking off the class struggle and disgracing the idea of socialism, have forfeited the right to speak or act in the name of the workers' International.

The Communist Party calls upon all revolutionary and socialist forces to seek to settle accounts with imperialism in their countries as quickly as possible and to build workers' and soldiers' councils, in order that world peace may be secured by the world proletariat marching under the banner of international socialism.

This congress holds that to be the only viable way to construct a new International, which must henceforth be the center of the proletariat's class organization — not an International of conferences and resolutions, but an International of revolutionary action. ☐

Levien commented that it might be useful, while boycotting the conference itself, to seek contact with any left-wing forces there who stood on the basis of bolshevism and communism. This might help prepare a subsequent "meeting of comrades with a Bolshevik position in the Entente countries and ourselves,"[68] he said, recommending that the Central Committee promote such a meeting. There was no further discussion, and the resolution was adopted without change.

A few hours earlier that day, Wilhelm Pieck had reported on a request from the Revolutionary Shop Stewards for immediate discussions with the KPD with the goal of rapid fusion. This was the first the congress had heard of such a possibility; many delegates had left, and others were skeptical. No observers from the Shop Stewards had been invited to the congress to help correct the misimpressions broadcast by the bourgeois press and shared by some Shop Steward leaders regarding KPD policy. Despite the lack of preparation, however, such a unification with the USPD's most prominent left-wing leaders promised to attract many radical-minded workers from that party into the KPD, as well as greatly increase the Communists' forces in Berlin's industrial proletariat. Pieck therefore proposed that the congress adjourn to permit a short meeting with the Shop Stewards.

The congress soon reconvened. Pieck reported that the Shop Stewards disagreed with the KPD's decisions on the party's name and on boycotting the national assembly elections and viewed these points as obstacles to a fusion. The KPD's representatives had explained that these questions had been settled by congress decision for the time being. No vote had been taken, however, on the details of the party's program and organizational structure, the KPD representatives had pointed out, inviting the Shop Stewards to elect three representatives to the Program and Organization Commission, which was to report on these questions to the next party congress.

The negotiations were still continuing, Pieck told the congress, and their outcome was still uncertain.[69]

The KPD delegates met the following morning with a seven-person commission chosen by the Shop Stewards. Pieck reported in 1920 that "we had almost come to agreement, when Ledebour appeared and demanded a separate meeting of the Shop Stewards without us. In it he formulated a number of conditions that revealed that incompatible differences of opinion existed between their commission and our viewpoint."[70]

The differences centered on five conditions presented by the Shop Stewards' representatives after their private meeting. As later summarized by Liebknecht, these were: (1) that the KPD congress retract its "decision regarding principled antiparliamentarism in general and nonparticipation in the national assembly elections"; (2) full parity for the two groups in the leadership and all commissions of the organization; (3) "a better definition of our policy on street actions and an agreement to undertake no such action in Berlin without first coming to agreement with the Shop Stewards"; (4) granting the Shop Stewards "full and decisive influence over our press and the party's leaflets"; and (5) a change in the party's name, eliminating the word "Spartacus."[71]

In response to these conditions the KPD delegates agreed that the party's name was open to discussion, although the KPD did not want to sacrifice the name "Communist." As for "principled antiparliamentarism," the KPD representatives explained that the KPD congress had taken no such stand. The congress decision concerned only the specific elections then pending, and it was not open to reconsideration. The KPD delegates also rejected the demand for parity as being out of proportion to the Shop Stewards' weight in a fused organization. Further, they stated, conditions three and four "reflected such a profound suspicion" of the Spartacists' "entire previous course" that they put in question whether the two organizations really stood on a common political footing.[72]

At the KPD's request, its response to the five conditions was submitted to a plenary meeting of the Shop Stewards. A lengthy discussion ensued. Richard Müller stressed the suspicions shared by many Shop Stewards that the Spartacists were inclined toward "putschist" actions such as the occupation of *Vorwärts*. The decisive role in the meeting, according to Liebknecht's later report to the congress, was played by Ledebour, a "downright fanatical enemy" of the Spartacists, who "had the effect of dynamite on this assembly."[73]

Ledebour's stubborn opposition to fusion carried the day among the Shop Stewards. His "conditions" were put to a vote and approved; the narrowest margin was twenty-six to sixteen on the national assembly elections. The KPD offer of five seats on the program commission was rejected by thirty-four votes to eight.

This meeting ended the unity talks. The KPD congress then recon-

vened and heard a report by Liebknecht on the course of the negotiations. Despite their failure, he stated, there was a positive side to the
outcome. A minority of seven Shop Stewards, representing large and
influential segments of the Berlin working class, had stated that they
supported the KPD. Much more could be won from this milieu, he
said, and the party should therefore redouble its educational work
among the masses.[74]

Following Liebknecht's report, the Hamburg delegate Fritz Sturm
stated that since the issues were clearly drawn, a resolution should be
adopted immediately without further discussion. "Berlin is not all of
Germany," Sturm said, "and this wing of the Shop Stewards of Greater
Berlin, which perhaps has the support of only a part of the workers,
and maybe not even that, is certainly not all of Germany. They are just
trying to use this business to cut themselves a bigger piece of the
pie."[75] The motion to end discussion was then adopted with two opposing votes.

The KPD congress concluded by unanimously adopting a resolution
on the breakdown of the unity negotiations. It regretted the "efforts of
fake-radical elements of the bankrupt USPD to confuse the ranks of
the Revolutionary Shop Stewards and to disrupt the fighting team they
and the Spartacus League have represented in Berlin." It greeted those
Shop Stewards (and those workers who elected them) who "stand together under the banner of world revolution, which is held aloft in
Germany by our party alone."

"The congress has no doubt," the statement concluded, "that faced
with the choice between the KPD and the USPD, the masses of the revolutionary proletariat of Greater Berlin will decide for the Communist
Party of Germany."[76]

Unity with the Shop Stewards crashed on the rocks of the KPD's ultraleftism and disunity, and, above all, the centrist vacillation of
Ledebour and other Shop Stewards' leaders. This failure was a serious
setback for the newly formed KPD. Moreover, this outcome left the
revolutionary-minded workers of Berlin divided and their leadership
split into two hostile and competing camps as they faced the onslaught
of Ebert's troops in early January. Not until 1920 was the KPD able to
achieve fusion with the revolutionary forces in the USPD.

Notes

1. Ya.S. Drabkin, *Die Novemberrevolution 1918 in Deutschland* (Berlin
[GDR]: Deutscher Verlag der Wissenschaften, 1968), p. 446.

2. Jacob Walcher, "Die deutsche Proletariat und seine Revolution," in *Die Kommunistische Internationale*, vol. 2 no. 14, (1920), p. 129.

3. Pieck, "Erinnerungen an die Novemberrevolution in Berlin," in *Gesammelte Reden und Schriften* (Berlin [GDR]: Dietz Verlag, 1959), vol. 1, p. 457.

4. *Protokoll des III Kongresses der Kommunistischen Internationale* (Hamburg: Verlag der Kommunistischen Internationale, 1921), vol. 2, p. 668.

5. Hermann Weber, ed., *Der Gründungsparteitag der KPD* (Frankfurt: Europäische Verlagsanstalt, 1969), p. 32.

6. Rosa Luxemburg, *Gesammelte Briefe* (Berlin [GDR]: Dietz Verlag, 1984), vol. 5, p. 422.

7. *Dokumente und Materialien zur Geschichte der deutschen Arbeiterbewegung* (Berlin [GDR]: Dietz Verlag, 1957), series 2, vol. 2, p. 653.

8. Ibid.

9. Excerpted from Karl Radek, "Noyabr'," in *Krasnaya Nov'*, October 1926, pp. 149-52.

10. Heinrich Laufenberg's caucus at the congress, the "United Revolutionaries," played an intermediate role between the Spartacists and the USPD.

11. Jogiches led the "Central Committee" wing of the Social Democracy of the Kingdom of Poland and Lithuania, whose political positions were close to those of the Luxemburg-led current in the German SPD. Radek and many other younger leaders, on the other hand, adhered to the "Regional Committee," a Warsaw-based public faction of the Polish Social Democracy, which had closer ties with the Bolsheviks and which rallied to the Zimmerwald Left in 1915. Jogiches and Luxemburg had backed Radek's expulson from the Polish party in 1912, and they were implicated in his expulsion from the SPD the following year. In 1918 she still did not conceal her mistrust of him.

12. Luxemburg's views on these questions before November 1918 are reflected in her draft essay, "The Russian Revolution." While not contesting the Soviet government's action in dispersing the Constituent Assembly, she had criticized the Soviets for not then calling elections to a new Constituent Assembly, which she believed would have been able to reflect the new reality of Russia after the October revolution. Under mass pressure, she held, such an assembly could evolve as the revolution marched forward and keep abreast of shifts in the masses. Her essay did not discuss the new, Soviet system of rule established by the October revolution, which the Bolsheviks held to be a form of democracy superior to the Constituent Assembly and other representative bodies found in capitalist societies. (See Mary-Alice Waters, ed., *Rosa Luxemburg Speaks* [New York: Pathfinder Press, 1980], pp. 384-87.)

Luxemburg's articles after the November 1918 revolution expressed quite a different viewpoint on this question, one closer to that of the Bolsheviks. See her article, "The National Assembly," printed in chapter 2 of the present work.

Luxemburg's manuscript on the Russian revolution also criticized the Bolshevik's agrarian policy; that portion of her essay is printed below in chapter 5.

13. Luxemburg's theory of accumulation is developed in her work, *The Accumulation of Capital*. This book aimed to explain the course of capitalist expansion and prove capitalism's economic need for an aggressive imperialist policy. Lenin, while agreeing with her general political conclusions, considered her explanation erroneous; a reply to her work was written by the Bolshevik leader Nikolai Bukharin in 1924. (Rosa Luxemburg, *The Accumulation of Capital — An Anti-critique*, and Nikolai Bukharin, *Imperialism and the Accumulation of*

Capital [New York: Monthly Review Press, 1972]).

14. Knief's city of Bremen and other North Sea port cities where the IKD was strong had been members during the late middles ages of the Hanseatic League, an association of merchant towns of northern Europe.

15. The USPD members of the Council of People's Representatives resigned on the night of December 28-29.

16. Rosa Luxemburg, "Die Wahlen zur Nationalversammelung," in *Gesammelte Werke* (Berlin [GDR]: Dietz Verlag, 1974), vol. 4, p. 476. An English translation of this article is printed in Robert Looker, ed., *Rosa Luxemburg, Selected Political Writings* (New York: Grove Press, 1974), pp. 287-90.

17. *Dokumente und Materialien,* series 2, vol. 2, p. 664.

18. Zetkin based her view of Luxemburg's position on a letter from Leo Jogiches. See Paul Frölich, *Rosa Luxemburg: Her Life and Work* (New York: Howard Fertig, 1969), p. 323.

19. In 1948 Heinrich Brandler estimated that in November 1918 the Spartacists had at most 3,000 members, "and a good half of them were moral pacifists not Marxists." (Isaac Deutscher, "Dialogue with Heinrich Brandler," in Tamara Deutscher, ed., *Marxism, Wars and Revolutions: Essays from Four Decades* [London: Verso, 1984], p. 133.)

20. Luxemburg's early polemic against Lenin, "Organizational Questions in Russian Social Democracy," is printed under the title "Leninism or Marxism" in Rosa Luxemburg, *The Russian Revolution and Leninism or Marxism* (Ann Arbor, Mich.: University of Michigan Press, 1961).

21. See John Riddell, ed., *Lenin's Struggle for a Revolutionary International: Documents, 1907-1916; The Preparatory Years* (New York: Monad Press, 1984), chapters 7, 8, 10, and 12, a volume of *The Communist International in Lenin's Time.*

22. V.I. Lenin, *Collected Works* (Moscow: Progress Publishers, 1964) (hereinafter *CW*), vol. 22, p. 307. Luxemburg's "Junius" pamphlet, criticized here by Lenin, is printed in Waters, *Rosa Luxemburg Speaks,* pp. 261-331.

23. Lenin, *CW,* vol. 22, p. 319.

24. For comments made by Lenin following Luxemburg's death on the evolution of German communism, see chapter 6 of this volume.

25. Paul Levi, "Report to the Second Congress of the Communist International," quoted in Pierre Broué, *Révolution en Allemagne: 1917-1923* (Paris: Les Editions de Minuit, 1971), p. 215.

26. Ernst Meyer, "Zur Geschichte der KPD," in *Die Kommunistische Internationale,* vol. 7 no. 15 (24), 1926, p. 679, quoted in Weber, *Gründungsparteitag,* p. 35.

27. *Protokoll des III Kongresses der Kommunistischen Internationale,* (Hamburg: Verlag der Kommunistischen Internationale, 1921) vol. 2, p. 669.

28. Hugo Eberlein, "Souvenirs sur la fondation de l'Internationale Communiste," in *La Correspondance internationale,* vol. 4, no. 15, February 27, 1924, p. 154. For Lenin's explanation of why he proposed that the Bolshevik party adopt the name "Communist," see "What Should Be the Name of Our Party — One That Will be Correct Scientifically and Help to Clarify the Mind of the Proletariat Politically?" in Lenin, *CW,* vol. 24, pp. 84-88.

29. The Free Socialist Youth originated in the SPD-oriented youth organization as a faction opposing the SPD's stand on the World War and favoring a class-struggle course. In the spring of 1916 this current held its first congress.

With the active assistance of Liebknecht and the Socialist Youth International, the congress launched a separate national organization, publishing *Freie Jugend* (Free youth) as its organ. Following the 1917 split in the SPD, the new youth organization was aligned with the USPD, but Spartacus supporters were dominant in its leadership. After the November revolution the Free Socialist Youth grew rapidly, and by February 1919 it counted 12,000 members. Its February 22-23, 1919, congress decided politically for the KPD and against the USPD but declined any organizational tie with the KPD. Not until October 1919 did the youth organization exclude USPD supporters from its ranks.

30. Weber, *Gründungsparteitag*, p. 37. Regarding the delegates' political activity after 1919, Weber calculates that of eighty-eight delegates about whom information could be obtained, twenty-nine remained in the KPD in 1933. Sixteen joined or sympathized with the ultraleft KAPD, which was formed in 1920; Paul Levi and three others broke away in 1921; ten joined Brandler's Communist Party (Opposition) after 1928; seven left or were expelled from the KPD but did not join another group; and ten were not politically active after 1919. Six delegates were murdered in 1919, and six others died before 1933. Weber records three delegates who were killed by Nazism and seven (including two fraternal delegates from Russia) who were killed in the Soviet Union during the Stalinist purge trials of the late 1930s.

31. Ibid., pp 63-66. No stenographic record of the congress proceedings was published at the time. Stenographic notes were later discovered in the papers of Paul Levi. Hermann Weber's edition of the congress proceedings is based on this record, supplemented by newspaper accounts.

32. The original draft of the resolution probably contained the name "Revolutionary Communist Party of Germany (Spartacus League)," which had been proposed by the commission established the previous day.

33. Weber, *Gründungsparteitag*, p. 83.

34. Ibid., p. 87. Liebknecht's introductory remarks in solidarity with the Russian revolution are printed in *Archiv für Sozialgeschichte*, vol. 13, 1973, pp. 393-97.

35. Excerpted from Weber, *Gründungsparteitag*, p. 88-96.

36. Levi is referring here to the nickname of Richard Müller, a central leader of the Revolutionary Shop Stewards, who had been dubbed by SPD members as "Dead-Body Müller." The nickname came from his speech to a November 19 assembly of Berlin workers' and soldiers' councils, where he said, "The national assembly is the road to bourgeois rule, the road to confrontation; the road to the national assembly will pass over my dead body." (Richard Müller, *Die Novemberrevolution*, vol. 2 of *Geschichte der deutschen Revolution* [Berlin: Olle und Wolter, 1979], p. 85).

37. Rhineland-Westphalia included the heavily industrialized Ruhr region.

38. "Schilda" is the proverbial name of an isolated rural town of narrow-minded provincials. There is no real place called Schilda.

39. Excerpted from Weber, *Gründungsparteitag*, pp. 96-131.

40. The reference is to Rosa Luxemburg's article, "The Elections to the National Assembly," published December 23.

41. The reference is to the Spartacists' decision in April 1917 to participate in the first USPD congress at Gotha.

42. The reference is to the resignation of the USPD members of the government.

43. The two resolutions are not found in the congress proceedings. The text of the resolution given here is taken from a newspaper report.

44. When 250,000 Berlin workers and soldiers demonstrated against the Ebert-Scheidemann government on December 16, the SPD organized a pro-government demonstration of comparable size.

45. Another delegate had moved that the party participate, casting ballots bearing the names of Liebknecht and Luxemburg. The report by Levi was not put to a vote.

46. Frölich, *Rosa Luxemburg,* p. 313.

47. Pieck, *Gesammelte Reden,* p. 459.

48. Lenin, *CW,* vol. 29, p. 562.

49. Excerpted from "Reichskonferenz des Spartakus-Bundes," in *Vorwärts,* December 31, 1918.

50. Radek stated that he wrote the Central Committee at the Heidelberg congress warning against the projected split, but that Levi suppressed his letter ("Noyabr'," p. 168).

When Lenin learned of the split, he immediately wrote to the KPD leadership and also to the breakaway group, affirming that "given agreement on the *basic issue* (for Soviet rule, against bourgeois parliamentarism), unity, in my opinion, is possible and necessary." He called on both sides to invite the Comintern's Executive Committee to mediate with a view to reunification. Despite the Comintern's efforts, the split was never healed. (Lenin, *CW,* vol. 30, pp. 87-90.)

51. See the second congress resolutions, "The Communist Party and Parliament" and "The Trade-Union Movement, Factory Committees and the Third International," in Alan Alder, ed., *Theses, Resolutions and Manifestos of the First Four Congresses of the Third International* (London: Pluto Press, 1983), pp. 97-113, and Lenin, " 'Left-Wing' Communism — an Infantile Disorder," in *CW,* vol. 31, pp. 17-118.

52. *Dokumente und Materialien,* pp. 393-94.

53. Ibid., pp. 397-99.

54. Excerpted from Weber, *Gründungsparteitag,* pp. 149-67.

55. The last great Ruhr miners' strike before the war took place not in 1913 but in March 1912, when 250,000 miners were defeated in a short but bitter conflict. Troops were sent in to break the strike. Legal reprisals against the workers reached unheard-of proportions, with criminal charges being brought against 1,500 workers.

56. See "What the Spartacus League Wants," section C, points 7 and 8, printed in chapter 3 of this volume.

57. See John Riddell, ed., *The Founding of the Communist International* (New York: Monad Press, 1986), chapter 4, a volume of *The Communist International in Lenin's Time.*

58. Karl Radek, *Die Entwicklung der Weltrevolution und die Taktik der Kommunistischen Internationale im Kampfe um die Diktatur des Proletariats* (Westeuropäisches Sekretariat der Kommunistischen Internationale, 1919).

59. Excerpted from Weber, *Gründungsparteitag,* pp. 172-200. An English translation of the complete text is printed in Waters, *Rosa Luxemburg Speaks,* pp. 400-427.

60. An English-language translation of the Erfurt program is printed in Richard T. Ely, *Socialism: an Explanation of its Nature, its Strength and its Weakness, with Suggestions for Social Reform* (New York: Thomas Y.

Crowell & Co. 1894), pp. 357-62.

61. *The Class Struggles in France, 1848-1850,* a history of the 1848 democratic revolution in France, was written by Marx in 1850. See Marx and Engels, *Collected Works* (New York: International Publishers, 1978) vol. 10, pp. 45-145. For Engels's introduction, see Marx and Engels, *Selected Works* (Moscow: Progress Publishers, 1969), vol. 1, pp. 186-204.

62. In his 1895 introduction to a new edition of Marx's *The Class Struggles in France,* Frederick Engels assessed the incorrect estimation he and Marx had made at that time that the revolutionary overthrow of the bourgeoisie was on the agenda. "History has proved . . . that the state of economic development on the Continent at that time was not, by a long way, ripe for the elimination of capitalist production," Engels wrote. By contrast, by the closing decade of the nineteenth century, accelerated capitalist industrial development and the growth and increasing economic and political organization of the working class had created new political conditions. These developments, Engels said, had forged "*one* great international army of Socialists, marching irresistibly on and growing daily in number, organisation, discipline, insight and certainty of victory."

Engels pointed out, however, that this victory could not be achieved by attempting to repeat the pattern of revolution described in Marx's pamphlet: the kind of spontaneous plebeian revolt seen in Paris in 1848, in which the defense of street barricades was the main form of combat. Writing at a time when the German Socialists were menaced by a new edition of Bismarck's anti-Socialist laws, Engels explained the bourgeoisie's increased ability to crush an uprising based on street barricades and pointed to the necessity for the proletarian party to build mass support among working people of city and countryside as a precondition for a successful revolution. He pointed to the German party's effective use of legal and parliamentary openings to help build such a popular base.

Engels's introduction emphasized that this preparatory propaganda and party-building work was necessary to ensure that "the decisive 'shock force' of the international proletarian army" would be "available at the critical moment" in order that "the decisive combat" not be "delayed, protracted, and attended by heavier sacrifices." (Marx and Engels, *Selected Works,* vol. 1, pp. 201-2.)

Given the crackdown threatened by the German government, Engels was cautious in his formulations about the need for revolutionary action to overthrow the state of the exploiters. Even so, leaders of the German party considered that his text went too far and wrote Engels asking for a series of changes. Engels replied, "I have complied with your serious objections where possible, although in about half the cases I cannot for the life of me see the grounds for these objections. I cannot accept that you will pledge yourselves body and soul to absolute legality, legality in all circumstances. . . . As I see it, you will gain nothing by preaching absolute abstention from force. Nobody will believe you, and *no* party in any country goes so far as to waive the right to resist illegality arms in hand." ("Engels to Richard Fischer," in Marx and Engels, *Werke* [Berlin (GDR): Dietz Verlag, 1978], vol. 39, p. 424.) This letter was not published in its entirety until 1967. See Hans-Josef Steinberg, "Ein unveröffentlichter Brief Friedrich Engels' an Richard Fischer," *International Review of Social History,* vol. 12, part 2, 1967, pp. 177-89.

Engels reluctantly agreed to delete several key passages from his original draft. He was then outraged to find that the party leaders in Berlin published in

Vorwärts a tendentious selection of quotations from his essay, which gave the impression that he favored only legal means of struggle. In response to Engels's protests, the fuller version of the introduction — with the deletions Engels had grudgingly accepted — was published in the party magazine, *Die Neue Zeit.*

In 1899, Eduard Bernstein cited Engels's truncated "Introduction" to buttress his revisionist thesis that socialism could be achieved without revolution through gradual peaceful change. Kautsky was aware that the published text was expurgated and publicly requested that Bernstein, who had been entrusted with Engels's papers, publish the original draft. Bernstein failed to do so. It thus remained possible in 1918 for Luxemburg to accept the published version as accurately reflecting Engels's views when it was written.

In the early 1920s Engels's original draft was found by the Soviet historian Riazanov among papers given by Bernstein at that time to the SPD party archives. In 1925 Riazanov published the deleted portions of the original manuscript in the German Communist journal, *Unter dem Banner des Marxismus,* vol. 1, no. 1, 1928, pp. 160-65.

The version of this article printed in Marx and Engels, *Selected Works,* vol. 1, pp. 186-204, contains the original text of the article, together with a listing of the changes made at the urging of the SPD leadership.

63. Excerpted from Weber, *Gründungsparteitag,* pp. 202-22.

64. The carmagnole was a militant song and street dance of the French revolution.

65. Weber, *Gründungsparteitag,* pp. 248-49.

66. The Comintern's statement on party functioning, "The Organizational Structure of the Communist Parties, the Methods and Content of Their Work: Theses," is printed in Adler, *Theses, Resolutions and Manifestos,* pp. 234-61.

67. Weber, *Gründungsparteitag,* p. 265.

68. Ibid., pp. 267-68.

69. Ibid., pp. 252-53.

70. Pieck, *Gesammelte Reden,* p. 273.

71. See Liebknecht's subsequent report to the KPD congress, in Weber, *Gründungsparteitag,* p. 273.

72. Ibid., p. 274.

73. Ibid., p. 275.

74. Ibid., p. 278.

75. Ibid., pp. 281-82.

76. Ibid., p. 290.

Left, Karl Liebknecht speaking in Berlin Tiergarten; right, Georg Ledebour.

Above, Paul Frölich, Emil Eichhorn; below, Käte Duncker, Hugo Eberlein.

-5-
Toward a Worker-Peasant Alliance

As the political crisis in Germany sharpened in the last weeks of 1918, revolutionary workers grew increasingly conscious of the need to find allies in the countryside among agricultural laborers and exploited peasants. Rosa Luxemburg told the German Communists' congress on December 31 that the November 9 upheaval was still "only an urban revolution . . . the countryside remains virtually unaffected." As for the peasantry, "precisely because it has not yet been touched by the revolution, it remains a reserve force for the counterrevolutionary bourgeoisie." She challenged the new party to "carry the class struggle to the countryside and mobilize the landless proletariat and the small peasants. . . ."[1]

To do this, however, the party required an agrarian program and political orientation for work among the peasantry. There was little in the experience of the German Socialist movement that could point the way. The Social Democratic Party had done little work among peasants. No current in the SPD, including its Marxist left wing, sought to incorporate and build on what Marx and Engels had learned and written about regarding the strategic importance of an alliance with the exploited peasants in the fight to conquer power and hold onto it.[2] This isolation from the rural producers and inattention to the forging of a worker-peasant alliance persisted among the revolutionists who broke with the SPD during the World War.

The November 1918 revolution, however, lent urgency to this question. The formation of a revolutionary government led by the proletariat, previously a distant perspective that received little attention, was now posed as a goal for action. But a lasting conquest of state power was impossible without an alliance with other victims of capitalist exploitation — above all among the peasantry.

Class Antagonisms in the Countryside

The German countryside had been less shaken than the cities by the

---

November 1918 revolution, but this was not because exploitation and oppression there were any less severe. Indeed, agricultural producers in large parts of the country still lived and labored under the heavy burden of what Engels in 1891 termed Germany's "colossal survivals of feudalism."[3]

Although there was no parallel in German history to the successful antifeudal revolution that swept France after 1789, southern and western Germany had directly felt the impact of the French revolution and the Napoleonic wars. Agrarian reforms were carried out by the French authorities in the German regions they annexed west of the Rhine and along the North Sea coast, and these changes were imitated in the independent German states west of the Elbe River. These regions therefore benefited during the opening decades of the nineteenth century from substantial measures to undermine feudal relations on the land. By the late nineteenth and early twentieth century there were few great estates in this region, and many peasants tilled their own plots.

In Germany east of the Elbe River, however, the opposite was true; in this, the historic heartland of Prussia, the big-estate system was still the rule. Here the Prussian "land reform" of the early nineteenth century had left many more aspects of feudal social relations intact, while adjusting modes of exploitation in a direction more suited to capitalist development. The junkers were becoming capitalist estate holders. The peasants were no longer legally bound to the land. But the law that had released them from direct feudal services had compelled them to pay the landlords compensation for this, and they could farm the land only through renting or purchasing it. Peasants were left deeply in debt to the landlords, or, in many cases, they had lost access to the land altogether.

In the 1848 revolution the peasantry had backed the liberal bourgeoisie in the struggle against the feudal institutions that were blocking capitalist development and national unification in Germany. Peasant revolts had swept across southern and western Germany, the areas where small peasants had gained from the reforms of Napoleon's time. These uprisings demanded the abolition of onerous rents and payments, compulsory feudal services, and other feudal privileges still maintained by the big landowners. The bourgeoisie, however, was frightened by the social upheaval unleashed by the revolution and was unwilling to break with large rural property owners, who were increasingly engaged in capitalist agriculture. The bourgeois liberals enacted only the most timid rural reforms, refused to enforce even these, and betrayed the rebellious peasantry, abandoning them to be crushed by the armies of Germany's reactionary princes.

As a result, in 1918 the landholding aristocracy still retained at least some of its privileges everywhere in Germany and remained the object of peasant hatred. The junkers still stood at the pinnacle of a sharply polarized rural class structure. Moreover, their control of institutions of local government in eastern Germany and their domination of the Prussian-German state as a whole served to defend and augment their wealth and privileges.

The junkers dominated a tiny class of ten thousand capitalist estate owners, less than one-half of one percent of agricultural property owners, who held some 20 percent of the cultivated land in Germany. These farms were worked almost entirely by wage labor. Adding in smaller capitalist farms, who used some family labor but relied mainly on exploited wage labor, about half the cultivated land was concentrated in 5 percent of the farms.

At the other extreme, about 60 percent of farm units were less than two hectares (about five acres) in size, and occupied only a little more than 5 percent of the total cultivated land. Nearly one-third of those working the land and one-quarter of all rural landowners toiled on these tiny plots. This data was based on an agricultural census that categorized farms by area while taking no account of variations in land fertility, land use, and the forms of labor employed in production, and it can therefore offer only an approximate reflection of class relations in the countryside. Nonetheless, it is safe to estimate that the big majority of the peasants farming these small plots employed almost no wage labor and, in fact, received most of their income from working a job, either on or off the land. These were the semiproletarian farmers, who made up the bulk of the rural inhabitants that owned any land at all and were spread across the entire country.

A layer of small to medium peasants, owning between two and ten hectares, made up some 30 percent of farm families, working a quarter of the land under cultivation in Germany. These farms relied primarily on family labor, hiring farmworkers only on a limited and occasional basis.

Between 5 and 10 percent of farm families held between ten and twenty hectares and could be counted as large peasants, that is, those employing wage labor on a regular basis.[4]

In addition, about 4.5 million agricultural workers labored on German farms.[5] Found in large numbers throughout Germany, they were concentrated in the east, where they were still subjected to their masters' whim by laws carried over from feudal times.

All told, exploited peasants and farm laborers made up, with their families, about one-fifth of Germany's population of 65 million. By comparison, about 12 million were urban wage workers.

In the decades before 1918, German agriculture faced increasingly stiff international competition, especially from North America and Russia, and prices of agricultural products tended to decline. During the decades before 1918, more and more peasants were being forced off the land into tenancy, or onto smaller farms where they had to work another job to make ends meet. They were driven deeper into poverty, indebtedness, and added toil.

In the years prior to 1914, V.I. Lenin followed the agrarian question in Germany closely and wrote about it frequently. Writing about German peasants in 1913, Lenin stated that independent commodity production "keeps going under capitalism only by *squeezing out* of the workers a *larger* amount of work than is squeezed out of the worker in large-scale production. The peasant is more tied up, more entangled in the complicated net of capitalist dependence than the wage worker. He thinks he is independent, that he can 'make good'; but as a matter of fact, in order to keep going, he must work (for capital) harder than the wage worker."[6]

Earlier that year, in an article commenting on Germany's 1907 agricultural census, Lenin stressed:

"The majority of the [German] peasants live in poverty, are ruined and become proletarians, while the minority trail after the capitalists and help keep the masses of the rural population dependent upon the capitalists. That is why the peasants in all capitalist countries have so far mostly kept aloof from the workers' socialist movement and have joined various reactionary and bourgeois parties. Only an independent organization of wage-workers which conducts a consistent class struggle can wrest the peasantry from the influence of the bourgeoisie and explain to them the absolute hopelessness of the small producers' position in capitalist society."[7]

The SPD's Agrarian Policy

The SPD's weakness in the countryside stood out in the years before the war as one of its most conspicuous political failures. While in the 1903 elections it had achieved second rank among political parties in the rural vote, it had still made only very modest organizational gains among rural proletarians and lacked any significant influence among the exploited small peasantry. Although repressive political conditions in the countryside hindered work by the SPD to win peasant support, the fundamental problem was the party's lack of a strategic orientation to building an alliance of exploited peasants with the proletariat to overthrow capitalist rule.

In the 1890s Karl Kautsky and other left-wing leaders of the party had fought opportunist pressure for a vote-catching orientation to the rich peasants, those who relied on the exploitation of farm labor.[8] The Kautsky-led left wing had explained that under capitalism the working peasants could not escape ruin and that their only future as agricultural producers lay in backing the proletariat's struggle for power. This current in the SPD, however, never developed a strategy for winning peasants as an ally in the fight for power through the course of joint struggles around demands against the common capitalist exploitation of workers and peasants.

German Marxists rejected any forcible expropriation of small-peasant property holders under a workers' government. Beyond that minimal guarantee, however, the left wing in the SPD had little to say to peasants except to extol the advantages of large-scale cooperative cultivation organized along socialist lines. The exploited peasants were assured that their lives would become much better as workers on such socialist-run farms than they currently were as small property holders and tenants at the mercy of the capitalist market. This abstract socialist propaganda offered small peasants no perspective of struggle against the effects of capitalist-imposed debt slavery facing them day in and day out.

Kautsky and his supporters in the SPD left wing considered the fight of working peasants to hold onto their land as fundamentally contrary to the proletarian struggle for socialism. Thus, it explicitly rejected support to immediate demands such as nationalization of mortgages and other land debts and cheap, state-provided credit to peasants, labeling these as reformist schemes to patch up capitalism. The SPD left wing also refused to advocate the more sweeping demand of nationalization of the land as a measure to guarantee peasants continued use of the soil in face of the threat of ruin under the capitalist rents and mortgages system.

The Marxists in the SPD also turned a blind eye toward the aspiration for land among large numbers of landless agricultural workers and semiproletarian peasants with tiny plots.

These programmatic and strategic shortcomings of Marxists in Germany left a political and organizational vacuum in the countryside that the junkers and rich peasants were quick to fill.

The Farmers' League (Bund der Landwirte) was formed in the 1890s under junker and Conservative Party influence to combat the SPD in the countryside by uniting exploiting and exploited farmers alike around their supposed common interests. It campaigned strongly for high tariffs on agricultural imports, especially grain. This mainly helped the estate owners, who specialized in grain production, rather than the small and middle peasants, who produced little grain and had to pay increased prices for food and for fodder for their livestock and poultry.

Nonetheless, the Farmers' League became the most prominent voice of "agriculture" on a national level. The Catholic Center Party also formed peasant organizations and was politically the dominant force in the countryside in the south and west. Other, more progressive peasant organizations also existed, such as the Bavarian Peasants' League (Bayerischer Bauernbund) based in southern Germany, which was influenced by liberal bourgeois and petty-bourgeois forces, and even to some extent by the SPD. But nowhere in Germany did the working class succeed in forming a fighting alliance with significant peasant forces in this period.

Rosa Luxemburg, one of the outstanding revolutionary leaders of the prewar SPD, while influenced on the peasant question by the earlier left-wing position defended by Kautsky, was also strongly affected by her background in the Polish and Russian Social Democratic movements.

Luxemburg recognized the peasantry as a revolutionary force in the tsarist empire, but only for carrying out the bourgeois-democratic revolutionary tasks that were posed in backward Russia in the struggle against absolutism and feudal landlordism. Speaking at the 1907 congress of the Russian Social Democratic Labor Party, she drew a sharp distinction in this respect between Russia and Germany.

"The peasantry ... constitutes an objectively revolutionary factor in our [Russian] revolution," Luxemburg said, "to the degree that, by sharply placing on the revolutionary agenda the question of an agrarian revolution, it poses a question that cannot be resolved within the framework of bourgeois society and that, by its very nature, goes beyond the limits of that society. It may very well be that if the revolutionary wave recedes and the agrarian question is finally settled in some manner consistent with bourgeois private property, wide layers of the peasantry will be transformed into an openly reactionary petty-bourgeois force."[9]

Luxemburg's Polish party, the SDKPiL, despite its recognition of the peasants' revolutionary role in the tsarist empire, did not share the Bolsheviks' strategic orientation toward a worker-peasant alliance in Russia and Poland. While favoring an alliance with the peasantry, the SDKPiL rejected the Bolsheviks' formula for the alignment of class forces in a provisional revolutionary government — the "revolutionary democratic dictatorship of the proletariat and the peasantry." Instead, the Polish party called in Russia and Poland for "the dictatorship of the proletariat supported by the peasantry."[10] Characteristic of this out-look was Leo Jogiches's statement to the 1908 SDKPiL congress that "when the proletariat comes to try and exploit the achievements of the revolution, its allies — the peasantry — will certainly turn against it . . . the political make-up of the peasantry disbars it from any active or in-dependent role and prevents it from achieving its own class represen-tation. . . . By nature it is bourgeois and shows its reactionary essence clearly in certain fields. . . . That is why the proposition before the con-gress speaks of the dictatorship of the proletariat alone *supported* by the peasantry. . . . The peasantry must assist the proletariat, not the proletariat the peasantry in the achievement of the latter's wishes."[11]

Luxemburg did not consider the question of the worker-peasant al-liance to be of strategic importance in industrial Germany, where she centered her activity after the defeat of the 1905-7 revolution in Russia and tsarist-occupied Poland. Right up to the November 1918 revolu-tion, the Luxemburg current remained largely within the framework of the limited and passive policy of the traditional SPD left wing.

Peasants and the November 1918 Revolution

The outbreak of the World War threw the German countryside into upheaval. Masses of peasants and agricultural laborers were torn from their work and thrust into the army; by the war's end more than half the male agricultural work force had been conscripted. Supplies of necessary fertilizer were cut in half, and tools, machinery, and other essential materials were unobtainable. Crop production fell sharply and by 1918 was down to only 45 percent of its prewar level. A dispro-portionate number of peasants were drafted and killed at the front, and among family members still at home hunger and deprivation, while less severe than in the cities, still raised mortality rates by a third.[12]

As hunger spread across Germany, government controls kept the prices of farm products low, while industrial goods the peasants needed soared in price, if they were available at all. Government offi-cials, who patrolled the countryside to requisition food and force tax payments, became the object of fierce hatred. Toward the end of the war, there was even talk in some areas of dividing the estates "like the Russians."[13]

Under these conditions, there was strong hostility to the war in the countryside just as in the cities. Moreover, for the millions of peasants and farm workers in the army, the war broke down barriers isolating them from urban workers and ultimately united peasants and workers in the army in common action to bring the slaughter to an end.

Because of this unity, the imperial government was not able in November 1918 to use rank-and-file soldiers anywhere against the revolutionary upsurge, and the revolution triumphed almost unopposed.

In Bavaria, top figures of the Peasants' League helped lead the mass movement. But victory came so quickly that even in Bavaria the rural population took no part in the overturn. The response to the revolution in the countryside differed from area to area and among the various layers within the peasantry. The big majority of peasants welcomed the return of peace. They felt no stake in defending the imperial regime, which was discredited by its identification with the war. Many were positive toward the republic and hoped that the new SPD-USPD government in Berlin would better serve their interests as toilers.[14]

Noticeably absent from the initial actions of the new government, however, were measures to benefit the small and middle peasantry. The abrogation — on paper — of the law on domestic servants was not accompanied by any other measures against the great landholders or other exploiters of the peasants.

Instead, on November 12, the new government announced its goals to be to "safeguard law and order in the countryside and the uninterrupted continuation of rural production," pledging to oppose all "arbitrary interference with property relationships." Moreover, it said it had reached an agreement with "the competent organizations of German agriculture" — the Farmers' League and other organizations of the junkers and rich peasants — to strive for these aims through the formation of "peasant councils" composed of all layers of the rural population. This provision provided cover for the formation of counterrevolutionary "peasant guards" that were later used against the revolution. The "peasant councils" were to be made up one-half of "independent farmers" and one-half of "workers and nonagricultural rural inhabitants"; the latter provision allowed petty-bourgeois professionals in the towns to occupy council seats and join with rich farmers to dominate these bodies. The Central Committee of the peasant councils was not to be elected but appointed by the right-wing farmers' organizations.[15]

While this policy was similar to that pursued by the SPD leadership to strengthen the procapitalist wing in the urban councils of workers and soldiers, it was more successful in the countryside. A Bavarian study showed that estate owners and rich peasants won disproportionate representation in the peasant councils, while mayors, civil servants, teachers, and other petty-bourgeois village inhabitants took over at least a quarter of the local council seats and about half the chairmanships of regional coordinating bodies.[16] Across Germany the pattern was similar.

The Spartacists' *Rote Fahne* denounced these bodies on December 1 as "junker councils." It called for their replacement by councils elected by small peasants and agricultural workers alone and for democratic election of their coordinating body.[17]

In March 1919, *Rote Fahne*'s position was taken up by Lenin in a report to the First Congress of the Communist International. Lenin agreed with *Rote Fahne* that it was "the bourgeoisie and their lackeys," the SPD leaders, who had raised the slogan of peasant councils, which was formulated so as to encompass the exploiters as well as the exploited. *Rote Fahne*, on the other hand, was "quite properly supporting Soviets of farm labourers and poor peasants." Lenin, however, considered that in the four months since the *Rote Fahne* article the German party had not given this course toward the exploited rural producers sufficient centrality in its political work. "Very little is being done to spread the Soviet system in the countryside," Lenin warned. "In this, perhaps, lies the real and quite serious danger threatening the . . . German proletariat."[18]

Although the Spartacists undertook no systematic work among peasants in the first months of the revolution, initiatives that were taken on a local level achieved some gains. Several local workers' and soldiers' councils, outraged that the peasants' councils were being bureaucratically organized by government authorities, took over this task and drove out the large landowners. In some cases, workers' and soldiers' councils won better working conditions for agricultural workers.[19]

It was in Bavaria that the revolutionary movement among peasants developed furthest. Its strength was rooted in the predominance of small and middle peasants there and in their strong traditions of antifeudal and democratic struggle. The junker-dominated Farmers' League had never gained more than a weak foothold in Bavaria. The dominant agrarian organization, with 170,000 members in 1918, was the Bavarian Peasants' Association (Bayerischer Bauernverein). Closely linked with the Catholic Church and the Center Party, its stated goal was to maintain a Christian, patriotic, and economically strong peasantry. Among its rivals, however, was the smaller, but more radical Bavarian Peasants' League, which arose in the economic crisis of the 1890s to provide an alternative to the locally dominant Center Party. The Peasants' League's program was antifeudal, pacifist, and protectionist. Primarily an electoral organization, it gained 70,000 votes in 1907 and won six seats in the Bavarian assembly.

When war broke out in 1914, the Peasants' League stood aside from the government's chauvinist campaign. It continued to oppose government policies during the war, calling for democratic reforms and measures to aid smaller peasants and defending the rights of rank-and-file soldiers. As the war crisis deepened, its course radicalized, and in mid-1918 its main leader, Ludwig Gandorfer, declared his outright opposition to the war, hinting in veiled language that the soldiers should overthrow the existing system.[20]

The overwhelming majority of the Bavarian peasant population welcomed the revolution in November 1918. Prorevolutionary feeling varied by region and was strongest in Lower (southern) Bavaria, the area close to Munich and a Peasants' League stronghold. The Peasants' League leadership joined the SPD and USPD in the Bavarian coalition government headed by USPD leader Kurt Eisner.

Peasant councils were organized across Bavaria, encompassing 90 percent of the rural communities by early 1919. The Eisner government instructed local town officials, who dated from the former royal administration, to take the organization of peasant councils in hand. The monarchist Peasants' Association gained control over many peasants' councils. Nonetheless, the Peasants' League was predominant in the councils in much of Bavaria; in some areas, the SPD was also a factor. The very existence of these councils, their efforts to get action on key peasant demands, and the competition among the various parties to gain control over them reflected the political ferment among the Bavarian peasantry.

Regional peasants' councils were established, as well as a Central Peasants' Council for Bavaria. Ludwig Gandorfer died in an accident a few days after the November revolution. His brother Karl then assumed leadership of the Peasants' League and represented it in the government, and it was Karl Gandorfer who chose the members of the Central Peasants' Council.

When the SPD pressed in late 1918 to end the formal sovereignty of the Bavarian councils and revert to conventional bourgeois parliamentary rule, the Peasants' League leadership supported this move. The league then scored major gains in the January 1919 Bavarian elections, more than doubling its representation in the Bavarian Assembly. It was also active at all levels of the peasants' councils, pressing for action on small peasants' longstanding grievances.

The Peasants' League went on to participate in the establishment of the short-lived Bavarian council republic in April 1919.

The November 1918 revolution in Germany did not unleash a peasant war in the countryside, as had happened in Russia the previous year. But the peasantry across Germany felt hatred and contempt toward the great landowners, whom they recognized as idlers who did not labor in their fields but drew profit from peasants' rent and labor. There was a movement by peasants to gain land. Many wished to take the estates and divide them up; others wanted to purchase portions of them. In either case this required abolition of the feudal law of entail, which blocked division of noble estates.

In Bavaria, where this movement was strongest, most peasant councils attempted to act on the land question, and there were some similar actions in other regions. But they ran into organized opposition from the ruling classes and gained no support from the new government. They also found no sympathy from revolutionary currents in the workers' movement, who counterposed socialization of agriculture to dividing up the estates. In Bavaria, Eisner of the USPD declared his support for the peasants' demands for land, but the government he headed failed to act on the question. In these unfavorable conditions, the peasants' efforts to gain land were rapidly blocked.[21]

Government spokesmen justified this hostile stance toward the peasantry with references to alleged proletarian principles. The Prussian minister of agriculture, Adolf Hofer, a USPD member, claimed that division of large estates "is diametrically opposed to our socialist ideals," and could "not be undertaken in the foreseeable future for practical and technical reasons."[22] SPD leader Otto Braun explained that "the destruction of the large landholdings and their division into many peasant holdings that is now being demanded so vigorously" was impossible, because it would lead to a reduction in agricultural production.[23]

Karl Kautsky argued similarly in a lengthy pamphlet, *Die Sozialisierung der Landwirtschaft* (The socialization of agriculture): "The revolution in the cities did not pass the workers in the countryside by without a trace. Unspeakable havoc would be caused if they were seized by strike fever or, even more, if they were to attempt socialization through direct action, by dividing the large estates among themselves, which could not take place without destruction and plunder.... Socialization must certainly not follow the Bolshevik model. The Bolsheviks erected a strict dictatorship in the cities and gave the peasants a free hand to ravage at will."[24]

As it became clear that the SPD-USPD government would do nothing to change social and property relationships in the countryside, enthusiasm for the revolution ebbed among exploited peasants. The landlords and their allies regained firm control in the villages. Many peasants became intimidated, apathetic, or even actively turned against the revolution. Counterrevolutionary forces sometimes succeeded in organizing blockades of food shipments to cities where the revolutionary workers' movement was strong or enlisted peasants in counterrevolutionary military units sent into those cities.

In the months following the revolution, a strong farm workers' movement also emerged, especially in Prussia, and continued to grow even after the workers' defeats of early 1919. The two unions of farm workers increased their membership in one year from only 17,000 before the revolution to more than 680,000.[25] In mid-1919 they launched powerful strikes for better social conditions, and in many districts, particularly in the Prussian province of Pomerania in northeast Germany, a state of siege was declared and troops were sent against them.[26]

Writing in July 1919, during the farm workers' mobilization, KPD leader August Thalheimer noted that "the rural population has so far been the last great reservoir of the counterrevolution, both through its passivity and through its active participation in counterrevolutionary actions and organizations." But the strike movement of farm workers had now broken the political calm of the countryside, Thalheimer said, and the advancing economic crisis would soon weaken the junkers' grip on the small peasants, as well.[27]

This upsurge occurred, however, at a time when the peasants' movement had been repulsed, and the industrial proletariat had not yet recovered from its defeat in the civil war of early 1919. The possibilities opened by this struggle for an alliance of farm workers, small peasants, and urban proletarians were not achieved.

Although their own procapitalist policies were largely responsible for the peasants' alienation from the workers' movement, the SPD and USPD leaders nonetheless demagogically sought to portray the peasantry as an inherently conservative brake on what the working class could accomplish. They argued that peasant opposition was too deep to be overcome and that any attempt to establish the power of the workers' and soldiers' councils was therefore doomed to defeat. One of the most forthright expositions of this argument was made by Otto Bauer, a central leader of the Social Democratic Party in German Austria, in the following extract from a series of articles written in April 1919, "Dictatorship of the Councils or Democracy?"

Peasants and a Workers' Dictatorship[28]
by Otto Bauer

All power to the councils. That is the Communists' basic demand. But which councils should seize power? Only the workers' and soldiers' councils? Or should power be shared with the peasant councils?

Only if the workers' and soldiers' councils alone grasp power would a real proletarian dictatorship be created. Only in this case would the proletariat alone rule, imposing its will on all other classes, not only the bourgeoisie, big and small, but also the peasantry. But is such a proletarian dictatorship possible? . . .

In the cities the workers' and soldiers' councils could certainly establish and maintain their supremacy; it would not be all that difficult to subjugate the bourgeoisie and petty bourgeoisie. But in the countryside a government of workers' and soldiers' councils would run into insurmountable difficulties. The peasants would refuse to obey the decrees. Rather than deliver food to the cities, they would bury it. They would counter forced requisitions with passive resistance and eventually venture even to armed opposition.

In provinces like Tirol and Styria, where there are far more peasants than industrial workers, the proletariat would certainly not be strong enough to quell the peasants' resistance. These provinces would break away from German Austria completely. Already they are cutting themselves off from us; already the slogan "break with Vienna" is very popular; already in Tirol and Carinthia the demand to break with German Austria and create an independent Tirolean and Carinthian republic is being raised.

If there were a government in Vienna composed only of workers' and soldiers' councils, one in which the peasants had absolutely no influence, then the peasant provinces of Tirol, Carinthia, Styria, and Upper Austria would secede from us. The power of the Viennese proletarian government would soon be limited to Lower Austria and the adjacent industrial regions in Upper Austria and Styria. But this small area could never feed its industrial population. As soon as the peasant provinces seceded and halted food supplies, the population would be delivered over to starvation. The attempt to set up a dictatorship of workers' and soldiers' councils in German Austria would end quickly and ignominiously in catastrophic famine.

In fact, such an undertaking has not been attempted anywhere, not even in Russia or Hungary. There, too, the revolution did not transfer power to councils of workers and soldiers, but rather to workers', soldiers', and peasants' councils. But that is no longer a true dictatorship of the proletariat. Instead it is a coalition of the proletariat with the peasantry against the bourgeoisie. The workers do not govern alone in these countries, but do so in league with the peasants. . . .

In Russia, the peasants were robbed of a large part of their land through the Emancipation Act of the 1860s. The peasant was freed from serfdom, but in exchange had to transfer a portion of the land that he worked to the lord of the manor. Thus the Russian peasants did not have enough land, and since then they have yearned to take the land of the nobility. The Russian Socialists took advantage of this. They won over the peasants by promising them the lord's land. That is how the Russian peasants became socialists. Those elected to the peasants' councils and to the congress of councils may be Bolsheviks or Socialist Revolutionaries, but in any case they are members of Socialist parties. . . .

The situation in German Austria is completely different. There are relatively few large landholdings, and they consist mostly of forest and grassland, not of arable land. Almost all the cultivated land in our country belongs not to large landowners, but to peasants. . . . Therefore, the peasant cannot hope to increase the size of his farm through a social revolution. . . .

The economic being of persons determines their political consciousness. The Russian peasant, whose farmland was too small for his extensive farming methods, was driven to become a revolutionary by his greed for the lord's land. The German-Austrian, who cannot hope to appreciably expand his farmland through a social revolution, is conservative. He farms much more intensively than the Russian peasant and has completely different concerns than that of a revolution in landed-property relations. He is angry about the flight of farm workers to the city, the *lack of people* on the land, and the growing *greed* of farm hands and dayworkers. So he ends up opposed to the workers. He wants high prices for grain, livestock, and milk and is furious at the workers, who demand lower prices. Thus he becomes an enemy of socialism. Therefore the majority of our peasants are conservative, hostile to workers, and antisocialist. In other words, they are Christian Socialists.[29]

So what would German-Austrian peasant councils look like? The peasants would send the same men to the peasant councils as they now elect to the municipal councils and agricultural cooperatives, that is, members of the Christian Socialist Party. And these peasant councils would elect to the congress of councils, the legislative body of the council republic, the same people as the peasants now send to the national assembly, that is, Christian Socialists once again. What would be the make up of the German-Austrian congress of councils? About half of its members would be Socialist representatives of the workers' councils, the other half would be Christian Socialist representatives of the peasant councils. In other words, the congress of councils would look much like the present national assembly, minus only the few Christian Socialist and German Nationalist representatives from the cities. But that really would not change much. In German Austria a council dictatorship certainly would not be an instrument for fundamental reorganization as in Russia or Hungary. Those people who think that a council dictatorship in German Austria would work just as in Russia or Hungary have forgotten a basic principle of Karl Marx, that is, the effectiveness of any governmental form depends upon the relationship of class forces. . . . □

Some currents in the revolutionary wing of the German workers' movement agreed with Bauer that it was impossible to forge an alliance with significant peasant forces in Germany and Austria. Characteristic of their outlook was Paul Frölich's pamphlet, *Der Weg zum Sozialismus* (The road to socialism), published in late January 1919 by the Hamburg branch of the KPD, a branch that came from the former IKD. After describing the revolutionary layer of poor peasants that existed in Russia, Frölich's pamphlet continued as follows.

The German Peasantry and the Revolution[30]
by Paul Frölich

In Germany this revolutionary layer was missing. The migration of farm workers from eastern Prussia [*Sachsengängerei*] has blocked the emergence of a strong rural proletariat in our country. Even if the victorious revolution wins over the existing rural proletarians, no revolutionary spirit can be detected among them, and they are also much too weak to secure the revolution in the countryside. That applies even for those regions of Germany in which the junkers' large holdings predominate. These areas have largely been separated from Germany by the revolution in the east. Actually, large landholdings still predominate only in old Prussia, Pomerania, and Mecklenburg. In the remaining regions it is not strong enough to leave its mark on agriculture.

The dissatisfied small peasant does not constitute a strong class in Germany either. There is no perspective for satisfying his hunger for land, because smashing the large landholdings in Germany in order to create a class of prosperous peasants is out of the question. Agrarian conditions are far too developed. The prosperous peasant is the predominant type in our agriculture. In German agriculture everyone who owns property, large or small, is outspokenly counterrevolutionary.

Although we need have no particular fear of a German *Vendée*, we do have to count on a determined passive resistance in the countryside against the revolution. The peasants, like the large landowners, will try to block food supplies to the big cities in order to starve out the revolution. Furthermore, an impairment of our transportation system can seriously endanger food supplies to the big cities. One of the first measures of the victorious revolution will be the resettlement of large numbers of industrial proletarians in the countryside to ease the burden on the urban labor market as well as the urban food market, to supply agriculture with necessary skilled labor, and to suppress the counterrevolution in the countryside. □

Unlike Frölich, the central leadership of the Spartacus current did not write off the peasantry as a reactionary bloc. Despite their serious political unclarity and strategic inadequacies in this regard, the Spartacists did aim to win the small peasants to an alliance with farm workers and the industrial proletariat. But they maintained their long-standing hostility to any policy that would meet the small peasants' land hunger. Their reasoning was most clearly explained by Rosa Luxemburg in her criticism of the land policy applied by the Bolsheviks in the Russian revolution, composed as part of her essay "The Russian Revolution."

The Bolsheviks' decree on land, adopted by the Soviet congress immediately following the October revolution, had nationalized the land without compensation to the former landlords. The landed estates were turned over to local peasants' land committees and peasants' soviets to be allocated according to the guidelines established by the All-Russian Soviet of Peasants' Deputies. According to these guidelines, lands where "high-level scientific farming" was practiced were to be converted intact into "model farms." The use of other lands was to be distributed to all peasants on an equal basis.[31]

Luxemburg wrote her analysis of Bolshevik land policy while still in prison in the early autumn of 1918, when she lacked access to reliable information on Russian conditions. It is an uncompleted draft, no more than rough notes in some places. Nonetheless, it echoes the viewpoint of her report to the 1907 RSDLP congress that where small peasants gain land as individual family units, they will tend to harden into a reactionary layer — the viewpoint that set her current's policy for both the Russian and German revolutions. The following is the portion of her draft essay, "The Russian Revolution," on the agrarian question.

The Bolshevik Land Policy[32]
by Rosa Luxemburg

The Bolsheviks are the historic heirs of the English Levellers and the French Jacobins.[33] But the concrete task they inherited in the Russian revolution after taking power was incomparably more difficult than that of their historical predecessors.[34] Certainly the slogan of direct, immediate seizure and division of the land by the peasants was the shortest, simplest, most clear-cut solution to accomplish two different things: to smash the large estates and to immediately bind the peasants to the revolutionary government. As a political measure to reinforce the proletarian, socialist government this was an excellent tactic. But unfortunately it was a two-sided one, and its flip side was that the direct seizure of the land by the peasants has nothing in common with socialist cultivation.

The socialist transformation of the economy presupposes two things with respect to agrarian relations. First is the nationalization specifically of the large estates, as the technically most advanced concentrations of the methods and means of agrarian production, which alone can be the starting point of the socialist economic order in the countryside. Of course there is no need to take away the small peasant's plot. He can be safely left to be won over voluntarily by the advantages of social production, first to cooperative integration and ultimately to incorporation into the collective socialist enterprise. Every socialist economic reform in the countryside therefore must obviously begin with the large and medium-sized holdings. Here property rights must be transferred to the nation, or — which is the same with a socialist government — to the state. For only in this way is it possible to organize agricultural production according to a coherent, broad, socialist viewpoint.

Second, however, one of the preconditions to this transformation is that the separation of agriculture and industry, that characteristic feature of bourgeois society, be abolished, giving way to their mutual penetration and fusion and to the comprehensive fashioning of both agrarian and industrial production according to a unified vision. However management may take place in individual cases, whether through municipal districts, as some suggest, or from the center of government, in any case a precondition for this is a reform, initiated and carried out from the center in a uniform manner, and, as its precondition, the nationalization of the land. Nationalization of the large and medium-sized land holdings and unification of industry and agriculture: these are two basic starting points of any socialist economic reform, without which there is no socialism.

But if the Soviet government in Russia has not carried out these immense reforms, who can reproach them? It would be a sorry jest to demand or expect that in the short span of their rule, amidst the raging maelstrom of battles within and without, beset on all sides by countless enemies and resistance, Lenin and his comrades should solve or even tackle one of the most difficult, yes, we can safely say, *the* most difficult task of the socialist transformation. Once we have come to power, even under the best of conditions, we too in the West will break a few teeth on this hard nut before we are over the worst of the thousand complicated difficulties of this gigantic undertaking.

When a socialist government comes to power, however, at all costs it must do one thing: take measures that lead toward these basic preconditions for a later socialist reform of agrarian relations. At the very least it must avoid anything that blocks the path to such measures.

Now the slogan that the Bolsheviks raised — for the peasants to immediately seize possession of and divide up the land — necessarily led in the opposite direction. Not only is it not a socialist measure, but it cuts off the path to such measures and heaps up insurmountable obstacles to transforming agrarian relations in a socialist manner.

When the peasants seized possession of landed property in accordance with Lenin and his friends' brief and clear-cut slogan, "Go and take the land!", it led simply to the sudden, chaotic transformation of the large estates into peasant holdings. What was created was not social property but new private property, and this, moreover, by breaking up the large holdings into middle and small-sized holdings, by breaking up relatively advanced large enterprises into primitive small enterprises, which are worked by methods from the time of the pharoahs.

And as if that were not enough, through this measure and the chaotic, purely arbitrary way it was carried out, the disparities in property in the countryside were not abolished, but rather sharpened. Although the Bolsheviks called upon the peasantry to build peasant committees in order to make taking possession of the aristocrats' estates somehow a collective action, it is clear that this general advice was not able to change the actual practice and the real relationship of forces in the countryside. With or without committees, the rich peasants and profiteers that make up the village bourgeoisie and control the real local power in every Russian village have become the main beneficiaries of the agrarian reform. Sight unseen, it is obvious that the result of dividing up the land is not to abolish the social and economic inequalities among the peasants, but rather to increase them. Class differences have become sharper. But this shift of power has taken place to the decisive *disadvantage* of proletarian and socialist interests.

Lenin's speech on the necessity of centralizing industry, nationalizing the banks, commerce, and industry. Why not the land? Here just the opposite — decentralization and private property.

Before the revolution Lenin's own agrarian program was different. The demand taken over from the much-reviled Socialist Revolutionaries, or, more accurately, from the spontaneous movement of the peasantry.

In order to introduce socialist principles into agrarian relations, the Soviet government has now tried to create agrarian communes with proletarians — mostly unemployed urban elements. However, it is easy to guess in advance that the results of these efforts, measured against the totality of agrarian relations, must remain insignificantly tiny and do not even enter into consideration in judging the question.[35] (After the most appropriate starting point for the socialist economy, the great estates, were broken up into small landholdings, now they want to build communist model enterprises from small beginnings.) Under present circumstances, these communes can only claim to be experiments, not a comprehensive social reform.

Previously a socialist reform in the countryside confronted at most the opposition of a small class of noble and capitalist large landholders and a small minority of the rich village bourgeoisie. Their expropriation by the revolutionary popular masses is child's play. Now, after "taking possession," any socialist nationalization of agriculture is confronted by an enormously swollen and strengthened mass of propertied peasants, who will defend their newly acquired property tooth and nail against any socialist assaults. Now the question of the future socialization of agriculture, and therefore of production as a whole in Russia, has become a matter of antagonism and struggle between the urban proletariat and the peasant masses.

How sharp this antagonism has already become is shown by the peasants' boycott of the cities, holding back food supplies from them in order to engage in profiteering, just like the Prussian junkers. The French peasant with his little plot became the most valiant defender of the Great French Revolution, which had given him land confiscated from emigrants. As Napoleon's soldier, he carried France's flag to victory, crossing all of Europe and smashing feudalism in one country after another. Lenin and his friends may have expected their agrarian slogan to have a similar effect. Nonetheless, the Russian peasant, once he had his hands on the land, did not dream of defending Russia and the revolution to which he owes the land. He clamped onto his new property and abandoned the revolution to its enemies, the state to ruin, and the urban population to hunger.

The Leninist agrarian reform created a new and powerful social layer of enemies in the countryside, whose opposition will be much more dangerous and tenacious than was that of the aristocratic large landholders. □

A few weeks before Luxemburg's release from jail, on October 7, 1918, a secret Spartacus conference published a brief program for the approaching revolution, which addressed the agrarian question. Its statement called for "expropriation of all large and middle-sized landholdings, and transfer of production management to delegates of the farm workers and the small peasants."[36]

The Spartacists said more on their agrarian program two months later in their programmatic pamphlet, *What the Spartacus League Wants*, published above in chapter 3. With regard to agriculture, they demanded "expropriation of the land of all large and middle-sized agricultural enterprises; formation of socialist agricultural cooperatives with a unified central administration for the whole country; small peasants' enterprises to remain the property of their owners until they voluntarily decide to join the socialist cooperatives." Just as in the earlier statement, the middle peasants were grouped with the junkers and rich peasants among those identified for expropriation.

Statements by Spartacus leaders from that period frequently attempted to assess the mood of the peasantry as a whole as an undifferentiated class, rather than a series of social layers with different and often conflicting class interests. Such a failure to distinguish between exploited and exploiting layers in the countryside often led to one-sided and impressionistic conclusions, overlooking prospects for winning layers of the peasants to the proletarian struggle. In a speech printed above, for example, Karl Liebknecht referred to the peasant councils as "councils of that layer of the population that has been among the most backward and bitter enemies of the proletariat, and which even today remains the most vehement foe of the rural proletariat."[37]

With reference to Luxemburg's criticisms of the Bolsheviks' land policy, Karl Radek's diary of the German revolution reported in the excerpt printed above in chapter 4 that by December 1918 she "had also recognized that it was wrong to oppose any division of the landed estates." No other record exists of Luxemburg's final position on this question. Her report to the KPD's December 1918 congress on the party program, however, maintained the core of her previous position, combining it with an urgent appeal to the new party to turn its face to the countryside. The following is a portion of her report.

Take the Class Struggle to the Countryside[38]
by Rosa Luxemburg

I would also like to remind you here of some of the deficiencies of the German revolution that were not overcome in the first stage. Instead, unfortunately, they clearly show that we are not yet far enough along to guarantee the victory of socialism by overturning the government. I have tried to show that the November 9 revolution was mainly a political revolution, which must become one that is primarily economic. But it was also only an urban revolution. The countryside remains virtually unaffected. It would be idiocy to think that socialism can be realized without agriculture. From the standpoint of a socialist economy, industry cannot be transformed at all unless it is directly and integrally connected with an agriculture that has been reorganized along socialist lines. The most important concept in the socialist economic system is the elimination of the contradiction and separation between city and countryside. This separation, this contradiction, this opposition, is an exclusively capitalist phenomenon, and the socialist standpoint indicates that it must be eliminated immediately. If we are serious about socialist reconstruction, we have to pay as much attention to the countryside as we do to the industrial centers, and in this respect I am afraid we are not even at the beginning of the beginning.

We must take this matter seriously not only because there can be no socialization without agriculture, but also because after we have taken stock of all the reserves which the counterrevolution can use against us, there is an important one which we have left out: the peasantry. Precisely because it has not yet been touched by the revolution, it remains a reserve force for the counterrevolutionary bourgeoisie. And the first thing the bourgeoisie will do when the flames of socialist strikes are licking at their heels is to mobilize the peasantry, who are the most fanatical supporters of private property. There is no way to counteract this dangerous counterrevolutionary force other than to carry the class struggle to the countryside and mobilize the landless proletariat and the small peasants against the peasantry. (*Shouts of "Bravo!" Applause*) □

Contributions to the discussion of Luxemburg's report, excerpted below, showed the range of views in the young German Communist movement on the peasant question, including some that were trying to go beyond the limitations of the previous positions of the SPD's left wing.

Congress Debate on the Peasantry[39]

Ludwig Bäumer (Bremen): . . . Comrades, if we are opposed to private property, opposed to private ownership, if the Communist Party promotes the expropriation of private property and private ownership, then we must not stop before the small landholder. If we are to expropriate, then it must be a radical expropriation. To expropriate large holdings and permit a certain number of small capitalists to survive is compromising with capitalism, which in the end will and must turn against us. Our socialism will then be compromised with capitalism. (*"Very true!"*) . . .

Eugen Leviné (Berlin): Now we come to another difference, which is how to resolve the agrarian question. It is a difference insofar as we cannot say that we agree with what is set out in the program. The question is exceptionally complicated and it would therefore be best to elect a separate agrarian commission. Comrade Luxemburg correctly emphasized how important it is for the revolution to also include the purely proletarian forces in the countryside. We must bring the rural working population over to our side if we want to organize the reconstruction, and in order to do this we must carry the class struggle into the countryside. Here we are told that the large and middle-sized farms should be expropriated, but at the same time that small owners may keep their property until they voluntarily join the socialist society.

I agree with the comrade from the former Communist Party [IKD], who said that everything must be socialized, everything must be expropriated, but that small property up to a certain size must be left to its owners for a transitional period. The ownership of agricultural land is quite another question. We have just learned from the Russian experience that the workers' power forced the bourgeoisie to submit to the socialization of industry. However, it then also became necessary to socialize agriculture on the basis that land ceased to be private property, could no longer be sold or inherited, and could be given only to individuals to cultivate; and rural wage labor was not allowed.

So the key question is: Can we apply these principles to Germany? It will be said that they had the right conditions in Russia because they had the communist peasants' communities, the so-called *mir*,[40] whereas we do not have anything like that in Germany. However, we do see in Germany an extraordinarily rapid spread of discontent against profiteering off the land. Moreover, workers who live in rural communities, many of whom are agricultural laborers, are joining the so-called homestead movement, the land reform movement,[41] and so forth, and this stems from dissatisfaction over the failure to solve the agrarian question. We also know that peasants in Pomerania are planning to divide up the land. If we want to prevent it from being divided up chaotically, which would lead only to the creation of a new layer of rich peasants, a new set of large enterprises, we must have a clear program to present to the public. We want to win the small peasants to our side, not by adapting to their capitalist private-property aspirations, but by giving them more land to till — precisely by dividing up the land of the large landowners and rich peasants.

Thus, I would strongly advise you to separate out this question from all the rest and form a special agrarian commission that can be responsible for gathering information as quickly as possible and clarifying the questions as competently as possible. . . .

Ernst Meyer (Berlin): . . . Since the first days of the revolution we have been accused of demanding the dictatorship of a minority. Nothing could be more false than this accusation. On the contrary, we must state what we want very sharply — we want rule by the majority, a dictatorship of the majority. As a result of Germany's particular economic and social relations, we are still a long way from this goal. On the one hand we have a strongly developed industry with a highly advanced proletariat, but on the other hand there are still large areas of the nation, namely the countryside, that do not yet have the self-confidence of the industrial proletariat. For this reason we must try to encompass these layers in our thinking.

I recently had the opportunity to visit several areas east of the Elbe River, and I was shocked at the openly counterrevolutionary atmosphere that is widespread there, permeating even into wide layers of the petty bourgeoisie. In train cars, cafés, and restaurants there is open talk of how the Berliners must be shown a thing or two, and that everything that was overturned on November 9 must be restored to its old glory. I was almost even more shocked by the fact that the workers in the cities themselves did not yet understand what is necessary in this situation. Therefore we must begin agitating with full force not only in the countryside, but also in the small and middle-sized towns. . . .

Karl Liebknecht: . . . One comrade has charged that we are making an exception of the peasantry. Comrades, remember that we are talking about immediate economic demands. We are not talking about creating the whole socialist system, but only about initial measures designed to give the proletariat the power to create socialism, to prepare the way for its creation. In view of that, we must restrict ourselves to the initial demands, whose implementation is what we are proposing as our program. That imposes a certain limitation. A second reason for imposing such a limitation is that certain sectors of the population are at the moment not yet ready to work for thoroughgoing socialization. We want to win them over and develop them as we work gradually toward socialization. That job is particularly difficult among small peasants.

Someone else said that we are making an error on precisely this point by not also putting pressure on the small peasants right away, confiscating their property, and giving them only the right to cultivate the land. Comrades, this is a transitional measure that is being proposed to you here. The idea behind it is that the cooperative system in the countryside ought to be developed along socialist lines and that by developing such socialist agricultural co-ops, the small peasants will come to see for themselves, little by little, the merit of such institutions and in that way be convinced to socialize their property as well. Basically, small peasants are nothing but proletarians in disguise; they just have a special psychology due to the fact that they appear to own property. . . .   □

The KPD Develops an Agrarian Policy

Although the Bolshevik leadership could obtain only the scantiest information on KPD activity in the countryside, they considered this a decisive arena of work for the German revolutionary proletariat. This was shown in their response to news of the establishment of the revolutionary workers' and peasants' government in Bavaria in April 1919.[42] When fragmentary radio reports of these events reached Moscow, there was no way to contact the new government directly. Lenin therefore twice radioed Hungarian Communist Party leader Béla Kun asking that he forward greetings to Bavaria along with a request for information. "What is the position in Bavaria as regards the agrarian programme of the [Bavarian] Soviet Government?",[43] Lenin asked. On April 27 he sent a message to the Bavarian councils, which included the following questions: "Has use been made of the stocks of clothing and other items for immediate and extensive aid to the workers, and especially to the farm labourers and small peasants; have the capitalist factories and wealth in Munich and the capitalist farms in its environs been confiscated; have mortgage and rent payments by small peasants been cancelled; have the wages of farm labourers and unskilled workers been doubled or trebled? ... The most urgent and most extensive implementation of these and similar measures, coupled with the initiative of workers', farm labourers' and — acting apart from them — small peasants' councils, should strengthen your position. An emergency tax must be levied on the bourgeoisie, and an actual improvement effected in the condition of the workers, farm labourers and small peasants at once and at all costs."[44]

The impact of the January workers' defeat in Berlin, and the civil war that subsequently spread across Germany, prevented the KPD for many months from acting on its congress decision to develop educational work in the countryside. The discussion on the peasantry bore fruit, however, in July 1919, when the KPD published an agrarian program that marked a distinct advance over the previous position of the German revolutionary workers' movement.

In this program German Marxists committed themselves to assist the "small peasants" in defending and developing their farms. They defined small peasants as all those who do not employ outside labor power, or, if they do, "integrate it into the family's life and work." The program declared "The economic position of small peasants, as small peasants, must be improved through the all-sided assistance of socialist industry and trade. The small peasants must be freed from the tutelage of bureaucratic scribblers. The road must be opened for them to manage their own affairs. Finally, the attempts at small-peasant cooperatives must be expanded, so that the small peasant, step by step, may proceed to large-scale cooperative production." A number of practical measures were proposed to this end, including the nationalization of all mortgages and a permanent ban on foreclosures.[45]

That same month the KPD established a central agricultural commission and began the publication of *Der Pflug* (The plow), a weekly publication for farm workers and small peasants edited by Edwin Hoernle. That fall, the party sold and distributed large numbers of a pamphlet by Hoernle directed to working peasants.[46]

An even more significant advance followed with the adoption of "Theses on the Agrarian Question" by the Second Congress of the Communist International in 1920. These theses built on the lessons of the Russian revolution. They restored Marx and Engels's emphasis on the strategic importance of an alliance with the peasantry in the fight for power and countered the hostility to small peasants' demands prevalent in big sections of the workers' movement prior to 1917.

The small peasants will gain from the victory of the proletariat, the Second Congress theses stated, through deliverance from rent, sharecropping, mortgages, and the diverse forms of oppression by big landowners; by immediate aid from the proletarian state for their farms; and in many other ways. Middle peasants, who rely mainly on family labor and employ wage labor only on a limited and occasional basis, will also benefit immediately through the abolition of the rents and mortgages system.

The theses challenged the assumption that Marxists — especially in the more economically advanced countries of western Europe — could in no case favor distribution of land of the great estates to the small peasantry. While distribution of the land might not be as extensive in central and western Europe as it had been in the Russian revolution, the theses stated, it was certainly in order in some circumstances:

"However, in areas where vestiges of the medieval system and feudal obligations result in special forms of exploitation, where personal servitude or sharecropping or the like still exist, it may under certain circumstances be necessary to transfer to the peasants a portion of the land of the great estates.

"In countries and regions where large agricultural enterprises play a relatively limited role, but where on the other hand there are a large number of small peasant owners who are trying to obtain land, dividing up the land of the large landowners will prove to be the surest means of winning the peasantry to the revolution, whereas preserving the large estates is not of particular significance for provisioning the cities.

"The first and most important duty of the proletariat is to secure its lasting victory, come what may. The proletariat should not stop at a temporary reduction in production for the sake of the success of the revolution. The lasting stability of proletarian power can only be achieved by managing to preserve the neutrality of the middle peasantry and winning the support of the big majority, if not all, of the small peasantry."[47]

Notes

1. Hermann Weber, *Der Gründungsparteitag der KPD* (Frankfurt/Main: Europäische Verlagsanstalt, 1969), pp. 196-97.

2. The following are some of the places in the writings of Karl Marx and Frederick Engels where they presented aspects of their thinking on the peasant question:

Marx, "The Class Struggles in France," in Marx and Engels, *Collected Works* (New York: International Publishers, 1979), vol. 10, pp. 120-23;

Marx, "The Eighteenth Brumaire of Louis Bonaparte," ibid., vol. 11, pp. 189-92;

Marx, "Share-Cropping and Small-Scale Peasant Ownership," in Marx, *Capital* (New York: Vintage Books, 1981), vol. 3, pp. 938-50.

Engels, "Preface to *The Peasant War in Germany*," in Marx and Engels, *Collected Works*, vol. 2, pp. 158-65.

Marx, "First Outline of 'The Civil War in France,' " in Marx and Engels, *On the Paris Commune* (Moscow: Progress Publishers, 1971), pp. 157-61;

Marx, "The Conspectus of Bakunin's Book, 'State and Anarchy,' " in Marx, Engels, and V.I. Lenin, *Anarchism & Anarcho-Syndicalism* (New York: International Publishers, 1974), pp. 147-48;

Engels, "The Peasant Question in France and Germany," in Marx and Engels, *Selected Works* (Moscow: Progress Publishers, 1977), vol. 3, pp. 457-76.

3. Karl Marx and Frederick Engels, *Selected Works* (Moscow: Progress Publishers, 1977), vol. 3, p. 431.

4. Statistics from the 1907 agricultural census are cited in V.I. Lenin, *Collected Works* (hereinafter *CW*) (Moscow: Progress Publishers, 1974), vol. 16, pp. 432-38; vol. 40, pp. 300, 306, 308. Comparable figures from the 1925 census are found in David Abraham, *The Collapse of the Weimar Republic* (Princeton, NJ: Princeton University Press, 1981), p. 57.

5. Lenin, *CW*, vol. 40, p. 364.

6. Lenin, *CW*, vol. 19, p. 282.

7. Lenin, *CW*, vol. 19, p. 208.

8. The debate on opportunism in the SPD moved to center stage in 1894 when the opportunist current, headed by Georg von Vollmar and Eduard David, challenged the party's basic principles by leading the Bavarian SPD in voting in favor of the budget proposed by the royal Bavarian government. The controversy on the peasant question dominated the party's convention in Breslau the following year.

9. *Protokoly, Londonskiy s"ezd RSDRP, izdaniye tsentralnogo komiteta* (Paris, 1909), p. 322.

10. J.P. Nettl, *Rosa Luxemburg* (London: Oxford University Press, 1966), vol. 2, p. 566.

11. Ibid.

12. Wilhelm Mattes, *Die bayerischen Bauernräte* (Stuttgart: J.G. Cotta'sche Buchhandlung Nachf., 1921), pp. 51-52.

13. Ya.S. Drabkin, *Die Novemberrevolution 1918 in Deutschland* (Berlin: [GDR]: Deutscher Verlag der Wissenschaften, 1968), p. 73.

14. Arthur Rosenberg, *A History of the German Republic* (London: Methuen & Co., 1936), p. 128.

15. *Dokumente und Materialien zur Geschichte der deutschen Arbeiterbewegung* (Berlin [GDR]: Dietz Verlag, 1957), pp. 367-68, 481-83.

16. Mattes, *Bauernräte*, pp. 101, 103.

17. *Dokumente und Materialien*, pp. 519-21.

18. Lenin, *CW*, vol. 28, p. 473.

19. Drabkin, *Die Novemberrevolution*, pp. 399-400.

20. Mattes, *Bauernräte*, pp. 57-58.

21. Mattes, *Bauernräte*, pp. 133-54; Drabkin, *Die Novemberrevolution*, pp. 227-28, 400.

22. Drabkin, *Die Novemberrevolution*, p. 228.

23. Ibid., pp. 400-401.

24. Karl Kautsky, *Die Sozialisierung der Landwirtschaft* (Berlin: Paul Cassirer, 1921), p. 10.

25. John Bradshaw Holt, *German Agricultural Policy, 1918-1934* (Chapel Hill, N.C.: University of North Carolina Press, 1936), p. 28.

26. "Das Agrarprogramm der Kommunistischen Partei Deutschlands (Spartakusbund)," in *Die Internationale*, vol. 1, no. 7-8, July 19, 1919, p. 6. (Reprinted by the Verlag Neue Kritik in Frankfurt/Main, 1971.)

27. Ibid., pp. 8-9.

28. Excerpted from "Rätediktatur oder Demokratie?" in Otto Bauer, *Werkausgabe*, (Vienna: Europaverlag, 1976), vol. 2, pp. 138-43.

29. The Christian Socialist Party was the dominant political party of the Austrian bourgeoisie after 1918.

30. Paul Frölich, *Der Weg zum Sozialismus* (Hamburg: Verlag der Kommunistischen Arbeiterzeitung, 1919), p. 17.

31. The decree on land is printed in Lenin, *CW*, vol. 26, pp. 258-60.

32. Rosa Luxemburg, "Die russische Revolution," in *Gesammelte Werke* (Berlin [GDR]: Dietz Verlag, 1974), vol. 4, pp. 342-45. An English translation of the entire article is printed in Mary-Alice Waters, ed., *Rosa Luxemburg Speaks* (New York: Pathfinder Press, 1980), pp. 365-95.

33. The Levellers, those accused of wanting to "level men's estates," were a republican and democratic party in England during the revolution of 1642-60. Originating in 1645-46 among the radical Parliamentarians, the party put forward a program of social and economic reform, seeking suffrage for all male freeholders and annual or biennial sessions of Parliament. Their proposals were rejected by Parliament, and they were suppressed in 1649.

The Jacobins were a political association that provided much of the leadership and organization for the French revolution. Its members were drawn in the main from the revolutionary bourgeoisie and urban petty bourgeoisie; its leaders included Maximilian Robespierre, Jean-Paul Marat, and Georges Danton. During 1793-94, the most radical period of the revolution, the Jacobins encompassed 5,000 to 8,000 clubs with 500,000 members throughout France. The clubs raised supplies for the revolutionary army, policed local markets, and often replaced local officials. The Jacobin clubs declined as a political force with the overthrow of Robespierre in late 1794.

34. Marginal note by Luxemburg: "Meaning of the agrarian question. Already 1905. Then in the Third Duma the *right-wing* peasants! Peasant question and defense, army."

35. Marginal note by Luxemburg: "Grain monopoly with bonuses. *Now, post festum* [after the fact], they want to carry the class struggle into the village."

36. *Documente und Materialien*, p. 232.

37. From Liebknecht's speech, "The Hour of Socialism Is Now," printed in chapter 3 of the present work.

38. Weber, *Gründungsparteitag*, pp. 196-97.

39. Ibid., pp. 207-21.

40. The *mir* in prerevolutionary Russia was a community of peasant households that held land in common and redistributed it periodically among its members.

41. Faced with urban rebellion and millions of unemployed, recently demobilized soldiers, the SPD government issued the Land Settlement ordinance on January 19. On its face, the measure promised land to the unemployed and rural toilers at the expense of the large estates. However, the law provided that it was to be implemented by the large landowners themselves. Actually, the measure corresponded with imperial Germany's long-standing attempt to promote settlements of ethnic Germans in the eastern provinces and thus strengthen German claims to land largely inhabited by Poles. The bill subsequently adopted by the National Assembly thus won the support of parties ranging from the SPD to the Germany National People's Party, which represented the junkers. The law was never implemented. See John B. Holt, *German Agricultural Policy, 1918-1934* (Chapel Hill, N.C.: University of North Carolina Press, 1936) p. 40.

42. Documents on the Bavarian Council Republic and the council republic established at that time in Hungary will be contained in a future volume of the Monad Press series, *The Communist International in Lenin's Time*.

43. Lenin, *CW*, vol. 44, p. 208.

44. Ibid., vol. 29, pp. 325-26.

45. "Das Agrarprogramm der Kommunistischen Partei Deutschlands (Spartakusbund)," pp. 8-15.

46. Edwin Hoernle, *Bauer! Wo fehlt's? Ein ernstes Wort von Spartakus an die deutschen Kleinbauern!* (Peasant, what's gone wrong? A serious word by Spartacus to the German small peasant) (Berlin: *Rote Fahne,* 1919).

47. *Der zweite Kongress der Kommunistischen Internationale* (Hamburg: Verlag der Kommunistischen Internationale, 1921), p. 775-76. A different English translation of the entire resolution can be found in *Second Congress of the Communist International* (London: New Park Publications, 1977), vol. 2, pp. 286-295. A new translation of the resolution will be printed in a forthcoming volume of the Monad Press series, *The Communist International in Lenin's Time*.

For the draft of these theses written by Lenin, which differs in significant respects, see Lenin, *CW*, vol. 31, pp. 152-64.

Karl Liebknecht, Rosa Luxemburg.

-6-

January 1919: Civil War in Berlin

No sooner was the German Communist Party formed than it had to meet its most severe test. In early January the Ebert-Scheidemann government launched a well-prepared armed assault on the Berlin workers' movement. The KPD, still a weak and poorly coordinated force in Berlin of only three hundred members,[1] could not prevent the working class from suffering a serious defeat. Yet its efforts to organize the Berlin workers' resistance and its courageous stand against the assault helped unify Germany's revolutionary workers and laid the basis to win growing numbers of them to the Communist movement in subsequent months.

The failure of the government's December 24 attack on the People's Naval Division left it temporarily with almost no reliable troops in the Berlin area. The big majority of soldiers in the city had refused to stand by the government in a confrontation with the working class. Friedrich Ebert evacuated the Reich chancellery, the seat of government, in a move that was at least in part a provocation. Gen. Wilhelm Groener, head of the army, later testified that Ebert told him on December 24, "If the Liebknecht group uses this opportunity to seize control of the government, no one can stop them. But if they find nothing there ... they will have fired their cannon with a blank shell, and in a few days we will be in a position to set up our government somewhere else."[2]

The repercussions of the Christmas fighting forced Berlin City Commander Otto Wels, who was a prominent SPD leader, to resign, and the government was for the moment unable to install a permanent replacement. On December 29, however, it was able to deploy near Berlin the first detachments of a new armed force organized for use against the working class. These were the Freikorps (Free Corps): volunteer battalions recruited privately by right-wing officers. The declared goal of the Friekorps was to defend Germany's eastern borders, challenged by the Polish minority within Germany that was clamoring

Footnotes to this chapter begin on page 291.

for union with the new Polish state, and to suppress Bolshevik-inspired unrest. During the first week of January, units containing many thousands of reactionary soldiers of fortune were integrated into the army's forces around Berlin. Meanwhile a veritable flood of right-wing propaganda stepped up the witch-hunt against the revolutionary movement.

The initial blow in the government offensive was directed against Emil Eichhorn, a USPD member and Berlin's chief of police. Appointed following the workers' November 9 victory, Eichhorn had organized a new police force of 2,000 Socialist workers and soldiers. On January 1 the SPD opened up in *Vorwärts* a campaign of charges against Eichhorn. On January 4 the Prussian government, headed by SPD member Paul Hirsch, dismissed Eichhorn from office, replacing him with an SPD member, Eugen Ernst. Ebert's cabinet had obviously orchestrated this move. Given Eichhorn's enormous popularity among Berlin workers, this move could be counted on to provoke resistance. Later, on January 16, Ernst himself explained the provocative nature of this action to a reporter: "The Spartacus people could not succeed because through our preparations we compelled them to strike prematurely. They had to make their move before they wanted to, and we were therefore in a position to counter them."[3]

The Communist Party's central leaders were aware of the dangers of a premature confrontation with the government, in which the vanguard of the working class could be isolated and slaughtered. In a leaflet published in the first days of January the KPD explained that "if Berlin workers were today to disperse the national assembly and throw the Ebert-Scheidemann people into prison, while the workers of the Ruhr and Upper Silesia and the rural workers of Germany east of the Elbe remained inactive, the capitalists would be able tomorrow to subdue Berlin through hunger."[4] But such warnings were insufficient to counter the illusions in the party's own ranks that the government could be successfully ousted in the near future by a Berlin uprising. These illusions were also strong among big layers of militant Berlin workers outside the party.

The KPD Central Committee met January 4 to discuss how to resist the move to oust Eichhorn. "All present agreed that it would be senseless to strive for 'government,'" a 1920 KPD account reported. "At that point, a government based on the proletariat would have lasted two weeks and no longer." The KPD's leaders agreed to raise limited demands that did not "in themselves imply the government's overthrow." This minimal program "had to be carried through with maximum energy . . . a colossal act of revolutionary will."[5]

The Revolutionary Shop Stewards and the Berlin USPD leadership also favored an energetic response, and they met with KPD leaders on January 4 to decide on a common course. It was agreed to support Eichhorn in his refusal to surrender his post. A joint leaflet distributed the next morning pointed out, "The blow against the Berlin police force is aimed at the entire German proletariat, the entire German revolution.... Come out in a massive demonstration! Show your power to the rulers.... Down with the tyranny of Ebert-Scheidemann, Hirsch, and Ernst!"[6]

The same morning, the following editorial in *Rote Fahne* explained the move against Eichhorn and proposed slogans for the action that day.

The Counterrevolution's Latest Blow[7]

Not a day passes without an attack by the Ebert government. This time it is aimed at Police Chief Eichhorn. He and his administration have long been a thorn in the side of the Scheidemann people. Now they have decided to bring him down forthwith.

The pretext is a long list of every conceivable sin: failure to file daily reports; arrest of a police official, who by the way was suspected of homicide; all sorts of "unauthorized actions"; distributing weapons to the Schwartzkopff workers; receiving the notorious "Russian money"; and so forth. The worst part comes at the end of *Vorwärts'* prosecutor's brief: "Eichhorn's Role on the Night of December 9," and "The Smear Campaign Against Wels." According to *Vorwärts*, on the night of December 9 Eichhorn alerted all stations to the advance of "allegedly counterrevolutionary troops" on Berlin.[8] Worse, Eichhorn permitted "an unbelievable smear campaign against Wels" to be carried on within the police force.

The issue is clear. Ebert-Scheidemann-Wels found Eichhorn to be a big problem. He disrupted their intrigues and conspiracies. The police force was trying to be a revolutionary police force, rather than actively or passively serving the counterrevolution.

It is easy to understand the Ebert people's anguish. Under the old regime, police headquarters was one of the most important bulwarks of the ruling classes. The infamous Seventh Section, the political police with their gangs of finks, was the most zealous of bloodhounds — baying and chasing after the revolutionary movement, sniffing about, snooping, bribing, informing on, and arresting the best and most active elements of the workers' movement. It threw them behind bars for months and years, tried to wear them down physically and spiritually, kept secret files on everyone who was in any way active in the revolutionary movement, and drained the workers' movement like a leech, especially under the wartime state of siege.

Since Eichhorn became police chief, these good old times are gone. While Ebert, Wels, and Co. spewed out graft and corruption in the service of the counterrevolution in a volume unsurpassed even in Stieber's time, they raged at having to do without such an effective and useful tool as the police department. They were faced with the unpleasant fact that the police headquarters and its operatives took seriously their calling as an organization to defend the revolutionary proletariat. This drastically upset the shady machinations of the Ebert-Wels creatures.

That could not be tolerated. If the Ebert-Scheidemann government was to proceed against the revolution with the necessary force, then Eichhorn and the revolutionary police force had to be cleared out of the way. All available sham pretexts were used to remove Eichhorn from his office.

The blow against Eichhorn was aimed not at him personally, but against the cause of the revolution. Eichhorn is not in our party, he is a member of the USPD. But as everyone can see, the blow against Eichhorn was aimed at the proletarian masses. Eichhorn's firing was a provocation directed against the revolutionary workers. Workers cannot take this brazen provocation lying down. They must respond to this attack with forceful revolutionary measures.

Disarm the counterrevolution! Arm the proletariat! Consolidate all troops that are true to the revolution! These must be the demands of the day. From every corner must resound the cry:

Down with Ebert-Scheidemann! □

When Eugen Ernst, accompanied by the acting city commander of the army, arrived on January 5 at the police headquarters to assume office, Eichhorn turned him away, explaining that he would surrender the post only to the executive bodies of the councils from which he had received it. Around 2:00 p.m. an enormous throng of 150,000 gathered in the Tiergarten park and proceeded across the city center to police headquarters near Alexanderplatz. Eichhorn, Georg Ledebour, Karl Liebknecht, and others addressed the crowd, which insistently demanded weapons. The Ebert cabinet had not expected such a massive response, and once again its members abandoned the government buildings for a private home, where they held anxious and inconclusive discussions.

The speakers at the police headquarters urged demonstrators to go home and to return for a renewed action the next day. Nonetheless, the demonstrators, determined to defend the police headquarters, remained in the area, waiting for further instructions from their leadership.[9] Then, in the evening, after the vast majority had returned home, the cry was raised: "Occupy *Vorwärts!*" Groups of workers headed spontaneously for the newspaper district, where they seized not only *Vorwärts* but several bourgeois newspapers. It was later revealed that progovernment provocateurs and agents of the High Command had played key roles in launching the leaderless workers into this action.[10] Although the KPD had no part in initiating the occupation, it took responsibility to defend it and assigned forces to take part in it.

While this took place, a meeting of leaders of the Berlin USPD, of the Shop Stewards, and of KPD leaders Liebknecht and Wilhelm Pieck was taking place inside police headquarters. Buoyed by the great success of that day's action, they received word of the newspaper occupations. They also heard reports that several key military detachments were ready to move into action to overthrow the Ebert-Scheidemann government.

Richard Müller's summary of the discussion states that Liebknecht intervened at this point, holding that, "Given this situation, not only must the blow against Eichhorn be warded off, but it was possible and absolutely necessary to overthrow the Ebert-Scheidemann government."[11]

Ledebour, recounting the meeting in later court testimony, said, "The idea came up that we could not limit ourselves to remaining so to speak on the defensive," merely protecting Eichhorn's post. For if the government used troops against Eichhorn, and these troops were repulsed, "then it would automatically lead to the result that the government would disappear. . . . I myself was convinced that if we launched a struggle, it would be all or nothing. . . . We therefore took a decision to resist the removal of Eichhorn and to attempt to overthrow the Ebert-Scheidemann government."[12]

The KPD's 1929 history of these events quotes Ledebour's version, and states that Liebknecht and Pieck intervened strongly in favor of this proposal. Pieck himself makes it clear that he and Liebknecht were acting independently of the rest of the party leadership, which disagreed with their stand.[13]

The meeting agreed on the need to continue the struggle and call the Berlin workers to general strike. A further proposal to maintain the newspaper occupation and, in Müller's words, "to undertake a struggle against the government up to and including its overthrow," was adopted by a substantial majority against the opposition of six votes, including the influential Shop Steward leaders Müller and Ernst Däumig.

A Revolutionary Committee of several dozen members was established. It convened at midnight. Pieck, one of its members, recalls that "in general there was little spirit of initiative" among his colleagues. "They sat, exhausted, slumped in their chairs, smoking cigarettes," and had no notion of what was to be done to achieve victory. A leadership committee was elected composed of Ledebour (for the USPD), Liebknecht (for the KPD), and Paul Scholze (for the Shop Stewards). Decisions were taken to occupy the key military buildings and to arm the workers.[14] A short appeal called the workers to an 11:00 a.m. demonstration. More was now at stake than the attack on Eichhorn, the appeal stated. "The door must be barred to all counterrevolutionary intrigues. . . . Arise and fight for the power of the revolutionary proletariat! Down with the Ebert-Scheidemann government!"[15] The committee members went home about 2:00 a.m., leaving Liebknecht and three others at committee headquarters in the Marstall, headquarters of the People's Naval Division.

Half a million workers took to the streets the next morning, and a great many of them brought weapons. All large factories were shut down. SPD leader Gustav Noske later wrote: "Great masses of workers . . . answered the call to struggle. Their favorite slogan 'Down, down, down' [with the government] resounded once more. I had to cross the procession at the Brandenburg Gate, in the Tiergarten, and again in front of general staff headquarters. Many marchers were armed. Several trucks with machine guns stood at the Siegessäule. Repeatedly, I politely asked to be allowed to pass, as I had an urgent errand. Obligingly, they allowed me to cross through. If the crowds had had determined, conscious leaders, instead of windbags, by noon that day Berlin would have been in their hands."[16]

Rote Fahne later called the demonstration "the greatest workers' mass action in history." The densely packed workers "were ready to do anything, to sacrifice anything for the revolution, even their lives. It was an army of 200,000 men, such as no Ludendorff had ever beheld.

"And then an outrage took place. From 9:00 a.m. the masses stood in the cold and light drizzle. And somewhere the leaders sat and deliberated. The drizzle intensified and still the masses stood there. But the leaders were deliberating. Midday arrived, and to the cold was now added hunger. And the leaders deliberated. The masses were feverish with excitement: they wanted a deed, even merely a word to appease their anxiety. But no one knew what to do. For the leaders were deliberating. The drizzle picked up again, and it was twilight. Sadly the masses went home. They had intended a great deed, but had accomplished nothing. For the leaders had been deliberating.... Deliberating, deliberating, and deliberating."[17]

Weapons had been procured and were distributed at the Marstall. Some three thousand workers were armed in this way, but no measures were taken to organize them into detachments, and many of them took no part in subsequent events. About 4:00 p.m. Ledebour, Liebknecht, and other leaders returned to the Marstall from the army barracks, where they had spent the day appealing to soldiers to back the Revolutionary Committee. They reported that the key military units whose support had been counted on, including the People's Naval Division, were unwilling to rally to the action. Most military detachments in the Berlin area declared themselves neutral.

One of the few initiatives taken by the Revolutionary Committee was to send a unit of three hundred sailors to occupy the war ministry. The officers in charge of the ministry however, explained that they would permit the occupation only if shown a written authorization. When they were shown an authorization, they pointed out that it was not signed. Lemmgen, the sailors' leader, therefore left his detachment posted in front of the ministry and hurried back to the Marstall to collect the signatures of the Revolutionary Committee. There he received the following typed statement signed by two members of the committee's leadership body.

Comrades! Workers!
Communiqué of the Revolutionary Committee[18]

Berlin, January 6, 1919

The Ebert-Scheidemann government is utterly compromised. It is hereby deposed by the undersigned Revolutionary Committee, the representatives of the revolutionary socialist workers and soldiers (Independent Social Democratic Party and Communist Party).

The undersigned Revolutionary Committee has provisionally taken over the affairs of state.

Comrades! Workers! Support the measures of the Revolutionary Committee.

The Revolutionary
Committee
Ledebour, Liebknecht,
Scholze
(signed in Ledebour's absence by Liebknecht) □

As he left the Marstall, Lemmgen heard that the People's Naval Division had declared against the Revolutionary Committee and had ordered it to leave the premises. "That cleared things up," he later testified. "I took the document ... went home, reported in sick, and stayed there for eight full days." The sailors in front of the war ministry waited for him in vain and gradually dispersed.[19] The communiqué ultimately came into the hands of the SPD, which published it January 14.

Rosa Luxemburg called on the leaders of the movement to halt their vacillations and indecision. The next day, January 7, her article in *Rote Fahne* read in part as follows.

What Are the Leaders Doing?[20]
by Rosa Luxemburg

The masses must learn through their own struggles to fight and to act. And you can sense it today; to a large extent the Berlin workers *have* learned to act. They thirst for decisive deeds, clear situations, and sweeping measures. They are not the same as they were on November 9, they *know* what they want and what they should do.

But are their leaders, the executive bodies of their will, up to the task? Have the Revolutionary Shop Stewards of the Large Factories and the radical forces in the USPD grown in determination and initiative? Has their willingness to act kept pace with the masses' growing determination?

We fear that we cannot answer this question with a categorical "yes." We fear that the leaders are the same as they were on November 9. They have learned little since then.

Twenty-four hours have elapsed since the Ebert government's attack on Eichhorn. The masses responded impetuously to their leaders' appeal. They spontaneously pushed through Eichhorn's reinstatement with their own forces and occupied *Vorwärts* on their own initiative, taking control of the bourgeois editorial office and of the Wolff Telegraph Bureau. To the extent possible, they armed themselves. They are awaiting further instructions and actions from their leaders.

What have these latter done in the meantime? What have they settled? What measures have they taken to assure the revolution's victory in this tense situation that will decide the fate of the revolution, at least for the next period? We see and hear nothing! The workers' representatives may well be thoroughly and extensively *discussing*, but now is the time to *act*. . . .

Act! Act! Courageously, decisively, consistently — that is the bounden duty and obligation of the Revolutionary Shop Stewards and honest Socialist party leaders. Disarm the counterrevolution, arm the masses, occupy all strategic positions. Act *quickly!* The revolution requires it. In world history the revolution's hours count for months and its days for years. The institutions of the revolution must be fully aware of their great responsibility! □

———

While the KPD vainly urged the Revolutionary Committee to act, the government was recovering its self-confidence. The SPD announced its own general strike in support of the regime and held a meeting of several thousand in front of the Reich chancellery. Scheidemann announced that all men with military experience loyal to the government would be armed and organized in its defense. The SPD also organized a meeting of the Berlin Executive Committee of the councils, which only two USPD members, Däumig and Müller, attended. Against their opposition, it voted support for the removal of Eichhorn and ordered an end to the newspaper occupations.

A joint meeting of the cabinet with the Central Committee of the councils (elected by their December congress and boycotted by the USPD) resolved to use military force to suppress the uprising and appointed Noske to command the government's troops in the Berlin area. He accepted the task, explaining, "One of us must be the bloodhound. I do not shirk the responsibility."[21] The following declaration of the Central Committee of the councils was published January 7.

Special Powers to the Government[22]

Berlin, January 6, 1919

To All Workers' and Soldiers' Councils of Germany:

As you know, the General Congress of Workers' and Soldiers' Councils of Germany appointed us as its executive body and entrusted us with its full powers. We have been forced to devote our attention in these first weeks almost exclusively to the outrageous situation in Berlin. A small minority there is striving to erect a brutal tyranny of violence against the will of the population as a whole and especially that of the people of Berlin, and against the express will of the workers' and soldiers' councils of all of Germany.

The criminal activity of armed bands, threatening all the gains of the revolution, has obliged us to confer extraordinary powers on the national government, so that order and respect for the law, especially necessary in the freest of societies, could finally be restored in Berlin. All differences of opinion on particulars must now be subordinated to the goal of protecting the people's hard-won freedom, to assure peace within and without, and thereby to protect the entire working population from renewed dreadful misfortune.

It is the duty of all workers' and soldiers' councils to support us and the national government with all available means. Stand ready with everything necessary to accomplish this. The more solidly the workers and soldiers of Germany and their elected councils stand together, the more quickly the fight to implement the will of the people will be won.

The Central Council of the
German Socialist Republic □

The national leadership of the USPD had taken no part in the decision to resist the dismissal of Eichhorn. It now contacted the government and the Revolutionary Committee, proposing negotiations between the two sides. The government agreed. Ledebour and the Berlin USPD leadership rallied to the idea. At a meeting of the Shop Stewards, Liebknecht and Pieck argued strongly against negotiations, which they said could only undercut the workers' struggle while allowing the government time to assemble its troops. The Shop Stewards, however, voted fifty-one to ten to begin negotiations with the very government that they had decided to overthrow twenty-four hours earlier. A joint negotiating committee was then established; the KPD refused to participate.[23]

When negotiations began January 6-7 at midnight, the government representatives demanded that the occupied newspaper buildings be evacuated as a precondition to any agreement. The USPD and Shop Stewards' negotiators said they were prepared to evacuate the bourgeois newspapers, but not *Vorwärts,* and the talks stalled at that point. In fact, the negotiators had little authority with the occupiers of *Vorwärts,* led among others by Eugen Leviné of the KPD. These militant workers were indignant with Ledebour for agreeing to negotiations. When Karl Liebknecht addressed the occupiers January 8, denouncing the inactivity of the Revolutionary Committee and its decision to negotiate, the meeting demanded that these leaders be removed.[24]

The USPD's *Freiheit* called on the workers January 7 to remain calm and await the outcome of negotiations, while *Rote Fahne* appealed for decisive action. Once again masses of workers assembled in downtown Berlin and waited in vain for directions on what to do. Spontaneously they moved to occupy a few additional positions, and there were initial clashes with progovernment troops. At a meeting of the Shop Stewards that evening Oskar Cohn of the USPD national leadership argued for immediate surrender of the occupied buildings, while Pieck insisted on the need to defend them. The Shop Stewards decided to continue both the occupations and the negotiations.[25]

Caught up in the swirl of events, Liebknecht and Pieck were functioning on their own, out of touch with the Central Committee of their party. Pieck later wrote that the leadership "could not always be immediately informed about my and Liebknecht's decisions." When the Central Committee was finally able to meet, on January 8, "it turned out that while these comrades agreed with the struggle against the government's measures, they did not agree with the goal set for the action: a fight to take the government." At the January 8 meeting, Pieck continued, Jogiches and Luxemburg "criticized the leadership of this action in the sharpest terms and categorically demanded that Liebknecht and I withdraw from the Revolutionary Committee. Liebknecht found it extraordinarily difficult to carry out this decision."[26]

Despite its disagreement with the decisions of the Revolutionary Committee, the KPD Central Committee felt it necessary that all Communists remain in the front ranks of the working class as it underwent the government assault. The KPD tried to give what leadership it could in organizing the resistance and shifting its demands toward more realistic and defensive goals than that of immediately toppling the Ebert-Scheidemann regime. Rosa Luxemburg's article in the January 8 *Rote Fahne*, excerpted below, made specific proposals to this end.

Neglect of Duty[27]
by Rosa Luxemburg

Since November 9 the revolutionary wave has repeatedly crashed against the same wall, the Ebert-Scheidemann government. The cause, form, and force of the collision are different in each of the revolutionary crises that we have experienced in the last eight weeks. But the cry, "Down with Ebert-Scheidemann!" is the theme of *all* the crises up to now and the slogan with which they all end up, the slogan that resounds ever louder, more forcefully, and more unanimously from the masses. . . .

But what is *not at all* clearly understood, and where the weaknesses and immaturity of revolution show through, is the question of *how* to conduct the fight to get rid of the Ebert government, *how* to convert the revolution's present level of maturity into actions and into a shift in the relationship of forces. Nothing has revealed these weaknesses and shortcomings more blatantly than these last three days.

Getting rid of the Ebert-Scheidemann government does not just mean storming the Reich chancellor's palace and arresting a few people or chasing them out the door. Above all, it means seizing all the positions of real power, *holding* them, and *using* them.

But what did we see in these three days? The positions that were really conquered — the reoccupation of the police headquarters, the occupations of *Vorwärts,* the Wolff Telegraph Bureau, and the editorial offices of the bourgeois newspapers — were all the spontaneous work of the masses. And those bodies who during these days stood or claimed to stand at the head of the masses — the Revolutionary Shop Stewards and the Central Executive Committee of the Greater Berlin USPD — what did they do? They ignored the most basic principles of revolutionary action that exist:

1. When the masses occupy *Vorwärts,* it is the duty of the Revolutionary Shop Stewards and the Central Executive Committee of the Greater Berlin USPD, who claim to officially represent the Berlin workers, to immediately provide an editorial leadership in line with the views of these revolutionary workers. Where were the editors? What were Däumig and Ledebour doing — journalists and editors by profession and repute? As the left wing of the USPD, they do not now have any paper. Why did they leave the masses in the lurch? Did they have some more important business to "discuss," instead of acting?

2. When the masses occupy the Wolff Telegraph Bureau, the most immediate duty of the workers' revolutionary organizations is to *use* the telegraph bureau for the cause of the revolution, to inform the public and the masses of comrades across the country about what is happening in Berlin, to orient them to the situation. This is the only way that the political connection between the Berlin workers and the revolutionary movement in the whole country can be established, without which the revolution can win neither here nor there.

3. While engaged in the sharpest battle with the Ebert-Scheidemann government, you do not at the same time open "negotiations" with this same government. The Haase people: Oskar Cohn, Luise Zietz, Kautsky, Breitscheid, and all the rest of those unstable

figures, whoever they are, jump at every opportunity to hastily reknit relations with the Ebert people, from whom they separated only with heavy hearts. As for the Revolutionary Shop Stewards, who have a feel for the masses, they know very well that Ebert and Scheidemann are mortal enemies of the revolution. Do you negotiate with mortal enemies? These negotiations can only lead to one of two things — either to a compromise or, more likely, simply to a delay, which the Eberts will use to prepare the most brutal repression.

4. When the masses are called into the streets in a state of alert, they must be told clearly and plainly what they have to do, or at least what is happening, what friend and foe are doing and planning. Obviously, in times of revolutionary crisis the masses belong in the streets. They are the revolution's only stronghold, its only security. When the revolution is in danger, *as it is now to the highest degree,* then the duty of the proletarian masses is to stand guard where their power can be flexed — in the streets! Their mere presence, their contact with each other is a threat and a warning to all overt and covert enemies of the revolution: Watch out!

However, the masses must not only be summoned; they must also be politically active. They must be called upon to decide upon all that is said and done. Did the Revolutionary Shop Stewards, did the Central Executive Committee of the Greater Berlin USPD not see that they had to appear before the masses assembled on the Siegesallee and present their decision to "negotiate" with Ebert and Scheidemann? Had they done so, they would have received a response so thunderous as to deprive them of any desire to negotiate! . . .

The experience of the last three days cries out to the leading bodies of the workers: Do not prattle! Do not discuss forever! Do not negotiate! Act! □

The KPD leadership stood by its January 4 decision that the action should be limited in its objectives. A leaflet issued by the party on January 8 called for arming all proletarians, unifying them in Red Guards, and disarming the counterrevolutionaries. It proposed a campaign to go to the barracks to persuade soldiers to support the action, and utilization of the occupied facilities for revolutionary education.[28]

On January 9 the KPD added a new demand, which came to grips with the SPD's domination of the executive committees of the councils and these bodies' support of the Ebert-Scheidemann government against the Berlin workers. "The task today is to reelect the workers' and soldiers' councils and the Berlin Executive Committee with the slogan, 'Throw out Ebert and his supporters!' " wrote *Rote Fahne* on January 9. The experiences of the last eight weeks must be used "to defeat Ebert-Scheidemann above all in the basic institutions of the revolution, the councils." Only then would the masses possess "revolutionary institutions that at the decisive moment can provide real leaders and real action centers that can conduct the fight and bring victory."[29]

But as Ebert's troops closed in, the KPD leadership was unable to lead the retreat that was in order, and some of its leaders were reluctant to accept responsibility for such a retreat. Instead, its January 8 leaflet concluded, "The road is the same, the goal is the same, the slogan is the same: Down with the Ebert-Scheidemann government! Long live the Red Guard!"[30]

A different course of action was suggested to the party leadership by Karl Radek, who had remained in hiding in Berlin after the party congress to assist the party leadership. On January 9 he wrote the following letter to the Central Committee proposing that it act to deny Ebert a crushing victory over Berlin workers by attempting to lead an organized retreat.

Letter to KPD Leaders[31]
by Karl Radek

Dear comrades!

The Berlin movement has landed in a blind alley. I was therefore compelled as early as Monday [January 6] to bring to the attention of various Central Committee comrades my opinion that it was necessary to break off the fight. You will now understand why, at the last minute, I turn to you, as leaders of the German Communist Party. I request that you report to all members of the party my modest opinion, in my capacity as a representative of a fraternal party that is just as interested in the German movement as in its own.

Your programmatic pamphlet, *What the Spartacus League Wants*, explains that you will take governmental power only when the majority of the German working class is behind you. The absolute correctness of this position is clearly demonstrated by the simple fact that a workers' government is unthinkable without the mass organization of the proletariat. Right now, the only mass organizations that come into consideration, the workers' councils, exist hardly more than in name. They have not led any struggles that could release the power of the masses. And corresponding to that, the party of struggle, the Communist Party, does not have the upper hand in them; instead, the social patriots or the Independents do. *In such a situation the seizure of power by the proletariat is out of the question.* Were the government to fall into your hands through a putsch, in a couple of days it would be cut off from the countryside and strangled.

In this situation, the action launched on Saturday by the Revolutionary Shop Stewards against the social-patriotic government's attack on the police headquarters, in all probability, can have the character only of a protest action. The most advanced Berlin workers, embittered by the government's policies, have been misled by the Revolutionary Shop Stewards, who lack any political experience and are not in a position to see the relationship of forces in the country as a whole. The Shop Stewards have impetuously turned the struggle from a protest movement into a fight for power. That allowed Ebert and Scheidemann to deal the Berlin movement a blow that can set it back months.

The only restraining force that can prevent this misfortune is you, the Communist Party. You have enough insight to know that the fight is hopeless. Your members, Comrades Levi and H. Duncker, told me that you really know this. Of course, I am aware of how difficult it is now, after so many sacrifices, to stand up before the masses and sound the retreat. I know that this will lead to a decline in morale. But such depression is nothing compared to what the masses will say to themselves after the bloodletting. They will say that blind leaders incited them to hopeless battle, or that leaders saw the abyss but that out of revolutionary egoism they could not make up their minds to call, "Halt!" All considerations of revolutionary egoism must take a secondary position to the real relationship of forces.

Nothing forbids the weaker side from withdrawing in the face of an enemy who represents a far superior force. In July 1917, when we were stronger than you are now, we held the masses back with all our strength. When this did not work, we intervened decisively to pull them back out of an impending hopeless battle. And despite temporary depression, despite the fact that our comrades threw down their weapons with tears and curses, afterward they showed even more confidence in us and saw the complete honesty of our policies toward them.

This, in my opinion, is what should be done now:

1. We must demand that the Shop Stewards break off the fight and withdraw the workers and soldiers from battle, arms in hand, if possible, or without arms if a gradual and peaceful retreat is not possible. A manifesto, which must point out the inescapability of a

bloody carnage, must demand immediate elections for new workers' councils. The betrayal by the Berlin Executive Committee opens the possibility of making this struggle a fight for the organs of power of the Berlin working class.

2. Should the Shop Stewards reject your proposal, we must break with them, tell the truth about their positions to the masses, and secure the replacement of the Shop Stewards' clique by real representatives of the Berlin revolutionary working class. The road forward is for your movement across the whole country to undertake a struggle for the councils of workers' deputies, without which there is no use in even thinking of taking power.

I took the liberty to communicate my opinions to you not because of my credentials — of course, I do not know what opinion is held now in the Russian Communist Party concerning the situation in Berlin — but because of the experience I have acquired in the Russian movement, as well as my knowledge of the situation in Germany. □

In 1921, after his expulsion from the KPD, Paul Levi said that he had supported Radek's proposal within the Central Committee, and that Jogiches had gone even further and called for an open repudiation of Liebknecht and Pieck by *Rote Fahne*. This was not done, however, and the majority of the Central Committee members continued to favor resolute defense of the *Vorwärts* building.[32]

Radek said that he received a reply from Rosa Luxemburg of the Central Committee saying that the USPD was heading toward an agreement with the government and "there was no point in our taking on ourselves the role of sounding the retreat."[33] Contrary to Luxemburg's expectations, however, the USPD did not carry out an organized retreat. Nor did the Communists. The groups of armed workers in Berlin were left to face the full force of the assault by Noske's Freikorps.

On Wednesday evening, January 8, the Revolutionary Committee broke off negotiations, having concluded that the government was not participating with a view to reaching an agreement, but merely to buy time. That night Noske's troops signaled the beginning of a full-scale assault on the centers of resistance with an attack on an occupied railway station, the railway headquarters, and other points. About that time Noske issued the following proclamation, which was pasted on the walls of Berlin.

Above, January 1919: barricades in Berlin newspaper quarter; below, Leo Jogiches, Wilhelm Pieck.

"I Aim to Cleanse, Not Destroy"[34]

Worker, Soldier, Citizen!

Today at one o'clock 3,000 men with heavy artillery and machine guns marched through Berlin and Charlottenburg. Through them the government showed that it has the power to carry out your will, which demands an end to the pillaging and bloodshed.

Today the government still hopes that your firm determination will *intimidate terrorism,* that the Spartacists will not launch a fight for the stolen buildings, but will instead vacate their shameful showcases.

Should the hope be dashed that, at the last moment, they will come to their senses, *then the government's and your patience will be exhausted.* You must chase them out if they delay even one day. In the east, Spartacus gangs drive from house to house plundering with drawn revolvers while Eichhorn's police force stands watch. The charade that this is a political movement has been exposed.

Robbery and plunder are revealed as the ultimate and single goal of the rioters.

Workers!

The Reich government has entrusted me with the leadership of the republican soldiers.

This means that a worker stands at the peak of power in the socialist republic.

You know me and my history in the party. I promise that no unnecessary blood will be spilled.

I aim to cleanse, not to destroy.

With the new republican army, I want to bring you freedom and peace.

The working class must stand united against Spartacus, if democracy and socialism are not to be lost.

> The Commander in Chief
> Noske □

The Revolutionary Committee responded to the January 8 fighting with a renewed call to battle. "Now the last mists have lifted; the situation is clear," it declared in a leaflet distributed January 9 and signed as before by the Berlin USPD, the KPD, and the Shop Stewards. "Everything is at stake.... We have no choice; we must fight to the end! ... Take up arms! Use your weapons against your deadly enemies, the Eberts and Scheidemanns. ... Join the general strike! Into the streets for the final struggle, for victory!"[35]

Thousands of Berlin workers answered the call. But once again, they were left with no directives for action. A participant in these events, Julius Ludwig, later recalled, "The general strike was carried through with unity in the Berlin factories, and the workers stood in the streets ready for battle. But the masses of working people had no understanding at all of what they were to do. Tired of roaming aimlessly through the streets without adequate knowledge of the real situation, in increasing numbers they grasped the slogan, 'Stop the fratricide! Unity of the workers without the leaders!'"[36]

The workers of the Humboldthain district, who counted among the militant vanguard of Berlin's proletariat, held a mass demonstration that day with the slogan, "Proletarians unite, if not through your leaders, then over their heads." They elected a parity committee to meet with the contending leaderships and proposed replacing existing leaders with figures who were "not compromised," dissolving the army High Command, abolishing ranks, and demobilizing the army. The next day 15,000 workers in the Spandau district called for resignation of Ebert's cabinet, formation of committees at every level made up of the three workers' parties on a parity basis, and reelection of the councils. Many other groups of workers were drawn into this "unity" movement, which the USPD national leadership had helped to initiate, and which attracted many SPD members. A frequent demand was formation of a united government of the three workers' parties. In reply to such initiatives, Communist Party spokespersons explained that it was the SPD's policies that were blocking workers' unity, and that condemning these policies and preventing their continuation was the only road to achieving unity.[37]

On the evening of January 9 the Revolutionary Committee, overriding the KPD's objections, resumed negotiations with the government yet again. The small groups of armed workers in the occupied buildings were left isolated in their strongholds, without coordinated leadership. Noske was free during the four days beginning January 9 to attack and subdue these groups one by one.

The KPD Central Committee met again January 10 and decided a second time, now with Liebknecht's agreement, to withdraw from the Revolutionary Committee. The party leadership adopted the following letter to explain its decision. The letter could not be delivered to the Revolutionary Committee, since it had now ceased functioning, but the document was published in the January 13 issue of *Rote Fahne*.

KPD Breaks With Revolutionary Committee[38]

Berlin,
Friday, January 10, 1919

To the Revolutionary Shop Stewards of the Large Factories of Greater Berlin and to the Revolutionary Committee, Berlin:

Comrades,

Given the failure of our repeated attempts to induce the Shop Stewards' assembly and the Revolutionary Committee to adopt a vigorous stance, clear in its goals; given the serious harm caused the revolutionary movement by the uncertainty and indecisiveness of both bodies; given the entry by the Revolutionary Shop Stewards, together with the Central Executive Committee of the USPD, into the procrastinating, bewildering, demoralizing, disorganizing, paralyzing negotiations with Ebert and Scheidemann, despite our strong protest; and given their shameful initiation, following Wednesday evening's strike call [January 8], of new unity talks on Thursday and their action today, Friday, in taking this disgraceful and harmful step for the fourth time, the leadership of the Communist Party of Germany (Spartacus League) has decided:

In the interests of the revolutionary movement's understanding and strength, an immediate change in our relationship with the Revolutionary Shop Stewards is absolutely necessary.

From now on we are no longer willing to participate in the Revolutionary Committee, not even as advisers. However, we continue to stand ready at all times to exchange opinions with the committee on request.

In the future we will send a delegation of two representatives to the Shop Stewards' meetings for the purpose of mutual information.

We are compelled to take this decision because we believe, after overabundant experience, that only if we maintain complete freedom of action and independence, even with respect to the Shop Stewards, can we fulfill entirely our duty to the revolution and the proletariat. We will nevertheless fight shoulder to shoulder with the Shop Stewards, despite all differences, if ever they proceed to effective revolutionary action.

(signed) Pieck □

Although three regiments of SPD supporters had been formed in preparation for the fighting, Noske chose to rely mainly on the Freikorps battalions, which were led by right-wing officers loyal to the old regime and bitterly hostile to the revolution and the working class.[39] The right-wing witch-hunt against the Spartacists reached a fever pitch, and included open calls for the murder of Communist leaders, such as the following anonymous poster:

"Workers, Citizens:

"The fatherland is close to destruction. Save it! It is not threatened from without but from within, *by the Spartacus group. Murder their leaders! KILL LIEBKNECHT!* Then you will have peace, work, and bread.

"The front soldiers"[40]

The SPD joined in building the witch-hunt atmosphere, provocatively claiming in a January 6 appeal that "Liebknecht has proclaimed a 'fight to the death' against the population. . . . Down with the murderers and criminals!"[41] In another statement on January 8 it declared that, "Force can only be fought by force. . . . The hour of reckoning is approaching!"[42] The Social Democratic Party leaders were not above utilizing rank racism and anti-Semitism against revolutionary workers. The following poem, which appeared in *Vorwärts* January 12, pointedly played on anti-Semitic feeling by using Germanized equivalents of the original Jewish names of Leon Trotsky (Bronstein) and Radek (Sobelson).

"I saw the masses marauding
Behind Karl, the blind war god,
Dancing to the Pied Piper's flute,
Who slyly promised them the world.
They bowed before bloodied idols,
Groveled before all that humanity scorns,
Before Russia's Asiatics and Mongols,
Before Braunstein, Luxemburg, and Sobelsohn.
Go back, you raging hoards!
You cry for freedom, only to kill it."[43]

The next day another poem appeared in *Vorwärts*, cynically noting that Liebknecht, Luxemburg, and Radek were not among those who fell victim in the battles supposedly unleashed by their own actions. The poem concluded:

"Many hundred corpses in a row,
Proletarians,
Karl, Rosa, Radek, and Co.,
Not one of them is there,
Proletarians."[44]

Nor did the SPD do anything to restrain the right-wing fanaticism and lust for revenge of the counterrevolutionary officers whose battalions were now unleashed against the Berlin population. Quite the contrary, Noske's proclamation printed above slandered the Spartacists as nothing more than looters and so justified using against them the standard punishment for those identified as "looters" under a state of siege: to be shot on sight. When Noske's troops assaulted the *Vorwärts* building on January 11 with cannons and mortars, negotiators sent by the defenders were killed on the spot. Many workers who surrendered to Noske's forces were summarily shot. The government figure of the number killed was 156; the actual toll was much higher.

With the taking of *Vorwärts* that day and of the police headquarters January 12 organized resistance ceased. The strikes ended January 13. But the pogrom atmosphere was maintained as troops began house-to-house searches of working-class districts. All Communist leaders located were arrested and the party in Berlin was for the moment driven underground.

In the last hours before their arrest and murder, Luxemburg and Liebknecht wrote the following statements of defiance against the government assault and of confidence in the proletariat's ultimate victory. Luxemburg's article appeared in *Rote Fahne* January 14, and Liebknecht's the following day.

Order is Restored in Berlin[45]
by Rosa Luxemburg

"Order is restored in Warsaw!" announced [French government] Minister Sebastiani to the French parliament in 1831, after Suvorov's marauding troops had savagely overrun the suburb of Praga and had invaded the Polish capital to begin their butchery of the insurgents.[46]

"Order is restored in Berlin!" exult the bourgeois press, Ebert and Noske, and the officers of the "victorious troops," who are welcomed in Berlin's streets by the petty-bourgeois mob with waving handkerchiefs and shouts of "Hurrah!" The glory and honor of German arms have been vindicated before the tribunal of world history. The pathetic, defeated forces from Flanders and the Argonne have regained their reputation with a brilliant victory — over three hundred "Spartacists" in the *Vorwärts* building.[47] The days when German troops first triumphantly crossed into Belgium, and the age of General von Emmich, the conqueror of Liège,[48] pale when compared with the exploits of Reinhardt and Co. in the streets of Berlin. The massacred mediators, who had been trying to negotiate the surrender of the *Vorwärts* building, were clubbed beyond recognition by the rifle butts of the government's rampaging troops so that their bodies cannot be identified. Prisoners were put against the wall and slaughtered so violently that bits of skull and brain tissue splattered everywhere. After glorious deeds like those, who would remember the ignominious defeat at the hands of the French, British, and Americans? Now "Spartacus" is the enemy, Berlin is the place where our officers can win, and Noske, "the worker," is the general who can organize victories where Ludendorff failed.

Who is not reminded of that delirious victory celebration by the "law and order" mob in Paris, that orgy the bourgeoisie celebrated over the bodies of the Communards?[49] Only a short while before, that same bourgeoisie had shamefully capitulated to the Prussians and abandoned the capital to the external enemy, taking to their heels like abject cowards. But oh, how the manly courage of those darling sons of the bourgeoisie, of the "golden youth," and of the officers blazed back to life against the poorly armed, starving Parisian proletariat and their defenseless women and children. How the courage of those sons of Mars, broken by the external enemy, raged with bestial cruelty against defenseless people, prisoners, and the wounded.

"Order is restored in Warsaw!" "Order is restored in Paris!" "Order is restored in Berlin!" Every half century, the bulletins from the guardians of "order" flash from one center of world-historic struggle to the next. And the jubilant "victors" never notice that any "order" that needs to be maintained through periodic bloody slaughters strides inexorably toward its historic fate and its own demise.

What was the recent "Spartacus week" in Berlin? What were its results? What can it teach us? While we are still in the heat of battle, while the counterrevolution is still crowing about victory, revolutionary proletarians must take stock of what happened; they must measure events and their results on the great yardstick of history. The revolution does not waste time; it rushes onward over still-open graves, over "victories" and "defeats," toward its great objectives. The first task of fighters for international socialism is to consciously follow the revolution's dictates and its path.

Could the revolutionary proletariat have expected a decisive victory in this battle? Could Ebert-Scheidemann have been overthrown and the socialist dictatorship inaugurated? Certainly not, if we carefully weigh all factors that bear upon the question. At this juncture, the sore spot in the revolutionary cause is the political immaturity of the masses of soldiers, who still permit their officers to use them against the people for counterrevolutionary ends. That alone shows that no *lasting* revolutionary victory was possible in this confrontation. On the other hand, the immaturity of the army is in itself but a symptom of the general immaturity of the German revolution.

The countryside, the source of a large percentage of the soldiers, is still scarcely affected by the revolution. So far, Berlin has remained virtually isolated from the rest of the country. To be sure, the revolutionary centers in the provinces support the Berlin proletariat, heart and soul: the Rhineland, the North Sea coast, Brunswick, Saxony, Württemberg. But at the present time they are still not advancing directly in step with one other; there is still no direct coordination of actions, which would render the thrust and striking power of the Berlin working class incomparably more effective. Furthermore, the economic struggle — the actual volcanic reservoir that constantly feeds the revolutionary class struggle — is only in its initial stage, and that is the underlying reason why the revolution has an unfinished political character.

It flows from all of this that a decisive, lasting victory was not in the cards at this time. Does that mean that the past week's struggle was an "error"? The answer would be yes if we were talking about a deliberate "offensive" or "putsch." But what started this week of battles? As in all previous cases, as on December 6 and December 24, it was a brutal provocation by the government. Like the bloodbath against defenseless demonstrators in Chausseestrasse,[50] like the butchery of the sailors, this time the attack on the Berlin police command precipitated all subsequent events. The revolution does not maneuver of its own volition, in a clear field of battle, according to a plan devised by clever "strategists." The revolution's opponents can *also* take the initiative, and indeed as a rule they make use of it far more frequently than does the revolution.

Given the impudent provocation by Ebert-Scheidemann, the revolutionary working class was *forced* to take up arms. Indeed, the *honor* of the revolution depended upon immediately and decisively repulsing the attack, in order to prevent the counterrevolution from being emboldened to try further assaults, and to prevent the revolutionary ranks of the proletariat and the moral credibility of the German revolution in the International from being shaken.

Sure enough there was such an immediate and spontaneous outpouring of resistance from the Berlin masses, so natural and determined, that in the first round the street actions won a moral victory.

Now, it is one of the fundamental, inner laws of revolution that it never stops, it never becomes passive or inactive at any stage. The best defensive maneuver is a good, strong blow. This elementary law governs all struggles, but is especially true at every stage of a revolution. Obviously, the Berlin proletariat was not going to be content with reinstating Eichhorn in office. It is testimony to their healthy instincts and the fresh, vital force that resides in them that they proceeded instead to occupy spontaneously other strongholds of the counterrevolution: the bourgeois press, the semiofficial news agency, and the *Vorwärts* building. The masses took these measures out of an instinctive understanding that the counterrevolution would not accept defeat, but would seek a general test of strength.

Here again we encounter one of history's great laws of revolution, which confuses all the petty, "revolutionary" hairsplitters and know-it-alls of the USPD variety, who always grasp at any excuse to retreat from struggle. Once the fundamental problem of the revolution has been clearly posed — and in *this* revolution it is overthrowing the Ebert-Scheidemann government, the primary obstacle to the victory of socialism — then that question will emerge repeatedly and acutely. With the inevitability of a natural law, every individual episode in the struggle will reveal this problem in its full scope regardless of whether the revolution is ready to resolve it or whether the situation is ripe for it. "Down with Ebert-Scheidemann!" — the slogan arises inevitably in every revolutionary crisis as the single formula summing up all partial struggles. Thus by itself, by its own inner, objective logic, it turns every episode in the struggle into a crisis, whether anyone likes it or not.

Because of the contradiction in the early stages of the revolutionary process between the task being sharply posed and the absence of any means to resolve it, individual struggles end in formal *defeat*. But another of history's peculiar laws is that revolution is the only form of "war" in which the ultimate victory can be prepared only by a series of "defeats."

What does the history of socialism and of all modern revolutions show? The first incidence of class struggle in Europe, the uprising of the silk weavers in Lyon in 1831, ended with a serious defeat; the Chartist movement in Britain ended in defeat; the uprising of the Parisian proletariat in the June days of 1848 ended with a crushing defeat;[51] and the Paris Commune ended with a terrible defeat. The whole history of socialism — where revolutionary struggles are concerned — is strewn with nothing but defeats.

Yet history is marching inexorably, step by step, toward ultimate victory! Where would we be today *without* those "defeats," which have given us historical experience, understanding, power, and idealism? Today, as we are about to go into the final battle in the proletarian class struggle, we stand on those very defeats; and we need every single one, because each forms a part of our strength and understanding.

Revolutionary struggles are the exact opposite of parliamentary struggles. In Germany for four decades we had nothing but parliamentary "victories." Why, we practically walked from victory to victory. And when the great historic test came on August 4, 1914, the result was a devastating political and moral defeat, an unprecedented debacle, a bankruptcy without parallel. To date, revolutions have given us nothing but defeats. Yet these unavoidable defeats pile guarantee upon guarantee of the ultimate victory of the future.

There is of course *one* condition. It is important to know why each defeat occurred: whether it happened because the onrushing combative energy of the masses collided with the barrier of insufficient historical conditions, or because the revolutionary act itself was paralyzed by indecision, vacillation, and internal weaknesses.

The February revolution in France on the one hand and the March revolution [of 1848] in Germany on the other are classic illustrations of each situation. The heroic action by the Parisian proletariat in 1848 has become a living source of energy for the class struggle of the entire international proletariat. The wretchedness of the German March revolution has hung on the whole development of modern Germany like a ball and chain. The peculiar history of official German Social Democracy caused the effects of that defeat to extend right up into the most recent developments in the German revolution and on into the dramatic crisis we have just lived through.

How does the "Spartacus week" defeat appear in the light of the above historical question? Was it a case of impetuous revolutionary energy running into an insufficiently developed situation, or was it a case of weak and indecisive action?

Both! The crisis had a dual character. The contradiction between the powerful, decisive, aggressive performance of the Berlin masses on the one hand and the indecisive, fainthearted vacillation of the Berlin leadership on the other is the peculiar characteristic of this latest episode.

The leadership failed. But a new leadership can and must be created by the masses and out of them. The masses are the deciding factor. They are the rock on which the ultimate victory of the revolution will be built. The masses were up to the mark, and out of this "defeat" they have forged a link in the chain of historic defeats, which is the pride and the power of international socialism. That is why future victories will spring from this "defeat."

"Order is restored in Berlin!" You ignorant stooges! Your "order" is built upon sand. Tomorrow the revolution will "rise up again, clashing its weapons," and terrify you with the clarion call:
I was, I am, I shall be![52] □

Despite Everything![53]
by Karl Liebknecht

All-out war on the Spartacus League! "Down with the Spartacists!" they howl through the streets. "Catch them! Whip them! Stab them! Shoot them! Run them through! Run them down! Tear them to shreds!" Atrocities are being committed that are far worse than those of the German troops in Belgium.

"Spartacus has been defeated!" crows everyone from the *Post* to *Vorwärts*.

"Spartacus has been defeated," and its defeat will be sealed by the sabers, revolvers, and carbines of the resurrected Teutonic police and by the disarming of the revolutionary workers. "Spartacus defeated!" Under the bayonets of Colonel Reinhardt and under the machine guns and cannons of General Lüttwitz the national assembly elections are to take place — a plebiscite for Napoleon Ebert.[54]

"Spartacus is defeated!"

Yes, indeed, the revolutionary workers of Berlin were beaten. Yes, upwards of a hundred of its best mowed down. Yes, many hundreds of its most loyal thrown in jail.

Yes, it is true, they were beaten — because they were abandoned by the sailors, by the soldiers, by the security forces and people's military units, on whose aid they had so firmly counted. And their power was paralyzed by the weakness and indecision of their leadership. And they were drowned in a huge, counterrevolutionary mudslide from the backward sectors of the population and the possessing classes.

Oh, yes! They were beaten, and it was ordained by history that they would be beaten, for the time was not ripe. Yet the battle could not be avoided, because to relinquish the police headquarters, that guardian of the revolution, to Eugen Ernst and Hirsch without a fight would have been defeat without honor. The fight was forced upon the proletariat by the Ebert gang, and it boiled up from the masses of Berlin with elemental force and spilled over the bounds of doubt and misgivings.

Yes! The revolutionary workers of Berlin were beaten.

And the Eberts, Scheidemanns, and Noskes won. They won because on their side they had the generals, the bureaucrats, the barons of steel mills and cabbage fields, the preachers, the moneybags, and everything else that was narrow-minded, stupid, and backward — and those forces won for them with gas, case shot, and mortars.

But there are defeats that are victories, and victories that are more disastrous than defeats.

Those who were vanquished in that bloody week in January stood up gloriously. They fought for a great ideal, for suffering humanity's noblest ideal, for the spiritual and material salvation of the starving masses. They have consecrated their blood by shedding it for a sacred ideal. And every drop of their blood is a seed of discord for today's victors, like dragon's teeth, because from them will grow those who will avenge the fallen; from every shredded fiber, new warriors will arise to carry on the lofty cause, a cause as eternal and everlasting as the firmament.

The vanquished of today shall be the victors of tomorrow, for they will learn from defeat. . . .

Those who were beaten today have learned. They have been cured of the delusion that they could look to the confused mass of soldiers for their salvation; cured of the delusion that they could depend upon their leaders, who proved impotent and incompetent; cured of their faith in the independent Social Democracy, which shamefully abandoned them in their hour of need. In the future, they will fight their battles and win their victories on their own. And from the bitter lessons of this week the motto that the liberatioñ of the working class can be achieved only by the working class itself has acquired a deeper meaning.

Those misguided soldiers will also quickly see through the game that is being played with them when they again feel on their backs the lash of restored militarism. They too will awaken from their present stupor.

"Spartacus has been defeated!"

Not so fast! We have not fled, we are not beaten. Though you lay us in bonds, we are still here and we will remain here, and victory will be ours.

Because Spartacus means fire and spirit, heart and soul, the will and the deed of the proletarian revolution. Spartacus means all the needs and aspirations, all the militancy and class consciousness of the proletariat. Spartacus means socialism and world revolution.

The German working class's journey to Calvary is not yet over, but the day of redemption is drawing nearer, and with it the day of judgment for the Eberts, Scheidemanns, and Noskes and for the capitalist rulers who still hide behind them today. The waves of history billow to the heavens, and we are accustomed to being tossed from the crest to the trough, but our ship sails steadily and proudly on a straight course toward its goal.

Whether or not we are alive when it arrives, our program will live, and it will reign in a world of redeemed humanity. Despite everything!

The thunder of the approaching economic catastrophe will awaken the slumbering proletarian host like the trumpets of the apocalypse, and the bodies of the slaughtered warriors will rise from the dead and call the accursed to account. Today, we hear the subterranean rumbling of the volcano; tomorrow will come the explosion that will bury them all in glowing ash and rivers of lava. □

On January 15, Liebknecht and Luxemburg were arrested in their hiding place and taken to the headquarters of one of the Freikorps divisions. There they were killed by soldiers acting according to a clearly prearranged plan.[55] The military command and the judicial authorities successfully concealed the origin of the order for their murder. Only token sentences of two years imprisonment were levied against two of the men who carried out the murder; the officers in command on the scene of the crime went free.[56] But for revolutionary workers at the time, ultimate responsibility for the crime was clear: it lay with the SPD government that had set the Freikorps murderers loose against the Berlin working class.

Four days later, the national assembly elections took place as planned. When the assembly met, the SPD formed a coalition regime with two bourgeois political parties. Unemployment increased rapidly in early 1919, and bread rations suffered further reductions. Workers' hopes for socialization came to nothing. Even the capitalist democratic reforms were not consolidated, since archreactionaries retained control of the officer corps and decisive influence in the judiciary and state administration. The Freikorps preserved much of their structures and influence in the Weimar republic. They were a factor in Hitler and Ludendorff's beer hall putsch of 1923, and most of their cadres ultimately fused into the Nazis' storm troopers.

Moreover, the civil war continued. In one region after another Noske sent his Freikorps against the workers. The Council Republic of Bremen was crushed in early February. When Ruhr workers, with considerable support from local SPD members, went into action that same month for expropriation of their employers, the army intervened. In scattered fighting on February 20 it killed seventy-two workers. The next day Kurt Eisner, head of the Bavarian government, was assassinated by a right-wing fanatic. On February 22 a general strike erupted in central Germany; troops moved against the workers on March 1, and the strike was over within a week. Just as these workers were returning to the job, Berlin erupted in a new general strike. Pitched street battles flared up once again, and this time an estimated 3,000 workers were massacred. Among the dead, shot while "trying to escape," was Leo Jogiches.

After this, Noske's troops attacked the Ruhr for the second time, then Saxony, and then the Bavarian council republic, which fell on May 1. The central leader of the Bavarian revolutionary workers' and peasants' government, Eugen Leviné, was executed by order of a military court.

The Communist Party was the main target of government repression and survived only with great difficulty. In four months four central leaders of the party were murdered by the counterrevolution: Liebknecht, Luxemburg, Jogiches, and Leviné. In the same period two other central figures, Knief from the IKD and Franz Mehring, died of natural causes. Almost all of the party's most authoritative leaders were gone. It was gagged and driven underground. Its membership was small and politically isolated. Nevertheless, the party's courageous stand in the civil war of early 1919 won it broader support in the working class and served as a basis for the KPD's subsequent fusion with the left-wing majority of the USPD in 1920.

Luxemburg's last letter, written January 11 to Zetkin, expressed her assessment of the young party's first congress and future prospects.

Letter to Clara Zetkin[57]
by Rosa Luxemburg

Dearest Clara,

I received your detailed letter today, was finally able to read it in peace, and more unbelievably, to answer it. I cannot describe the way I — all of us — have been living for the past weeks: the turmoil, the constant changing of apartments, the incessant reports of new emergencies, and in between all that, intense work, meetings, and so on and so forth. I literally could not write you. I see my apartment only occasionally for a few hours at night. Maybe today I'll manage to get this letter written. But I do not know where to begin, I have so much to tell you.

First of all, on the question of not participating in the elections. You enormously overestimate the significance of this decision. There are no "Rühlites"; Rühle was not at all a leader at the conference. Our "defeat" was only the triumph of a somewhat childish, half-bakcd, simplistic radicalism. But that was only the beginning of the conference. As it proceeded, communication between us (the Central Committee) and the delegates was established. When I briefly returned in my report to the question of participating in the elections, I already sensed a completely different response than at the beginning. Do not forget that the "Spartacists" are in large part a new generation, free from the mind-numbing traditions of "the old party, tried and true,"[58] and that has its good and bad sides. We unanimously decided not to go to court over the matter or to take it to heart.

In practice the question of the national assembly is being pushed completely into the background by the storm of events. If things continue as they have been up to now, it looks very questionable whether we will ever get to the elections or the national assembly. You view the question (I mean the unfortunate decision on the resolution) completely differently than we do because unfortunately you do not now have close contact with us, or better, you do not have the feel for the situation that can only come from first-hand contact. As I read your letter and your telegram on the election question, my first impulse was to telegraph you to come here immediately. I am *certain* that a week's stay here and direct participation in our work and discussions would be enough to produce total agreement between you and us on all questions. But now I see that I am compelled to tell you the opposite: wait a while before you come, until things settle down a bit. Living in this tumult and hourly danger, changing apartments, this hunt and chase is not for you and anyway, there is no opportunity for orderly work or even to confer. I hope that the situation will be clearer one way or another in a week and regular work will again be possible. Then your move here would be the beginning of the systematic collaboration from which communication and agreement flow automatically.

By the way, we did not admit any "Borchardtites."[59] On the contrary, the "International Communists" threw Borchardt out — at our insistence, by the way. The "Communists" were mostly those from Hamburg and Bremen. They are a thorny acquisition, to be sure, but these are secondary matters that we must get over and that will be smoothed out as the movement progresses.

On the whole our movement is developing magnificently, and across the entire country, at that. The split with the USPD had become absolutely unavoidable for *political* reasons, because even if the *people* are the same as they were in Gotha, the *situation* has changed completely.

The fierce political crises that we go through here in Berlin every two weeks, or even more frequently, seriously limit the course of systematic educational and organizational work, but at the same time they are themselves an excellent school for the masses. And in the end we have to take history as it comes. That you receive the *Rote Fahne* so rarely is really terrible! I will see to it that I send it to you daily. At this very minute the battles in Berlin continue. Many of our brave youth have fallen; Meyer, Ledebour and (we fear) Leo [Jogiches] have been arrested.

I have to close for now.

A thousand hugs,

yours,

Rosa □

Karl Radek's memoirs of January 1919, which follow, show the impact of the Berlin defeat and of the murder of Liebknecht and Luxemburg on the KPD leadership.

The Defeat in Berlin and the Murder of Rosa and Karl[60]
by Karl Radek

On January 4 the Prussian government removed the left-Independent police chief, Eichhorn, from office. He had armed the Berlin workers, Independents, and Communists. Ebert knew very well that the workers would not take this action lying down, but he was seeking a confrontation as a pretext for disarming them. General Groener has now testified to this before the court,[61] but we suspected it all along.

The day after Eichhorn's removal, *Daily Herald* correspondent Philips Price, who had become a Communist in Russia in 1918, rushed up to me and said that Ernst had been appointed in Eichhorn's place. Price also reported that when asked about his views on the dispute, Ernst said if the Eichhorn people did not give up their arms he would disarm them himself. The Central Committee [of the KPD] met and voted to proclaim a general strike and to call the workers into the streets. I asked Rosa Luxemburg what tasks we had set for ourselves. Rosa replied that this was a protest strike. We would watch what Ebert decided to do, how the workers from the provinces responded to events in Berlin, and then we would see. Liebknecht told me in a private conversation: "While it is still impossible for us to form a government, nonetheless a Ledebour government, supported by the Revolutionary Shop Stewards, may yet be possible."

Mass participation in the demonstrations was so great that it was quite possible in those days to take power in Berlin. On Wilhelmstrasse only an unarmed crowd of Social Democratic workers defended the government.[62] There were no military troops at all around the government buildings, and we now know from Groener's testimony that Ebert was ready to flee Berlin so he could return with troops. However, no one provided the masses in the streets with a battle plan. Rosa thought that taking power in Berlin would be senseless if the provinces did not rise up. The masses were taking over buildings that had no strategic importance, such as that of *Vorwärts*.

There was a group of Russian Communists, prisoners of war, in Berlin. I organized them into a reconnaissance service and sent them to a few key points on the railroad near Berlin and its environs. They reported to me that some kind of military headquarters was being set up near Dahlem, with bicyclists and automobiles going to and fro. At midmorning they told me that Noske was encamped there. It was clear that the government was planning a military attack on Berlin. By order of the Central Committee I did not leave my apartment, for Liebknecht maintained that my arrest would make the situation much more difficult: rumor had it that the Russians were orchestrating the movement. Through Central Committee member [Hermann] Duncker I sent a letter notifying the committee of Noske's military preparations, and pointing out that if we did not intend to take power, there was no point in having armed confrontations which would end in the disarming of unorganized workers. My proposal was to end the protest strike and to advance the slogan of reelecting the councils, which had handed over power to the bourgeoisie. Paul Levi delivered Rosa's response to me. She thought that the Independents would reach an agreement with the government and there was no point in our taking on ourselves the role of sounding the retreat.

Both the Central Committee and I had lost contact with Liebknecht. He had become utterly absorbed in the movement and was sitting somewhere in the Bötzow brewery with representatives of the Independent workers. On Thursday night [January 9] when Levi came to see me, we agreed that given the complete disorganization of the Central Committee we had to take the initiative.

On Friday morning a large workers' rally was supposed to assemble on Friedrichstrasse. We decided to go there, lead the crowd to the worker-occupied buildings, primarily *Vorwärts,* and get the occupiers to withdraw in order to prevent the inevitable armed conflict with government forces.

We received news that some troops were already in the city and decided to change into military uniforms. Comrades from Rixdorf had brought me such a fantastically tattered soldier's outfit that when Levi and I came on to the street the next day, everyone stared at us. We had to return home. While I was trying to assume a more respectable image, we received word that the *Vorwärts* building was surrounded and troops were storming it. Small outbreaks in Kiel and in Bremen were already suppressed.

In the *Rote Fahne* editorial offices Rosa was sitting most calmly, while Levi took great pains to persuade her to leave the premises, since an attack was imminent. There was a flurry of activity as they searched for a hiding place for Rosa and Karl. Karl insisted on calling a public meeting for Tuesday, where he and Rosa would speak. But suddenly we received a copy of *Vorwärts* which included a reproduction of a document signed by Liebknecht and Ledebour. It stated that the Ebert government had been overthrown and a government had been formed by Liebknecht and Ledebour. This document was signed on Wednesday, the sixth,[63] without the knowledge of the Central Committee.

After Rosa's and Karl's deaths, Levi related to me the impression that this document produced in Rosa. She was sitting with Liebknecht in an apartment in hiding when they brought the paper; the movement had already been defeated. When she caught sight of the ill-fated document, she asked Liebknecht what it meant.[64] Embarrassed, he answered that he had wanted to take over the Ministry of War building and that when our people needed a piece of paper to prove the overthrow of the old government, he just dictated the document and signed it. It was a military ruse. All evening Rosa did not say a word. It was obvious that Liebknecht had been carried away with the idea of forming a transitional government of left Independents and undertook this step without the knowledge of the Central Committee.

Shots were heard in the city. Everywhere workers were being disarmed. On the morning of the sixteenth we learned that Liebknecht

Armed workers and soldiers demonstrate in Berlin, January 6, 1919.

and Rosa had been arrested during the night. A meeting of the Central Committee was called for six that evening and a number of comrades were assigned to find out quickly how the arrest took place and where the arrested had been taken. On the way to the meeting I bought a newspaper and learned that our comrades were no longer among the living.

Thalheimer, Eberlein, Levi, and if I am not mistaken, Pieck sat in silence in the waiting room of a Communist doctor. I went to the next room to write an appeal to the workers about what had transpired. The Berlin workers were so badly defeated that they could not possibly think about an immediate strike. The whole city was in the hands of a raging army of brutes, former officers and subofficers and some student goons armed to the teeth, enlisted by Konrad Haenisch, Prussian minister of education, formerly a comrade and friend to us all.

Our first task was to bring together the party central leadership in order to restore communications and find out just how our comrades were murdered. Levi took the latter task in hand. Eberlein worked at reorganizing ties with the provinces. We began to search the prisons for Tyszka [Jogiches], but he soon showed up in person; he had escaped arrest. The old man came to my apartment. He had aged by ten years. He began to speak very anxiously about our old quarrels; he said that since Rosa was not here anymore, we had to pull together the old leadership again. He was anxious about when Marchlewski would return.[65]

We arranged to meet the next day at a little Dutch teahouse on Nollendorfplatz. As soon as we met, he urged me to leave for Bremen or Munich for a time, pointing out that the Social Democrats were headed for disaster, and it was necessary to wait this one out. I asked him if he intended to leave. Smiling he replied that there was no question of that: someone had to stay and write their obituary. I refused to go, for it was clear that we had to assemble some comrades to publish the party's central newspaper. As we were leaving the teahouse, Tyszka suddenly grabbed me by the arm and brought me to a pillar with posters on it. I read a poster announcing a reward for information as to my whereabouts. Tyszka insisted that if I refused to leave the city, I must not leave my apartment during the day. □

For several weeks after the Berlin workers' defeat Radek remained in hiding, and during that time he wrote an essay entitled, "The Lessons of the Civil War in Berlin." On February 12 he was arrested and his manuscript was confiscated. It was not published until 1921, when it was included in a Soviet collection of his articles on the German revolution. It was the only extended critical analysis by a Bolshevik leader of the Communists' role in the January 1919 events ever published.

Radek's 1919 essay reflects in part what he learned as a member of the Bolshevik leadership team after he arrived in Russia in late 1917. It is also marked by his earlier experiences as an active participant in the left wing of the German Socialist movement. When Radek's article appeared in Soviet Russia in 1921, it was not presented as the collective viewpoint of the Bolshevik leadership. Nonetheless, Radek was at that time the Comintern Executive Committee's leading spokesperson on Germany, and his analysis carried weight as that of the only Bolshevik who participated in these events.

Lessons of the Civil War in Berlin[66]
by Karl Radek

"The Spartacus League will never take governmental power until that is the clear, unambiguous will of the great majority of the proletarian masses of Germany. It will never take power until the masses are in conscious agreement with its aims, goals, and methods of struggle."

How is it that this point of view, which concludes the program of the Spartacus League and must be a guiding principle for the proletarian party in a time of proletarian revolution, played such an insignificant role in the civil war in Berlin that even one of the Spartacus League's founders momentarily forgot it, and also that workers joining the struggle on the call of the Spartacus League did not comprehend it?

This is explained by the newness of the Communist Party, by the absence of a rounded Communist organization, in which tactical principles are firmly rooted as a result of prolonged collective work and have entered into the flesh and blood of the masses. Our basic tactical principle, that the proletarian party has the right to take power only when the majority of the proletariat stands behind it, was expressed in the Spartacus League program as a result of the theoretical convictions of its leaders. However, it did not flow from the membership having thought the question through, if only simply because the organization of the Communist Party was still quite young and had not managed to acquire any kind of experience in mass struggle.

The Spartacus League propaganda up to now has had for the most part an *agitational character*. As the propaganda of a minority that did not yet venture to contemplate the conquest of political power, it took as its primary task urging the masses forward. It assumed that for the time being it could neglect the countervailing forces. Nowhere does its literature indicate the fact that the majority of the working class still stands on the side of the bourgeoisie; nowhere does it stop to consider the meaning and cause of this fact. Nowhere do we find any indication that the urban proletariat cannot possibly win unless it creates at least the embryo of an organization of the village proletariat throughout the countryside. Nowhere is it mentioned that in contrast to the situation in Russia, in Germany the peasants and the soldiers who are not demobilized or who are volunteers must be counted with the forces of counterrevolution. Not only the agitational character of the Spartacus League's policies in the first period of revolution, when it was necessary above all to gather the vanguard forces of the proletariat, but also the whole *character of its activity* could only call forth among Communists an inclination toward a *policy of rebellion*.

The Communist Party bases its politics on the council system. On a theoretical level it regards the councils not only as the form of state structure toward which it strives but also as a path to victory: as organs of proletarian struggle the councils are for them a means of winning a council republic. But so far this theoretical conviction has had no influence on the Communist Party's activity. *Nowhere do we see a systematic and dogged aspiration to win the majority in local workers' councils.*

From the very beginning of the revolution the social patriots took it into their hands to form the councils — not to organize the masses but to deceive and pacify them. Thus we see that in the majority of cities they establish councils not only through elections in factories and mills but also by means of parity representation of the parties. We see how everywhere they reduce the councils to the level of the former electoral associations, how they force these councils to waste time in futile discussions just so that the representatives not take into their heads to begin leading the economic and political struggle, not to speak of governmental or municipal matters. This tactic is quite natural from the point of view of the Social Democracy: like the bourgeoisie, it regards the working masses as idiots, who can best be cared for by the enlightened trade union and party bureaucrats through negotiations with representatives of the ruling class. Worker deputies elected in the factories and mills and subject at any moment to recall by their comrades would serve to express mass aspirations, while the workers' bureaucracy sees itself as a brake on the workers' movement and that is exactly how it hopes to affect it. This is why Noske's order limits the activity of the soldiers' councils and turns them into "housekeeping councils," and the official draft of the new constitution *entirely omits mention of the workers' councils*. This transformation of councils of worker deputies into weak-willed and powerless mannequins tempts the Spartacus League *to turn its back on them*, and not even to try to make them organs of struggle for council power.

At the first congress of the councils the Spartacus fraction held to a completely passive policy. Never did it act independently. It did not counterpose its policy to the policy of castrating the councils. It did not present the councils with a program showing *the role they must play*. When the congress of the councils, exceeding its authority, gave all power to the Ebert clique, the *Rote Fahne* in a brilliant article called for a mobilization of local councils of worker deputies against this action of self-castration by the congress, but this was the limit of it — *the mobilization was not carried out*.

If the social patriots' perversion of the councils can serve to explain why the Communist Party did not turn its attention to them, this inattention could only have *disastrous results* for the party. Having rejected a struggle to win a majority in the councils of workers' deputies and to broaden the scope of their activity, party members could not help but lose a feel for the living relationship of forces. This optical illusion pushed them to move out on their own in actions that far exceeded their strength.

There is nothing that deludes revolutionaries like a successful demonstration. They do not perceive the dimensions of the mass actions and they may go wrong in estimating their size, even by a factor of ten. They forget that the masses represent a solid force only when they are organizationally linked together. In particular, it is easy for a revolutionary to fall into error in Germany, where the revolutionaries did not give adequate weight to the importance of organization as a source of strength, and consequently the social patriots' organization enabled them to take power. Relying on the masses demonstrating under the banner of communism, the revolutionary is inclined to bring the struggle to a head with the strength of these forces alone.

If the Communists had waged a day-to-day struggle in the Berlin council of workers' deputies, even though a minority, if they had striven to win the majority in it, this would then have given them a solid basis to resist the thrusts of the social-patriot government and they would not have been compelled to turn every partial battle into a fight for state power before the time was ripe. By forcing the council of workers' deputies to speak out against the government attack on the workers' demonstration, they could have appealed to the factories and mills, pillorying the council if it began covering up for the government. Without a doubt reelections would thus have become necessary in a whole series of factories and mills. At the time of the conflict with the sailors, they would have already achieved dominance in the council and, given the strong pressure generated by the demonstrations, they undoubtedly could have forced the council to take up the question of city self-government. With every day they would approach being able to oppose the government with the organized strength of the working class. Giving their own independent actions at first only the character of protest and agitation, they would in addition steadily instill in the masses the basic rule that *insurrections can be carried out only when they are backed by the organized strength of the working class, the councils of workers' deputies.* In this way, they would not end up being in the position where a struggle for political power was foisted on them against their will when the conditions for it had not yet matured and when they had not taken political responsibility for this fight.

Precisely because the Communist Party was not united with the council system in its agitation or in fact, urging it forward, even while restraining it from assault, the Spartacus League's theoretical conviction that the time had not yet come for the seizure of power remained a dead letter. As early as January 7 news of the formation of a provisional government reached the Spartacus Central Committee, which opposed the activity of leading figures of the Berlin movement in that formation. Nevertheless, the committee did not look honestly enough at the facts that showed an evolution toward a conscious movement to overthrow the government.

In this situation you could choose between only two possible goals: either demonstrating the polarization between the vanguard layers of Berlin workers and the government, or pressuring the government in order to resolve the disputed questions. The first goal was already attained. The protests were diminishing; it goes without saying that they could not continue endlessly. And as this happened, so too the means of exerting pressure were also disappearing. Negotiations with the government were necessary to strive quickly for a compromise. However, in this case the plans of the Spartacus Central Committee were disturbed by an attitude that often arises in battle situations but which is also the source of *tactical errors that can be easily repeated.* For the sake of our future, *this must be stopped.*

Pressure on the enemy presupposes a desire to negotiate with him after the pressure has been applied. But the enemy in this case was not the usual bourgeois government, from which you can expect any kind of atrocity. This was a traitorous workers' government, each of whose crimes produced a feeling of pain, as if caused by a red-hot iron. Stricken by this mood, the Spartacus League stopped taking the reality into consideration and assumed that they did not have the right to negotiate with a government of traitors. This attitude lent strength to the deceptive policy whereby the Independents began negotiations, but transformed them in fact from what they should have been — an agreement with the enemy required by the circumstances — into an initial step toward the unification of Socialist parties. But refusal of false unity with the social patriots did not have to lead to a refusal to understand the real situation.

The social-patriot government was a capitalist government, like any other. In the absence of sufficient strength to overthrow this government, it has to be reckoned with as a fact, and insofar as necessary it should be negotiated with on an equal footing. If the Spartacus League did not want this, then there was nothing left for them but simply to end the struggle, openly admit their defeat, and order the Red workers and soldiers to evacuate the positions they had taken. That is, of course, if the Spartacists were not secretly still counting on the Independents to conclude an agreement with the government on their own responsibility. If that kind of speculation really took place, then it was an attempt to evade responsibility and unload it onto others. A party with such significant prospects for the future, a party of Communists, did not have the right to act that way. The party that wants to lead the revolutionary struggle of the masses *must give them an absolutely clear analysis of the situation, however woeful it may be at the present time.* An attempt to unload onto others' shoulders, for reasons of expediency, responsibility for a decision that the party itself might secretly desire, might seem on the surface to be very cunning. But this will only hurt the movement, preventing it from understanding that as long as it possesses insufficient forces for victory, negotiations with the enemy are appropriate.

The *rebellious mood* of one part of the revolutionary working class, easily explained by the newness of the German revolutionary movement, will induce certain workers to disagree with what has just been said. They conceive of the revolution as a wave continuously surging forward. For them, the task of a revolutionary leader is constantly and blindly to drive it on. In view of the authority the Russian workers' revolution and its leaders rightfully enjoy among the revolutionary working class of Germany, it is necessary to recall here the July events of 1917 in Petrograd and the role in them of the Russian Communist Party. Four months had passed since the March revolution. Economic ruin, the government's inaction on the question of peace, the policy of continuous compromise with the bourgeoisie all gave the Communist Party (Bolsheviks) greatly increased political weight. It was much stronger then than the German Communist Party is now, in January 1919. On its side stood the whole urban proletariat, the entire Petrograd garrison, and forty or so influential newspapers in the provinces. Nevertheless the party still considered the seizure of power to be premature. Outside the capital only a very small fraction was on its side.

At the front matters were no different. The peasants were still expecting the Menshevik–Socialist Revolutionary government to give them land. Therefore, when the working masses and the Petrograd garrison, in response to the new government crisis, came out on the streets and surrounded the government buildings, *the party with all its strength resisted the attempt to thrust power on it.* For the party knew how easy it was to get cut off from food supplies and be crushed by the troops recalled from the front. And this would mean the destruction of the Petrograd proletariat and the beheading of the revolution as well. In *Pravda Lenin, Trotsky,* and *Zinoviev* spoke out very strongly against the actions of the popular masses. When Kerensky assembled his troops and the confrontation was thus at hand between the soldiers from the front on the one hand and the Petrograd garrison and Kronstadt sailors on the other, and there was no hope of winning, the leaders of the Communist Party insisted not only on breaking off the fighting but even on giving up arms, since there was no way of escaping this.

Our best troops, who were later sent off to the front, dispersed with tears and curses against the Communist leaders' "betrayal." But very soon they themselves became convinced that the Bolshevik leaders had been right to hold back the movement, thereby avoiding the premature waste of fighting forces. It turned out that confidence in these leaders, far from being undermined by this defeat, increased with every day.

We are convinced that *Rosa Luxemburg and Karl Liebknecht* would have led in helping the workers understand the lessons of the Berlin defeat, had they not been torn out of the ranks of the struggling proletariat by Ebert's mercenaries. A whole series of historical circumstances compelled these true revolutionaries, filled with the will to victory, to press further than the situation permitted and to miscalculate, not allowing them to strain every effort to correct their errors, which they recognized. Yet they were too critical toward themselves, they strove too selflessly toward the truth, to conceal the reason for their errors and these errors themselves. They knew and constantly taught *that the proletariat requires self-criticism and that a basic principle of revolutionary working class politics is to know how, with the aid of self-criticism, to transform a defeat into a source of new strength.* As Karl Liebknecht wrote on the day the treacherous bullet of his assassin killed him, *"The vanquished of today shall be the victors of tomorrow, for they will learn from defeat."*[67] □

Radek was not the only Soviet Communist leader of the time to compare the Berlin events of January 1919 to the 1917 "July days" in Petrograd. In the following article, written in April 1919, Trotsky pointed to the key difference between the German events and the July days in Russia: the lack in Germany of an experienced, authoritative, and disciplined revolutionary party to argue clearly and unambiguously against premature confrontation, organize and lead the workers in a retreat, and unify them for the next round of struggle.

A Creeping Revolution[68]
by Leon Trotsky

The German revolution bears clear traits of similarity to the Russian. But no less instructive are its traits of dissimilarity. At the beginning of October a "February" revolution took place in Germany.[69] Two months later the German proletariat was already going through its "July days," that is, the first open clash on the new "republican" foundation with the bourgeois-compromisers' imperialist forces. In Germany, as in our country, the July days were neither an organized uprising, nor a decisive battle spontaneous in origin. This was the first stormy demonstration of the class struggle in pure form on soil reclaimed by the revolution, an action accompanied by clashes between vanguard detachments. In our country the experience of the July days served and aided the proletariat in further concentrating its forces and in organized preparations for the decisive battle. In Germany, after the Spartacists' first open revolutionary action was crushed and after their leaders were murdered, no breathing spell followed, truly not even of a single day. Strikes, uprisings, and open battles followed one after another in various places throughout the country. No sooner had Scheidemann's government succeeded in restoring order in the suburbs of Berlin than the valiant guardsmen, inherited from the Hohenzollerns, had to rush to Stuttgart or Nuremberg. Essen, Dresden, Munich in turn became the arena of bloody civil war. Each new victory of Scheidemann was only the point of departure for a new uprising of the Berlin workers. The revolution of the German proletariat has taken on a protracted, creeping character and, at first sight, this might arouse fears lest the ruling scoundrels succeed in bleeding it white, section by section, through a series of countless skirmishes. At the same time the following question seems to suggest itself: Has the leadership perhaps committed serious tactical blunders which threaten the entire movement with destruction?

In order to understand the German proletarian revolution one must judge it not simply by analogy with the Russian October revolution, but by taking the internal conditions of Germany's own evolution as the starting point.

History has been so shaped that in the epoch of imperialist war the German Social Democracy proved — and this can now be stated with complete objectivity — to be the most counterrevolutionary factor in world history. The German Social Democracy, however, is not an accident; it did not fall from the skies but was created by the efforts of the German working class in the course of decades of uninterrupted construction and adaptation to conditions under the capitalist-junker state. The party organization and the trade unions connected with it drew from the proletarian milieu the most outstanding, energetic elements and molded them psychologically and politically. The moment war broke out, that is to say, when the moment arrived for the greatest historical test, it turned out that the official working-class organization thought and acted not as the proletariat's organization of combat against the bourgeois state but as an auxiliary organ of the bourgeois state, designed to discipline the proletariat. The working class was paralyzed, since bearing down upon it was not only the full weight of capitalist militarism but also the apparatus of its own party. The hardships of war, its victories, its defeats, broke the paralysis of the German working class, freed it from the discipline of the official party. The party split asunder. But the German proletariat remained without a revolutionary combat organization. History once again exhibited to the world one of its dialectical contradictions. The German working class had expended most of its energy in the previous epoch on building self-sufficient organizations, and its party and trade union apparatus ranked first in the Second International. But precisely because of this, in this new epoch, at the moment of its transition to open revolutionary struggle for power, the German working class proved to be extremely defenseless organizationally.

The Russian working class which accomplished its October revolution received a priceless legacy from the previous epoch: a centralized revolutionary party. The pilgrimage of the Narodnik intelligentsia to the peasantry; the terrorist struggle of the *Narodovoltsi;*[70] the underground agitation of the pioneer Marxists; the revolutionary actions of the early years of this century; the October general strike and the barricades of 1905; the revolutionary "parliamentarism" of the Stolypin epoch,[71] so closely tied with the underground movement — all this prepared a large staff of revolutionary leaders, tempered in struggle and bound together by the unity of the revolutionary socialist program.

History bequeathed nothing like this to the German working class. It is compelled not only to fight for power but to create its organization and train future leaders in the very course of this struggle. True, under the conditions of a revolutionary epoch this work of education is being done at a feverish pace, but time is nevertheless needed to accomplish it. Absent was a centralized revolutionary party with a combat leadership whose authority is universally accepted by the working masses; absent was a leading combat nucleus and leaders, tried in action and tested in experience throughout the various centers and regions of the proletarian movement. Thus, this movement, upon breaking out into the streets, by necessity became intermittent, chaotic, and creeping in character. These erupting strikes, insurrections, and battles represent at present the only available form to openly mobilize the forces of the German proletariat, freed from the old party's yoke. At the same time they represent the sole means under these conditions of educating new leaders and of building the new party. It is self-evident that such a road calls for enormous exertion and demands countless sacrifices. But there is no choice. It is the one and only road along which the class uprising of the German proletariat can develop to its final victory.

After Bloody Sunday, January 9, 1905,[72] when the workers of Petrograd and after them, gradually, the workers throughout the country came to understand the necessity of struggle and at the same time sensed how dispersed their forces were, there ensued in the land a powerful but extremely chaotic strike movement. Sages then arose to shed tears over such expenditures of energy by the Russian working class, foretelling its exhaustion and, as a result of this, the defeat of the revolution. In reality, however, the spontaneous, creeping strikes in the spring and summer months of 1905 were the only possible form of revolutionary mobilization and of organizational education. These strikes laid the groundwork for the great October strike [of 1905] and for building the first soviets.

There is a certain analogy between what is now occurring in Germany and the period of the first Russian revolution I have just indicated. But the German revolutionary movement is, of course, developing on incomparably higher and mightier foundations. While the old official party has suffered complete bankruptcy and has become converted into an instrument of reaction, this naturally does not mean that the work accomplished by it in the preceding epoch has disappeared without a trace. The political and cultural level of the German workers, their organizational habits and capabilities, are superlative. Tens and hundreds of thousands of worker-leaders, who had been absorbed during the previous epoch by the political and trade union organizations and seemingly assimilated by them, in reality were only putting up for the time being with the violence done to their revolutionary conscience. Today in the course of open though limited clashes, through the hardships of this revolutionary mobilization, in the harsh experience of this creeping revolution, tens of thousands of temporarily blinded, deceived, and intimidated worker leaders are awakening and rising to their full stature. The working class is seeking them out, just as they themselves are finding their places in the new struggle of the working class. If the historical task of Kautsky-Haase's Independent Party consists in introducing vacillation among the ranks of the government party and supplying a refuge for its frightened, desperate, or indignant elements, then on the other hand, the stormy movement in which our Spartacist brothers-in-arms are playing such a heroic role will, as one of its consequences, lead to the uninterrupted demolition of the Independent Party from the left, since its best and most self-sacrificing elements are being drawn into the Communist movement.

The difficulties, the partial defeats, and the great sacrifices of the German proletariat should not for a moment dishearten us. History does not offer the proletariat a choice of ways. The stubborn, unabated, creeping revolution, erupting again and again, is clearly approaching the critical moment when, having mobilized and trained all its forces in advance for combat, the revolution will deal the class enemy the final mortal blow. □

In 1921 Lenin explained to German Communists how he viewed their experience following the November 1918 revolution. He considered that the fundamental error of German revolutionists was their failure, between 1914 and 1918, to make a clean political break from centrism and to begin construction of an independent revolutionary party. As a result, in the months following the November revolution, the organization lacked the strength, class struggle experience, and political homogeneity required for it to develop a correct course and implement it in a centralized manner. At the Comintern's third congress in 1921, Lenin stated that "the sufferings the whole of the German working class has had to endure during this long and weary post-war period in the history of the German revolution are due to the fact that the German party did not break with the Mensheviks."[73] Lenin returned to the question in a letter to the German Communists in August 1921, excerpted below, in which he reviewed the difficult early days of their party.

A Letter to German Communists[74]
by V.I. Lenin

From the end of 1918, the international position of Germany very quickly and sharply aggravated her internal revolutionary crisis and impelled the vanguard of the proletariat towards an immediate seizure of power. At the same time, the German and the entire international bourgeoisie, excellently armed and organized, and taught by the "Russian experience", hurled itself upon the revolutionary proletariat of Germany in a frenzy of hate. Tens of thousands of the best people of Germany — her revolutionary workers — were killed or tortured to death by the bourgeoisie, its heroes, Noske and Co., its servants, the Scheidemanns, etc. and by its indirect and "subtle" (and therefore particularly valuable) accomplices, the knights of the "Two-and-a-Half International", with their despicable spinelessness, vacillations, pedantry and philistinism. The armed capitalists set traps for the unarmed workers; they killed them wholesale, murdered their leaders, ambushing them one by one, and making excellent use to this end of the counter-revolutionary howling of both shades of Social-Democrats, the Scheidemannites and the Kautskyites. When the crisis broke out, however, the German workers lacked a genuine revolutionary party, owing to the fact that the split was brought about too late, and owing to the burden of the accursed tradition of "unity" with capital's corrupt (the Scheidemanns, Legiens, Davids and Co.) and spineless (the Kautskys, Hilferdings and Co.) gang of lackeys. The heart of every honest and class-conscious worker who accepted the Basle Manifesto of 1912 at its face value and not as a "gesture" on the part of the scoundrels of the "Second" and the "Two-and-a-Half" grades, was filled with incredibly bitter hatred for the opportunism of the old German Social-Democrats, and this hatred — the greatest and most noble sentiment of the best people among the oppressed and exploited masses — blinded people and prevented them from keeping their heads and working out a correct strategy with which to reply to the excellent strategy of the Entente capitalists, who were armed, organised and schooled by the "Russian experience", and supported by France, Britain and America. This hatred pushed them into premature insurrections.

That is why the development of the revolutionary working-class movement in Germany has since the end of 1918 been treading a particularly hard and painful road. But it has marched and is marching steadily forward. □

———————

Despite these criticisms, Lenin always pointed to the revolutionary intransigence of Luxemburg, Liebknecht, and their comrades as an example to all working-class militants. Lenin rejected the attempts of some to seize upon the leftist errors of Luxemburg and Liebknecht to justify an opportunist course.

When Paul Levi left the German Communist Party in 1921, he published Luxemburg's 1918 manuscript on the Russian revolution in an attempt to portray her as an opponent of Bolshevism. In response, Lenin in February 1922 wrote the following brief assessment of Luxemburg's contribution:

"Paul Levi now wants to get into the good graces of the bourgeoisie — and, *consequently*, of its agents, the Second and the Two-and-a-Half Internationals — by republishing precisely those writings of Rosa Luxemburg in which she was wrong. We shall reply to this by quoting two lines from a good old Russian fable: 'Eagles may at times fly lower than hens, but hens can never rise to the height of eagles.' Rosa Luxemburg was mistaken on the question of the independence of Poland; she was mistaken in 1903 in her appraisal of Menshevism; she was mistaken on the theory of the accumulation of capital; she was mistaken in July 1914, when, together with Plekhanov, Vandervelde, Kautsky and others, she advocated unity between the Bolsheviks and Mensheviks; she was mistaken in what she wrote in prison in 1918 (she corrected most of these mistakes at the end of 1918 and the beginning of 1919 after she was released). But in spite of her mistakes she was — and remains for us — an eagle. And not only will Communists all over the world cherish her memory, but her biography and her *complete* works (the publication of which the German Communists are inordinately delaying, which can only be partly excused by the tremendous losses they are suffering in their severe struggle) will serve as useful manuals for training many generations of Communists all over the world. 'Since August 4, 1914, German Social-Democracy has been a stinking corpse' — this statement will make Rosa Luxemburg's name famous in the history of the international working-class movement. And, of course, in the backyard of the working-class movement, among the dung heaps, hens like Paul Levi, Scheidemann, Kautsky and all that fraternity will cackle over the mistakes commited by the great Communist. To every man his own."[75]

Notes

1. Ya.S. Drabkin, *Die Novemberrevolution 1918 in Deutschland* (Berlin [GDR]: Deutscher Verlag der Wissenschaften, 1968), p. 512.

2. *Illustrierte Geschichte der deutschen Revolution* (Berlin: Internationaler Arbeiter-Verlag, 1929), p. 272.

3. Ibid., p. 271.

4. Richard Müller, *Der Bürgerkrieg in Deutschland*, vol. 3 of *Geschichte der deutschen Revolution*, (West Berlin: Verlag Olle und Wolter, 1979), p. 30.

5. "George Ledebour, die Revolution und die Anderen," in *Die Rote Fahne*, September 5, 1920.

6. *Dokumente und Materialien zur Geschichte der deutschen Arbeiterbewegung* (Berlin [GDR]: Dietz Verlag, 1958), series 2, vol. 3, pp. 9-10.

7. Ibid., pp. 7-8.

8. On December 9, 1918, three days after the attempted military coup, reports reached Berlin workers that heavily armed counterrevolutionary troops under the command of General Lequis were about to march into the city to subdue revolutionary workers and soldiers. Lequis's troops entered Berlin December 10, but proved unwilling to be used in battle against the Berlin workers and soldiers.

9. Wilhelm Pieck, "Erinnerungen an die Novemberrevolution in Berlin," in *Gesammelte Reden und Schriften* (Berlin [GDR]: Dietz Verlag, 1959), vol. 1, p. 466; and Müller, *Bürgerkrieg*, p. 32.

10. Müller, *Bürgerkrieg*, pp. 41-43.

11. Ibid., pp. 32-34.

12. *Illustrierte Geschichte*, pp. 274-75.

13. *Illustrierte Geschichte*, pp. 275; Pieck, *Gesammelte Reden*, p. 472.

14. Pieck, *Gesammelte Reden*, p. 467.

15. *Dokumente und Materialien*, p. 11.

16. Gustav Noske, *Von Kiel bis Kapp: zur Geschichte der deutschen Revolution* (Berlin: Verlag für Politik und Wirtschaft, 1920) p. 69.

17. *Die Rote Fahne,* September 5, 1920.
18. Karl Liebknecht, *Gesammelte Reden und Schriften* (Berlin [GDR]: Dietz Verlag, 1974), vol. 9, p. 707.
19. *Illustrierte Geschichte,* p. 276; Müller, *Bürgerkrieg,* p. 37-38.
20. Excerpted from Rosa Luxemburg, *Gesammelte Werke* (Berlin [GDR]: Dietz Verlag, 1974), vol. 4, pp. 518-20. Another translation of the full article can be found in Robert Looker, ed., *Rosa Luxemburg, Selected Political Writings,* (New York: Grove Press, 1974), pp. 291-94.
21. Noske, *Von Kiel bis Kapp,* p. 68.
22. *Dokumente und Materialien,* pp. 16-17.
23. Pieck, *Gesammelte Reden,* p. 470.
24. Drabkin, *Novemberrevolution,* pp. 494-95.
25. Pieck, *Gesammelte Reden,* p. 471.
26. Ibid., 472-73.
27. Excerpted from Luxemburg, *Gesammelte Werke,* pp. 521-24.
28. *Dokumente und Materialien,* p. 22.
29. *Illustrierte Geschichte,* p. 283.
30. *Dokumente und Materialien,* pp. 21-22.
31. Karl Radek, *Germanskaya revolyutsiya* (Moscow: Gosizdat., 1925), vol. 1, pp. 93-95; excerpted in *Illustrierte Geschichte,* p. 282.
32. Pierre Broué, *Révolution en Allemagne: 1917-1923,* (Paris: Les Editions de Minuit, 1971), p. 251.
33. See Karl Radek, "The Defeat in Berlin and the Murder of Rosa and Karl," printed below in this chapter.
34. *Illustrierte Geschichte,* p. 276.
35. *Dokumente und Materialien,* p. 34-35.
36. Drabkin, *Novemberrevolution,* p. 498.
37. Broué, *Révolution en Allemagne,* p. 250; Drabkin, *Novemberrevolution,* pp. 498-99; Pieck, *Gesammelte Reden,* pp. 473-74.
38. *Dokumente und Materialien,* pp. 41-42.
39. Arthur Rosenberg, *A History of the German Republic* (London: Methuen & Co., 1936), pp. 81-82.
40. *Illustrierte Geschichte,* p. 241.
41. Müller, *Bürgerkrieg,* pp. 223-24.
42. Gerhard A. Ritter and Susanne Miller, *Die deutsche Revolution 1918-1919: Dokumente* (Frankfurt: Fischer Taschenbuch Verlag, 1983), pp. 184-85.
43. *Vorwärts,* January 12, 1919.
44. Ibid., January 13, 1919. The poem's full text is printed in J.P. Nettl, *Rosa Luxemburg* (London: Oxford University Press, 1966), vol. 2, p. 770.
45. Luxemburg, *Gesammelte Werke,* pp. 533-38.
46. In November 1830 an insurrection for national independence broke out in Russian-ruled Poland. Russian troops were dispatched in February 1831, and Warsaw finally fell on September 8 of that year. Thousands of Poles were killed, imprisoned, or banished in retaliation. Luxemburg erred in identifying the Russian general in command; it was not Suvorov but I.F. Paskevich.
47. The Argonne Forest of northeast France and the Belgian province of Flanders were the scenes of major Allied victories in the final weeks of the First World War.
48. German forces captured the Belgian city of Liège in August 1914, in one of the first major battles of the war.

49. Following the defeat of the Paris Commune in May 1871, the government carried out indiscriminate massacres of Parisian workers; at least 17,000 were executed.

50. Demonstrators led by the Spartacists were proceeding along the Chausseestrasse on December 6 when they were fired upon by government troops.

51. Chartism was a mass movement of the British working class for political democracy and social equality that began in 1838 but was largely demobilized in the 1850s.

After the Paris workers' uprising was defeated in 1848, more than 3,000 captured workers were executed.

52. The words "rise up again, clashing its weapons" are taken from Ferdinand Freiligrath's poem, "Abschiedswort," printed in the final issue of Marx's *Neue Rheinische Zeitung,* May 19, 1849.

The words "I was, I am, I shall be" can be found in Freiligrath's popular poem "Die Revolution," written in 1851.

53. Excerpted from Liebknecht, *Gesammelte Reden,* pp. 709-13.

54. Napoleon Bonaparte used a plebiscite in 1800 to gain popular ratification for his military dictatorship. His successor Louis Bonaparte employed the same method to gain a popular mandate for his coup of December 2, 1851, and his institution of the "Second Empire."

55. The circumstances of the murder of Liebknecht and Luxemburg are described in Paul Frölich, *Rosa Luxemburg* (New York: Howard Fertig, 1969), pp. 326-33; and Nettl, *Rosa Luxemburg,* pp. 770-77.

56. A trooper named Otto Runge, who struck the first blow against Rosa Luxemburg, was sentenced to two years imprisonment for attempted manslaughter.

Lieutenant Vogel, who transmitted the order for Luxemburg's murder and fired the fatal shot, was sentenced to two years imprisonment for "neglect of duty while on active service" and for disposing illegally of a corpse. Thanks to the intervention of his superiors, Vogel was able to escape from prison in May 1919 and reach safety in the Netherlands.

Captains Horst and Heinz von Pflugk-Hartung and Captain Pabst, the three superior officers who had planned, ordered, and helped carry out the killings, went free. Exactly how the three officers had received instructions or approval for carrying out the murders was never revealed.

In 1921 Runge made a confession of his role in the murders in which he declared the officers' responsibility for ordering the crime. Nonetheless, no action was taken against the officers. Runge's confession pointed out that "The investigation has been a comedy," and described the repeated private meetings before the trial with Jörns, the public prosecutor, in which Jörns assured him, "Be calm, take everything on your shoulders, it will only be four months and afterwards you can always address yourself to us when you are in need." (*January Fifteenth: The Murder of Karl Liebknecht and Rosa Luxemburg, 1919* [London: Young Communist League of Great Britain, n.d.], pp. 60-62.) Jörns went on to a successful career after 1933 in the Nazi People's Court.

In 1962, Pabst, who had prospered through the years of Nazi rule and after, published an account of the murders, stating that "in practice the authority of the state was in the hands of the Freikorps, but they had the full support of Noske." The resulting controversy elicited a statement from the Press and Information Office of the Federal Republic of Germany that the murder of the two revolutionary leaders was "an execution in accordance with martial law." (Nettl, *Rosa Luxemburg,* vol. 2, p. 773.)

57.   Rosa Luxemburg, *Gesammelte Briefe* (Berlin [GDR]: Dietz Verlag, 1984), vol. 5, pp. 426-27.

58.   Luxemburg's words recall August Bebel's famous phrase, "the old policies, tried and true," which was linked to his stubborn defense of the SPD's traditions against anti-Marxist revisionism, and also, in his last years, against the proposals of the SPD's revolutionary left wing. See John Riddell, ed., *Lenin's Struggle for a Revolutionary International: Documents, 1907-1916; The Preparatory Years* (New York: Monad Press, 1984), p. 95, a volume of *The Communist International in Lenin's Time.*

59.   The leader of a small revolutionary group in Berlin, Julian Borchardt joined the Zimmerwald Left in 1915 and collaborated with the Bolsheviks. After 1916 he adopted anarchist views and broke with Marxism. His Berlin group fused without him into the IKD in 1918.

60.   Excerpted from Karl Radek, "Noyabr'," in *Krasnaya Nov',* October 1926, pp. 152-54.

61.   Groener testified in October 1925 in a trial that examined the causes of Germany's 1918 military collapse.

62.   The Reich chancellery and other key government buildings were located on Wilhelmstrasse.

63.   January 6, 1919, was a Monday, not a Wednesday.

64.   Another report often repeated in the early KPD was that when Liebknecht came to the party offices after a meeting of the Revolutionary Committee, Luxemburg challenged him: "But Karl, how could you, and what about our program?" See Nettl, *Rosa Luxemburg,* vol. 2, p. 767.

65.   Marchlewski, a Polish revolutionary socialist, had also been a leader of Luxemburg's current in the pre-1914 German SPD. In January 1919 he was in Russia, where he was a prominent member of the RCP.

66.   Excerpted from Karl Radek, "Uroki grazhdanskoy voyny v Berline," in *Germanskaya Revolyutsiya,* vol. 2, pp. 122-30.

67.   The quotation is from Liebknecht's article, "Despite Everything," printed above in this chapter.

68.   Leon Trotsky, "Polzuchaya Revolyutsiya," in *Pyat' let Kominterna* (Moscow: Gosizdat., 1924), pp. 25-28.

69.   At the beginning of October Max von Baden was appointed Reich chancellor, replacing a de facto military dictorship with a regime supported by the Reichstag majority. Simultaneously Germany made a peace offer to the Allied powers. These actions announced the opening of the German revolution. They were followed two months later by the first major confrontation between government troops and Berlin workers.

The month of October is given in both the 1919 *Pravda* text of Trotsky's article, and the reprinted version from 1924. Nonetheless, the context of Trotsky's article indicates that he is referring to Germany's November revolution, when a workers' and soldiers' insurrection overthrew the monarchy, as its "February," and the January fighting in Berlin as its "July days."

70.   The Narodniks (populists), a revolutionary democratic movement aimed at the overthrow of tsarism, arose in Russia in the 1870s. In 1879 the principal populist organization, Land and Liberty (Zemlya i Volya) split in two; the majority formed the People's Will (Narodnaya Volya), the minority the Black Redis-

tribution (Chërnyy Peredel). The followers of the majority were known as the Narodovoltsi.

Many of the Narodovoltsi were influenced by Marx and Engels's writings and organized their translation into Russian. Marx and Engels corresponded with leaders of this current and respected its commitment to the revolutionary overthrow of the autocracy.

Many of the Narodovoltsi later oriented toward an alliance with the liberal bourgeoisie and turned to individual terrorism. This current gave birth in 1900 to the Socialist Revolutionary Party.

A few years after the 1879 split, the leaders of the minority group, including Georgiy Plekhanov, evolved toward Marxism, and in 1883 founded Russia's first Marxist organization, the Emancipation of Labor group.

71. The Stolypin epoch covers the period of reaction following the defeat of the 1905 revolution in Russia. Stolypin headed the tsarist cabinet until his assassination in 1911.

72. On this date tsarist troops fired on a peaceful march of 100,000 Petersburg (Leningrad) workers bearing a petition for democratic rights. Several hundred were killed.

73. V.I. Lenin, *Collected Works* (Moscow: Progress Publishers, 1973), vol. 32, p. 464.

74. Excerpted from Lenin, *Collected Works*, vol. 32, pp. 512-13.

75. Ibid., vol. 33, pp. 210-11.

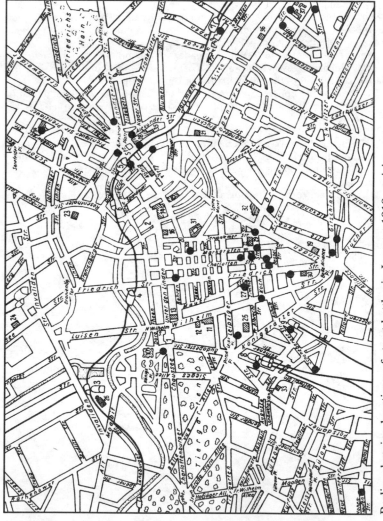

Berlin, showing locations of street battles in January 1919 uprising.

Part Two:
Toward Launching the
Communist International

-7-
The Debate on the Soviet Republic

Following the November 9, 1918, revolution in Germany, the Russian revolution moved to the center of the debate in the workers' movement there. The Spartacists and other revolutionists called for a second, anticapitalist revolution in Germany like that of the Russian October. They advocated internationalist solidarity and cooperation with the young Soviet republic. The German bourgeoisie, on the other hand, denounced the horrors of Bolshevism and called for Germany to take up the struggle against Soviet Russia. The SPD joined in this anticommunist campaign, portraying Russia as the tormented victim of Bolshevik terror and tyranny. These slanders of the Soviet regime were facilitated by the German government's refusal to allow diplomatic representation by the Soviet republic or the free entry of its citizens and publications. German troops continued to occupy wide areas of eastern Europe, where they clashed with revolutionary workers' detachments. The German High Command began to create special volunteer units, supposedly intended to defend the eastern borders, and on December 13 it proposed renewing full-scale war against Soviet Russia.

Well-financed right-wing propaganda agencies produced scare propaganda in press runs of millions. A leaflet of the Alliance to Combat Bolshevism, for example, announced that "Bolshevism means the socialization of women"; it printed a supposed Soviet decree beginning, "(1) The right to hold as property women between seventeen and thirty-two years old is abolished. (2) By this decree, all women are the property of the people." The faked document continued with lurid details of how use of this "people's property" was to be allocated.[1]

The SPD press also hammered away at the Bolshevik menace. It warned persistently against Soviet militarism, picking up the theme of the "Russian menace" previously used to justify Germany's war against its former imperialist rival to the east. The Social Democrats charged

Footnotes to this chapter begin on page 399.

that the Spartacists intended to install such a military tyranny in Germany. The following full-page statement in *Vorwärts* was typical.

Bolshevism: The Militarism of the Loafers[2]

It was hunger that forced the Russian people under the yoke of militarism. Russia's workers went on strike, destroyed the economy through overhasty socialization, deprived themselves of the means of making a living through unrealizable demands, and sacrificed their freedom to militarism. Bolshevik militarism is the violent despotism of a clique, the dictatorship of the idlers and those unwilling to work. Russia's army, made up of masses of unemployed workers, is today already waging another bloody war.

Let the Russian example be a warning. Do we also want another war? Do we want terror, the bloody reign of a caste?

NO!

We want no more bloodshed and no militarism. We want to achieve peace through work. We want peace, in order not to degenerate into a militarism dictated by the unemployed, as in Russia. Bolshevik bums call the armed masses into the streets, and armed masses, bent on violence, are militarism personified. But we do not want militarism of the right or of the left.

Bolshevism, the lazy man's militarism, knows no freedom or equality. It is vandalism and terror by a small group that arrogates power. So do not follow Spartacus, the German Bolsheviks, unless you want to ruin our economy and trade.

The collapse of German industry and trade means the downfall of the German people.

So, no to terror, no to militaristic rule by loafers and deserters.

Not militarism, but *freedom!* □

The majority leadership of the USPD also took up the cudgels against Bolshevism, seeking to counter the widespread support for Soviet Russia in the working-class ranks of the party. Karl Kautsky undertook to refute the theoretical foundations of Bolshevism in his August 1918 pamphlet, *The Dictatorship of the Proletariat*. He condemned the Bolsheviks for establishing a revolutionary dictatorship of the exploited based on the soviets of workers', peasants', and soldiers' deputies. Much of his critique of the Soviet regime, printed later in this chapter, rested on a distortion of the Bolsheviks' policy toward the Russian

Constituent Assembly, written from a bourgeois-liberal point of view. The dispersal of this body in January 1918 by the Bolshevik-led Soviet government became a central issue in the international debate between defenders of "democratic" capitalist rule and those who favored a revolutionary government of the exploited.

During the days of tsarist absolutism all Russian Social Democrats, including the Bolsheviks, had demanded a Constituent Assembly elected by universal, equal suffrage. Its primary task would be to establish a constitution for a democratic republic. After the February revolution in 1917, the bourgeois Provisional Government, which by May included the Menshevik and Socialist Revolutionary (SR) parties, repeatedly delayed election of such an assembly.

The new regime's steps to subvert a representative election were part and parcel of its efforts to postpone and eventually ditch implementation of all the most radical democratic demands of the workers and peasants — above all an immediate peace and renunciation of annexationist war aims, and a thoroughgoing confiscation of the landlords' estates and redistribution of land to those who tilled it.

Voting for the Constituent Assembly did not take place until mid-November, after the Soviet government was established. By that time, the Socialist Revolutionary Party, which still enjoyed the support of most peasants, had split on the question of Soviet power. The Left SRs opposed the party majority leadership's betrayal of the peasantry's aspiration for land. The Left SR deputies backed the Bolshevik majority in the October Soviet congress, which enacted a sweeping agrarian reform as one of its first acts upon taking power. Voting for the Constituent Assembly was based on lists of candidates drawn up by the right-wing party leadership before the split. As a result, most of the SR candidates who were elected to the assembly were Right SRs, whose policies were in more and more open conflict with the party's peasant base.

The elections gave the Bolsheviks a majority in Moscow and Petrograd, while in the country as a whole they obtained 25 percent of the vote. Fifty-eight percent of the vote went to the SRs, 13 percent to the bourgeois Constitutional Democrats (Cadets), and 4 percent to the Mensheviks.

The opponents of the Soviet majority thus had won well more than half the seats in the election. These procapitalist forces agitated for the Constituent Assembly to be granted political sovereignty in place of the Bolshevik-led workers' and peasants' government, which included several Left SR members. The slogan, "All power to the Constituent

Assembly" became a rallying cry for the first counterrevolutionary armies then launching civil war against the soviets, such as the "volunteer army" in the south headed by General A.M. Kaledin. In Petrograd, initial steps were taken to organize a military insurrection in support of the assembly.[3]

In response to this challenge, V.I. Lenin defined the Bolshevik position on the Constituent Assembly in the following article, printed in *Pravda* December 26 (13), 1918.

Theses on the Constituent Assembly[4]
by V.I. Lenin

1. The demand for the convocation of a Constituent Assembly was a perfectly legitimate part of the programme of revolutionary Social-Democracy, because in a bourgeois republic the Constituent Assembly represents the highest form of democracy and because, in setting up a Pre-parliament,[5] the imperialist republic headed by Kerensky was preparing to rig the elections and violate democracy in a number of ways.

2. While demanding the convocation of a Constituent Assembly, revolutionary Social-Democracy has ever since the beginning of the Revolution of 1917 repeatedly emphasised that a republic of Soviets is a higher form of democracy than the usual bourgeois republic with a Constituent Assembly.

3. For the transition from the bourgeois to the socialist system, for the dictatorship of the proletariat, the Republic of Soviets (of Workers', Soldiers' and Peasants' Deputies) is not only a higher type of democratic institution (as compared with the usual bourgeois republic crowned by a Constituent Assembly), but is the only form capable of securing the most painless transition to socialism.

4. The convocation of the Constituent Assembly in our revolution on the basis of lists submitted in the middle of October 1917 is taking place under conditions which preclude the possibility of the elections to this Constituent Assembly faithfully expressing the will of the people in general and of the working people in particular.

5. Firstly, proportional representation results in a faithful expression of the will of the people only when the party lists correspond to the real division of the people according to the party groupings reflected in those lists. In our case, however, as is well known, the party which from May to October had the largest number of followers among the people, and especially among the peasants—the Socialist-Revolutionary Party—came out with united election lists

for the Constituent Assembly in the middle of October 1917, but split in November 1917, after the elections and before the Assembly met.

For this reason, there is not, nor can there be, even a formal correspondence between the will of the mass of the electors and the composition of the elected Constituent Assembly.

6. Secondly, a still more important, not a formal nor legal, but a socio-economic, class source of the discrepancy between the will of the people, and especially the will of the working classes, on the one hand, and the composition of the Constituent Assembly, on the other, is due to the elections to the Constituent Assembly having taken place at a time when the overwhelming majority of the people could not yet know the full scope and significance of the October, Soviet, proletarian-peasant revolution, which began on October 25, 1917, i.e., after the lists of candidates for the Constituent Assembly had been submitted.

7. The October Revolution is passing through successive stages of development before our very eyes, winning power for the Soviets and wresting political rule from the bourgeoisie and transferring it to the proletariat and poor peasantry.

8. It began with the victory of October 24-25 in the capital, when the Second All-Russia Congress of Soviets of Workers' and Soldiers' Deputies, the vanguard of the proletarians and of the most politically active section of the peasants, gave a majority to the Bolshevik Party and put it in power.

9. Then, in the course of November and December, the revolution spread to the entire army and peasants, this being expressed first of all in the deposition of the old leading bodies (army committees, gubernia peasant committees, the Central Executive Committee of the All-Russia Soviet of Peasants' Deputies, etc.)—which expressed the superseded, compromising phase of the revolution, its bourgeois, and not proletarian, phase, and which were therefore inevitably bound to disappear under the pressure of the deeper and broader masses of the people—and in the election of new leading bodies in their place.

10. This mighty movement of the exploited people for the reconstruction of the leading bodies of their organisations has not ended even now, in the middle of December 1917, and the Railwaymen's Congress,[6] which is still in session, represents one of its stages.

11. Consequently, the grouping of the class forces in Russia in the course of their class struggle is in fact assuming, in November and December 1917, a form differing in principle from the one that the party lists of candidates for the Constituent Assembly compiled in

the middle of October 1917 could have reflected.

12. Recent events in the Ukraine (partly also in Finland and Byelorussia, as well as in the Caucasus) point similarly to a regrouping of class forces which is taking place in the process of the struggle between the bourgeois nationalism of the Ukrainian Rada, the Finnish Diet, etc., on the one hand,[7] and Soviet power, the proletarian-peasant revolution in each of these national republics, on the other.

13. Lastly, the civil war which was started by the Cadet-Kaledin counter-revolutionary revolt against the Soviet authorities, against the workers' and peasants' government, has finally brought the class struggle to a head and has destroyed every chance of settling in a formally democratic way the very acute problems with which history has confronted the peoples of Russia, and in the first place her working class and peasants.

14. Only the complete victory of the workers and peasants over the bourgeois and landowner revolt (as expressed in the Cadet-Kaledin movement), only the ruthless military suppression of this revolt of the slave-owners can really safeguard the proletarian-peasant revolution. The course of events and the development of the class struggle in the revolution have resulted in the slogan "All Power to the Constituent Assembly!"—which disregards the gains of the workers' and peasants' revolution, which disregards Soviet power, which disregards the decisions of the Second All-Russia Congress of Soviets of Workers' and Soldiers' Deputies, of the Second All-Russia Congress of Peasants' Deputies, etc.—*becoming in fact* the slogan of the Cadets and the Kaledinites and of their helpers. The entire people are now fully aware that the Constituent Assembly, if it parted ways with Soviet power, would inevitably be doomed to political extinction.

15. One of the particularly acute problems of national life is the problem of peace. A really revolutionary struggle for peace began in Russia only after the victory of the October 25 Revolution, and the first fruits of this victory were the publication of the secret treaties, the conclusion of an armistice, and the beginning of open negotiations for a general peace without annexations and indemnities.

Only now are the broad sections of the people actually receiving a chance fully and openly to observe the policy of revolutionary struggle for peace and to study its results.

At the time of the elections to the Constituent Assembly the mass of the people had no such chance.

It is clear that the discrepancy between the composition of the elected Constituent Assembly and the actual will of the people on the question of terminating the war is inevitable from this point of view too.

16. The result of all the above-mentioned circumstances taken together is that the Constituent Assembly, summoned on the basis of the election lists of the parties existing prior to the proletarian-peasant revolution under the rule of the bourgeoisie, must inevitably clash with the will and interests of the working and exploited classes which on October 25 began the socialist revolution against the bourgeoisie. Naturally, the interests of this revolution stand higher than the formal rights of the Constituent Assembly, even if those formal rights were not undermined by the absence in the law on the Constituent Assembly of a provision recognising the right of the people to recall their deputies and hold new elections at any moment.

17. Every direct or indirect attempt to consider the question of the Constituent Assembly from a formal, legal point of view, within the framework of ordinary bourgeois democracy and disregarding the class struggle and civil war, would be a betrayal of the proletariat's cause, and the adoption of the bourgeois standpoint. The revolutionary Social-Democrats are duty bound to warn all and sundry against this error,[8] into which a few Bolshevik leaders, who have been unable to appreciate the significance of the October uprising and the tasks of the dictatorship of the proletariat, have strayed.

18. The only chance of securing a painless solution to the crisis which has arisen owing to the divergence between the elections to the Constituent Assembly, on the one hand, and the will of the people and the interests of the working and exploited classes, on the other, is for the people to exercise as broadly and as rapidly as possible the right to elect the members of the Constituent Assembly anew, and for the Constituent Assembly to accept the law of the Central Executive Committee on these new elections, to proclaim that it unreservedly recognises Soviet power, the Soviet revolution, and its policy on the questions of peace, the land and workers' control, and to resolutely join the camp of the enemies of the Cadet-Kaledin counter-revolution.

19. Unless these conditions are fulfilled, the crisis in connection with the Constituent Assembly can be settled only in a revolutionary way, by Soviet power adopting the most energetic, speedy, firm and determined revolutionary measures against the Cadet-Kaledin counter-revolution, no matter behind what slogans and institutions (even participation in the Constituent Assembly) this counter-revolution may hide. Any attempt to tie the hands of Soviet power in this struggle would be tantamount to aiding counter-revolution. □

When the Constituent Assembly met on January 18 (5), 1919, the Bolshevik leader Y.M. Sverdlov proposed the following declaration, drafted by Lenin and submitted by the all-Russian soviet executive committee.

Declaration of Rights of the Working and Exploited People[9]
by V.I. Lenin

The Constituent Assembly resolves:

I. 1. Russia is hereby proclaimed a Republic of Soviets of Workers', Soldiers' and Peasants' Deputies. All power, centrally and locally, is vested in these Soviets.

2. The Russian Soviet Republic is established on the principle of a free union of free nations, as a federation of Soviet national republics.

II. Its fundamental aim being to abolish all exploitation of man by man, to completely eliminate the division of society into classes, to mercilessly crush the resistance of the exploiters, to establish a socialist organisation of society and to achieve the victory of socialism in all countries, the Constituent Assembly further resolves:

1. Private ownership of land is hereby abolished. All land together with all buildings, farm implements and other appurtenances of agricultural production, is proclaimed the property of the entire working people.

2. The Soviet laws on workers' control and on the Supreme Economic Council are hereby confirmed for the purpose of guaranteeing the power of the working people over the exploiters and as a first step towards the complete conversion of the factories, mines, railways, and other means of production and transport into the property of the workers' and peasants' state.

3. The conversion of all banks into the property of the workers' and peasants' state is hereby confirmed as one of the conditions for the emancipation of the working people from the yoke of capital.

4. For the purpose of abolishing the parasitic sections of society, universal labour conscription is hereby instituted.

5. To ensure the sovereign power of the working people, and to eliminate all possibility of the restoration of the power of the exploiters, the arming of the working people, the creation of a socialist Red Army of workers and peasants and the complete disarming of the

propertied classes are hereby decreed.

III. 1. Expressing its firm determination to wrest mankind from the clutches of finance capital and imperialism, which have in this most criminal of wars drenched the world in blood, the Constituent Assembly whole-heartedly endorses the policy pursued by Soviet power of denouncing the secret treaties, organising the most extensive fraternisation with the workers and peasants of the armies in the war, and achieving at all costs, by revolutionary means, a democratic peace between the nations, without annexations and indemnities and on the basis of the free self-determination of nations.

2. With the same end in view, the Constituent Assembly insists on a complete break with the barbarous policy of bourgeois civilisation, which has built the prosperity of the exploiters belonging to a few chosen nations on the enslavement of hundreds of millions of working people in Asia, in the colonies in general, and in the small countries.

The Constituent Assembly welcomes the policy of the Council of People's Commissars in proclaiming the complete independence of Finland, commencing the evacuation of troops from Persia, and proclaiming freedom of self-determination for Armenia.

3. The Constituent Assembly regards the Soviet law on the cancellation of the loans contracted by the governments of the tsar, the landowners and the bourgeoisie as a first blow struck at international banking, finance capital, and expresses the conviction that Soviet power will firmly pursue this path until the international workers' uprising against the yoke of capital has completely triumphed.

IV. Having been elected on the basis of party lists drawn up prior to the October Revolution, when the people were not yet in a position to rise *en masse* against the exploiters, had not yet experienced the full strength of the resistance of the latter in defence of their class privileges, and had not yet applied themselves in practice to the task of building socialist society, the Constituent Assembly considers that it would be fundamentally wrong, even formally, to put itself in opposition to Soviet power.

In essence the Constituent Assembly considers that now, when the people are waging the last fight against their exploiters, there can be no place for exploiters in any government body. Power must be vested wholly and entirely in the working people and their authorised representatives — the Soviets of Workers', Soldiers' and Peasants' Deputies.

Supporting Soviet power and the decrees of the Council of People's Commissars, the Constituent Assembly considers that its own task is confined to establishing the fundamental principles of the socialist reconstruction of society.

At the same time, endeavouring to create a really free and voluntary, and therefore all the more firm and stable, union of the working classes of all the nations of Russia, the Constituent Assembly confines its own task to setting up the fundamental principles of a federation of Soviet Republics of Russia, while leaving it to the workers and peasants of each nation to decide independently at their own authoritative Congress of Soviets whether they wish to participate in the federal government and in the other federal Soviet institutions, and on what terms. □

A motion to discuss this proposed declaration was defeated by 237 votes to 138. After further debate, the Bolshevik and Left SR deputies left the assembly. They declared that the Right SR majority had shown its determination to use the assembly to fight against Soviet power and against the gains achieved by the exploited under Soviet rule.[10] The rump of the assembly continued its debates into the night, until at 5:00 a.m. they were asked to leave by the guards and did so without resistance. The next day the Soviet government decreed the assembly's dissolution. This action was treated as a sensation by the bourgeois press abroad, but it passed almost unnoticed among the Russian masses.[11] The following is the text of the Soviet decree.

Draft Decree on the Dissolution of the Constituent Assembly[12]
by V.I. Lenin

At its very inception, the Russian revolution produced the Soviets of Workers', Soldiers' and Peasants' Deputies as the only mass organisation of all the working and exploited classes capable of leading the struggle of these classes for their complete political and economic emancipation.

During the whole of the initial period of the Russian revolution the Soviets multiplied in number, grew and gained strength and were taught by their own experience to discard the illusions of compromise with the bourgeoisie and to realise the deceptive nature of the forms of the bourgeois-democratic parliamentary system; they arrived by practical experience at the conclusion that the emancipation of the oppressed classes was impossible unless they broke with these forms and with every kind of compromise. The break came with the October Revolution, which transferred the entire power to the Soviets.

The Constituent Assembly, elected on the basis of electoral lists drawn up prior to the October Revolution, was an expression of the old relation of political forces which existed when power was held by the compromisers and the Cadets. When the people at that time voted for the candidates of the Socialist-Revolutionary Party, they were not in a position to choose between the Right Socialist-Revolutionaries, the supporters of the bourgeosie, and the Left Socialist-Revolutionaries, the supporters of socialism. The Constituent Assembly, therefore, which was to have crowned the bourgeois parliamentary republic, was bound to become an obstacle in the path of the October Revolution and Soviet power.

The October Revolution, by giving power to the Soviets, and through the Soviets to the working and exploited classes, aroused the desperate resistance of the exploiters, and in the crushing of this resistance, it fully revealed itself as the beginning of the socialist revolution. The working classes learned by experience that the old bourgeois parliamentary system had outlived its purpose and was absolutely incompatible with the aim of achieving socialism, and that not national institutions, but only class institutions (such as the Soviets) were capable of overcoming the resistance of the propertied classes and of laying the foundations of socialist society. To relinquish the sovereign power of the Soviets, to relinquish the Soviet Republic won by the people, for the sake of the bourgeois parliamentary system and the Constituent Assembly, would now be a step backwards and would cause the collapse of the October workers' and peasants' revolution.

Owing to the above-mentioned circumstances, the Party of Right Socialist-Revolutionaries, the party of Kerensky, Avksentyev and Chernov, obtained the majority in the Constituent Assembly which met on January 5. Naturally, this party refused to discuss the absolutely clear, precise and unambiguous proposal of the supreme organ of Soviet power, the Central Executive Committee of the Soviets, to recognise the programme of Soviet power, to recognise the Declaration of Rights of the Working and Exploited People, to recognise the October Revolution and Soviet power. By this action the Constituent Assembly severed all ties with the Soviet Republic of Russia. It was inevitable that the Bolshevik group and the Left Socialist-Revolutionary group, who now patently constitute the overwhelming majority in the Soviets and enjoy the confidence of the workers and the majority of the peasants, should withdraw from such a Constituent Assembly.

The Right Socialist-Revolutionary and Menshevik parties are in fact carrying on outside the Constituent Assembly a most desperate struggle against Soviet power, calling openly in their press for its overthrow and describing as arbitrary and unlawful the crushing of the resistance of the exploiters by the forces of the working classes, which is essential in the interests of emancipation from exploitation. They are defending the saboteurs, the servants of capital, and are going as far as undisguised calls to terrorism, which certain "unidentified groups" have already begun. It is obvious that under such circumstances the remaining part of the Constituent Assembly could only serve as a screen for the struggle of the counter-revolutionaries to overthrow Soviet power.

Accordingly, the Central Executive Committee resolves that the Constituent Assembly is hereby dissolved. □

The following are the portions of Kautsky's pamphlet, *The Dictatorship of the Proletariat,* that deal with the Constituent Assembly and offer an appraisal of Soviet rule in Russia.

The Dictatorship of the Proletariat[13]
by Karl Kautsky
6. Constituent Assembly and Soviets

The foundation of the Bolshevik revolution was the assumption that it would be the starting point of a general European revolution, that this bold Russian initiative would summon the proletariat of all Europe to rise up.

Given that assumption, it was of course irrelevant what form Russia's separate peace took, what humiliations and burdens it placed on the Russian people, and what interpretation it gave to the right to self-determination. It was also irrelevant whether Russia could defend itself. From this point of view, the European revolution constituted the Russian revolution's best defense and would provide full and true self-determination for all the peoples in the formerly Russian territories.

A revolution in Europe that established and consolidated socialism would also be the means with which to overcome the obstacles posed by Russia's economic backwardness to implementing socialist production there.

This was all reasonable and logically thought out, provided you conceded the underlying premise, that the Russian revolution would definitely unleash the European. But what if that did not happen?

That precondition has not yet been fulfilled. And now the European proletariat is being accused of having abandoned and betrayed the Russian revolution. . . .

However, the Bolsheviks cannot be overly blamed for having expected a European revolution. Other socialists did likewise and we certainly will encounter conditions that could produce a sharpening of the class struggle, with many surprises. And if the Bolsheviks have been wrong so far in expecting a revolution, did not Bebel, Engels, and Marx sometimes make the same mistake? We cannot deny that. But they never had in mind a *specific deadline* for a revolution. They never shaped their tactics so as to make the party's existence and the advance of the proletarian class struggle contingent upon the revolution occurring. They never forced the proletariat to chose between revolution or bankruptcy.

Like all politicians, they too were mistaken in their expectations from time to time. But never did such an error lure them onto a false course, into a dead end.

Our Bolshevik comrades staked everything on the general European revolution. When this gamble did not pay off, they were forced onto a course strewn with insoluble problems. Without an army they had to defend Russia against powerful and ruthless enemies. They were supposed to establish a reign of prosperity for all in a situation of general disintegration and impoverishment. The more that the material and intellectual requirements for all their goals were lacking, the more, of necessity, they felt forced to substitute the use of naked power — the dictatorship. This substitution increased as the popular masses' opposition to them grew. Thus dictatorship inexorably displaced democracy.

The Bolsheviks deluded themselves first with the expectation that they needed only to form the government in order to touch off the European revolution, and equally by thinking that they needed only to seize the rudder of state, and the majority of the population would rejoice and rally around them. As we have noted, while in opposition they certainly developed great propagandistic strength, given the conditions in Russia. Only a handful at the beginning of the revolution, they eventually became strong enough to seize state power. But did they have the support of the mass of the population?

The Constituent Assembly was supposed to determine that. The Bolsheviks, like the other revolutionaries, had called for and at times vehemently demanded a constituent assembly elected by general, equal, direct, and secret ballot.

Immediately after the Bolsheviks' conquest of power, the new regime was confirmed by the Second All-Russian Congress of Soviets, although over the opposition of a strong minority that bolted the congress in protest. But even the majority did not yet reject the idea of a constituent assembly. The resolution confirming the Soviet government began with the words, *"Until the Constituent Assembly is convoked,* a provisional workers' and peasants' government, called the *Council of People's Commissars,* shall constitute *the national government."*

Thus the Constituent Assembly was recognized as having authority over the Council of People's Commissars.

On November 3 the Petrograd city council was dissolved on the grounds that it did not represent the views of the population as expressed by the November 7 revolution and *"the Constituent Assembly elections."* The new elections were called on the basis of the existing general franchise. But soon a flaw was discovered in the Constituent Assembly elections. On December 7 the All-Russian Executive Committee of the Soviets published a resolution that read:

"However the election machinery may be devised, a body composed of elected representatives can be seen as truly democratic and actually representing the will of the people only if the voters' right to recall the deputies is recognized and utilized. This basic principle of true democracy applies to all representative bodies, including the *Constituent Assembly.* . . . The Congress of Soviets of the Workers', Soldiers', and Peasants' Deputies, convened on the basis of equality of representation, has the right to call new elections for all urban, rural, and other representative bodies, including the Constituent Assembly. At the request of more than half the voters of any electoral district, the soviets must call a new election."

The demand that the majority of the voters be able to recall a deputy whenever he no longer reflects their views corresponds fully with democratic principles. But that does not explain why the soviets came to order new elections. Moreover, they did not yet make any further move against the Constituent Assembly. Neither the institution of the assembly itself nor the franchise was touched.

Nevertheless, it became increasingly clear that the Bolsheviks had not won a majority in the elections. Therefore, on December 26, 1917, *Pravda* published a series of theses on the Constituent Assembly that Lenin had drafted and the Central Committee had adopted. Two of them are particularly important. One stated that the elections had taken place shortly after the Bolshevik victory, before the Socialist Revolutionaries had split. So the Left and the Right Socialist Revolutionaries had a common candidates' list. Therefore, the elections did not give a clear picture of the masses' real mood.

Logically, the December 7 decree would lead to calling new Constituent Assembly elections in those districts where Socialist Revolutionaries had been elected. What other purpose could the resolution have? Nevertheless, by December 26, it was already forgotten, and suddenly an entirely different song was heard, found in the second of Lenin's sentences that concern us. Having shown that the recently elected Constituent Assembly was invalid because it did not express the real mood of the popular masses, he explains that the general franchise itself, that is, any Constituent Assembly, elected by the masses, is also invalid:

"The Republic of Soviets (of Workers', Soldiers' and Peasants' Deputies) is not only a higher type of democratic institution (as compared with the usual bourgeois republic crowned by a Constituent Assembly), but is the only form capable of securing the most painless transition to socialism."

Pity that they did not realize this until after they had been placed in a minority in the Constituent Assembly. Before that, no one had demanded it more vehemently than Lenin.

Now a collision with the Constituent Assembly was unavoidable. It ended in victory for the soviets, whose dictatorship was proclaimed as Russia's permanent form of government. . . .[14]

10. The New Theory

We have seen that the method of dictatorship does not promise good results for the proletariat either from the standpoint of theory in general or in the particular Russian conditions. Nevertheless, it is precisely these conditions that enable us to understand the dictatorship.

The struggle against tsarism was long directed against a governmental system that no longer had a base in social relations, that maintained itself only with naked force, and that had to be overthrown by force. That could easily lead to a cult of violence among the revolutionaries and to an overestimation of what could be accomplished with sheer power that is not sustained by the economic relations, but rather is elevated above these relations by special circumstances. In addition, the fight against tsarism had to be carried out in secrecy. But conspiracy bred the customs and habits of dictatorship, not democracy.

Granted, another effect of the struggle against absolutism counteracted these factors. We have already noted that contrary to democracy, with its profusion of painstaking labor for ephemeral goals, dictatorship awakens interest in the big picture and noble aims — it arouses interest in theory. But today there is still only one revolutionary social theory, that of Karl Marx.

This became the theory of Russian socialism. It teaches how our will and power depend upon material conditions. It shows the helplessness of even the strongest will to rise above these conditions. It sharply opposed the cult of naked power and led to agreement among the Social Democrats that their actions in the coming revolution would be confined by certain limits. Given Russia's economic backwardness, it initially could only be a bourgeois revolution.

Then the second revolution came and brought the Socialists enormous power that surprised even them, since this revolution led to the complete disintegration of the army, the sturdiest pillar of property and bourgeois order. And with the repressive apparatus went the moral buttresses of this order, which collapsed completely. Neither the church nor the intellectuals could maintain their authority. Power fell to the nation's lowest classes, the workers and peasants. But the peasants are not a class that can govern alone. They willingly allowed themselves to be led by a proletarian party that promised them immediate peace, whatever the cost, and immediate satisfaction of their hunger for land. The proletarian masses also streamed to this same party, which promised them peace and bread.

That is how the Bolsheviks were able to achieve power. With the proletariat's conquest of power, was not the precondition set by Marx and Engels for the coming of socialism finally met? True, economic theory held that socialist production was not immediately attainable under Russian social conditions. This conclusion was confirmed by the fact that the new government was by no means a dictatorship of the proletariat alone, but rather was a coalition of proletarian and bourgeois forces, which maintained itself by allowing each side free rein in its respective domain. The proletariat did nothing to obstruct the peasants on the land, and the peasants did nothing to obstruct the proletariat in the factories.

Nevertheless, for the first time in world history, a Socialist party had gained mastery in a big country. Certainly a tremendous, glorious event for the struggling proletariat.

But what is a Socialist party to use its power for, if not to implement socialism? It must immediately get to work, ruthlessly and without second thoughts clearing all obstacles that stand in the way. If in the process democracy comes into conflict with the new regime, if despite the great popularity it has newly won, it still cannot get a majority of the votes in the country, then so much the worse for democracy. Then it must be replaced by dictatorship, a substitution more easily accomplished in Russia where popular freedom was very new and had not yet sunk deep roots in the masses of the people. The task of the dictatorship was now to implement socialism. This concrete example would not only sweep away all resistant elements in their own country, but would also arouse the proletariat of the other capitalist countries to do likewise, inflaming them to revolution.

This grandiose and audacious line of reasoning certainly held a captivating appeal for every proletarian and every socialist. At last, we supposedly had attained what we had fought a half century for and so often thought was so close, but which had always eluded us. No wonder the proletariat of all countries cheered the Bolsheviks. The fact of proletarian power carried more weight than theoretical considerations. And the general triumphant mentality was promoted by the people's mutual ignorance of their neighbor's conditions. Only a few are able to study foreign lands. Most assume that things in other countries are much like at home, and that whoever did not accept this must have some pretty fanciful ideas about other countries.

Hence the comfortable view that the same imperialism ruled everywhere. From this came the Russian Socialists' expectation that Europe's peoples were as close to political revolutions as Russia's, and likewise the expectation that conditions for socialism were as ripe in Russia as in western Europe.

What then transpired, once the army was completely dissolved and the Constituent Assembly had been given the boot, was only the logical consequence of the course that had been chosen.

This is all very understandable, if not agreeable. But it is not so comprehensible why our Bolshevik comrades did not stick to explaining their conduct within the peculiar Russian situation and to justifying it in light of the pressure from the special conditions that, in their opinion, left them no options other than dictatorship or abdication. Instead, they went on to justify their actions by erecting a whole new theory that they claim has general application.

We believe this comes from their great interest in theory, a characteristic of theirs that we can only appreciate.

The Bolsheviks are Marxists. They have inspired proletarian layers with an enthusiasm for Marxism. Nevertheless, their dictatorship is inconsistent with the Marxist doctrine that objectively a people cannot skip or abolish by decree stages of historical development. So how do they come up with a contrary Marxist argument?

At this point they recollect, most opportunely, that Marx once used the term "dictatorship of the proletariat" in a letter in 1875.[15] However, he was only trying to describe a political *situation,* not a *form of government.* But now it is suddenly used to describe a form of government, namely, that created under Soviet rule.

But Marx did not merely say that a dictatorship of the proletariat might arise under certain circumstances, but rather he described that situation as inevitable for the transition to socialism. However, at almost the same time he explained that in countries like Britain and America, a peaceful transition to socialism is possible.[16] Since that could be achieved only democratically and not by means of a dictatorship, he showed that what he meant by dictatorship did not imply abolishing democracy. The advocates of dictatorship did not allow that to stop them. Since Marx once said that the dictatorship of the proletariat was unavoidable, they proclaim that the Soviet constitution, disfranchising opponents of the soviets, was recognized by Marx himself as the intrinsically proletarian governmental form, necessary to its supremacy. As such, it must last as long as proletarian rule itself, until socialism has been generally accomplished and all class differences have disappeared. Thus the dictatorship emerges not as a stopgap that gives way to democracy as soon as quieter times arrive. Instead, it is a state of affairs that we must accept as being of lengthy duration. . . .

Turning to dictatorial methods not to save an endangered democracy but to stay in power against democracy is shortsighted politics of expediency on the part of the Russian revolutionaries. But it is understandable.

What is not understandable is that German Social Democrats, who are not yet in power but at this point still represent a weak opposition, adopt this theory. Instead of seeing dictatorship and disfranchisement of broad masses of people as methods that in general we condemn, or at most we view as the product of exceptional circumstances such as confront Russia, they go so far as to praise these methods as something that even German Social Democracy aspires to.

This claim is not only totally false; it is extremely damaging. If generally believed, it would seriously cripple our party's propagandistic strength, because except for a small gang of sectarian fanatics, the entire German and the entire international proletariat adhere to the principle of universal democracy. The proletariat will indignantly repudiate any thought of beginning its reign by establishing a new privileged class and a new subject class. It will repudiate any thought of accepting only with a mental reservation the people's longing for general civil rights, while in reality merely seeking privileges for itself. And it will equally repudiate the comical impertinence that it solemnly declare today that its demand for democracy is a lie.

The dictatorship as a form of government in Russia is just as understandable as was Bakunin's anarchism previously. But understanding is not approving, and we must reject the one just as decisively as the other. Dictatorship is not a means that a socialist party can use to achieve and preserve power against the popular majority. Rather it is only a means of confronting problems that are beyond its strength, whose resolution exhausts and wears it down. But the socialist ideal is thereby all too easily compromised, and its progress is hindered, not advanced.

Fortunately, the failure of a dictatorship does not have to be synonymous with the revolution's collapse. That would be true only if the Bolshevik dictatorship were a mere prelude to a bourgeois dictatorship. The essential gains of this revolution will be saved if the dictatorship can be replaced with democracy in time. □

Kautsky's opposition to Bolshevism was not shared by broad sectors of the working-class ranks of the USPD, where sympathy with the Soviet government was strong. The party's cochairman, Hugo Haase, took this fact into account in his widely read December 14 article, "A German Policy for the German Revolution." Rather than taking the Bolsheviks' course head on, Haase argued that their policies could not succeed in Germany because conditions there differed so greatly from those in Russia, particularly with respect to the land question, the mood of the army, and workers' attitudes to democracy.

In Russia, wrote Haase, "once the peasants had their land, they were no longer concerned with the fate of the revolution and became either counterrevolutionary or indifferent. If the Russian proverb earlier held that 'the tsar is far away,' now the Bolsheviks were far away. The peasants' indifference largely explains why the Bolsheviks have been able to hold power so long. Their rule extends only over the industrial centers and does not touch the great peasant masses." Against this, Haase contrasted the German peasant, whom he held to be almost irreversibly prone to conservative views.

The force that brought the Bolsheviks to power, Haase continued, was "a rebellion of the army, which wanted peace at any price, while the Kerensky government had begun a new offensive, demanding heavy sacrifices." In Germany, however, the soldiers' rebellion had already taken place before November 9, and the new government was at one with the soldiers in its commitment to peace.

Thirdly, "the Bolsheviks proclaimed a permanent Soviet dictatorship. They then had to expand this dictatorship through the terror, which was not instituted of their own free will, but was forced on them by the course of events. This terror was directed not only against the bourgeoisie, but against representatives of the peasants and proletarians, the Socialist Revolutionaries and the Mensheviks."

Because of the profound democratic convictions of the German working class, however, "an attempt to erect such a dictatorship in Germany would cause the outbreak of war within the working class itself, precisely at the moment when the counterrevolution undertook its first attempts to strangle the revolution."[17]

Despite their differences in approach and argumentation, *Vorwärts*, Kautsky, and Haase all supported the SPD-USPD government's hostile moves against the Russian Soviet republic.

The Spartacus current, by contrast, stood in full solidarity with the Soviet government. Nonetheless, its leaders, to varying degrees, held criticisms of Bolshevik policy, particularly of the Soviet government's decision in early 1918 to sign a separate peace with the German regime. The first comment on the October revolution in the Spartacists' underground newspaper, which appeared in its January 1918 issue, warned that the Bolsheviks were overestimating the revolution's impact on workers in the warring imperialist powers. The article also cautioned that a separate Russian peace with Germany, far from leading to a general peace, would simply give a second wind to German imperialism. But if the Bolsheviks felt compelled to seek such a peace, the Spartacists continued, this was fundamentally due to the failure of the western and above all the German proletariat to rise in support of the Soviet peace offer.[18]

Subsequently, the Spartacus leadership refrained from public criticism of the Bolsheviks. Rosa Luxemburg, who was still in Breslau prison at the time, disagreed with this policy, and an exception was made for her in the September 1918 issue of *Spartacus* with the publication of her unsigned article, "The Russian Tragedy."[19] It criticized the Brest-Litovsk peace as "a capitulation of the Russian revolutionary proletariat before German imperialism." Signing this treaty had lessened the chances for a German revolution, she wrote, without preventing continued German conquests in the East that were strangling the Soviet republic.[20] An editor's note expressed agreement with the fears expressed in the article, but underlined that these problems had arisen "because of the objective situation of the Bolsheviks, not because of their subjective conduct."[21]

The Spartacus leadership rejected a second article by Luxemburg. She reluctantly accepted this decision, but wrote a fuller exposition of her criticisms of Bolshevik policy, which was intended only for leadership circulation. Entitled "The Russian Revolution,"[22] this manuscript was never edited to completion and was not published until after her death, in 1922. In addition to her criticisms of Bolshevik agrarian policy, printed above in chapter 5, it reiterated her criticisms of the Bolsheviks' decision to conclude a separate peace with Germany. It also opposed Bolshevik application of the principle of self-determination to nations oppressed within the old tsarist empire, criticized the dissolution of the Constituent Assembly, and warned against the Bolsheviks' political and military course (the "Red Terror") in quelling the armed counterrevolution.

Yet Luxemburg reemphasized that the problems of the Russian revolution flowed from "an inevitable chain of causes and effects," resulting from "the failure of the German proletariat and the occupation of Russia by German imperialism." The Bolsheviks, "by their determined revolutionary stand, their exemplary strength in action, and their unswerving loyalty to international socialism . . . have truly accomplished all that could possibly be accomplished under such devilishly hard conditions. . . . The Bolsheviks have shown that they can do everything that a genuine revolutionary party is capable of within the limits of the historical possibilities."[23]

Following her release from prison, Luxemburg did not raise her criticisms of Bolshevik policies either in the party's press or in its internal discussions. She explained her conduct in a November 1918 letter to Adolf Warszawski, a Polish Communist leader long associated with her wing of the Polish Social Democracy:

"If our party [the SDKPiL] is full of enthusiasm for Bolshevism and at the same time has opposed the peace of Brest-Litovsk that the Bolsheviks signed and also their propagation of national self-determination as a solution, then it is no more than enthusiasm coupled with the spirit of criticism — what more can we want? . . .

"I shared all your reservations and doubts, but have dropped them on the most important questions, and in many others I never went as far as you. True, terrorism is evidence of grave weakness, but it is directed against internal enemies who base their hopes on capitalism's existence outside Russia and draw support and encouragement from it. Once the European revolution comes, the Russian counterrevolutionaries will lose not only this support, but — what is more important — all their courage. Bolshevik terror is above all the expression of the weakness of the European proletariat. Naturally the new agrarian conditions just created there are the weak spot of the Russian revolution, which will cause the most trouble. But as is shown once again, even the greatest revolution can achieve only that for which social conditions are ripe. This weakness too can only be healed through the European revolution. And it is coming!"[24]

Following the German revolution of November 9, there was no reflection in the Spartacists' public statements of their initial hesitations toward and criticisms of the Bolshevik revolution. On some questions, such as that of constituent assemblies, the experience of the German revolution led the Spartacists toward agreement with Bolshevik positions. Differences persisted on other questions. The Spartacists' congress at the end of 1918 and the subsequent debates in the Communist International registered the varying degrees to which particular individuals and currents within the German revolutionary movement had come to understand and agree with the course advocated and implemented by the Russian Communist Party, as well as the extent to which key differences persisted.

Kautsky's articles attacking Soviet power began to appear in the German press in the months following the dissolution of the Russian Constituent Assembly in 1918, but no reply from the Spartacist leaders was published. In part, this was due to the imprisonment of Liebknecht, Luxemburg, and other Spartacus leaders. Yet Lenin was impatient for publication of a reply and believed it would have the most impact if written by a leading German Marxist.

"Kautsky's disgraceful rubbish, childish babble and shallowest opportunism impel me to ask," Lenin wrote on September 20 to three Soviet envoys in western Europe, "why do we do nothing to fight the *theoretical* vulgarisation of Marxism by Kautsky?" Referring to two Spartacus leaders still at liberty, Lenin asked, "Can we tolerate that even such people as Mehring and Zetkin keep away from Kautsky more 'morally' (if one may put it so) than *theoretically*." He called on the Soviet representatives to "have a detailed talk with the Left (Spartacists and others), stimulating them to make a statement *of principle,* of *theory,* in the press, that on the question of dictatorship Kautsky is producing philistine Bernsteinism, not Marxism."[25]

In the subsequent weeks, Lenin himself took up the task of writing a conclusive reply to Kautsky, based on Kautsky's pamphlet, *The Dictatorship of the Proletariat,* which had just arrived in Russia. Initially, Lenin wrote a brief article entitled, "The Proletarian Revolution and the Renegade Kautsky," which was rushed to the Soviet embassy in Berlin for publication in leaflet form. A shortened version of it appeared in the October 25, 1918, issue of *Vorwärts* — a rare case where masses of German workers heard an authentic voice from Soviet Russia.[26] On November 10 Lenin completed a fuller reply with the same title, and it was published in Russia by the end of the year and in a German edition in 1919. In answering Kautsky's criticisms of the Bolsheviks, Lenin also took up the substance of the arguments leveled by Kautsky against the Spartacists in his article on the national assembly, published in chapter 2 of the present work. Lenin's pamphlet thus represents the main Bolshevik contribution to the debate in the workers' movement between those advocating a revolutionary government of the exploited and those favoring some form of continued capitalist rule — the disagreement that divided the world workers' movement in 1919 into rival organized Internationals.

The Proletarian Revolution and the Renegade Kautsky[27]
by V. I. Lenin
Preface

Kautsky's pamphlet, *The Dictatorship of the Proletariat*, recently published in Vienna (Wien, 1918, Ignaz Brand, pp. 63) is a most lucid example of that utter and ignominious bankruptcy of the Second International about which all honest socialists in all countries have been talking for a long time. The proletarian revolution is now becoming a practical issue in a number of countries, and an examination of Kautsky's renegade sophistries and his complete renunciation of Marxism is therefore essential.

First of all, it should be emphasised, however, that the present author has, from the very beginning of the war, repeatedly pointed to Kautsky's rupture with Marxism. A number of articles published between 1914 and 1916 in *Sotsial-Demokrat* and *Kommunist*, issued abroad, dealt with this subject. These articles were afterwards collected and published by the Petrograd Soviet under the title *Against the Stream*, by G. Zinoviev and N. Lenin (Petrograd, 1918, pp. 550). In a pamphlet published in Geneva in 1915 and translated at the same time into German and French I wrote about "Kautskyism" as follows:

"Kautsky, the leading authority in the Second International, is a most typical and striking example of how a verbal recognition of Marxism has led in practice to its conversion into 'Struvism' or into 'Brentanoism' [i.e., into a bourgeois-liberal theory recognising the non-revolutionary "class" struggle of the proletariat, which was expressed most clearly by Struve, the Russian writer, and Brentano, the German economist]. Another example is Plekhanov. By means of patent sophistry, Marxism is stripped of its revolutionary living spirit; *everything* is recognised in Marxism *except* the revolutionary methods of struggle, the propaganda and preparation of those methods, and the education of the masses in this direction. Kautsky reconciles in an unprincipled way the fundamental idea of social-chauvinism, recognition of defence of the fatherland in the present war, with a diplomatic sham concession to the Lefts — his abstention from voting for war credits, his verbal claim to be in opposition, etc. Kautsky, who in 1909 wrote a book on the approaching epoch of revolutions and on the connection between war and revolution, Kautsky, who in 1912 signed the Basle Manifesto on taking revolutionary advantage of the impending war,[28] is outdoing himself in justifying and embellishing social-chauvinism and, like Plekhanov, joins the bourgeoisie in ridiculing any thought of revolution and all steps towards the immediate revolutionary struggle.

"The working class cannot play its world-revolutionary role unless it wages a ruthless struggle against this backsliding, spinelessness, subservience to opportunism, and unparalled vulgarisation of the theories of Marxism. Kautskyism is not fortuitous; it is the social product of the contradictions within the Second International, a blend of loyalty to Marxism in word and subordination to opportunism in deed" (G. Zinoviev and N. Lenin, *Socialism and War*, Geneva, 1915, pp. 13-14).[29]

Again in my book *Imperialism, the Latest Stage of Capitalism*,[30] written in 1916 and published in Petrograd in 1917, I examined in detail the theoretical fallacy of all Kautsky's arguments about imperialism. I quoted Kautsky's definition of imperialism: "Imperialism is a product of highly developed industrial capitalism. It consists in the striving of every industrial capitalist nation to bring under its control or to annex all large areas of *agrarian* [Kautsky's italics] territory, irrespective of what nations inhabit it." I showed how utterly incorrect this definition was, and how it was "adapted" to the glossing over of the most profound contradictions of imperialism, and then to reconciliation with opportunism. I gave my own definition of imperialism: "Imperialism is capitalism at that stage of development at which the dominance of monopolies and finance capital is established; at which the export of capital has acquired pronounced importance; at which the division of the world among the international trusts has begun; at which the division of all territories of the globe among the biggest capitalist powers has been completed." I showed that Kautsky's critique of imperialism is on an even lower plane than the bourgeois, philistine critique.

Finally, in August and September 1917 — that is, before the proletarian revolution in Russia (October 25 [November 7], 1917), I wrote a pamphlet (published in Petrograd at the beginning of 1918) entitled *The State and Revolution. The Marxist Theory of the State and the Tasks of the Proletariat in the Revolution.*[31] In Chapter VI of this book, entitled "The Vulgarisation of Marxism by the Opportunists", I devoted special attention to Kautsky, showing that he had completely distorted Marx's ideas, tailoring them to suit opportunism, and that he had "repudiated the revolution in deeds, while accepting it in words".

In substance, the chief theoretical mistake Kautsky makes in his pamphlet on the dictatorship of the proletariat lies in those opportunist distortions of Marx's ideas on the state — the distortions which I exposed in detail in my pamphlet, *The State and Revolution.*

These preliminary remarks were necessary for they show that I openly accused Kautsky of being a renegade *long before* the Bolsheviks assumed state power and were condemned by him on that account.

How Kautsky Turned Marx Into a Common Liberal

The fundamental question that Kautsky discusses in his pamphlet is that of the very essence of proletarian revolution, namely, the dictatorship of the proletariat. This is a question that is of the greatest importance for all countries, especially for the advanced ones, especially for those at war, and especially at the present time. One may say without fear of exaggeration that this is the key problem of the entire proletarian class struggle. It is, therefore, necessary to pay particular attention to it.

Kautsky formulates the question as follows: "The contrast between the two socialist trends" (i.e., the Bolsheviks and non-Bolsheviks) "is the contrast between two radically different methods: the *dictatorial* and the *democratic*" (p. 3).

Let us point out, in passing, that when calling the non-Bolsheviks in Russia, i.e., the Mensheviks and Socialist-Revolutionaries, socialists, Kautsky was guided by their *name*, that is, by a word, and not by the *actual place* they occupy in the struggle between the proletariat and the bourgeoisie. What a wonderful understanding and application of Marxism! But more of this later.

For the moment we must deal with the main point, namely, with Kautsky's great discovery of the "fundamental contrast" between "democratic and dictatorial methods". That is the crux of the matter; that is the essence of Kautsky's pamphlet. And that is such an awful theoretical muddle, such a complete renunciation of Marxism, that Kautsky, it must be confessed, has far excelled Bernstein.

The question of the dictatorship of the proletariat is a question of the relation of the proletarian state to the bourgeois state, of proletarian democracy to bourgeois democracy. One would think that this is as plain as a pikestaff. But Kautsky, like a schoolmaster who has become as dry as dust from quoting the same old textbooks on history, persistently turns his back on the twentieth century and his face to the eighteenth century, and for the hundredth time, in a number of paragraphs, in an incredibly tedious fashion chews the old cud over the relation of bourgeois democracy to absolutism and medievalism!

It sounds just like he were chewing rags in his sleep!

But this means he utterly fails to understand what is what! One cannot help smiling at Kautsky's effort to make it appear that there are people who preach "contempt for democracy" (p.11) and so forth. That is the sort of twaddle Kautsky uses to befog and confuse the issue, for he talks like the liberals, speaking of democracy in general, and not of *bourgeois* democracy; he even avoids using this precise, class term, and, instead, tries to speak about "pre-socialist" democracy. This windbag devotes almost one-third of his pamphlet, twenty pages out of sixty-three, to this twaddle, which is so agreeable to the bourgeoisie, for it is tantamount to embellishing bourgeois democracy, and obscures the question of the proletarian revolution.

But, after all, the title of Kautsky's pamphlet is *The Dictatorship of the Proletariat*. Everybody knows that this is the very *essence* of Marx's doctrine; and after a lot of irrelevant twaddle Kautsky *was obliged* to quote Marx's words on the dictatorship of the proletariat.

But the *way* in which he the "Marxist" did it was simply farcical! Listen to this:

"This view" (which Kautsky dubs "contempt for democracy") "rests upon a single word of Karl Marx's." This is what Kautsky literally says on page 20. And on page 60 the same thing is repeated even in the form that they (the Bosheviks) "opportunely recalled the little word" (that is literally what he says — *des Wörtchens*!!) "about the dictatorship of the proletariat which Marx once used in 1875 in a letter".

Here is Marx's "little word":

"Between capitalist and communist society lies the period of revolutionary transformation of the one into the other. Corresponding to this is also a political transition period in which the state can be nothing but the revolutionary dictatorship of the proletariat". [32]

First of all, to call this classical reasoning of Marx's, which sums up the whole of his revolutionary teaching, "a single word" and even "a little word", is an insult to and complete renunciation of Marxism. It must not be forgotten that Kautsky knows Marx almost by heart, and, judging by all he has written, he has in his desk, or in his head, a number of pigeon-holes in which all that was ever written by Marx is most carefully filed so as to be ready at hand for quotation. Kautsky *must know* that both Marx and Engels, in their letters as well as in their published works, *repeatedly* spoke about the dictatorship of the proletariat, before and especially after the Paris Commune. Kautsky must know that the formula "dictatorship of the proletariat" is merely a more historically concrete and scientifically exact formulation of the proletariat's task of "smashing" the bourgeois state machine, about which both Marx and Engels, in summing up the experience of the Revolution of 1848, and, still more so, of 1871, spoke *for forty years*, between 1852 and 1891.

How is this monstrous distortion of Marxism by that Marxist pedant Kautsky to be explained? As far as the philosophical roots of this phenomenon are concerned, it amounts to the substitution of eclecticism and sophistry for dialectics. Kautsky is a past master at this sort of substitution. Regarded from the point of view of practical politics, it amounts to subservience to the opportunists, that is, in the last analysis to the bourgeoisie. Since the outbreak of the war, Kautsky has made increasingly rapid progress in this art of being a Marxist in words and a lackey of the bourgeoisie in deeds, until he has become a virtuoso at it.

One feels even more convinced of this when examining the remarkable way in which Kautsky "interprets" Marx's "little word" about the dictatorship of the proletariat. Listen to this:

"Marx, unfortunately, neglected to show us in greater detail how he conceived this dictatorship. . . . (This is an utterly mendacious phrase of a renegade, for Marx and Engels gave us, indeed, quite a number of most detailed indications, which Kautsky, the Marxist pedant, has deliberately ignored.)

Literally, the word dictatorship means the abolition of democracy. But, of course, taken literally, this word also means the undivided rule of a single person unrestricted by any laws — an autocracy, which differs from despotism only insofar as it is not meant as a permanent state institution, but as a transient emergency measure.

The term, 'dictatorship of the proletariat', hence not the dictatorship of a single individual, but of a class, *ipso facto* precludes the possibility that Marx in this connection had in mind a dictatorship in the literal sense of the term.

He speaks here not of a *form of government*, but of a *condition*, which must necessarily arise wherever the proletariat has gained political power. That Marx in this case did not have in mind a form of government is proved by the fact that he was of the opinion that in Britain and America the transition might take place peacefully, i.e., in a democratic way" (p. 20).

We have deliberately quoted this argument in full so that the reader may clearly see the methods Kautsky the "theoretician" employs.

Kautsky chose to approach the question in such a way as to begin with a definition of the "*word*" dictatorship.

Very well. Everyone has a sacred right to approach a question in whatever way he pleases. One must only distinguish a serious and honest approach from a dishonest one. Anyone who wants to be serious in approaching the question in this way ought to give *his own definition* of the "word". Then the question would be put fairly and squarely. But Kautsky does not do that. "Literally," he writes, "the word dictatorship means the abolition of democracy."

In the first place, this is not a definition. If Kautsky wanted to avoid giving a definition of the concept dictatorship, why did he choose this particular approach to the question?

Secondly, it is obviously wrong. It is natural for a liberal to speak of "democracy" in general; but a Marxist will never forget to ask: "for what class?" Everyone knows, for instance (and Kautsky the "historian" knows it too), that rebellions, or even strong ferment, among the slaves in ancient times at once revealed the fact that the ancient state was essentially a *dictatorship of the slaveowners*. Did this dictatorship abolish democracy *among*, and *for*, the slaveowners? Everybody knows that it did not.

Kautsky the "Marxist" made this monstrously absurd and untrue statement because he "*forgot*" the class struggle. . . .

To transform Kautsky's liberal and false assertion into a Marxist and true one, one must say: dictatorship does not necessarily mean the abolition of democracy for the class that exercises the dictatorship over other classes; but it does mean the abolition (or very material restriction, which is also a form of abolition) of democracy for the class over which, or against which, the dictatorship is exercised.

But, however true this assertion may be, it does not give a definition of dictatorship.

Let us examine Kautsky's next sentence:

". . . But, of course, taken literally, this word also means the undivided rule of a single person unrestricted by any laws. . . ."

Like a blind puppy sniffing at random first in one direction and then in another, Kautsky accidentally stumbled upon *one* true idea (namely, that dictatorship is rule unrestricted by any laws), *nevertheless*, he *failed* to give a definition of dictatorship, and, moreover, he made an obvious historical blunder, namely, that dictatorship means the rule of a single person. This is even grammatically incorrect, since dictatorship may also be exercised by a handful of persons, or by an oligarchy, or by a class, etc.

Kautsky then goes on to point out the difference between dictatorship and despotism, but, although what he says is obviously incorrect, we shall not dwell upon it, as it is wholly irrelevant to the question that interests us. Everyone knows Kautsky's inclination to turn from the twentieth century to the eighteenth, and from the eighteenth century to classical antiquity, and we hope that the German proletariat, after it has attained its dictatorship, will bear this inclination of his in mind and appoint him, say, teacher of ancient history at some Gymnasium. To try to evade a definition of the dictatorship of the proletariat by philosophising about despotism is either crass stupidity or very clumsy trickery.

As a result, we find that, having undertaken to discuss the dictatorship, Kautsky rattled off a great deal of manifest lies, but has given no definition! Yet, instead of relying on his mental faculties he could have used his memory to extract from "pigeon-holes" all those instances in which Marx speaks of dictatorship. Had he done so, he would certainly have arrived either at the following definition or at one in substance coinciding with it:

Dictatorship is rule based directly upon force and unrestricted by any laws.

The revolutionary dictatorship of the proletariat is rule won and maintained by the use of violence by the proletariat against the bourgeoisie, rule that is unrestricted by any laws.

This simple truth, a truth that is as plain as a pikestaff to every class-conscious worker (who represents the people, and not an upper section of petty-bourgeois scoundrels who have been bribed by the capitalists, such as are the social-imperialists of all countries), this truth, which is obvious to every representative of the exploited classes fighting for their emancipation, this truth, which is beyond dispute for every Marxist, has to be "extracted by force" from the most learned Mr. Kautsky! How is it to be explained? Simply by that spirit of servility with which the leaders of the Second International, who have become contemptible sycophants in the service of the bourgeoisie, are imbued.

Kautsky first committed a sleight of hand by proclaiming the obvious nonsense that the word dictatorship, in its literal sense, means the dictatorship of a single person, and then — on the strength of this sleight of hand — he declared that "hence" Marx's words about the dictatorship of a class were *not* meant in the literal sense (but in one in which dictatorship does not imply revolutionary violence, but the "peaceful" winning of a majority under bourgeois — mark you — "democracy").

One must, if you please, distinguish between a "condition" and a "form of government". A wonderfully profound distinction; it is like drawing a distinction between the "condition" of stupidity of a man who reasons foolishly and the "form" of his stupidity.

Kautsky *finds it necessary* to interpret dictatorship as a "condition of domination" (this is the literal expression he uses on the very next page, p. 21), because then *revolutionary violence, and violent revolution, disappear*. The "condition of domination" is a condition in which any majority finds itself under . . . "democracy"! Thanks to such a fraud, *revolution* happily *disappears*!

The fraud, however, is too crude and will not save Kautsky. One cannot hide the fact that dictatorship presupposes and implies a "condition", one so disagreeable to renegades, of *revolutionary violence* of one class against another. It is patently absurd to draw a distinction between a "condition" and a "form of government". To speak of forms of government in this connection is trebly stupid, for every schoolboy knows that monarchy and republic are two different forms of government. It must be explained to Mr. Kautsky that *both* these forms of government, like all transitional "forms of government" under capitalism, are only variations of the *bourgeois state*, that is, of the *dictatorship of the bourgeoisie*.

Lastly, to speak of forms of government is not only a stupid, but also a very crude falsification of Marx, who was very clearly speaking here of this or that form or type of *state*, and not of forms of government.

The proletarian revolution is impossible without the forcible destruction of the bourgeois state machine and the substitution for it of a *new one* which, in the words of Engels, is "no longer a state in the proper sense of the word".[33]

Because of his renegade position, Kautsky, however, has to befog and belie all this.

Look what wretched subterfuges he uses.

First subterfuge. "That Marx in this case did not have in mind a form of government is proved by the fact that he was of the opinion that in Britain and America the transition might take place peacefully, i.e., in a democratic way."

The *form of government* has absolutely nothing to do with it, for there are monarchies which are not typical of the bourgeois *state*, such, for instance, as have no military clique, and there are republics which are quite typical in this respect, such, for instance, as have a military clique and a bureaucracy. This is a universally known historical and political fact, and Kautsky cannot falsify it.

If Kautsky had wanted to argue in a serious and honest manner he would have asked himself: Are there historical laws relating to revolution which know of no exception? And the reply would have been: No, there are no such laws. Such laws only apply to the typical, to what Marx once termed the "ideal", meaning average, normal, typical capitalism.

Further, was there in the seventies anything which made England and America exceptional *in regard to what we are now discussing*? It will be obvious to anyone at all familiar with the requirements of science in regard to the problems of history that this question must be put. To fail to put it is tantamount to falsifying science, to engaging in sophistry. And, the question having been put, there can be no doubt as to the reply: the revolutionary dictatorship of the proletariat is *violence* against the bourgeoisie; and the necessity of such violence is *particularly* called for, as Marx and Engels have repeatedly explained in detail (especially in *The Civil War in France* and in the preface to it),[34] by the existence of *militarism and a bureaucracy.* But it is precisely these institutions that were *non-existent* in Britain and America in the seventies, when Marx made his observations (they *do* exist in Britain and in America *now*)!

Kautsky has to resort to trickery literally at every step to cover up his apostasy!

And note how he inadvertently betrayed his cloven hoof when he wrote: "peacefully, *i.e., in a democratic way*"!

In defining dictatorship, Kautsky tried his utmost to conceal from the reader the fundamental feature of this concept, namely, revolutionary *violence*. But now the truth is out: it is a question of the contrast between *peaceful* and *violent revolutions*.

That is the crux of the matter. Kautsky has to resort to all these subterfuges, sophistries and falsifications only to *excuse* himself from *violent* revolution, and to conceal his renunciation of it, his desertion to the side of the *liberal* labour policy, i.e., to the side of the bourgeoisie. That is the crux of the matter.

Kautsky the "historian" so shamelessly falsifies history that he "forgets" the fundamental fact that pre-monopoly capitalism — which actually reached its zenith in the seventies — was by virtue of its fundamental *economic* traits, which found most typical expression in Britain and in America, distinguished by a, relatively speaking, maximum fondness for peace and freedom. Imperialism, on the other hand, i.e., monopoly capitalism, which finally matured only in the twentieth century, is, by virtue of its fundamental *economic* traits, distinguished by a minimum fondness for peace and freedom, and by a maximum and universal development of militarism. To "fail to notice" this in discussing the extent to which a peaceful or violent revolution is typical or probable is to stoop to the level of a most ordinary lackey of the bourgeoisie.

Second subterfuge. The Paris Commune was a dictatorship of the proletariat, but it was elected by *universal* suffrage, i.e., without depriving the bourgeoisie of the franchise, i.e., "*democratically*". And Kautsky says triumphantly: " . . . The dictatorship of the proletariat was for Marx" (or: according to Marx) "a condition which necessarily follows from pure democracy, if the proletariat forms the majority" (*bei überwiegendem Proletariat*, S. 21).

This argument of Kautsky's is so amusing that one truly suffers from a veritable *embarras de richesses* (an embarrassment due to the wealth . . . of objections that can be made to it). Firstly, it is well known that the flower, the General Staff, the upper sections of the bourgeoisie, had fled from Paris to Versailles. In Versailles there was the "socialist" Louis Blanc — which, by the way, proves the falsity of Kautsky's assertion that "all trends" of socialism took part in the Paris Commune. Is it not ridiculous to represent the division of the inhabitants of Paris into two belligerent camps, one of which embraced the entire militant and politically active section of the bourgeoisie, as "pure democracy" with "universal suffrage"?

Secondly, the Paris Commune waged war against Versailles as the workers' government of *France* against the bourgeois government.

What have "pure democracy" and "universal suffrage" to do with it, when Paris was deciding the fate of France? When Marx expressed the opinion that the Paris Commune had committed a mistake in failing to seize the bank, which belonged to the whole of France, did he not proceed from the principles and practice of "pure democracy"?[35]

In actual fact, it is obvious that Kautsky is writing in a country where the police forbid people to laugh "in crowds", otherwise Kautsky would have been killed by ridicule.

Thirdly, I would respectfully remind Mr. Kautsky, who has Marx and Engels off pat, of the following appraisal of the Paris Commune given by Engels from the point of view of . . . "pure democracy":

"Have these gentlemen" (the anti-authoritarians) "ever seen a revolution? A revolution is certainly the most authoritarian thing there is; it is an act whereby one part of the population imposes its will upon the other by means of rifles, bayonets and cannon — all of which are highly authoritarian means. And the victorious party must maintain its rule by means of the terror which its arms inspire in the reactionaries. Would the Paris Commune have lasted more than a day if it had not used the authority of the armed people against the bourgeoisie? Cannot we, on the contrary, blame it for having made too little use of that authority?"[36]

Here is your "pure democracy"! How Engels would have ridiculed the vulgar petty bourgeois, the "Social-Democrat" (in the French sense of the forties and the general European sense of 1914-18), who took it into his head to talk about "pure democracy" in a class-divided society!

But that's enough. It is impossible to enumerate all Kautsky's various absurdities, since every phrase he utters is a bottomless pit of apostasy.

Marx and Engels analysed the Paris Commune in a most detailed manner and showed that its merit lay in its attempt *to smash, to break up* the "ready-made state machinery". Marx and Engels considered this conclusion to be so important that this was the *only* amendment they introduced in 1872 into the "obsolete" (in parts) programme of the *Communist Manifesto*. Marx and Engels showed that the Paris Commune had abolished *parliamentarism*, had destroyed "that parasitic excrescence, the state", etc. But the sage Kautsky, donning his nightcap, repeats the fairy-tale about "pure democracy", which has been told a thousand times by liberal professors.

No wonder Rosa Luxemburg declared, on August 4, 1914, that German Social-Democracy was a *stinking corpse*.

Third subterfuge. "When we speak of the dictatorship as a form of government we cannot speak of the dictatorship of a class, since a class, as we have already pointed out, can only rule but not govern. . . ." It is "organisations" or "parties" that govern.

That is a muddle, a disgusting muddle, Mr. "Muddle-headed Counsellor"! Dictatorship is not a "form of government"; that is ridiculous nonsense. And Marx does not speak of the "form of government" but of the form or type of *state*. That is something altogether different, entirely different. It is altogether wrong, too, to say that a *class* cannot govern: such an absurdity could only have been uttered by a "parliamentary cretin", who sees nothing but bourgeois parliaments and notices nothing but "ruling parties". Any European country will provide Kautsky with examples of government by a ruling *class*, for instance, by the landowners in the Middle Ages, in spite of their insufficient organisation.

To sum up: Kautsky has in a most unparalleled manner distorted the concept dictatorship of the proletariat, and has turned Marx into a common liberal; that is, he himself has sunk to the level of a liberal who utters banal phrases about "pure democracy", embellishing and glossing over the class content of *bourgeois* democracy, and shrinking, above all, from the use of *revolutionary violence* by the oppressed class. By so "interpreting" the concept "revolutionary dictatorship of the proletariat" as to expunge the revolutionary violence of the oppressed class against its oppressors, Kautsky has beaten the world record in the liberal distortion of Marx. The renegade Bernstein has proved to be a mere puppy compared with the renegade Kautsky.

Bourgeois and Proletarian Democracy

The question which Kautsky has so shamelessly muddled really stands as follows.

If we are not to mock at common sense and history, it is obvious that we cannot speak of "pure democracy" as long as different *classes* exist; we can only speak of *class* democracy. (Let us say in parenthesis that "pure democracy" is not only an *ignorant* phrase, revealing a lack of understanding both of the class struggle and of the nature of the state, but also a thrice-empty phrase, since in communist society democracy will *wither away* in the process of changing and becoming a habit, but will never be "pure" democracy.)

"Pure democracy" is the mendacious phrase of a liberal who wants to fool the workers. History knows of bourgeois democracy which takes the place of feudalism, and of proletarian democracy which takes the place of bourgeois democracy.

When Kautsky devotes dozens of pages to "proving" the truth that bourgeois democracy is progressive compared with medievalism, and that the proletariat must unfailingly utilise it in its struggle against the bourgeoisie, that in fact is just liberal twaddle intended to fool the workers. This is a truism, not only for educated Germany, but also for uneducated Russia. Kautsky is simply throwing "learned" dust in the eyes of the workers when, with a pompous mien, he talks about Weitling and the Jesuits of Paraguay and many other things,[37] *in order to avoid* telling about the *bourgeois* essence of modern, i.e., *capitalist*, democracy.

Kautsky takes from Marxism what is acceptable to the liberals, to the bourgeoisie (the criticism of the Middle Ages, and the progressive historical role of capitalism in general and of capitalist democracy in particular), and discards, passes over in silence, glosses over all that in Marxism which is *unacceptable* to the bourgeoisie (the revolutionary violence of the proletariat against the bourgeoisie for the latter's destruction). That is why Kautsky, by virtue of his objective position and irrespective of what his subjective convictions may be, inevitably proves to be a lackey of the bourgeoisie.

Bourgeois democracy, although a great historical advance in comparison with medievalism, always remains, and under capitalism is bound to remain, restricted, truncated, false and hypocritical, a paradise for the rich and a snare and deception for the exploited, for the poor. It is this truth, which forms a most essential part of Marx's teaching, that Kautsky the "Marxist" has failed to understand. On this — the fundamental issue — Kautsky offers "delights" for the bourgeoisie instead of a scientific criticism of those conditions which make every bourgeois democracy a democracy for the rich.

Let us first remind the most learned Mr. Kautsky of the theoretical propositions of Marx and Engels which that pedant has so disgracefully "forgotten" (to please the bourgeoisie), and then explain the matter as popularly as possible.

Not only the ancient and feudal, but also "the modern representative state is an instrument of exploitation of wage-labour by capital" (Engels, in his work on the state).[38] "As, therefore, the state is only a transitional institution which is used in the struggle, in the revolution, to hold down one's adversaries by force, it is sheer nonsense to talk of a 'free people's state'; so long as the proletariat still needs the state, it does not need it in the interests of freedom but in order to hold down its adversaries, and as soon as it becomes possible to speak of freedom the state as such ceases to exist" (Engels, in his letter to Bebel, March 28, 1875).[39] "In reality, however, the state is nothing but a machine for the oppression of one class by another, and indeed in the democratic republic no less than in the monarchy" (Engels, Introduction to *The Civil War in France* by Marx).[40] Universal suffrage is "the gauge of the maturity of the working class. *It cannot and never will be anything more in the present-day state*". (Engels, in his work on the state.[41] Mr. Kautsky very tediously chews over the cud in the first part of this proposition, which is acceptable to the bourgeoisie. But the second part, which we have italicised and which is not acceptable to the bourgeoisie, the renegade Kautsky passes over in silence!) "The Commune was to be a working, not a parliamentary, body, executive and legislative at the same time. . . . Instead of deciding once in three or six years which member of the ruling class was to represent and suppress (*ver- und zertreten*) the people in Parliament, universal suffrage was to serve the people, constituted in Communes, as individual suffrage serves every other employer in the search for workers, foremen and accountants for his business" (Marx, in his work on the Paris Commune, *The Civil War in France*).[42]

Every one of these propositions, which are excellently known to the most learned Mr. Kautsky, is a slap in his face and lays bare his apostasy. Nowhere in his pamphlet does Kautsky reveal the slightest understanding of these truths. His whole pamphlet is a sheer mockery of Marxism!

Take the fundamental laws of modern states, take their administration, take freedom of assembly, freedom of the press, or "equality of all citizens before the law", and you will see at every turn evidence of the hypocrisy of bourgeois democracy with which every honest and class-conscious worker is familiar. There is not a single state, however democratic, which has no loopholes or reservations in its constitution guaranteeing the bourgeoisie the possibility of dispatching troops against the workers, of proclaiming martial law, and so forth, in case of a "violation of public order", and actually in case the exploited class "violates" its position of slavery and tries to behave in a non-slavish manner. Kautsky shamelessly embellishes bourgeois democracy and omits to mention, for instance, how the most democratic and republican bourgeoisie in America or Switzerland deal with workers on strike.

The wise and learned Kautsky keeps silent about these things! That learned politician does not realise that to remain silent on this matter is despicable. He prefers to tell the workers nursery tales of the kind that democracy means "protecting the minority". It is incredible, but it is a fact! In the year of our Lord 1918, in the fifth year of the world imperialist slaughter and the strangulation of internationalist minorities (i.e., those who have not despicably betrayed socialism, like the Renaudels and Longuets, the Scheidemanns and Kautskys, the Hendersons and Webbs et al.) in all "democracies" of the world, the learned Mr. Kautsky sweetly, very sweetly, sings the praises of "protection of the minority". Those who are interested may read this on page 15 of Kautsky's pamphlet. And on page 16 this learned . . . individual tells you about the Whigs and Tories in England in the eighteenth century!

What wonderful erudition! What refined servility to the bourgeoisie! What civilised belly-crawling before the capitalists and boot-licking! If I were Krupp or Scheidemann, or Clemenceau or Renaudel, I would pay Mr. Kautsky millions, reward him with Judas kisses, praise him before the workers and urge "socialist unity" with "honourable" men like him. To write pamphlets against the dictatorship of the proletariat, to talk about the Whigs and Tories in England in the eighteenth century, to assert that democracy means "protecting the minority", and remain silent about *pogroms* against internationalists in the "democratic" republic of America — isn't this rendering lackey service to the bourgeoisie?

The learned Mr. Kautsky has "forgotten" — accidentally forgotten, probably — a "trifle", namely, that the ruling party in a bourgeois democracy extends the protection of the minority only to another *bourgeois* party, while the proletariat, on all *serious, profound and fundamental* issues, gets martial law or pogroms, instead of the "protection of the minority". *The more highly developed a democracy is, the more imminent are pogroms or civil war in connection with any profound political divergence which is dangerous to the bourgeoisie*. The learned Mr. Kautsky could have studied this "law" of bourgeois democracy in connection with the Dreyfus case in republican France,[43] with the lynching of Negroes and internationalists in the democratic republic of America, with the case of Ireland and Ulster in democratic Britain,[44] with the baiting of the Bolsheviks and the staging of pogroms against them in April 1917 in the democratic republic of Russia. I have purposely chosen examples not only from wartime but also from pre-war time, peacetime. But mealy-mouthed Mr. Kautsky prefers to shut his eyes to these facts of the twentieth century, and instead to tell the workers wonderfully new, remarkably interesting, unusually edifying and incredibly important things about the Whigs and Tories of the eighteenth century!

Take the bourgeois parliament. Can it be that the learned Kautsky has never heard that the *more highly* democracy is developed, the *more* the bourgeois parliaments are subjected by the stock exchange and the bankers? This does not mean that we must not make use of bourgeois parliament (the Bolsheviks made better use of it than probably any other party in the world, for in 1912-14 we won the entire workers' curia in the Fourth Duma). But it does mean that only a liberal can forget the *historical limitations and conventional nature* of the bourgeois parliamentary system as Kautsky does. Even in the most democratic bourgeois state the oppressed people at every step encounter the crying contradiction between the *formal* equality proclaimed by the "democracy" of the capitalists and the thousands of *real* limitations and subterfuges which turn the proletarians into *wage-slaves*. It is precisely this contradiction that is opening the eyes of the people to the rottenness, mendacity and hypocrisy of capitalism. It is this contradiction that the agitators and propagandists of socialism are constantly exposing to the people, *in order to prepare* them for revolution! And now that the era of revolution *has begun*, Kautsky turns his back upon it and begins to extol the charms of *moribund* bourgeois democracy.

Proletarian democracy, of which Soviet government is one of the forms, has brought a development and expansion of democracy unprecedented in the world, for the vast majority of the population, for the exploited and working people. To write a whole pamphlet about democracy, as Kautsky did, in which two pages are devoted to dictatorship and dozens to "pure democracy", and *fail to notice* this fact, means completely distorting the subject in liberal fashion.

Take foreign policy. In no bourgeois state, not even in the most democratic, is it conducted openly. The people are deceived everywhere, and in democratic France, Switzerland, America and Britain this is done on an incomparably wider scale and in an incomparably subtler manner than in other countries. The Soviet government has torn the veil of mystery from foreign policy in a revolutionary manner. Kautsky has not noticed this, he keeps silent about it, although in the era of predatory wars and secret treaties for the "division of spheres of influence" (i.e., for the partition of the world among the capitalist bandits) this is of *cardinal* importance, for on it depends the question of peace, the life and death of tens of millions of people.

Take the structure of the state. Kautsky picks at all manner of "trifles", down to the argument that under the Soviet Constitution elections are "indirect", but he misses the point. He fails to see the *class* nature of the state apparatus, of the machinery of state. Under bourgeois democracy the capitalists, by thousands of tricks — which are the more artful and effective the more "pure" democracy is developed — *drive* the people away from administrative work, from freedom of the press, freedom of assembly, etc. The Soviet government is the *first* in the world (or strictly speaking, the second, because the Paris Commune began to do the same thing) to *enlist* the people, specifically the *exploited* people, in the work of administration. The working people are *barred* from participation in bourgeois parliaments (they *never decide* important questions under bourgeois democracy, which are decided by the stock exchange and the banks) by thousands of obstacles, and the workers know and feel, see and realise perfectly well that the bourgeois parliaments are institutions *alien* to them, *instruments for the oppression* of the workers by the bourgeoisie, institutions of a hostile class, of the exploiting minority.

The Soviets are the direct organisation of the working and exploited people themselves, which *helps* them to organise and administer their own state in every possible way. And in this it is the vanguard of the working and exploited people, the urban proletariat, that enjoys the advantage of being best united by the large enterprises; it is easier for it than for all others to elect and exercise control over those elected. The Soviet form of organisation automatically *helps* to unite all the working and exploited people around their vanguard, the proletariat. The old bourgeois apparatus — the bureaucracy, the privileges of wealth, of bourgeois education, of social connections, etc. (these real privileges are the more varied the more highly bourgeois democracy is developed) — all this disappears under the Soviet form of organisation. Freedom of the press ceases to be hypocrisy, because the printing-plants and stocks of paper are taken away from the bourgeoisie. The same thing applies to the best buildings, the palaces, the mansions and manorhouses. Soviet power took thousands upon thousands of these best buildings from the exploiters at one stroke, and in this way made the right of assembly — without which democracy is a fraud — *a million times* more democratic for the people. Indirect elections to non-local Soviets make it easier to hold congresses of Soviets, they make the *entire* apparatus less costly, more flexible, more accessible to the workers and peasants at a time when life is seething and it is necessary to be able very quickly to recall one's local deputy or to delegate him to a general congress of Soviets.

Proletarian democracy is *a million times* more democratic than any bourgeois democracy; Soviet power is a million times more democratic than the most democratic bourgeois republic.

To fail to see this one must either deliberately serve the

bourgeoisie, or be politically as dead as a doornail, unable to see real life from behind the dusty pages of bourgeois books, be thoroughly imbued with bourgeois-democratic prejudices, and thereby objectively convert oneself into a lackey of the bourgeoisie.

To fail to see this one must be incapable of *presenting the question* from the point of view of the *oppressed* classes:

Is there a single country in the world, even among the most democratic bourgeois countries, in which the *average rank-and-file* worker, the average rank-and-file *farm labourer*, or village semi-proletarian generally (i.e., the representative of the oppressed, of the overwhelming majority of the population), enjoys anything approaching such *liberty* of holding meetings in the best buildings, such *liberty* of using the largest printing-plants and biggest stocks of paper to express his ideas and to defend his interests, such *liberty* of promoting men and women of his own class to administer and to "knock into shape" the state, as in Soviet Russia?

It is ridiculous to think that Mr. Kautsky could find in any country even one out of a thousand of well-informed workers or farm labourers who would have any doubts as to the reply. Instinctively, from hearing fragments of admissions of the truth in the bourgeois press, the workers of the whole world sympathise with the Soviet Republic precisely because they regard it as a *proletarian* democracy, *a democracy for the poor*, and not a democracy for the rich that every bourgeois democracy, even the best, actually is.

We are governed (and our state is "knocked into shape") by bourgeois bureaucrats, by bourgeois members of parliament, by bourgeois judges — such is the simple, obvious and indisputable truth which tens and hundreds of millions of people belonging to the oppressed classes in all bourgeois countries, including the most democratic, know from their own experience, feel and realise every day.

In Russia, however, the bureaucratic machine has been completely smashed, razed to the ground; the old judges have all been sent packing, the bourgeois parliament has been dispersed — and *far more accessible* representation has been given to the workers and peasants; *their* Soviets have replaced the bureaucrats, or *their* Soviets have been put in control of the bureaucrats, and *their* Soviets have been authorised to elect the judges. This fact alone is enough for all the oppressed classes to recognise that Soviet power, i.e., the present form of the dictatorship of the proletariat, is a million times more democratic than the most democratic bourgeois republic.

Kautsky does not understand this truth, which is so clear and obvious to every worker, because he has "forgotten", "unlearned" to put the question: democracy *for which class*? He argues from the point of view of "pure" (i.e., non-class? or above-class?) democracy. He argues like Shylock: my "pound of flesh" and nothing else. Equality for all citizens — otherwise there is no democracy.

We must ask the learned Kautsky, the "Marxist" and "socialist" Kautsky:

Can there be equality between the exploited and the exploiters?

It is dreadful, it is incredible that such a question should have to be put in discussing a book written by the ideological leader of the Second International. But "having put your hand to the plough, don't look back", and having undertaken to write about Kautsky, I must explain to the learned man why there can be no equality between the exploiter and the exploited.

Can There Be Equality Between the Exploited and the Exploiter?

Kautsky argues as follows:

(1) "The exploiters have always formed only a small minority of the population" (p. 14 of Kautsky's pamphlet).

This is indisputably true. Taking this as the starting point, what should be the argument? One may argue in a Marxist, a socialist way. In which case one would proceed from the relation between the exploited and the exploiters. Or one may argue in a liberal, a bourgeois-democratic way. And in that case one would proceed from the relation between the majority and the minority.

If we argue in a Marxist way, we must say: the exploiters inevitably transform the state (and we are speaking of democracy, i.e., one of the forms of the state) into an instrument of the rule of their class, the exploiters, over the exploited. Hence, as long as there are exploiters who rule the majority, the exploited, the democratic state must inevitably be a democracy for the exploiters. A state of the exploited must fundamentally differ from such a state; it must be a democracy for the exploited, and a means of *suppressing the exploiters*; and the suppression of a class means inequality for that class, its exclusion from "democracy".

If we argue in a liberal way, we must say: the majority decides, the minority submits. Those who do not submit are punished. That is all. Nothing need be said about the class character of the state in general, or of "pure democracy" in particular, because it is irrelevant; for a majority is a majority and a minority is a minority. A pound of flesh is a pound of flesh, and that is all there is to it.

And this is exactly how Kautsky argues.

(2) "Why should the rule of the proletariat assume, and necessarily assume, a form which is incompatible with democracy?" (p. 21.) Then follows a very detailed and a very verbose explanation, backed by a quotation from Marx and the election figures of the Paris Commune, to the effect that the proletariat is in the majority. The conclusion is: "A regime which is so strongly rooted in the people has not the slightest reason for encroaching upon democracy. It cannot always dispense with violence in cases when violence is employed to suppress democracy. Violence can only be met with violence. But a regime which knows that it has popular backing will employ violence only to *protect* democracy and not to *destroy* it. It would be simply suicidal if it attempted to do away with its most reliable basis — universal suffrage, that deep source of mighty moral authority" (p. 22).

As you see, the relation between the exploited and the exploiters has vanished in Kautsky's argument. All that remains is majority in general, minority in general, democracy in general, the "pure democracy" with which we are already familiar.

And all this, mark you, is said *apropos of the Paris Commune*! To make things clearer I shall quote Marx and Engels to show what they said on the subject of dictatorship *apropos of the Paris Commune*:

Marx: " . . . When the workers replace the dictatorship of the bourgeoisie by their revolutionary dictatorship . . . to break down the resistance of the bourgeoisie . . . the workers'invest the state with a revolutionary and transitional form. . . ."[45]

Engels: " . . . And the victorious party" (in a revolution) "must maintain its rule by means of the terror which its arms inspire in the reactionaries. Would the Paris Commune have lasted more than a day if it had not used the authority of the armed people against the bourgeoisie? Cannot we, on the contrary, blame it for having made too little use of that authority? . . . "[46]

Engels: "As, therefore, the state is only a transitional institution which is used in the struggle, in the revolution, to hold down one's adversaries by force, it is sheer nonsense to talk of a 'free people's state'; so long as the proletariat still needs the state, it does not need it in the interests of freedom but in order to hold down its adversaries, and as soon as it becomes possible to speak of freedom the state as such ceases to exist. . . ."[47]

Kautsky is as far removed from Marx and Engels as heaven is from earth, as a liberal from a proletarian revolutionary. The pure democracy and simple "democracy" that Kautsky talks about is merely a paraphrase of the "free people's state", i.e., *sheer nonsense*. Kautsky, with the learned air of a most learned armchair fool, or with the innocent air of a ten-year-old schoolgirl, asks: Why do we need a dictatorship when we have a majority? And Marx and Engels explain:

— to break down the resistance of the bourgeoisie;

— to inspire the reactionaries with fear;

— to maintain the authority of the armed people against the bourgeoisie;

— that the proletariat may forcibly hold down its adversaries.

Kautsky does not understand these explanations. Infatuated with the "purity" of democracy, blind to its bourgeois character, he "consistently" urges that the majority, since it is the majority, need not "break down the resistance" of the minority, nor "forcibly hold it down" — it is sufficient to suppress *cases* of infringement of democracy. Infatuated with the "purity" of democracy, Kautsky *inadvertently* commits the little error that all bourgeois democrats always commit, namely, he takes formal equality (which is nothing but a fraud and hypocrisy under capitalism) for actual equality! Quite a trifle!

The exploiter and the exploited cannot be equal.

This truth, however unpleasant it may be to Kautsky, nevertheless forms the essence of socialism.

Another truth: there can be no real, actual equality until all possibility of the exploitation of one class by another has been totally destroyed.

The exploiters can be defeated at one stroke in the event of a successful uprising at the centre, or of a revolt in the army. But except in very rare and special cases, the exploiters cannot be destroyed at one stroke. It is impossible to expropriate all the landowners and capitalists of any big country at one stroke. Furthermore, expropriation alone, as a legal or political act, does not settle the matter by a long chalk, because it is necessary to *depose* the landowners and capitalists in actual fact, to *replace* their management of the factories and estates by a different management, workers' management, in actual fact. There can be no equality between the exploiters — who for many generations have been better off because of their education, conditions of wealthy life, and habits — and the exploited, the majority of whom even in the most advanced and most democratic bourgeois republics are downtrodden, backward, ignorant, intimidated and disunited. For a long time after the revolution the exploiters inevitably continue to retain a number of great practical advantages: they still have money (since it is impossible to abolish money all at once); some movable property — often fairly considerable; they still have various connections, habits of organisation and management; knowledge of all the "secrets" (customs, methods, means and possibilities) of management; superior education; close connections with the higher technical personnel (who live and think like the bourgeoisie); incomparably greater experience in the art of war (this is very important), and so on and so forth.

If the exploiters are defeated in one country only — and this, of course, is typical, since a simultaneous revolution in a number of countries is a rare exception — they *still* remain *stronger* than the exploited, for the international connections of the exploiters are enormous. That a section of the exploited from the least advanced middle-peasant, artisan and similar groups of the population may, and indeed does, follow the exploiters has been proved by *all* revolutions, including the Commune (for there were also proletarians among the Versailles troops, which the most learned Kautsky has "forgotten").[48]

In these circumstances, to assume that in a revolution which is at all profound and serious the issue is decided simply by the relation between the majority and the minority is the acme of stupidity, the silliest prejudice of a common liberal, an attempt to *deceive the people* by concealing from them a well-established historical truth. This historical truth is that in every profound revolution, the *prolonged, stubborn and desperate* resistance of the exploiters, who for a number of years retain important practical advantages over the exploited, is the *rule*. Never — except in the sentimental fantasies of the sentimental fool Kautsky — will the exploiters submit to the decision of the exploited majority without trying to make use of their advantages in a last desperate battle, or series of battles.

The transition from capitalism to communism takes an entire historical epoch. Until this epoch is over, the exploiters inevitably cherish the hope of restoration, and this *hope* turns into *attempts* at restoration. After their first serious defeat, the overthrown exploiters — who had not expected their overthrow, never believed it possible, never conceded the thought of it — throw themselves with energy grown tenfold, with furious passion and hatred grown a hundredfold, into the battle for the recovery of the "paradise", of which they were deprived, on behalf of their families, who had been leading such a sweet and easy life and whom now the "common herd" is condemning to ruin and destitution (or to "common" labour . . .). In the train of the capitalist exploiters follow the wide sections of the petty bourgeoisie, with regard to whom decades of historical experience of all countries testify that they vacillate and hesitate, one day marching behind the proletariat and the next day taking fright at the difficulties of the revolution; that they become panic-stricken at the first defeat or semi-defeat of the workers, grow nervous, run about aimlessly, snivel, and rush from one camp into the other — just like our Mensheviks and Socialist-Revolutionaries.

In these circumstances, in an epoch of desperately acute war, when history presents the question of whether age-old and thousand-year-old privileges are to be or not to be — at such a time to talk about majority and minority, about pure democracy, about dictatorship being unnecessary and about equality between the exploiter and the exploited! What infinite stupidity and abysmal philistinism are needed for this!

However, during the decades of comparatively "peaceful" capitalism between 1871 and 1914, the Augean stables of philistinism, imbecility, and apostasy accumulated in the socialist parties which were adapting themselves to opportunism. . . .

*   *   *

The reader will probably have noticed that Kautsky, in the passage from his pamphlet quoted above, speaks of an attempt to encroach upon universal suffrage (calling it, by the way, a deep source of mighty moral authority, whereas Engels, apropos of the same Paris Commune and the same question of dictatorship, spoke of the authority of the armed people against the bourgeoisie — a very characteristic difference between the philistine's and the revolutionary's views on "authority" . . .).

It should be observed that the question of depriving the exploiters of the franchise is a *purely Russian* question, and not a question of the dictatorship of the proletariat in general. Had Kautsky, casting aside hypocrisy, entitled his pamphlet *Against the Bolsheviks*, the title would have corresponded to the contents of the pamphlet, and Kautsky would have been justified in speaking bluntly about the franchise. But Kautsky wanted to come out primarily as a "theoretician". He called his pamphlet *The Dictatorship of the Proletariat — in general.* He speaks about the Soviets and about Russia specifically only in the second part of the pamphlet, beginning with the sixth paragraph. The subject dealt with in the first part (from which I took the quotation) is *democracy* and *dictatorship in general*. In speaking about the franchise, Kautsky *betrayed himself* as an opponent of the

Bolsheviks, *who does not care a brass farthing for theory*. For theory, i.e., the reasoning about the general (and not the nationally specific) class foundations of democracy and dictatorship, ought to deal not with a special question, such as the franchise, but with the general question of whether democracy can be *preserved for the rich, for the exploiters* in the historical period of the overthrow of the exploiters and the replacement of their state by the state of the exploited.

That is the way, the only way, a theoretician can present the question.

We know the example of the Paris Commune, we know all that was said by the founders of Marxism in connection with it and in reference to it. On the basis of this material I examined, for instance, the question of democracy and dictatorship in my pamphlet, *The State and Revolution*, written before the October Revolution. *I did not say anything at all* about restricting the franchise. And it must be said now that the question of restricting the franchise is a nationally specific and not a general question of the dictatorship. One must approach the question of restricting the franchise by studying the *specific conditions* of the Russian revolution and the *specific path* of its development. This will be done later on in this pamphlet. It would be a mistake, however, to guarantee in advance that the impending proletarian revolutions in Europe will all, or the majority of them, be necessarily accompanied by restriction of the franchise for the bourgeoisie. It may be so. After the war and the experience of the Russian revolution it probably will be so; but it is *not absolutely necessary* for the exercise of the dictatorship, it is not an *indispensable* characteristic of the logical concept "dictatorship", it does not enter as an *indispensable* condition in the historical and class concept "dictatorship".

The indispensable characteristic, the necessary condition of dictatorship is the *forcible* suppression of the exploiters as a *class*, and, consequently, the *infringement* of "pure democracy", i.e., of equality and freedom, *in regard to* that *class*.

This is the way, the only way, the question can be put theoretically. And by failing to put the question thus, Kautsky has shown that he opposes the Bolsheviks not as a theoretician, but as a sycophant of the opportunists and the bourgeoisie.

In which countries, and given what national features of capitalism, democracy for the exploiters will be in one or another form restricted (wholly or in part), infringed upon, is a question of the specific national features of this or that capitalism, of this or that revolution.

The theoretical question is different: Is the dictatorship of the proletariat possible *without infringing democracy* in relation to the *exploiting* class?

It is precisely this question, the *only* theoretically important and essential one, that Kautsky has evaded. He has quoted all sorts of passages from Marx and Engels, *except those* which bear on this question, and which I quoted above.

Kautsky talks about anything you like, about everything that is acceptable to liberals and bourgeois democrats and does not go beyond their circle of ideas, but he does not talk about the main thing, namely, the fact that the proletariat cannot achieve victory *without breaking the resistance* of the bourgeoisie, *without forcibly suppressing its adversaries*, and that, where there is "forcible suppression", where there is no "freedom", *there is, of course, no democracy*.

This Kautsky has not understood.

*   *   *

We shall now examine the experience of the Russian revolution and that divergence between the Soviets of Deputies and the Constituent Assembly which led to the dissolution of the latter and to the withdrawal of the franchise from the bourgeoisie.

The Soviets Dare Not Become State Organisations

The Soviets are the Russian form of the proletarian dictatorship. If a Marxist theoretician, writing a work on the dictatorship of the proletariat, had really studied the subject (and not merely repeated the petty-bourgeois lamentations against dictatorship, as Kautsky did, singing to Menshevik tunes), he would first have given a general definition of dictatorship, and would then have examined its peculiar, national, form, the Soviets; he would have given his critique of them as one of the forms of the dictatorship of the proletariat.

It goes without saying that nothing serious could be expected from Kautsky after his liberalistic "interpretation" of Marx's teaching on dictatorship, but the manner in which he approached the question of what the Soviets are and the way he dealt with this question is highly characteristic.

The Soviets, he says, recalling their rise in 1905, created "the most all-embracing (*umfassendste*) form of proletarian organisation, for it embraced all the wage-workers" (p. 31). In 1905 they were only local bodies; in 1917 they became a national organisation.

"The Soviet form of organisation," Kautsky continues, "already has a great and glorious history behind it, and it has a still mightier future before it, and not in Russia alone. It appears that everywhere the old methods of the economic and political struggle of the proletariat are inadequate (*versagen*; this German expression is somewhat stronger than "inadequate" and somewhat weaker than "impotent") against the gigantic economic and political forces which finance capital has at its disposal. These old methods cannot be discarded; they are still indispensable for normal times; but from time to time tasks arise which they cannot cope with, tasks that can be accomplished successfully only as a result of a combination of all the political and economic instruments of force of the working class" (p. 32).

Then follows a reasoning on the mass strike and on "trade union bureaucracy" — which is no less necessary than the trade unions — being "useless for the purpose of directing the mighty mass battles that are more and more becoming a sign of the times. . . ."

"Thus," Kautsky concludes, "the Soviet form of organisation is one of the most important phenomena of our time. It promises to acquire decisive importance in the great decisive battles between capital and labour towards which we are marching.

"But are we entitled to demand more of the Soviets? The Bolsheviks, after the November Revolution (new style, or October, according to our style) 1917, secured in conjunction with the Left Socialist-Revolutionaries a majority in the Russian Soviets of Workers' Deputies, and after the dispersion of the Constituent Assembly, they set out to transform the Soviets from a *combat organisation* of one *class*, as they had been up to then, into a *state organisation*. They destroyed the democracy which the Russian people had won in the March (new style, or February, our style) Revolution. In line with this, the Bolsheviks have ceased to call themselves Social-*Democrats*. They call themselves *Communists*" (p. 33, Kautsky's italics).

Those who are familiar with Russian Menshevik literature will at once see how slavishly Kautsky copies Martov, Axelrod, Stein and Co. Yes, "slavishly", because Kautsky ridiculously distorts the facts in order to pander to Menshevik prejudices. Kautsky did not take the trouble, for instance, to ask his informants (Stein of Berlin, or Axelrod of Stockholm) *when* the questions of changing the name of the Bolsheviks to Communists and of the significance of the Soviets as state organisations were first raised. Had Kautsky made this simple inquiry he would not have penned these ludicrous lines, for both these questions were raised by the Bolsheviks *in April 1917*, for example, in my "Theses" of April 4, 1917, i.e., *long before* the Revolution of October 1917 (and, of course, long before the dissolution of the Constituent Assembly on January 5, 1918).

But Kautsky's argument which I have just quoted in full represents the *crux* of the whole question of the Soviets. The crux is: should the Soviets aspire to become state organisations (in April 1917 the Bolsheviks put forward the slogan: "All Power to the Soviets!" and at the Bolshevik Party Conference held in the same month they declared they were not satisfied with a bourgeois parliamentary republic but demanded a workers' and peasants' republic of the Paris Commune or Soviet type); *or* should the Soviets not strive for this, refrain from taking power into their hands, refrain from becoming state organisations and remain the "combat organisations" of one "class" (as Martov expressed it, embellishing by this innocent wish the fact that under Menshevik leadership the Soviets were *an instrument for the subjection of the workers to the bourgeoisie*)?

Kautsky slavishly repeats Martov's words, picks out *fragments* of the theoretical controversy between the Bolsheviks and the Mensheviks, and uncritically and senselessly transplants them to the general theoretical and general European field. The result is such a hodge-podge as to provoke Homeric laughter in every class-conscious Russian worker had he read these arguments of Kautsky's.

When we explain what the question at issue is, every worker in Europe (barring a handful of inveterate social-imperialists) will greet Kautsky with similar laughter.

Kautsky has rendered Martov a backhanded service by developing his mistake into a glaring absurdity. Indeed, look what Kautsky's argument amounts to.

The Soviets embrace all wage-workers. The old methods of economic and political struggle of the proletariat are inadequate against finance capital. The Soviets have a great role to play in the future, and not only in Russia. They will play a decisive role in great decisive battles between capital and labour in Europe. That is what Kautsky says.

Excellent. But won't the "decisive battles between capital and labour" decide which of the two classes will assume state power?

Nothing of the kind! Heaven forbid!

The Soviets, which embrace all the wage-workers, *must not become state organisations* in the "decisive" battles!

But what is the state?

The state is nothing but a machine for the suppression of one class by another.

Thus, the oppressed class, the vanguard of all the working and exploited people in modern society, must strive towards the "decisive battles between capital and labour", *but must not touch* the machine by means of which capital suppresses labour! — *It must not break up* that machine! — *It must not make use* of its all-embracing organisation *for suppressing the exploiters!*

Excellent, Mr. Kautsky, magnificent! "We" recognise the class struggle — in the same way as all liberals recognise it, i.e., without the overthrow of the bourgeoisie. . . .

This is where Kautsky's complete rupture both with Marxism and with socialism becomes obvious. Actually, it is desertion to the camp of the bourgeoisie, who are prepared to concede everything except the transformation of the organisations of the class which they oppress into state organisations. Kautsky can no longer save his position of trying to reconcile everything and of getting away from all profound contradictions with mere phrases.

Kautsky either rejects the assumption of state power by the working class altogether, or he concedes that the working class may take over the old, bourgeois state machine. But he will by no means concede that it must break it up, smash it, and replace it by a new, proletarian machine. Whichever way Kautsky's arguments are "interpreted", or "explained", his rupture with Marxism and his desertion to the bourgeoisie are obvious.

Back in the *Communist Manifesto*, describing what sort of state the victorious working class needs, Marx wrote: "the state, i.e., the proletariat organised as the ruling class."[49] Now we have a man who claims still to be a Marxist coming forward and declaring that the proletariat, fully organised and waging the "decisive battle" against capital, *must not* transform its class organisation into a state organisation. Here Kautsky has betrayed that "superstitious belief in the state" which in Germany, as Engels wrote in 1891, "has been carried over into the general thinking of the bourgeoisie and even of many workers".[50] Workers, fight! — our philistine "agrees" to this (as every bourgeois "agrees", since the workers are fighting all the same, and the only thing to do is to devise means of blunting the edge of their sword) — fight, but *don't dare win*! Don't destroy the state machine of the bourgeoisie, don't replace the bourgeois "state organisation" by the proletarian "state organisation"!

Whoever sincerely shared the Marxist view that the state is nothing but a machine for the suppression of one class by another, and who has at all reflected upon this truth, could never have reached the absurd conclusion that the proletarian organisations capable of defeating finance capital must not transform themselves into state organisations. It was this point that betrayed the petty bourgeois who believes that "after all is said and done" the state is something outside classes or above classes. Indeed, why should the proletariat, *"one class"*, be permitted to wage unremitting war on *capital*, which rules not only over the proletariat, but over the whole people, over the whole petty bourgeoisie, over all the peasants, yet this proletariat, this *"one class"*, is not to be permitted to transform its organisation into a state organisation? Because the petty bourgeois is *afraid* of the class struggle, and does not carry it to its logical conclusion, *to its main object*.

Kautsky has got himself completely mixed up and has given himself away entirely. Mark you, he himself admits that Europe is heading for decisive battles between capital and labour, and that the old methods of economic and political struggle of the proletariat are inadequate. But these old methods were precisely the utilisation of *bourgeois* democracy. It therefore follows. . . ?

But Kautsky is afraid to think of what follows.

. . . It therefore follows that only a reactionary, an enemy of the working class, a henchman of the bourgeoisie, can now turn his face to the obsolete past, paint the charms of bourgeois democracy and babble about pure democracy. Bourgeois democracy *was* progressive compared with medievalism, but it had to be utilised. But now it is *not sufficient* for the working class. Now we must look forward instead of backward — to replacing the bourgeois democracy by *proletarian* democracy. And while the preparatory work for the proletarian revolution, the formation and training of the proletarian army were possible (and necessary) *within the framework* of the bourgeois-democratic state, now that we have reached the stage of "decisive battles", to confine the proletariat to this framework means betraying the cause of the proletariat, means being a renegade.

Kautsky has made himself particularly ridiculous by repeating Martov's argument *without noticing* that in Martov's case this argument was based on *another* argument which he, Kautsky, does not use! Martov said (and Kautsky repeats after him) that Russia is not yet ripe for socialism; from which it logically follows that it is too early to transform the Soviets from organs of struggle into state organisations (read: it is timely to transform the Soviets, with the assistance of the Menshevik leaders, into instruments for *subjecting* the workers to the imperialist bourgeoisie). Kautsky, however, *cannot* say outright that Europe is not ripe for socialism. In 1909, when he was not yet a renegade, he wrote that there was then no reason to fear a *premature* revolution, that whoever had renounced revolution for fear of defeat would have been a traitor. Kautsky does not dare renounce this *outright*. And so we get an absurdity, which completely reveals the stupidity and cowardice of the petty bourgeois: on the one hand, Europe is ripe for socialism and is heading towards decisive battles between capital and labour; but, on the other hand, the *combat organisation* (i.e., the organisation which arises, grows and gains strength in combat), the organisation of the proletariat, the vanguard and organiser, the leader of the oppressed, *must not* be transformed into a state organisation!

*   *   *

From the point of view of practical politics the idea that the Soviets are necessary as combat organisations but must not be transformed into state organisations is infinitely more absurd than from the point of view of theory. Even in peacetime, when there is no revolutionary situation, the mass struggle of the workers against the capitalists — for instance, the mass strike — gives rise to great bitterness on both sides, to fierce passions in the struggle, the bourgeoisie constantly insisting that they remain and mean to remain "masters in their own house", etc. And in time of revolution, when political life reaches boiling point, an organisation like the Soviets, which embraces *all* the workers in *all* branches of industry, *all* the soldiers, and all the working and poorest sections of the rural population — such an organisation, of its own accord, with the development of the struggle, by the simple "logic" of attack and defence, comes inevitably to pose the question *point-blank*. The attempt to take up a middle position and to "reconcile" the proletariat with the bourgeoisie is sheer stupidity and doomed to miserable failure. That is what happened in Russia to the preachings of Martov and other Mensheviks, and that will inevitably happen in Germany and other countries if the Soviets succeed in developing on any wide scale, manage to unite and strengthen. To say to the Soviets: fight, but don't take all state power into your hands, don't become state organisations — is tantamount to preaching class collaboration and "social peace" between the proletariat and the bourgeoisie. It is ridiculous even to think that such a position in the midst of fierce struggle could lead to anything but ignominious failure. But it is Kautsky's everlasting fate to sit between two stools. He pretends to disagree with the opportunists on everything in theory, but *in practice* he agrees with them on everything essential (i.e., on everything pertaining to revolution).

The Constituent Assembly and the Soviet Republic

The question of the Constituent Assembly and its dispersal by the Bolsheviks is the crux of Kautsky's entire pamphlet. He constantly reverts to it, and the whole of this literary production of the ideological leader of the Second International is replete with innuendoes to the effect that the Bolsheviks have "destroyed democracy" (see one of the quotations from Kautsky above). The question is really an interesting and important one, because the relation between bourgeois democracy and proletarian democracy here confronted the revolution in a *practical* form. Let us see how our "Marxist theoretician" has dealt with the question.

He quotes the "Theses on the Constituent Assembly", written by me and published in *Pravda* on December 26, 1917. One would think that no better evidence of Kautsky's serious approach to the subject, quoting as he does the documents, could be desired. But look *how* he quotes. He does not say that there were nineteen of these theses; he does not say that they dealt with the relation between the ordinary bourgeois republic with a Constituent Assembly and a Soviet republic, as well as with the *history* of the divergence in our revolution between the Constituent Assembly and the dictatorship of the proletariat. Kautsky ignores all that, and simply tells the reader that "two of them" (of the theses) "are particularly important": one stating that a split occurred among the Socialist-Revolutionaries after the elections to the Constituent Assembly, but before it was convened (Kautsky does not mention that this was the fifth thesis), and the other, that the republic of Soviets is in general a higher democratic form than the Constituent Assembly (Kautsky does not mention that this was the third thesis).

Only from this third thesis does Kautsky quote a part in full, namely, the following passage:

"The republic of Soviets is not only a higher type of democratic institution (as compared with the *usual* bourgeois republic crowned by a Constituent Assembly), but is the only form capable of securing the most painless* transition to socialism" (Kautsky omits the word

---

* Incidentally, Kautsky, obviously trying to be ironical, repeatedly quotes the expression "most painless" transition; but as the shaft misses its mark, a few pages farther on he commits a slight forgery and falsely quotes it as a "painless" transition! Of course, by such means it is easy to put any absurdity into the mouth of an opponent. The forgery also helps him to evade the

"usual" and the introductory words of the thesis: "For the transition from the bourgeois to the socialist system, for the dictatorship of the proletariat").

After quoting these words, Kautsky, with magnificent irony, exclaims:

"It is a pity that this conclusion was arrived at only after the Bolsheviks found themselves in the minority in the Constituent Assembly. Before that no one had demanded it more vociferously than Lenin."

This is literally what Kautsky says on page 31 of this book!

It is positively a gem! Only a sycophant of the bourgeoisie could present the question in such a false way as to give the reader the impression that all the Bolsheviks' talk about a higher type of state was an invention which saw light of day *after* they found themselves in the minority in the Constituent Assembly! Such an infamous lie could only have been uttered by a scoundrel who has sold himself to the bourgeoisie, or, what is absolutely the same thing, who has placed his trust in Axelrod and is concealing the source of his information.

For everyone knows that on the very day of my arrival in Russia, on April 4, 1917, I publicly read my theses in which I proclaimed the superiority of the Paris Commune type of state over the bourgeois parliamentary republic.[51] Afterwards I *repeatedly* stated this in print, as, for instance, in a pamphlet on political parties, which was translated into English and was published in January 1918 in the New York *Evening Post*.[52] More than that, the Conference of the Bolshevik Party held at the end of April 1917 adopted a resolution to the effect that a proletarian and peasant republic was superior to a bourgeois parliamentary republic, that our Party would not be satisfied with the latter, and that the Party Programme should be modified accordingly.[53]

In face of these facts, what name can be given to Kautsky's trick of assuring his German readers that I had been vigorously demanding the convocation of the Constituent Assembly, and that I began to "belittle" the honour and dignity of the Constituent Assembly only after the Bolsheviks found themselves in the minority in it? How can

---

substance of the argument, namely, that the most painless transition to socialism is possible only when all the poor are organised to a man (Soviets) and when the core of state power (the proletariat) helps them to organise.

one excuse such a trick?* By pleading that Kautsky did not know the facts? If that is the case, why did he undertake to write about them? Or why did he not honestly announce that he was writing on the strength of information supplied by the Mensheviks Stein and Axelrod and Co.? By pretending to be objective, Kautsky wants to conceal his role as the servant of the Mensheviks, who are disgruntled because they have been defeated.

This, however, is a mere trifle compared with what is to come.

Let us assume that Kautsky would not or could not (?) obtain from his informants a translation of the Bolshevik resolutions and declarations on the question of whether the Bolsheviks would be satisfied with a bourgeois parliamentary democratic republic or not. Let us assume this, although it is incredible. But Kautsky *directly mentions* my theses of December 26, 1917, on page 30 of his book.

Does he not know these theses in full, or does he know only what was translated for him by the Steins, the Axelrods and Co.? Kautsky quotes the *third* thesis on the *fundamental* question of whether the Bolsheviks, *before* the elections to the Constituent Assembly, realised that a Soviet republic is superior to a bourgeois republic, and whether they told the *people* that. *But he keeps silent about the second thesis.*

The second thesis reads as follows:

"While demanding the convocation of a Constituent Assembly, revolutionary Social-Democracy has ever since the beginning of the revolution of 1917 *repeatedly emphasised that a republic of Soviets is a higher form of democracy than the usual bourgeois republic with a Constituent Assembly*" (my italics).

In order to represent the Bolsheviks as unprincipled people, as "revolutionary opportunists" (this is a term which Kautsky employs somewhere in his book, I forget in which connection), Mr. Kautsky *has concealed from his German readers* the fact that the theses contain a direct reference to "*repeated*" declarations!

These are the petty, miserable and contemptible methods Mr. Kautsky employs! That is the way he has evaded the *theoretical* question.

Is it true or not that the bourgeois-democratic parliamentary republic is *inferior* to the republic of the Paris Commune or Soviet type? This is the whole point, and Kautsky has evaded it. Kautsky has "forgotten" all that Marx said in his analysis of the Paris Commune. He has also "forgotten" Engels's letter to Bebel of March 28, 1875, in

---

* Incidentally, there are many Menshevik lies of this kind in Kautsky's pamphlet! It is a lampoon written by an embittered Menshevik.

which this same idea of Marx is formulated in a particularly lucid and comprehensible fashion: "The Commune was no longer a state in the proper sense of the word."[54]

Here is the most prominent theoretician of the Second International, in a special pamphlet on *The Dictatorship of the Proletariat*, specially dealing with Russia, where the question of a form of state that is higher than a democratic bourgeois republic has been raised directly and repeatedly, ignoring this very question. In what way does this differ *in fact* from desertion to the bourgeois camp?

(Let us observe in parenthesis that in this respect, too, Kautsky is merely trailing after the Russian Mensheviks. Among the latter there are any number of people who know "all the quotations" from Marx and Engels. Yet not a single Menshevik, from April to October 1917 and from October 1917 to October 1918, has *ever* made a *single* attempt to examine the question of the Paris Commune type of state. Plekhanov, too, has evaded the question. *Evidently he had to.*)

It goes without saying that to discuss the dispersal of the Constituent Assembly with people who call themselves socialists and Marxists, but who in fact desert to the bourgeoisie on the *main* question, the question of the Paris Commune type of state, would be casting pearls before swine. It will be sufficient to give the complete text of my theses on the Constituent Assembly as an appendix to the present book. The reader will then see that the question was presented on December 26, 1917, in the light of theory, history and practical politics.

If Kautsky has completely renounced Marxism as a theoretician he might at least have examined the question of the struggle of the Soviets with the Constituent Assembly as a historian. We know from many of Kautsky's works that he *knew how* to be a Marxist historian, and that *such* works of his will remain a permanent possession of the proletariat in spite of his subsequent apostasy. But on this question Kautsky, even as a historian, *turns his back* on the truth, ignores *well-known* facts and behaves like a sycophant. He *wants* to represent the Bolsheviks as being unprincipled and he tells his readers that they tried to *mitigate* the conflict with the Constituent Assembly before dispersing it. There is absolutely nothing wrong about it, we have nothing to recant; I gave the theses in full and there it is said as clear as clear can be: Gentlemen of the vacillating petty bourgeoisie entrenched in the Constituent Assembly, either reconcile yourselves to the proletarian dictatorship, or else we shall defeat you by "revolutionary means" (theses 18 and 19).

That is how a really revolutionary proletariat has always behaved and always will behave towards the vacillating petty bourgeoisie.

Kautsky adopts a formal standpoint on the question of the Constituent Assembly. My theses say clearly and repeatedly that the interests of the revolution are higher than the formal rights of the Constituent Assembly (see theses 16 and 17). The formal democratic point of view is precisely the point of view of the *bourgeois* democrat who refuses to admit that the interests of the proletariat and of the proletarian class struggle are supreme. As a historian, Kautsky would not have been able to deny that bourgeois parliaments are the organs of this or that class. But now (for the sordid purpose of renouncing revolution) Kautsky finds it necessary to forget his Marxism, and he *refrains from putting the question*: the organ of what *class* was the Constituent Assembly of Russia? Kautsky does not examine the concrete conditions; he does not want to face facts; he does not say a single word to his German readers about the fact that the theses contained not only a theoretical elucidation of the question of the limited character of bourgeois democracy (theses 1-3), not only a description of the concrete conditions which determined the discrepancy between the party lists of candidates in the middle of October 1917 and the real state of affairs in December 1917 (theses 4-6), but also *a history of the class struggle and the Civil War* in October-December 1917 (theses 7-15). From this concrete history we drew the conclusion (thesis 14) that the slogan "All Power to the Constituent Assembly!" had, *in reality*, become the slogan of the Cadets and the Kaledin men and their abettors.

Kautsky the historian fails to see this. Kautsky the historian has never heard that universal suffrage sometimes produces petty-bourgeois, sometimes reactionary and counter-revolutionary parliaments. Kautsky the Marxist historian has never heard that the form of elections, the form of democracy, is one thing, and the class content of the given institution is another. This question of the class content of the Constituent Assembly is directly put and answered in my theses. Perhaps my answer is wrong. Nothing would have been more welcome to us than a Marxist criticism of our analysis by an outsider. Instead of writing utterly silly phrases (of which there are plenty in Kautsky's book) about somebody preventing criticism of Bolshevism, he ought to have set out to make such a criticism. But the point is that he offers no criticism. He does not even *raise the question* of a class analysis of the Soviets on the one hand, and of the Constituent Assembly on the other. It is therefore *impossible* to argue, to debate with Kautsky. All we can do is *demonstrate* to the reader why Kautsky cannot be called anything else but a renegade.

The divergence between the Soviets and the Constituent Assembly has its history, which even a historian who does not share the point of view of the class struggle could not have ignored. Kautsky would not *touch* upon this actual history. Kautsky has concealed from his German readers the universally known fact (which only malignant Mensheviks now conceal) that the divergence between the Soviets and the "general state" (that is, bourgeois) institutions existed even under the rule of the Mensheviks, i.e., from the end of February to October 1917. Actually, Kautsky adopts the position of conciliation, compromise and collaboration between the proletariat and the bourgeoisie. However much Kautsky may repudiate this, it is a fact which is borne out by his whole pamphlet. To say that the Constituent Assembly should not have been dispersed is tantamount to saying that the fight against the bourgeoisie should not have been fought to a finish, that the bourgeoisie should not have been overthrown and that the proletariat should have made peace with them.

Why has Kautsky kept quiet about the fact that the Mensheviks were engaged in this inglorious work between February and October 1917 and did not achieve anything? If it was possible to reconcile the bourgeoisie with the proletariat, why didn't the Mensheviks succeed in doing so? Why did the bourgeoisie stand aloof from the Soviets? Why did the *Mensheviks* call the Soviets "revolutionary democracy", and the bourgeoisie the "propertied elements"?

Kautsky has concealed from his German readers that it was the Mensheviks who, in the "epoch" of their rule (February to October 1917), called the Soviets "revolutionary democracy", *thereby* admitting their superiority over all other institutions. It is only by concealing this fact that Kautsky the historian made it appear that the divergence between the Soviets and the bourgeoisie had no history, that it arose instantaneously, without cause, suddenly, because of the bad behaviour of the Bolsheviks. Yet, in actual fact, it was *the more than six months'* (an enormous period in time of revolution) *experience* of Menshevik compromise, of their attempts to reconcile the proletariat with the bourgeoisie, that convinced the people of the fruitlessness of these attempts and drove the proletariat away from the Mensheviks.

Kautsky admits that the Soviets are an excellent combat organisation of the proletariat, and that they have a great future before them. But, that being the case, Kautsky's position collapses like a house of cards, or like the dreams of a petty bourgeois that the acute struggle between the proletariat and the bourgeoisie can be avoided. For revolution is one continuous and moreover desperate struggle, and the proletariat is the vanguard class of *all* the oppressed, the focus and centre of all the aspirations of all the oppressed for their emancipation! Naturally, therefore, the Soviets, as the organ of the struggle of the oppressed people, reflected and expressed the moods and changes of opinions of these people ever so much quickly, fully, and faithfully than any other institution (that, incidentally, is one of the reasons why Soviet democracy is the highest type of democracy).

In the period between February 28 (old style) and October 25, 1917, the Soviets managed to convene *two* all-Russia congresses of representatives of the overwhelming majority of the population of Russia, of all the workers and soldiers, and of 70 or 80 per cent of the peasants, not to mention the vast number of local, uyezd, town, gubernia, and regional congresses. During this period the bourgeoisie did not succeed in convening a single institution representing the majority (except that obvious sham and mockery called the "Democratic Conference",[55] which enraged the proletariat). The Constituent Assembly reflected *the same* popular mood and *the same* political grouping as the First (June) All-Russia Congress of Soviets. By the time the Constituent Assembly was convened (January 1918), the Second (October 1917) and Third (January 1918) Congresses of Soviets had met, both of which had *demonstrated as clear as clear could be* that the people had swung to the left, had become revolutionised, had turned away from the Mensheviks and the Socialist-Revolutionaries, and had passed over to the side of the Bolsheviks; *that is*, had turned away from petty-bourgeois leadership, from the illusion that it was possible to reach a compromise with the bourgeoisie, and had joined the proletarian revolutionary struggle for the overthrow of the bourgeoisie.

So, even the *external history* of the Soviets shows that the Constituent Assembly was a *reactionary* body and that its dispersal was inevitable. But Kautsky sticks firmly to his "slogan": let "pure democracy" prevail though the revolution perish and the bourgeoisie triumph over the proletariat! *Fiat justitia, pereat mundus!* [Let justice be done, even though the world may perish.]

Here are the brief figures relating to the all-Russia congresses of Soviets in the course of the history of the Russian revolution:

All-Russia Congress of Soviets	Number of Delegates	Number of Bolsheviks	Percentage of Bolsheviks
First (June 3, 1917)	790	103	13
Second (October 25, 1917)	675	343	51
Third (January 10, 1918)	710	434	61
Fourth (March 14, 1918)	1,232	795	64
Fifth (July 4, 1918)	1,164	773	66

One glance at these figures is enough to understand why the defence of the Constituent Assembly and talk (like Kautsky's) about the Bolsheviks not having a majority of the population behind them are just ridiculed in Russia.

The Soviet Constitution

As I have already pointed out, the disfranchisement of the bourgeoisie is not a necessary and indispensable feature of the dictatorship of the proletariat. And in Russia, the Bolsheviks, who long before October put forward the slogan of proletarian dictatorship, did not say anything in advance about disfranchising the exploiters. *This* aspect of the dictatorship did not make its appearance "according to the plan" of any particular party; it *emerged* of itself in the course of the struggle. Of course, Kautsky the historian failed to notice this. He failed to understand that even when the Mensheviks (who compromised with the bourgeoisie) still ruled the Soviets, the bourgeoisie cut themselves off from the Soviets of their own accord, boycotted them, put themselves up in opposition to them and intrigued against them. The Soviets arose without any constitution and existed without one for *more than a year* (from the spring of 1917 to the summer of 1918). The fury of the bourgeoisie against this independent and omnipotent (because it was all-embracing) organisation of the oppressed; the fight, the unscrupulous, self-seeking and sordid fight, the bourgeoisie waged against the Soviets; and, lastly, the overt participation of the bourgeoisie (from the Cadets to the Right Socialist-Revolutionaries, from Milyukov to Kerensky) in the Kornilov mutiny — all this *paved the way* for the formal exclusion of the bourgeoisie from the Soviets.[56]

Kautsky has heard about the Kornilov mutiny, but he majestically scorns historical facts and the course and forms of the struggle which determine the *forms* of the dictatorship. Indeed, who should care about facts where "pure" democracy is involved? That is why Kautsky's "criticism" of the disfranchisement of the bourgeoisie is distinguished by such . . . sweet naïveté, which would be touching in a child but is repulsive in a person who has not yet been officially certified as feeble-minded.

" . . . If the capitalists found themselves in an insignificant minority under universal suffrage they would more readily become reconciled to their fate" (p. 33). . . . Charming, isn't it? Clever Kautsky has seen many cases in history, and, generally, knows perfectly well from his own observations of life of landowners and capitalists reckoning with the will of the majority of the oppressed. Clever Kautsky firmly advocates an "opposition", i.e., parliamentary struggle. That is literally what he says: "opposition" (p. 34 and elsewhere).

My dear learned historian and politician! It would not harm you to know that "opposition" is a concept that belongs to the peaceful and only to the parliamentary struggle, i.e., a concept that corresponds to a non-revolutionary situation, a concept that corresponds to an *absence of revolution*. During revolution we have to deal with a ruthless enemy in civil war; and no reactionary jeremiads of a petty bourgeois who fears such a war, as Kautsky does, will alter the fact. To examine the problems of ruthless civil war from the point of view of "opposition" at a time when the bourgeoisie are prepared to commit any crime — the example of the Versailles men and their deals with Bismarck must mean something to every person who does not treat history like Gogol's Petrushka[57] — when the bourgeoisie are summoning foreign states to their aid and intriguing with them against the revolution, is simply comical. The revolutionary proletariat is to put on a nightcap, like "Muddle-headed Counsellor" Kautsky, and regard the bourgeoisie, who are organising Dutov, Krasnov and Czech counter-revolutionary insurrections and are paying millions to saboteurs, as a legal "opposition". Oh, what profundity!

Kautsky is exclusively interested in the formal, legal aspect of the question, and, reading his disquisitions on the Soviet Constitution, one involuntarily recalls Bebel's words: Lawyers are thoroughbred reactionaries. "In reality," Kautsky writes, "the capitalists alone cannot be disfranchised. What is a capitalist in the legal sense of the term? A property-owner? Even in a country which has advanced so far along the path of economic progress as Germany, where the proletariat is so numerous, the establishment of a Soviet republic would disfranchise a large mass of people. In 1907, the number of persons in the German Empire engaged in the three great occupational groups — agriculture, industry and commerce — together with their families amounted roughly to thirty-five million in the wage-earner's and salaried employees' group, and seventeen million in the independent group. Hence, a party might well form a majority among the wage-workers but a minority among the population as a whole" (p. 33).

That is an example of Kautsky's mode of argument. Isn't it the counter-revolutionary whining of a bourgeois? Why, Mr. Kautsky, have you relegated all the "independents" to the category of the disfranchised, when you know very well that the overwhelming majority of the Russian peasants do not employ hired labour, and do not, therefore, lose their franchise? Isn't this falsification?

Why, learned economist, did you not quote the facts with which you are perfectly familiar and which are to be found in those same German statistical returns for 1907 relating to hired labour in agriculture according to size of farms? Why did you not quote these facts to enable the German workers, the readers of your pamphlet, to see *how many exploiters there are*, and how few they are compared with the total number of "farmers" who figure in German statistics?

You did not because your apostasy has made you a mere sycophant of the bourgeoisie.

The term capitalist, Kautsky argues, is legally a vague concept, and on several pages he thunders against the "arbitrariness" of the Soviet Constitution. This "serious scholar" has no objection to the British bourgeoisie taking several centuries to work out and develop a new (new for the Middle Ages) bourgeois constitution, but, representative of lackey's science that he is, he will allow no time to us, the workers and peasants of Russia. He expects us to have a constitution all worked out to the very last letter in a few months. . . .

"Arbitrariness!" Just imagine what a depth of vile subservience to the bourgeoisie and most inept pedantry is contained in *such* a reproach. When thoroughly bourgeois and for the most part reactionary lawyers in the capitalist countries have for centuries or decades been drawing up most detailed rules and regulations and writing scores and hundreds of volumes of laws and interpretations of laws to *oppress* the workers, to bind the *poor man* hand and foot and to place thousands of hindrances and obstacles in the way of any of the common labouring people — there the bourgeois liberals and Mr. Kautsky see no "arbitrariness"! That is "law" and "order"! The ways in which the poor are to be "kept down" have all been thought out and written down. There are thousands of bourgeois lawyers and bureaucrats (about them Kautsky says nothing at all, probably just because Marx attached enormous significance to *smashing* the bureaucratic machine . . .) — lawyers and bureaucrats who know how to interpret the laws in such a way that the worker and the average peasant can never break through the barbed-wire entanglements of these laws. This is not "arbitrariness" on the part of the bourgeoisie, it is not the dictatorship of the sordid and self-seeking exploiters who are sucking the blood of the people. Nothing of the kind! It is "pure democracy", which is becoming purer and purer every day.

But now that the toiling and exploited classes, while cut off by the imperialist war from their brothers across the border, have for the first time in history set up their *own* Soviets, have called to the work of political construction *those people* whom the bourgeoisie used to oppress, grind down and stupefy, and have begun *themselves* to build a *new*, proletarian state, have begun in the heat of furious struggle, in the fire of civil war, to *sketch* the fundamental principles of a state *without exploiters* — all the bourgeois scoundrels, the whole gang of bloodsuckers, with Kautsky echoing them, howl about "arbitrariness"! Indeed, how will these ignorant people, these workers and peasants, this "mob", be able to interpret their laws? How can these common labourers acquire a sense of justice without the counsel of educated lawyers, of bourgeois writers, of the Kautskys and the wise old bureaucrats?

Mr. Kautsky quotes from my speech of April 28, 1918, the words: "The people themselves determine the procedure and the time of elections." And Kautsky, the "pure democrat", infers from this:

"... Hence, it would mean that every assembly of electors may determine the procedure of elections at their own discretion. Arbitrariness and the opportunity of getting rid of undesirable opposition in the ranks of the proletariat itself would thus be carried to the extreme" (p. 37).

Well, how does this differ from the talk of a hack hired by capitalists, who howls about the people oppressing industrious workers who are "willing to work" during a strike? Why is the *bourgeois* bureaucratic method of determining electoral procedure under "pure" bourgeois democracy *not* arbitrariness? Why should the sense of justice *among the masses who have risen to fight* their age-old exploiters and who are being educated and steeled in this desperate struggle be less than that of a *handful* of bureaucrats, intellectuals and lawyers brought up in *bourgeois* prejudices?

Kautsky is a true socialist. Don't dare suspect the sincerity of this very respectable father of a family, of this very honest citizen. He is an ardent and convinced supporter of the victory of the workers, of the proletarian revolution. All he wants is that the honey-mouthed, petty-bourgeois intellectuals and philistines in nightcaps should *first* — *before* the masses begin to move, *before* they start a furious battle with the exploiters, and certainly *without* civil war — draw up a moderate and precise *set of rules for the development of the revolution*. ...

Burning with profound moral indignation, our most learned Judas Golovlyov tells the German workers that on June 14, 1918, the All-

Russia Central Executive Committee of Soviets resolved to expel the representatives of the Right Socialist-Revolutionary Party and the Mensheviks from the Soviets.[58] "This measure," writes Judas Kautsky, all afire with noble indignation, "is not directed against definite persons guilty of definite punishable offences. . . . The Constitution of the Soviet Republic does not contain a single word about the immunity of Soviet deputies. It is not definite *persons*, but definite *parties* that are expelled from the Soviets" (p. 37).

Yes, it is really awful, an intolerable departure from pure democracy, according to the rules of which our revolutionary Judas Kautsky will make the revolution. We Russian Bolsheviks should first have guaranteed immunity to the Savinkovs and Co., to the Lieberdans, Potresovs ("activists") and Co.,[59] then drawn up a criminal code proclaiming participation in the Czech counter-revolutionary war, or in the alliance with the German imperialists in the Ukraine or in Georgia *against* the workers of one's own country, to be "punishable offences", and *only then*, on the basis of this criminal code, would we be entitled, in accordance with the principles of "pure democracy", to expel "definite persons" from the Soviets. It goes without saying that the Czechs, who are subsidised by the British and French capitalists through the medium (or thanks to the agitation) of the Savinkovs, Potresovs and Lieberdans, and the Krasnovs who receive ammunition from the Germans through the medium of the Ukranian and Tiflis Mensheviks, would have sat quietly waiting until we were ready with our proper criminal code, and, like the purest democrats they are, would have confined themselves to the role of an "opposition". . . .

No less profound moral indignation is aroused in Kautsky's breast by the fact that the Soviet Constitution disfranchises all those who "employ hired labour with a view to profit". "A home-worker, or a small master employing only one journeyman," Kautsky writes, "may live and feel quite proletarian, but he has no vote" (p. 36).

What a departure from "pure democray"! What an injustice! True, up to now all Marxists have thought — and thousands of facts have proved it — that the small masters were the most unscrupulous and grasping exploiters of hired labour, but our Judas Kautsky takes the small masters not as a *class* (who invented that pernicious theory of the class struggle?) but as single individuals, exploiters who "live and feel quite like proletarians". The famous "thrifty Agnes", who was considered dead and buried long ago, has come to life again under Kautsky's pen. This "thrifty Agnes" was invented and launched into German literature some decades ago by that "pure" democrat, the bourgeois Eugen Richter. He predicted untold calamities that would follow the dictatorship of the proletariat, the confiscation of the capital of the exploiters, and asked with an innocent air: What is a capitalist in the legal sense of the term? He took as an example a poor, thrifty seamstress ("thrifty Agnes"), whom the wicked "proletarian dictators" rob of her last farthing. There was a time when all German Social-Democrats used to poke fun at this "thrifty Agnes" of the pure democrat, Eugen Richter. But that was a long, long time ago, when Bebel, who was quite frank and open about there being many national-liberals in his party, was still alive; that was very long ago, when Kautsky was not yet a renegade.[60]

Now "thrifty Agnes" has come to life again in the person of the "small master who employs only one journeyman and who lives and feels quite like a proletarian". The wicked Bolsheviks are wronging him, depriving him of his vote. It is true that "every assembly of electors" in the Soviet Republic, as Kautsky tells us, may admit into its midst a poor little master who, for instance, may be connected with this or that factory, if, by way of an exception, he is not an exploiter, and if he *really* "lives and feels quite like a proletarian". But can one rely on the knowledge of life, on the sense of justice of an irregular factory meeting of common workers acting (how awful!) without a written code? Would it not clearly be better to grant the vote to *all* exploiters, to *all* who employ hired labour, rather than risk the possibility of "thrifty Agnes" and the "small master who lives and feels quite like a proletarian" being wronged by the workers?

*   *   *

Let the contemptible renegade scoundrels, amidst the applause of the bourgeoisie and the social-chauvinists,* abuse our Soviet Constitution for disfranchising the exploiters! That's fine because it will accelerate and widen the split between the revolutionary workers of Europe and the Scheidemanns and Kautskys, the Renaudels and Longuets, the Hendersons and Ramsay MacDonalds, the old leaders and old betrayers of socialism.

---

* I have just read a leading article in *Frankfurter Zeitung* (No. 293, October 22, 1918), giving an enthusiastic summary of Kautsky's pamphlet. This organ of the stock exchange is satisfied. And no wonder! And a comrade writes to me from Berlin that *Vorwärts*, the organ of the Scheidemanns, has declared in a special article that it subscribes to almost every line Kautsky has written. Hearty congratulations!

The mass of the oppressed classes, the class-conscious and honest revolutionary proletarian leaders will be *on our side*. It will be enough to acquaint such proletarians and such people with our Soviet Constitution for them to say at once: "These are really *our people*, this is a real workers' party, this is a real workers' government, for it does not deceive the workers by talking about reforms in the way *all the above-mentioned leaders have done*, but is fighting the exploiters in real earnest, making a revolution in real earnest and *actually* fighting for the complete emancipation of the workers.

The *fact* that after a year's "experience" the Soviets have deprived the exploiters of the franchise *shows* that the Soviets are really organisations of the oppressed and not of social-imperialists and social-pacifists who have sold themselves to the bourgeoisie. The *fact* that the Soviets have disfranchised the exploiters *shows* they are not organs of petty-bourgeois compromise with the capitalists, not organs of parliamentary chatter (on the part of the Kautskys, the Longuets and the MacDonalds), but organs of the genuinely revolutionary proletariat which is waging a life-and-death struggle against the exploiters.

"Kautsky's book is almost unknown here," a well-informed comrade wrote to me from Berlin a few days ago (today is October 30). I would advise our ambassadors in Germany and Switzerland not to stint thousands in buying up this book and *distributing it gratis* among the class-conscious workers so as to trample in the mud this "European" — read: imperialist and reformist — Social-Democracy, which has long been a "stinking corpse".

*   *   *

At the end of his book, on pages 61 and 63, Mr. Kautsky bitterly laments the fact that the "new theory" (as he calls Bolshevism, fearing to touch Marx's and Engels's analysis of the Paris Commune) "finds supporters even in old democracies like Switzerland, for instance". "It is incomprehensible" to Kautsky "how this theory can be adopted by German Social-Democrats".

No, it is quite comprehensible; for after the serious lessons of the war the revolutionary masses are becoming sick and tired of the Scheidemanns and the Kautskys.

"We" have always been in favour of democracy, Kautsky writes, yet we are supposed suddenly to renounce it!

"We", the opportunists of Social-Democracy, have always been opposed to the dictatorship of the proletariat, and Kolb and Co. proclaimed this *long ago*. Kautsky knows this and vainly expects that he will be able to conceal from his readers the obvious fact that he has "returned to the fold" of the Bernsteins and Kolbs.

"We", the revolutionary Marxists, have never made a fetish of "pure" (bourgeois) democracy. As is known, in 1903 Plekhanov was a revolutionary Marxist (later his unfortunate turn brought him to the position of a Russian Scheidemann). And in that year Plekhanov declared at our Party Congress, which was then adopting its programme, that in the revolution the proletariat would, if necessary, disfranchise the capitalists and *disperse any parliament* that was found to be counter-revolutionary.[61] That this is the only view that corresponds to Marxism will be clear to anybody even from the statements of Marx and Engels which I have quoted above; it patently follows from all the fundamental principles of Marxism.

"We", the revolutionary Marxists, never made speeches to the people that the Kautskyites of all nations love to make, cringing before the bourgeoisie, adapting themselves to the bourgeois parliamentary system, keeping silent about the *bourgeois* character of modern democracy and demanding only *its* extension, only that *it* be carried to its logical conclusion.

"We" said to the bourgeoisie: You, exploiters and hypocrites, talk about democracy, while at every step you erect thousands of barriers to prevent the *oppressed people* from taking part in politics. We take you at your word and, in the interests of these people, demand the extension of *your* bourgeois democracy *in order to prepare the people for revolution* for the purpose of overthrowing you, the exploiters. And if you exploiters attempt to offer resistance to our proletarian revolution we shall ruthlessly suppress you; we shall deprive you of all rights; more than that, we shall not give you any bread, for in our proletarian republic the exploiters will have no rights, they will be deprived of fire and water, for we are socialists in real earnest, and not in the Scheidemann or Kautsky fashion.

That is what "we", the revolutionary Marxists, said, and will say — and that is why the oppressed people will support us and be with us, while the Scheidemanns and the Kautskys will be swept into the renegades' cesspool.

What Is Internationalism?

Kautsky is absolutely convinced that he is an internationalist and calls himself one. The Scheidemanns he calls "government socialists". In defending the Mensheviks (he does not openly express his solidarity with them, but he faithfully expresses their views),

Kautsky has shown with perfect clarity what kind of "internationalism" he subscribes to. And since Kautsky is not alone, but is spokesman for a trend which inevitably grew up in the atmosphere of the Second International (Longuet in France, Turati in Italy, Nobs and Grimm, Graber and Naine in Switzerland, Ramsay MacDonald in Britain, etc.), it will be instructive to dwell on Kautsky's "internationalism".

After emphasising that the Mensheviks also attended the Zimmerwald Conference (a diploma, certainly, but . . . a tainted one), Kautsky sets forth the views of the Mensheviks, with whom he agrees, in the following manner:

" . . . The Mensheviks wanted a general peace. They wanted all the belligerents to adopt the formula: no annexations and no indemnities. Until this had been achieved, the Russian army, according to this view, was to stand ready for battle. The Bolsheviks, on the other hand, demanded an immediate peace at any price; they were prepared, if need be, to make a separate peace; they tried to force it by increasing the state of disorganisation of the army, which was already bad enough" (p. 27). In Kautsky's opinion the Bolsheviks should not have taken power, and should have contented themselves with a Constituent Assembly.

So, the internationalism of Kautsky and the Mensheviks amounts to this: to demand reforms from the imperialist bourgeois government, but to continue to support it, and to continue to support the war that this government is waging until everyone in the war has accepted the formula: no annexations and no indemnities. This view was repeatedly expressed by Turati, and by the Kautsky supporters (Haase and others), and by Longuet and Co., who declared that they stood *for* defence of the fatherland.

Theoretically, this shows a complete inability to dissociate oneself from the social-chauvinists and complete confusion on the question of defence of the fatherland. Politically, it means substituting petty-bourgeois nationalism for internationalism, deserting to the reformists' camp and renouncing revolution.

From the point of view of the proletariat, recognising "defence of the fatherland" means justifying the present war, admitting that it is legitimate. And since the war remains an imperialist war (both under a monarchy and under a republic), irrespective of the country — mine or some other country — in which the enemy troops are stationed at the given moment, recognising defence of the fatherland means, *in fact*, supporting the imperialist, predatory bourgeoisie, and completely betraying socialism. In Russia, even under

Kerensky, under the bourgeois-democratic republic, the war continued to be an imperialist war, for it was being waged by the bourgeoisie as a ruling class (and war is a "continuation of politics"); and a particularly striking expression of the imperialist character of the war were the secret treaties for the partitioning of the world and the plunder of other countries which had been concluded by the tsar at the time with the capitalists of Britain and France.

The Mensheviks deceived the people in a most despicable manner by calling this war a defensive or revolutionary war. And by approving the policy of the Mensheviks, Kautsky is approving the popular deception, is approving the part played by the petty bourgeoisie in helping capital to trick the workers and harness them to the chariot of the imperialists. Kautsky is pursuing a characteristically petty-bourgeois, philistine policy by pretending (and trying to make the people believe the absurd idea) that *putting forward a slogan* alters the position. The entire history of bourgeois democracy refutes this illusion; the bourgeois democrats have always advanced all sorts of "slogans" to deceive the people. The point is to *test* their sincerity, to compare their words with their *deeds*, not to be satisfied with idealistic or charlatan *phrases*, but to get down to *class reality*. An imperialist war does not cease to be imperialist when charlatans or phrase-mongers or petty-bourgeois philistines put forward sentimental "slogans", but only when the *class* which is conducting the imperialist war, and is bound to it by millions of economic threads (and even ropes), is really *overthrown* and is replaced at the helm of state by the really revolutionary class, the proletariat. *There is no other way of getting out of an imperialist war, as also out of an imperialist predatory peace.*

By approving the foreign policy of the Mensheviks, and by declaring it to be internationalist and Zimmerwaldist, Kautsky, first, reveals the utter rottenness of the opportunist Zimmerwald majority (no wonder we, the *Left* Zimmerwaldists, at once dissociated ourselves from such a majority!), and, secondly — and this is the chief thing — passes from the position of the proletariat to the position of the petty bourgeoisie, from the revolutionary to the reformist.

The proletariat fights for the revolutionary overthrow of the imperialist bourgeoisie; the petty bourgeoisie fights for the reformist "improvement" of imperialism, for adaptation to it, while *submitting* to it. When Kautsky was still a Marxist, for example, in 1909, when he wrote his *Road to Power*, it was the idea that war would inevitably lead to *revolution* that he advocated, and he spoke of the approach of an *era of revolutions*. The Basle Manifesto of 1912 plainly and definitely speaks of a *proletarian revolution* in connection with that very imperialist war between the German and the British groups which actually broke out in 1914. But in 1918, when revolutions did begin in connection with the war, Kautsky, instead of explaining that they were inevitable, instead of pondering over and thinking out the *revolutionary* tactics and the ways and means of preparing for revolution, began to describe the reformist tactics of the Mensheviks as internationalism. Isn't this apostasy?

Kautsky praises the Mensheviks for having insisted on maintaining the fighting strength of the army, and he blames the Bolsheviks for having added to "disorganisation of the army", which was already disorganised enough as it was. This means praising reformism and submission to the imperialist bourgeoisie, and blaming and renouncing revolution. For under Kerensky maintaining the fighting strength of the army meant its preservation under *bourgeois* (albeit republican) command. Everybody knows, and the progress of events has strikingly confirmed it, that this republican army preserved the *Kornilov* spirit because its officers were Kornilov men. The bourgeois officers could not help being Kornilov men; they could not help gravitating towards imperialism and towards the forcible suppression of the proletariat. All that the Menshevik tactics amounted to *in practice* was to leave all the foundations of the imperialist war and all the foundations of the *bourgeois* dictatorship intact, to patch up details and to daub over a few trifles ("reforms").

On the other hand, not a single great revolution has ever taken place, or ever can take place, without the "disorganisation" of the army. For the army is the most ossified instrument for supporting the old regime, the most hardened bulwark of bourgeois discipline, buttressing up the rule of capital, and preserving and fostering among the working people the servile spirit of submission and subjection to capital. Counter-revolution has never tolerated, and never could tolerate, armed workers side by side with the army. In France, Engels wrote, the workers emerged armed from every revolution: "therefore, the disarming of the workers was the first commandment for the bourgeoisie, who were at the helm of the state."[62] The armed workers were the embryo of a new *army*, the organised nucleus of a *new* social order. The first commandment of the bourgeoisie was to crush this nucleus and prevent it from growing. The first commandment of every victorious revolution, as Marx and Engels repeatedly emphasised, was to smash the old army, dissolve it and replace it by a new one.[63] A new social class, when rising to power, never could, and cannot now, attain power and consolidate it except by completely disintegrating the old army ("Disorganisation!" the reactionary or just cowardly philistines howl on this score), except by passing through a most difficult and painful period without any army (the great French Revolution also passed through such a painful period), and by gradually building up, in the midst of hard civil war, a new army, a new discipline, a new military organisation of the new class. Formerly, Kautsky the historian understood this. Now, Kautsky the renegade has forgotten it.

What right has Kautsky to call the Scheidemanns "government socialists" if he *approves* of the tactics of the Mensheviks in the Russian revolution? In supporting Kerensky and joining his Ministry, the Mensheviks were also government socialists. Kautsky could not escape this conclusion if he were to put the question as to which is the *ruling class* that is waging the imperialist war. But Kautsky avoids raising the question about the ruling class, a question that is imperative for a Marxist, for the mere raising of it would expose the renegade.

The Kautsky supporters in Germany, the Longuet supporters in France, and Turati and Co. in Italy argue in this way: socialism presupposes the equality and freedom of nations, their self-determination, *hence*, when our country is attacked, or when enemy troops invade our territory, it is the right and duty of socialists to defend their country. But theoretically such an argument is either a sheer mockery of socialism or a fraudulent subterfuge, while from the point of view of practical politics it coincides with the argument of the quite ignorant country yokel who has even no conception of the social, class character of the war, and of the tasks of a revolutionary party during a reactionary war.

Socialism is opposed to violence against nations. That is indisputable. But socialism is opposed to violence against men in general. Apart from Christian anarchists and Tolstoyans, however, no one has yet drawn the conclusion from this that socialism is opposed to *revolutionary* violence. So, to talk about "violence" in general, without examining the conditions which distinguish reactionary from revolutionary violence, means being a philistine who renounces revolution, or else it means simply deceiving oneself and others by sophistry.

The same holds true of violence against nations. Every war is violent against nations, but that does not prevent socialists from being *in favour* of a revolutionary war. The class character of war — that is the fundamental question which confronts a socialist (if he is not a renegade). The imperialist war of 1914-18 is a war between two groups of the imperialist bourgeoisie for the division of the world, for the division of the booty, and for the plunder and strangulation of small and weak nations. This was the appraisal of the impending war given in the Basle Manifesto in 1912, and it has been confirmed by the facts. Whoever departs from this view of war is not a socialist.

If a German under Wilhelm or a Frenchman under Clemenceau says, "It is my right and duty as a socialist to defend my country if it is invaded by an enemy", he argues not like a socialist, not like an internationalist, not like a revolutionary proletarian, but like a *petty-bourgeois nationalist*. Because this argument ignores the revolutionary class struggle of the workers against capital, it ignores the appraisal of the war as a *whole* from the point of view of the world bourgeoisie and the world proletariat, that is, it ignores internationalism, and all that remains is miserable and narrow-minded nationalism. My country is being wronged, that is all I care about — that is what this argument amounts to, and that is where its petty-bourgeois, nationalist narrow-mindedness lies. It is the same as if in regard to individual violence, violence against an individual, one were to argue that socialism is opposed to violence and therefore I would rather be a traitor than go to prison.

The Frenchman, German or Italian who says: "Socialism is opposed to violence against nations, *therefore* I defend myself when my country is invaded," *betrays* socialism and internationalism, because such a man *sees only* his own "country", he puts "his own" . . . *bourgeoisie* above everything else and does not give a thought to the *international connections* which make the war an imperialist war and *his* bourgeoisie a link in the chain of imperialist plunder.

All philistines and all stupid and ignorant yokels argue in the same way as the renegade Kautsky supporters, Longuet supporters, Turati and Co.: "The enemy has invaded my country, I don't care about anything else."*

---

* The social-chauvinists (the Scheidemanns, Renaudels, Hendersons, Gomperses and Co.) absolutely refuse to talk about the "International" during the war. They regard the enemies of "*their*" respective bourgeoisies as "traitors" to . . . socialism. They *support* the policy of conquest pursued by *their* respective bourgeoisies. The social-pacifists (i.e., socialists in words and petty-bourgeois pacifists in practice) express all sorts of "internationalist" sentiments, protest against annexations, etc., but *in practice* they continue to *support their* respective imperialist bourgeoisies. The difference between the two types is unimportant; it is like difference between two capitalists — one with bitter, and the other with sweet, words on his lips.

The socialist, the revolutionary proletarian, the internationalist, argues differently. He says: "The character of the war (whether it is reactionary or revolutionary) does not depend on who the attacker was, or in whose country the 'enemy' is stationed; it depends on *what class* is waging the war, and on what politics this war is a continuation of. If the war is a reactionary, imperialist war, that is, if it is being waged by two world groups of the imperialist, rapacious, predatory, reactionary bourgeoisie, then every bourgeoisie (even of the smallest country) becomes a participant in the plunder, and my duty as a representative of the revolutionary proletariat is to prepare for the *world proletarian revolution* as the *only* escape from the horrors of a world slaughter. I must argue, not from the point of view of 'my' country (for that is the argument of a wretched, stupid, petty-bourgeois nationalist who does not realise that he is only a plaything in the hands of the imperialist bourgeoisie), but from the point of view of *my share* in the preparation, in the propaganda, and in the acceleration of the world proletarian revolution."

That is what internationalism means, and that is the duty of the internationalist, the revolutionary worker, the genuine socialist. That is the *ABC* that Kautsky the renegade has "forgotten". And his apostasy becomes still more obvious when he passes from approving the tactics of the petty-bourgeois nationalists (the Mensheviks in Russia, the Longuet supporters in France, the Turatis in Italy, and Haase and Co. in Germany) to criticising the Bolshevik tactics. Here is his criticism:

"The Bolshevik revolution was based on the assumption that it would become the starting-point of a general European revolution, that the bold initiative of Russia would prompt the proletarians of all Europe to rise.

"On this assumption it was, of course, immaterial what forms the Russian separate peace would take, what hardships and territorial losses (literally: mutilation or maiming, *Verstümmelungen*) it would cause the Russian people, and what interpretation of the self-determination of nations it would give. At that time it was also immaterial whether Russia was able to defend herself or not. According to this view, the European revolution would be the best protection of the Russian revolution, and would bring complete and genuine self-determination to all peoples inhabiting the former Russian territory.

"A revolution in Europe, which would establish and consolidate socialism there, would also become the means of removing the obstacles that would arise in Russia in the way of the introduction of the socialist system of production owing to the economic backwardness of the country.

"All this was very logical and very sound — only if the main assumption were granted, namely, that the Russian revolution would infallibly let loose a European revolution. But what if that did not happen?

"So far the assumption has not been justified. And the proletarians of Europe are now being accused of having abandoned and betrayed the Russian revolution. This is an accusation levelled against unknown persons, for who is to be held responsible for the behaviour of the European proletariat?" (p. 28.)

And Kautsky then goes on to explain at great length that Marx, Engels and Bebel were more than once mistaken about the advent of revolution they had anticipated, but that they never based their tactics on the expectation of a revolution "*at a definite date*" (p. 29), whereas, he says, the Bolsheviks "staked everything on one card, on a general European revolution".

First, to ascribe to an opponent an obviously stupid idea and then to refute it is a trick practised by none too clever people. If the Bolsheviks had based their tactics on the expectation of a revolution in other countries *by a definite date* that would have been an undeniable stupidity. But the Bolshevik Party has never been guilty of such stupidity. In my letter to American workers (August 20, 1918), I expressly disown this foolish idea by saying that we count on an American revolution, but not by any definite date. I dwelt at length upon the very same idea more than once in my controversy with the Left Socialist-Revolutionaries and the "Left Communists" (January-March 1918).[64] Kautsky has committed a slight . . . just a very slight forgery, on which he in fact based his criticism of Bolshevism. Kautsky has confused tactics based on the expectation of a European revolution in the more or less near future, but not at a definite date, with tactics based on the expectation of a European revolution at a definite date. A slight, just a very slight forgery!

The last-named tactics are foolish. The first-named *are obligatory* for a Marxist, for every revolutionary proletarian and internationalist — *obligatory*, because they alone take into account in a proper Marxist way the objective situation brought about by the war in all European countries, and they alone conform to the international tasks of the proletariat.

By substituting the petty question about an error which the Bolshevik revolutionaries might have made, but did not, for the important question of the foundations of revolutionary tactics in general, Kautsky adroitly abjures all revolutionary tactics!

A renegade in politics, he is *unable even to present the question* of the objective prerequisites of revolutionary tactics theoretically.

And this brings us to the second point.

Secondly, it is obligatory for a Marxist to count on a European revolution if a *revolutionary situation* exists. It is the *ABC* of Marxism that the tactics of the socialist proletariat cannot be the same both when there is a revolutionary situation and when there is no revolutionary situation.

If Kautsky had put this question, which is obligatory for a Marxist, he would have seen that the answer was absolutely against him. Long before the war, all Marxists, all socialists were agreed that a European war would create a revolutionary situation. Kautsky himself, before he became a renegade, clearly and definitely recognised this — in 1902 (in his *Social Revolution*) and in 1909 (in his *Road to Power*). It was also admitted in the name of the entire Second International in the Basle Manifesto. No wonder the social-chauvinists and Kautsky supporters (the "Centrists", i.e., those who waver between the revolutionaries and the opportunists) of all countries shun like the plague the declarations of the Basle Manifesto on this score!

So, the expectation of a revolutionary situation in Europe was not an infatuation of the Bolsheviks, but the *general opinion* of all Marxists. When Kautsky tries to escape from this indisputable truth using such phrases as the Bolsheviks "always believed in the omnipotence of violence and will", he simply utters a sonorous and empty phrase to *cover up* his evasion, a shameful evasion, to put the question of a revolutionary situation.

To proceed. Has a revolutionary situation actually come or not? Kautsky proved unable to put this question either. The economic facts provide an answer: the famine and ruin created everywhere by the war imply a revolutionary situation. The political facts also provide an answer: ever since 1915 a splitting process has been evident in *all* countries within the old and decayed socialist parties, a process of *departure of the mass* of the proletariat from the social-chauvinist leaders to the left, to revolutionary ideas and sentiments, to revolutionary leaders.

Only a person who dreads revolution and betrays it could have failed to see these facts on August 5, 1918, when Kautsky was writing his pamphlet. And now, at the end of October 1918, the revolution is growing *in a number* of European countries, and growing under everybody's eyes and very rapidly at that. Kautsky the "revolutionary", who still wants to be regarded as a Marxist, has proved to be a short-sighted philistine, who, like those philistines of 1847 whom Marx ridiculed, failed to see the approaching revolution!

Now to the third point.

Thirdly, what should be the specific features of revolutionary tactics when there is a revolutionary situation in Europe? Having become a renegade, Kautsky feared to put this question, which is obligatory for a Marxist. Kautsky argues like a typical petty bourgeois, a philistine, or like an ignorant peasant: has a "general European revolution" begun or not? If it has, then *he too* is prepared to become a revolutionary! But then, mark you, every scoundrel (like the scoundrels who now sometimes attach themselves to the victorious Bolsheviks) would proclaim himself a revolutionary!

If it has not, then Kautsky will turn his back on revolution! Kautsky does not display a shade of understanding of the truth that a revolutionary Marxist differs from the philistine and petty bourgeois by his ability to *preach* to the uneducated masses that the maturing revolution is necessary, to *prove* that it is inevitable, to *explain* its benefits to the people, and to *prepare* the proletariat and all the working and exploited people for it.

Kautsky ascribed to the Bolsheviks an absurdity, namely, that they had staked everything on one card, on a European revolution breaking out at a definite date. This absurdity has turned against Kautsky himself, because the logical conclusion of his argument is that the tactics of the Bolsheviks would have been correct if a European revolution had broken out by August 5, 1918! That is the date Kautsky mentions at the time he was writing his pamphlet. And when, a few weeks after this August 5, it became clear that revolution was coming in a number of European countries, the whole apostasy of Kautsky, his whole falsification of Marxism, and his utter inability to reason or even to present questions in a revolutionary manner, became revealed in all their charm!

When the proletarians of Europe are accused of treachery, Kautsky writes, it is an accusation levelled at unknown persons.

You are mistaken, Mr. Kautsky! Look in the mirror and you will see those "unknown persons" against whom this accusation is levelled. Kautsky assumes an air of naïveté and pretends not to understand *who* levelled the accusation, and its *meaning*. In reality, however, Kautsky knows perfectly well that the accusation has been and is being levelled by the German "Lefts", by the Spartacists, by Liebknecht and his friends. This accusation expresses a *clear appreciation* of the fact that the German proletariat betrayed the Russian (and world) revolution when it strangled Finland, the Ukraine, Latvia and Estonia.[65] This accusation is levelled primarily and above all, not against the *masses*, who are always downtrodden, but against those *leaders* who, like the Scheidemanns and the Kautskys, *failed* in their duty to carry on revolutionary agitation, revolutionary propaganda, revolutionary work among the masses to overcome their inertness, who in fact worked *against* the revolutionary instincts and aspirations which are always aglow deep down among the mass of the oppressed class. The Scheidemanns bluntly, crudely, cynically, and in most cases for selfish motives betrayed the proletariat and deserted to the side of the bourgeoisie. The Kautsky and the Longuet supporters did the same thing, only hesitatingly and haltingly, and casting cowardly side-glances at those who were stronger at the moment. In all his writings during the war Kautsky tried to *extinguish* the revolutionary spirit instead of fostering and fanning it.

The fact that Kautsky does not even understand the enormous *theoretical* importance, and the even greater agitational and propaganda importance, of the "accusation" that the proletarians of Europe have betrayed the Russian revolution will remain a veritable historical monument to the philistine stupefaction of the "average" leader of German official Social-Democracy! Kautsky does not understand that, owing to the censorship prevailing in the German "Reich", this "accusation" is perhaps the only form in which the German socialists who have not betrayed socialism — Liebknecht and his friends — can express *their appeal to the German workers* to throw off the Scheidemanns and the Kautskys, to push aside such "leaders", to free themselves from their stultifying and debasing propaganda, to rise in revolt *in spite of* them, *without* them, and march over their heads *towards revolution*!

Kautsky does not understand this. And how could he understand the tactics of the Bolsheviks? Can a man who renounces revolution in general be expected to weigh and appraise the conditions of the development of revolution in one of the most "difficult" cases?

The Bolsheviks' tactics were correct; they were the *only* internationalist tactics, because they were based, not on the cowardly fear of a world revolution, not on a philistine "lack of faith" in it, not on the narrow nationalist desire to protect one's "own" fatherland (the fatherland of one's own bourgeoisie), while not "giving a damn" about all the rest, but on a correct (and, before the war and before the apostasy of the social-chauvinists and social-pacifists, a universally accepted) *estimation* of the revolutionary situation in Europe. These tactics were the only internationalist tactics, because they did the utmost possible in one country *for* the development, support and awakening of the revolution *in all countries*. These tactics have been justified by their enormous success, for Bolshevism (not by any means because of the merits of the Russian Bolsheviks, but because of the most profound sympathy of the *people* everywhere for tactics that are revolutionary in practice) has become *world* Bolshevism, has produced an idea, a theory, a programme and tactics which differ concretely and in practice from those of social-chauvinism and social-pacifism. Bolshevism *has given a coup de grâce* to the old, decayed International of the Scheidemanns and Kautskys, Renaudels and Longuets, Hendersons and MacDonalds, who from now on will be treading on each other's feet, dreaming about "unity" and trying to revive a corpse. Bolshevism *has created* the ideological and tactical foundations of a Third International, of a really proletarian and Communist International, which will take into consideration both the gains of the tranquil epoch and the experience of the *epoch of revolutions, which has begun*.

Bolshevism has popularised throughout the world the idea of the "dictatorship of the proletariat", has translated these words from the Latin, first into Russian, and then into *all* the languages of the world, and has shown by the example of *Soviet government* that the workers and poor peasants, *even* of a backward country, even with the least experience, education and habits of organisation, *have been able* for a whole year, amidst gigantic difficulties and amidst a struggle against the exploiters (who were supported by the bourgeoisie of the *whole* world), to maintain the power of the working people, to create a democracy that is immeasurably higher and broader than all previous democracies in the world, and to *start* the creative work of tens of millions of workers and peasants for the practical construction of socialism.

Bolshevism has actually helped to develop the proletarian revolution in Europe and America more powerfully than any party in any other country has so far succeeded in doing. While the workers of the whole world are realising more and more clearly every day that the tactics of the Scheidemanns and Kautskys have not delivered them from the imperialist war and from wage-slavery to the imperialist bourgeoisie, and that these tactics cannot serve as a model for all countries, the mass of workers in all countries are realising more and more clearly every day that Bolshevism *can serve as a model of tactics for all*.

Not only the general European, but the world proletarian revolution is maturing before the eyes of all, and it has been assisted, accelerated and supported by the victory of the proletariat in Russia. All this is not enough for the complete victory of socialism, you say? Of course it is not enough. One country alone cannot do more. But this one country, thanks to Soviet government, has done so much that even if Soviet government in Russia were to be crushed by world imperialism tomorrow, as a result, let us say, of an agreement between German and Anglo-French imperialism — even granted that very worst possibility — it would still be found that Bolshevik tactics have brought enormous benefit to socialism and have assisted the growth of the invincible world revolution.

Subservience to the Bourgeoisie in the Guise of 'Economic Analysis'

As has already been said, if the title of Kautsky's book were properly to reflect its contents, it should have been called, not *The Dictatorship of the Proletariat*, but *A Rehash of Bourgeois Attacks on the Bolsheviks*.

The old Menshevik "theories" about the bourgeois character of the Russian revolution, i.e., the old distortion of Marxism by the Mensheviks (*rejected* by Kautsky in 1905!), are now once again being rehashed by our theoretician. We must deal with this question, however boring it may be for Russian Marxists.

The Russian revolution is a bourgeois revolution, said all the Marxists of Russia before 1905. The Mensheviks, substituting liberalism for Marxism, drew the following conclusion from this: the proletariat therefore must not go beyond what is acceptable to the bourgeoisie and must pursue a policy of compromise with them. The Bolsheviks said this was a bourgeois-liberal theory. The bourgeoisie were trying to bring about the reform of the state on bourgeois, *reformist*, not revolutionary lines, while preserving the monarchy, the landlord system, etc., as far as possible. The proletariat must carry through the bourgeois-democratic revolution to the end, not allowing itself to be "bound" by the reformism of the bourgeoisie. The Bolsheviks formulated the alignment of *class* forces in the bourgeois revolution as follows: the proletariat, winning over the peasants, will neutralise the liberal bourgeoisie and utterly destroy the monarchy, medievalism and the landlord system.

It is the alliance between the proletariat and the peasants *in general* that reveals the bourgeois character of the revolution, for the peasants in general are small producers who exist on the basis of commodity production. Further, the Bolsheviks then added, the proletariat will win over *the entire semi-proletariat* (all the working and exploited people), will neutralise the middle peasants and *overthrow* the bourgeoisie; this will be a socialist revolution as distinct from a bourgeois-democratic revolution. (See my pamphlet *Two Tactics*, published in 1905 and reprinted in *Twelve Years*, St. Petersburg, 1907.)[66]

Kautsky took an indirect part in this controversy in 1905, when, in reply to an inquiry by the then Menshevik Plekhanov, he expressed an opinion that was essentially *against* Plekhanov, which provoked particular ridicule in the Bolshevik press at the time. But now Kautsky does *not* say *a single word* about the controversies of that time (for fear of being exposed by his own statements!), and thereby makes it utterly impossible for the German reader to understand the essence of the matter. Mr. Kautsky *could not* tell the German workers in 1918 that in 1905 he had been in favour of an alliance of the workers with the peasants and not with the liberal bourgeoisie, and on what conditions he had advocated this alliance, and what programme he had outlined for it.

Backing out from his old position, Kautsky, under the guise of an "economic analysis", and talking proudly about "historical materialism", now advocates the subordination of the workers to the bourgeoisie, and, with the aid of quotations from the Menshevik Maslov, chews over the old liberal views of the Mensheviks. Quotations are used to prove the new idea of the backwardness of Russia. But the deduction drawn from this new idea is the old one, that in a bourgeois revolution one must not go farther than the bourgeoisie! And this in spite of all that Marx and Engels said when comparing the bourgeois revolution of 1789-93 in France with the bourgeois revolution of 1848 in Germany![67]

Before passing to the chief "argument" and the main content of Kautsky's "economic analysis", let us note that Kautsky's very first sentences reveal a curious confusion, or superficiality, of thought.

"Agriculture, and specifically small peasant farming," our "theoretician" announces, "to this day represents the economic foundation of Russia. About four-fifths, perhaps even five-sixths, of the population live by it" (p. 45). First of all, my dear theoretician, have you considered how many exploiters there may be among this mass of small producers? Certainly not more than one-tenth of the total, and in the towns still less, for there large-scale production is more highly developed. Take even an incredibly high figure; assume that one-fifth of the small producers are exploiters who are deprived of the franchise. Even then you will find that the 66 per cent of the votes held by the Bolsheviks at the Fifth Congress of Soviets represented the *majority of the population*. To this it must be added that there was always a considerable section of the Left Socialist-Revolutionaries who were in favour of Soviet power — in principle *all* the Left Socialist-Revolutionaries were in favour of Soviet power, and when a section of them, in July 1918, started an adventurous revolt, two new parties split away from the old party, namely, the "Narodnik Communists" and the "Revolutionary Communists" (of the prominent Left Socialist-Revolutionaries who had been nominated for important posts in the government by the old party, to the first-mentioned belongs Zax, for instance, and to the second Kolegayev). So, Kautsky has himself — inadvertently — refuted the ridiculous fable that the Bolsheviks only have the backing of a minority of the population.

Secondly, my dear theoretician, have you considered the fact that the small peasant producer *inevitably* vacillates between the proletariat and the bourgeoisie? This Marxist truth, which has been confirmed by the whole modern history of Europe, Kautsky very conveniently "forgot", for it simply demolishes the Menshevik "theory" that he keeps repeating! Had Kautsky not "forgotten" this he could not have denied the need for a proletarian dictatorship in a country in which the small peasant producers predominate.

Let us examine the main content of our theoretician's "economic analysis".

That Soviet power is a dictatorship cannot be disputed, says Kautsky. "But is it a dictatorship of *the proletariat*?" (p. 34.)

"According to the Soviet Constitution, the peasants form the majority of the population entitled to participate in legislation and administration. What is presented to us as a dictatorship of *the proletariat* would prove to be — if carried out consistently, and if, generally speaking, a class could directly exercise a dictatorship, which in reality can only be exercised by a party — a dictatorship of *the peasants*" (p. 35).

And, highly elated over so profound and clever an argument, our good Kautsky tries to be witty and says: "It would appear, therefore, that the most painless achievement of socialism is best assured when it is put in the hands of the peasants" (p. 35).

In the greatest detail, and citing a number of extremely learned quotations from the semi-liberal Maslov, our theoretician labours to prove the new idea that the peasants are interested in high grain prices, in low wages for the urban workers, etc., etc. Incidentally, the enunciation of these new ideas is the more tedious the less attention our author pays to the really new features of the post-war period — for example, that the peasants demand for their grain, not money, but goods, and that they have not enough agricultural implements, which cannot be obtained in sufficient quantities for any amount of money. But more of this later.

Thus, Kautsky charges the Bolsheviks, the party of the proletariat, with having surrendered the dictatorship, the work of achieving socialism, to the petty-bourgeois peasants. Excellent, Mr. Kautsky! But what, in your enlightened opinion, should have been the attitude of the proletarian party towards the petty-bourgeois peasants?

Our theoretician preferred to say nothing on this score — evidently bearing in mind the proverb: "Speech is silver, silence is gold." But he gives himself away by the following argument:

"At the beginning of the Soviet Republic, the peasants' Soviets were organisations of the *peasants* in general. Now this Republic proclaims that the Soviets are organisations of the proletarians and the *poor* peasants. The well-to-do peasants are deprived of the suffrage in the elections to the Soviets. The poor peasant is here recognised to be a permanent and mass product of the socialist-agrarian reform under the 'dictatorship of the proletariat'" (p. 48).

What deadly irony! It is the kind that may be heard in Russia from any bourgeois: they all jeer and gloat over the fact that the Soviet Republic openly admits the existence of poor peasants. They ridicule socialism. That is their right. But a "socialist" who jeers at the fact that after four years of a most ruinous war there remain (and will remain for a long time) poor peasants in Russia — such a "socialist" could only have been born at a time of wholesale apostasy.

And further:

". . . The Soviet Republic interferes in the relations between the rich and poor peasants, but not by redistributing the land. In order to relieve the bread shortage in the towns, detachments of armed workers are sent into the countryside to take away the rich peasants' surplus stocks of grain. Part of that stock is given to the urban population, the other — to the poorer peasants" (p. 48).

Of course, Kautsky the socialist and Marxist is profoundly indignant at the idea that such a measure should be extended beyond the environs of the large towns (and we have extended it to the whole of the country). With the matchless, incomparable and admirable coolness (or pigheadedness) of a philistine, Kautsky the socialist and Marxist sermonises: . . . "It [the expropriation of the well-to-do peasants] introduces a new element of unrest and civil war into the process of production" . . . (civil war introduced into the "process of production" — that is something supernatural!) . . . "which stands in urgent need of peace and security for its recovery" (p. 49).

Oh, yes, of course, Kautsky the Marxist and socialist must sigh and shed tears over the subject of peace and security for the exploiters and grain profiteers who hoard their surplus stocks, sabotage the grain monopoly law, and reduce the urban population to famine. "We are all socialists and Marxists and internationalists," the Kautskys, Heinrich Webers (Vienna),[68] Longuets (Paris), MacDonalds (London), etc., sing in chorus. "We are all in favour of a working-class revolution. Only . . . only we would like a revolution that does not infringe upon the peace and security of the grain profiteers! And we camouflage this sordid subservience to the capitalists by a 'Marxist' reference to the 'process of production'. . . ." If this is Marxism, what is servility to the bourgeoisie?

Just see what our theoretician arrives at. He accuses the Bolsheviks of presenting the dictatorship of the peasants as the dictatorship of the proletariat. But at the same time he accuses us of introducing civil war into the rural districts (which we think is to our *credit*), of dispatching into the countryside armed detachments of workers, who publicly proclaim that they are exercising the "dictatorship of the proletariat and the poor peasants", assist the latter and confiscate from the profiteers and the rich peasants the surplus stocks of grain which they are hoarding in contravention of the grain monopoly law.

On the one hand, our Marxist theoretician stands for pure democracy, for the subordination of the revolutionary class, the leader of the working and exploited people, to the majority of the population (including, therefore, the exploiters). On the other hand, as an argument *against* us, he explains that the revolution must inevitably bear a bourgeois character — bourgeois, because the life of the peasants as a whole is based on bourgeois social relations — and at the same time he pretends to uphold the proletarian, class, Marxist point of view!

Instead of an "economic analysis" we have a first-class hodgepodge. Instead of Marxism we have fragments of liberal doctrines and the preaching of servility to the bourgeoisie and the kulaks.

The question which Kautsky has so tangled up was fully explained by the Bolsheviks as far back as 1905. Yes, our revolution is a bourgeois revolution *as long* as we march *with* the peasants *as a whole*. This has been as clear as clear can be to us; we have said it hundreds and thousands of times since 1905, and we have never attempted to skip this necessary stage of the historical process or abolish it by decrees. Kautsky's efforts to "expose" us on this point merely expose his own confusion of mind and his fear to recall what he wrote in 1905, when he was not yet a renegade.

Beginning with *April* 1917, however, long before the October Revolution, that is, long before we assumed power, we publicly declared and explained to the people: the revolution cannot now stop at this stage, for the country has marched forward, capitalism has advanced, ruin has reached fantastic dimensions, which (whether one likes it or not) *will demand* steps forward, *to socialism.* For there is *no* other way of advancing, of saving the war-weary country and of *alleviating* the sufferings of the working and exploited people.

Things have turned out just as we said they would. The course taken by the revolution has confirmed the correctness of our reasoning. *First,* with the "whole" of the peasants against the monarchy, against the landowners, against medievalism (and to that extent the revolution remains bourgeois, bourgeois-democratic). *Then,* with the poor peasants, with the semi-proletarians, with all the exploited, *against capitalism,* including the rural rich, the kulaks, the profiteers, and to that extent the revolution becomes a *socialist* one. To attempt to raise an artificial Chinese Wall between the first and second, to separate them *by anything else* than the degree of preparedness of the proletariat and the degree of its unity with the poor peasants, means to distort Marxism dreadfully, to vulgarise it, to substitute liberalism in its place. It means smuggling in a reactionary defence of the bourgeoisie against the socialist proletariat by means of quasi-scientific references to the progressive character of the bourgeoisie in comparison with medievalism.

Incidentally, the Soviets represent an immensely higher form and type of democracy just because, by uniting and drawing the *mass of workers and peasants* into political life, they serve as a most sensitive barometer, the one closest to the "people" (in the sense in which Marx, in 1871, spoke of a real people's revolution),[69] of the growth and development of the political, class maturity of the people. The Soviet Constitution was not drawn up according to some "plan"; it was not drawn up in a study, and was not foisted on the working people by bourgeois lawyers. No, this Constitution *grew up* in the course of the development of *the class struggle* in proportion as *class antagonisms* matured. The very facts which Kautsky himself has to admit prove this.

At first, the Soviets embraced the peasants as a whole. It was owing to the immaturity, the backwardness, the ignorance of the poor peasants that the leadership passed into the hands of the kulaks, the rich, the capitalists and the petty-bourgeois intellectuals. That was the period of the domination of the petty bourgeoisie, of the Mensheviks and Socialist-Revolutionaries (only fools or renegades like Kautsky can regard either of these as socialists). The petty bourgeoisie inevitably and unavoidably vacillated between the dictatorship of the bourgeoisie (Kerensky, Kornilov, Sakinkov) and the dictatorship of the proletariat; for owing to the basic features of its economic position, the petty bourgeoisie is incapable of doing anything independently. Kautsky, by the way, completely renounces Marxism by confining himself in his analysis of the Russian revolution to the legal and formal concept of "democracy", which serves the bourgeoisie as a screen to conceal their domination and as a means of deceiving the people, and by *forgetting* that in practice "democracy" sometimes stands for the *dictatorship of the bourgeoisie,* sometimes for the impotent reformism of the petty bourgeoisie who submit to that dictatorship, and so on. According to Kautsky, in a capitalist country there were bourgeois parties and there was a proletarian party (the Bolsheviks), which led the majority, the mass of the proletariat, but *there were no* petty-bourgeois parties! The Mensheviks and Socialist-Revolutionaries had no *class roots*, no petty-bourgeois roots!

The vacillations of the petty bourgeoisie, of the Mensheviks and the Socialist-Revolutionaries, helped to enlighten the people and to repel the overwhelming majority of them, all the "lower sections", all the proletarians and semi-proletarians, from such "leaders". The Bolsheviks won predominance in the Soviets (in Petrograd and Moscow by October 1917); the split among the Socialist-Revolutionaries and the Mensheviks became more pronounced.

The victorious Bolshevik revolution meant the end of vacillation, meant the complete destruction of the monarchy and of the landlord system (which had *not* been destroyed before the October Revolution). We carried the *bourgeois* revolution *to its conclusion.* The peasants supported us *as a whole.* Their antagonism to the socialist proletariat could not reveal itself all at once. The Soviets united the peasants *in general.* The class divisions among the peasants had not yet matured, had not yet come into the open.

That process took place in the summer and autumn of 1918. The Czech counter-revolutionary mutiny roused the kulaks. A wave of kulak revolts swept over Russia. The poor peasants learned, not from books or newspapers, *but from life itself*, that their interests were irreconcilably antagonistic to those of the kulaks, the rich, the rural bourgeoisie. Like every other petty-bourgeois party, the "Left Socialist-Revolutionaries" reflected the vacillation of the people, and in the summer of 1918 they split: one section joined forces with the Czechs (the rebellion in Moscow, when Proshyan, having seized the Telegraph Office — for one hour! — announced to Russia that the Bolsheviks had been overthrown; then the treachery of Muravyov, Comander-in-Chief of the army that was fighting the Czechs, etc.),[70] while the other section, that mentioned above, remained with the Bolsheviks.

The growing food shortage in the towns lent increasing urgency to the question of the grain monopoly (this Kautsky the theoretician completely "forgot" in his economic analysis, which is a mere repetition of platitudes gleaned ten years ago from Maslov's writings!).

The old landowner and bourgeois, and even democratic-republican, state had sent to the rural districts armed detachments which were practically at the beck and call of the bourgeoisie. Mr. Kautsky does not know this! He does not regard that as the "dictatorship of the bourgeoisie" — Heaven forbid! That is "pure democracy", especially if endorsed by a bourgeois parliament! Nor has Kautsky "heard" that, in the summer and autumn of 1917, Avksentyev and S. Maslov, in company with the Kerenskys, the Tseretelis and other Socialist-Revolutionaries and Mensheviks, arrested members of the Land Committees; he does not say a word about that!

The whole point is that a bourgeois state which is exercising the dictatorship of the bourgeoisie through a democratic republic cannot confess to the people that it is serving the bourgeoisie; it cannot tell the truth, and has to play the hypocrite.

But the state of the Paris Commune type, the Soviet state, openly and frankly tells the people the *truth* and declares that it is the dictatorship of the proletariat and the poor peasants; and by this truth it wins over scores and scores of millions of new citizens who are kept down in any democratic republic, but who are drawn by the Soviets into political life, *into democracy*, into the administration of the state. The Soviet Republic sends into the rural districts detachments of armed workers, primarily the more advanced, from the capitals. These workers carry socialism into the countryside, win over the poor, organise and enlighten them, and help them to *suppress the resistance of the bourgeoisie*.

All who are familiar with the situation and have been in the rural districts declare that it is only now, in the summer and autumn of 1918, that the rural districts *themselves* are passing through the "October" (i.e., proletarian) Revolution. Things are beginning to change. The wave of kulak revolts is giving way to a rise of the poor, to a growth of the "Poor Peasants' Committees". In the army, the number of workers who become commissars, officers and commanders of divisions and armies is increasing. And at the very time that the simple-minded Kautsky, frightened by the July (1918) crisis and the lamentations of the bourgeoisie,[71] was running after the latter like a cockerel, and writing a whole pamphlet breathing the conviction that the Bolsheviks are on the eve of being overthrown by the peasants; at the very time that this simpleton regarded the secession of the Left Socialist-Revolutionaries as a "narrowing" (p. 37) of the circle of those who support the Bolsheviks — at that very time the *real* circle of supporters of Bolshevism was *expanding enormously,* because scores and scores of millions of the village poor were freeing themselves from the tutelage and influence of the kulaks and village bourgeoisie and were awakening to *independent* political life.

We have lost hundreds of Left Socialist-Revolutionaries, spineless intellectuals and kulaks from among the peasants; but we have gained millions of poor people.*

A year after the proletarian revolution in the capitals, and under its influence and with its assistance, the proletarian revolution began in the remote rural districts, and it has finally consolidated the power of the Soviets and Bolshevism, and has finally proved there is no force in the country that can withstand it.

Having completed the bourgeois-democratic revolution in alliance with the peasants as a whole, the Russian proletariat finally passed on to the socialist revolution when it succeeded in splitting the rural population, in winning over the rural proletarians and semi-proletarians, and in uniting them against the kulaks and the bourgeoisie, including the peasant bourgeoisie.

Now, if the Bolshevik proletariat in the capitals and large industrial centres had not been able to rally the village poor around itself against the rich peasants, this would indeed have proved that Russia was "unripe" for socialist revolution. The peasants would then have remained an "integral whole", i.e., they would have remained under the economic, political, and moral leadership of the kulaks, the rich, the bourgeoisie, and the revolution would not have passed beyond

---

* At the Sixth Congress of Soviets (November 6-9, 1918), there were 967 voting delegates, 950 of whom were Bolsheviks, and 351 delegates with voice but no vote, of whom 335 were Bolsheviks, i.e., 97 per cent of the total number of delegates were Bolsheviks.

the limits of a bourgeois-democratic revolution. (But, let it be said in parenthesis, even if this had been the case, it would not have proved that the proletariat should not have taken power, for it is the proletariat alone that has really carried the bourgeois-democratic revolution to its conclusion, it is the proletariat alone that has done something really important to bring nearer the world proletarian revolution, and the proletariat alone that has created the Soviet state, which, after the Paris Commune, is the second step towards the socialist state.)

On the other hand, if the Bolshevik proletariat had tried at once, in October-November 1917, without waiting for the class differentiation in the rural districts, without being able to *prepare* it and bring it about, to "decree" a civil war or the "introduction of socialism" in the rural districts, had tried to do without a temporary bloc with the peasants in general, without making a number of concessions to the middle peasants, etc., that would have been a *Blanquist* distortion of Marxism, an attempt by the *minority* to impose its will upon the majority; it would have been a theoretical absurdity, revealing a failure to understand that a general peasant revolution is *still* a bourgeois revolution, and that *without a series of transitions, of transitional stages*, it cannot be transformed into a socialist revolution in a backward country.

Kautsky has confused *everything* in this very important theoretical and political problem, and has, in practice, proved to be nothing but a servant of the bourgeoisie, howling against the dictatorship of the proletariat.

*   *   *

Kautsky has introduced a similar, if not greater, confusion into another extremely interesting and important question, namely: was the *legislative* activity of the Soviet Republic in the sphere of agrarian reform — that most difficult and yet most important of socialist reforms — based on sound principles and then properly carried out? We should be boundlessly grateful to any West-European Marxist who, after studying at least the most important documents, gave a *criticism* of our policy, because he would thereby help us immensely, and would also help the revolution that is maturing throughout the world. But instead of criticism Kautsky produces an incredible theoretical muddle, which converts Marxism into liberalism and which, in practice, is a series of idle, venomous, vulgar sallies against the Bolsheviks. Let the reader judge for himself:

"Large landed estates could not be preserved. This was a result of the revolution. That was at once clear. The transfer of the large estates to the peasant population became inevitable. . . ." (That is not true, Mr. Kautsky. You substitute what is "clear" to you for the attitude of the different *classes* towards the question. The history of the revolution has shown that the coalition government of the bourgeois and the petty bourgeois, the Mensheviks and the Socialist-Revolutionaries, pursued a policy of preserving big land-ownership. This was proved particularly by S. Maslov's bill and by the arrest of the members of the Land Committees.[72] Without the dictatorship of the proletariat, the "peasant population" would not have vanquished the landowners, who had joined forces with the capitalists.)

" . . . But as to the forms in which it was to take place, there was no unity. Various solutions were conceivable. . . ." (Kautsky is most of all concerned about the "unity" of the "socialists", no matter who called themselves by that name. He forgets that the principal classes in capitalist society are bound to arrive at different solutions.)

" . . . From the socialist point of view, the most rational solution would have been to convert the large estates into state property and to allow the peasants who hitherto had been employed on them as wage-labourers to cultivate them in the form of co-operative societies. But such a solution presupposes the existence of a type of farm labourer that did not exist in Russia. Another solution would have been to convert the large estates into state property and to divide them up into small plots to be rented out to peasants who owned little land. Had that been done, at least something socialistic would have been achieved. . . ."

As usual Kautsky confines himself to the celebrated: on the one hand it cannot but be admitted, and on the other hand it must be confessed. He places different solutions *side by side* without a thought—the only realistic and Marxist thought—as to what must be the *transitional stages* from capitalism to communism in such-and-such *specific* conditions. There are farm labourers in Russia, but not many; and Kautsky did not touch on the question—which the Soviet government *did raise*—of the method of transition to a communal and co-operative form of land cultivation. The most curious thing, however, is that Kautsky claims to see "something socialistic" in the renting out of small plots of land. In reality, this is a *petty-bourgeois* slogan, and there is *nothing* "socialistic" in it. If the "state" that rents out the land is *not* a state of the Paris Commune type, but a parliamentary bourgeois republic (and that is exactly Kautsky's constant assumption), the renting of land in small plots is a typical *liberal reform*.

Kautsky says nothing about the Soviet government having abolished *all* private ownership of land. Worse than that: he resorts to an incredible forgery and quotes the decrees of the Soviet government in such a way as to omit the most essential.

After stating that "small production strives for complete private ownership of the means of production", and that the Constituent Assembly would have been the "only authority" capable of preventing the dividing up of the land (an assertion which will evoke laughter in Russia, where everybody knows that the Soviets *alone* are recognised as authoritative by the workers and peasants, while the Constituent Assembly has become the slogan of the Czechs and the landowners), Kautsky continues:

"One of the first decrees of the Soviet Government declared that: (1) Landed proprietorship is abolished forthwith without any compensation. (2) The landed estates, as also all crown, monastery and church lands, with all their livestock, implements, buildings and everything pertaining thereto, shall be placed at the disposal of the volost Land Committees of the uyezd Soviets of Peasants' Deputies pending the settlement of the land question by the Constituent Assembly."[73]

Having quoted *only these two clauses*, Kautsky concludes:

"The reference to the Constituent Assembly has remained a dead letter. In point of fact, the peasants in the separate volosts could do as they pleased with the land" (p.47).

Here you have an example of Kautsky's "criticism"! Here you have a "scientific" work which is more like a fraud. The German reader is induced to believe that the Bolsheviks capitulated before the peasants on the question of private ownership of land, that the Bolsheviks permitted the peasants to act locally ("in the separate volosts") in whatever way they pleased!

But in reality, the decree Kautsky quotes—the first to be promulgated, on October 26, 1917 (old style)—consists not of two, but of five clauses, *plus* eight clauses of the Mandate, which, it was expressly stated, "shall serve as a guide".

Clause 3 of the decree states that the estates are transferred "*to the people*", and the "exact inventories of all property confiscated" shall be drawn up and the property "protected in the strictest revolutionary way". And the Mandate declares that "private ownership of land shall be abolished forever", that "lands on which high-level scientific farming is practised . . . *shall not be divided up*", that "all livestock and farm implements of the confiscated estates shall pass into the exclusive use of the state or a commune, depending on size and importance, and no compensation shall be paid for this", and that "all land shall become part of the national land fund".

Further, simultaneously with the dissolution of the Constituent Assembly (January 5, 1918), the Third Congress of Soviets adopted the *Declaration of Rights* of the Working and Exploited People, which now forms part of the Fundamental Law of the Soviet Republic. Article 2, paragraph 1 of this Declaration states that "private ownership of land is hereby abolished", and that "model estates and agricultural enterprises are proclaimed national property".

So the reference to the Constituent Assembly did *not* remain a dead letter, because another national representative body, immeasurably more authoritative in the eyes of the peasants, took upon itself the solution of the agrarian problem.

Again, on February 6 (19), 1918, the land socialisation law was promulgated, which once more confirmed the abolition of all private ownership of land, and placed the land and *all private* stock and implements at the disposal of the Soviet authorities *under the control of the federal Soviet government*. Among the duties connected with the disposal of the land, the law prescribed:

"the development of collective farming as more advantageous from the point of view of economy of labour and produce, at the expense of individual farming, with a view to transition to socialist farming (Article 11, paragraph *e*)."

The same law, in establishing the principle of *equal* land tenure, replied to the fundamental question: "Who has a right to the use of the land?" in the following manner:

"(Article 20.) Plots of land surface within the borders of the Russian Soviet Federative Republic may be used for public and private needs. A. For cultural and educational purposes: (1) by the state as represented by the organs of Soviet power (federal, as well as in regions, gubernias, uyezds, volosts, and villages), and (2) by public bodies (under the control, and with the permission, of the local Soviet authorities); B. For agricultural purposes: (3) by agricultural communes, (4) by agricultural co-operative societies, (5) by village communities, (6) by individual families and persons. . . ."

The reader will see that Kautsky has completely distorted the facts, and has given the German reader an absolutely false view of the agrarian policy and agrarian legislation of the proletarian state in Russia.

Kautsky proved even unable to formulate the theoretically important fundamental questions!

These questions are:

(1) Equal land tenure and

(2) Nationalisation of the land — the relation of these two measures to socialism in general, and to the transition from capitalism to communism in particular.

(3) Farming in common as a transition from small scattered farming to large-scale collective farming; does the manner in which this question is dealt with in Soviet legislation meet the requirements of socialism?

On the first question it is necessary, first of all, to establish the following two fundamental facts: (a) in reviewing the experience of 1905 (I may refer, for instance, to my work on the agrarian problem in the First Russian Revolution), the Bolsheviks pointed to the democratically progressive, the democratically revolutionary meaning of the slogan "equal land tenure", and in 1917, *before* the October Revolution, they spoke of this quite definitely; (b) when enforcing the land socialisation law — the "spirit" of which is equal land tenure — the Bolsheviks most explicitly and definitely declared: this is not our idea, we do not agree with this slogan, but we think it our duty to enforce it because this is the demand of the overwhelming majority of the peasants. And the idea and demands of the majority of the working people are things that the working people must *discard of their own accord:* such demands cannot be either "abolished" or "skipped over". We Bolsheviks shall *help* the peasants to discard petty-bourgeois slogans, to *pass* from them as quickly and as easily as possible to socialist slogans.

A Marxist theoretician who wanted to help the working-class revolution by his scientific analysis should have answered the following questions: first, is it true that the idea of equal land tenure has a democratically revolutionary meaning of carrying the *bourgeois*-democratic revolution to its conclusion? Secondly, did the Bolsheviks act rightly in helping to pass by their votes (and in most loyally observing) the petty-bourgeois equal land tenure law?

Kautsky failed even to *perceive* what, theoretically, was the crux of the problem!

Kautsky will never be able to refute the view that the idea of equal land tenure has a progressive and revolutionary value in the bourgeois-democratic revolution. Such a revolution cannot go beyond this. By reaching its limit, it *all the more clearly, rapidly* and *easily* reveals to the people the *inadequacy* of bourgeois-democratic solutions and the necessity of proceeding beyond their limits, of passing on to *socialism.*

The peasants, who have overthrown tsarism and the landowners, dream of equal land tenure, and no power on earth could have stopped the peasants, once they had been freed both from the land-owners and from the *bourgeois* parliamentary republican state. The workers say to the peasants: We shall help you reach "ideal" capitalism, for equal land tenure is the idealisation of capitalism by the small producer. At the same time we shall prove to you its in-adequacy and the necessity of passing to farming in common.

It would be interesting to see Kautsky's attempt to disprove that *this kind* of leadership of the peasant struggle by the proletariat was right.

Kautsky, however, preferred to evade the question altogether. . . .

Next, Kautsky deliberately deceived his German readers by with-holding from them the fact that in its *land law* the Soviet government gave *direct* preference to communes and co-operative societies.

With all the peasants right through to the end of the bourgeois-democratic revolution; and with the poor, the proletarian and semi-proletarian section of the peasants, forward to the socialist revolu-tion! That has been the policy of the Bolsheviks, and it is the only Marxist policy.

But Kautsky is all muddled and incapable of formulating a single question! On the one hand, he *dare not* say that the workers should have parted company with the peasants over the question of equal land tenure, for he realises that it would have been absurd (and, moreover, in 1905, when he was not yet a renegade, he himself clearly and explicitly advocated an alliance between the workers and peasants as a condition for the victory of the revolution). On the other hand, he sympathetically quotes the liberal platitudes of the Men-shevik Maslov, who "proves" that petty-bourgeois equal land tenure is utopian and reactionary *from the point of view of socialism*, but hushes up the progressive and revolutionary character of the petty-bourgeois struggle for equality and equal tenure *from the point of view of the bourgeois-democratic revolution.*

Kautsky is in a hopeless muddle: note that he (in 1918) *insists* on the *bourgeois* character of the Russian revolution. He (in 1918) peremptorily says: Don't go beyond these limits! Yet this very same Kautsky sees "something *socialistic*" (for a *bourgeois* revolution) in the *petty-bourgeois* reform of renting out small plots of land to the *poor* peasants (which is an approximation to equal land tenure)!

Understand this if you can!

In addition to all this, Kautsky displays a philistine inability to take into account the real policy of a definite party. He quotes the empty *phrases* of the Menshevik Maslov and *refuses to see the real* policy the Menshevik Party pursued in 1917, when, in "coalition" with the landowners and Cadets, they advocated what was virtually a *liberal agrarian reform and compromise with the landowners* (proof: the arrest of the members of the Land Committees and S. Maslov's land bill).

Kautsky failed to notice that P. Maslov's phrases about the reactionary and utopian character of petty-bourgeois equality are really a screen to conceal the Menshevik policy of *compromise* between the peasants and the landowners (i.e., of supporting the landowners in duping the peasants), instead of the *revolutionary* overthrow of the landowners by the peasants.

What a "Marxist" Kautsky is!

It was the Bolsheviks who strictly differentiated between the bourgeois-democratic revolution and the socialist revolution: by carrying the former through, they opened the door for the transition to the latter. This was the only policy that was revolutionary and Marxist.

It would have been wiser for Kautsky not to repeat the feeble liberal witticism: "Never yet have the small peasants anywhere adopted collective farming under the influence of theoretical convictions" (p. 50).

How very smart!

But never as yet and nowhere have the small peasants of any large country been under the influence of a proletarian state.

Never as yet and nowhere have the small peasants engaged in an open class struggle reaching the extent of a civil war between the poor peasants and the rich peasants, *with* propagandist, political, economic and military support given to the poor by a proletarian state.

Never as yet and nowhere have the profiteers and the rich amassed such wealth out of war, while the mass of peasants have been so utterly ruined.

Kautsky just reiterates the old stuff, he just chews the old cud, afraid even to give thought to the new tasks of the proletarian dictatorship.

But what, dear Kautsky, if the peasants *lack* implements for small-scale farming and the proletarian state *helps* them to obtain machines for collective farming — is that a "theoretical conviction"?

We shall now pass to the question of nationalisation of the land. Our Narodniks, including all the Left Socialist-Revolutionaries, deny that the measure we have adopted is nationalisation of the land. They are wrong in theory. Insofar as we remain within the framework of commodity production and capitalism, the abolition of private ownership of land is nationalisation of the land. The term "socialisation" merely expresses a tendency, a desire, the preparation for the transition to socialism.

What should be the attitude of Marxists towards nationalisation of the land?

Here, too, Kautsky fails even to formulate the theoretical question, or, which is still worse, he deliberately evades it, although one knows from Russian literature that Kautsky is aware of the old controversies among the Russian Marxists on the question of nationalisation, municipalisation (i.e., the transfer of the large estates to the local self-government authorities), or division of the land.

Kautsky's assertion that to transfer the large estates to the state and rent them out in small plots to peasants who own little land would be achieving "something socialistic" is a downright mockery of Marxism. We have already shown that there is nothing socialistic about it. But that is not all; it would not even be carrying the *bourgeois-democratic* revolution to its conclusion. Kautsky's great misfortune is that he placed his trust in the Mensheviks. Hence the curious position that while insisting on our revolution having a bourgeois character and reproaching the Bolsheviks for taking it into their heads to proceed to socialism, he *himself* proposes a liberal reform under the guise of socialism, *without carrying this reform* to the point of completely clearing away all the survivals of medievalism in agrarian relations! The arguments of Kautsky, as of his Menshevik advisers, amount to a defence of the liberal bourgeoisie, who fear revolution, instead of defence of consistent bourgeois-democratic revolution.

Indeed, why should only the large estates, and not all the land, be converted into state property? The liberal bourgeoisie thereby achieve the maximum preservation of the old conditions (i.e., the least consistency in revolution) and the maximum facility for a reversion to the old conditions. The radical bourgeoisie, i.e., the bourgeoisie that want to carry the bourgeois revolution to its conclusion, put forward the slogan of *nationalisation of the land*.

Kautsky, who in the dim and distant past, some twenty years ago, wrote an excellent Marxist work on the agrarian question,[74] cannot but know that Marx declared that land nationalisation is in fact a *consistent* slogan of the *bourgeoisie*.[75] Kautsky cannot but be aware of Marx's controversy with Rodbertus, and Marx's remarkable passages in his *Theories of Surplus Value* where the revolutionary significance — in the bourgeois-democratic sense — of land nationalisation is explained with particular clarity.

The Menshevik P. Maslov, whom Kautsky, unfortunately for himself, chose as an adviser, denied that the Russian peasants would agree to the nationalisation of all the land (including the peasants' lands). To a certain extent, this view of Maslov's could be connected with his "original" theory (which merely parrots the bourgeois critics of Marx), namely, his repudiation of absolute rent and his recognition of the "law" (or "fact", as Maslov expressed it) "of diminishing returns".

In point of fact, however, already the 1905 Revolution revealed that the vast majority of the peasants in Russia, members of village communes as well as homestead peasants, were in favour of nationalisation of all the land. The 1917 Revolution confirmed this, and after the assumption of power by the proletariat this was done. The Bolsheviks remained loyal to Marxism and never tried (in spite of Kautsky, who, without a scrap of evidence, accuses us of doing so) to "skip" the bourgeois-democratic revolution. The Bolsheviks, first of all, helped the most radical, most revolutionary of the bourgeois-democratic ideologists of the peasants, those who stood closest to the proletariat, namely, the Left Socialist-Revolutionaries, to carry out what was in effect nationalisation of the land. On October 26, 1917, i.e., on the very first day of the proletarian, socialist revolution, private ownership of land was abolished in Russia.

This laid the foundation, the most perfect from the point of view of the development of capitalism (Kautsky cannot deny this without breaking with Marx), and at the same time created an agrarian system which is the *most flexible* from the point of view of the transition to socialism. From the bourgeois-democratic point of view, the revolutionary peasants in Russia *could go no farther: there can be nothing* "more ideal" from this point of view, nothing "more radical" (from this same point of view) than nationalisation of the land and equal land tenure. It was the Bolsheviks, and only the Bolsheviks, who, thanks only to the victory of the *proletarian* revolution, helped the peasants to carry the bourgeois-democratic revolution really to its conclusion. And only in this way did they do the utmost to facilitate and accelerate the transition to the socialist revolution.

One can judge from this what an incredible muddle Kautsky offers to his readers when he accuses the Bolsheviks of failing to understand the bourgeois character of the revolution, and yet himself betrays such a departure from Marxism that he *says nothing* about nationalisation of the land and presents the least revolutionary (from the bourgeois point of view) liberal agrarian reform as "something socialistic"!

We have now come to the third question formulated above, namely, to what extent the proletarian dictatorship in Russia has taken into account the necessity of passing to farming in common. Here again, Kautsky commits something very much in the nature of a forgery: he quotes only the "theses" of one Bolshevik which speak of the task of passing to farming in common! After quoting one of these theses, our "theoretician" triumphantly exclaims:

> "Unfortunately, a task is not accomplished by the fact that it is called a task. For the time being, collective farming in Russia is doomed to remain on paper only. Never yet have the small peasants anywhere adopted collective farming under the influence of theoretical convictions" (p. 50).

Never as yet and nowhere has a literary swindle been perpetrated equal to that to which Kautsky has stooped. He quotes "theses", but says nothing about the *law* of the Soviet government. He talks about "theoretical convictions", but says nothing about the proletarian state power which holds in its hands the factories and goods! All that Kautsky the Marxist wrote in 1899 in his *Agrarian Question* about the means at the disposal of the proletarian state for bringing about the gradual transition of the small peasants to socialism has been forgotten by Kautsky the renegade in 1918.

Of course, a few hundred state-supported agricultural communes and state farms (i.e., large farms cultivated by associations of workers at the expense of the state) are very little, but can Kautsky's ignoring of this fact be called "criticism"?

The nationalisation of the land that has been effected in Russia by the proletarian dictatorship has best ensured the carrying of the bourgeois-democratic revolution to its conclusion — even in the event of a victory of the counter-revolution causing a reversion from land nationalisation to land division (I made a special examination of this possibility in my pamphlet on the agrarian programme of the Marxists in the 1905 Revolution).[76] In addition, the nationalisation of the land has given the proletarian state the maximum opportunity of passing to socialism in agriculture.

To sum up, Kautsky has presented us, as far as theory is concerned, with an incredible hodge-podge which is a complete renunciation of Marxism, and, as far as practice is concerned, with a policy of servility to the bourgeoisie and their reformism. A fine criticism indeed!

*　　*　　*

Kautsky begins his "economic analysis" of industry with the following magnificent argument:

Russia has a large-scale capitalist industry. Cannot a socialist system of production be built up on this foundation? "One might think so if socialism meant that the workers of the separate factories and mines made these their property" (literally appropriated these for themselves) "in order to carry on production separately at each factory" (p. 52). "This very day, August 5, as I am writing these lines," Kautsky adds, "a speech is reported from Moscow delivered by Lenin on August 2, in which he is stated to have declared: 'The workers are holding the factories firmly in their hands, and the peasants will not return the land to the landowners.' Up till now, the slogan: the factories to the workers, and the land to the peasants, has been an anarcho-syndicalist slogan, not a Social-Democratic one" (pp. 52-53).

I have quoted this passage in full so that the Russian workers, who formerly respected Kautsky, and quite rightly, might see for themselves the methods employed by this deserter to the bourgeois camp.

Just think: on August 5, when numerous decrees on the nationalisation of factories in Russia had been issued — and not a single factory had been "appropriated" by the workers, but had *all* been converted into the property of the Republic — on August 5, Kautsky, on the strength of an obviously crooked interpretation of one sentence in my speech, tries to make the German readers believe that in Russia the factories are being turned over to individual groups of workers! And after that Kautsky, at great length, chews the cud about it being wrong to turn over factories to individual groups of workers!

This is not criticism, it is the trick of a lackey of the bourgeoisie, whom the capitalists have hired to slander the workers' revolution.

The factories must be turned over to the state, or to the municipalities, or the consumers' co-operative societies, says Kautsky over and over again, and finally adds:

"This is what they are now trying to do in Russia. . . ." Now! What does that mean? In August? Why, could not Kautsky have commissioned his friends Stein or Axelrod, or any of the other friends of the Russian bourgeoisie, to translate at least one of the decrees on the factories.

"How far they have gone in this direction, we cannot yet tell. At all events, this aspect of the activity of the Soviet Republic is of the greatest interest to us, but it still remains entirely shrouded in darkness. There is no lack of decrees. . . . (That is why Kautsky ignores their *content*, or conceals it from his readers!) But there is no reliable information as to the effect of these decrees. Socialist production is impossible without all-round, detailed, reliable and rapidly informative statistics. The Soviet Republic cannot possibly have created such statistics yet. What we learn about its economic activities is highly contradictory and can in no way be verified. This, too, is a result of the dictatorship and the suppression of democracy. There is no freedom of the press, or of speech" (p. 53).

This is how history is written! From a "free" press of the capitalists and Dutov men Kautsky would have received information about factories being taken over by the workers. . . . This "serious savant" who stands above classes is magnificent, indeed! About the countless facts which show that the factories are being turned over to the Republic *only*, that they are managed by an organ of Soviet power, the Supreme Economic Council, which is constituted mainly of workers elected by the trade unions, Kautsky refuses to say a single word. With the obstinacy of the "man in the muffler",[77] he stubbornly keeps repeating one thing: give me peaceful democracy, without civil war, without a dictatorship and with good statistics (the Soviet Republic has created a statistical service in which the best statistical experts in Russia are employed, but, of course, ideal statistics cannot be obtained so quickly). In a word, what Kautsky demands is a revolution without revolution, without fierce struggle, without violence. It is equivalent to asking for strikes in which workers and employers do not get excited. Try to find the difference between this kind of "socialist" and common liberal bureaucrat!

So, relying upon such "factual material", i.e., deliberately and contemptuously ignoring the innumerable facts, Kautsky "concludes":

"It is doubtful whether the Russian proletariat has obtained more in the sense of real practical gains, and not of mere decrees, under the Soviet Republic than it would have obtained from a Constituent Assembly, in which, as in the Soviets, socialists, although of a different hue, predominated" (p. 58).

A gem, is it not? We would advise Kautsky's admirers to circulate this utterance as widely as possible among the Russian workers, for

Kautsky could not have provided better material for gauging the depth of his political degradation. Comrade workers, Kerensky, too, was a "socialist", only of a "different hue"! Kautsky the historian is satisfied with the name, the title which the Right Socialist-Revolutionaries and the Mensheviks "appropriated" to themselves. Kautsky the historian refuses even to listen to the facts which show that under Kerensky the Mensheviks and the Right Socialist-Revolutionaries supported the imperialist policy and marauding practices of the bourgeoisie; he is discreetly silent about the fact that the majority in the Constituent Assembly consisted of these very champions of imperialist war and bourgeois dictatorship. And this is called "economic analysis"!

In conclusion let me quote another sample of this "economic analysis".

". . .After nine months' existence, the Soviet Republic, instead of spreading general well-being, felt itself obliged to explain why there is general want" (p. 41).

We are accustomed to hear such arguments from the lips of the Cadets. All the flunkeys of the bourgeoisie in Russia argue in this way: show us, after nine months, your general well-being — and this after four years of devastating war, with foreign capital giving all-round support to the sabotage and rebellions of the bourgeoisie in Russia. *Actually,* there has remained absolutely no difference whatever, not a shadow of difference, between Kautsky and a counterrevolutionary bourgeois. His honeyed talk, cloaked in the guise of "socialism", only repeats what the Kornilov men, the Dutov men and Krasnov men in Russia say bluntly, straightforwardly and without embellishment.

*   *   *

The above lines were written on November 9, 1918. That same night news was received from Germany announcing the beginning of a victorious revolution, first in Kiel and other northern towns and ports, where power has passed into the hands of Councils of Workers' and Soldiers' Deputies, then in Berlin, where, too, power has passed into the hands of a Council.

The conclusion which still remained to be written to my pamphlet on Kautsky and on the proletarian revolution is now superfluous. □

Notes

1. *Illustrierte Geschichte der deutschen Revolution* (Berlin: Internationaler Arbeiter-Verlag, 1929), p. 236.

2. *Vorwärts*, December 24, 1918, as reprinted in Hermann Weber, *Der Gründungsparteitag der KPD* (Frankfurt: Europäische Verlagsanstalt, 1969), p. 267.

3. Marcel Liebman, *Leninism Under Lenin* (London: Merlin Press: 1980), p. 233; Victor Serge, *Year One of the Russian Revolution* (Chicago: Holt, Rinehart and Winston, 1972), pp. 129-31.

4. V.I. Lenin, *Collected Works* (hereinafter *CW*) (Moscow: Progress Publishers, 1972), vol. 26, pp. 379-83.

5. The "Preparliament" was established by the All-Russian Democratic Conference, which was convened in Petrograd in September 1917 by the Central Executive Committee of the Soviets, then controlled by the Mensheviks and Socialist Revolutionaries. These parties ensured themselves a majority in the Democratic Conference by granting exaggerated representation to petty-bourgeois and bourgeois organizations. The soviets received only 230 of the more than 1,500 delegates. The Democratic Conference decided to establish the Preparliament to serve as an advisory body to the government.

The Preparliament consisted of about 15 percent of the delegates to the Democratic Conference, plus about 120 representatives of organizations of the possessing classes. Heavily weighted in composition against the workers and soldiers, only 15 percent of its members were Bolsheviks, who made up the majority at the October 1917 congress of soviets. The Preparliament met in Petrograd in October. It proved to be an indecisive and unauthoritative body, and was swept away by the October revolution.

6. The Extraordinary All-Russian Congress of Railwaymen convened in Petrograd on December 25 (12), 1918, on the initiative of the Moscow and Petrograd railwaymen's unions. Confronted by the hostility to the October revolution of the railway union's executive committee, Vikzhel, the congress rallied in support of the Soviet government.

7. The Menshevik-controlled Ukranian Rada proclaimed a Ukrainian People's Republic on November 20 (7), 1917, which was recognized by the Soviet government in Petrograd. The Rada commenced aiding counterrevolutionary forces opposing the Soviet regime, however, and soviets within the Ukraine began to contest its rule. The Rada was ousted February 8 (January 26), 1918, and a Soviet government established, although it was soon overthrown in turn by the invading German army.

Soviet recognition of Finnish independence on December 31 (18), 1917, led to a similar chain of events.

In Belorussia a bourgeois regime was ousted in December 1917 and a Soviet government established.

In Transcaucasia a regional government that held sway at that time was anti-Bolshevik and rejected the authority of the Soviet government.

8. The Bolsheviks were known as the Russian Social Democratic Labor Party (Bolsheviks) until March 1918. They then assumed the name Russian Communist Party (Bolsheviks).

9. Lenin, *CW*, vol. 26, pp. 423-25.

10. The declaration of the Bolshevik fraction is printed in Lenin, *CW,* vol. 26, pp. 429-30.

11. Serge, *Year One,* p. 135. See also W.H. Chamberlin, *The Russian Revolution* (New York: Grosset & Dunlap, 1977), vol. 1, p. 370.

12. Lenin, *CW,* vol. 26, pp. 434-36.

13. Excerpted from Karl Kautsky, *Die Diktatur des Proletariats* (Vienna: Volksbuchhandlung Ignaz Brand & Co., 1918), pp. 28-31 and 58-63. The complete text of Kautsky's pamphlet is printed in a different English translation in Karl Kautsky, *The Dictatorship of the Proletariat* (Ann Arbor, Michigan: University of Michigan Press, 1964).

14. Sections 7, 8, and 9 of Kautsky's work, not translated here, are quoted extensively in Lenin's reply printed below in this chapter. In section 7, Kautsky argued that the Soviets' assumption of governmental power led to their destruction as instruments of workers' democracy. Section 8 discussed the Soviet republic's failure to bring an improvement in the living standards of the Russian masses. Section 9 took up the Soviet government's agrarian and industrial policies.

15. Kautsky is referring to a passage in Marx's "Critique of the Gotha Program," which reads, "Between capitalist and communist society lies the period of the revolutionary transformation of the one into the other. Corresponding to this is also a political transition period in which the state can be nothing but *the revolutionary dictatorship of the proletariat.*" See Karl Marx, "Marginal Notes to the Programme of the German Workers' Party" (Critique of the Gotha Program), in Karl Marx and Frederick Engels, *Selected Works* (hereinafter *SW*) (Moscow: Progress Publishers, 1977), vol. 3, p. 26.

As Lenin points out in his reply to Kautsky, "Both Marx and Engels, in their letters as well as in their published works, *repeatedly* spoke about the dictatorship of the proletariat." (*CW,* vol. 28, p. 233.) Probably the first written use of the term occurs in Marx's 1850 work, *The Class Struggles in France, 1848 to 1850.* (Marx and Engels, *Collected Works* [New York: International Publishers, 1978] vol. 10, p. 127.)

Marx underlined the central importance of this strategic perspective to the line of march of the proletariat in a letter written March 5, 1852, to Joseph Weydemeyer. There Marx stated, "Now as for myself, I do not claim to have discovered either the existence of classes in modern society or the struggle between them. Long before me, bourgeois historians had described the historical development of this struggle between the classes, as had bourgeois economists their economic anatomy. My own contribution was 1. to show that the *existence of classes* is merely bound up with *certain historical phases in the development of production;* 2. that the class struggle necessarily leads to the *dictatorship of the proletariat;* 3. that this dictatorship itself constitutes no more than a transition to the *abolition of all classes* and to a *classless society.*" (Marx and Engels, *Collected Works* [New York: International Publishers, 1982], vol. 39, pp. 62-65.)

This letter was published in 1907 by Franz Mehring in the SPD's journal, *Die neue Zeit,* which was edited by Kautsky.

16. Kautsky's reference is to Marx's "Speech on the Hague Congress" of the First International, delivered September 8, 1872 in Amsterdam. A French newspaper reported Marx as saying:

"The workers will have to seize political power one day in order to construct the new organization of labour; they will have to overthrow the old politics which bolster up the old institutions, unless they want to share the fate of the early Christians, who lost their chance of heaven on earth because they rejected and neglected such action.

"We do not claim, however, that the road leading to this goal is the same everywhere.

"We know that heed must be paid to the institutions, customs, and traditions of the various countries, and we do not deny that there are countries, such as America and England, and if I was familiar with its institutions, I might include Holland, where the workers may attain their goal by peaceful means. That being the case, we must recognize that in most continental countries the lever of the revolution will have to be force; a resort to force will be necessary one day in order to set up the rule of labour." (Karl Marx, *The First International and After*, vol. 3 of *Political Writings* [New York:Vintage Books, 1974], p. 324.)

A year earlier, Marx told a reporter of the New York *World* that "the English middle class has always shown itself willing enough to accept the verdict of the majority so long as it enjoyed the monopoly of the voting power. But mark me," he continued, "as soon as it finds itself outvoted on what it considers vital questions we shall see here a new slave-owners' war." The "slave-owners' war" he referred to was the U.S. Civil War, which was sparked by the refusal of southern slaveowners to accept the outcome of the 1860 presidential election. (Ibid., p. 400).

Engels recalled Marx's views on this question in his 1886 introduction to the English edition of *Capital*. Marx's studies led him to the conclusion, Engels wrote, that "at least in Europe, England is the only country where the inevitable social revolution might be effected entirely by peaceful and legal means. He certainly never forgot to add that he hardly expected the English ruling classes to submit, without a 'pro-slavery rebellion', to this peaceful and legal revolution." (Karl Marx, *Capital* [New York: Vintage Books, 1977], vol. 1, p. 113.)

17. *Die Freiheit*, December 14, 1918.

18. "Die geschichtliche Verantwortung," in *Spartakusbriefe* (Berlin [GDR]: Dietz Verlag, 1958), pp. 406-11. The Spartacists' response to the Russian revolution will be documented more fully in the volume of the present series, *The Communist International in Lenin's Time* covering the years 1917-18.

19. J.P. Nettl, *Rosa Luxemburg* (London: Oxford University Press, 1966), vol. 2, p. 695.

20. *Spartakusbriefe*, p. 454.

21. Ibid., p. 453.

22. An English translation of Luxemburg's "The Russian Revolution" can be found in Mary-Alice Waters, ed., *Rosa Luxemburg Speaks* (New York: Pathfinder Press, 1980), pp. 367-95.

23. Rosa Luxemburg, *Gesammelte Werke* (Berlin [GDR]: Dietz Verlag, 1974), vol. 4, pp. 364-65.

24. Rosa Luxemburg, *J'étais, je suis, je serai! Correspondance 1914-1919* (Paris: François Maspéro, 1977), p. 366.

25. Lenin, "To Y.A. Berzin, V.V. Vorovsky and A.A. Joffe," in *CW*, vol. 35, pp. 362-63.

26. Lenin, "The Proletarian Revolution and the Renegade Kautsky," in *CW*, vol. 28, pp. 105-13.

27. Lenin, "The Proletarian Revolution and the Renegade Kautsky," in *CW*, vol. 28, pp. 227-318.

28. The Basel Manifesto was unanimously adopted by the November 1912 emergency congress of the Second International, called as a demonstration of Socialist unity against the Balkan War and the imperialist war drive as a whole. It reaffirmed the call of the International's 1907 congress to utilize the crisis created by war to rouse the masses and speed social revolution and pointed to many examples where this had taken place. The manifesto is printed in John Riddell, ed., *Lenin's Struggle for a Revolutionary International: Documents, 1907-1916; The Preparatory Years* (New York: Monad Press, 1984), p. 88-90, a volume of *The Communist International in Lenin's Time*.

29. The pamphlet, *Socialism and War*, a rounded explanation of the Marxist position on the First World War, was written by Gregory Zinoviev and Lenin for circulation to the delegates at the September 1915 Zimmerwald conference. It is printed in Lenin, *CW*, vol. 21, pp. 295-338.

30. See Lenin, *CW*, vol. 22, pp. 185-304.

31. See Lenin, *CW*, vol. 25, pp. 385-497.

32. Marx, "Critique of the Gotha Program," in Marx and Engels, *SW*, vol. 3, p. 26.

33. See Engels's "Letter to A. Bebel" of March 18-28, 1875, printed in Marx and Engels, *SW*, vol. 3, p. 34.

34. Marx and Engels, *SW*, vol. 2, pp. 178-244.

35. See Engels's introduction to Marx's, "The Civil War in France," in Marx and Engels, *SW*, vol. 2, p. 186.

36. Engels, "On Authority," in Marx and Engels, *SW*, vol. 2, p. 379.

37. Wilhelm Weitling (1808-1871) was an early German proletarian writer and a utopian socialist. In a portion of his pamphlet not printed in this chapter, Kautsky compared the Bolsheviks' views with those of Weitling, who "wanted the greatest geniuses to govern. They would be selected by competitions before scientific assemblies." Kautsky held the Bolsheviks' supposed contempt for democracy to be "quite an old conception, [which] corresponds to a primitive stage in the working-class movement." In this stage many socialists, like Weitling, considered that "the proletariat, which was too ignorant and demoralized to organize and rule itself, should be organized and ruled from the top down by a government comprised of its educated elite," Kautsky continued, "something like the way the Jesuits in Paraguay organized and governed the Indians." (Kautsky, *Die Diktatur des Proletariats,* pp. 9-11.)

38. Engels, "Origin of the Family, Private Property and the State" in Marx and Engels, *SW*, vol. 3, p. 328.

39. Engels, "Letter to A. Bebel," in Marx and Engels, *SW*, vol. 3. pp. 34-35.

40. Marx and Engels, *SW*, vol. 2, p. 189.

41. Engels, "Origin of the Family," in Marx and Engels, *SW*, vol. 3, p. 161.

42. Marx and Engels, *SW*, vol. 2, p. 220-21. The German words italicized by Lenin are inaccurately translated in the *Selected Works.* They are translated correctly by Lenin.

43. In 1894 reactionary monarchist circles in France instituted proceedings against Alfred Dreyfus, a general staff officer and a Jew, on trumped-up charges of espionage and high treason. A campaign in his defense by democrats and Socialists met intransigent opposition from reactionary circles, but ultimately won his release and reinstatement into the army.

44. Official statistics admit to the lynching of more than three thousand Blacks in the seven decades after 1882. Revolutionary workers such as Frank Lit-

tle and Wesley Everest of the IWW also fell victim to this practice. The British government suppressed the Irish Easter Rebellion of 1916, executing many Irish patriots.

45. Marx, "Indifference to Politics," in *Anarchism and Anarcho-Syndicalism: Selected Writings by Marx, Engels, and Lenin* (New York: International Publishers, 1974), p. 95.

46. Engels, "On Authority," in Marx and Engels, *SW*, vol. 2, p. 379.

47. Engels, "Letter to A. Bebel," in Marx and Engels, *SW*, vol. 3, pp. 34-35.

48. During the Paris Commune of 1871, the bourgeois national government fled to Versailles, where it organized counterrevolutionary troops to destroy the revolutionary uprising.

49. Marx and Engels, *Collected Works* (New York: International Publishers, 1976), vol. 6, p. 504.

50. The reference is to Engels's introduction to "The Civil War in France," in Marx and Engels, *SW*, vol. 2, p. 188.

51. See "Tasks of the Proletariat in the Present Revolution," known as the "April Theses" in Lenin, *CW*, vol. 24, pp. 19-26.

52. See Lenin, "Political Parties in Russia and the Tasks of the Proletariat," written in April 1917 and printed in Lenin, *CW*, vol. 24, pp. 93-106.

53. See "Resolution on the Question of Revising the Party Programme," in Lenin, *CW*, vol. 24, pp. 280-81.

54. Engels, "Letter to A. Bebel," in Marx and Engels, *SW*, vol. 3, p. 34.

55. See footnote 5 in this chapter.

56. The tsarist general Kornilov led a counterrevolutionary conspiracy and insurrection in August-September 1917, which aimed at replacing the Provisional Government with a military dictatorship and dissolving the soviets. The Kornilov revolt was crushed by the resistance of Petrograd workers, soldiers, and sailors.

57. Petrushka, a character in Gogol's novel *Dead Souls*, could read only by syllables. He enjoyed the process of reading, but could not understand what he had read.

58. Judas Golovlyov is a hypocritical and sanctimonious feudal landowner in Saltykov-Shchedrin's novel *The Golovlyov Family*.

59. *Lieberdans* was an epithet for the followers of the Menshevik leaders M.I. Lieber and F.I. Dan.

The "activists" were a group of Mensheviks who resorted to armed struggle against Soviet power after the October Revolution.

60. In the German Empire before 1918, the National Liberals were the party of the German big bourgeoisie. August Bebel referred to right wingers in his party as "National Liberals" at the SPD's 1910 congress in Magdeburg. Lenin reports on Bebel's remarks in "Two Worlds," in Lenin, *CW*, vol. 16, p. 308.

61. *1903: Second Congress of the Russian Social Democratic Labour Party* (London: New Park Publications, 1978), p. 220.

62. Engels, "Introduction" to Marx's "The Civil War in France," in Marx and Engels, *SW*, vol. 2, pp. 179-80.

63. See, for example, Marx and Engels's preface to the 1872 German edition of the "Communist Manifesto," in Marx and Engels, *SW*, vol. 1, p. 99; Marx, "The Civil War in France," in Marx and Engels, *SW*, vol. 2, p. 217; and Engels's introduction to the 1891 edition, ibid., p. 187.

64. The "Left Communists" were a current in the Bolshevik party, led by

Nikolai Bukharin, who in early 1918 opposed the conclusion of a separate peace with Germany. The Left Socialist Revolutionaries also opposed signing such a treaty.

65. In 1918, German imperialism occupied Finland, the Ukraine, Latvia, and Estonia and overturned the revolutionary governments that existed in these countries. While German workers had shown their hostility to German expansionism in the mass strikes of January 1918, the organized German workers' movement did little or nothing in solidarity with the workers and peasants oppressed by German militarism in these countries.

66. See "Two Tactics of Social-Democracy in the Democratic Revolution," in Lenin, *CW*, vol. 9, pp. 15-140.

67. See for example part two of Marx's December 15, 1848, article, "The Bourgeoisie and the Counter-revolution," in Marx and Engels, *Collected Works*, vol. 8, pp. 159-63.

68. Heinrich Weber was a pseudonym of Otto Bauer.

69. In a letter to Ludwig Kugelmann of April 12, 1871, Marx wrote, "the next French Revolution will no longer attempt to transfer the bureaucratic-military apparatus from one hand to another, but *to smash* it, and this is the precondition for every real people's revolution on the Continent." (Marx and Engels, *Selected Correspondence* [Moscow: Progress Publishers, 1975], p. 247.)

70. The Soviet commander M.A. Muravyov led an unsuccessful revolt against the Soviet government in July 1918, which was closely connected to the uprising that month of the Left Socialist Revolutionaries.

71. The July 1918 crisis was a series of counterrevolutionary revolts against the Soviet government in the central provinces, the Volga area, the Urals, and Siberia.

72. A few days before the October revolution, Minister of Agriculture S.L. Maslov submitted to the Provisional Government a bill that preserved the holdings of the large landholders and failed to meet the demands of small peasants.

Members of the Land Committees were arrested under the Provisional Government as a reprisal against peasant revolts and seizures of landed estates.

73. For the Soviet government's decree on land, see Lenin, *CW*, vol. 26, pp. 258-61.

74. Kautsky, *Die Agrarfrage* (Zurich: Limmat Verlag, 1966). First published in 1899.

75. Marx, *Theories of Surplus Value* (Moscow: Progress Publishers, 1968), part 2, pp. 44-45.

76. See "The Agrarian Programme of Social-Democracy in the First Russian Revolution, 1905-07," in Lenin, *CW*, vol. 13, pp. 217-431.

77. The "man in the muffler" is a character in the story with that title by A.P. Chekhov, describing a narrow-minded philistine, afraid of initiative and new ideas.

-8-

The Bern Conference:
A Revived Second International?

Two months after the German revolution erupted, the political parties claiming to represent the German working class were arrayed against each other in armed battles in the streets of Berlin. The wartime split in German socialism had now created two currents pursuing diametrically opposed goals: the SPD leadership, with the USPD leaders in tow, striving to defend and reform capitalism, and the KPD working to replace capitalist rule with a revolutionary government of the exploited. The German revolution thus quickly reproduced the situation in Russia, where right-wing "Socialists" faced Bolsheviks on opposite sides of a civil war. This split cut through virtually all the parties of the old International.

Late in 1918, the reformist current moved to regroup and reorganize the forces in the world labor movement who opposed the Russian October revolution and supported capitalist reconsolidation. The proclaimed goal of this current was to revive the Second International, which had ceased to function with the outbreak of World War in August 1914. The initiative to achieve this aim, however, did not come from any elected bodies of the old International, but from the chauvinist-led Social Democratic parties in the victorious Allied powers. The Third Inter-Allied Labor and Socialist Conference in February 1918 established a committee to secure representation of the leaderships of its component organizations in any future conference of the Allied governments and "to organize Labour and Socialist representatives to sit concurrently with the official conference."[1] The committee was composed of Albert Thomas of France, Emile Vandervelde of Belgium, and Arthur Henderson of Britain — all of whom had participated in the governments of their respective ruling classes.

While the war lasted, nothing was done to call such an international conference, but following the triumph of the Allied armies the com-

---

Footnotes to this chapter begin on page 427.

mittee moved into action. It drew into its work Camille Huysmans, who had been the secretary of the Second International, and broadened the framework to include all Social Democratic and labor organizations. Since the victorious imperialist powers were to confer in Paris on the terms of the "peace" they intended to impose, the committee's initial proposal was to hold the parallel conference there, where it could most effectively fulfill its central goal of lobbying the Allied governments. Due to objections by the French government, however, the Social Democratic conference was transferred to Switzerland. There, too, the initially favored site, Lausanne, had to be abandoned because of official objections, and the conference was held in Bern February 3-10, 1919. Invitations were sent to the organizations of the pre-1914 Second International, whether from the Allied countries or the Central Powers, and whether or not their leaderships had supported their governments in the war. Invitations also went out to trade union bodies not affiliated with Social Democratic parties, such as the American Federation of Labor.

The Bern conference did not pretend to be a decision-making body of an International. Its goals were to strengthen the reformists' influence at the Allied "peace" conference, to establish a united front against Bolshevism, and to set in motion the reconstruction of an international organization.

Attendance was spotty. The Belgian party persisted in refusing to meet in the same room with leaders of parties from the Central Powers who had backed their countries' war effort. The American Federation of Labor took a similar stand. Moreover, the Bolsheviks called on revolutionary forces not to attend, and many left-wing parties stayed away, including the German KPD, the Bulgarian Tesnyaki, and the official Socialist parties of Italy, Switzerland, Serbia, and Romania. The final attendance was 102 delegates from twenty-six countries.[2]

The English-language magazine of the Communist International, launched later in the year, reported the explanation of Italian Socialist leader Costantino Lazzari on his party's refusal to participate:

"The Italian Socialists cannot take part in the meetings of such parties and groups, that have united their cause with the cause of the bourgeois governments, and especially of those, whose conscience is burdened with the double murder of Karl Liebknecht and of Rosa Luxemburg. . . .

"With this sort of International we have nothing in common; and all our comrades throughout the world who stand on the basis of class struggle are with us. The socialistic proletariat will not allow itself to be deceived: it sees the abyss yawning between these men and itself.

Everything must and will be built up afresh. This concerns the International also. But that new International will be the International of the proletarian socialists, the first spark of which was struck in gloomy, tragic days in the small village of Zimmerwald, amidst the accusations and persecution of that bourgeoisie, which has turned the world into a sea of blood; amidst calumny and animosity from the greater part of those, who yesterday at Bern dared to play the role of Defenders of Socialism."[3]

Those currents that did attend the Bern conference were themselves separated by deep divisions. USPD delegates from Germany challenged the SPD's conduct during the war. The French delegation was divided between the centrist forces led by Jean Longuet, now a majority in the party, and the former majority, the right wing led by Albert Thomas and Pierre Renaudel. Longuet joined with Friedrich Adler of Austria to lead a centrist minority at the conference against a right-wing majority.[4]

The openly chauvinist delegates were further divided according to their allegiance to rival groups of imperialist powers. These interimperialist rivalries threatened to blow the conference apart soon after it convened. Thomas, who as French minister of munitions had been an outspoken proponent of all-out war, proclaimed that "the resolutions of the Bern conference will have no authority and no effect" because of the absence of "mutual confidence" caused by the German SPD's support of Berlin's war effort.[5]

A bitter debate followed, marked by sharp recriminations between the German and French delegates. The final outcome, however, was a compromise. The SPD submitted a declaration that "the German proletariat has overthrown and destroyed through revolution the old system responsible for the war," and that however one judged the SPD's actions during the war, it had thus "shown in action its determined will . . . to fight together with Socialists of all countries in the League of Nations for socialism." The conference then hailed the German declaration and referred the question of ultimate responsibility for the war to some subsequent gathering.[6]

The conference united more readily on the question of how to avoid future world wars. Its resolution marked a sharp break from those of the Second International before 1914, which had projected a course — at least in words — of countering the war danger through independent working-class action and the struggle for socialism. The Bern resolution, by contrast, presented the bourgeois-pacifist notion that the evil of war "can be banished only through the establishment of the League of Nations," the permanent imperialist alliance that the Allied powers proposed to establish. It then specified measures to enable the proposed league to achieve this task, such as "representation of nations in its council not by delegates of governments, but by delegates of parliaments." It also demanded disarmament, arbitration of international disputes, free trade, and an "open door" to all powers to trade in the colonies.[7]

In its resolutions, the pre-1914 International had formally opposed any type of colonialism, although right-wing leaders of many Socialist parties had argued against this position. The Bern conference went completely over to the racist stance long held by these right-wingers. It entrusted colonial peoples to the "protection" of the League of Nations, which was to "promote their development, so that they might become capable of membership in the league of free peoples."

A further resolution on territorial disputes specified that colonial peoples were to be helped toward self-determination by "establishing schools, ensuring as a first step local autonomy and ... political rights." Nothing was said about granting them independence or ending the exploitation and oppression of these peoples. Territorial disputes among imperialist countries were to be resolved by a referendum "under the supervision of the League of Nations, which shall make the final decision."[8]

The resolution on international labor legislation complained of "the unfair competition of backward countries which endangered labor and industry in the more advanced states." It proposed to press for reforms in labor legislation through the League of Nations's permanent labor commission. A catalog of such reforms was provided, ranging from free education and the eight-hour day to establishing national boards to regulate minimum wages and other questions, with equal representation of labor and employers.[9]

The political heart of the Bern conference, however, was its closing discussion on the Russian revolution, Bolshevism, and democracy. Long hours of wrangling in a commission had produced a compromise majority text, which failed to oppose Allied intervention against Soviet Russia, while outlining theoretical reasons why the revolutionary regime had no right to exist.[10] An alternative resolution was introduced by the centrist forces at the conference, led by Adler and Longuet. Given the strong sympathy for Bolshevism within the ranks of most Social Democratic parties, these centrists felt that taking an open stand against the Soviet government would obstruct the reconstruction of the International. A third point of view was advanced by Fernand Loriot, leader of the pro-Bolshevik tendency in the French Socialist Party, the only revolutionary current that had decided to attend the conference.

The debate in the conference, excerpts of which follow, was opened by the Swedish Social Democratic leader Hjalmar Branting, the reporter for the majority draft resolution.

The Bern Debate on Democracy and Soviet Rule[11]

Hjalmar Branting (Sweden): The remaining point on the agenda is entitled: "Democracy or Dictatorship of the Proletariat."

Currently, this is one of the most burning questions in almost all countries. It is the question of Bolshevism, which has called forth very divergent opinions within our ranks.

We place ourselves in the framework of democracy, as the International has always done. But many among us think that we are not yet in a position to make a fair judgment. The events in Russia are still too little known for us to be able to express an opinion with full knowledge of the facts.

Moreover, the issue is much too important to be dealt with by soothing declarations. If we are still democrats, if we are still against all oppression, whether by majorities or by minorities, then we need a frank and clear position. We want to proceed to socialism by the straight and narrow path of democracy.

We do not question in any way the good intentions and sincerity of the comrades who have a different opinion. But today when we are reconstituting the workers' International, we should speak openly. . . .

We all recognize that there exist revolutionary junctures in the lives of nations. But just because revolutionary movements may be necessary and we may all be led to approve of them, we cannot say: We adopt this revolutionary dictatorship as a lasting political system and we abandon our old democratic principles, hallowed by socialism up to now. We should always allow ourselves to be guided by the conviction that, if revolutionary movements command recognition under certain circumstances, only democracy can create stable conditions for the people.

Only when we have the support of the masses — that is all sectors of the population; workers, peasants, and intellectuals — only then can we be sure of having achieved a lasting improvement in the lot of the entire people.

The commission's task was to express these two tendencies. We can neither exclude revolution nor abandon democracy. We Socialists shall remain democrats. For the sake of socialism, we expect lasting security only from democracy. Only with democracy can we build a solid foundation for the new society. All other roads are wrong and will lead us away from democracy. The people's happiness cannot be achieved through dictatorship. . . .

But we send a warning to the world's reactionary forces: do not push the working class of the entire world to upheavals of despair. We do not expect salvation from such upheavals. However, White reaction is just as detestable as Red Terror and the workers will endure any suffering to rid themselves of this White Terror. □

Majority Resolution: Democracy and Dictatorship[12]

The conference salutes the mighty political revolutions that have shattered the old imperialist and militarist system in Russia, Austria-Hungary, and Germany and have swept away their governments.

The conference urges the workers of all countries to develop democratic, republican institutions that will provide the framework for the socialist transformation of society.

In these decisive days, when the socialist reorganization of society is posed more immediately than ever before, the working people must be united in understanding the course that must be followed to their liberation.

The Bern conference is rooted intransigently in the principles of democracy, in full agreement with all the International's congresses. A reorganized society, increasingly influenced by socialism, cannot be created, much less defended, if it is not anchored in free principles won and extended through democracy. These democratic principles — freedom of speech, press, and assembly, universal suffrage, accountability of government to a parliamentary system, institutions that ensure public participation and decisions, freedom of association, and so forth — also give the proletariat the democratic tools for its struggles.

The conference wishes to strongly emphasize that, in contrast to some current phenomena, the socialist economic order is constructive in character. Socialization entails the planned development of the various branches of industry under the control of a democratic society. The arbitrary seizure of individual factories by a small group of workers is not socialization, it is capitalism with more stockholders.

The conference believes that since true socialism can only evolve through democracy, methods of socialization that have no perspective of winning over a popular majority must therefore be rejected from the outset. Any attempt at such a dictatorship is even more dangerous if it is based on only part of the proletariat. That can lead only to wearing the proletariat down through civil war. The end result would be the dictatorship of reaction.

The Russian delegates have suggested that the conference send a commission of representatives of all the Socialist tendencies to Russia in order to impartially inform the International about Russia's political and economic situation. The conference is fully aware of the difficulties involved in such a mission, but given the proletariat's universal interest in learning the truth about the revolutionary ferment there, the conference recommends that the permanent commission send such a delegation to Russia.

The conference places the question of Bolshevism on the agenda of the next congress and instructs the commission to undertake the necessary preliminary work.

However, the conference cannot fail to emphasize that the poverty and misery that afflicts the entire world, especially in the defeated countries as a result of the war, can give rise only to conditions of social breakdown. Instead of utilizing Bolshevism as a bogeyman, using this label to slander every resistance by desperate proletarians, the governments should recognize their own responsibility.

Counterrevolutionary forces are on the move everywhere. The conference warns the present rulers, who hold the world's destiny in their hands, against an imperialist policy of military or economic suppression of peoples. It urges the world's Socialists to close ranks, not to abandon the revolutionary peoples to international reaction, but rather to make every possible effort to ensure the victory of socialism and democracy, which are inseparable. ☐

Discussion (Continued)

J. Ramsay MacDonald (Great Britain):[13] This resolution is in many respects the most important considered by the conference, and it is very unfortunate that it has to be discussed so late in the proceedings. It is essential that a pronouncement should be made on this subject for three reasons. First, the Socialist movement must guard itself. Second, the governments of Europe must be warned of what is going on inside Europe. That warning can best be given by men attending the conference, many of whom have become personally responsible for new governments and all of whom are in contact with the great working-class movements that make and unmake states.

Third, it is necessary to make a pronouncement in order that those who look forward to some new, rapid way of establishing socialism in the world may be challenged, not in a hostile but in a friendly way, to reconsider their theories and their tactics.

We are living in absolutely abnormal times. There is a reaction toward conservatism on the one side and to revolution on the other. Reaction comes when the fabric of society has been so shattered by some great social crisis such as the recent war — and when principles that are usually used for the purpose of criticizing the old and established order become suddenly released from responsibility and threaten themselves to become new sources of disorder and anarchy. In such times are we living today, and the duty of the Socialist movement is to keep a calm mind, a sane judgment, a steady lead, and to tell the people how they are to act, what goals they are to aim at and what paths they are to pursue.

War compelled them to revise some of their theories. Before the war we all assumed that democratic expression, on its governmental side, could be expressed only through parliaments. The war has shown that that conception of democratic liberty may now be supplemented. What is democracy? How can it express itself? What is the responsibility of aggressive minorities in the state? We used to use an old-fashioned socialist saying that "the tyranny of the minority in some circumstances might be justified." Under what circumstances can it be justified? Can it set itself up as an end in itself? Can anything like continual government be established on such a principle? It is the duty of Socialists to say "No." Such might be a temporary and limited phase of the revolution, but the moment that the conception of the tyranny of the minority becomes the basis of a continued policy, then that policy and theory must be condemned by every Socialist who believes in the liberty of the individual and by those who desire to exercise their liberty within the states to which they belong.

We welcome all the revolutions that have been achieved in Europe, but these revolutions must not create conditions which might be accurately described as a transition from one form of tyranny to another. Liberty, democracy, freedom must be their steady and unchangeable goal. A revolution that does not establish liberty is not a revolution toward socialism and is not a revolution for which Socialists ought to make themselves responsible or allow the outside bourgeois reaction to impose the responsibility for upon them.

Unrest is to be seen on every hand. It may be welcomed as an indication that the society affected requires change, but unrest must always be constructive and not destructive, and inspired by a definite conception of social reorganization. It must be architectural in the positive sense and not merely concern itself with destroying that to which it is opposed. The moment the vision of an unsettled democracy is limited by negations, then the working-class leadership ceases to be safe and begins to be unsafe.

The characteristic of socialism is its constructive side, not its destructive side. We, as Socialists, are anticapitalist, but that attitude does not compose socialism. There are many other theories and movements which are equally anticapitalist. Socialism is a construction of society, and the International must always place this before it as the special characteristic of the working-class movement which it voices and solidifies. We must always place before us that constructive view of society which alone entitles an organization or an individual to be called Socialist. . . . □

<hr />

After MacDonald's address, a confused procedural wrangle broke out over the speakers' list, the authenticity of the majority draft resolution, and whether any resolution should be voted at all. The dispute continued until adjournment at 1:00 a.m., at which point the conference seemed near collapse. This was averted later that morning when the majority gave way and accepted Adler's motion that no resolutions on this question be put to a vote. When discussion resumed, Loriot, the next speaker, began by reading a declaration.

Declaration[14]
by Fernand Loriot

Many of you have come here today as proxies for the bourgeois diplomats gathered in Paris in an attempt to determine, according to their own class interests, the destiny of nations. Many of you seek not the socialist solution to the tragic problems posed for humanity by the great capitalist crime, but to have the International vindicate the governmental, nationalist, chauvinist neosocialism of war that we saw break out everywhere after the declaration of war on the ruins of true socialism. You have gathered not to declare your loyalty to the Amsterdam resolution,[15] which before the war was a charter for us all, nor to affirm in the face of raging reaction your desire to implement socialism, but rather to give the International's formal approval to the policies of the bourgeois democrat Wilson, who answers to the American billionaires. (*"Very good"*) Finally, and above all, you have gathered to condemn in complete agreement the mighty effort at proletarian liberation that has begun in Russia and is moving irresistibly across Europe toward the western nations.

By that action the assassinations of Karl Liebknecht and Rosa Luxemburg would be absolved; the subsequent repression of the Spartacus movement in Germany would be legitimized; and the revolutionary efforts of the French, English, and Italian proletarians would be placed under suspicion and paralyzed.

We will be neither dupes nor accomplices to this antisocialist, counterrevolutionary undertaking. The new life you are striving to give the Second International is an illusion. Capitalist war wounded it mortally and social-nationalist policies finished it off as a class organization. All attempts to infuse this lost character back into it will be futile. Socialist history is not written at congresses; it is written by the proletarians page by page, day by day, and today those proletarians and their revolutionary, conscious vanguard are no longer with you. Experience has shown them the danger that capitalist anarchy poses to world peace and job security. They know what the supposed concessions of the ruling bourgeoisie are worth, and they expect salvation for the proletariat only through the revolutionary establishment of a new form of government based on the elimination of private property — a socialist regime.

Therefore, the ruined and starving workers and peasants are not looking to the Bern conference. Those who are watching you, those who expect something useful from you are the capitalist governments you are supposed to abolish, but to which you have hitched your destiny.

We know that there are sincere Socialists here with glorious revolutionary pasts, but they have not dissociated themselves from the actions of the others and thus bear a heavy share of the responsibility. History will judge them severely.

As for us, forever attached to socialism and its glorious traditions of class struggle and revolution, we send our fraternal greetings and the assurance of our active solidarity to the Russian communist republic, which is fighting a world of bourgeois and pseudosocialist enemies. Condemning the murderers of Liebknecht and Rosa Luxemburg, (*Cheers from the rear*) and the so-called socialist government that, with the complicity of the imperial generals, placed weapons in murderers' hands, we send the proletariat of Germany and of all countries our hopes for their final, total victory, which will be the victory of the entire proletariat. □

Discussion (Continued)

Loriot (France): Citizens, I would like to add but a word to this declaration, since the question of Bolshevism is being discussed. I am pleased at least with the effort made here at clarity in defining what Bolshevism is. I am pleased that, under the heading, "Democracy or Dictatorship," the resolution clarified the problem somewhat. This was necessary because so many definitions have been given for Bolshevism in the last year. I will not dwell here on all the slanders spread about Bolshevism by our class adversaries. That is their role. I only want to speak of what the International thinks about Bolshevism.

Until today's conference, tremendous confusion reigned in all minds on what significance should be given to Bolshevism. Let me repeat that I am happy to see that finally, today, Bolshevism is characterized as being the dictatorship of the proletariat. This being the case, one cannot deny that it is true socialism, because the dictatorship of the proletariat is not a specifically Russian invention. It is also found in the writings of the founders of modern scientific socialism. Is it a question of the form taken by this dictatorship? Speaking to me last night Citizen Rubanovich said, "But I support, as do you, the dictatorship of the proletariat . . . "

I.A. Rubanovich (Russia, Socialist Revolutionaries): Under certain conditions.

Loriot [continuing to paraphrase Rubanovich]: " . . . but what exists in Russia, as you can see for yourself if you go there, is not the dictatorship of the proletariat."

Rubanovich: It is the dictatorship of the sword!

Loriot: Perhaps. Citizens, we will go to Russia. If I do not go, others will, and their task there will be to find out if the forms of dictatorship that the Bolsheviks have been obliged to use were not caused precisely by the political conditions created by the counterrevolutionary propaganda of certain Socialists. They would need to find out if your own propaganda among the masses did not inevitably cause Lenin and Trotsky to exacerbate a dictatorship that is not in the spirit of their system, a dictatorship that they admit to being transitional, and which they maintain only as a result and to the degree of your counterrevolutionary efforts. (*Interruption*)

In any case, today two methods to achieve socialism have appeared on the stage. The first, which presupposes the dictatorship, is not new to socialism. It was foreseen and accepted by the International before the war. The second way to achieve socialism is that associated with the neosocialism of the war, which maintains that we can succeed in instituting socialism through a progressive evolution within democracy. But we know from experience all that we can expect from democracy. We are completely opposed to repeating that experience. If these were peaceful times, if these were still just theoretical discussions, we could perhaps examine whether the founders of the old International and of socialism might have made a mistake in visualizing the possibility of dictatorship. But, Russian citizens,[16] we are not at peace. This is not just the realm of theory. The dictatorship exists and the socialist regime is developing rapidly. The Russian proletariat has taken power — it has it, and holds it, (*"No!"*) and you who stand in contradiction to theory, in contradiction to all of historical determinism, you want to snatch away this power that the Russian proletariat holds in its hands. You want to wrench this power out of its hands in order to then reorganize the proletariat into an instrument of struggle to ultimately reconquer the power that it already holds in its hands! That is an anachronism.

"Of course," you say, "the revolution is premature, you cannot establish socialism in a country so economically disorganized." So then tell us, what is the criterion for establishing socialism in a democratic system? (*"Very good"*) I look forward with greatest interest to your coming up to this podium to tell us at what precise moment of economic development the proletariat may take power and if, on that day, the bourgeoisie, which controls the means of production and leisure, will consent to this substitution. There are no examples in history of a social class that was voluntarily dispossessed. Neither will the bourgeois masters simply give away their power, no matter what the level of development. And today I tell you this, Russian citizens: Never will the Russian proletariat, which holds power today, give it up. It will give up power only by force, only through counterrevolution. It will lose power only because of the Entente armies if they go to Russia. But they will go in vain.

Today the Russian proletariat has done so much for its socialist education, despite its prewar ignorance, that whatever the circumstances, whatever blows you deliver to what you call Bolshevism, the revolution and the socialism created by Bolshevism will rise from the ashes, whatever conditions you are able to inflict upon this unfortunate, impoverished proletariat. It is well-known that Russia lives in poverty, but poverty is found elsewhere and is not a specifically Russian phenomenon. The Bolsheviks have achieved a great deal in the last year and these accomplishments are what you want to destroy. (*"Such as what?"*) This achievement is what you want to put back into the hands of the bourgeoisie, only then to call on the proletariat to take it back again. That's a utopia! Whatever the circumstances, you will never succeed in destroying what the Russian revolution has accomplished! □

A resolution in defense of the Soviet republic had been submitted to the commission by Loriot, together with the French delegates Paul Faure, Louis-Oscar Frossard, and Raoul Verfeuil. At first Longuet also supported the resolution and proposed it in the commission session, but he then withdrew it, and it never reached the plenary session. The text of the resolution follows.

Draft Resolution of Frossard, Faure, Verfeuil, and Loriot[17]

The International Socialist Conference refuses to conduct a debate for the purpose of condemning dictatorship in the name of democracy, just as it would refuse to condemn democracy in the name of dictatorship, if such a proposal were made.

As the conference is neither empowered nor, because of the absence of several national sections, presently qualified to properly conduct a debate calling into question the legitimacy of the system established by the Soviet government, and considering that in some countries the state of siege and censorship would prevent gathering the information necessary to form an authoritative opinion, the conference believes that such a debate could not result in theoretical or practical conclusions of any real value.

But most importantly, the conference is of the opinion that even the act of questioning the legitimacy of a government that the capitalist classes of all countries are gunning for with implacable hatred would serve the purposes of those governments who dream of annihilating by economic blockade and military intervention that which we call Bolshevism, which is an attempt at liberation by the Russian workers and peasants.

In any case, given on the one hand that the blockade and intervention threaten the security and existence of the Russian revolution and its orderly development and, on the other, that the international proletariat has the right to be impartially informed about the socialist experiment that is taking place in the Soviet republic;

The conference declares that the duty of Socialist parties is to fight with all their energy to force their governments to withdraw from Russia and to discharge the troops still stationed there and to lift the blockade that is economically smothering the Russian people. The conference resolves that an international Socialist and workers' commission shall be charged as soon as possible to go to Russia to obtain there all the facts that alone will permit the International to form an informed and definitive opinion on the achievements and methods of the Russian revolution. □

Discussion (Continued)

Pavel Axelrod (Russia, Mensheviks): It seems that there are many comrades present who do not see us Russian Socialists as irrelevant. How else can I explain the applause that you have given me? Some people, out of bias or misunderstanding, try to construe our goals as if we came here to sit in judgment of the Bolsheviks and to provoke you to condemn them. And yet as long as six months ago we stressed that our proposal to send a commission to Russia aimed above all at ascertaining the truth and reporting to us according to the principle *audiatur et altera pars* [the other party should also be heard]. The Bolshevik press, above all their mouthpiece *Politiken* in Stockholm, tried to distort this opportunistic proposal of ours, as did the Berlin *Vorwärts*.[18] The proposal was presented as if we were prosecutors. I do not want to deny by this that I believe the Bolsheviks' entire conduct to show them to be in reality counterrevolutionaries who want to exercise a dictatorship over the proletariat. But it will not do for us simply to claim such a thing without investigating. We first must study the facts on the spot in Russia and get to the bottom of things. But it is far from our intention to make accusations. We do not want to sit in judgment of the Bolsheviks. . . .

We do not want to allow our proposal to be mixed up with a question of principle that really should be discussed for months in advance in order to be properly answered. Revolution and democracy are not contradictory in the Marxist view. It was Bolshevism that caused the confusion that we must now challenge. By tying our resolution to this question of principle, we will be robbed of the only opportunity to allow our hearts to speak. . . .

Friedrich Adler (Austria): . . . Since the problem of Bolshevism has been reopened here and the question of the East is under discussion, we must say that we are pained to see that not a word has been said against the barrier in the West or the imperialists there, and that we are unable to join together to discuss the blockade.[19] (*"Very true"*) We who are affected by it cannot raise the question. It was the duty of comrades from other countries to raise such a motion. That would have been real internationalism. (*Applause*) . . .

Comrades, the fact that the Italian Socialist Party is not represented here is a problem for us. Their conduct during the war was exemplary for the proletariat of all countries, and they refused to participate in this conference for reasons of principle. We want to keep the door open for the Italian comrades, so that we really can again unify the truly proletarian, class-conscious, Socialist forces into one International. And just as the Italian Socialists are not represented, so too even the Socialists of the country in which we meet, the Swiss comrades, are not represented. We do not want to embitter the Swiss comrades with rash judgments. Instead we want to make it possible for the comrades of all countries to return to and rejoin the International.

I know, comrades, there are those who would like to see the International split. There are such people among the Bolsheviks, just as there are among the right-wing comrades, who during this crisis want to continue working among peace-loving citizens for an International that is not disturbed by any thoughts of revolution.

And therefore comrades, we, as internationalists who during the war based all our policies upon internationalism, have a duty to struggle so that nothing happens at this conference that damages the International. . . .

We thought that no decision should be made here, because only one side can be heard and the accused are not present. I too have strong misgivings about the comrades in Russia who call themselves Bolsheviks, and I know that they are making mistakes. But it is one thing for me as a comrade to form a personal opinion and quite another for the International to take a position after hearing only one side. . . .

And when we hear that comrades in Russia are suffering, I am convinced that much injustice is being perpetrated. However, in the process we must not forget that before the October revolution there were also Russian comrades in jail under the government of those comrades who went with the Entente. So, Comrade Axelrod, you say it is fine to lock up others, and only bad if you yourself are locked up.

Pavel Axelrod: No, back then there were only a few, but now there are thousands.

Adler: Comrade Axelrod confirms that it is not only a question of quality, but of quantity. . . .

The question of Bolshevism is certainly very important, but we must note that the conference has passed over a much more fundamental issue. The important question is not so much the tactical method that the Bolsheviks have erroneously made into a principle. A much more important matter, in my opinion, is the historical question that we must understand today if the International is to remain capable of action — namely the question of whether capitalism can reconsolidate itself after the shock of the war. Then what methods are used to abolish capitalism becomes an extremely small question, and the issue becomes whether these people's chain of reasoning was correct.

Recently, I happened to come upon this question again in the minutes of the Stuttgart congress. It was Comrade Luxemburg who said, "If a world war breaks out, then the dominant system is digging its own grave; it will not recover again. Not only will the reaction and the monarchal system in Europe collapse, but the bell will toll for European capitalism as well."[20]

So, comrades, that is the problem that actually confronts us. I cannot say more on this subject since it is not on the agenda. But if I may touch on it briefly, the crux of the problem facing socialism really lies in the fact that the war so weakened capitalism in all of Europe, indeed in the whole world, that the dominant powers are ripe for overthrow. But on the other hand the war so ravaged and economically oppressed Europe that it certainly would be very difficult to build socialism under such war conditions. That is the problem, and the question is whether we should allow capitalism to recover, regain its strength, and restore its system; or whether those people are right who say that we should seize the moment and move now.

That is the central question. However, it is unfortunately not up for discussion at this conference. But that would be the main question that Socialists who have remained internationalists should take up first. □

Adler-Longuet Resolution[21]

The most important aspect of the policies that we tirelessly and vigorously championed throughout the war's long duration was to reestablish the international unity of the revolutionary class-conscious proletariat. This basic position of ours also determined our conduct at the Bern conference.

We note that the Bern conference invites criticism not so much because of the *content* of its resolutions as by the fact that these self-evident truths *came too late,* coming not *during* the war, but only *after* its conclusion.

The "Democracy and Dictatorship" resolution is an exception. The same forces that for four and a half years passively and actively obstructed international actions against the war, who felt they could forgo all international conferences, now hurry to use the conference in such a way that must necessarily multiply the International's problems. We protest against every attempt — however formulated — to decry the situation in the Russian Soviet republic, because we have nothing near a sufficient basis to make a judgment. We only know one thing for certain, which is that the disgraceful competition during the war between the press agencies of the Central Powers and the Entente to generate lies about the Russian Soviet republic is continuing unabatedly. In judging a political movement we do not want to become victims of the official slandermongers. Unfortunately, we also cannot rely solely on the reports of the Russian comrades present at the conference either, for they represent only a minority of the Russian proletariat. Without meaning to question their good faith, we must demand that the International stick to the old principle that both sides must be heard before a decision can be made.

The Bern conference is an initial and still very weak attempt at international collaboration. Entire parties, such as the Italian, Serbian, Romanian, and Swiss stayed away. Others decided to participate only very reluctantly. We cautioned against every resolution that would interfere with the future reunification of the proletariat of all countries. We wanted to keep the door open to class conscious, revolutionary, Socialist parties of all countries. No one listened to our warning. We do not want to become accomplices in schemes against the International and will therefore vote against the resolution, because certain sections can be exploited by the bourgeoisie against the Russian revolution. □

Discussion (Continued)

Rubanovich: With all our heart and soul we tell you that it is wrong to believe that an experiment in implementing socialism is being carried out in Russia. Even before the war the economy there was very backward, and now the war has heaped ruins upon ruins. In order to avert the sad disillusionment that threatens socialism in the most advanced countries, it is our duty to tear off the false labels and show reality as it is, so that socialism does not fall victim to false appearances.

We speak of the dictatorship of the proletariat. What conscious

Socialist, be he a disciple of Peter Lavrov or of Karl Marx,[22] does not know that the evolution of modern capitalist society must at a given moment culminate in the dictatorship of the working class? History teaches us, and it is a truth that has become trite, that every class, once it arrives at a certain stage of development, overturns the old equilibrium and secures new forms of economic, legal, and social life, using constraints whose forms depend upon the general level of this or that country. But this dictatorship is possible only to break the resistance of a minority, to proclaim the new order accepted by the conscious majority.

Loriot: In a private conversation you told me you were a supporter of the dictatorship of the proletariat.

Rubanovich: Yes, I told you more than that. Lenin, who dreams of soon becoming the Dalai Lama of the world dictatorship, considers only you to be worthy of being his representative in the French Soviet Republic.

Loriot: That would be an honor for me, but I regret that we are not that far along yet.

Rubanovich: I agree with you, Loriot. We are not that far along yet.

Scientific socialism, which yesterday Lenin still supported, as opposed to "utopian and sentimental" socialism, explained that the dictatorship of the proletariat could arise only after the ripening of conditions and of men. First, production has to have attained a superior level of development, stimulating modern creative forces to the maximum. Second, the working class itself, developing within a democratic society that guarantees all freedoms, developing its autonomous trade union organizations and cooperatives, must attain a sufficient level of maturity to feel able to assume responsibility for administering this high level of production under conditions that would assure to the overwhelming majority of the nation, and all the producers of wealth, a life of physical and intellectual well-being superior to that which bourgeois society is capable of offering them.

These are the two preconditions. Without them — as the disciples of Karl Marx, Frederick Engels, Kautsky, and others have repeated quite sufficiently — any attempt to establish the dictatorship of the proletariat can only end in disaster.

"The worst misfortune that could befall us," Engels said, "is to take power prematurely."[23]

That is the misfortune that has befallen Soviet Russia. Taking advantage of the destruction, the weariness of the Russian people, and the triumph of the Prussian armies, a handful of fanatics seized power and, currying the favor of a crazed mob of lumpens and of the army in rout, proclaimed the dictatorship of the proletariat. A bureaucracy surpassing that of the tsarist regime installed itself with an abundance of red tape and a veritable frenzy of decrees to impose an arbitrary course onto the life of a nation of 150 million people.

Instead of socializing the land, which our party was preparing to carry out in the Constituent Assembly and which required a strong organization of democratic self-government and a strong class-consciousness, the land was given to lumpen day-laborers with instructions to plunder. It was nothing less than a declaration of war against the working peasants aimed at snatching the product of their labors.

And the irony is that, under the label of communism, we already see the appearance of a strong class of enriched peasants who seek refuge from the pillage in private property and a strong reactionary power.

In the cities, industry is dying, workers' control is reduced to naught, and these impotent dictators already dream of replacing this workers' control with some kind of dictatorship by the foremen. Incapable of running the factories, they make desperate appeals to intellectuals whom yesterday they were shooting in droves, and to whom exorbitant promises are made today, provided that they lend their assistance not to the dictatorship *of* the proletariat but, as Axelrod said, to the dictatorship *over* the proletariat. And this proletariat has become nothing less than a parasite vegetating at the expense of the national treasury, which in turn manipulates the level of promissory notes and prints fake money by the hundreds of billions.

Workers' control on paper; in reality the collapse of production and closing of factories. Socialization of the land on paper; in reality plunder and massacre of working peasants. Soviet rule on paper; in reality the arbitrary bureaucracy of an army of petty tyrants and the submission of short-lived assemblies to mercenary Red Guards made up of Chinese and Letts, of Hungarian, German, Turkish, and Bulgarian prisoners. The leaders, who look like statesmen from afar, up close are nothing but followers of the vacillating moods of the masses, who through war are familiar with death, which they inflict and accept with a common contempt for human life.

That is why the genuine theoreticians of scientific socialism declared that a premature seizure of power would be a disaster for the working class. This Bolshevik power is not a dictatorship; it is tyranny by the lumpen mobs. This is not working-class power, it is a hideous mixture of panic and naive candor, of terrorism feeding on fear. . . .

Karl Kautsky: . . . The situation today is that production has been entirely disrupted and we have been reduced to dire poverty. What the workers need is to get production going again, and so they ask themselves which system is better suited to this: capitalism or socialism. The question now is whether capitalism or socialism proves itself to be the more productive system. If socialism cannot do it, then it has lost its case. If socialism is not capable of getting production going again, and that means getting it going better than capitalism can, then capitalism will rise again. That is why we must ask ourselves whether the Bolshevik method of getting production moving again was correct. Theoretical considerations speak against it.

I have also received a range of information that totally corresponds with facts that the Bolsheviks themselves concede. It is said that the Bolsheviks have not instituted socialism, but instead have nearly destroyed those foundations for socialism as already existed in Russia. . . . The Bolsheviks have also both demoralized and corrupted the proletariat. A portion of the proletariat has drifted into the countryside and become peasants. Another portion leads a grueling existence under a reign of terror, while a third portion enjoys the status of a privileged class, living at the cost of society — a class similar to the proletariat in ancient Rome. The only thing the Bolsheviks have managed to do, and this has been their big success, is to create a strong army. The Bolsheviks wanted to institute socialism but instead created a new form of militarism. . . .

But I do not consider it out of the question for the Bolsheviks to return to the fold. I hope they will, as they have many comrades who are very effective and knowledgeable, and who would enrich the International. How do we hold the door open for them? On the one hand they are very intolerant and ruthless, but on the other hand they are not at all dogmatists who cling to convictions. On the contrary, they have shown themselves to be very flexible. They showed that by supporting democratic principles until the day that they failed to win a majority in the Constituent Assembly. Since then they have made one concession after another, not concessions to democracy mind you, but, for now, to capitalism and militarism. However, I am convinced that they will also make concessions to democracy and will eventually arrive at the same standpoint as us. Then those in western Europe who support Bolshevism will also come over.

It is said that we should not supply arms against the Russian revolution. No, we should not, but the Bolsheviks are not the Russian revolution, and the Entente does not come to us looking for the arguments they need against the Russian revolution. We are conducting this discussion here in full consideration of the impact on the Russian revolutionaries themselves. We must not forget that there are two tendencies in Russia, and that the trial between them is not being conducted here. The dispute between the Russian Bolsheviks and the other Socialists revolves around which of the two methods is better. The more we support Russia's democratic Socialists, the stronger they will be. Today they feel weak because they feel abandoned by the German Socialists. But if we strengthen them, then we are strengthening the democratic forces against the Bolsheviks and thereby removing the Entente's best pretext for intervening against Russia. We are not supplying weapons to the Entente, instead we are supplying weapons to Russia's democratic Socialists, with which to fight against the internal as well as the external enemy. Therein, I believe, lies our duty. . . .

Eduard Bernstein (Germany):[24] At the beginning of his speech, Comrade Kautsky raised an objection to identifying or equating Bolshevism with the revolution and the proletariat. I can only concur, as Bolshevism is at best a certain form of the revolution or a certain phase, but never the revolution itself.

Bolshevism is only a certain phase, and not a pretty one at that. And how did this phase begin? The Bolshevik government was the first socialist regime that had peacefully demonstrating workers shot down with machine guns.[25] The Bolshevik government was the first to simply lock up Socialists of other persuasions — Socialists who are not putschists, but who were robbed of their rights outside the law and in breach of the law, repeating in all this things previously done by reactionary governments. In Russia Socialists, comrades who were at many international congresses and who have fought for socialism all their lives, are locked up and robbed of their rights. I am astonished that at a Socialist congress, which certainly otherwise stands up for the rights of all citizens, not a word of indignation is to be heard over this.

In the spring of 1918 the reactionaries in the Reichstag held up the Bolsheviks to us, the German Socialists and said, "those are your people who are locking people up and suppressing freedom of the press." Our friend Haase took the floor and defended the Bolsheviks. For this the Bolsheviks cut him down and explained, "Oh yes, we do suppress, we do lock up, we do all that. We have two sets of standards for justice and morality." The Bolsheviks have an excuse, of course; they claim that the Mensheviks and Socialist Revolutionaries are the counterrevolutionaries. Now that is easy to say, but in truth the Bolsheviks were the counterrevolutionaries. They were in Russia then and they are in Germany today.

No matter how savage, how radical, how destructive they are, destruction alone is never the revolution. In fact, the Bolshevik system is the death of the revolution's gains. It means disorganization, wrack, and ruin for the country. Now you want to send a fact-finding commission to Russia. Fine; I am not against it, but it is not necessary. We need only to read the Bolsheviks' own reports, we need only to read their government's own statistics on the state of finances and of social life as a whole, to see that a rotten, fraudulent system is at the helm, a system that compromises itself further by trying, after having bankrupted its own country, to pull other countries into this bankruptcy. . . .

You have seen that in Russia the Bolsheviks, who thought they had dealt militarism a deathblow, have actually created, strengthened, and expanded a new militarism, with tsarist generals and tsarist officers,[26] a praetorian guard, to hold the revolution down in their own country and expand their activity across the world.

But then those who thought they could deal capitalism a deathblow find themselves forced to reestablish it. A new capitalist class has arisen, truly not better, but instead considerably worse, consisting of those who speculate on the people's misery. They have become Russia's new bourgeoisie, in part with the help of the Bolsheviks. That is the truth of the matter. The Bolsheviks did not get rid of corruption in Russia, but rather strengthened it and now want to extend it to the International, to all countries. This must also be mentioned, because when we look around, we find that we already have this corruption in Germany: beliefs are for sale, rubles for travel, just like under the tsar.

I regret having to speak in such terms, but from this podium I must protest against the way Bolshevism has been equated with socialism.

Once again I say to you that many of us have seen Bolshevism at work; how in Russia it has led to depopulating the cities and to ruining the factories — a situation that would be even worse if it happened to us and reduced our proletariat to misery by the millions.

Once again I protest against the identification of Socialists with the Bolsheviks in any way, as has happened here. □

After the discussion, each delegation stated which resolution it supported, and the resulting list was published as a form of indicative vote. The minority text from the commission, submitted by Adler and

Longuet, was supported by the majority of French delegates, half the Austrian delegates, by the delegations of Ireland, the Netherlands, Norway, and Spain, and by a Greek delegate. The resolution of the commission majority received the support of both the SPD and USPD delegations from Germany, as well as the French minority, half the Austrians, and delegates from Sweden, Russia (in exile), Britain, and several smaller countries.[27]

The conference established a special commission to visit Soviet Russia to investigate political and economic conditions. The Soviet Government agreed to permit this commission to come, but the Allied governments refused to issue passports, and the mission did not take place.

A Standing Committee was also established, formed of two representatives from each party, and led by an Action Committee of Branting, Henderson, and Huysmans. The Standing Committee held two conferences in 1919 and prepared an international congress that was ultimately convened in July 1920. By that time, the fears of Adler and Longuet had been confirmed regarding the depth of sympathy for Soviet Russia in the ranks of Socialist parties outside Russia. The left-wing and centrist parties that refused to attend the Bern conference were now joined by the USPD and the French, Norwegian, Spanish, United States, and Austrian parties in rejecting invitations to the 1920 congress. The congress did give birth to an international organization that claimed to be a revived "Second International," but whose positions had little in common with those of the Second International before 1914. Its membership was limited, initially at least, to a narrow range of Social Democratic parties grouped around the SPD and the British Labour Party.

Notes

1. Merle Fainsod, *International Socialism and the World War* (Garden City, N.Y.: Anchor Books, 1969), p. 243

2. Fainsod, *International Socialism*, p. 249-50. The Bolsheviks' appeal of December 24, 1918, concerning the Bern conference is printed in chapter 9 of the present work.

3. Excerpted from a statement by Oddino Morgari, quoting Lazzari, printed in *The Communist International*, no. 2, June 1919, col. 232.

4. For a Bolshevik account of the conference, see Zinoviev's report, "The Bern Conference and Our Attitude to the Socialist Currents," printed in John Riddell, ed., *The Founding of the Communist International* (New York: Monad Press, 1986), chapter 7, a volume of *The Communist International in Lenin's Time*. Other accounts can be found in Fainsod, *International Socialism*, pp.

247-57; and Arno J. Mayer, *Politics and Diplomacy of Peacemaking: Containment and Counterrevolution at Versailles, 1918-1919* (New York: Alfred A. Knopf, 1967), pp. 373-409.

5. Gerhard A. Ritter, ed., *Die II Internationale 1918/1919: Protokolle, Memoranden, Berichte und Korrespondenzen* (West Berlin: Verlag J.H.W. Dietz Nachf., 1980), p. 202.

6. Ritter, *Die II Internationale*, p. 316; Fainsod, *International Socialism*, pp. 250-51.

7. *Die Resolutionen der Internationalen Arbeiter- und Sozialistenkonferenz in Bern (3.-10. Februar, 1919)* (Basel: A.C. Jünger, [1919]), pp. 4-5. For the resolutions of the Second International on this topic adopted between 1907 and 1912, see John Riddell, ed., *Lenin's Struggle for a Revolutionary International: Documents, 1907-1916; The Preparatory Years,* (New York: Monad Press, 1984), pp. 33-35, 69-70, 88-90, a volume of *The Communist International in Lenin's Time.*

8. *Die Resolutionen*, pp. 5-7. For the 1907 resolution and debate of the Second International on colonialism, see Riddell, *Lenin's Struggle*, pp. 7-9.

9. Mayer, *Politics and Diplomacy*, pp. 399-400.

10. The proceedings of the commission are described in Robert F. Wheeler, "The Failure of 'Truth and Clarity' at Berne: Kurt Eisner, the Opposition and the Reconstruction of the International," in *International Review of Social History,* vol. 18, part 2, 1973, pp. 185-190.

11. Except as noted, all Bern conference resolutions and excerpts from proceedings have been translated from Ritter, *Die II Internationale*, pp. 500-553.

12. According to the French Socialist leader Pierre Renaudel, this resolution was approved by a five-to-two vote in the subcommission, receiving his support and that of Branting, Eisner, Sukhomlin, and Wels. Adler and Longuet voted against, while Axelrod and MacDonald abstained. (Pierre Renaudel, *L'Internationale à Berne: Faits et Documents* [Paris: Bernard Grasset, 1919], p. 133.)

13. MacDonald's speech is recorded in English in the conference proceedings.

14. The translation of Loriot's declaration and his remarks to the conference have been compared with the version printed in *L'Internationale Communiste*, no. 2, 1919, pp. 269-70 and edited accordingly.

15. The reference is to the resolution condemning reformism that was adopted by the 1904 congress of the Second International in Amsterdam.

16. Loriot is addressing the Russian emigré delegates in the hall.

17. Translated from Renaudel, *L'Internationale à Berne*, pp. 131-32. Faure's name as a sponsor of the resolution is omitted by Renaudel, but included with the resolution in *The Communist International*, no. 2, June 1919, col. 235-38.

18. The August 28, 1918, issue of the SPD daily *Vorwärts* commented on the Menshevik proposal by stating, "Should the International soon display renewed viability, as we hope it does, it would be the worst imaginable misuse of it for it to become the prosecutor of those of its members who first made the practical attempt to convert socialism into reality for an entire people. We have frequently and emphatically criticized the mistakes and errors of the Bolsheviks in these columns. But however little we agree with the Bolsheviks' methods, we highly respect their courage and the purity of their convictions. A new International that began by prosecuting the Bolsheviks would thereby put itself in the worst possible light from the outset."

This response by *Vorwärts* reflected the SPD's attempts, at a time when German imperialism neared collapse, to rebuild its base among working people, among whom the Soviet republic was very popular.

19. The reference is to the continuing Allied blockade against the Central Powers.

20. No such statement by Rosa Luxemburg can be found in the proceedings of the 1907 Stuttgart International Socialist Congress. Only one intervention by her was recorded, made in the commission on militarism and international conflicts. (See Riddell, *Lenin's Struggle*, pp. 31-32.)

Adler and Luxemburg both participated in the subcommission on this topic, where no stenographic record was made. He is possibly referring to a comment made by Luxemburg in that subcommission.

21. The Adler-Longuet resolution was also signed by Marcel Cachin, Paul Faure, Louis-Oscar Frossard, Paul Mistral, Adrien Pressemane, and Raoul Verfeuil (France), Olav Scheflo and Martin Tranmael (Norway), Johnson and O'Shannon (Ireland), Petridis (Greece), and Joseph Herzfeld (Germany).

22. Peter Lavrov was a spokesman for nineteenth-century Russian populism.

23. In 1850 Frederick Engels wrote: "The worst thing that can befall the leader of an extreme party is to be compelled to assume power at a time when the movement is not yet ripe for the domination of the class he represents and for the measures this domination implies." (Engels, "The Peasant War in Germany," in Marx and Engels *Collected Works* [New York: International Publishers, 1978], vol. 10, p. 469.)

Three years later, Engels wrote Joseph Weydemeyer that, "I have a feeling that one fine day, thanks to the helplessness and spinelessness of all the others, our party will find itself forced into power, whereupon it will have to enact things that are not immediately in our own, but rather in the general, revolutionary and specifically petty-bourgeois interest; in which event, spurred on by the proletarian *populus* and bound by our own published statements and plans — more or less wrongly interpreted and more or less impulsively pushed through in the midst of party strife — we shall find ourselves compelled to make communist experiments and leaps which no one knows better than ourselves to be untimely." (Marx and Engels, *Collected Works*, vol. 39, pp. 308-9.)

24. Bernstein, while not an official delegate to the conference, spoke on behalf of the SPD delegation, which had been compelled to leave the conference before its conclusion. A USPD member since 1917, Bernstein had rejoined the SPD in December 1918 and was a member of both parties at the time of the Bern conference. The following month, a ruling of a USPD congress obliged him to choose between the two parties, and he chose the SPD.

25. While Bernstein did not say what "workers' demonstration" he was referring to, he probably had in mind the most publicized case of action taken against an anti-Soviet demonstration: the dispersal of the Right Socialist Revolutionary march held on January 18 (5), 1918, the day the Constituent Assembly convened in Petrograd. Right SRs had seen in the assembly's convocation an opening to overturn the Soviet government and had made preparations for an armed insurrection. These were cancelled late in the day by the Right SR leadership. Nonetheless, it decided to go forward with a mass demonstration on an "unarmed" basis.

Socialist Revolutionary historian Boris Sokolov, a partisan of the Constituent Assembly, admitted that most demonstrators came from privileged sections of the population and were motivated more by hatred of Bolshevism than by sympathy for the Constituent Assembly.

Regarding the debate over the Constituent Assembly, Bolshevik writer Victor Serge stated that in factories where Socialist Revolutionary influence was predominant, "the SRs who came to urge a struggle against the Bolsheviks were rudely received. They were asked if they couldn't reach some better understanding with the Bolsheviks, who are devoted to the people's cause."

On January 18, the day of the SR march, "petty-bourgeois citizens ... thronged the main thoroughfares of the city." The SR-sponsored march was "both numerous and pathetic," Serge wrote. "A few rifle-shots fired here and there by the sailors scattered this ineffectual crowd, deserted and disarmed as it was by irresolute leaders. In Sokolov's words, 'it was absurd, ridiculous.'" (Victor Serge, *Year One of the Russian Revolution* [Chicago: Holt, Rinehart and Winston, 1972], pp. 130-31.)

Although the demonstration was supposed to be "unarmed," the January 20 (7) issue of *Pravda* reported that a quantity of revolvers and bombs had been collected from arrested participants.

26. The Soviet Red Army enlisted many thousands of former officers from the tsarist army, who served under the supervision of political commissars.

27. Renaudel, *L'Internationale à Berne,* p. 133.

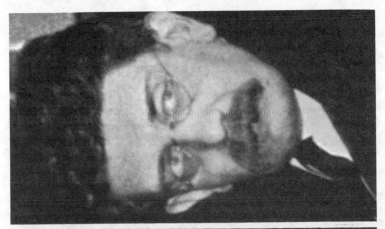

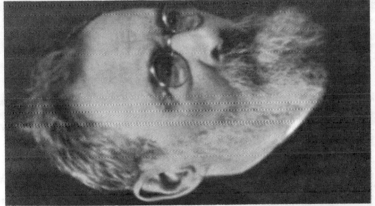

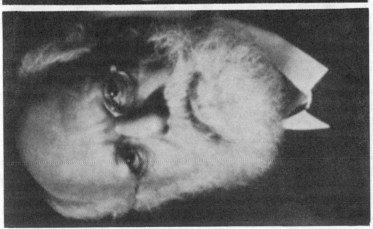

Karl Kautsky, Pavel Axelrod, Friedrich Adler.

Lenin dedicates Marx-Engels monument, November 7, 1918.

-9-
Preparing the First Communist Congress

The Bolsheviks viewed the establishment of a workers' and peasants' regime in Russia as only one link in the chain of world revolution. "The final victory of socialism in a single country is of course impossible," V.I. Lenin explained to a Soviet congress on January 24 (11), 1918. "Our contingent of workers and peasants which is upholding Soviet power is one of the contingents of the great world army, which at present has been split by the world war, but which is striving for unity."[1]

Doing everything possible to organize and inspire that world army was an urgent task of the new Soviet government. "Every piece of information," Lenin continued, "every fragment of a report about our revolution, every name, the proletariat greets with loud and sympathetic cheers, because it knows that in Russia the common cause is being pursued, the cause of the proletariat's uprising, the international socialist revolution."[2]

Leon Trotsky, who had been the first people's commissar for foreign affairs, emphasized this same theme in an address to a Soviet congress in March 1919. "If the peoples of Europe do not arise and crush imperialism," he stated, "we shall be crushed — that is beyond doubt. Either the Russian revolution will raise the whirlwind of struggle in the west, or the capitalists of all countries will stifle our struggle."[3]

In the first year of Soviet rule, the work of the foreign affairs commissariat combined three tasks. It conducted the Soviet republic's diplomatic affairs with other governments. It coordinated the mobilization of international solidarity with Soviet Russia. And it sought to advance the organization of revolutionary political forces around the world into a new International with a communist program and strate-

---

Footnotes to this chapter begin on page 466.

gy.[4] After the founding of the Communist International in March 1919, these tasks were increasingly divided among various bodies of the Soviet state, the Communist Party, and the new world revolutionary organization.

In December 1917 the Soviet government placed two million rubles at the disposal of the newly formed foreign affairs commissariat for the needs of the international revolutionary movement. A few weeks later the commissariat established a section for international propaganda headed by Karl Radek. In Stockholm, the Bolshevik Party's secretariat abroad published information on Soviet Russia. Inside the Soviet republic, newspapers were published in Czech, German, Hungarian, Romanian, Serbian, and Turkish to reach the more than two million prisoners of war held in Russia, and to encourage the formation of Communist currents among them.[5] Educational work was also directed at the large numbers of foreign workers in Russia, some of them from western Europe, but many more from Persia, China, and Korea.

On February 6 (January 24), 1918, a small conference was held in Russia of representatives of left Socialist parties. Present were central leaders of the Bolsheviks and the Left Socialist Revolutionaries from Russia and of the Swedish Left Social Democrats, and representatives from parties in Norway, Poland, Romania, Serbia, and other countries. The conference decided to reject invitations to the upcoming Third Inter-Allied Labor and Socialist Conference, organized by the Social Democratic parties backing the war, and to convene rapidly an international conference of revolutionary Socialists. These plans soon had to be suspended, however, because of the offensive against the Soviet republic opened by the German imperial regime on February 18 and the subsequent military intervention of the Allied powers against Soviet Russia.[6]

Defense of the world's first workers' and peasants' republic against imperialist intervention and internal counterrevolution was a pressing task not only of Russian workers and peasants but of the entire international proletariat. Thus, during 1918 more than 50,000 workers and soldiers in Soviet Russia from outside the old tsarist empire enlisted in the ranks of the Red Army.[7]

That same year the Russian Communist Party established the Federation of Foreign Groups, which included nine organizations: Czech, British-American, French, Romanian, German, Hungarian, South Slav, Polish, and Bulgarian. In their educational work, these groups reached out not only to workers of these countries resident in Russia but to the soldiers of the imperialist armies invading Soviet territory.

During 1918 the revolution that opened with the victory in Russia rapidly spread eastward among the oppressed Asian peoples of the old tsarist empire. Various communist organizations emerged among these peoples and came together in Soviet-wide conferences in March and June 1918. In November 1918 they affiliated to the Russian party, forming the Central Bureau of Muslim Organizations of the RCP. Revolutionary organizations were also established among the more than 200,000 Chinese workers in Russia, who had been condemned by tsarism to a pariah status. Chinese workers won to communism formed the first Chinese communist cells and built the 60,000-member Union of Chinese Workers in Russia.

The few diplomatic outposts that Soviet Russia had been able to establish abroad were mobilized in an urgent educational effort to rally solidarity and support for the Soviet government. In August 1918, for example, a small group of revolutionary Italians, former prisoners of war, left Russia to do political work in their homeland. They carried with them a letter from Lenin asking the Soviet ambassador in Switzerland, J.A. Berzin, to assist them.

"It is necessary to exercise the maximum caution and help them in every way to organise work *and publications* among Italians, in the Italian language," Lenin wrote. "For God's sake, *do not grudge* money for publications (in German, French, Italian and English) and be quick, be quick.

"It is a critical moment here: the struggle against the British and Czechoslovaks, and the kulaks. The fate of the revolution is being decided."[8]

As the revolutionary wave mounted in central Europe in October 1918, Lenin appealed again to Berzin to press this work forward:

"Too little! Too little!! Too little!!! *Engage* a group of translators and publish ten times as much. . . .

"You have *plenty* of money. . . . We shall give *more and still more, in plenty.* Write how much.

"*N.B.* Collect a set of Spartakusbund . . . and republish the entire set *in 4 languages.* Also Junius and Liebknecht."[9]

This internationalist work encompassed collaboration with working-class organizations abroad, including some whose leadership opposed Bolshevik policies. The Soviet ambassador in Germany, A.A. Joffe, supplied the USPD leadership there with material for parliamentary speeches, and, as Joffe later explained, with "material assistance from us for the publishing projects on which our writers collaborated with them." He also supplied significant sums of money for the purchase of arms.[10] In December 1918, when the USPD leadership was participating in Germany's capitalist government and defending the exclusion of the Soviet ambassador from Germany, Joffe wrote a detailed account of this collaboration and support for the Soviet daily, *Izvestiya*.

The outbreak of revolution in central Europe in October and November 1918 led to the formation of Communist parties and currents in many countries of central and western Europe. In German Austria a Communist party was founded on November 3. Returning prisoners of war established the Hungarian Communist Party on November 24. The Polish party was launched on December 15 through a unification of three currents with a long revolutionary tradition: the two wings of the Social Democracy of the Kingdom of Poland and Lithuania and the Polish Socialist Party–Left. The organization of a party in Germany followed on December 30.

In Bulgaria, the Netherlands, and Sweden revolutionary parties that had split away from opportunist currents before October 1917 declared their support for Bolshevism. In Norway, Italy, and Serbia the mass parties of the old Second International had been propelled in their majority toward revolutionary positions and claimed sympathy with Bolshevik principles. In Switzerland, a pro-Bolshevik current was contesting for leadership of the Socialist Party. Minority pro-Bolshevik currents were gaining influence in the Socialist parties of France and the United States. Many currents of anarcho-syndicalist origin were now attracted to Bolshevism, such as the tendency in France led by Pierre Monatte and Alfred Rosmer and the Industrial Workers of the World (IWW) in the United States and some other countries.

Communist parties were being formed among the oppressed peoples on the borderlands of the old tsarist empire, reflecting Bolshevism's growing influence among the oppressed masses of Asia. The Communist movement's expansion outside Europe was also symbolized by the foundation early in January 1919 by Argentinian revolutionists of the Internationalist Socialist Party, which was to become the Communist party of that country.

The Bolsheviks now speeded efforts to organize these forces into a new International. Large internationalist rallies were held in Moscow (December 5) and Petrograd (December 19), featuring speakers from many national Communist groups within Russia. The proceedings of the Petrograd meeting were translated into several languages for international distribution.[11]

The renowned Russian Socialist author Maxim Gorky chaired the Petrograd rally, and the speakers included the Bolshevik leader Gregory

Zinoviev; members of Socialist parties in the United States and six countries of Europe; representatives of German and Austrian prisoners of war; and speakers of six nationalities from revolutionary groups recently formed among Asian workers in Russia. In addition, soldiers from the United States, England, and Scotland, who had been sent with armies of intervention to overturn Soviet power and then captured by the Red Army, spoke in defense of the Soviet government.

Most of these speakers also addressed the first Comintern congress held in Moscow four months later, and their reports can be found in the proceedings of that congress.[12] The following are the remarks of three of the speakers at the Petrograd rally who did not attend the later congress.

"The Russian People Have an Ally in India"[13]

Achmed (representative of India): I speak in the name of 330,000,000 Indian people oppressed by British imperialism. And I wish to express my deep gratitude for the opportunity to visit with you, to see the success of the Russian proletarian movement, and to speak to you about my country. I only regret that I do not have time to reveal to you all the terrible details on how the British oppress the many millions of Indian people. Please understand that however difficult it was for you to get the better of your autocracy, it will be even more difficult for the unfortunate Indian people to beat back foreign imperialism! In India every year millions of Indians literally die of hunger, despite the fact that the country is fertile and unlike Russia today is not being blockaded on all sides by her enemies. If the Indian people are perishing, it is solely because British imperialism is squeezing out our life blood. Everything that the Indian people need, they export to Europe.

I have heard and I know what a fearful struggle is being waged against the Russian liberation movement, but the words of the preceding speaker, the British representative, have convinced me that the Russian people have not only enemies but allies as well, and such an ally is the people in whose name I now speak. This people, worn out and exhausted with suffering, thirsting for freedom from imperialist oppression, understands the aspirations and sufferings of the Russian people, shares their ideals, and hopes that the time will come when they will be able to provide real help. I want to call your attention to the following: the British representative, Comrade Fineberg, had the floor before me. I do not see him as an enemy, but on the contrary, as my brother in struggle. For the enemy of the Indian and

British toiling peoples is not the British but the British imperialists.

Once again, thank you for your hospitality. I am confident that the united efforts of all oppressed peoples will succeed in securing the triumph of justice, freedom, and socialism on this earth. □

"The Flames Ignited by the Soviets Will Spread to Iran"[14]

Rejeb Bombi (Heydar Khan 'Amu Ughli): Comrades and brothers, I bring you greetings from the revolutionary toilers of Iran. I bring greetings to Soviet Russia, which has raised the banner of the liberation of the toiling classes and peoples of the world against the oppression and exploitation of international capital.

Comrades, our national poet has composed the following lines against the exploiting classes:

"By turning your face to the wicked
Relying on them for your betterment,
You sacrifice your own birthright
You nurture vipers at your bosom."

Comrades, to conciliate with the bourgeoisie, to look to it in hopes of betterment, is to nurture a viper.

Comrades, we are the children of the people, and we fight for the rights of the people. The capitalists are our enemies, and we seek no reconciliation with them. They strangle the revolutionary movement and suck the blood of the toiling masses. In the struggle against the oppressors, there is only death or victory. We are certain that the flames ignited by the land of the soviets will spread to revolutionary Iran.

Since Russia was ruled by a tsarist autocracy during the recent upheaval in Iran,[15] the people of Russia are not acquainted with these events. Therefore, I must tell you a bit about the aggression of your bourgeoisie against us and about some aspects of Iranian history.

Comrades, our country, Iran, was plundered from two sides: on one side by a clique of European capitalists and on the other by a clique of Asiatic plunderers. The European clique was composed of Russian and British capitalists who came to Iran. They were granted concessions by the government, and they rented whole villages and regions from the state or from landowners and feudal lords. They proceeded to arm some hoodlums and common criminals and to obtain arms from their respective embassies. These armed thugs were then sent to threaten the lives, property, and dignity of the people. During the harvest season, they would steal the whole crop, leaving nothing for the peasants. These peasants had to join the refugees who were forced to leave their country for foreign lands in search of work and a piece of bread for their families. Most of these impoverished peasant families died of hunger or cold.

The Asiatic clique was worse. The shah's friends and servants occupied themselves plundering provinces and regions. A large region would be sold to an influential person. He, in turn, through his bailiffs and servants, could deal with the peasants in any way he desired. The people became increasingly discontented with that situation. Soon, various constitutionalist and republican groups were formed.[16] The first goal of these freedom fighters was to eliminate the most heartless of all enemies of the people, the shah.[17] After his assassination, the regime launched a campaign of persecution and terror throughout Iran. Liberation was blocked, but underground and secret activity continued. Ten years later, Iran saw this movement rise again; the modern revolution was organized, and after a series of revolutionary struggles, the constitution was adopted and constitutional government was established.

The imperialists could not tolerate such freedom and the constitution for long. They decided to put an end to democracy and crush the revolution in Iran. The situation there was not acceptable to British imperialism because it could no longer extract major concessions. Trying with all their power to destroy the first Iranian revolution, the British imperialists used the tsar's arms and soldiers on occasion to suppress the Iranian revolution. This policy continued after the February revolution, since Kerensky, the head of the Provisional Government, was a puppet of British imperialism. Only the October revolution granted liberty to the peoples of the East.

The emergence of socialist Russia proved to the world the truth and essence of Bolshevism.

The October revolution annulled the 1907 agreement between Britain and Russia.[18] It ended all expansionist designs of imperialist Russia and recalled the Russian army from Iran, thus beginning to lay the foundation for a socialist world.

Comrades! Today, after the victory of the October revolution, we count you as our friends and brothers. And as brothers, we must help each other. Dear comrades, we have succeeded in organizing 13,800 Iranians into the ranks of our Red Army. We are pleased that we can look forward to enjoying further relations between today's Russia and revolutionary Iran.

Comrades, let us fight our common enemy shoulder to shoulder. We will be able to organize up to a hundred thousand into the Iranian

Red Army. (*Shouts of "Hurrah!" Prolonged, standing ovation*)

We will struggle in your ranks. Meanwhile, we will send groups of propagandists and agitators from Iran to India. When the Iranian and Indian revolutions unite, British imperialism will be destroyed. (*Applause*) Comrades, we, the delegates from the East at this gathering, have a common goal in this struggle against our common enemy. We thank you for the opportunity to present these facts to the Soviet peoples. (*Prolonged ovation*) □

"We Were Sent from America to Fight the Russian People"[19]

Halders (a young American worker, the first American soldier to be taken as a prisoner from the camp where capitalism holds sway and brought into the socialist camp): I left America thinking we were being sent to fight Germany. Our transport of twelve vessels left New York for Liverpool on July 16. In England we were told that we would be taken to London and then to the French front, in order to avoid sailing on British waters because of the mines. On August 21, however, our Eighty-fifth Division was sent to Arkhangelsk instead of to France. They claimed to be taking us there to guard the railroad. As a matter of fact, after our arrival in Arkhangelsk on September 16, we were sent to the Russian front to fight against the Russian people. We were assured that the Russians were stealing provisions, ammunition, metals, and arms, and in general everything they could carry off in order to take it to Germany. "If you are taken prisoner by them," they said about the Russians, "they will have no mercy on you whatsoever; they'll finish you off, like animals."

In November we were surrounded by Russians and taken prisoner. We thought the end was near. When I was turned over to the Russians by order of an officer, to my great surprise, I got a reception such as I had never known in the division. It was then that I realized why they were fabricating wild stories about the Russians!

I had the great pleasure of being in Vologda on the anniversary of the October revolution, and I must express my surprise at the work that the Russian people did during those months, despite the long time they spent in ignorance and backwardness and without schools under the former government. In conclusion, I only want to say that I wish the greatest future success to the Russian Soviet Federated Socialist Republic. Through your example the red flag soon will be waving everywhere, all over the world, for the good of all the toiling people! Whatever happens when I return to America, for my part, I will do everything possible to help raise this banner there too and to win for American workers the means to enjoy true freedom and the fruits of their labor. □

By December 1918 the Russian Communist Party leadership judged that the formation of Communist parties in a significant number of countries over the previous year had already created the new revolutionary International as a living, fighting force. Thus, they explained, the time had arrived to give their new International an organizational structure. That same month the Social Democratic parties in the Entente countries issued the call for their international conference, then planned for Lausanne, Switzerland, and ultimately held in Bern. The reformists clearly hoped to claim for themselves the political continuity of the pre-1914 Second International. This challenge was an additional reason to convene a Communist conference with dispatch. The RCP responded on December 24 with the following appeal sent out by radio, the only means of rapid communication with its cothinkers in the West.

Against an International of Traitors[20]

The British Labour Party's proposal to call an international Socialist conference in Lausanne on January 6, forwarded by Arthur Henderson to Branting, is in no sense an attempt to restore the Second International. In fact, the latter ceased to exist at the beginning of August 1914, when representatives of the majority in almost every Socialist party sided with their respective imperialist governments. The attempts to restore the Second International came from fainthearted elements in the movement, who conducted continuous agitation to this end in almost every country throughout the World War.[21] While not following an openly social-imperialist course, at the same time they did not recognize the need to launch the revolutionary Third International in opposition to the official majority parties, which have turned into instruments of pressure by the imperialist oligarchy on the working class. Their attempts to restore the workers' movement to its prewar status ran counter to the openly imperialist policy of the official majorities. At that time these majorities rejected anything that could create even the impression that the International had been reconstructed. This, they believed, would weaken the workers' dependence on their governments' military policies.

In order to deal a blow to such efforts, the open social imperialists changed the very composition of international delegations of the national sections of the former International. These so-called inter-Allied socialist conferences of parties from the Entente countries were already convened on this new basis. Great Britain was represented by a motley conglomerate called the "Labour Party," and the Socialist parties in Britain were denied direct representation.[22] Italy was represented by reformists who had never before joined the International, while the Italian Socialist Party was not represented. Gompers from America attended, representing the trade unions, which to a great extent have nothing in common with socialism. The social imperialists are preparing to convene an international conference on the basis of this manipulated representation. They are cheered on by the German pseudosocialist, counterrevolutionary newspaper *Vorwärts,* which joyfully hails the proposed formation of a Yellow International.

An International of traitors and counterrevolutionaries is being formed with the obvious intent of creating a stronghold against the rapidly developing world proletarian revolution. To oppose this, Communists of all countries must rally around the revolutionary Third International, which, for all intents and purposes, has already been launched. It has nothing in common either with the open social imperialists or with the vacillators, who in practice aid the social traitors and do not even stop at participating in their conferences.

The Russian Communist Party (Bolsheviks) refuses to take part in conferences of enemies of the working class, who hide behind the name of socialism. We call on all those who stand on the ground of the revolutionary Third International, which has set before the proletariat of all countries the task of seizing power, to do the same. The Communist parties of Lithuania and Belorussia, the Ukraine, Poland, and Holland stand in solidarity with the Russian Communist Party. We also regard as our cothinkers the German Spartacists, the Communist Party of German Austria, and other proletarian revolutionaries of the former Austro-Hungarian state; the Swedish Left Social Democrats, the Norwegian Social Democracy, and the revolutionary Social Democrats of Switzerland and Italy; the cothinkers of MacLean in England, of Debs in America, and of Loriot in France. In them the Third International already exists and leads the world revolution.

During the war, the social imperialists of the Entente countries constantly extolled Liebknecht and heaped the harshest criticisms on the Scheidemannites. Now they are allying with the latter and breaking with the former. Communists of all countries understand the necessity for close unity on the basis of our world revolutionary tasks

for the successful development of the revolution. Our most dangerous enemy today is the treacherous Yellow International, through
which capitalism has managed to keep a significant part of the working class under its influence. The road to power for the proletariat lies
in an uncompromising fight with its betrayers, the social traitors.

Central Committee,
Communist Party
of Russia (Bolsheviks) □

An opportunity to expedite the official launching of the new revolutionary International was provided by the arrival in Moscow in December of a leader and representative of the German Spartacus
League, Eduard Fuchs.[23] He brought with him a short note to Lenin
from Luxemburg, written to pass inspection by suspicious German
border guards, which read, "I am profiting from uncle's [Fuchs] journey to send you all hearty greetings from the family, Karl [Liebknecht],
Franz [Mehring], and the others. May God grant that the coming year
will fulfill all our wishes. All the best! Uncle will report about our life
and doings, meantime I press your hand."[24]

Not since the expulsion of the Soviet embassy from Germany nearly
two months earlier had Bolshevik leaders received firsthand news
of the work of their German comrades. Lenin talked with Fuchs on
December 25 and two or three days later Lenin wrote the following
memorandum to Georgiy Chicherin, the commissar for foreign affairs.

To G.V. Chicherin[25]

Comrade Chicherin,

We must *urgently* (to be endorsed in the C.C. before departure of
the Spartacist) prepare an international socialist conference for
founding the Third International. (in Berlin (openly) or in Holland
(secretly), *say, for 1. II. 1919*

[generally *very* soon]

For this we must
(a) formulate platform *principles* (I think we could
    (A) take the theory and practice of *Bolshevism*—have *Bukharin*
        set this forth in theses, as briefly as possible. Talk it over
        with Bukharin—perhaps *take part of them* from my draft
        programme[26]

(B) then take *"Was will der Spartacusbund?"*). A + B give sufficiently clear *platform principles;*

(b) define the *basis* (organisational) of the *Third International* (nothing in common with the social-patriots);

(c) give a list of parties, roughly under three headings

AA) parties and groups we have good reason to consider as *already sharing the platform of the Third International and as being sufficiently unanimous on the question of formally* founding the Third International;

BB) parties *close* to this, from whom we *expect* alignment and affiliation;

CC) *groups* and currents *within* the social-patriotic parties more or less close to *Bolshevism.*

I am offering a tentative list (p. 4); additions should be made **with care**.

Who are we *inviting* to our conference? Only AA + BB + CC and only those (1) who resolutely stand up for a break with the social-patriots (i.e., the people who, directly or indirectly, supported the bourgeois governments during the imperialist war of 1914-1918); 2) who are *for* a socialist revolution *now* and *for* the dictatorship of the proletariat; 3) who are *in principle* for "Soviet power" and against *subordination* to it, and who recognise the fact that the Soviet *type* of government is *higher* and *closer* to *socialism.*

Perhaps we should add that we do not suggest that the *whole* of the Third International immediately start calling itself "communist", but we **do place** *on the order of the day (for discussion)* the *question* of resolutely rejecting the names of "Social-Democratic" and "socialist" parties, and adopting that of "communist" parties.

Arguments	*theoretical*	Engels and Marx
	historical	breakdown of the Second International
		disgrace of social-patriotism
	practical	already accepted by

Russia
Finland
German Austria
Holland
Hungary

Please tackle this job *urgently*, and together with Bukharin draw up a *draft* on all these points. *Answer me at once, if only briefly.*

Greetings! *Lenin*

On no account must the Zimmerwaldists be taken as a gauge.

(AA) *Spartacusbund* (Germany)

The Communist Party of Finland

		"	"	German Austria
		"	"	Hungary
Social-		"	"	Holland
Democrats		"	"	Russia
AA of Poland		"	"	Ukraine
and		"	"	Estonia
Lithuania		"	"	Latvia

BB   The Tesnyaki of Bulgaria
Rumanian Party?

CC   the Lefts and the young in
the Swiss Social-Democratic Party

BB   The Socialist Party of Scotland

AA   the Left S.D. of Sweden

BB   the Norwegian S.D. Party

BB   the Danish S.D. group (Marie Nielsen) and
the syndicalists, close to Bolshevism

CC   Loriot's group in France

BB   the "League" in the United States
(or followers of Debs?)

We count on closer
alignment and   [[the British Socialist Party . . . BB
affiliation with   [[the Italian Socialist Party . . . BB

Following the discussions with Fuchs, the Bolsheviks drew up a statement of solidarity with the Communists of Germany and Austria, where the revolutionary struggle was now entering its decisive phase. The declaration, which follows, was written by Trotsky and printed in *Pravda* January 5, 1919.

Letter to the Spartacus Group in Germany and the Communist Party of German Austria[27]

Dear Comrades,

With the greatest joy we are following your struggle and the actions you are carrying out under the banner of revolutionary socialism. It has fallen to you to conduct your struggle in unusually difficult conditions.

The barbarous invasion of Anglo-French-American imperialism, sending even nonwhite troops against the raging world revolution;[28] the treacherous policy carried out by the governmental Socialists, who are working behind the mask of a socialist republic to preserve the capitalist "order" and the sacred inviolability of private ownership; the quick mobilization of counterrevolutionary forces, who lean directly upon official Social Democracy for support; and finally, the presence of ostensibly "left" and "independent" groups, who in fact obstruct unleashing the forces of the socialist revolution and by their participation in the government support the criminals from the yellow Social Democracy — all this creates an extremely difficult situation for our common cause.

We, however, not only believe, but *know* that the German and Austrian proletariat must throw off the chains in which their bourgeoisie, acting through its Social Democratic agents, holds them prisoner.

The German and Austrian proletariat will soon see that a celebrated democratic republic and national assembly are nothing but a dam to hold back the force of the revolutionary wave.

The German and Austrian proletariat will come to understand that their only way out lies in relying on their own power to mercilessly suppress all opposition of the bourgeoisie — a power which will become a mighty lever for the socialist reconstruction of society, not just in words but in action.

The actual power in Germany and German Austria now rests in the hands of the old officials of the monarchy. Messrs. Ebert and Renner, who all their lives have been saturated with deferential fear of the police as representatives of bourgeois state power, have left the old apparatus fully inviolable, an apparatus which was shaped and built over centuries as an instrument of struggle against the popular masses.

The real power today — that of the bourgeoisie, which is now preserved only thanks to their "socialist" puppets — must be replaced — and it will inevitably be replaced — by the real power of the proletariat, its iron *revolutionary dictatorship*. This must be done despite, and in opposition to, the social traitors, who handed over power to the bourgeoisie at the first congress of German councils.

The Russian working class has survived a period of agreements with the bourgeoisie, onslaughts of counterrevolution, and partial defeats. It has been convinced by experience that in our era of the greatest social battles, the like of which world history has hardly ever known, only one of two things is possible: either a rabid, unruly, savage, and bloody *dictatorship of the generals* to rescue the capitalist world, or the *dictatorship of the workers,* building a new world on the ruins of countries laid waste by war.

And our party, the party of the proletariat — which at the beginning of the revolution was considered a "bunch of madmen" and which now has held state power with a firm hand for more than a year — sees with joy that in both Germany and Austria fraternal parties are growing and marching toward our common goal, socialism, along our common road, the *dictatorship of the working class.*

The destruction of the bourgeoisie and the victory of the proletariat are equally inevitable. *Your* victory is inevitable, comrades! We believe and we know that together with you we shall win out. On the ruins of capitalist robbery we shall build a new world of real human brotherhood and solidarity among the peoples.

Long live the world revolution!

Long live the dictatorship of the proletariat!

Long live the international socialist republic!

Long live communism!

By order of the Central Committee of the Russian Communist Party,
> Lenin, Trotsky, Sverdlov,
> Stalin, Bukharin □

Fuchs arrived back in Germany in the first week of January, just as fighting broke out in Berlin. The events of the following ten days cut off contact for the moment between the leaderships of the German and Russian parties. Without waiting for a reply from the KPD, the Bolsheviks therefore convened on January 21 a meeting of revolutionary leaders from several countries then living in Russia to draft a call for an international Communist congress.

The meeting was small and informal, occupying only one corner of the former tsar's royal bedchamber. It was probably attended only by the nine Communists who signed the call and a few others from the Russian party. Those present discussed and agreed on an appeal drafted by Trotsky; its final text, published January 24, was as follows.

Letter of Invitation to the
First Congress of the Communist International[29]

Dear Comrades,

The undersigned parties and organizations consider it necessary and urgent to convoke the first congress of our new revolutionary International. Not only has the course of war and revolution made it absolutely clear that the old Socialist and Social Democratic parties, and with them the Second International, were completely bankrupt; not only have the intermediate elements of the old Social Democracy (the so-called center) been shown to be incapable of effective revolutionary action; but in addition we now see the truly revolutionary International taking a definitive shape and outline.

The tremendously swift advance of world revolution constantly poses new challenges, and the danger is great that it will be strangled by the counterrevolutionary alliance of capitalist governments organized under the hypocritical banner of the "League of Nations." The social-traitor parties are attempting to grant each other an "amnesty" and are joining together to help their governments and their bourgeoisies deceive the working class yet again. Finally, there has been an accumulation of a vast experience in revolution, and the revolution has expanded to international dimensions. All these factors compel us to take the initiative in placing on the agenda for discussion the calling of an international congress of revolutionary proletarian parties.

I. Goals and Tactics

The new International must be based, in our view, on the recognition of the following principles, drawn up here as a platform and based on the program of the Spartacus League in Germany and the Communist Party (Bolsheviks) in Russia:*

1. The present period is one of the disintegration and collapse of the entire world capitalism system, which will also entail the collapse of European civilization as a whole if capitalism itself, with its insurmountable contradictions, is not eliminated.

2. The task of the proletariat today is to seize state power quickly. Taking state power consists in destroying the bourgeois state apparatus and organizing a new apparatus of proletarian power.

3. This new apparatus must embody the dictatorship of the working class (and in some places, of the semiproletariat in the coun-

---

*The Spartacus League program is published in their pamphlet, *What Is the Spartacus League?* We are reprinting it immediately in all the most important languages.

tryside, that is, the poor peasants); that is to say, it must be an instrument for systematically suppressing the exploiting classes and expropriating them. Not a false, bourgeois democracy — that hypocritical form of rule by the financial oligarchy — with its purely formal equality but a proletarian democracy, which can realize freedom for the toiling masses; not parliamentarism but self-administration of these masses through their elected bodies; not capitalist bureaucracy but administrative bodies created by the masses themselves with their real participation in managing the country and in socialist construction. Such must be the form of the proletarian state. Its concrete expression is the power of the soviets and similar organizations.

4. The dictatorship of the proletariat must be a lever for the immediate expropriation of capital and the abolition of private ownership of the means of production and its transformation into social property. The socialization of large-scale industry and its organizing centers, the banks (socialization signifies the abolition of private property and its transfer to proletarian state ownership and to the socialist administration of the working class); the confiscation of landed estates and the socialization of capitalist rural agricultural production; establishment of a state monopoly of large-scale trade; the socialization of large buildings in the cities and on the estates; the introduction of workers' administration and the centralization of economic functions in the hands of the organizations of proletarian dictatorship: these are the most vital tasks of the day.

5. In order to secure the socialist revolution, defend it from internal and external enemies, aid other national sections of the struggling proletariat, and so forth, it is necessary to completely disarm the bourgeoisie and its agents and to arm the entire proletariat.

6. The world situation at this time requires maximum contact among the different sections of the revolutionary proletariat and complete unity among those countries where the socialist revolution has already triumphed.

7. The basic method of struggle is mass actions of the proletariat, up to and including open armed conflict with the state power of capital.

II. Relations with the Socialist Parties

8. The old "International" split into three basic groups: the open social chauvinists, who, throughout the imperialist war of 1914-18, supported their own bourgeoisies and reduced the working class to

the role of executioner of world revolution; the "center," whose leading theoretician is Kautsky and which is a conglomerate of eternal vacillators, incapable of following any definite course of action and at times acting as outright traitors; and finally the revolutionary left wing.

9. Toward the social chauvinists who appear everywhere and at the most critical moments take up arms against the proletariat, merciless struggle is the only conceivable response. Toward the "center," our tactic is to break away from it the most revolutionary forces, while ruthlessly criticizing and exposing its leaders. At a certain stage of development an organizational separation from the centrists is absolutely necessary.

10. It is further necessary to form a bloc with those elements of the revolutionary workers' movement who earlier did not join the Socialist parties but now completely support proletarian dictatorship in the form of Soviet power. This applies above all to syndicalist forces in the working class.

11. Finally, all those proletarian groups and organizations must be won over that, although they have not openly sided with the left revolutionary current, nevertheless manifest a tendency to develop in that direction.

12. Concretely, we propose that representatives of the following parties, groups, and currents participate in the congress. (Membership in the Third International with full rights will be granted to parties which, as a whole, are fully committed to its principles.)

(1) The Spartacus League (Germany); (2) the Communist Party (Bolsheviks) (Russia); (3) the Communist Party of German Austria; (4) the Communist Party of Hungary; (5) the Communist Party of Poland; (6) the Communist Party of Finland; (7) the Communist Party of Estonia; (8) the Communist Party of Latvia; (9) the Communist Party of Lithuania; (10) the Communist Party of Belorussia; (11) the Communist Party of the Ukraine; (12) the revolutionary forces of the Czech Social Democracy; (13) the Bulgarian Social Democratic Party (Tesnyaki); (14) the Romanian Social Democratic Party (15) the left wing of the Serbian Social Democratic Party; (16) the Swedish Left Social Democracy; (17) the Norwegian Social Democratic Party; (18) the *Klassekampen* [Class Struggle] group in Denmark; (19) the Dutch Communist Party; (20) the revolutionary forces in the Belgian Workers Party; (21) and (22) the groups and organizations within the French socialist and syndicalist movement in basic solidarity with Loriot; (23) the left Swiss Social Democracy (24) the Italian Socialist Party; (25) the left forces in the Spanish Socialist

Party; (26) left forces in the Portuguese Socialist Party; (27) the left forces in the British Socialist Party (in particular, representatives of the MacLean current); (28) the Socialist Labour Party (Britain); (29) the Industrial Workers of the World (Britain); (30) the Industrial Workers (Britain); (31) revolutionary forces in the shop stewards' movement (Britain); (32) revolutionary forces in Irish workers' organizations; (33) Socialist Labor Party (America); (34) left forces of the American Socialist Party (especially the current represented by Debs and that represented by the Socialist Propaganda League); (35) Industrial Workers of the World (America); (36) Industrial Workers of the World (Australia); (37) Workers International Industrial Union (America); (38) Socialist groups in Tokyo and Yokohama (represented by Comrade Katayama); (39) the Socialist Youth International (represented by Comrade Münzenberg).

III. The Question of Organization and the Party's Name

13. The creation of the Third International has been made possible by the formation in different parts of Europe of groups and organizations of cothinkers who stand on a common platform and generally use the same tactical methods. These are first of all the Spartacists in Germany and the Communist parties in many other countries.

14. The congress must propose an overall fighting body, the center of the Communist International, that has permanent relations with the movement and gives it systematic leadership, subordinating the interests of the movement in each country to the common interests of the revolution on an international scale. The precise form of organization, representation, and so forth, will be worked out at the congress.

15. The congress must take the name "First Congress of the Communist International," while the various parties become its sections. Marx and Engels had already thought the name "social democratic" theoretically incorrect. Moreover, the shameful collapse of the Social Democratic "International" requires a dissociation. Finally, the fundamental core of the great movement is already constituted in a number of parties that have taken that name.

In view of the above, we propose that all fraternal parties and organizations place on the order of the day consideration of the convening of an international Communist congress.

With comradely greetings,

The Central Committee of the Russian Communist Party (Lenin, Trotsky)

The Bureau of the Polish Communist Workers Party Abroad (Karski)

The Bureau of the Communist Workers Party of Hungary Abroad (Rudnyánsky)

The Bureau of the Communist Workers Party of German Austria Abroad (Duda)

The Russian Bureau of the Central Committee of the Latvian Communist Party (Rozin)

The Central Committee of the Communist Party of Finland (Sirola)

The Central Committee of the Revolutionary Balkan Federation (Rakovsky)

The Socialist Labor Party of America (Reinstein) □

Lenin's "Letter to the Workers of Europe and America," which reviewed progress in building a new International, was also published January 24. The principal section of this letter has been printed as a prologue to the present volume. After its completion, Lenin received news of the murder of Liebknecht and Luxemburg, and wrote the following postscript to his letter, taking up the significance of this blow.

After the Murder of Liebknecht and Luxemburg[30]
by V.I. Lenin

The foregoing lines were written before the brutal and dastardly murder of Karl Liebknecht and Rosa Luxemburg by the Ebert and Scheidemann government. Those butchers, in their servility to the bourgeoisie, allowed the German whiteguards, the watchdogs of sacred capitalist property, to lynch Rosa Luxemburg, to murder Karl Liebknecht by shooting him in the back on the patently false plea that he "attempted to escape" (Russian tsarism often used that excuse to murder prisoners during its bloody suppression of the 1905 Revolution). At the same time those butchers protected the whiteguards with the authority of the government, which claims to be quite innocent and to stand above classes! No words can describe the foul and abominable character of the butchery perpetrated by alleged socialists. Evidently, history had chosen a path on which the role of "labour lieutenants of the capitalist class" must be played to the "last degree" of brutality, baseness and meanness. Let those simpletons, the Kautskyites, talk in their newspaper *Freiheit* about a "court" of representatives of "all" "socialist" parties (those servile souls insist that the Scheidemann executioners are socialists)! Those heroes of philistine stupidity and petty-bourgeois cowardice even fail to understand that the courts are organs of state power, and that the issue in the struggle and civil war now being waged in Germany is precisely one of who is to hold this power — the bourgeoisie, "served" by the Scheidemanns as executioners and instigators of pogroms, and by the Kautskys as glorifiers of "pure democracy", or the proletariat, which will overthrow the capitalist exploiters and crush their resistance.

The blood of the best representatives of the world proletarian International, of the unforgettable leaders of the world socialist revolution, will steel ever new masses of workers for the life-and-death struggle. And this struggle will lead to victory. We in Russia, in the summer of 1917, lived through the "July days", when the Russian Scheidemanns, the Mensheviks and Socialist-Revolutionaries, also provided "state" protection for the "victory" of the whiteguards over the Bolsheviks, and when Cossacks shot the worker Voinov in the streets of Petrograd for distributing Bolshevik leaflets. We know from experience how quickly such "victories" of the bourgeoisie and their henchmen cure the people of their illusions about bourgeois democracy, "universal suffrage", and so forth.

*   *   *

The bourgeoisie and the governments of the Allied countries seem to be wavering. One section sees that demoralization is already setting in among the Allied troops in Russia, who are helping the whiteguards and serving the blackest monarchist and landlord reaction. It realises that continuation of the military intervention and attempts to defeat Russia — which would mean maintaining a million-strong army of occupation for a long time — is the surest and quickest way of carrying the proletarian revolution to the Allied countries. The example of the German occupation forces in the Ukraine is convincing enough of that.

Another section of the Allied bourgeoisie persists in its policy of military intervention, "economic encirclement" (Clemenceau) and strangulation of the Soviet Republic. The entire press in the service of that bourgeoisie, i.e., the majority of the capitalist-bought daily newspapers in Britain and France, predicts the early collapse of the Soviet government, draws lurid pictures of the horrors of the famine in Russia, lies about "disorders" and the "instability" of the Soviet Government. The whiteguard armies of the landowners and capitalists, whom the Allies are helping with officers, ammunition, money and auxiliary detachments, are cutting off the starving central and northern parts of Russia from the most fertile regions, Siberia and the Don.

The distress of the starving workers in Petrograd and Moscow, in Ivanovo-Voznesensk and other industrial centres is indeed great. If the workers did not understand that they are defending the cause of socialism in Russia and throughout the world they would never be able to bear the hardships, the torments of hunger to which they are doomed by the Allied military intervention, (often covered up by hypocritical promises not to send their "own" troops, while continuing to send "black" troops, and also ammunition, money and officers).

The "Allied" and other whiteguard troops hold Archangel, Perm, Orenburg, Rostov-on-Don, Baku and Ashkhabad, but the "Soviet movement" has won Riga and Kharkov. Latvia and the Ukraine are becoming Soviet republics. The workers see that their great sacrifices are not in vain, that the victory of Soviet power is approaching, spreading, growing and gaining strength the world over. Every month of hard fighting and heavy sacrifice strengthens the cause of Soviet power throughout the world and weakens its enemies, the exploiters.

The exploiters are still strong enough to murder the finest leaders of the world proletarian revolution, to increase the sacrifices and suffering of the workers in occupied or conquered countries and regions. But the exploiters all over the world are not strong enough to prevent the victory of the world proletarian revolution, which will free mankind from the yoke of capital and the eternal menace of new imperialist wars, which are inevitable under capitalism. □

Although the German Communist leaders welcomed the invitation to an international Communist conference, the majority of them favored postponing formation of a new world organization. In an article published in English in 1929, Hugo Eberlein recounted a discussion with Rosa Luxemburg on this topic, which took place only three days before her death.

A Conversation with Rosa Luxemburg on the New International[31]
by Hugo Eberlein

One night, as I was accompanying Rosa from the editorial offices of *Rote Fahne* to her house in the southern district, she told me that the invitation had come, and discussed the question of who should be sent. She and Karl Liebknecht were not to be considered, for it was impossible for them to leave Berlin. Apart from that Rosa thought that the C.P.G. [KPD] should be represented at this Conference by a German comrade whose political judgment would not be influenced by previous disagreements with Russian comrades. She referred now and again to the differences of opinion between herself and Leo Jogiches, and the Bolsheviks. Rosa suggested that I should go.

During our conversation, she referred to the importance of the conference in the following terms: the Bolsheviks will probably propose that a new international should be founded immediately, even if only a few delegates turn up. The foundation of the Communist International is obviously and unconditionally necessary, but it should not be premature. The Communist International should only be definitely founded when, in the revolutionary mass movements sweeping over almost all the countries of Europe, Communist Parties have arisen. It is also particularly necessary to choose the exact time of its foundation so as to accelerate the separation of the revolutionary masses from the United Social-Democratic Party.[32] Rosa therefore suggested that at the Conference I should propose the establishment of a commission consisting of representatives of the different countries, and that the inaugural Congress should take place some time between Easter and Whitsun [seven weeks after Easter].

Three days later Rosa and Karl were dead. We all felt the pain of the irreparable loss of our leaders — there were no discussions among us in those days. Then there was a meeting in the Kochstrasse, in which Jogiches, Karski, Pieck, Levi and Eberlein took part (Meyer was under arrest). I reported to the comrades my last conversation with Rosa, and Leo Jogiches, who shared her opinion, confirmed it. It was agreed that I should be the delegate, on the unconditional mandate that I put forward the opinion of Rosa and Leo. □

In another account, written five years earlier, Eberlein had paraphrased Luxemburg's arguments on the question as follows:

"It is absolutely necessary to create a new revolutionary International clearly opposed to the Second, reformist International. But the time to found it has not yet come. For the existence of a new, revolutionary International capable of action was dependent on that of several revolu-

tionary parties in western Europe. Immediately founding the International when there was still only one Communist Party in the West, our own — and it only just formed — could only weaken the idea of a revolutionary International."[33]

When Eberlein arrived in Moscow on February 25, preparations were well advanced for the congress to launch the new International, which was to convene the following week. Draft programmatic statements were being circulated and revised. One example of these that has been released from the Moscow archives is a set of outline theses by Zinoviev, extracts of which follow.

Foundations of the Third International: Theses[34]
by Gregory Zinoviev

1. . . . The struggle among the predator states to divide and redivide the world, culminating in an unprecedented destruction of productive forces and in world hunger, is now being transformed into a civil war within this country and a class war of capitalism's united forces against both the organized proletarian state of Russia and the proletariat striving toward power in other countries.

2. The social-patriotic slogan "defense of the fatherland" is definitively exposed as a gross deception of the masses and a defense of the predatory policies of imperialism. . . . The newer imperialist slogan of the "League of Nations" . . . is even more dangerous. It is revealing itself to be a cover for the Holy Alliance of capitalists of all countries against the proletarian uprising. . . .[35]

3. The entire world situation . . . places on the agenda for the European and American working class a communist workers' revolution that must destroy and break up the bourgeois state machine and organize a new power, the dictatorship of the proletariat.

4. What now emerges first and foremost, therefore, is an intensification of the tactic of mass action through the development of street demonstrations, of general strikes, and so forth, toward an armed uprising of the proletarian masses, winning over to its side the masses of armed soldiers.

The foremost duty of all the parties that stand for a socialist revolution, not in word but in deed, is to do the most energetic work to prepare for the insurrection, especially among soldiers.

5. It is essential to utilize parliament . . . as a tribune for revolutionary agitation, uniting parliamentary actions with action in the streets. . . .

6. It is necessary to create an underground revolutionary ap-

paratus, capable of transmitting insurrectionary slogans in their entirety and generating the necessary cadres to lead the proletarian revolutionary struggle.

7. . . . The movement's political goal and slogan is not a bourgeois democracy . . . but a dictatorship of the proletariat. . . . This *proletarian* democracy is not confined to a *proclamation* of freedoms, but rather shifts its center of gravity to establishing *guarantees of their realization for the toiling classes.* . . .

8. This democracy of *proletarians* is at the same time its *dictatorship*, that is, an organ of the strictest repression against the enemies of the proletariat. The experience of the *Russian* revolution . . . showed that the bourgeoisie does not stop before any methods of struggle. . . . The proletariat must crush these actions ruthlessly. . . .

9. The real organs of mass revolutionary struggle, which will be transformed after the victory of insurrection into organs of *power*, are the soviets of worker deputies. . . . Therefore in every country our slogan must be . . . for a *Soviet republic*.

10. The Social Democratic parties, and also Marxism, as the movement's official ideology, have definitively broken up into three basic groups: the right, the center, and the left radicals. . . . □

Lenin wrote critical notes on Zinoviev's theses, which aimed to make them more specific and relate them more concretely to conditions of the day. They are not found in the current English-language edition of Lenin's *Collected Works*. The paragraph numbers correspond to those of Zinoviev's theses.

Remarks on Theses "Foundations of the Third International"[36]
by V.I. Lenin

For the theses:

1. Rework so that it becomes a *thesis* on practical politics. Recognition of the *ripeness* of proletarian socialist revolution; its *necessity* today; *transformation* into civil war as a confirmation of our historical slogan.

2. Add: in *this* 1914-1918 war.

2b. Separate out the role of the "League of Nations" and "social pacifism" as slogan of liberal betrayal.

3. Emphasize "smashing" the state machine — and dictatorship

— in contrast to the *opportunists* and the *center*.

4. *Preparation* of revolution and armed uprising. Conduct all propaganda and agitation in this spirit. (Elaborate.)

5. Insert: categorically (à la Liebknecht).

6. Add: In view of violations and limitations of bourgeois legality found everywhere and typical (of imperialism).

7. and 8. Place together with the dictatorship.

9. *Of the type* of the Commune and the Soviets. (Not necessarily "Soviets.")

10. Add: Right = class enemy. Center = vacillating petty bourgeoisie. + add: Marxism has split, (a) and (b) are not Marxist. + Worthlessness of Zimmerwald and the necessity of uniting the left. □

On his arrival Eberlein immediately explained to the Bolshevik leaders the KPD leadership's opposition to forming the new International at that time. "In our discussions, which for the most part took place in Lenin's office," Eberlein related in 1924, "the question was immediately brought up as to whether the conference was going to preside over the founding of the International. I was the only one who spoke out against the idea, as my party had instructed me to. The Russian comrades — especially Trotsky, Bukharin, and Rakovsky — tried to convince me of the need for immediate action. They demolished all my arguments, one by one. Lenin finally decided that, if the German party persisted in its view, the founding of the International would be postponed."[37] Ernst Meyer told a KPD congress in 1920 that Eberlein had announced in these discussions that he would walk out of the conference if it decided to launch the Third International at once.[38]

According to Zinoviev, speaking to the Russian Communist Party congress two weeks after the international congress closed, the German Communists had demanded, "almost as an ultimatum, that we remain merely a conference and not proclaim ourselves a congress." The Bolshevik Central Committee "considered it absolutely clear that it was necessary immediately to found the Third International. But we also said that since the German Communists were against this, and since they posed the question as an ultimatum, we did not want to permit the slightest strain to arise in relations with the German Spartacists," and had therefore given way. Zinoviev added that with the arrival of other delegates from abroad and the progress of reports and discussions, Eberlein's stance became more flexible.[39]

Forced to retreat for the moment regarding the goals of the coming conference, the Bolshevik leaders reiterated their arguments publicly in the form of theses proposed to their Russian party congress, which was scheduled to convene a few weeks later. These theses, which follow, were drafted by Zinoviev and published in *Pravda* on March 2, the day the international conference convened.

The Hour for a Genuine Communist International Has Struck[40]
by Gregory Zinoviev

I

As early as the 1907 International Socialist Congress at *Stuttgart*, when the Second International came up against the questions of colonial policy and imperialist wars, it was revealed that a good half of the Second International — and the majority of its leadership — stood much closer to the views of the bourgeoisie on these questions than to the communist viewpoint of Marx and Engels.

At Stuttgart the revisionists' proposed "recognition" of bourgeois colonial policy — that is, support for imperialist wars — was rejected by only a very narrow majority. The leading parties of the Second International — the German, French, and British — and especially the trade union leaders in these countries — spoke out there definitely and absolutely *against* revolutionary policies.

Nevertheless, the Stuttgart congress accepted an amendment, introduced by Lenin and Rosa Luxemburg, stating: "In case war should break out anyway, it is [Socialists'] duty to intervene for its speedy termination and to strive with all their power to utilize the economic and political crisis created by the war to rouse the masses and thereby hasten the downfall of capitalist class rule."[41]

II

The Balkan War of 1912 could only be the prelude to an imperialist world war. That was clear to all socialists.

At the *Basel* congress (November 1912), convened during the Balkan War, the Second International announced: "Let [the bourgeois governments] remember that the Franco-Prussian War was followed by the revolutionary outbreak of the Commune; that the Russo-Japanese War set into motion the revolutionary energies of the peoples of the Russian Empire. . . . Proletarians consider it a crime to fire at each other for the profits of the capitalists, the ambitions of dynasties, or the greater glory of secret diplomatic treaties."[42]

III

As late as the end of July and the beginning of August 1914, twenty-four hours before the beginning of the imperialist war, the leading bodies and institutions of the Second International's chief parties continued to denounce the impending war as a monstrous crime. Statements of these parties dating from those days and collected by the Viennese professor Carl Grünberg serve as the most eloquent indictment against the leaders of the Second International.[43] These documents show more convincingly than anything else that on August 4, 1914, the leaders of the Second International called "white" what they themselves on August 3 had called "black."

IV

As the first shots rang out on the fields of the imperialist war, the leading parties of the Second International betrayed the working class. Under the guise of "defending the fatherland" each party crossed over to the side of "its own" bourgeoisie. In Germany Scheidemann and Ebert, in France Thomas and Renaudel, in England Henderson and Hyndman, in Belgium Vandervelde and de Brouckère, in Austria Renner and Pernerstorfer, in Russia Plekhanov and Rubanovich, in Sweden Branting and his party, in America Gompers and his accomplices, in Italy Mussolini and Co. — they all called for the proletariat to conclude "civil peace" with the bourgeoisie of "its own" country, that is, to reject the struggle against the exploiters, to reject a war against the war — in reality, to become cannon fodder for the imperialists.

At that moment the Second International went completely bankrupt and perished.

V

This sudden conversion of the Second International into an organization carrying out the program of the imperialists was, in reality, not so sudden. It was prepared little by little in the course of over thirty years of "peaceful" capitalist development — roughly from the defeat of the Paris Commune in 1871 until the first Russian revolution in 1905.

Thanks to the general course of economic development, the

bourgeoisie of the wealthiest countries acquired the ability to bribe and corrupt the upper layers of the working class — the labor aristocracy — with crumbs from their superprofits. The *petty-bourgeois "camp followers"* of socialism flooded into the ranks of the official Social Democratic parties and gradually shifted their political course in a bourgeois direction. The leaders of the conciliatory parliamentary workers' movement, the leaders of the narrow-minded trade unions, the party secretaries, the editors, and the functionaries of Social Democracy came together into a whole caste, the *workers' bureaucracy,* having its own self-satisfied group interests even to the point of being hostile to socialism.

As a result of all this, official Social Democracy degenerated into an *anti*socialist and chauvinist party.[44]

The war wiped out all conventions, tore away all verbal covers. It shook up all humanity, and compelled all the parties and groups to show their true colors. What had been concealed was now in plain view. The Second International showed itself for what it really was: an organization dominated by the petty bourgeoisie and agents of the big bourgeoisie, who played the part of workers' leaders. Solemn vows to fight to the death and internationalist resolutions were forgotten. Each "leading" party of the Second International began to call on the workers of its country to kill the workers of other countries — to serve the interests of a gang of bankers and generals. Each of the "Social Democratic" parties began to carry out whatever tasks that had been entrusted to them by the bourgeoisie of their respective country or imperialist coalition.

VI

Three fundamental groupings had already taken shape in the heart of the Second International. During the war years and up to the onset of proletarian revolution in Europe these three groupings took shape quite clearly.

VII

1. The *social-chauvinist* tendency (the "majority" tendency). Its most characteristic representatives are the German Social Democrats, who now share power with the German bourgeoisie and are the murderers of leaders of the Communist International, Karl Liebknecht and Rosa Luxemburg.

During the entire war partisans of this tendency in Germany,

France, Britain, Russia, Austria,and all the other countries supported finance capital and monarchy, inflamed chauvinistic passions, participated in the murderous extermination of the flower of the working class, preached "war to the finish," converted the workers' press into a tool of bourgeois corruption of the proletariat and the workers' party into a housemaid of the imperialists.

The "majority Socialists" carry the same share of responsibility for all the crimes committed during the war against the working class of all countries as do the kings, bourgeois ministers, heroes of secret diplomacy, and bankers.

Now that the imperialist war is over, now that it is at last being replaced by the *civil* war of the oppressed classes against their ancient oppressors, the social chauvinists assume the role of the out-and-out butchers of the international proletarian revolution.

The social chauvinists have now fully revealed themselves as the class opponents of the proletariat and are carrying out the program to "liquidate" the war urged on them by the bourgeoisie: burdening the working masses with the main weight of taxes; preserving the inviolability of private property and bourgeois control of the army; dissolving the workers' councils rising up everywhere; keeping political power in bourgeois hands; and counterposing bourgeois "democracy" to socialism.

Majority "Social Democrats" are one of the main obstacles to the workers' victory over the bourgeoisie in the present epoch. The bourgeoisie deliberately installs the social chauvinists in power, in order to facilitate massacring the workers. In Germany, Austria, and Hungary the bourgeoisie at this very moment is carrying this out, trying to defeat the Communist proletariat under the banner of the "Social Democratic" Party. This confirms the words of Engels in his foreword to *Revelations about the Cologne Communist Trial:*

"Petty-bourgeois democracy in Germany is even now the party which must certainly be the first to come to power in Germany as the saviour of society from the communist workers."[45]

Up to this point the Communists have not struggled sharply against the "majority Social Democrats," since we still did not all recognize the scope of the danger these traitors posed to the international proletariat. Opening the eyes of all working people to the Judas-like role of the social chauvinists and neutralizing arms in hand this counterrevolutionary party is a most important task of the international proletarian revolution.

VIII

2. *The center tendency* (social pacifists, Kautskyites, Independents). This tendency began to take shape even before the war, mainly in Germany. At the beginning of the war the center almost everywhere was in fundamental solidarity with the social chauvinists. The theoretical leader of the center, Kautsky, came out with a justification of the policy conducted by German and French social chauvinists. The International became "an instrument for peacetime," as Kautsky wrote at the beginning of 1915. Once the war has broken out, only one thing is left for us to do, he added: "Struggle for peace, class struggle in peacetime."[46]

During four years of war the center sometimes wavered to the left, but in general it remained true to the policies outlined above. During the January uprising of the Berlin proletariat, the center played a very ambiguous role and weakened the workers with the prospect of negotiations with the government hangmen.

From the very start of the war the center insisted on "unity" with the social chauvinists. After the murder of Liebknecht and Luxemburg, the center continued to preach the same "unity" — that is, unity of the worker-communists with the murderers of the Communist leaders Liebknecht and Luxemburg.

As soon as the war began the center (Kautsky, Victor Adler, Turati, MacDonald) started to preach for a "mutual amnesty" of the leaders of the social-chauvinist parties of Germany and Austria, on the one hand, and of France and England, on the other. The center preaches this amnesty even now at the end of the war, and that hinders the workers from understanding the reasons for the collapse of the Second International.

The center sent its representatives to the Bern international conference of class collaborators, making it that much easier for the Scheidemanns and Renaudels to deceive the workers.

The center continues its petty-bourgeois–pacifist propaganda for "disarmament" under capitalism, courts of arbitration under imperialism, and so on, easing the counterrevolutionary work organized by the allied imperialists' infamous "League of Nation."

It is of the utmost importance to clear a path for the international proletariat through the reactionary rubbish heaped on the road of revolution by the leaders of the center. It is necessary to break away the most revolutionary forces from the center, and that requires ruthless criticism and exposure of the center's leaders. An organizational break with the center is a historical necessity. The timing of this break must be determined by the Communists of each country, according to the movement's stage of development.

IX

3. *Communists*. This tendency remained in the minority in the Second International, where it defended Marxist views on war and the tasks of the proletariat (at Stuttgart in 1907, through the resolution of Lenin and Luxemburg). The "left radical" group in Germany (later the Spartacus League), the Bolshevik Party in Russia, the "Tribunists" in Holland, the youth group in Sweden, and the left wing of the Youth International in a number of countries constituted the initial nucleus of the new International.

Since the start of the war this tendency, true to the interests of the working class, has proclaimed the slogan: "Turn the imperialist war into a civil war!"

At the Zimmerwald conference (1915), the *Zimmerwald Left* was formed, the first nucleus of the Third, Communist International. Since then, and especially since the victory of the proletarian revolution in Russia, communism has grown in a number of countries.

In *Germany* the Spartacus League, which had won worldwide fame and affection from the workers of all countries, formed the Communist Party. It is growing with every passing day, marching to power at a rapid pace.

In *Russia* the Communist Party has won the sympathy of the entire working class of city and country, united 700,000 members in its ranks, worked out a scientifically based program, held power for fifteen months, created a strong Red Army, and aroused the warm sympathy of the proletarians of all the world.

In *Austria* an influential group of Communists has been formed, which has a great future.

In *Hungary* the Communist Party already has won the majority of the town proletariat, and in the near future it will also win the majority of soldiers and peasants.

In *Italy* at the last congress of the Socialist Party a victory went to the Communist forces, who led a heroic struggle against imperialism during the war and who have won the sympathy of an enormous majority of the Italian proletariat.[47]

In *France* sympathy for communism is growing, which is indirectly reflected in the conduct of the French center group. The statement of such a man as Henri Barbusse that he considers himself a

French Spartacist is an extraordinarily significant sign of the times.

In *Britain* the British Socialist Party as well as the MacLean group are moving toward the early formation of a Communist party.

Likewise, in a whole number of other countries (Romania, Sweden, Holland, Bulgaria, Denmark, Norway) and in territories formerly part of the Russian Empire (Poland, Latvia, the Ukraine, Lithuania, Belorussia, Estonia), strong Communist parties have formed.

X

The *program* of the RCP, which will receive the approval of the eighth party congress, will on the whole undoubtedly be acceptable for all the enumerated parties, and will become the program of the Communist International.

The tactics of the Communist International are defined for the most part in fifteen theses, published in the name of eight Communist parties on January 25, 1919, with a specific proposal for calling the first congress of the Communist International.

These tactics are determined by a profound conviction that the present-day epoch is one of the decay and collapse of the entire world capitalist system, and that the proletariat's task is now to seize state power rapidly, to realize the dictatorship of the laboring classes, and to create a proletarian state on the basis of soviets or similar organizations.

The *organizational forms* of the Third International must be determined at the first congress of the Communist parties. It must establish a strong leading center able to direct the movement ideologically and organizationally in all countries.

XI

At present we invite the following parties to join the Communist International: . . . [48]

All other workers' organizations that stand on the published platform and whose work shows dedication to the cause of the Third International have the right to join its ranks.

XII

The League of Nations, now being organized by the imperialists, is in fact the "International" of the *bourgeoisie* whose aim is to *strangle nations*. The League of Nations is a cooperative society founded by the Entente imperialists to exploit the entire civilized world and to drown in blood the workers now initiating the proletarian revolution in all the main countries.

The Bern International "Socialist" Conference, which attempted to reanimate the corpse of the Second International, is in fact a tool of the imperialist League of Nations.

As a counterweight to the international organization of the exploiters and their lackeys, the Eighth Congress of the Russian Communist Party decides to organize the *International Organization of the Toilers — the Communist International*.

The Federation of Foreign Communist Groups affiliated with the RCP, groups of Communists who were prisoners of war, must receive the most ardent support from our party.

The RCP must do everything it can to help achieve all that is undertaken by the First Congress of the Communist International and its executive body.

The international league of Communist parties announces a decisive struggle with the international league of the imperialists.

The Eighth Congress of the RCP is unshakably convinced of the imminent victory of communism. The Communist International will triumph as the *international union of Soviet republics*. In the name of this great goal the Communist proletariat of the entire world proclaims *revolutionary war* against the bourgeoisie. The Russian proletariat, the first to win power in its own country, *began* this war, with the help of its socialist Red Army. The international proletariat, organized in the Communist International, will wage it to its conclusion.

At the end of 1873, when the First International — founded by Marx and Engels — fell apart after the smashing of the Paris Commune, Marx predicted: "Events and the inevitable development and complication of things will of themselves see to it that the International shall rise again improved in form."[49]

Now this prediction is coming true. The hour of the creation of a genuine Communist International has struck. In the near future it will unite suffering humanity in a worldwide league of Soviet republics and abolish the state itself in the old sense of the word. □

Notes

1. V.I. Lenin, *Collected Works* (hereinafter *CW*) (Moscow: Progress Publishers, 1972), vol. 26, pp. 470-71.

2. Ibid., p. 471.

3. E.H. Carr, *The Bolshevik Revolution 1917-1923* (London: Penguin Books, 1971), vol. 3, p. 29.

4. The preparatory work during 1917 and 1918 for the launching of the new International will be documented in a forthcoming volume of the Monad Press series, *The Communist International in Lenin's Time.*

5. Carr, *The Bolshevik Revolution,* p. 30; Ya.G. Tëmkin and B.M. Tupolev, *Ot vtorogo k tret'emu internatsionalu* (Moscow: Mysl', 1978), p. 225.

6. Tëmkin and Tupolev, *Ot vtorogo k tret'emu,* p. 223-24.

7. Ibid., p. 231.

8. Lenin, *CW,* vol. 44, pp. 123-24.

9. Lenin, *CW,* vol. 44, p. 154. "Junius" was the pseudonym used by Rosa Luxemburg for her 1916 pamphlet, "The Crisis in the German Social Democracy." See Mary-Alice Waters, ed., *Rosa Luxemburg Speaks* (New York: Pathfinder Press, 1980), pp. 257-331.

10. Victor Serge, *Year One of the Russian Revolution* (Chicago: Holt, Rinehart and Winston, 1972), pp. 325-26.

11. The Russian edition was entitled, *Sovetskaya Rossiya i narody mira* (Soviet Russia and the peoples of the world) (Petrograd: Izdaniye Petrogradskogo Soveta Rabochikh i Krasnoarmeyskikh Deputatov, 1919). No English-language edition was published. An English translation was done, however, by the New York State Joint Legislative Committee Investigating Seditious Activities as part of its report, *Revolutionary Radicalism: Its History, Purpose and Tactics, with an Exposition and Discussion of the Steps Being Taken and Required to Curb It* (Albany, N.Y.: J.B. Lyon, 1920), part 1, vol. 1, pp. 421-58.

12. The congress proceedings can be found in John Riddell, ed., *The Founding of the Communist International* (New York: Monad Press, 1986), a volume of *The Communist International in Lenin's Time.*

13. *Sovetskaya Rossiya,* pp 14-15.

14. Excerpted from D. Bozorgue, ed., *Asnad-e Tarikhi: Jonbesh-e Kargari, Sosial Demokrasy va Kommunisti-e Iran 1903-1963* [Historical documents: The workers', social democratic, and communist movement in Iran 1903-1963] (Florence: Mazdak, [1970]), vol. 8, pp. 67-68. Iran was then known in the West as Persia. In this document, however, the designation "Iran," which had been used within the country for many centuries, has been preserved.

15. The reference is to the 1905-11 Constitutional Revolution in Persia. The massive wave of protest that swept the country in the summer of 1906 forced Muzzafar al-Din Shah to agree to the election of a Constituent Assembly that eventually adopted a constitution. The shah soon died, and his son Mohammed Ali Shah — a staunch opponent of the revolution — assumed power. In 1908 a mercenary force supplied by Russia marched on Tehran, crushed the assembly, and annulled the constitution. Civil war ensued. In the summer of 1909 a "Grand Assembly" deposed Mohammed Ali Shah and named his son as the next shah. In contrast, in Tabriz, center of the Azerbaijani nationality, a revolutionary provisional government was established that held out until the tsarist army marched on Tabriz in 1911.

16. These first nationalist groups, still weakly organized, were formed by bourgeois and petty-bourgeois forces toward the end of the nineteenth century.

17. The reference is to the assassination of Naser al-Din Shah in 1896.

18. By this treaty, Iran was divided into three spheres of influence. The oil-rich South and Southwest was carved out for Britain, the North and Northwest (the most developed sector) was taken by Russia, and the remaining territory was declared "neutral."

19. *Sovetskaya Rossiya*, pp. 16-17.

20. *Pervyy kongress Kominterna* (Moscow: Partiynoye Izdat., 1933), pp. 252-53.

21. This viewpoint was advanced during the war by centrist forces such as those led by Kautsky in Germany and Longuet in France. The openly chauvinist leaderships, particularly in the Allied countries, opposed any resumption of ties with their counterparts in the opposed imperialist camp. When the war ended it was these same right-wing forces who initiated the formation of a reformist International.

22. The British Labour Party was a federated organization composed of affiliated Socialist organizations, trade unions, and other groups. Some affiliated Socialist organizations, such as the Independent Labour Party and the British Socialist Party, were directly represented at international gatherings of the Second International. When both these organizations radicalized under the impact of the war and the Russian revolution, the Labour Party's right-wing leadership countered by moving against those groups' right to direct international representation.

23. Lenin, *Polnoye sobraniye sochineniy* (Moscow: Izdat. Politicheskoy Literatury, 1969), vol. 37, p. 719.

24. J.P. Nettl, *Rosa Luxemburg* (London: Oxford University Press, 1966), vol. 2, p. 782.

25. Lenin, *CW*, vol. 42, pp. 119-21.

26. A pamphlet by Lenin containing proposals for a revision of the party program had been published in June 1917 (see Lenin, *CW*, vol. 24, pp. 455-79). Further proposals for the program were published in March 1918 (ibid., vol. 27, pp. 152-58). Later, in February 1919, a final draft was prepared and submitted to the party congress the following month. The program as adopted by the March 1918 congress is printed as a appendix to this volume.

27. L.D. Trotsky, *Sochineniya* (Moscow: Gosizdat., 1926), vol. 13, pp. 91-93.

28. The imperialist governments in several European countries experimented after 1918 with using non-European troops from the colonies to repress workers' struggles. The European rulers reckoned that since most of these troops were unacquainted with European languages and less directly affected by the class struggle in Europe, they would not be as easily influenced by the working class as were the mass armies conscripted from among European workers and peasants.

These moves aroused indignation in the workers' movement of several European countries, in which fear of this new ruling-class attack was combined with elements of racism promoted by the ruling classes against the colonial peoples.

The Bolsheviks had long been the Socialist party most strongly identified with the demand for immediate independence of colonial peoples and with resolute defense of their struggles. (See John Riddell, ed., *Lenin's Struggle for a Revolutionary International: Documents, 1907-1916; The Preparatory Years* [New York, Monad Press, 1984], pp. 97-102, a volume of *The Communist International in Lenin's Time*.) Several statements by leading Bolsheviks attacked this new move by the imperialist powers to exploit the colonial peoples and set them against workers and peasants in Europe.

After its formation in 1919, the Communist International was successful in winning broad layers of workers across Europe to active defense of the colonial freedom struggle. At the same time, revolutionary Marxism began to win considerable support among oppressed colonial peoples in Asia and Africa. Mass struggles for independence and for a national democratic revolution gathered strength in these continents, blasting the myth that workers and peasants in the colonies were inherently more politically backward than those in Europe.

As a consequence, the imperialist governments subsequently made little use of colonial troops in European social struggles. After the mid-1920s, little more was heard of such threats.

29. *Pervyy kongress Kominterna,* pp. 253-56.

The fact that Trotsky was the author of the draft call is easily accessible to Soviet publishers and academic scholars since this call was included in the collection of Trotsky's writings on the Communist International published in the Soviet Union by the State Publishing House in 1926. Nonetheless, Soviet historical writing of the Stalin and post-Stalin period has chosen to omit mention of Trotsky's authorship.

(See Leon Trotsky, *Kommunisticheskiy Internatsional,* vol. 13 of *Sochineniya* [Moscow: Gosizdat., 1926], pp. 33-37; the fifth Russian-language edition of Lenin, *Polnoye sobraniye sochineniy,* vol. 50, p. 460-62; and Ruth Stoljarowa's study of the origin of this call, "Zur Entstehungsgeschichte des Aufrufs 'Zum 1. Kongress der Kommunistischen Internationale' vom Januar 1919," in the German Democratic Republic journal, *Zeitschrift für Geschichtswissenschaft,* 1968, no. 11, pp. 1381-1401.)

Trotsky's draft of this call was submitted to Lenin December 31 for editing. Lenin's changes are indicated in Lenin, *Polnoye sobraniye sochineniy,* vol. 50, pp. 460-62. The following are the paragraphs altered by Lenin. The words deleted by Lenin are enclosed in square brackets; the words that he added are printed in italics.

"I. Goals and Tactics

"1. The new International must be based, in our view, on the recognition of the following principles, drawn up here as a platform and based on the program of the Spartacus League *in Germany* and the Communist Party (Bolsheviks) in Russia:...

"2. The task of the proletariat today is to seize state power quickly. Taking state power consists in destroying the [old] bourgeois state apparatus and organizing a new apparatus of proletarian power.

"3. This new apparatus must embody the dictatorship of the working class (and in some places, of *the semiproletariat in the countryside, that is,* the poor peasants); that is to say, it must be an instrument for systematically suppressing the exploiting classes and expropriating them. Not a false, bourgeois democracy — that hypocritical form of rule by the financial oligarchy — with its purely formal equality but a proletarian democracy, which can realize freedom for the *toiling* [broad] masses; not parliamentarism but self-administration of *these masses* [the masses themselves] through their elected bodies; not capitalist bureaucracy but administrative bodies created by the masses themselves with their *real* [broad] participation in managing the country and in socialist construction. Such must be the form of the proletarian state. Its concrete expression is the power of the soviets and similar organizations.

"4. The dictatorship of the proletariat must be a lever for the immediate expropriation of capital and *the abolition of private ownership of the means of production and its transformation into social property* [the socialization of the means of production without any compensation]. The socialization of large-scale industry and its organizing centers, the banks *(socialization signifies the abolition of private property and its transfer to proletarian state ownership and to the socialist administration of the working class)*; the confiscation of landed estates and the socialization of capitalist rural agricultural production; establishment of a state monopoly of large-scale trade; the socialization of large buildings in the cities and on the estates; the introduction of workers' administration and the centralization of economic functions in the hands of the organizations of proletarian dictatorship: these are the most vital tasks of the day. . . .

"11. Finally, all those *proletarian* groups and organizations must be won over that, although they have not openly sided with the left revolutionary current, nevertheless manifest a tendency to develop in that direction. . . ."

In addition, in the list of groups and parties invited to the congress (thesis 12), Lenin proposed changing the designation of the invited French revolutionists from "the Loriot group" to "the cothinkers of Loriot" or "the groups and organizations within the French socialist and syndicalist movement in basic solidarity with Loriot."

Lenin's editing raised the question of adding the "Japanese party" to the list of invited groups.

Lenin also proposed adding to the first paragraph of the first section, "Goals and Tactics" the following:

"The Spartacus League program is published in their pamphlet, *What is the Spartacus League?* We are reprinting it immediately in *all* languages (in the *following languages).*"

The suggestion was incorporated in modified form as a footnote.

30. Lenin, *CW*, vol. 28, pp. 434-36.

31. Hugo Eberlein, "The Foundation of the Comintern and the Spartakusbund," in *The Communist International,* vol. 6, nos. 9-10, [1929] pp. 436-37.

32. The reference is to the Independent Social Democratic Party of Germany (USPD).

33. Eberlein, "Souvenirs sur la fondation de l'Internationale Communiste," in *La Correspondance internationale,* vol. 4, no. 15, February 27, 1924, p. 154.

34. Excerpted from "Osnovy III Internatsionala," in V.I. Lenin, *Polnoye sobraniye sochineniy* (Moscow: Izdat. Politicheskoy Literatury, 1970), vol. 54, pp. 734-36. The author of the notes is identified in Tëmkin and Tupolev, *Ot vtorogo k tret'emu,* p. 258.

35. The "Holy Alliance" was formed in 1815 by the victorious powers of continental Europe (except Turkey) after their victory over Napoleon. By this agreement, they pledged to act together to defend "Christian principles," that is, to protect the established order and block revolutionary change.

36. Lenin, *Polnoye sobraniye sochineniy,* p. 502.

37. Eberlein, "Souvenirs sur la fondation," p. 155.

38. *Bericht über den 5. Parteitag der Kommunistischen Partei Deutschlands vom 1. bis 3. November 1920 in Berlin* (Berlin, 1921), p. 28.

39. *Vos'moy S"ezd RKP(b). Protokoly* (Moscow: Gosizdat., 1959), p. 135.

40. "Kommunisticheskiy Internatsional," in *Pravda,* March 2, 1919.

41. Riddell, *Lenin's Struggle*, p. 35.

42. Ibid., p. 89.

43. Carl Grünberg, "Die Internationale und der Weltkrieg, Materialien," in *Archiv für die Geschichte des Sozialismus und der Arbeiterbewegung,* vol. 6, 1916, pp. 373-541, and vol. 7, 1917, pp. 99-248. A selection of these documents are printed in Riddell, *Lenin's Struggle,* pp. 111-39.

44. This question is discussed in Zinoviev's article, "The Social Roots of Opportunism," and Lenin's article, "Imperialism and the Split in Socialism," both printed in Riddell, *Lenin's Struggle,* pp. 475-504.

45. Frederick Engels, "On the History of the Communist League," in Marx and Engels, *Selected Works* (Moscow: Progress Publishers, 1977), vol. 3, p. 187.

46. The reference is to Karl Kautsky's article, "Internationalism and the War," where he wrote, "The International is at its strongest in peacetime and its weakest in wartime. While we must certainly regret this, it does not lessen in the slightest the International's importance in times of peace, that is, in times of normal social development.

"The International is not merely at its strongest in peacetime. It is also the most powerful instrument to keep the peace. . . .

"Our partisanship in the war will not prevent the International, firm and united, from fulfilling its great historical tasks: Struggle for peace, class struggle in peacetime." (Riddell, *Lenin's Struggle,* pp. 148-49.)

47. A congress of the Italian Socialist Party in Rome, September 1-5, 1918, approved a left-wing resolution hailing Soviet Russia and calling for the dictatorship of the proletariat in Italy.

48. The list of organizations that follows in the original text is identical to that given in the "Letter of Invitation to the First Congress of the Communist International," printed above in this chapter.

49. Karl Marx, "To Friedrich Adolph Sorge," in *Selected Correspondence* (Moscow: Progress Publishers, 1975), p. 269.

Above: left, Leon Trotsky; right, Gregory Zinoviev; below: Karl Radek.

Appendix

Program of the Russian Communist Party (Bolsheviks)[1]

Adopted March 22, 1919, by the Eighth Party Congress

The dictatorship of the proletariat established by the Russian revolution of November 7 (October 25), 1917, began, with the support of the poorest peasantry or semiproletariat, to lay the foundations of communist society. The course of the revolutions in Germany and in Austria-Hungary; the growth of the proletarian revolutionary movement in all advanced countries; the spread of the soviet form of this movement, a form directly aimed at establishing the dictatorship of the proletariat — all this proclaimed the beginning of the era of world proletarian communist revolution.

This revolution resulted inevitably from the development of capitalism, which is still dominant in most civilized countries. Except for incorrectly designating the party as the "Social Democratic Party," our old program correctly characterized the nature of capitalism and of bourgeois society as follows:

"The chief characteristic of such a society is commodity production based on capitalist relations of production, where the most important and substantial part of the means of production and exchange belongs to a numerically small class. The enormous majority of the population are proletarians and semiproletarians, whose economic position compels them permanently or periodically to sell their labor power. They must hire themselves out to the capitalists and create by their own labor the income of the upper classes of society.

"The constant improvement in technology more and more extends the sphere of dominion of capitalist productive relations. This increases the economic weight of large enterprises and leads to the displacement of petty independent producers, some of whom are turned into proletarians. Others play a diminishing role in social and eco-

---

Footnotes to the appendix begin on page 495.

nomic life and are subjected to a dependence on capital that may be more or less total, more or less obvious, more or less burdensome.

"Moreover, this same technological progress enables the capitalists to increase the involvement of female and child labor in the production and exchange of goods. Since this technological progress also brings about a relative decrease in the capitalists' demand for human labor power, the demand for labor necessarily lags behind its supply. This increases wage labor's dependence on capital and raises the level of exploitation of labor.

"This situation in the bourgeois countries and the growing competition among them in the world market make it increasingly difficult for them to sell the goods that are produced in ever larger quantities. Overproduction, manifested in more or less acute industrial crises, followed by periods of industrial stagnation of varying length, is an inevitable consequence of the development of productive forces in bourgeois society. Crises and periods of industrial stagnation in turn further ruin the small producers, deepen the dependence of wage labor on capital, and lead even more rapidly to a relative and sometimes absolute deterioration of the conditions of the working class.

"Thus while improvement in technology increases the productivity of labor and expands social wealth in bourgeois society, it also brings about an increase in social inequality. The disparity between those with property and those without it grows. An ever increasing layer of the toiling masses experiences a greater precariousness of existence, unemployment, and other hardships.

"But the more that these contradictions inherent in bourgeois society grow and develop, the greater is the discontent of the toilers and exploited masses with the existing state of affairs. The number of toilers and their solidarity expands, and their struggle against the exploiters sharpens. The improvement of technology, by concentrating the means of production and exchange and socializing the process of labor in capitalist enterprises, more and more rapidly creates the material basis for replacing capitalist productive relations with communist ones. That is, it creates the basis for social revolution — the final goal of the entire activity of the international Communist Party, the conscious exponent of the class movement of the proletariat.

"The proletarian social revolution will replace private property in the means of production and exchange with social property. It will introduce planned organization of the social productive process in order to secure the well-being and many-sided development of all the members of society. In this way, the revolution will abolish the division of society into classes. It will liberate the whole of oppressed humanity, for it will put an end to all forms of exploitation of one sector of society by another.

"The necessary prerequisite for this social revolution is the dictatorship of the proletariat, that is, the proletariat's conquest of such political power as will enable it to suppress all resistance of the exploiters.

"The international Communist Party assumes the task of making the proletariat capable of performing its great historic mission. It organizes the proletariat into an independent political party opposed to all the bourgeois parties. It leads all expressions of the proletariat's class struggle, reveals to the proletariat the irreconcilable opposition between the interests of the exploiters and those of the exploited, and explains to the proletariat the historic importance and necessary prerequisites of the coming social revolution. At the same time the party shows all the other toiling and exploited masses the hopelessness of their position in capitalist society and the necessity for a social revolution to win their own liberation from capital's yoke. The Communist Party, the party of the working class, calls on all strata of the toiling and exploited population who accept the proletarian point of view to join its ranks."[2]

The process of concentration and centralization of capital destroyed free competition. It thus led at the beginning of the twentieth century to the creation of powerful monopolistic associations of capitalists — syndicates, cartels, and trusts. These have acquired decisive importance in all economic life. This same process led to the merging of banking capital with industrial capital, which was enormously concentrated, and to an increase in the export of capital to foreign countries. Trusts covering entire groups of capitalist powers began the economic partition of the world, which had already been territorially divided among the richest countries. This epoch of finance capital, which inevitably intensifies the struggle between the capitalist countries, is the epoch of imperialism.

This leads inevitably to imperialist wars for markets, spheres for capital investment, raw materials, and labor, that is, for world domination and for power over small and weak nationalities. That was precisely the nature of the first great imperialist war of 1914-18.

Many factors make capitalism's collapse and the transition to a higher type of social economy inevitable. World capitalism in general has achieved an extremely high level of development. Free competition has been replaced by state monopoly capitalism. The banks along with the capitalist corporations are creating an apparatus for social regulation of the production and distribution of products. As a result of the growth of capitalist monopolies, prices have increased and the oppression of the working class by the cartels has deepened. The working class has been enslaved by the imperialist state and gigantic handicaps have been imposed on its economic and political struggle. The imperialist war has caused horrors, calamities, and ruin.

The imperialist war could not be ended either by a just peace or by the conclusion of a more or less stable peace among the bourgeois governments. Capitalism reached the point where the imperialist war was and is being transformed of necessity before our eyes into a civil war against the bourgeoisie by the exploited toiling masses led by the proletariat.

The growing pressure from the proletariat, especially when it is victorious in individual countries, increases the exploiters' resistance and compels them to create new forms of international capitalist unity (the League of Nations, and so on). While these bodies organize the systematic exploitation of all peoples on a world scale, they direct their immediate efforts at suppressing the revolutionary movement of the proletariat of all countries.

All this inevitably leads to combining the civil war within separate countries with revolutionary wars both by the proletarian countries acting in self-defense and by the oppressed peoples against the yoke of imperialist powers.

Under such conditions, the slogans of pacifism, international disarmament under capitalism, arbitration, and so forth are not only reactionary utopias but an outright deception of the toilers. They are intended to disarm the proletariat and to divert it from the task of disarming the exploiters.

Only a proletarian communist revolution can lead humanity out of the deadlock created by imperialism and imperialist wars. No matter what difficulties the revolution may encounter and despite temporary setbacks or possible waves of counterrevolution, the final victory of the proletariat is inevitable.

This victory of the world proletarian revolution requires the greatest confidence, the closest fraternal unity, and the greatest possible coordination of revolutionary activities of the working class in the advanced countries.

These conditions cannot be realized without a determined break from the bourgeois perversion of socialism that gained the upper hand in the leading bodies of the official Social Democratic and Socialist parties and a ruthless struggle against it.

One side of this perversion is the opportunist and social-chauvinist current, which is socialist in words yet chauvinist in practice. It disguises defense of the predatory interests of its national bourgeoisie under the false slogan of defense of the fatherland both as a general concept and specifically during the imperialist war of 1914-18. This current arose because the surplus profits resulting from the robbery by the advanced capitalist governments of the colonial and weak nations enable the bourgeoisie to bribe the upper layer of the proletariat. This layer is placed in a privileged position where it is guaranteed tolerable petty-bourgeois conditions of life during peacetime. The bourgeoisie also takes the leaders of this layer into its service. As servants of the bourgeoisie, the opportunists and social chauvinists are the direct class enemies of the proletariat. This is especially true now, when together with the capitalists they are suppressing, with armed force, the revolutionary movement of the proletariat in their own as well as in foreign countries.

The other form of this bourgeois perversion of socialism is the "centrist" movement, which is also found in all capitalist countries. It vacillates between the social chauvinists and the Communists, advocates union with the former, and strives to revive the bankrupt Second International.

The only leader in the proletarian struggle for emancipation is the new Third Communist International, of which the Russian Communist Party (Bolsheviks) (RCP) is a component. This International was actually created when the real proletarian elements of former Socialist parties in different countries, particularly in Germany, formed Communist parties. It was formally established in March 1919 at its First Congress held in Moscow. The Communist International is winning increasing sympathy among the masses of the proletariat of all countries. It returns to Marxism not only through its name but also through its entire ideological and political content. All its activities apply the teachings of Marx, cleansed of all bourgeois opportunist perversions.

The RCP defines the concrete tasks of the proletarian dictatorship in Russia, where the outstanding characteristic is the numerical preponderance of the petty-bourgeois layers of the population, in the following manner.

In the Sphere of General Politics

1. Because of the existence of private property in land and in other means of production, even the most democratic bourgeois republic, sanctified by slogans like "will of the people," "will of the

nation," or "will of all classes," has inevitably proved to be a dictatorship of the bourgeoisie. It is a machine for the exploitation and suppression of the overwhelming majority of the toilers by a handful of capitalists. Proletarian or Soviet democracy, by contrast, has transformed the mass organizations of precisely those classes oppressed by capitalism, the proletarians and the poorest peasants (semiproletarians), who are the enormous majority of the population, into the sole and permanent basis of the entire state apparatus, local and central, from top to bottom. In this way, the Soviet government introduced (and, incidentally, in a much wider form than anywhere else) local and regional self-government, without any official authorities appointed from above. The party's task is to work untiringly for the complete realization of this highest form of democracy, which requires for its proper functioning a steady improvement in the level of the masses' culture, organization, and activity.

2. In contrast to bourgeois democracy, which conceals the class nature of its state, the Soviet government openly recognizes that every state must inevitably be a class state until the division of society into classes and along with it all state power finally disappears. By its very essence, the Soviet state aims at crushing the resistance of the exploiters. The Soviet constitution proceeds from the standpoint that freedom of any kind is a deception if it stands opposed to the liberation of labor from the yoke of capital.[3] It therefore does not hesitate to deprive the exploiters of their political rights. The task of the proletarian party is to suppress the exploiters' resistance decisively and to combat ideologically the deep-rooted prejudices concerning the absolute nature of bourgeois rights and liberties. At the same time the party must explain that any curtailment of political rights or restrictions of freedom are necessary only as temporary measures to fight any attempts of the exploiters to maintain or restore their privileges. To the extent that the objective possibility of exploitation of one human being by another disappears, the necessity for such temporary measures will also vanish. The party will strive to reduce these measures and to abolish them completely.

3. Bourgeois democracy has limited itself to extending political rights and liberties, such as freedom of assembly, association, and the press, formally to all citizens alike. But in reality, administrative practice and above all the economic enslavement of the toilers under bourgeois democracy have always prevented them from making any wide use of these rights and liberties.

Instead of formally proclaiming rights and liberties, proletarian democracy achieves them in reality, primarily and mainly for those classes that were oppressed by capitalism, namely the proletariat and the peasantry. For this purpose the Soviet government expropriates the bourgeoisie's buildings, printing plants, paper supplies, and so on, and places them at the complete disposal of the workers and their organizations.

The task of the RCP is to involve the masses of the toiling population on an ever wider basis in utilizing thcsc dcmocratic rights and liberties and to broaden the material possibilities for this.

4. For centuries bourgeois democracy has proclaimed the equality of persons regardless of sex, religion, race, or nationality. But capitalism never allowed this equality to be realized in practice anywhere, and in its imperialist stage it has intensified racial and national oppression. Only because the Soviet government is the government of the toilers was it able for the first time in history to introduce this equality of rights totally and in all spheres of life. It has absolutely eliminated the last traces of women's inequality in the realm of marriage and general family law. The party's task at the present time is mainly to carry on ideological and educational work aimed at finally stamping out all traces of the former inequality and prejudices, especially among the backward layers of the proletariat and the peasantry.

Not satisfied with the formal equality of women, the party strives to free women from the material burden of obsolete housework by replacing it with residential communes, public dining halls, central laundries, nurseries, and so on.

5. The Soviet government guarantees the toiling masses incomparably greater opportunities than under bourgeois democracy and parliamentarism to elect and recall deputies. It provides this in a form much easier and more accessible to workers and peasants. At the same time it abolishes the negative features of parliamentarism, especially the separation of the legislative and executive powers, the isolation of the representative institutions from the masses, and so forth.

The Soviet government also brings the state apparatus closer to the masses by making the industrial division (factories, mills) rather than geographical district the electoral constituency and the basic unit of the state.

The task of the party in all its activities is to bring the organs of power and the masses of toilers even closer together on the basis of the masses' ever more vigorous and full implementation of democracy in practice. In particular, functionaries must be made responsible and accountable for their actions.

6. Bourgeois democracy, in spite of all its declarations, has converted its army into a weapon of the propertied classes by separating it from the toiling masses and opposing it to them. It has made it difficult if not impossible for soldiers to exercise their rights. The Soviet state, on the other hand, merges together its organs, the soviets of the workers and those of the soldiers, on a basis of complete equality of rights and identity of interests. The party's task is to maintain and develop this unity of workers and soldiers in the soviets, strengthening the indissoluble ties between the armed forces and the organizations of the proletariat and semiproletariat.

7. The urban industrial proletariat played a leading role throughout the revolution because it was the most concentrated, united, enlightened section of the toiling masses, the most hardened in struggle. It assumed the leading role from the very inception of the soviets and throughout the whole course of their evolution into organs of power. Our Soviet constitution reflects this fact by preserving certain privileges for the industrial proletariat in comparison with the more scattered petty-bourgeois masses in the countryside.

The RCP must explain the temporary character of these privileges, which are historically connected with the difficulties of organizing the countryside along socialist lines. The party must strive persistently and systematically to utilize this position of the industrial workers to unite the advanced workers more closely with the most backward and scattered masses of rural proletarians, semiproletarians, and the middle peasantry as well, counteracting the narrow craft and trade union interests fostered by capitalism among the workers.

8. Only with the Soviet organization of the state was the proletarian revolution able at one stroke to destroy and root out the old bourgeois, bureaucratic, and juridical state apparatus. However, a partial revival of bureaucratism within the Soviet system has been brought about by the inadequate cultural level of the broad masses, the lack of necessary experience in administrative affairs among the workers appointed by the masses to responsible posts, the necessity of appointing specialists of the old school quickly and under difficult conditions, and the drafting into military service of the most advanced sector of the urban workers.

The RCP is conducting a most determined struggle against bureaucratism and advocates the following measures to completely eliminate this evil:

(1) Obligatory participation by every member of the soviet in performing a defined duty in administering the state;

(2) Consecutive rotation of these duties so as gradually to embrace all branches of administration;

(3) The gradual involvement of the entire toiling population in the work of state administration.

These measures represent further progress along the road taken by the Paris Commune. Their complete and rounded application and the simplification of administrative functions, together with raising the cultural level of the toilers, will lead to the abolition of state power.

In the Sphere of National Relations

9. On the national question the RCP is guided by the following propositions:

(1) The cornerstone of our policy is to draw together the proletarians and semiproletarians of different nationalities in waging a joint revolutionary struggle to overthrow the landowners and the bourgeoisie.

(2) The distrust felt by the working masses of the oppressed countries toward the proletariat of states that used to oppress those countries must be overcome. To do this it is necessary to abolish each and every privilege enjoyed by any national group whatsoever. Complete equality of rights for all nationalities must be established, and the right of colonies and dependent nations to separate must be recognized.

(3) To this end, the party proposes a federation of states organized along Soviet lines as one of the transitional forms on the road to complete unity.

(4) As regards to who is to express the desire of the nation to separate, the RCP adopts a historical class viewpoint. It takes into consideration the given nation's stage of historical development — whether it is evolving from medievalism to bourgeois democracy, or from bourgeois democracy to Soviet or proletarian democracy, and so on.

In any case, the proletariat of those nations that were oppressor nations must exercise special care and pay special attention to the remnants of national sentiment among the toiling masses of oppressed or dependent nations. Only by following such a policy will it be possible to create conditions for really durable, voluntary unity among nationally heterogeneous elements of the international proletariat, as was shown by the experience of uniting a number of Soviet republics around Soviet Russia.

In the Military Sphere

10. The tasks of the party in the military sphere are outlined in the following fundamental propositions:

(1) In the period of imperialist decay and expanding civil war, it is impossible either to retain the old army or build a new one on the so-called nonclass or all-national basis. As a weapon of the proletarian dictatorship, the Red Army must of necessity bear an openly class character. It must be exclusively composed of the proletariat and the semiproletarian strata of peasantry that are akin to the proletariat. Only when classes are abolished will this class army be transformed into a nationwide socialist militia.

(2) Military training must be widely extended to all proletarians and semiproletarians, and the teaching of corresponding subjects must be introduced in the schools.

(3) The work of military training and education of the Red Army is conducted on the basis of class solidarity and socialist education. Therefore reliable and devoted Communists must be appointed as political commissars alongside the military commanders. Communist cells must be organized in each unit in order to maintain internal ideological ties and conscious discipline.

(4) In contrast to the old army, the period of barracks training must be reduced to the shortest possible time. The military barracks must come to resemble military or military-political schools, and the closest possible contact must be established between military units and factories, mills, trade unions, and organizations of the rural poor.

(5) For the young revolutionary army to achieve the necessary organizational contacts and stability, it requires a commanding staff drawn from among class-conscious workers and peasants, although this may initially apply only to its lower levels. Therefore, one of the principal tasks in the construction of the army is to train the most capable and energetic soldiers devoted to the socialist cause for positions of command.

(6) Operational and technical experience from the last World War must be widely used and applied. In this regard, military specialists trained in the old army must be drawn in to organize the Red Army and its operational leadership. At the same time, the necessary condition for utilizing such specialists is that political leadership of the army and full control over the military command remain concentrated in the hands of the working class.

(7) The demand for the election of commanding officers had enormous significance with regard to the bourgeois army. There the mil-

itary commanders were selected and trained as an apparatus of class subjection of the soldiers and through them of the working masses. This demand completely loses its principled significance when applied to the class-based Red Army of workers and peasants. The possibility of combining election and appointment of commanders for the revolutionary class army is dictated exclusively by practical considerations. It depends upon the level of organization reached, the degree of solidarity of army units, the availability of commander cadres, and so forth.

In the Judicial Sphere

11. Proletarian democracy takes power into its own hands and completely abolishes the organs of bourgeois domination — the courts of the former system. It thereby replaces the bourgeois democratic slogan, "judges elected by the people," with the class slogan, "judges elected from the toilers and by them alone." This slogan is applied throughout the judicial system, while equal rights are extended to both sexes in electing judges and exercising judicial functions.

In order to involve the broadest masses of the proletariat and the poorest peasantry in the administration of justice, temporary judge-assessors have been introduced into the courts on a rotating basis.[4] The mass workers' organizations, the trade unions, and so on, should take part in compiling the lists of these judge-assessors.

The Soviet government has replaced the formerly endless series of courts of justice, with their various divisions, with a very simplified, uniform system of people's courts. These are accessible to the population and free of all red tape in legal procedure.

The Soviet government has repealed the laws of the deposed governments and charged the judges elected by the soviets to carry out the will of the proletariat and apply its decrees. In cases where such decrees may be absent or incomplete, judges must be guided by their socialist understanding of justice.

Courts constructed on this basis have already brought about a radical change in the character of penalties. They have introduced suspended sentences on a wide scale and public censure as a form of punishment. They have substituted compulsory labor without confinement in place of imprisonment. They have turned prisons into educational institutions and made possible the introduction of comrades' courts.

While advocating the further development of the courts along this road, the RCP must draw the entire toiling population into exercising judicial duties and must ultimately replace the system of punishment with measures of an educational character.

In the Sphere of Public Education

12. In the field of public education, the RCP has set itself the task of finishing the work begun by the October Revolution of 1917. It seeks to transform the school from an instrument of bourgeois class rule into an instrument for the abolition of class divisions in society and for its communist regeneration.

During the period of proletarian dictatorship, that is, while the conditions for the full realization of communism are being prepared, the school must be not only for communist principles in general, but for the ideological, organizational, and educational influence of the proletariat over the semiproletarian and nonproletarian strata of the toiling masses. This is necessary in order to educate a generation completely capable of establishing communism. In doing this, the immediate task is to develop further the following school and educational principles, already decreed by the Soviet government:

(1) Introduce free and compulsory general and polytechnical education (which acquaints the students with all the main branches of industry in theory and practice) for all children of both sexes up to the age of seventeen;

(2) Establish a network of preschool institutions, nurseries, kindergartens, children's homes, and so forth, in order to improve social education and emancipate women;

(3) Fully realize the principle of uniform industrial schools with instruction in the native language; with coeducation for children of both sexes; unconditionally secular, that is, free from any religious influence; schools where education, closely connected with socially productive work, turns out rounded, developed members of communist society;

(4) Provide all pupils with food, clothing, footwear, and school supplies at state expense;

(5) Train new cadres of educational workers imbued with the ideas of communism;

(6) Involve the toiling population in active participation in the work of education (the development of "councils of public education," mobilization of literate persons);

(7) Provide general state assistance to self-education and self-

development of workers and peasants (establish a network of institutions for education outside of school, such as libraries, schools for adults, people's clubs and universities, courses, lectures, cinemas, studios, and so on);

(8) Extensively develop vocational education for persons from the age of seventeen and up in connection with polytechnical knowledge;

(9) Make universities widely available to all who wish to study, in the first place to workers; draw all competent persons into the universities as instructors; remove all artificial obstacles preventing young scientific workers from aspiring to university chairs; materially provide for students so that workers and peasants are able to attend the universities;

(10) Provide the toilers with access to all art treasures, which were created through the exploitation of their labor and have been hitherto at the exclusive disposal of the exploiters;

(11) Develop the most far-reaching propaganda of communist ideas and utilize the machinery and resources of state power to this end.

In the Sphere of Religion

13. With regard to religion, the RCP does not confine itself to the already decreed separation of church and state and of church and school. These are measures that bourgeois democracy includes in its program but has nowhere consistently carried out because of numerous connections between capital and religious propaganda.

The RCP is guided by the conviction that only achieving consciousness and planning in the social and economic activity of the masses will cause religious prejudices to die out. The party strives for complete dissolution of the ties between the exploiting classes and the religious propaganda organizations. It facilitates the real emancipation of the working masses from religious prejudices and organizes the broadest possible scientific educational and antireligious propaganda. At the same time it is necessary to carefully avoid offending the religious sentiments of believers, which would lead only to strengthening religious fanaticism.

In the Sphere of Economics

1. The RCP seeks to continue steadfastly to bring about the complete expropriation of the bourgeoisie. This expropriation has begun and to a large extent it has already been completed. The means of

production and exchange must be made the property of the Soviet republic, that is, the common property of all the toilers.

2. The main and fundamental goal determining Soviet economic policy as a whole must be to increase to the utmost the productive forces of the country. In view of the serious dislocation the country has experienced, everything must be subordinated to the practical aim of increasing immediately and at all costs the quantity of the products most needed by the population. The successful functioning of each Soviet institution connected with the economy must be measured by the practical results achieved to this end.

Moreover, it is necessary first of all to note the following:

3. The collapse of the imperialist economy left a notorious legacy of chaos in organization and management of production during the first period of the Soviet state. It is therefore all the more imperative to advance, as one of the most fundamental tasks, the consolidation of all the country's economic activity into a general state plan. Production must be centralized to the maximum by unifying it into branches and groups of branches and concentrating it in the most productive units and in the rapid fulfillment of economic tasks. The greatest coordination of the entire productive apparatus, the rational and economical utilization of all material resources of the country is required.

Furthermore, efforts must be made to establish economic cooperation and political contact with other nations while striving simultaneously to establish a single economic plan with those nations that have already adopted the Soviet system.

4. Small and handicraft industries must be widely utilized by placing government orders with the artisans. They must be included in the general plan for supplying raw materials and fuel and also must be supported financially on condition that individual artisans, their associations, producers' cooperatives, and small enterprises amalgamate into larger productive and industrial units. Such amalgamations must be encouraged by offers of economic advantages that together with other measures are aimed at paralyzing the aspirations of the artisans to become small industrialists. In this way a painless transition from these backward methods of production to the higher forms of big mechanized industry can be brought about.

5. The organized apparatus of socialized industry must rest above all on the trade unions. They must increasingly free themselves from the narrow craft outlook and transform themselves into large productive associations, involving the majority and gradually all the workers of a given branch of production.

According to the laws of the Soviet republic and by established practice, the trade unions already participate in all the local and central organs of management of industry. They must eventually concentrate in their hands the management of the whole national economy as a single economic unit. In this way, establishing indissoluble ties among the central state administration, the national economy, and the broad masses of toilers, the trade unions must involve the latter as much as possible in direct management of the economy. Participation by the trade unions in managing the economy and their involvement of the broad masses in this work also is the principal means of struggle against bureaucratization of the Soviet economic apparatus. This also makes it possible to establish real popular control over the output of production.

6. An immediate task of Soviet economic policy must be to maximize utilization of all the state's available labor power and ensure its proper distribution and redistribution among the various geographical regions and branches of the economy. This is essential for the planned development of the national economy and can be achieved only through close collaboration with the trade unions. In order to fulfill certain social tasks, the complete mobilization of all able-bodied people by the Soviet government is needed, with the participation of the trade unions. This mobilization must be carried out on a much wider scale and more systematically that has been done so far.

7. The capitalist methods of organizing labor are in decay. Thus the productive forces of the country can be restored and developed and a socialist mode of production consolidated only through the comradely discipline of workers, a maximum degree of initiative on their part, a sense of responsibility, and the strictest mutual control over labor productivity.

Persistent, systematic work to reeducate the masses is needed to reach this goal. This work is made easier because they can see that the capitalists, landowners, and merchants are being removed. The masses can come through their own practical experience to the conclusion that the level of their prosperity depends entirely on disciplining their own labor.

The trade unions must play the principal role in creating the new socialist discipline. Breaking with the old pattern, they must put into practice and test various measures to realize this goal, such as establishing accountability and production norms, introducing responsibility to special workers' (comrades') courts, and so on.

8. Developing the productive forces requires the immediate,

broad, and full utilization of those specialists in science and technology left to us as a legacy of capitalism. This is the case even though the majority of them are inescapably steeped in a bourgeois world outlook and bourgeois habits. The party believes that the period of acute struggle with this layer that was caused by its organized sabotage is over, because such sabotage in general has been overcome.

The RCP, in close alliance with the trade unions, must pursue its former policy. On the one hand, the party must not make the slightest political concession to this bourgeois layer and must ruthlessly suppress all counterrevolutionary impulses on its part. On the other hand, the party must also carry out a relentless struggle against the pseudoradical, genuinely ignorant, and conceited idea that workers can overcome capitalism and the bourgeois order without the help of bourgeois specialists and their knowledge or without going through a long period of education alongside them.

While striving to equalize wages for every type of labor and to fully realize communism, the Soviet government cannot set itself the immediate task of bringing about this equality today. Only the first steps are now being made in the transition from capitalism to communism. It will therefore be necessary for some time for specialists to receive higher wages so that they can work not worse but better than before. For the same reason it is impossible to dispense with the system of bonuses for the most successful and well-organized work.

Equally important is situating the bourgeois specialists in a comradely environment of common work, side by side with the masses of rank-and-file workers and led by class-conscious communists. This would facilitate mutual understanding and closer relations between workers doing physical labor and those doing intellectual labor, who were formerly separated by capitalism.

9. The Soviet government has already taken a number of measures to develop science and bring it closer to production. A whole network of new institutes of applied science, laboratories, experimental stations, experimental testing of new technical methods, improvements and inventions, and registration and organization of all scientific resources and methods have been established. The RCP supports all these measures and strives to develop them further. It seeks to create the most favorable conditions for scientific work in order to increase the country's productive forces.

In the Sphere of Agriculture

10. Having completely abolished private property in land, the

Soviet government has already started to carry out a great many measures toward organizing large-scale socialist agriculture. The most important of these are the following:

(1) Organization of Soviet farms, that is, large socialist enterprises;

(2) Support of societies and associations for cooperative land cultivation;

(3) A state organization to cultivate all uncultivated land, no matter to whom it belongs;

(4) State mobilization of all agronomists to carry out energetic measures to raise the level of agriculture;

(5) Support of agricultural communes as completely voluntary associations of those who work the land for common, large-scale agricultural production.

The RCP regards these measures as the only road to the absolutely necessary increase in the productivity of agricultural labor. The party strives to apply them as fully as possible, spread them to the more backward regions of the country, and take further steps in this direction. In particular the RCP advocates:

(1) The utmost encouragement by the state of agricultural cooperatives engaged in processing agricultural products;

(2) An extensive system of land improvement;

(3) A broad and systematic supply of agricultural implements to the poor and middle peasants through special depots.

The RCP realizes that small-peasant farming will exist for a long time. It therefore strives for a number of measures directed toward raising the productivity of peasant farming. These measures are:

(1) Regulate peasant land tenure (eliminate strip farming, and so forth);

(2) Supply the peasants with improved seeds and artificial fertilizer;

(3) Improve livestock breeding;

(4) Spread knowledge of agricultural science;

(5) Provide peasants with agronomic aid;

(6) Repair peasants' agricultural implements in Soviet workshops;

(7) Establish experimental stations, model fields, centers for equipment rental, and so forth;

(8) Improve peasant lands.

11. The counterposition of town and country is one of the most far-reaching causes of village economic and cultural backwardness.

In a period of great crisis like the present, both town and country face the immediate danger of degeneration and ruin. In view of this, the RCP regards eliminating this counterposition as one of the fundamental tasks of communist construction. In addition to general measures, the party considers it necessary to systematically involve industrial workers in communist construction in agriculture and to develop the activity of the national "Workers' Assistance Committees" already organized by the Soviet government for this purpose.

12. In all its work in the countryside, the RCP continues, as before, to rely on the proletarian and semiproletarian layers there. First of all, the party organizes these sectors into an independent force by setting up party cells in the countryside, organizations of the poor, special types of trade unions of rural proletarians and semiproletarians, and so forth. The party then brings them closer in every possible way to the urban proletariat and wrests them from the influence of the village bourgeoisie and small-property interests.

The policy of the RCP toward the kulak class, the village bourgeoisie, is to resolutely combat their tendency to exploit and to suppress their resistance to the Soviet policy.

The policy of the RCP toward the middle peasantry is to gradually and systematically draw them into the work of socialist construction. The party sets itself the task of separating them from the kulaks and winning them to the side of the working class by carefully attending to their needs. The party fights their backwardness with ideological weapons rather than measures of repression. It strives, in all cases where the middle peasantry's vital interests are concerned, to come to practical agreements with them and make concessions on the ways and means of carrying out the socialist transformation.

In the Sphere of Distribution

13. In the sphere of distribution, the task of the Soviet government today is to continue undeviatingly to replace private trade by a planned distribution of products on a national scale. The aim is to organize the entire population into a single network of consumers' communes, capable of distributing all the necessary products with the maximum speed, planning, and economy and with the least expenditure of labor, strictly centralizing the whole distribution process.

The consumers' communes and their associations must be based on the existing general and workers' cooperatives, which are the largest organizations of consumers and constitute the best apparatus for mass distribution created by the history of capitalism.

The RCP believes in principle that the only correct line is not to abolish the cooperative apparatus, but to further its communist development. The party must systematically continue this policy. All party members are obligated to work in the cooperatives; to lead them, with the help of the trade unions, to a communist spirit; to develop the initiative and discipline of the working population organized in cooperatives. Party members must try to organize the entire population into cooperatives and unite all these cooperatives into a single cooperative, embracing the entire Soviet republic. Finally and most importantly, the predominant influence of the proletariat over the other sections of the toilers must constantly be maintained. Also various measures to facilitate and implement the transition from petty-bourgeois cooperatives of the old capitalist type to the consumer communes led by the proletarians and semiproletarians must be tested in practice.

In the Sphere of Money and Banking

14. Avoiding the mistakes of the Paris Commune,[5] the Soviet government immediately seized the state bank and proceeded to nationalize private commercial banks. It united the nationalized banks, savings banks, and treasuries with the state bank. In this way the government laid the basis for a single national bank of the Soviet republic. The bank was transformed from a center of finance capital's economic domination and a weapon for the exploiters' political rule into a weapon for the workers' government and a lever for economic revival. The RCP, having set itself the aim of consistently carrying through to conclusion the work begun by the Soviet government, emphasizes the following principles:

(1) The entire banking system is a monopoly of the Soviet state.

(2) A radical change and simplification of banking operations is instituted by transforming the banks into an apparatus for uniform bookkeeping and general accounting in the Soviet republic. The organization of a planned national economy will lead to the abolition of banking and to its transformation into the central bookkeeping department of communist society.

15. During the initial stages of the transition from capitalism to communism, pending the full organization of communist production

and distribution, it is impossible to abolish money. Under these circumstances the bourgeois elements of the population continue to utilize the money that remains in private hands for the purposes of speculation, profiteering, and robbing the toilers. Resting its policy on the nationalization of the banks, the RCP strives to implement a number of measures that will extend the sphere of nonmonetary transactions. These measures to prepare for the abolition of money include the compulsory deposit of money in the people's bank, introduction of budget books, replacement of money with checks and short-term notes entitling the possessor to receive products, and so forth.

In the Sphere of Finance

16. In the epoch when the socialization of the means of production expropriated from the capitalists has begun, the state ceases to be a parasitic apparatus over the means of production. It begins to be transformed into an organization directly performing the function of managing the country's economy, and to that extent the state budget becomes the budget of the national economy as a whole.

Under such conditions state revenues and expenditures can be balanced only if there are proper systems of planned state production and distribution of products. To meet immediate state expenditures in the transitional period, the RCP will advocate a transition from the system of levies imposed upon capitalists, which was historically necessary and lawful in the initial period of the socialist revolution, to a progressive income and property tax. As this tax becomes obsolete due to large-scale expropriation of the propertied classes, state expenditures must be met by the direct conversion of part of the revenue from various state monopolies into state revenue.

In the Sphere of Housing

17. In trying to solve the housing problem, which became particularly acute during the war, the Soviet government completely expropriated all the houses owned by capitalist landlords and turned them over to the city soviets. It transferred masses of workers from the outskirts of town into bourgeois homes. The government turned over the best houses to the workers' organizations, maintaining them at state expense. It has started to provide the workers' families with furniture.

The RCP's task is to follow this course by exerting the greatest effort to improve the housing conditions of the toiling masses without infringing on the interests of noncapitalist home ownership. It seeks to abolish overcrowding and unsanitary conditions in old residential areas, to remove houses unfit for habitation, to reconstruct old houses and construct new ones corresponding to the new conditions of life of the working masses, and to resettle the working population in a rational manner.

In the Sphere of Labor Protection and Social Security

The establishment of the dictatorship of the proletariat has made it possible for the first time to fully realize the minimum program of socialist parties in the sphere of labor protection.

The Soviet government has passed legislation, embodied in the Code of Labor Laws, that secures a maximum eight-hour working day for all toilers; a working day not to exceed six hours for persons under eighteen years of age, for those working in unhealthy branches of production, and for miners working underground; a forty-two-hour uninterrupted rest per week for all toilers; the prohibition of overtime as a general rule; the prohibition of employment of children and youth under sixteen; the prohibition of night work and of work in unhealthy branches of production for all women and for men under eighteen; an exemption from work for women eight weeks before and eight weeks after giving birth, with full wages and free medical treatment and medicine; the guarantee to working women of not less than half an hour every three hours for nursing their babies and of additional subsidies to nursing mothers; and the election by trade union councils of factory and sanitary inspection teams.

The Soviet government has passed legislation extending complete social insurance to all toilers who do not exploit the labor of others. This provides insurance against all cases of loss of ability to work and introduces unemployment insurance for the first time in the world at the expense of the employers and the state. The insured are granted complete self-administration of their affairs with broad trade union participation.

Moreover the Soviet government, in some respects, has gone further than the minimum program and provided in the same Code of Labor Laws for the participation of workers' organizations in questions of hiring and discharging workers. The code also provides for one month's vacation with full pay for all toilers who have worked without interruption for not less than one year, state regulation of wages based on rates worked out by the trade unions, and departments to distribute and regulate the work force under the soviets and trade unions in order to find work for the unemployed.

However the extreme destruction caused by the war and the pressure of world imperialism have forced the Soviet government to retreat in the following cases: to allow overtime in exceptional cases, with a limit of fifty days in one year; to permit youth between fourteen and sixteen to work, limiting their working day to four hours; to temporarily reduce the one month vacation to two weeks; and to increase night work hours to seven.

The RCP must carry out an extensive propaganda campaign to secure active participation of the toilers themselves in energetically fulfilling all these measures to protect labor, for which it is necessary to:

(1) Strengthen the work to organize and extend labor inspection by choosing and training active workers from the ranks, and to extend the inspection to small and cottage industries;

(2) Spread job protection to all fields of work (construction workers, land and water transport, domestic servants, and agricultural workers);

(3) Take all minors out of the work force completely and further decrease working hours for youth.

In addition, the RCP must take on the task of establishing the following:

(1) A maximum six-hour day without reduction of wages as general productivity increases, on condition that all workers devote two additional hours a day without compensation to studying the theory of their trade or industry, to practical study of the technique of state administration, and to military training;

(2) A bonus system to encourage labor productivity.

In the sphere of social security, the RCP strives to organize state support on a large scale not only for war victims and victims of natural calamities, but also for victims of abnormal social relations. The party is waging a determined struggle against all parasites and idlers and takes on the task of restoring to useful work all those who have dropped out of the work force.

In the Sphere of Public Health

The RCP proposes as the basis of its work in protecting the public health above all to implement broad health and sanitary measures with the goal of preventing the spread of disease. The dictatorship of the proletariat has already made possible carrying out a whole series of health and medical measures, unrealizable within the framework of bourgeois society. Drugstores, large privately owned medical institutions, and health resorts have been nationalized; compulsory work for all medical personnel has been introduced; and so on.

Accordingly the RCP sets itself the following immediate tasks:

(1) Broad measures for sanitation on behalf of the toilers must be resolutely applied. These include:

(a) improved sanitation in populated areas (protection of soil, water, and air);

(b) organizing communal meals on a scientific-hygienic basis;

(c) adopting measures to prevent the outbreak and spread of infectious diseases;

(d) introducing legislation on sanitation.

(2) Social diseases (tuberculosis, venereal disease, alcoholism, and so on) must be fought.

(3) Free, qualified medical care to all must be guaranteed. □

Notes

1. *Kommunisticheskaya Partiya Sovetskogo Soyuza v rezolyutsiyakh i resheniyakh s"ezdov, konferentsiy i plenumov TsK* (Moscow: Izdat. Politicheskoy Literatury, 1970), vol. 2, pp. 37-59. The numbering of sections in this program follows that in the original text.

2. For another translation of the complete 1903 program of the Russian Social Democratic Labor Party, see R.C. Elwood, ed., *The Russian Social Democratic Labour Party 1898-October 1917*, vol. 1 of R.H. McNeal, ed., *Resolutions and Decisions of the Communist Party of the Soviet Union* (Toronto: University of Toronto Press, 1974), pp. 39-45.

3. The "Constitution (Fundamental Law) of the Russian Socialist Federal Soviet Republic" was first published in *Izvestiya*, July 19, 1918. The Declaration of Rights of the Working and Exploited People, printed in chapter 7 of the present work, was incorporated into the constitution as a preamble.

4. Under Soviet law, two nonprofessional "people's assessors" serve together with a professional judge in hearing all civil and criminal cases in the first instance. The people's assessors have equal rights with the judge during hearings and in reaching decisions.

5. Karl Marx and Frederick Engels criticized the Paris Commune for its failure to nationalize the Bank of France. "The bank in the hands of the Commune — this would have been worth more than ten thousand hostages," Engels commented. See Engels, "Introduction to The Civil War in France," in Marx and Engels, *Selected Works* (Moscow: Progress Publishers, 1977), vol. 2, p. 186.

Chronology

	an end but rejects German annexationist terms, quits peace negotiations.
February 18	New German offensive against Soviet Russia begins.
March 3	Brest-Litovsk peace treaty signed between Germany and Soviet government.
March 21	Beginning of German offensive on western front.
May 2	Prussian House of Deputies rejects equal voting rights bill.
June-September	Strike wave grows throughout Germany.
July 15-17	Last German offensive at the Marne and in Champagne fails.
July 18	English-French-U.S. counteroffensive on western front begins.
August 14	German army command admits to government that the war cannot be won.
September 15-21	Central Powers' front in Bulgaria collapses.
September 29	Bulgaria surrenders to Entente powers.
October 3	Prince Max von Baden appointed imperial chancellor. SPD leaders join government next day.
October 7	Spartacus group holds clandestine national conference in Berlin.
October 16	Five thousand participate in USPD demonstration in Berlin, demanding overthrow of government.
October 23	After release from Luckau prison, Liebknecht arrives in Berlin; welcomed by 20,000.
October 26	Discussions begin between Spartacists, Revolutionary Shop Stewards, and Berlin USPD to organize Berlin insurrection.
October 27	Austria-Hungary informs U.S. government of readiness to make separate peace. Mutinies begin in German fleet.
October 28	Czechoslovakia declares independence from Austria-Hungary. Kaiser Wilhelm II signs constitutional amendment "parliamentarizing" Germany.
October 30	Mass demonstrations, strikes sweep Austro-Hungarian Empire. Social Democrat Renner forms coalition government in Vienna.
October 31	Hungarian revolution begins. Count Mihály Károlyi forms government in Budapest. Turkey surrenders to Allied powers.
November 3	Austria-Hungary surrenders to Allied powers. Austrian Communist Party formed.
November 4	Workers' and soldiers' council formed in Kiel, controls city. Revolution spreads to all major

	German cities in next five days.
November 5	German government closes Soviet embassy in Berlin and deports staff
November 7	Bavarian monarchy overthrown, republic founded, headed by SPD-USPD-Peasants' League coalition.
November 9	Revolution reaches Berlin. Kaiser ousted. Max von Baden appoints Ebert imperial chancellor. Revolution triumphant across Germany.
	Luxemburg released from Breslau prison, arrives in Berlin November 10.
November 10	Busch Circus meeting of Berlin workers' and soldiers' delegates endorses SPD-USPD Council of People's Representatives government. The former kaiser flees to Holland. General Groener and Ebert agree to cooperate to hold back revolution.
	Lenin finishes pamphlet *The Proletarian Revolution and the Renegade Kautsky*.
November 11	Cease-fire signed between Germany and Allied powers, formally ending World War I.
	Spartacus League founded.
November 12	Republic declared in Austria, deposing Hapsburg monarchy.
November 13	Soviet government annuls Brest-Litovsk treaty.
November 16	Republic proclaimed in Hungary, abolishing monarchy.
November 18	SPD-USPD government refuses to reestablish diplomatic ties with Russian Soviet government.
November 19= December 17	Strikes in coalfields of Saxony and Ruhr region.
November 24	Hungarian Communist Party founded.
December 6	Right-wing putsch attempt in Berlin fails.
December 14	Spartacus League publishes program *What the Spartacus League Wants*.
December 15	Berlin USPD general assembly debates national assembly and Spartacus proposal for immediate party congress.
December 15-17	First national IKD congress in Berlin.
December 16-21	First General Congress of the Workers' and Soldiers' Councils of Germany meets in Berlin.
December 24	Government troops in Berlin launch unsuccessful attack on People's Naval Division.
	Second IKD national congress votes for fusion with Spartacus League.
December 27 or 28	After meeting with Spartacus envoy Fuchs, Lenin

	writes letter to Chicherin on calling international Communist congress.
December 29– January 1	KPD founding congress.
Late December	Government begins bringing Freikorps divisions into Berlin environs.

1919

January 4	SPD government of Prussia fires popular Berlin police chief Eichhorn, provoking January fighting.
January 5	Revolutionary Committee elected to lead fight in Berlin; calls for mass demonstrations and overthrow of government.
January 8	Noske's troops begin assault on positions held by revolutionary workers.
January 10	Council republic proclaimed in Bremen.
January 12	Last armed resistance by Berlin workers crushed by Noske's troops.
January 15	Rosa Luxemburg and Karl Liebknecht murdered by Freikorps.
January 18	Victorious Allied powers open Paris conference that will dictate terms of "peace."
January 19	Elections to German National Assembly take place.
January 24	Invitation to Comintern congress published in *Pravda*.
February 3-10	International Socialist Conference takes place in Bern.
February 4	Bremen council republic crushed.
February 21	Kurt Eisner, USPD prime minister of Bavaria, assassinated by monarchist.
March 2-6	Founding congress of Communist International in Moscow.

Glossary

Adler, Friedrich (1879-1960) — son of Victor Adler, the founding leader of Austrian Social Democracy; elected secretary of Austrian party 1911; led centrist opposition to party's policy on World War; in 1916 assassinated Austrian Prime Minister Stürgkh as protest against war; condemned to death, sentence later commuted to imprisonment; freed by 1918 revolutionary upsurge; leader of centrist opposition at 1919 Bern conference; opponent of Comintern; secretary of centrist Two-and-a-Half International 1921-23, of Second International 1923-39.

All-Russian Central Executive Committee — elected June 1917 at First All-Russian Congress of Soviets of Workers', Soldiers', and Peasants' Deputies; predominantly composed of Mensheviks and Socialist Revolutionaries until Bolsheviks won majority at second soviet congress November 7-9 (October 25-27), 1917; highest body of Soviet government after October revolution.

Austerlitz, Friedrich (1862-1931) — leader of Austrian Social Democratic Party, editor-in-chief of *Arbeiter Zeitung;* chauvinist during war.

Avksentyev, N.D. (1878-1943) — Right Socialist Revolutionary; minister of interior in Russian Provisional Government 1917; emigrated to France 1919.

Axelrod, Pavel (1850-1928) — early Russian Social Democrat; leading Menshevik after 1903; supporter of Zimmerwald right during war; opposed October 1917 revolution; delegate to 1919 Bern conference.

Bakunin, Mikhail (1814-1876) — Russian revolutionist; founder of anarchist movement and opponent of Marx in First International.

Barbusse, Henri (1873-1935) — prominent French pacifist; wrote novels depicting horrors of World War; joined French CP in 1923; later a follower of Stalin.

Barth, Emil (1879-1941) — anarchist before 1910; later active in SPD and USPD; chairman of Revolutionary Shop Stewards February-November 1918; member of Ebert government November-December 1918; rejoined SPD 1921.

Bauer, Otto (Heinrich Weber) (1881-1938) — leader of Austrian Social Democratic Party and theoretician of Austro-Marxism; Austrian foreign minister 1918-19; opposed Comintern and helped found centrist Two-and-a-Half International.

Bäumer, Ludwig (b. 1892?) — IKD delegate from Bremen to German

Communist Party founding congress, member of Council of People's Representatives of Bremen Council Republic 1919; subsequently left political activity.

Bavarian Peasant Association (Bayerisches Bauernverein) — conservative Bavarian Catholic peasant organization; 170,000 members in 1918.

Bavarian Peasant League (Bayerisches Bauernbund) — arose in 1890s during agricultural crisis; composed mostly of small and medium peasants; joined SPD and USPD in provisional government of Bavaria; participated briefly in the revolutionary government of April 1919.

Bebel, August (1840-1913) — collaborator of Marx and Engels; founder and central leader of SPD; prominent in Second International; opposed revisionist current in SPD but eventually adopted centrist positions.

Belgian Workers Party — founded 1879 as Socialist Party of Belgium; in 1885 merged with trade unions and cooperative societies to form Workers Party; took chauvinist position during World War; 450,000 individual members and 650,000 affiliated through unions and cooperatives in May 1920; left-wing currents within party broke away in 1919 and 1921 to form two Communist groups that fused in September 1921 as Communist Party of Belgium.

Berger, Victor (1860-1929) — right-wing leader of U.S. SP from Milwaukee; held extreme chauvinist, anti-immigrant, and racist positions; opposed SP joining Comintern and argued for rejoining Second International.

Berliner Tageblatt und Handelszeitung (Berlin daily and commerce gazette) — liberal bourgeois paper founded 1871.

Bernstein, Eduard (1850-1932) — early German Social Democrat and Engels's literary executor; became leading advocate of revisionism; author of *Evolutionary Socialism* (1899); adopted pacifist stand during war; joined USPD 1917; rejoined SPD in December 1918 and briefly a member of both parties; attended 1919 Bern conference as USPD member; reelected to Reichstag from SPD 1920-28.

Berzin, J.A. (1881-1941) — joined Latvian Social Democratic Party 1902; emigrated 1908; represented Latvian party at Zimmerwald where he supported Zimmerwald Left; moved to Russia and elected to Bolshevik Central Committee 1917; Soviet ambassador to Switzerland until expelled after general strike November 1918; active in Comintern and Soviet diplomatic service until recalled by Stalin 1929; arrested during Stalin purges 1937.

Beseler, Hans Hartwig von (1850-1921) — German general; commanded troops that conquered Antwerp 1914; governor of Poland 1915-18; attempted to organize Polish government and army under German control.

Bismarck, Otto von (1815-1898) — German baron, later prince; prime minister of Prussia 1862-71; chancellor of Germany 1871-90; achieved a unified German national state under Prussian domination in Franco-Prussian War 1871; collaborated in crushing Paris Commune 1871; instituted anti-Socialist laws 1878.

Blanqui, Louis-August (1805-1881) — French proletarian revolutionist; spent over thirty-three years in prison; name associated with strategy of armed insurrection by small groups to overturn capitalist rule.

Bolsheviks — see Russian Communist Party (Bolsheviks).

Borchardt, Julian (1868-1932) — left-wing Social Democrat before war; leader of International Socialists of Germany; member of Zimmerwald Left; shifted toward anarchist positions after 1916; expelled from IKD prior to KPD founding congress December 1918.

Brandler, Heinrich (1881-1967) — joined SPD in 1901; leader of Spartacus group in Chemnitz; central leader of KPD 1921-24; expelled in 1929 as supporter of right opposition led by Bukharin; maintained independent left-wing organization in 1930s and after 1945.

Branting, Hjalmar (1860-1925) — longtime leader of Swedish Social Democrats and editor of *Social-Demokraten; right-wing leader of Second International; leading organizer and chairman of 1919 Bern conference; won Nobel Peace Prize 1921; Swedish prime minister 1921-23.*

Braun, Otto (1872-1955) — SPD agriculture minister of Prussia 1918; later SPD prime minister of Prussia.

Breitscheid, Rudolf (1874-1944) — founding member of USPD; Prussian interior minister 1918-19; rejoined SPD in 1922; killed by Nazis at Buchenwald.

Bremen Left — revolutionary Socialist current in SPD in Bremen; broke from SPD during war; refused to enter USPD; known as Left Radicals; joined with other groups in International Communists of Germany in December 1918.

Brentano, Lujo (1844-1931) — German economist; advocated class reconciliation through reformist trade unions.

Brest-Litovsk Treaty — signed March 3, 1918; ended hostilities between Germany and Russia; terms were exceedingly unfavorable to the Soviet republic.

British Labour Party — founded in 1906 as federation of trade unions and Socialist organizations and societies; affiliated to Second International; over 1.6 million members in 1914, predominantly through union affiliation; supported British imperialism in World War; 3.5 million members in 1919.

British Socialist Party — founded 1911 out of fusion of Social Democratic Federation and other groups; right-wing pro-war minority split off in 1916; 10,000 members in early 1919; joined Comintern 1919; majority participated in founding British CP through fusion with other groups in 1920.

Brouckère, Louis de (1870-1951) — leader and theoretician of Belgian Workers Party; left-winger before war, became chauvinist in 1914 and subsequently entered Belgian government; president of Second International 1937-39.

Bukharin, Nikolai (1888-1938) — joined Bolsheviks 1906; emigrated to western Europe in 1911; during war helped edit *Kommunist* in 1915 and *Novy Mir* (New world) in New York 1916-17; returned to Russia in 1917 and was leading member of Bolshevik Central Committee; led Left Communists in 1918; editor of *Pravda* 1919-29; one of main Bolshevik leaders of Comintern; head of Comintern 1926-29; headed Right Opposition and was expelled from Soviet CP in 1929; later recanted views and was readmitted; executed on Stalin's orders after third Moscow frame-up trial.

Cadets (Constitutional Democrats) — liberal bourgeois party in Russia founded 1905; supported constitutional monarchy; participated in Provisional Government in 1917; after October Revolution, worked for overthrow of Soviet government.

Cavaignac, Louis-Eugène (1802-1857) — French general and republican politician; as war minister, responsible for suppression of Paris workers in June 1848 revolution, for which was appointed prime minister.

Center Party (Zentrum) — German bourgeois party founded 1870, supported privileges for Catholic hierarchy and opposed reform in general.

Central Committee of the German Socialist Republic (Zentralrat) — elected December 1918 by congress of councils as the source of governmental authority pending election of national assembly; boycotted by USPD and composed solely of SPD.

Central Peasants Council (Bavaria) — highest body of Bavarian peasant councils, consisted of fifty delegates chosen by Karl Gandorfer.

Cheka — Russian acronym for All-Russia Extraordinary Commission for Combating Counterrevolution and Sabotage, first Soviet internal security police department set up in 1917; first headed by F. Dzerzhinsky; renamed GPU (State Political Administration) 1922.

Chernov, V.M. (1876-1952) — Russian Socialist Revolutionary leader and theoretician; attended Zimmerwald conference; minister of agriculture in Provisional Government 1917; organized anti-Soviet revolts after October revolution.

Chicherin, Georgiy (1872-1936) — tsarist diplomat until 1904; supported 1905 revolution and joined RSDLP in exile; Menshevik before 1914; internationalist during war; returned to Russia in January 1918 and joined Bolsheviks; People's Commissar of Foreign Affairs 1918-30; played key role in organizing first Comintern congress.

Clemenceau, Georges (1841-1929) — French prime minister, 1906-9. 1917-20; chief organizer of 1919 Paris conference and Treaty of Versailles.

Cohn, Oskar (1869-1937) — joined USPD 1917; adviser to Soviet embassy in Berlin 1918; rejoined SPD 1922; lawyer for Trotsky's son Leon Sedov early 1930s; fled Nazism and took exile in Soviet Union 1933; arrested and disappeared during Moscow trials.

Communist Party of Belorussia — founded as component of RCP December 30-31, 1918, with 17,800 members; led establishment of Belorussian Soviet republic January 1919; functioned as united organization with Lithuanian CP from February 1919 until 1920.

Communist Party of Estonia — founded 1918 by Estonian section of RCP; led Estland Working People's Commune (Estonian Soviet republic)

November 1918-January 1919; first congress November 1920 representing 700 members.

Communist Party of Finland — founded in Moscow August 29, 1918, by members of Finnish Social Democratic Party left wing forced into exile by White Terror; helped found Comintern 1919.

Communist Party of German Austria — founded November 3, 1918, in Vienna by Left Radical group that emerged from January 1918 strikes; 10,000 members in 1919.

Communist Party of Germany (KPD) — founded December 30, 1918, by Spartacus League with participation of International Communists of Germany; joined Comintern 1919; lost half its membership in 1919 split of ultraleft forces that later formed the Communist Workers Party of Germany (KAPD); 78,000 members at time of fusion with USPD left wing in 1920.

Communist Party of Hungary — founded November 24, 1918, in Budapest by returned members of Hungarian Communist Group in Russia, left-wing currents in Social Democratic Party, and other forces; fused with Social Democratic Party of Hungary to form SP March 1919, which led Hungarian revolutionary government March-July 1919; SP disintegrated; CP reorganized 1925.

Communist Party of Latvia — founded by Social Democracy of the Latvian Territory, which had affiliated to RSDLP in 1904 and was allied with Bolsheviks thereafter; led Latvian Soviet republic 1919; name changed to CP in March 1919; 7,500 members in 1919.

Communist Party of Lithuania — founded August 1918 as component of RCP; held first conference October 1-3, 1918, representing 800 members; led Lithuanian Soviet republic December 1918-April 1919; functioned as united organization with Belorussian CP until 1920.

Communist Party of Romania — see Socialist Party of Romania.

Communist Party of Switzerland — revolutionary grouping that originated around *Forderung* newspaper; expelled from Swiss Social Democratic Party October-November 1918; known as the "old Communists"; claimed 1,200 members in Zürich 1919; fused with left wing of Social Democracy to form Swiss CP 1921.

Communist Party of the Netherlands — founded November 17, 1918; traced origin to formation in 1909 of Social Democratic Party (SDP) by expelled left-wing members (Tribunists) of Social Democratic Workers Party; SDP adopted internationalist position during war and aligned with Zimmerwald Left; 1,000 members in late 1918; joined Comintern April 1919.

Communist Party of the Ukraine — formed July 1918 as autonomous component of RCP with 4,000 members; grew out of RSDLP(B) of the Social Democracy of the Ukraine, which had led Ukranian Soviet republic January-February 1918.

Communist Workers Party of Germany (KAPD) — founded 1920 by ultraleft wing of KPD expelled in October 1919.

Communist Workers Party of Poland — founded December 16, 1918, in Warsaw by fusion of SDKPiL with Polish Socialist Party–Left.

Council of People's Representatives — name taken by Ebert's cabinet after November 9; consisted originally of three representatives each from SPD and USPD.

Dan, F.I. (1871-1947) — central leader of Russian Mensheviks; leading opponent of October revolution; deported in 1922; edited emigré Menshevik journal.

Däumig, Ernst (1866-1922) — an editor of *Vorwärts,* 1911-16; dismissed for opposing SPD war policy; leader of USPD and Revolutionary Shop Stewards in 1918; member of Berlin Executive Committee of Workers' and Soldiers' Councils; became cochairman of USPD in December 1919 and cochairman of German CP in 1920; left CP in 1921.

David, Eduard (1863-1930) — leader of SPD revisionists and outspoken supporter of German imperialism; worked in imperial colonial ministry in Max von Baden government 1918; first president of National Assembly 1919; minister without portfolio 1919-20.

Debs, Eugene V. (1855-1926) — founder and spokesman for U.S. SP and five-time presidential candidate; leader of party's left wing; helped found IWW; imprisoned for antiwar statements 1918-21; solidarized with Bolshevik revolution but remained in SP following 1919 split and establishment of U.S. Communist Party.

Denikin, A.I. (1872-1947) — tsarist general; commander-in-chief of White Army in southern Russia in civil war; emigrated 1920 after defeat by Red Army.

Deutsche Tageszeitung (German daily gazette) — conservative organ of Farmers' League; appeared 1894-1934 in Berlin.

Dittmann, Wilhelm (1874-1954) — SPD Reichstag deputy from 1912; joined centrist opposition in 1915; USPD party secretary 1917-22; imprisoned February-October 1918; member of Ebert cabinet November-December 1918; USPD delegate to second Comintern congress 1920; opposed Twenty-one Conditions and unification with KPD; returned to SPD in 1922.

Dreyfus, Alfred (1859-1935) — French officer framed for treason in 1894 as part of anti-Semitic campaign; conviction later overturned after long defense campaign.

Duda, G.A. — became Communist while Austrian war prisoner in Russia; signed invitation to first Comintern congress for Austrian Communists; on return to Austria joined Social Democrats and was denounced as traitor by CP.

Duma — Russian parliament under the tsar; had extremely limited powers.

Duncker, Hermann (1874-1960) — joined SPD 1893; founding member of Spartacus group; member of Spartacus and KPD Central Committees from 1918; arrested by Nazis 1933; fled Germany 1936; settled in German Democratic Republic after WWII where he joined SED.

Duncker, Käte (1871-1953) — joined SPD 1890; worked with Zetkin on

SPD women's paper; member of Spartacus and KPD Central Committees; responsible for party's work among women; held no leading posts after 1920; fled Germany 1938; settled in German Democratic Republic after WWII.

Dutov, A.I. (1864-1921) — tsarist colonel; general in Kolchak's White army 1918-19; defeated by Red Army; fled to China 1920; killed by own troops.

Dzerzhinsky, Feliks (Józef) (1877-1926) — Polish revolutionary, founder of SDKPiL; member Bolshevik Party central committee 1917-26; headed Cheka after revolution.

Eberlein, Hugo (1887-1944) — joined SPD 1906; member of Spartacus and KPD central committees; delegate to first Comintern congress; played leading role in Comintern until stripped of leadership posts 1928; fled Germany 1933; arrested 1937 in Soviet Union during Moscow purge trials; died in prison.

Ebert, Friedrich (1871-1925) — SPD leader, close collaborator of Bebel from 1906; cochairman of SPD 1913-19; supported chauvinist positions during war; appointed imperial chancellor by Max von Baden 1918; led Council of People's Representatives 1918-19; worked with army High Command to crush January uprising; German president 1919-25.

ECCI — Executive Committee of the Communist International, the elected leadership body of the Communist International.

Eichhorn, Emil (1863-1925) — headed SPD press bureau 1908-17; member of USPD 1917-20; Berlin chief of police 1918-19; dismissal by SPD sparked January uprising; joined KPD 1920.

Eisner, Kurt (1867-1919) — German Social Democrat; *Vorwärts* editor 1900-1906; revisionist before war; convinced of German responsibility for war, he opposed SPD pro-war policy and founded Munich USPD; led November 1918 revolution in Munich; prime minister of Bavarian republic 1918-19; helped organize right wing at Bern conference; assassinated by monarchist in February.

Emmich, Otto von (1848-1915) — German general; a key commander of army that invaded Belgium 1914.

Engels, Frederick (1820-1895) — lifelong collaborator of Karl Marx; coauthor of *Communist Manifesto* and cofounder of scientific socialism; leader of revolutionary democratic forces in 1848 German revolution; lived in England 1841-44 and again from 1849 to his death; in his last years the outstanding figure in the Second International.

Ernst, Eugen (1864-1954) — member of SPD Executive Committee during November 1918 revolution; Prussian interior minister 1918-19; replaced Eichhorn as Berlin police chief 1919-20.

Erzberger, Matthias (1875-1921) — member of German bourgeois Center Party; headed armistice commission for Max von Baden government; retained in that capacity by Ebert; minister in Scheidemann, Bauer governments 1919-20; assassinated by right-wing nationalist.

Executive Committee of the Berlin Workers' and Soldiers' Councils (Vollzugsrat) — elected November 10, 1918, at Busch Circus meeting of Berlin workers' and soldiers' councils; Berlin executive body of councils; until December congress of councils it acted as their national executive committee and thus, in theory, as the source of governmental authority.

Farmers' League (Bund der Landwirte) — reactionary agrarian organization led by monarchist large landowners; founded 1893.

Faure, Paul (1878-1960) — leader of centrist opposition in French SP during war; opposition delegate to 1919 Bern conference; opposed SP affiliation to Comintern in 1920; general secretary of French SP 1920-40; supported pro-Nazi Vichy government during World War II; expelled from SP 1944.

Federation of Foreign Communist Groups — formed May 1918 by Russian CP to organize among prisoners of war and immigrant workers in Russia; dissolved 1920.

Fineberg, Joseph (1886-1957) — member of British SP 1908-18; moved to Russia, joined RCP; helped prepare Comintern founding congress 1919; subsequently worked for Soviet state publications.

Foch, Ferdinand (1851-1929) — WWI marshal of French army; supreme commander of Allied armies 1918; set armistice conditions; participated in organizing intervention against Russia.

Die Forderung: Organ für Sozialistische Endzielpolitik (The demand: Organ for the politics of socialism, the final goal) — publication of first group of Swiss Communists; nine issues from October 1917 to March 1918.

Frässdorf, Julius (1857-1932) — German Social Democrat; Saxon state minister 1919; president of Saxon state parliament 1919-22.

Free Socialist Youth — founded October 1918 by delegates representing 3,000 Spartacus- and USPD-influenced youth; grew to 35,000 members by October 1919; adhered to Communist Youth International shortly thereafter.

Die Freiheit (Freedom) — daily organ of German USPD published in Berlin 1918-22.

Friedberg, Robert (1851-1920) — chairman of German bourgeois National Liberal Party from 1917; vice-president of Prussian state ministry 1917-18; joined German Democratic Party in 1918.

Friedrich Wilhelm IV (1795-1861) — king of Prussia 1840-61; forced by 1848 revolution to grant constitution; reimposed autocratic regime shortly thereafter.

Frölich, Paul (1884-1953) — SPD member 1902; leader of Bremen Left; supported Zimmerwald Left at 1916 Kienthal conference; elected to KPD Central Committee at founding congress; participated in Bavarian council republic 1919; expelled from KPD 1928 and joined Brandler's right opposition; rejoined SPD 1950; biographer of Luxemburg.

Frossard, Louis-Oscar (1889-1946) — leader of centrist opposition in French SP during war; became general secretary of party October 1918; opposition delegate to 1919 Bern conference; SP representative to second

Comintern congress 1920; general secretary of French CP 1920-23; split from CP 1923; SP member 1923-32; minister in several governments in 1930s and subsequently in pro-Nazi Pétain government 1940.

Fuchs, Eduard (1870-1940) — longtime SPD member; leader of Spartacus group during war; met with Bolshevik leadership 1918 on founding Comintern; later worked in Comintern apparatus; left KPD 1929.

Galliffet, Gaston-Alexandre-Auguste (1830-1909) — French general; commanded massacre of Paris Communards in 1871.

Gandorfer, Karl (b. 1875) — head of Bavarian Peasants' League after brother Ludwig's death in 1918; chairman of Central Peasant Council; member of Eisner's Bavarian government 1918-1919; briefly a member of Bavarian revolutionary government April 1919.

Garnier-Pagès, Louis-Antoine (1803-1878) — member of French provisional government and mayor of Paris in 1848; member of republican government 1870-71.

Gelwitzki — delegate from Berlin to KPD founding congress; believed to have joined ultraleft split 1919; subsequently left politics.

German Democratic Party — liberal bourgeois party founded in November 1918 by former Progressive Party and left wing of National Liberals.

German Nationalist Party — bourgeois party in Austria.

Göhre, Paul (1864-1928) — SPD member; undersecretary of war 1918; Prussian minister 1919-23.

Gompers, Samuel (1850-1924) — founder and president of American Federation of Labor 1886-1924 (except 1895); advocated class collaboration, supported U.S. entry into war; chairman of Labor Commission at 1919 Versailles conference; refused to attend Bern conference for chauvinist reasons.

Graber, Ernst Paul (1875-1956) — leading Swiss Social Democrat; signed left statement at Kienthal conference; supported right wing in Swiss party after 1917.

Grimm, Robert (1881-1958) — leader of Swiss Social Democratic Party and longtime editor of *Berner Tagwacht;* took centrist position during war; participated in Zimmerwald and Kienthal conferences; chairman of International Socialist Commission 1915-17; helped organize Two-and-a-Half International in 1920; later returned to Second International.

Groener, Wilhelm (1867-1939) — head of Prussian war ministry 1916-17; succeeded Ludendorff as Quartermaster General 1918-19; collaborated with Ebert to preserve bourgeois rule and authority of officer corps after November revolution.

Grünberg, Carl (1861-1940) — Austrian Social Democrat; edited *Archiv für die Geschichte des Sozialismus und der Arbeiterbewegung,* prominent socialist historical journal.

Haase, Hugo (1863-1919) — elected SPD Reichstag member 1897; in SPD center current before war; SPD cochairman 1911-16; voted against war credits in Reichstag 1916; cochairman of USPD; member of Council of People's Representatives November-December 1918; assassinated by monarchist.

Haenisch, Konrad (1876-1925) — SPD member; in left wing before 1914; chauvinist during war; Prussian minister of culture 1918-21.

Hammer, Arthur — Spartacus delegate to KPD founding congress from Essen; member of Essen Workers' and Soldiers' Council; left KPD 1925.

Hapsburg — ruling dynasty of Austro-Hungarian Empire.

Hauschild, Herbert (1880-1928) — secretary, then acting consul-general of German legation in Moscow 1918.

Haydar Khan 'Amu Ughli (Rejeb Bombi) (d. 1921) — Iranian Socialist; joined RSDLP; helped found Iranian Social Democratic Party in 1904 in Baku; participant in Iranian Constitutional revolution; after 1916 a leader of Adalet (Justice) Party, which became Iranian CP in 1920; murdered in Gilan while in captivity by the Nationalist forces of Mirza Kuchech Khan.

Heckert, Fritz (1884-1936) — joined SPD in 1902; leading Spartacist in Chemnitz [Karl-Marx-Stadt] during war; chairman of Chemnitz Workers' and Soldiers' Council 1918; delegate to general congress of councils 1918; founding member of KPD; member of KPD central committee 1919; member of ECCI from 1921; KPD representative in Moscow 1932-36.

Henderson, Arthur (1863-1935) — general secretary of British Labour Party 1911-34; chauvinist during war; cabinet minister 1916-17; central organizer of 1919 Bern conference; president of Second International 1925-29; British foreign secretary 1929-31.

Heydebrandt und der Lasa, Ernst von (1851-1924) — leader of German Conservative Party in Prussian parliament; member of Reichstag.

Hilferding, Rudolf (1877-1941) — Austro-Marxist and economic theorist; supporter of SPD centrist opposition during war; member of USPD 1917; editor-in-chief of *Freiheit* 1918-22; anti-Bolshevik; returned to SPD in 1922; German finance minister 1923, 1928-29; killed by Hitler's gestapo.

Hindenburg, Paul von (1847-1934) — German general; army chief of staff 1916-18; president 1925-34; appointed Hitler chancellor.

Hintze, Paul von (1864-1941) — German admiral; foreign minister under kaiser 1918.

Hirsch, Paul (1868-1938) — SPD member; Prussian prime minister 1918-20 and interior minister 1918-19; helped plan suppression of January uprising.

Hirsch, Werner (1899-1937) — German revolutionist; member of Hamburg Workers' and Soldiers' Council; an organizer of People's Naval Division; delegate to KPD founding congress from Cuxhaven; from mid-1920s editor-in-chief of Vienna, then Berlin, *Rote Fahne;* imprisoned by Nazis 1933-34; arrested in Soviet Union during Moscow purge trials and probably shot.

Hoernle, Edwin (1883-1952) — SPD member 1910; active in youth work; supporter of left wing; Spartacist; chairman Württemburg KPD 1919;

editor of KPD farm weekly *Der Pflug* (The plow); KPD Central Committee 1923; exile in Moscow 1933-45; held important posts in GDR after 1945.

Hofer, Adolf (1868-1935) — joined SPD 1880s; USPD 1917; member USPD executive committee; Prussian minister of agriculture after November revolution; rejoined SPD 1922.

Hoffmann, Max (1869-1927) — German general; commander of eastern front 1916-18; part of German delegation at Brest-Litovsk negotiations 1918.

Hohenzollern — ruling dynasty of Prussia and German Empire until 1918.

Huysmans, Camille (1871-1968) — leader of Belgian Workers' Party; secretary of International Socialist Bureau from 1904; took chauvinist stand 1914; helped organize 1919 Bern conference; subsequently served in Belgian government.

IKD — see International Communists of Germany.

Independents — see Independent Social Democratic Party of Germany.

Independent Social Democratic Party of Germany (USPD) — formed at April 1917 congress by centrist opposition expelled from SPD; 120,000 members in 1917; participated in provisional government under Ebert November-December 1918; included Spartacists until they broke to form KPD December 1918; grew to 300,000 members by March, 750,000 by November 1919; majority fused with KPD and joined Comintern after 1920 congress; minority retained party name until rejoining SPD in 1922.

Industrial Workers of Great Britain — founded 1911; led significant local strikes that year.

Industrial Workers of the World (Australia) — formed 1907, with particular influence among mine and transport workers; during war active in struggle against war and conscription; main leaders convicted of "high treason"; renamed One Big Union in 1918.

Industrial Workers of the World (Britain) — formed 1910 following tour by U.S. IWW leader Bill Haywood; significant influence among dock workers and in shop stewards' movement.

Industrial Workers of the World (U.S.) — founded 1905 as revolutionary industrial union movement; led numerous strikes; rejected electoral participation and work in AFL; opposed U.S. participation in World War and suffered severe repression; went into decline after formation of CP in 1919; rejected affiliation to Comintern-led Red International of Labour Unions in 1921; participated in 1922 attempt to set up anarcho-syndicalist rival to it.

International Communists of Germany (IKD) — formed in December 1918 by Left Radicals of Bremen and groups in other cities which had broken with SPD during World War and had disagreed with Spartacists' tactic of remaining in USPD; joined KPD at founding congress.

Internationale Group — see Spartacus League.

Internationalist Socialist Party (Argentina) — split from Argentine Socialist Party January 1918; joined Comintern and changed name to CP.

International Socialist Bureau — formed in 1900 as executive body of

Second International with headquarters in Brussels; its secretariat moved to The Hague with outbreak of war, but the bureau did not meet again.

IWW — see Industrial Workers of the World (U.S.).

Izvestiya (News) — daily organ of All-Russian Central Executive Committee of the soviets from 1917.

Jacob — Berlin delegate to KPD founding congress; part of 1919 ultraleft split.

Jacob, Mathilde (1873-1943?) — German Socialist; Rosa Luxemburg's secretary; killed by Nazis in Theresienstadt concentration camp.

Jezierska, Fanny — Spartacist collaborator in Berlin; worked in Comintern apparatus in western Europe and Soviet Union 1919-29; emigrated to France.

Joffe, A.A. (1883-1927) — joined Russian Social Democracy before 1900; during war with Mezhrayontsi, a current intermediate between Bolsheviks and Mensheviks; joined Bolsheviks June 1917 and elected to Central Committee August 1917; member of Soviet delegation to Brest-Litovsk 1918; Soviet ambassador to Berlin April-November 1918; supported left opposition to Stalin led by Trotsky; committed suicide when refused visa to receive medical treatment.

Jogiches, Leo (Tyszka) (1867-1919) — a founding leader and central organizer of Polish Social Democracy; imprisoned but escaped to Germany 1907; central organizer of Spartacists during war; member Spartacus and KPD central committees; arrested and murdered in March.

Kahlert, Bruno — Spartacist during war; Berlin delegate to KPD founding congress; left party in 1920, supported ultralefts.

Kahmann, Hermann (b. 1881) — trade union and SPD functionary; member of Central Committee of the German Socialist Republic 1918-19.

Kaledin, A.M. (1861-1918) — tsarist general; leader of a cossack counterrevolutionary army during Russian civil war; committed suicide.

KAPD — see Communist Workers Party of Germany.

Kapp, Wolfgang (1858-1922) — cofounder of extreme chauvinist German Fatherland Party 1917; led 1920 putsch attempt to reestablish monarchy and military dictatorship.

Karski — see Marchlewski, Julian.

Kautsky, Karl (1854-1938) — Czech by origin; Marxist theorist and collaborator of Engels; founder and editor of *Die Neue Zeit;* a leader of "Marxist Center" in SPD before 1914; adopted pacifist stand 1914, apologist for chauvinist majority; founding member USPD and supporter of its right wing; undersecretary in foreign ministry after November 1918 revolution; delegate to 1919 Bern conference; vehement opponent of Russian October revolution; rejoined SPD 1922.

Kerensky, A.F. (1881-1970) — Russian Socialist Revolutionary; leader of Trudovik group in Fourth State Duma; prime minister of Russian Provisional Government overthrown by October 1917 revolution; emigrated 1918.

Klassekampen (Class struggle) — organ of Danish Socialist Workers Party, founded October 1918; edited by Marie-Sophie Nielson.

Knief, Johann (1880-1919) — leader of Bremen Left and IKD; member of Council of People's Representatives in short-lived 1919 Bremen council republic; founding member of KPD.

Kolb, Wilhelm (1870-1918) — right-wing German Social Democrat; chairman of SPD fraction in Baden state parliament.

Kolegayev, A.L. (1887-1937) — Russian revolutionist; Left SR; member of Council of People's Commissars December 1917-March 1918; opposed July 1918 Left SR uprising and joined RCP in November 1918.

Kommunist (Communist) — Bolshevik journal launched in 1915; only one double issue appeared in September 1915; discontinued because of disagreements between publishers and Central Committee.

Kornilov, L.G. (1870-1918) — tsarist general; commander-in-chief under Provisional Government 1917; led attempted putsch in September 1917; later led White armies until killed in battle.

KPD — see Communist Party of Germany.

Krasnov, P.N. (1869-1947) — tsarist general; led White army in south Russia 1918-19.

Kreuz-Zeitung — see *Neue Preussische Kreuz-Zeitung*.

Krupp von Bohlen und Halbach — family of leading German steel and armaments capitalists; during World War I, firm run by Gustav (1870- 1950) and Bertha (1886-1957); helped finance Nazis.

Kun, Béla (1886-1939) — joined Bolsheviks while war prisoner in Russia; chairman of Federation of Foreign Communist Groups 1918; returned to Hungary November 1918, organized and headed CP; head of Hungarian Soviet government March-June 1919; later worked in Comintern apparatus; arrested and killed during Moscow frame-up trials.

Lamartine, Alphonse de (1790-1869) — French poet and republican; minister of foreign affairs of French provisional government in 1848.

Landsberg, Otto (1869-1957) — German Social Democrat; open proimperialist during war; member of Council of People's Representatives November 1918; minister of justice in Scheidemann government 1919.

Lange, Paul (1880-1951) — joined SPD in 1900; member of Spartacus group during war; member of Spartacus and KPD central committees 1918-19; trade union functionary; rejoined SPD 1922; joined SED 1946.

Laufenberg, Heinrich (1872-1932) — German Socialist; Hamburg Left Radical during war; chairman of Hamburg workers' council in 1918-19; headed Unified Communists fraction at general congress of councils December 1918; KPD founding member; leader of 1919 ultraleft split.

Lavrov, Peter (1823-1900) — prominent Russian Narodnik writer.

Lazzari, Costantino (1857-1927) — general secretary of Italian SP 1912-19; attended Zimmerwald and Kienthal conferences; joined Comintern along with Italian SP in 1919, but left Comintern with SP majority in 1921; represented SP at third Comintern congress 1921.

League of Nations — imperialist alliance created by 1919 Paris conference convened by Entente powers to defend division of world imposed by that conference; U.S. refused to join; Soviet Union joined in 1934; disappeared with World War II.

Ledebour, Georg (1850-1947) — longtime SPD leader; opposed SPD majority position during war; led right wing of Zimmerwald movement; cochairman of USPD 1917-19; leader of Revolutionary Committee during January 1919 uprising; opposed USPD majority's fusion with Communists in 1920; refused to rejoin SPD and led a small left-wing group throughout 1920s; emigrated to Switzerland 1933.

Ledru-Rollin, Alexandre Auguste (1807-1874) — leader of petty-bourgeois liberal republicans in 1848 French revolution; member of 1848 provisional government; supported crushing of Paris workers in June 1848.

Left Communists — faction of the Bolshevik Party in 1918 that opposed Brest-Litovsk treaty; led by Bukharin.

Left Social Democratic Party of Sweden — founded 1917 by expelled left-wing minority of Social Democratic Workers Party; 17,000 members in 1919; affiliated to Comintern; majority became CP in 1921.

Left Socialist Revolutionary Party — split from Socialist Revolutionaries in 1917 over questions of war, land policy, and Soviet power; joined Bolshevik coalition government November 28 (15), 1917; broke from Soviet government and organized attempted insurrection July 1918.

Legien, Carl (1861-1920) — Social Democratic head of German trade unions from 1890; avowed reformist; supported SPD right wing during war; played central role in defeating Kapp putsch in 1920.

Leipziger Volkszeitung (Leipzig people's gazette) — Social Democratic newspaper; appeared 1894-1932; USPD organ 1917-22.

Lenin, V.I. (1870-1924) — founder of St. Petersburg League for the Emancipation of the Working Class 1893; exiled to Siberia 1896; went abroad and helped publish *Iskra* 1900-1903; central leader of Bolsheviks from 1903; developed strategy for proletarian leadership in fight for provisional revolutionary government to establish revolutionary democratic dictatorship of proletariat and peasantry; participated in 1905-7 Russian revolution; after 1907 defended revolutionary organization against liquidationism; RSDLP representative on International Socialist Bureau 1908-12; issued call for new, revolutionary International 1914; organized Zimmerwald Left to fight for this goal 1915-17; returned to Russia and led Bolsheviks' struggle for Soviet power 1917; chairman of People's Commissars 1917-24; central leader of Comintern.

Lequis, Arnold — German general; commanded troops brought into Berlin in December 1918 in unsuccessful attempt to put down revolution.

Levi, Paul (1883-1930) — left-wing German Social Democrat; worked with Lenin in Switzerland during war; member of Spartacus League and KPD central committees; central leader of party after Jogiches's murder in 1919; expelled 1921 for breach of discipline; rejoined USPD in 1922 and later SPD; leader of SPD left wing until his death.

Levien, Max (1885-1937) — Russian emigré; collaborated with Bolsheviks; settled in Germany; leader of Munich Spartacists; chairman of soldiers' council; with Leviné, leader of Munich council republic 1919; later returned to Russia and worked in Comintern apparatus; ECCI 1922; arrested and presumably shot during Moscow trials.

Leviné, Eugen (1883-1919) — born in Russia and participant in 1905 revolution; subsequently settled in Germany; member of Spartacus group and leader of KPD; delegate to general congress of councils 1918; central leader of Bavarian council republic in 1919; arrested, tried, and shot after its overthrow.

Lieber, M.I. (1880-1937) — leader of Jewish Bund and leading Menshevik during 1917; opponent of Russian October revolution; executed during Moscow trials.

Liebknecht, Karl (1871-1919) — son of Wilhelm Liebknecht, a founder of German socialism; helped found Socialist Youth International 1907; jailed same year for book *Militarism and Anti-Militarism;* only member of Reichstag to vote against war credits in December 1914; helped found Spartacus current; jailed 1916 for antiwar propaganda; released by November 1918 revolution; leader of Revolutionary Committee during Berlin January uprising; arrested and murdered by SPD-instigated Freikorps.

Lloyd George, David (1863-1945) — British Liberal politician; prime minister 1916-22; coauthored Versailles treaty and organized British intervention against Soviet republic.

Longuet, Jean (1876-1938) — grandson of Karl Marx; leader of centrist minority in French SP after 1916 although consistently voted for war credits in Chamber of Deputies; leader of centrist opposition at 1919 Bern conference; opposed SP joining Comintern; when it did so in 1920 he split along with right-wing minority that retained SP's name.

Loriot, Fernand (1870-1932) — leader of revolutionary left in French SP during war; secretary of Committee for the Third International; presented revolutionary viewpoint at 1919 Bern conference; international secretary of French CP 1921; opposed Stalinization of CP and left party 1926; subsequently collaborated with opposition communist groups.

Lüdemann, Hermann (b. 1880) — SPD delegate to General Congress of Workers' and Soldiers' Councils.

Ludendorff, Erich (1865-1937) — German general; Quartermaster General, real head of army and virtual dictator 1916-18; participated in 1920 right-wing coup attempt and 1923 Hitler putsch; Nazi delegate to Reichstag 1924-28.

Lüttwitz, Walther von (1859-1942) — German baron and general; commander-in-chief 1919-20; leading participant in 1920 right-wing coup attempt.

Luxemburg, Rosa (1871-1919) — founding leader of SDKP 1893; later lived in Germany and joined SPD 1898; Polish representative on International Socialist Bureau from 1903; leader of left wing against revisionist right and, after 1910, against "Marxist Center" led by Kautsky; leader of Spartacus group during war; imprisoned by German government 1915; chief writer for *Die Rote Fahne* November 1918-January 1919; founding leader of German CP; arrested and murdered by SPD-instigated Freikorps after January uprising.

MacDonald, James Ramsay (1866-1937) — leader of British Labour Party from 1906; forced to resign as head of Labour Party 1914 because of pacifist position on war; opposed to Bolshevik revolution; delegate to 1919 Bern conference; Labour prime minister in 1924, 1929-31; split from party 1931 to found coalition government with Conservatives and Liberals.

MacLean, John (1879-1923) — Scottish working-class leader; imprisoned for opposition to war; leader of left wing in British Socialist Party; editor of *Vanguard* 1915; supporter of Third International, although never joined CP.

Marchlewski, Julian (Karski) (1866-1925) — cofounder of SDKP; a leader of Spartacists during war; jailed by German government 1916-18; freed with Soviet government intervention; subsequently based in Russia, helped reorganize KPD after January defeat; played leading role in Comintern.

Martov, L. (Julius) (1873-1923) — a central leader of Russian Social Democrats and, from 1903, of Mensheviks; leader of "Menshevik-Internationalists" during Russian revolution; opposed October revolution; emigrated in 1920.

Marx, Karl (1818-1883) — leader of Communist League 1847-52; coauthor of "Communist Manifesto" and cofounder of scientific socialism; editor of *Neue Rheinische Zeitung* in 1848-49 revolution; central leader of International Working Men's Association (First International) 1864-1876; published first volume of *Capital* 1867; partisan and defender of Paris Commune.

Maslov, P.P. (1867-1946) — prominent Russian economist; member of Menshevik right wing; defensist during war; left politics 1917.

Maslov, S.L. (b. 1873) — Right Socialist Revolutionary; minister of agriculture in Russian Provisional Government 1917; opposed peasants' demand for land reform; later collaborated with Soviet government.

Max von Baden (1867-1929) — German prince, politician, and heir to throne of Baden; appointed imperial chancellor October 3, 1918; named Ebert as successor on November 9.

Mehring, Franz (1846-1919) — German Marxist historian and scholar; opposed revisionism; an editor of SPD magazine *Die Neue Zeit;* leader of Spartacus group; imprisoned 1916; founding member of Spartacus League and KPD.

Mensheviks — originated in 1903 as faction of RSDLP at its second congress; moved increasingly to right after 1907; during war, contained open chauvinist and centrist wings; participated in Provisional Government 1917; opposed October 1917 revolution; during civil war, one wing openly supported White armies, the other claimed to oppose Whites; after 1921 functioned primarily in exile.

Merges, August (1870-1933) — Spartacist leader of Brunswick Workers' and Soldiers' Council and president of Brunswick Council of People's Representatives 1918-19; represented ultraleft KAPD at second Comintern congress; later joined KPD; murdered by Nazis.

Meyer, Ernst (1887-1930) — left-wing SPD member from 1908; delegate to Zimmerwald and Kienthal conferences; leader of Spartacists; KPD Central Committee from 1918; chairman of its Political Bureau 1921-22; removed from leadership positions 1929 for opposition to Stalin's policies.

Milyukov, P.N. (1859-1943) — leader of Russian Cadet Party; ardent supporter of war; foreign minister in 1917 Provisional Government; active opponent of October revolution.

Monatte, Pierre (1881-1960) — French anarcho-syndicalist from 1904; leader of antichauvinist opposition in unions during war; secretary of Committee for Third International; advocated revolutionary syndicalists joining Comintern; did not join French CP until 1923; expelled 1924 for opposing anti-Trotsky campaign; returned to syndicalism.

Morgari, Oddino (1865-1929) — cofounder of Italian SP; became chief editor of *Avanti!* in 1908; member of International Socialist Committee elected at Zimmerwald; centrist; briefly supported Russian revolution and sympathetic to Bolsheviks; observer for ISP at 1919 Bern conference; subsequently became right-wing social democrat.

Müller, Hermann (1876-1931) — member SPD executive committee; SPD cochairman from 1919; member Executive Committee of Berlin councils; German foreign minister 1919-20; chancellor 1920, 1928-30.

Müller, Richard (b. 1880) — USPD member; chairman of Revolutionary Shop Stewards and of Executive Committee of Berlin councils; briefly in KPD 1920-21; delegate to first congress of Red Trade Union International in Moscow 1921; subsequently left politics.

Münzenberg, Willi (1889-1940) — German Socialist; moved to Switzerland 1910; secretary of reconstituted Socialist Youth International 1915-19; editor of *Jugend-Internationale;* rallied to Zimmerwald Left; founding member KPD; secretary of Communist Youth International 1919-21; KPD central committee 1927; broke with Stalinism and expelled from KPD 1938; killed during Nazi conquest of France.

Muravyov, M.A. (1880-1918) — former tsarist officer who sided with Left SRs after October revolution; led attempted mutiny of Red troops in 1918; killed during arrest.

Mussolini, Benito (1883-1945) — coeditor of Italian SP organ *Avanti!* 1912-14; adopted chauvinist position in 1914 and expelled from party; founded fascist movement 1919; Italian dictator 1922-43.

Nadolny, Rudolf (1873-1953) — member of German foreign office from 1902; head of its Russian department 1918-19.

Naine, Charles (1874-1926) — a leader of Swiss SP; member of International Socialist Committee elected at Zimmerwald; joined right wing of Swiss party 1917.

Narodnik Communists — founded September 1918 as split from Left SRs following July uprising against Soviet power; fused with RCP in November 1918.

Narodniks — movement among Russian intelligentsia in late nineteenth century dedicated to revolutionary overthrow of tsarism; saw the liberation of peasants and distribution of landed estates to them as key to opening road to socialist development; split in 1879; majority Narodovoltsi wing later oriented to alliance with liberal bourgeoisie and individual terrorism; these forces formed Socialist Revolutionary Party in 1901-2.

Narodovoltsi — see Narodniks.

National Democrats — Polish right-wing, anti-Semitic, capitalist party.

Neue Preussische Kreuz-Zeitung (New Prussian cross gazette) — main organ of reactionary Prussian junkers; published from 1848 in Berlin under various names.

New York Evening Post — bourgeois paper founded 1801; then under liberal editorship, it published the secret treaties between Entente and tsarist government after October revolution.

Nielson, Marie-Sophie (1875-1951) — leader of Danish Social Democratic Party 1916-18; helped found Socialist Workers Party in 1918 and Left Socialist Party in 1919; editor of *Klassekampen;* founding member of Danish CP 1919; expelled from party 1928 for not supporting campaign against Trotsky.

Nobs, Ernst (1886-1957) — leading Swiss Social Democrat; supported Zimmerwald Left at Kienthal conference; adopted centrist position in 1917 and became right-wing Social Democrat after 1920; president of Switzerland 1949.

Norwegian Workers Party — founded 1887; left-wing current won majority in 1918; 105,000 members in 1919; affiliated to Comintern June 1919, minority of 3,000 split in 1921 to form Social Democratic Workers Party; majority disaffiliated from Comintern in 1923; minority founded Norwegian CP with 15,000 members.

Noske, Gustav (1868-1946) — right-wing SPD leader and supporter of German colonial policy; member of Council of People's Representatives 1918-19; organized suppression of January 1919 uprising; German war minister 1919-20.

Pankhurst, Sylvia (1882-1928) — joined British Independent Labour Party at age sixteen; repeatedly arrested for activity in labor and suffrage movements; held antichauvinist position on war; took ultraleft stand at second Comintern congress; founding member British CP; expelled 1921.

Pannekoek, Anton (1873-1960) — joined Dutch Social Democrats in 1902; leader of left-wing Tribune current 1907; member of Zimmerwald Left during war; cofounder of Dutch CP 1918; part of 1921 ultraleft split, subsequently left political activity.

Party of Revolutionary Communism — founded September 1918 as split from Left SRs following July uprising against Soviet power; supported Soviet government but at first denied need for proletarian dictatorship; joined RCP in fall of 1920.

People's Naval Division — detachment of sailors stationed in Berlin after November 9, 1918, to defend republican government; radicalized and came into conflict with government; clashed with government forces December 24, 1918; formally declared neutrality in January 1919 fighting.

Der Pflug (The plow) — KPD farm weekly, published in Württemburg 1919.

Pieck, Wilhelm (1876-1960) — joined SPD in 1895; founding member of Spartacus current; imprisoned 1915; member of Spartacus League and KPD Central Committee; cochairman of KPD founding congress; member Comintern Executive Committee from 1928; chairman KPD from 1935; lived in Soviet Union 1933-45; leader of SED after World War II; president of German Democratic Republic 1949-60.

Plekhanov, Georgiy (1856-1918) — founder of Russian Marxism and of Emancipation of Labor group 1883; influential Marxist theorist; leader of RSDLP from its formation; Menshevik after 1903; took extreme chauvinist position during war; opposed October revolution.

Politiken (Politics) — daily organ of Swedish Left Social Democratic Party.

Die Post — reactionary Berlin newspaper; organ of Imperial Free Conservative Party; published 1866-1919.

Potresov, A.N. (1869-1934) — early Russian Marxist; right-wing Menshevik; chauvinist during war; opposed October revolution; emigrated 1922.

Price, M. Philips — *Manchester Guardian* reporter in Petrograd during Russian revolution; won to communism; *Daily Herald* correspondent in Berlin during German revolution; early publicist for Communist movement.

Proshyan, P.P. (1883-1918) — leader of Left SRs; participated in July 1918 revolt against Bolsheviks.

Radek, Karl (1885-1939) — joined SDKPiL 1904; moved to Germany in 1908 and was active in German Socialist left; expelled from SPD in factional purge 1913; a member of Zimmerwald Left bureau with Lenin and Zinoviev 1915; joined Bolsheviks 1917; Bolshevik and Soviet emissary to Germany December 1918; arrested February 1919; released January 1920; elected to Bolshevik Central Committee 1919; played prominent role in Comintern; member of ECCI presidium; with Trotsky, part of Bolshevik-Leninist opposition to Stalin 1923-29; expelled from CP 1927; capitulated 1929; arrested 1937 during Moscow frame-up trials and died in prison.

Rakovsky, Christian (1873-1941) — prominent Romanian Socialist since 1890s; organized antiwar conference of Balkan Socialist parties summer 1915; elected secretary of Revolutionary Balkan Social Democratic Labor Federation 1915; attended Zimmerwald conference; joined Bolsheviks 1918; became head of Ukrainian Soviet government January 1919;

elected to Bolshevik central committee 1919; member of Bolshevik-Leninist opposition to Stalin 1923-34; expelled from party and arrested 1927; capitulated 1934; died in prison following Moscow frame-up trials.

RCP — see Russian Communist Party.

Red Army — organized by Soviet government in early 1918, after disintegration of tsarist army; defended revolution from invasion by fifteen imperialist powers and from counterrevolutionary White Guards; led by Trotsky from March 4, 1918.

Red Soldiers' League — founded by Spartacus League November 1918; carried out political education and organization among soldiers.

Reinhard, Wilhelm (1869-1954) — German colonel; headed Freikorps troops that crushed January 1919 Berlin uprising.

Reinhardt, Walther (1872-1930) — German colonel; named Prussian war minister by SPD in December 1918.

Reinstein, Boris (1866-1947) — originally from Russia, moved to U.S. 1901; joined Socialist Labor Party; sent to abortive Stockholm conference 1917; went to Russia and joined Bolsheviks in April 1918; attended first Comintern congress as SLP delegate; subsequently worked in Comintern and Profintern apparatus.

Renaudel, Pierre (1871-1935) — prior to war an associate of Jean Jaurès, central leader of French SP; after 1914 central leader of SP rightwing majority; editor of *L'Humanité* 1914-18; delegate at 1919 Bern conference; opposed Comintern; part of 1920 right-wing split that retained name SP; led right-wing split from SP in 1933.

Renner, Karl (1870-1950) — prominent revisionist in Austrian Social Democracy; chauvinist during war; Austrian chancellor 1919-20, and president 1931-33.

Reventlow, Ernst von (1869-1943) — German count; journalist for *Deutsche Tageszeitung* during WWI; extreme chauvinist.

Revolutionary Balkan Social Democratic Federation — formed 1910 by Social Democrats from Serbia, Bulgaria, Romania, and Greece; 1915 conference elected Central Bureau with Christian Rakovsky as secretary; became Balkan Communist Federation in 1920.

Revolutionary Committee — formed by KPD, Revolutionary Shop Stewards, and Berlin USPD to lead January Berlin uprising; chairmen were Karl Liebknecht, Paul Scholze, and Georg Ledebour.

Revolutionary Shop Stewards of the Large Factories of Greater Berlin (Die revolutionäre Obleute und Vertrauensmänner der Grossbetriebe Gross-Berlins) — loose association of leaders of January 1918 strikes; composed of workers' delegates who were also members of USPD; rejected fusion with KPD on January 1, 1919; participated in January 1919 Berlin uprising; ceased functioning thereafter.

Richter, Eugen (1838-1906) — German bourgeois liberal politician.

Rieger — Berlin delegate to KPD founding congress; part of 1919 ultraleft split.

Rodbertus-Jagetzow, Johann Karl (1805-1875) — German economist and politician; leader of Left Center in Prussian National Assembly in 1848 revolution; advocated "state socialism."

Rosmer, Alfred (1877-1964) — French revolutionary syndicalist; joined Zimmerwald movement during war; joined CP on its formation 1920; editor of *L'Humanité;* leading member of Red International of Labor Unions; expelled from CP in 1924 as supporter of left opposition to Stalin; broke with International Left Opposition in 1930 but collaborated with Trotsky and Fourth International after 1936.

Die Rote Fahne (The red flag) — founded by Liebknecht and Luxemburg as daily central organ of Spartacus League and German CP; began publishing November 9, 1918.

Rozin, Fritz (1870-1919) — Latvian Bolshevik; member of RSDLP central committee 1907; Soviet commissar for Latvian affairs 1918-19.

RSDLP — see Russian Social Democratic Labor Party.

Rubanovich, I.A. (1860-1920) — a leader of Russian Socialist Revolutionary Party and its representative on International Socialist Bureau; chauvinist during war; delegate to 1919 Bern conference.

Rudnyánszky, Endre (1885-1943) — Hungarian prisoner of war in Russia; joined RCP 1917; took part in founding Hungarian Communist Group; chairman of Federation of Foreign Communist Groups in late 1918; attended first and second Comintern congresses; elected to ECCI; Moscow representative of Hungarian soviet republic; expelled from Hungarian CP 1921.

Rühle, Otto (1874-1943) — joined SPD in 1900; voted with Liebknecht against war credits in Reichstag in 1915; member of Spartacus group until 1917; refused to join USPD; leader of IKD in Dresden; original chairman of Dresden Workers' and Soldiers' Council; delegate to KPD founding congress; part of 1919 ultraleft split; served on Dewey commission to investigate Moscow frame-up trial against Trotsky 1937.

Russian Communist Party (Bolsheviks) (RCP) — originated as majority (Bolshevik) faction of RSDLP at 1903 second congress; led 1917 October revolution and Soviet government; changed name to RCP(B) in March 1918.

Russian Social Democratic Labor Party (RSDLP) — founded 1898; divided at 1903 congress into Bolshevik (majority) and Menshevik (minority) factions.

Savinkov, B.V. (1879-1925) — Russian Socialist Revolutionary; vice-minister of war in Provisional Government 1917; joined attempted Kornilov coup; led counterrevolutionary uprisings after October; captured and imprisoned.

Scheidemann, Philipp (1865-1939) — German SPD member; elected to Reichstag 1898; became a secretary of SPD executive committee 1911; with Ebert central leader of party after Bebel's death in 1913; led SPD into support for war 1914; SPD cochairman from 1917; appointed minister without portfolio by kaiser October 1918; member of Ebert's Council of People's

Representatives; presided over suppression of 1918-19 revolution; chancellor 1919; forced into exile by Nazis 1933.

Schiemann, Theodor (1847-1921) — German professor of Russian history, known for hostility to Russia.

Scheüch, Heinrich (b. 1864) — German general; chief of War Office from 1917; Prussian war minister 1918-19.

Scholze, Paul — chairman of Berlin Revolutionary Shop Stewards; cochairman with Liebknecht and Ledebour of Revolutionary Committee in January 1919 uprising; later joined KPD.

SDKP, SDKPiL — see Social Democracy of the Kingdom of Poland and Lithuania.

SED — Socialist Unity Party, ruling party of German Democratic Republic.

Serrati, Giacinto Menotti (1874-1926) — central leader of Italian SP during war; editor of *Avanti!* 1915-20; attended Zimmerwald and Kienthal conferences; led SP into Comintern; elected to ECCI; opposed break with Italian reformists and was expelled from International in 1921 along with party majority; led SP left wing into fusion with CP in 1924.

Severing, Carl (1875-1952) — right-wing SPD member; as commissioner for Rhineland and Westphalia 1919-20, helped suppress workers rebellions in Ruhr; Prussian interior minister 1920-26 and 1930-32; German interior minister 1928-30.

Sirola, Yrjö (1876-1936) — longtime leader of Finnish Social Democratic Party; commissar of foreign affairs in revolutionary government 1918; founding leader of Finnish CP 1918; elected to ECCI 1921; worked in Comintern apparatus; Comintern emissary to U.S. CP 1925-27.

Skoropadsky, P.P. (1873-1945) — tsarist general; head of German puppet government of Ukraine 1918.

Social Democracy of the Kingdom of Poland and Lithuania (SDKPiL) — founded 1893 as Polish organization (SDKP); fused with Lithuanian Social Democracy in 1899; affiliated to RSDLP in 1906; split into two wings 1911; reunited 1916; fused with PPS-Left to form Polish CP in 1918.

Social Democratic Party of Bulgaria — founded 1891; known as Bulgarian Workers' Social Democratic Party from 1894; split into revolutionary Tesnyaki (Narrow) and opportunist Shiroki (Broad) wings 1903; Tesnyaki won mass support during war and had 35,000 members in 1919; joined Comintern and changed name to CP May 1919. Shiroki voted to quit Second International 1919 and against joining Comintern 1920; left wing split and joined CP, Shiroki then had 8,000 members.

Social Democratic Party of Denmark — founded 1878; refused to participate in Zimmerwald; 60,000 members October 1915; 92,000 members January 1919; left wing split November 1919 and fused with other groups to form Left Socialist Party, which accepted terms of admission to Comintern November 1920 and changed name to CP.

Social Democratic Party of Germany (SPD) — founded 1875 as Social

Democratic Workers Party from fusion of Marxist and Lassallean parties; changed name to SPD in 1891; largest and most influential party within Second International; more than one million members 1914; leadership supported German imperialist war effort; expelled oppositionists 1917; 250,000 members in March 1918; headed bourgeois provisional government 1918-19; received 38% of vote to national assembly January 1919; membership rose from 250,000 in 1918 to one million members in 1919.

Social Democratic Party of Lithuania — founded 1896; left wing joined SDKP 1899; worked with RSDLP groups from 1901; formed CP August 1918 with 800 members.

Social Democratic Party of Norway — see Norwegian Workers Party.

Social Democratic Party of Romania — see Socialist Party of Romania.

Social Democratic Party of Serbia — founded 1903; took internationalist position during war; endorsed January 1919 call for formation of Comintern; helped organize founding of Socialist Workers Party (Communist) of Yugoslavia in April 1919 which had 50,000 members by late 1919.

Social Democratic Party of Switzerland — founded 1888; leadership took centrist position during war, helping to lead Zimmerwald movement; withdrew from Second International 1919 with 52,000 members; voted for Comintern affiliation at 1919 congress, but membership referendum later that year reversed decision; left wing split and fused with other Communist groups to form Swiss CP March 1921.

Social Democratic Party of the Netherlands — see Communist Party of the Netherlands.

Social Democratic Workers Party of Austria — formed in 1874 as United Social Democratic Party but soon broke apart; refounded 1888; loose federation of six autonomous national parties from 1896 until breakup of Austro-Hungarian Empire in 1918, then functioned solely within German Austria; led governmental coalition with bourgeois parties in November 1918; 335,000 members in 1920.

Social Democratic Workers Party of Czechoslovakia — founded 1878 as a wing of Austrian party; separated from it in 1918; 500,000 members at time of internal split in 1920; left wing formed Czech CP in 1921 with 400,000 members.

Socialist Christian Party — right-wing Austrian bourgeois party.

Socialist Labor Party (U.S.) — founded 1876; during 1890s came under leadership of Daniel De Leon; adopted increasingly sectarian positions; took internationalist position during war; 2,000-3,000 members in 1916; initially sympathetic to October revolution; represented at Comintern founding congress; some in left wing joined in forming CP; SLP later rejected Soviet workers' state; degenerated into sect.

Socialist Labour Party (Britain) — formed 1903 as split from Social Democratic Federation; looked to U.S. SLP; 1,000 members at end of war.

Socialist Party of America — formed in 1901; opposed war; more than

100,000 members in January 1919; majority left wing split in August 1919 to form Communist Party and Communist Labor Party, which united in 1921.

Socialist Party of France (Section Française de l'Internationale ouvrière) — founded by merger of Guesde's Socialist Party of France and Juarès's French Socialist Party 1905; all SP deputies voted for war credits at outbreak of war; 72,000 members 1914; dropped to 17,000 December 1915; centrist minority won leadership July 1918; party voted to join Comintern with over 120,000 members December 1920; changed name to French Communist Party; right-wing minority of 50,000 split away, retaining name SP.

Socialist Party of Italy — founded 1892; openly reformist and chauvinist wing expelled at 1912 congress; initiated Zimmerwald conference; 81,000 members 1919, 216,000 in 1920; voted to affiliate to Comintern 1919, but refused to exclude party's reformist wing; minority split in January 1921 to form Italian CP.

Socialist Party of Portugal — founded 1875; adopted pacifist position during war, supporting Zimmerwald movement; left-wing elements split off, helping to form CP in 1921.

Socialist Party of Romania — founded 1893 as Social Democratic Party of the Workers of Romania; right wing joined National Liberal Party 1899; party ceased to function; revived 1910 as Social Democratic Party; internationalist during war; participated in Zimmerwald; renamed SP November 1918; 24,000 members 1919; right wing split 1921 over call to join Comintern; majority took name CP.

Socialist Propaganda League — formed 1915 in Boston by members of U.S. SP's Latvian Federation; strongly influenced by Pannekoek and Dutch Tribunists; held ultraleft views; supported Bolsheviks and formation of Third International; published *New International,* renamed *Revolutionary Age,* with Louis Fraina as editor; played important role in birth of U.S. Communist movement 1919.

Socialist Revolutionary Party (Russia) — came together 1901-2 through fusion of Narodnik currents; affiliated to Second International; divided during war between defensist and nondefensist wings; in 1917 had majority support of peasantry; split between supporters and opponents of Provisional Government; Right SRs fought in civil war against Soviet rule; Left SRs participated in Soviet government until July 1918, when majority of leadership led anti-Bolshevik uprising; minority currents split away and eventually joined RCP.

Socialist Workers Party of Spain — founded 1879; took pro-Entente position during war; 15,000 members 1918, 52,000 by 1920; several left-wing groupings began to form mid-1918; left-wing forces among youth split 1920; a larger current split 1921; these two groups united November 1921 to form united Spanish CP.

Socialist Youth International (International Union of Socialist Youth Organizations) — founded 1907; fell apart during war; reconstituted 1915 by left-wing forces; organized 1915 Bern International Socialist Youth Conference, which took position opposed to war; published *Jugend-Internationale;* central leaders later aligned with Zimmerwald Left; formed Communist Youth International in November 1919 with 300,000 members.

Solf, Wilhelm Heinrich (1862-1936) — German colonial minister 1911-18; foreign minister 1918.

Sotsial-Demokrat (Social Democrat) — published 1908-17 as central organ of RSDLP; controlled by Bolsheviks after 1910; published abroad except first issue; main editors, Lenin and Zinoviev.

Spartacus League — originated December 1914 as revolutionary current in SPD opposed to majority support for war; organized as Internationale Group January 1916; known as Spartacus group from name of newsletter and leaflets; joined USPD 1917; formed Spartacus League on November 11, 1918, as public faction of USPD; split from USPD and formed KPD December 30, 1918.

SPD — see Social Democratic Party of Germany.

SR — see Socialist Revolutionary Party.

Stampfer, Friedrich (1874-1957) — right-wing SPD member; chief editor of *Vorwärts* 1916-33.

Stein, A. (1881-1948) — Russian Menshevik; emigrated to Germany in 1906 and joined SPD; founding member of USPD; an editor of *Freiheit.*

Stieber, Wilhelm (1818-1882) — head of Prussian political police; helped organize 1852 Cologne Communist trial.

Stinnes, Hugo (1870-1924) — leading German capitalist; headed industrial production during war.

Stolypin, P.A. (1862-1911) — Russian politician and big landowner; implemented agrarian reform aimed at creating kulak layer as bulwark for tsarist autocracy in countryside; associated with harsh political reaction following 1905 revolution.

Ströbel, Heinrich (1869-1944) — an editor of *Vorwärts* 1900-1916; joined USPD 1917; member of Prussian government 1918-19; rejoined SPD 1922.

Struve, P.B. (1870-1944) — Russian bourgeois economist; prominent "Legal Marxist"; Cadet party theorist after 1905; opposed Soviet power; member of Wrangel's White government; emigrated and eventually became monarchist.

Sturm, Fritz (Samuel Markovich Sachs-Gladjev) (1890?-1937?) — Bolshevik; moved to Hamburg 1918; IKD delegate to KPD founding congress; deported to Soviet Union 1920; supported Bukharin against Stalin 1928; arrested and presumably shot during Moscow frame-up trials.

Sukhomlin, V.V. (b. 1885) — editor of SR central organ *Delo Naroda;* member of SR central committee.

Sverdlov, Y.M. (1885-1919) — joined RSDLP 1901; head of secretariat of Bolshevik Central Committee; chairman of All-Russian Central Executive Committee of the soviets 1917-19.

Le Temps (The times) — French bourgeois daily 1861-1944; unofficial voice of French government.

Tesnyaki — see Social Democratic Party of Bulgaria.

Thalheimer, August (1884-1948) — joined SPD 1904; founding member of Spartacus group; member of Spartacus and KPD central committees; expelled 1929 as supporter of Right Opposition to Stalin.

Thiers, Louis-Adolphe (1797-1877) — French president 1871-73; organized crushing of Paris Commune.

Thomas, Albert (1878-1932) — leader of French SP right wing; chauvinist during war; held key government posts 1914-17 organizing railroads, artillery, and munitions; visited Russia April 1917 to promote war effort; leading organizer of 1919 Bern conference; first director of League of Nations' International Labour Organization.

Thyssen, Fritz (1873-1951) — German industrialist; controlled gigantic iron and steel manufacturing plants; helped finance Hitler's rise to power.

Tirpitz, Alfred von (1849-1930) — German admiral of the fleet; minister of imperial naval office 1897-1916; helped found German Fatherland Party 1917.

Tories — name for Conservative Party in Britain.

De Tribune (The tribune) — founded 1907 as publication of left wing of Dutch Social Democratic Workers Party by Pannekoek, Henriette Roland-Holst, and others; became paper of Social Democratic Party of Holland 1909 and of CP 1919.

Trotsky, Leon (1879-1940) — Russian Social Democrat; aligned with Mensheviks 1903-4; president of St. Petersburg soviet 1905; took intermediate position between Bolsheviks and Mensheviks 1904-17; joined Bolsheviks 1917 and elected to Bolshevik Central Committee; commissar of foreign affairs 1917-18; organized and led Red Army 1918-25; prominent leader of Comintern; led Bolshevik-Leninist opposition to Stalin from 1923; expelled from party 1927; exiled abroad 1929; in 1933 launched fight for Fourth International, which was founded 1938; main defendant, in absentia, at 1936-38 Moscow frame-up trials; assassinated by agent of Stalin.

Turati, Filippo (1857-1932) — a founder of Italian SP; avowed reformist; during war voted against war credits in Chamber of Deputies, but supported Woodrow Wilson's proposals; opposed Comintern; led right-wing split from SP 1922.

Two-and-a-Half International — derogatory name applied to the International Association of Socialist Parties; formed 1921 by centrist parties that had left the Second International, with which it reunited 1923.

Tyszka — see Jogiches, Leo.

USPD — see Independent Social Democratic Party of Germany.

Vandervelde, Emile (1866-1938) — Belgian Socialist; chairman of International Socialist Bureau from 1900; defended chauvinist positions during war; cabinet minister throughout war; an organizer of 1919 Bern conference; president of Second International 1929-36.

Verfeuil, Raoul (1887-1927) — leader of centrist opposition within French SP; supported opposition at Bern conference; left party when it joined Comintern and became CP 1920; later rejoined CP but was expelled 1922 for collaborating with party's right-wing opponents.

Vollmar, Georg von (1850-1922) — former German army officer; opposed SPD Erfurt program 1891; led Bavarian SPD in voting for budget of capitalist government 1894; advocated reformist program for peasantry; leader of openly anti-Marxist wing of SPD; chauvinist during war.

Vorwärts (Forward) — main daily organ of German SPD from 1876; during first part of war was in hands of oppositional Berlin organization; closed by government October 1916 on request of SPD majority leadership and reopened under the latter's control; chief editor, Friedrich Stampfer.

Vossische Zeitung — liberal bourgeois newspaper associated with Progressive Party; published in Berlin 1704-1934.

Warski — see Warszawski, Adolf.

Warszawski, Adolf (Warski) (1868-1937) — founding leader of SDKP; member of RSDLP Central Committee 1906-12; collaborator of Rosa Luxemburg; a founder of Polish CP; fled to Soviet Union 1929; executed during Moscow trials along with entire Polish CP leadership.

Webb, Sidney (1859-1947) and **Beatrice** (1858-1943) — leading figures in Fabian Society; supported British war policy; Sidney Webb became colonial minister in Labour government 1929-31; both hostile to Bolshevik government of early 1920s but admirers of Stalin's regime.

Weber, Heinrich — see Bauer, Otto.

Der Weckruf (Reveille) — published in Vienna November 1918-January 1919 as central organ of Austrian CP; replaced by *Die Soziale Revolution* and then *Die Rote Fahne.*

Wels, Otto (1873-1939) — right-wing SPD leader; member of SPD Executive Committee from 1913; Berlin city commander November-December 1918; elected SPD chairman 1931.

Whigs — British political group in eighteenth and nineteenth centuries seeking to limit royal authority and increase parliamentary power.

White Guards — counterrevolutionary armies during Russian civil war 1918-21.

Wilhelm II (1859-1941) — German kaiser and king of Prussia 1888-1918; fled to Holland to escape revolution; abdicated November 28, 1918.

Wilson, Woodrow (1856-1924) — U.S. president 1913-21; led U.S. into war; announced "fourteen points" as response to Soviet program for democratic peace 1918; participated in organizing invasion of Soviet republic 1919.

Workers' International Industrial Union (U.S.) — formed 1908 by supporters of SLP who left IWW; adopted name in 1915; disappeared in 1925.

Zaks, G.D. (1882-1937) — leader of Left SRs; member of Petrograd Military Revolutionary Committee 1917; opposed Left SR uprising in July

1918 and helped organize Narodnik-Communists, who fused with RCP in November 1918.

Zetkin, Clara (1857-1933) — founding member of Second International; editor of SPD women's paper; secretary of International Bureau of Socialist Women; helped organize International Conference of Socialist Women in Bern 1915; Spartacist during war; joined KPD in 1919; elected to ECCI in 1921; remained a prominent figure in Stalinized KPD and Comintern.

Zietz, Luise (1865-1922) — a party secretary of SPD from 1908 and of USPD 1917-22; as member of USPD Executive Committee, supported right-wing current led by Haase.

Zimmerwald conference — first gathering of antiwar socialist parties and currents after collapse of Second International; held September 1915 in Switzerland.

Zimmerwald Left — formed by left-wing delegates who supported Bolsheviks' revolutionary draft resolution at Zimmerwald conference; precursor of Communist International.

Zinoviev, Gregory (1857-1936) — joined RSDLP 1901; supporter of Bolsheviks; elected to RSDLP Central Committee 1907; lived in exile in western Europe 1908-17; member of Zimmerwald Left Bureau together with Lenin and Radek; disagreed with Lenin on timing of October 1917 insurrection; chairman of Petrograd soviet 1917-26; president of Communist International 1919-26; aligned with Stalin and Kamenev in 1923-25, aligned with Trotsky and Kamenev in United Opposition 1926-27; capitulated 1928; executed following first Moscow frame-up trial.

Further Reading

Only a very limited range of writings from 1917-18 by the leading figures in this volume has been translated into English. The following is an indication of writings related to this volume that have been published in English.

Communist International. New York: Greenwood Reprint Corporation, 1968. The organ of the Communist International Executive Committee, this journal began publication in May 1919.

Kamenev, Leon. *The Dictatorship of the Proletariat*. Detroit: Marxian Educational Society, [1920].

Kautsky, Karl. *The Dictatorship of the Proletariat*. Ann Arbor, Michigan: University of Michigan Press, 1964.

— *Terrorism and Communism*. London, 1920.

Lenin, V.I. *Collected Works*. Moscow: Progress Publishers, 1962-75. Translated from the fourth Russian edition.

Liebknecht, Karl. *The Future Belongs to the People*. New York: Macmillan Company, 1918. Contains a selection of his wartime speeches.

— *Speeches of Karl Liebknecht*. New York: International Publishers, 1927.

Luxemburg, Rosa. *Rosa Luxemburg Speaks*. Edited by Mary-Alice Waters. New York: Pathfinder Press, 1970.

— *Rosa Luxemburg: Selected Political Writings*. Edited by Robert Looker. New York: Grove Press, 1974.

— *Selected Political Writings*. New York: Monthly Review Press, 1971.

— *The Letters of Rosa Luxemburg*. Edited by Stephen Eric Bonner. Boulder, Colorado: Westview Press, 1978.

Radek, Karl: *Proletarian Dictatorship and Terrorism*. Detroit: Marxian Educational Society, [1921].

Arthur Rosenberg. *Imperial Germany: The Birth of the German Republic 1871-1918*. Boston: Beacon Press, 1964. An historical account by a participant in the early Communist Party.

— *A History of the German Republic*. London: Methuen & Co., 1936.

Trotsky, Leon. *The First Five Years of the Communist International*. New York: Monad Press, 1972.

— *Portraits, Personal and Political*. New York: Pathfinder Press, 1977. Contains a speech delivered January 18, 1919, in memory of Liebknecht and Luxemburg.

— *Terrorism and Communism*. Ann Arbor, Michigan: University of Michigan Press, 1961.

Index

529